MASTERPLOTS II

AMERICAN FICTION SERIES, REVISED EDITION

MASTERPLOTS II

AMERICAN FICTION SERIES, REVISED EDITION

3

Gre - Los

Edited by
STEVEN G. KELLMAN
The University of Texas at San Antonio

SALEM PRESS

Pasadena, California   Hackensack, New Jersey

Editor in Chief: Dawn P. Dawson
Managing Editor: Christina J. Moose
Project Editor: Robert A. McClenaghan   *Research Editor:* Jeffrey Jensen
Acquisitions Editor: Mark Rehn   *Research Assistant:* Jun Ohnuki

Library of Congress Cataloging-in-Publication Data
Masterplots II. American fiction series / edited by Steven G. Kellman.—Rev. ed.
    p.   cm.
Includes bibliographical references and index.
    ISBN 0-89356-871-6 (set) — ISBN 0-89356-872-4 (v. 1) — ISBN 0-89356-873-2 (v. 2) — ISBN 0-89356-874-0 (v. 3) — ISBN 0-89356-875-9 (v. 4) — ISBN 0-89356-876-7 (v. 5) — ISBN 0-89356-877-5 (v. 6)
    1. American fiction—Stories, plots, etc. I. Title: Masterplots 2. II. Title: Masterplots two. III. Title: American fiction series. IV. Kellman, Steven G., 1947-
PS373 .M37   2000
809.3′0097—dc21   99-053295

First Printing

LIST OF TITLES IN VOLUME 3

LIST OF TITLES IN VOLUME 3

MASTERPLOTS II

AMERICAN FICTION SERIES, REVISED EDITION

THE GREAT AMERICAN NOVEL

Author: Philip Roth (1933-   )
Type of plot: Social satire
Time of plot: 1943-1944, with flashbacks to the early decades of the twentieth
    century
Locale: Various cities in the eastern and midwestern United States
First published: 1973

> *Principal characters:*
> WORD SMITH (SMITTY), a retired baseball writer
> GENERAL DOUGLAS O. OAKHART, president of the Patriot Baseball
>   League
> GIL GAMESH, an all-star pitcher, banished from the league for
>   purposely injuring an umpire
> ULYSSES S. FAIRSMITH, the manager of the Ruppert Mundys
> MIKE MASTERSON, the umpire injured by Gil Gamesh
> ROLAND AGNI, a young star centerfielder for Ruppert Mundys
> ANGELA WHITLING TRUST, the owner of the Tri-City Tycoons

The Novel

The Great American Novel is the story of the bumbling Ruppert Mundys baseball
club and of the Patriot Baseball League. In a lengthy prologue, aging sportswriter
Word Smith (Smitty) recalls the greatness of the league, hints at the reasons for its demise, and bemoans the attempts by Americans of all walks of life to erase the league
from memory. His mission is to preserve this part of American history: The story
which makes up the novel proper is his account of the league's demise.

The main action of the novel occurs in 1943 and 1944, though numerous flashbacks
provide a sense of history necessary for the reader to understand the relationship of
the Patriot League to the other major leagues and to provide the rationale for much of
the action which takes place during this fateful baseball season. In these flashbacks,
interspersed throughout the novel, the reader learns of the tragedy of umpire Mike
Masterson, whose child was kidnapped and killed; the banishment of legendary
pitcher Gil Gamesh; the missionary zeal of Mundys manager Ulysses S. Fairsmith;
the conversion of Tri-City Tycoons owner Angela Whitling Trust from sexual profli-
gate to dedicated American Communist hunter.

In 1943, the Ruppert Mundys find themselves without a home ballpark; the War
Department has taken over their stadium as a training camp, and they are forced to
play their entire season on the road. The ballplayers who make this season-long odyssey are a collection of men too old, too young, misfit, malformed, or maladapted for
life in the big leagues. As they travel from city to city losing game after game and
making fools of themselves, Roth offers numerous character studies of the people associated with the team and the league, both on and off the field. Consequently, the

story of the Mundys' miserable season is told in a series of episodic vignettes, each aimed at highlighting the pathetic nature of the club and those who are doomed to play for it.

The Mundys' season is peppered with embarrassment both on and off the field, and a series of zany incidents makes the chronicle even more amusing. Big John Baal takes fourteen-year-old Nickname Damur to a special kind of prostitute who literally treats him like a baby, bathing and diapering him and singing lullabies to him. The Mundys play an exhibition game against inmates at an insane asylum. A rival owner introduces two dwarfs into the league; when one is traded to the Mundys, a major rivalry begins, leading to a tragedy of national consequence.

Having to suffer the ignominy of playing daily with such inept teammates wears down Roland Agni, the team's only legitimate major leaguer. Roland schemes with the son of the owner of a rival team to doctor his teammates' cereal with atomic-powered Wheaties; as a result, the Mundys start winning. Roland, who plays for no salary because his father wants to break his excessive pride, begins earning money so that he can buy his way off the club. The scheme fails, however, when he aborts the project because many high-ranking Americans, including the president, begin taking an interest in the team. On the day that the Mundys' winning streak is finally broken, however, manager Fairsmith dies of a stroke, brought on by Nickname Damur's attempt to steal a base with the club thirty-one runs behind.

Fairsmith is replaced by Gil Gamesh, who is restored to baseball because he convinces league president General Douglas O. Oakhart and Tycoons owner Angela Trust that he is the only man who can save the league from a Communist plot. In fact, Gamesh, while claiming to be a reformed Communist agent, infects the Mundys with a hatred of other teams, the fans, and everything American. There is a congressional investigation of the league, and numerous agents of the Red Menace are identified; the Mundys turn out to be a particular hotbed of Communism. The Patriot League is unable to withstand the scandal; fans desert the teams, and finally, in the late 1940's, the league dies.

The Characters

Roth populates his novel with dozens of characters, no one of whom can be said to have a dominant role. None is drawn realistically; rather, all are exaggerations, tools of the satirist's pen in this pointed fable about a mythical baseball league.

The character who first garners the reader's attention is the narrator, Word Smith, a retired baseball writer who transcribes the story that forms the heart of the novel. Smitty is confined to an asylum, ostensibly because he suffers from a chronic and fatal affliction: He alliterates too much. His excessive concern with wordplay is a source of humor in the novel; moreover, it provides a forum for some of Roth's more serious comments regarding the nature of fiction and the power of words to shape reality and convey truth.

A series of larger-than-life heroes and villains populate the playing field and the behind-the-scenes operations of the Patriot Baseball League. Many of the characters are modeled loosely on real-life figures from the game: Luke Gofannon, the legendary hitter of the post-World War I era, is a composite of Babe Ruth and Lou Gehrig. The dwarfs who are introduced into the league by Frank Mazuma have their real-life counterpart in three-foot-seven-inch Eddie Gaedel, who was brought into the real major leagues in 1951 in a short-lived experiment by entrepreneur and self-professed iconoclast Bill Veeck. (In Gaedel's only big-league at bat, he walked.) The avid baseball fan will recognize the outlines of many other real major leaguers in several of the characters in the novel. A few historical figures, such as President and Mrs. Franklin D. Roosevelt, and Commissioner Kenesaw Mountain Landis, are included in the story to maintain the facade of realism which is a prerequisite of good satire.

By far the greater concern that Roth shows in his portraits is in developing parallels to literary characters and generic personality types. Roland Agni, the perfectly built and remarkably talented center fielder for the Ruppert Mundys team, suggests both Achilles (in his pride) and Coriolanus (in his vacillation to preserve his honor). The saintly Mundys Manager Ulysses S. Fairsmith is a mixture of Moses and the typical fundamentalist preacher, drawn to an extreme.

Gil Gamesh, whose name is taken from the Babylonian epic, has the perfections and faults that make him a superb archvillain. Stung by a mistake made by umpire Mike Masterson—a mistake that costs him a perfect season on the mound—Gamesh retaliates by breaking the rules and throwing at Masterson; the blow robs Masterson of his voice, and Gamesh is banished from the league. He returns, however, to manage the Mundys; a changed man, he brings with him to the job a Communist-inspired hatred for all things American and successfully topples the league that had not treated him with the respect that his skills so obviously warranted.

Roth's Communist haters bear all the traits that Americans have come to associate with the worst aspects of McCarthyism. Self-righteous to a fault, General Douglas O. Oakhart and Angela Whitling Trust pursue the enemy relentlessly throughout the league. The lame and inept misfits of the Ruppert Mundys team are no match for their crusading vigilantism. Readers will recognize that these are not intended as realistic portraits; nevertheless, their actions will bring a shudder of recognition to those familiar with the historical events on which these satiric sketches are based.

Themes and Meanings

In *The Great American Novel*, Roth uses the method of the satirist to explore two widely diverse subjects: the nature of American society and the nature of fiction, particularly American fiction.

Beneath the comic scenario, the book presents a no-nonsense look at the American Dream: It examines what makes America what it is, and how it got to be that way. Stereotypes, some of them ugly, are poignant reminders that America has achieved its place of eminence in the world at the expense of individuals and groups who have been made to suffer for their race, creed, appearance, or political beliefs. Roth capitalizes on the notion that baseball is America's national pastime, and that American life is mirrored in its sport. As great satirists often do, he takes such metaphoric language literally and constructs his novel on the premise that not only is baseball inextricably intertwined with the country of its birth, but the future of the country is also linked to the health of the national sport. Hence, the real subject of this novel is America itself and the values which Americans hold dearest.

The rules that govern the game of baseball become a metaphor for the rules of American living. Situations occurring in the world of sport are intended to suggest activities that affect the status of the nation as a whole. Thus, individual prejudices, institutional discrimination and favoritism, individual and team attitudes toward such things as winning, fair play, dignity, and spectacle all serve to do more in this novel than merely give insight into the way baseball exists in America. There is constant interplay between the world of sport and the world of politics. Set during the war years, the novel offers insight into the serious way in which Americans regard their sport and suggests that sport is no mere diversion from what may be deemed by some to be the more important matters of life. Indeed, baseball is presented as America's religion, and the parallels between the rituals of faith and the rituals of sport are presented with striking similarity.

A second major concern of Roth is with the nature of fiction itself and with the desire that haunts every American novelist, to write "the great American novel." Roth consciously parodies the tradition of fiction, especially American fiction, and introduces numerous elements of the epic tradition into the work to leave no doubt in the reader's mind that he is dealing with issues beyond the story. His narrator remarks in the prologue and at the end of the work that this book is an attempt to preserve history before it is rewritten by those bent on perverting the truth. On more than one occasion, either the narrator or a character in the novel comments on the relationship between fiction and truth. Roth comes down strongly in favor of the literary postulate that fiction does offer a vision of the truth, the kind of vision outlined by Aristotle in the *Poetics*: Fiction (like poetry in Aristotle's famous essay) can be more effective than history at explaining human nature because it is able to go beyond the actual to explore the possible, thereby revealing aspects of human nature that may not be apparent in particular events of the past.

Roth parodies many literary conventions and makes references to dozens of other novels and novelists. The epic tradition comes under attack most frequently, as Roth includes almost all of its conventions: catalogs of heroes (the bumbling Ruppert Mundys team), men of great pride whose lives end in tragedy (Gil Gamesh and Roland Agni), issues of national importance (the survival of the Patriot League), epic bombast (the sermons of Mr. Ulysses S. Fairsmith and the vitriolic propaganda of the "reformed" Gil Gamesh), and many more. The introduction of the dwarfs into the story as full-fledged ballplayers gives the work a distinct mock epic flavor.

Authors mentioned or alluded to include Ernest Hemingway, James Joyce, Joseph Conrad, Sherwood Anderson, Geoffrey Chaucer, William Faulkner, Henry David Thoreau, Alexander Solzhenitsyn, Samuel Taylor Coleridge, and Percy Bysshe Shelley. The prologue, which contains an extended discussion of the problem of writing the Great American Novel, is a clear imitation of Nathaniel Hawthorne's "Prologue" to *The Scarlet Letter* (1935). Mr. Fairsmith's journey to Africa to bring baseball to the natives is an open parody of Conrad's *Heart of Darkness* (1902). Throughout, Roth engages in literary games and wordplay: Two politicians are called "Mr. Efghi" and "Mr. Stuvwyxz," baseball players accused of being Russian agents are given the names of heroes of famous Russian novels, a group of ministers are all named after bakery products. The comedy of wordplay is a constant reminder that this is a fiction, but one whose purpose is to comment on the real world.

Critical Context

Roth had already achieved a place in contemporary American fiction when *The Great American Novel* was published. *Goodbye, Columbus* (1959), had been made into a film, and *Portnoy's Complaint* (1969) had been a best-seller several years earlier. This novel is quite different, however, from earlier ones, in that autobiographical elements are less prevalent, and the satiric elements more pronounced.

Possibly the greatest significance of this novel lies in the author's attempt to explore the notion of the American epic. It has long been a commonplace among critics and authors that American novelists have been especially desirous of creating a major American novel that would stand with works such as Homer's *Odyssey* or Dante's *The Divine Comedy* as exemplary of the best work of an age and a civilization. Roth pokes fun at this notion throughout the novel, but he is careful to include in his own work all the elements one might expect to find in an epic about America. He is particularly conscious of the epic tradition in literature, including most of the elements of the classical epic—modified to meet his contemporary needs.

Roth's book is another reminder that sports can be the subject of serious literature, and that in sport Americans exhibit freely the characteristics—both good and bad—that make them distinct among peoples of the world.

Bibliography

Cooper, Alan. *Philip Roth and the Jews*. Albany: State University of New York Press, 1996. Cooper explores the spectrum of Roth's writing, including his early works, the "post-Portnoy seventies," and the Zuckerman novels. An excellent overall critical view.

Gentry, Marshall B. "Ventriloquists' Conversations: The Struggle for Gender Dialogue in E. L. Doctorow and Philip Roth." *Contemporary Literature* 34 (Fall, 1993): 512-537. Gentry contends that both Doctorow and Roth are different from other Jewish authors because of their incorporation of feminist thought into traditionally patriarchal Jewish literature. He notes that their reconciliation of feminism and Judaism could alienate them from both groups, but he commends their attempt.

Greenberg, Robert M. "Transgression in the Fiction of Philip Roth." *Twentieth Century Literature* 43 (Winter, 1997): 487-506. Greenberg argues that the theme of transgression pervades Roth's novels, and he demonstrates how this idea of infraction allows the author to penetrate places where he feels socially and psychologically excluded. An intriguing assessment of Roth's work.

Halio, Jay L. *Philip Roth Revisited.* New York: Twayne, 1992. Halio offers a brief biographical sketch of Roth, as well as in-depth discussions of his works. Includes a chapter entitled "Tour de Farce: The Comedy of the Grotesque in *The Great American Novel.*" Also includes helpful notes and a selected bibliography for further reading.

Halkin, Hillel. "How to Read Philip Roth." *Commentary* 97 (February, 1994): 43-48. Offering critical analyses of several of Roth's books, Halkin explores Roth's personal view of Jewishness, as well as other biographical elements in his works.

Podhoretz, Norman. "The Adventure of Philip Roth." *Commentary* 106 (October, 1998): 25-36. Podhoretz discusses the Jewish motifs in Roth's writing and compares Roth's work to that of other Jewish authors, including Saul Bellow and Herman Wouk. He also voices his disappointment concerning Roth's preoccupation with growing old as expressed in his later novels.

Laurence W. Mazzeno

GREEN GRASS, RUNNING WATER

Author: Thomas King (1943-   )
Type of plot: Social criticism
Time of plot: The 1960's to the 1980's
Locale: Blossom, Alberta, Canada
First published: 1993

> *Principal characters:*
> LIONEL RED DOG, a Blackfoot Indian
> CHARLIE LOOKING BEAR, Lionel's cousin
> ALBERTA FRANK, a professor, lover of Lionel and Charlie
> NORMA, Charlie's mother, Lionel's aunt
> ELI STANDS ALONE, Norma's brother
> KAREN, Eli's deceased wife
> BILL BURSUM, Lionel's employer, Charlie's former employer
> LATISHA, Lionel's sister, owner of the Dead Dog Café
> COYOTE, a trickster
> ROBINSON CRUSOE,
> ISHMAEL,
> THE LONE RANGER, and
> HAWKEYE, escapees from a mental hospital
> DR. HOVAUGH, a doctor in a mental hospital
> BABO, a worker in a mental hospital

The Novel

In *Green Grass, Running Water*, the line between reality and fantasy is blurred. The novel opens and closes with short sections devoted to Coyote, the trickster, who accounts for many of the book's inexplicable incidents.

The story then turns briefly to four characters—Robinson Crusoe, Ishmael, the Lone Ranger, and Hawkeye—all presumably Blackfoot Indians who have escaped from the mental institution in which they were confined. Their mission, with the help of Coyote, is to fix the world. These five add considerable humor to the story, but they may leave some readers baffled initially, both because it is not always clear where reality ends and fantasy begins with them and because they overstep linear time lines.

These characters present various creation stories drawn from Greek, Christian, and Native American mythologies. King's Ahdamn-First Woman story is the Adam and Eve story in contemporary garb; the first two humans on earth eat both fried chicken and the Edenic apple. Young Man Walking On Water (King's version of Christ) articulates King's beliefs about the conflict between the Indian culture and the dominant white culture—a major reason for his having written this novel—when he proffers his interpretation of Christian rules: "the first rule is that no one can help me. The second rule is that no one can tell me anything. Third, no one is allowed to be in two places at once. Except me."

The essence of *Green Grass, Running Water* is that a know-it-all white culture has intruded insensitively—sometimes dangerously, usually stupidly—upon the folkways of Native American cultures, which have conserved a land and a way of life by means that make environmental sense. These folkways are misunderstood and disrespected by those in nominal power, who refuse to observe long-standing treaties. Such people do not respect native festivals such as the Sun Dance, which they try to photograph—behavior that is an insult to the Indians.

On the fantastic level, Coyote helps the Blackfoot by using his trickster powers to thwart much of what the white people wish to do in order to, in their terms, advance civilization. Coyote and the escapees from the mental institution collaborate on fixing the world.

Two major structural challenges faced King in *Green Grass, Running Water*. First, he needed to mix mythology with reality, a quintessential ingredient in his revisionist history of his subjects. He achieved this end by using the Coyote trickster and his cronies to handle the mythic content of the novel; in so doing, the author infused the book with considerable humor. Second, he had to find a way to interweave eight interrelated yet individual stories.

King approaches this structural task by writing in short segments, sometimes a few lines, sometimes three or four pages, occasionally, but rarely, longer. Within the longer, more linear segments, King successfully experiments with a device that provides readers with necessary background. A segment may begin in the here and now, but the second paragraph will be a reflection on some past event; the third will continue the presentation of the here and now, the fourth will take up the presentation of the past event, and so forth to the end of the segment.

King handles this complicated structure deftly; reading these segments is neither confusing nor annoying. King frequently ends his paragraphs with cliffhanger sentences. One hates to leave a here and now paragraph and retreat to the past, but a few lines later, the here and now takes over again. This style provides King's narrative with a unique forward momentum.

Two major story lines dominate King's novel: Alberta's desire to become pregnant and Eli's struggle to keep the government from taking his mother's property. Nearly everything else in the novel stems from these two basic lines of development. When King departs from one story line to move into another, readers remain oriented, because each story line is connected to one or both of the main stories King is developing. Although five or six segments may be interposed between two elements of one of King's main narrative threads, it is never difficult to pick up that thread when King resumes telling that part of the story.

Two events bring the novel to its resolution. First, Alberta gets her wish. She becomes pregnant, but by neither Lionel nor Charlie. Then, an earthquake hits the area around Blossom, destroying the dam that Eli has been fighting and, in the process, returning the tribal waterway to its rightful owners and drowning Eli. Both events are Coyote's doing. The trickster has prevailed.

The Characters

The central figure in *Green Grass, Running Water* is Lionel Red Dog, who as a youth had a promising future that, through a series of misadventures not of his own doing, was foreclosed to him. During a trip to Salt Lake City to read a professional paper for a colleague in the Department of Indian Affairs, which employed him, Lionel was unwittingly drawn into an Indian activist group, and he landed in jail.

When he returned to Blossom, he was fired. His conviction made it difficult for him to get another job. Finally, Bill Bursum, the white owner of a local store, offered to hire Lionel to replace his cousin Charlie, who had left Bill's employ to attend law school. Twenty years later, Lionel is still at work in the store; he is Bill's best salesman, but he has never had a salary increase. Bill Bursum's story is closely connected to Lionel's.

The same is true of Charlie's story. Charlie, having completed law school, is a Porsche-driving success, employed by Duplessis International Associates, the construction firm commissioned to dam a tribal river. When the dam is finally destroyed, Duplessis, no longer needing its token Indian, fires Charlie.

Alberta Frank is a college professor in Calgary who, realizing that her biological clock is running down, wants desperately to have a baby but has no desire to have a husband. She engages in simultaneous affairs with Charlie and Lionel, and her story is intricately tied to theirs.

Norma is Lionel and Latisha's aunt and Eli Stands Alone's sister. Latisha, owner of the Dead Dog Café, is a successful businessperson who was married to George Morningstar, a good-looking, immature, unsuccessful white man from Ohio, who has left his wife and children.

Eli left the reservation some thirty years earlier to attend the University of Toronto. He married Karen, a white woman, and has spent his life teaching literature at the university. He and Karen returned to Blossom once before their marriage and attended the Sun Dance. Karen always wanted to attend another Sun Dance, but more than two decades later, recovering from cancer, she is killed in an automobile accident, never having been able to realize her wish.

Eli, learning through Norma of his mother's death some weeks after its occurrence, returns to Blossom to find that the tribal river has been dammed and that a power plant is about to be put into operation. He retires and becomes a man with a mission. When the dam is opened, the house that Eli and Norma's mother built with her own hands will be washed away. Eli exercises every legal remedy available to prevent the dam from becoming operative. He defies the government agency and Duplessis International Associates that have built the dam.

Clifford Sifton, who works for the builders of the dam, comes daily to ask Eli officially to leave. Eli daily refuses, also officially. He and Sifton become friends. Eli gives Sifton coffee; Sifton brings Eli books. Because of Eli's stubbornness, people, including Bill Bursum, who have bought property on what will be the lakefront created by the dam are kept from developing that property.

Straddling the line between the real and the fantastic are Dr. Hovaugh, a psychiatrist at a mental hospital, and Babo, who works in the hospital. Four of their patients have escaped. These four are delusional, and their association with Coyote brings out the mythical elements in the story.

Themes and Meanings

Thomas King lives with a foot in two worlds, the Native American world that is part of his heritage and the world of the white society of which he is fundamentally a part despite his Cherokee lineage. He understands both worlds well. He writes in *Green Grass, Running Water*, as he did in his first novel, *Medicine River* (1990), with a greater sympathy for the underdog society than for the dominant society.

Green Grass, Running Water directs its social commentary to current topics, including the feminist cause. Alberta is a liberated woman, bright, well-educated, and financially independent. She wants motherhood but denies any necessary connection between motherhood and marriage. She is a nurturing sort, more drawn to Lionel than to Charlie because Lionel is the less successful of the two, the one who needs nurturing. This, however, does not make Alberta want to marry him.

Throughout the novel, white society transgresses upon the native culture in ways both small and large. The small transgressions occur in insensitive acts: for example, a white tourist happens upon the Sun Dance and begins photographing it. Even worse, George, who is married to Latisha, a successful, independent Native American, wants to photograph the Sun Dance and, in an abortive reunion with Latisha, makes slighting remarks about her culture—something that Eli's white wife, Karen, never did.

In one heartbreaking vignette, King tells of how Alberta's parents, Ada and Amos, drove south to the United States to participate in a sacred tribal dance with relatives. At the border, they encountered arrogant customs agents who forced them to unpack their car. When the agents discovered their tribal costumes, they spread them on the asphalt and then, because the costumes were decorated with eagle feathers, confiscated them.

After considerable negotiation, the costumes were returned in plastic garbage bags with the feathers broken. The return of the costumes could not make amends for what had happened. The initial insult at the border, which results in Amos's arrest, was horrible. To have the costumes defiled as they were was an added insult. The greatest insult, however, was that the border agents robbed Alberta's parents of their dignity.

Among the larger affronts the Blackfoots suffered from white society was the building of the dam and its plans to operate a power plant and develop a recreational area on tribal land. Eli Stands Alone has left his people and gone to Toronto, seemingly forsaking his forebears. On the surface, he has repudiated his heritage.

King shows, however, that in the end, Eli cannot forsake his past. He returns to the house his mother built and, using knowledge and self-confidence he gained in the white world, he obstructs the operation of the dam for years. He keeps the project in limbo until, through the intervention of the trickster, nature reclaims the project.

In this novel, a symbiosis exists between the two societies King depicts. Among the ills the natives face is that their young people leave the reserve (King's preferred term for a reservation) and go out into the broader world beyond. They never really leave home, however, and when they return, they do so better equipped to defeat those who would suppress native culture.

Critical Context

Green Grass, Running Water was written at a time when considerable attention was being paid to Native American history. Advances in knowledge have resulted in considerable revisions of American history, which had largely been written from the perspective of a white establishment dominated by people with Western European outlooks.

The Columbus quincentenary in 1992 became, rather than a celebration of the discovery of the New World, a year of strident questioning. People asked such questions as, "How does one discover a world that has already been settled for centuries and that has a culture in many ways as advanced as that in Europe?" The Inca, the Aztec, and the Mayan Indians were exceptionally advanced in mathematics and such related areas of physics as astronomy. In the fields of art and architecture, these cultures had produced works of great sophistication.

Another prominent Native American novelist, Gerald Vizenor, addressed such questions in *Bearheart: The Heirship Chronicles* (1990) and *The Heirs of Columbus* (1991); he, like King, emphasized the trickster tradition. King is artistically dependent on this tradition in *Green Grass, Running Water*, using it to bring about the dual resolution of his novel.

King addresses a number of compelling social concerns in this novel. He presents independent, self-possessed women quite capable of functioning productively without men. Alberta Frank and Latisha Morningstar are prototypical modern women. They are too busy to march in parades or burn bras in public protests, but they forge ahead as contributing members of society, with minds of their own. They have no qualms about defying convention. They fit well into the context of women's liberation.

King is also concerned with the contemporary problem of the flight of young Native Americans to cities. He seems even more concerned, however, about what happens to someone like Lionel, who remains in Blossom in a dead-end job, accepting his fate all too willingly even though he has for two decades harbored vague, at times unrealistic, plans for continuing his education.

Bibliography

Berner, Robert L. "World Literature in Review: Native American." *World Literature Today* 67 (Autumn, 1993): 869. A short but interesting analysis of the satiric and mythic complexities of *Green Grass, Running Water*. Affirms the novel as "a permanent addition to the corpus of American Indian literature which will serve as a benchmark in the history of that subject."

Blair, Elizabeth. "Setting the Story Straight." *World and I* 8 (June, 1993): 284-295. Blair offers a brief comparison of King's *Medicine River* and *Green Grass, Run-*

ning Water. She presents an intriguing analysis of various components of the narrative, including the historical, mythic, and religious elements.

Eder, Richard. "Indian Spirits at Large in the World Today." *Newsday* (March 25, 1993): 66. Eder gives a brief overview of the plot of *Green Grass, Running Water* and highlights important events. His analysis of the mythic aspects of the story is helpful but not comprehensive.

Low, Denise. Review of *Green Grass, Running Water,* by Thomas King. *American Indian Quarterly* 18 (Winter, 1994): 104-106. Low discusses the four characters who launch the "cosmic farce" characterizing the story line of *Green Grass, Running Water.* She concludes that although King's humor can be gently scathing concerning the relationship between Native Americans and Europeans, its ultimate message is hopeful.

McManus, James. "Has Red Dog Gone White?" *The New York Times Book Review* 98 (July 25, 1993): 21. McManus comments on King's control of the diverse stories developed in *Green Grass, Running Water.* He calls the book "ambitious and funny" but criticizes King for spending too much time developing some of the book's less interesting characters.

Turbide, Diane. "A Literary Trickster: Thomas King Conjures Up Comic Worlds." *Maclean's* 106 (May 3, 1993): 43-44. Turbide explores the trickster aspect of the novel, focusing on the cultural and religious conflicts between American Indian and Christian viewpoints.

R. Baird Shuman

GRENDEL

Author: John Gardner (1933-1982)
Type of plot: Fantasy literature
Time of plot: The early Middle Ages
Locale: The Scandinavian countryside
First published: 1971

Principal characters:

GRENDEL, the monster who terrorizes the Scandinavian countryside
GRENDEL'S MOTHER, a monster to whom Grendel is attached but who
    is clearly not as intellectually advanced as her son
HROTHGAR, a petty king who unites several warring factions and builds
    a magnificent fortress
WEALTHEOW, Hrothgar's wife
THE DRAGON, a creature with exceptional philosophical insight into
    human affairs
UNFERTH, a hero in Hrothgar's court
THE GEAT HERO, a man of exceptional prowess who comes to
    Hrothgar's court to kill Grendel

The Novel

    Grendel is the story of the battle between the monster Grendel and the Scandinavian King Hrothgar, told through the eyes of the monster. The story highlights the various encounters between the monster and the men who hate and fear him but who are powerless to do anything to him, until a stranger from across the waters comes to end Grendel's life.

    Grendel lives in an undersea cave with his mother but spends most of his time wandering through the forests, observing the men and women in the various villages and fortresses built across the countryside. Angered by a rebuff that he receives from Hrothgar and his thanes, Grendel vows to make life miserable for the king. At will, he raids human dwellings, destroying life and property with delight. He takes particular pleasure in wreaking havoc in Hart, the hall that Hrothgar builds as a showplace and from which he reigns as a kind of overlord.

    None of Hrothgar's warriors can match the monster's strength, and Grendel mocks them because they are boastful at banquets but unable to live up to their claims when put to the test. He is especially harsh on Unferth, Hrothgar's greatest warrior; when Unferth follows the monster to his underwater lair, Grendel taunts him about the poor state of men who claim to be heroes, then renders him unconscious and delivers him back to Hart, unharmed, so he must suffer shame before his peers.

    Grendel is not the only enemy Hrothgar faces. Even while he fights the monster, the king strives to subdue the warring clans that populate the countryside around him and to organize them into a primitive nation. Hrothgar's efforts are largely successful; the king balances his efforts between warfare and diplomacy to attain a tenuous peace in his land. One of the results of his policy is a political marriage to Wealtheow, the sister of a powerful adversary. Grendel is taken with Wealtheow's beauty, and though he engages in particularly lurid acts with her to display his mastery over Hrothgar, he feels genuine remorse for his monstrous behavior.

Grendel's actions against the men he hates are carried out intermittently; the monster spends much of his time merely watching the humans and musing on the foibles of mankind. He consults the Dragon, a creature possessed of philosophical powers far superior to his own and to those of men, engaging him in an extended conversation about the meaning of life and about the place of men and monsters on earth. From the Dragon, Grendel learns what the future holds, but he is unable to apprehend what he is told.

Finally, a hero arrives from over the water, from the nation of the Geats, a world-renowned fighter and athlete. To Grendel, this presents simply another opportunity to humiliate Hrothgar. He makes a night raid on Hart and attacks the hero. Much to his surprise, however, the hero proves more than his match; in the fight, Grendel's arm is wrenched from its socket. Suffering with pain such as he has never felt before, the monster drags himself off to die.

The Characters

Gardner's novel is primarily a character study of the monster Grendel and the men who live in fear of him. Through the eyes of the monster, Gardner offers his readers an assessment of the human condition; the picture is not always nice and is in fact more often a scathing commentary on the essentially animalistic qualities that persist in men even as they delude themselves into thinking that they have risen above the beast.

Since Grendel tells his own story, the reader is allowed great insight into the loneliness that the monster feels as he tries to communicate with men. Grendel possesses superhuman strength, and though his size is never specified, he is clearly gargantuan: He is capable of seizing and tearing apart the warriors who oppose him and, with cannibalistic delight, devouring them. This same creature whose behavior strikes terror into the hearts of Hrothgar's thanes is, nevertheless, also capable of relatively subtle thought; his commentaries on the way that men treat one another show that he understands what mercy, charity, love, hate, and revenge mean. Additionally, he possesses an existentialist view of the world, musing on more than one occasion that all that happens is merely accidental; there is no god prompting the actions of men or monsters, or giving purpose to the world.

Because this is a first-person novel, the reader's impression of the other characters is colored by the descriptions offered by Grendel. Hrothgar appears pompous and egotistical, but a careful analysis of his actions suggests that he is a kind of King Arthur figure, trying to bring order to a troubled land and give those subordinate to him ideals toward which to strive. He is politically astute and less fatalistic than the monster about the value of life. Similarly, Unferth is treated with contempt by Grendel, but his speech in the monster's cave about the real meaning of heroism suggests that he has insight into human nature denied to Grendel. When Grendel makes fun of him, Unferth urges that they fight unobserved: "A hero is not afraid to face cruel truth," he tells the monster. No one will know how Unferth behaved in the underwater cave. "Only you and I and God will know the truth. That's inner heroism." Grendel treats this profundity as simply another embarrassing contradiction in human character.

Other characters appear undeveloped, almost stereotypes. Some attempt is made to personalize the young queen, Wealtheow, though she is little more than a combination sex object and lost child. Again, one must remember that she is viewed exclusively through the eyes of the monster, who lusts for her and yet is overcome by her charm and sincerity.

The hero who defeats and finally kills Grendel is hardly developed at all. Rather, he appears as an instrument of fate, a messenger of God or destiny sent to terminate the monster's life. He brings a final lesson to the monster (and the reader) about the nature of life: It is what each person (or each monster) makes it. Hence, the hero functions as simply a kind of existential angel of death. As he lies dying in the forest, Grendel expresses an understanding of the stranger's mission and his message; the whole incident, like life itself, is no more than a cruel accident.

Themes and Meanings

Beneath this fantasy story lies a serious metaphysical novel. Gardner's chief concerns are the nature of man and the meaning of life itself. The musings of the monster and his interactions with the Scandinavian warriors provide a vehicle for the reader's journey through the maze of philosophical issues confronting twentieth century man as he, too, searches for the rationale of human existence.

Gardner's position on the ultimate meaning of life remains unclear. Grendel is openly existentialist. (Indeed, many of his ideas and some of his very words are slyly adapted from the writings of Jean-Paul Sartre.) To him, life is merely an accident, unplanned and purposeless. No benevolent (or malevolent) deity presides over human destiny. Hence, there is no ultimate judge to pronounce men's actions good or evil. Throughout the novel, Grendel learns that lesson, which is made most clear to him by the hero who kills him: "You make the world by whispers, second by second," the hero tells him; "Whether you make it a grave or a garden of roses is not the point." Life is what each man, or each monster, makes of it. To Grendel, man's behavior seems merely ludicrous and hypocritical. Nevertheless, he sympathizes with those who display what the reader recognizes as man's highest and most human qualities, one of which is to act with some regard to the afterlife. Hence, it would be naïve to assume simply that the monster's fatalistic approach to life is the one that Gardner wants the reader to adopt.

What is clear is that men behave in strange ways, often at odds with what they profess. That dichotomy provides much of the grim humor that characterizes this novel: The monster, whom the reader assumes to be less than human, actually appears to possess a better understanding of and appreciation for the best qualities that characterize the species *Homo sapiens*. Men are constantly defining themselves against other men, or against ideals. That is a central lesson of the book: Man becomes man, establishes his unique identity, only by engaging in such comparisons. Grendel—and the reader—discovers that monsters have existence as foils for men; everything in the world is defined, ultimately, by contrast with its opposite.

An important minor theme in this novel is the significance of poetry (representative here of literature as a whole) in preserving and defining what is best in mankind. Grendel is enthralled with the Shaper, the old poet at Hrothgar's hall who immortalizes the deeds of great heroes in his songs each evening. Men live on after death in the songs of the poet; great poets, Grendel discovers, create reality. On this powerful pronouncement Grendel and his modern-day creator seem to agree.

Critical Context

The source for *Grendel*, and the primary inspiration for both its characters and its story line, is the medieval heroic poem *Beowulf*. That work recounts the major triumphs of Beowulf, hero of the Geats, whose immortality is assured by his actions to rid King Hrothgar's lands of the monster Grendel and to save his own kingdom from a fierce dragon. The details of Beowulf's encounter with Grendel are presented with exceptional fidelity in this twentieth century account of the story—with one important difference. Gardner, who was a scholar and teacher of medieval literature as well as a novelist, retold this most famous Old English story from the point of view of the monster. By shifting the novel's focus to the much-maligned villain of the earlier tale, Gardner highlighted the essential themes of *Beowulf* and allowed the reader familiar with both works to develop a better appreciation for the medieval classic.

Those not familiar with *Beowulf* may appreciate *Grendel* for itself: a tale of fantasy underpinned by metaphysical questioning. Readers who know the original, however, will immediately recognize the larger subject with which Gardner is dealing: the contrast between medieval and modern worldviews. The nature of heroism, and man's understanding of the purpose of life, have changed radically in the ten centuries intervening between the creation of these two works. By simply turning the story on its head, so to speak, Gardner has illustrated the way in which human nature has itself been radically changed.

With *Grendel*, Gardner joined a long line of modern authors who have recast medieval legends and woven into them contemporary themes. Since the revival of interest in medieval literature that began in the late eighteenth and early nineteenth centuries, authors have found in the sagas and legends first conceived in the so-called Dark Ages fertile ground for materials with which to create their own tales. Stories of King Arthur and his knights, of the German and French heroes, and of countless other figures who form a part of the national history of various European countries have become the source for modern investigations of universal human questions. Authors as various as Alfred, Lord Tennyson, Edwin Arlington Robinson, Charles Williams, and John Steinbeck have produced important modern works by mining the works of medieval authors for both story line and theme. Gardner's novel of the monster Grendel is exceptional among the thousands of these types of stories not only for its fidelity to its source, but also for its remarkable combination of medieval legend with contemporary psychology and philosophy.

Bibliography

Butts, Leonard. *The Novels of John Gardner: Making Life Art as a Moral Process.* Baton Rouge: Louisiana State University Press, 1988. Butts draws his argument from Gardner himself, specifically *On Moral Fiction* (that art is a moral process) and discusses the ten novels in pairs, focusing on the main characters as either artists or artist figures who to varying degrees succeed or fail in transforming themselves into Gardner's "true artist." As Butts defines it, moral fiction is not didactic but instead a matter of aesthetic wholeness.

Chavkin, Allan, ed. *Conversations with John Gardner.* Jackson: University Press of Mississippi, 1990. Reprints nineteen of the most important interviews (the majority from the crucial *On Moral Fiction* period) and adds one never before published interview. Chavkin's introduction, which focuses on Gardner as he appears in these and his other numerous interviews, is especially noteworthy. The chronology updates the one in Howell (below).

Cowart, David. *Arches and Light: The Fiction of John Gardner.* Carbondale: Southern Illinois University Press, 1983. Discusses the published novels through *Mickelsson's Ghosts*, the two story collections, and the tales for children. As good as Cowart's intelligent and certainly readable chapters are, they suffer (as does so much Gardner criticism) insofar as they are concerned with validating Gardner's position on moral fiction as a valid alternative to existential despair.

Henderson, Jeff. *John Gardner: A Study of the Short Fiction.* Boston: Twayne, 1990. Part 1 concentrates on Gardner's short fiction, including his stories for children; part 2 contains excerpts from essays and letters in which Gardner defines his role as a writer; part 3 provides excerpts from important Gardner critics. Includes chronology and bibliography.

_____, ed. *Thor's Hammer: Essays on John Gardner.* Conway: University of Central Arkansas Press, 1985. Presents fifteen original essays of varying quality, including three on *Grendel*. The most important are John M. Howell's biographical essay, Robert A. Morace's on Gardner and his reviewers, Gregory Morris's discussion of Gardner and "plagiarism," Samuel Coale's on dreams, Leonard Butts's on *Mickelsson's Ghosts*, and Charles Johnson's "A Phenomenology of *On Moral Fiction*."

Howell, John M. *John Gardner: A Bibliographical Profile.* Carbondale: Southern Illinois University Press, 1980. Howell's detailed chronology and enumerative listing of works by Gardner (down to separate editions, printings, issues, and translations), as well as the afterword written by Gardner, make this an indispensable work for any Gardner student.

McWilliams, Dean. *John Gardner.* Boston: Twayne, 1990. McWilliams includes little biographical material, does not try to be at all comprehensive, yet has an interesting and certainly original thesis: that Gardner's fiction may be more fruitfully approached via Mikhail Bakhtin's theory of dialogism than via *On Moral Fiction*. Unfortunately, the chapters (on the novels and *Jason and Medeia*) tend to be rather introductory in approach and only rarely dialogical in focus.

Morace, Robert A. *John Gardner: An Annotated Secondary Bibliography*. New York: Garland, 1984. An especially thorough annotated listing of all known items (reviews, articles, significant mentions) about Gardner through 1983. The annotations of speeches and interviews are especially full (a particularly useful fact given the number of interviews and speeches the loquacious as well as prolific Gardner gave). A concluding section updates Howell's *John Gardner: A Bibliographical Profile*.

Morace, Robert A., and Kathryn VanSpanckeren, eds. *John Gardner: Critical Perspectives*. Carbondale: Southern Illinois University Press, 1982. This first critical book on Gardner's work covers the full range of his literary endeavors, from his dissertation-novel "The Old Men" through his then most recent fictions, "Vlemk, The Box Painter" and *Freddy's Book*, with separate essays on his "epic poem" *Jason and Medeia*; *The King's Indian: Stories and Tales*; his children's stories; libretti; pastoral novels; use of sources, parody, and embedding; and theory of moral fiction. The volume concludes with Gardner's afterword.

Morris, Gregory L. *A World of Order and Light: The Fiction of John Gardner*. Athens: University of Georgia Press, 1984. Like Butts and Cowart, Morris works well within the moral fiction framework which Gardner himself established. Unlike Cowart, however, Morris emphasizes moral art as a process by which order is discovered rather than (as Cowart contends) made. More specifically the novels (including Gardner's dissertation novel "The Old Men") and two collections of short fiction are discussed in terms of Gardner's "luminous vision" and "magical landscapes."

Laurence W. Mazzeno

GRIEVER
An American Monkey King in China

Author: Gerald Vizenor (1934-   )
Type of plot: Neorealism
Time of plot: The early 1980's
Locale: Tianjin and Beijing, China; Minnesota
First published: 1987

>*Principal characters:*
>GRIEVER DE HOCUS, an American "crossbreed" teaching in China
>EGAS ZHANG, the director of the foreign affairs bureau
>HESTER HUA DAN, Zhang's daughter
>KANGMEI, Zhang's stepdaughter, sired by an American
>SHITOU, a Chinese shaman who crushes stone
>CHINA BROWNE, Griever's friend in America
>MATTEO RICCI, Griever's symbolic rooster

The Novel

Early in *Griever: An American Monkey King in China*, Gerald Vizenor informs his readers that "imagination is the real world, all the rest is bad television." Four pages later, he reinforces this contention, which is essential to an understanding of what Vizenor hopes to accomplish artistically: Imagination, he writes "is what burns in humans. We are not methods to be discovered, we are not freeze-dried methodologies. We remember dreams, never data, at the wild end." As *Griever* alternates between reality and fantasy, between consciousness and the dream world, readers need to remember these early admonitions. They have direct artistic import and, in light of Vizenor's subject, penetrating political implications.

Based on several months of language teaching that Vizenor and his wife did in post-Maoist Tianjin, China, *Griever* continually moves between documentable history and overt fantasy. This is one of the few novels that provides readers with a bibliography of historical sources in its final pages.

One might call *Griever* a nonfiction novel, a term applied by critics to such works as Truman Capote's *In Cold Blood* (1966). Yet Vizenor, unlike Capote, departs unapologetically from his facts, intermixing reveries with consciousness; he thereby creates a fantastic tale that borrows from his traditions as a "crossbreed" Chippewa, and he links these traditions, particularly that of the trickster, to similar traditions in Chinese legend.

Griever is essentially a tale about its protagonist's experiences in China during the period leading up to the Tiananmen Square uprising. Vizenor does not relate these experiences linearly but rather focuses on Griever de Hocus, a trickster whose last name suggests the sort of role he plays. As the novel develops, Griever becomes more and more outrageous, sneering at the bureaucracy, outwitting it at every turn, usually in highly humorous episodes that suggest the lighthearted effectiveness of tricksters—always humorous characters—in the Native American tradition.

Griever's first major move in this direction is heterodox but not openly defiant of China's structured official bureaucracy: On his first day in Tianjin, when he observes a butcher slaughtering chickens in the open market, he puts a handful of Chinese money on the butcher's blood-covered slaughtering block to buy all the chickens he can. When the accommodating butcher seeks to slaughter Griever's chickens for him, Griever protests that he wants them alive.

Having made this point, he then releases them, and they flutter off—except for one rooster, a handsome cock with orange wattles whom Griever names Matteo Ricci. Matteo figures prominently and symbolically throughout the rest of novel. The slaughter also foreshadows much more shocking slaughters on which Vizenor reports later in the book: the brutal, inhuman torture and slaying of the Lazarist Sisters of Saint Vincent de Paul in 1982, and an execution caravan, in which two trucks carrying prisoners drive their captives slowly through the streets to their executions—which, in a fanciful turn in the story, do not occur. The prisoners, like the chickens Griever buys, somehow escape their fate.

Egas Zhang is Griever's first official contact in China. Egas meets Griever at the airport and takes him to the guest house that he will share with a ragtag group of seven other teachers, some of whom—notably Carnegie Morgan and Colin Marport Gloome—are symbolically named. Egas Zhang has reared two daughters, Hester Hua Dan and Kangmei. Kangmei, however, is not his child; Egas hates her. Kangmei issued from a liaison between Egas's wife and an American who, through a series of mischances, became stateless and finally died in an earthquake that killed three hundred thousand people in Tianjin.

Kangmei has blonde hair that she usually hides under a scarf. Her stepfather is despotic. He has spies who observe the people around him and report their activities. Egas finally drowns Hester Hua Dan and her daughter, his grandchild, in the pond behind the guest house during the carnival. Kangmei escapes to Macao with Griever in an ultralight airplane that he has assembled.

Griever enacts a final vengeance in his last meeting with the detested Egas Zhang. Egas has continually prodded Griever to give him bear paws, gall bladders, and other aphrodisiacs. Shortly before his escape to Macao, Griever offers Egas a concoction that the depraved man accepts hungrily. This potion, however, contains estrogen, which in a short time will give Egas pendulous breasts and the high voice of a woman. He will go through life "walking and talking like a mutant hermaphrodite."

The Characters

Griever de Hocus, an autobiographical character, is a bright, well-educated crossbreed Chippewa Indian half a world away from his Minnesota roots. In Tianjin, he teaches English. Vizenor constructs in Griever the traditional trickster of Native American legend, a figure that occurs in most of his writing. Griever is mischievous but resolute in his defiance of despotism. He prefers to outwit rather than outfight his opponents. Griever almost singlehandedly creates the action that propels the novel. He is an omniscient third-person narrator as well as the perpetrator of all the book's crucial events.

Egas Zhang is the slippery villain. He is the quintessential bureaucrat, an obedient man devoid of independent values or principles. He appears accommodating, but behind this façade, his xenophobia lurks. This xenophobia is heightened by his knowledge that his wife conceived a child by an American who had lost his citizenship. She insisted on delivering this child, Kangmei, and Egas had to rear Kangmei as his own despite her blonde hair, a badge of illegitimacy. History repeats itself when Egas's own daughter, Hester Hua Dan, becomes pregnant after an encounter with Griever, who is Egas's virtual opposite in every fundamental respect.

China Browne is the friend back home. She is a sounding board to whom Griever writes regularly. Letters to her begin and end the book, creating a frame for the novel.

Kangmei, Egas Zhang's stepdaughter, becomes Griever's lover and his companion on his flight out of China to Macao. The trip takes several days in the ultralight aluminum plane, propelled by a snowmobile motor, that Griever has assembled. Kangmei is caught between two cultures and has lived a life of rejection. Is she in love, or is she simply desperate for a better life? Vizenor does not reveal her real motives.

Shitou is a shaman who crushes stone with his bare hands. He has many of the mystical attributes of both the shaman and the trickster in Native American legend. By allowing him to figure prominently throughout the novel, Vizenor holds the mirror to the folklore of two cultures separated by half a world but sharing comparable beliefs about the supernatural, preconscious state.

Matteo Ricci, although a rooster rather than a human, occupies a prominent place in the novel. Rescued from the chicken slaughter, his freedom (and survival) purchased with a few pieces of paper money, Matteo accompanies Griever everywhere, even to the auspicious opening of Maxim de Beijing's. Griever's rescue of Matteo is a reenactment of his rescue of frogs from a science experiment when he was a schoolboy and also is a foreshadowing of the freeing of the prisoners from the execution caravan. The essence of these rescues provides a veiled statement about the rights of all living things.

Hester Hua Dan, the dutiful daughter of Egas Zhang, is a translator. She bears the shame of an illegitimate pregnancy in a country where, according to Vizenor's repeated mantras, one child is all that is permitted. Hester could escape with Griever, but she is so used to conforming to her father's authority that she stays in Tianjin and is murdered.

Themes and Meanings

Skillfully juxtaposing himself between two worlds, the Native American culture from which he sprang and the post-Maoist culture with which he became involved as a language teacher in China, Vizenor discovers common threads that unite the two. He does not and cannot, nevertheless, blind himself to the excesses of the Chinese government, to the cruel control of every aspect of human existence with which the government concerns itself. Opposition is squelched summarily, frequently by the execution of dissidents, and a hypocritical, puritanical bureaucracy deals with moral turpitude in equally unforgiving ways.

Griever's rooster, Matteo Ricci, serves as an alarm clock to the residents in the guest house of the language institute. Vizenor wonders, however, whether such an alarm clock is needed: The beginning of each day is heralded by blasts from loudspeakers that play the propagandistic anthem "The East Is Red," which is broadcast throughout China every morning as the sun slowly appears on the distant horizon.

Late one night in Tianjin, however, Griever steals from the guest house, climbs on a bamboo ladder to a broken window in the security-tight administration building, and patches his own tape into the recording of the song to which one-fifth of the world's population awakens every morning. In that section of Tianjin, "The East Is Red" is replaced that morning by the rousing strains of John Philip Sousa's "The Stars and Stripes Forever" and the U.S. Marine hymn.

Egas Zhang officiously storms the guest house in an attempt to find out how this atrocity has happened. Griever, having stolen back into his quarters, answers the knock on his door like any just-awakening person working methodically through his morning ablutions. The exchange between him and Egas is one of the most humorous in the book, but it also shows the trickster at work outwitting the methodical, unimaginative bureaucrat. Griever is equally skillful in retrieving his ultralight airplane from the bureaucrats at the customs office, who try to extract two thousand dollars duty from him before giving him his property.

In these encounters, Griever, as a representative of Western society, demonstrates how futile are governmental attempts to subjugate human beings. The themes of individual freedom and individual accomplishment underlie nearly every major episode in the novel.

As the narrative progresses, Griever becomes increasingly flippant and outrageous. Toward the book's end, when he is sitting on the ground viewing a propagandistic film with one of his language students, the student asks Griever if, in his country, there are vicious mosquitoes like the ones that are at the moment sucking the blood from Griever's veins. Griever replies that American mosquitoes own television sets; he then goes on to expose the student to obscenities that do not appear in the innocent boy's English-Chinese dictionary. Finally, Griever makes the student blush by asking him if there are any sex scenes in the film the two are about to see.

Some students watch the film from behind a large white sheet that is strung up for use as a projecting screen. Griever notes how those behind the screen see blurred images, reversals, more romantic impressions than the ones seen by those who look at the film from the front. This observation suggests the duality of vision of the entire novel, the two perspectives of which Griever, now on the reverse side of his usual venue, is fast becoming aware.

Griever sets intelligent wit against bureaucratic gravity, and in the conflict it is wit, in the best trickster tradition, that triumphs. "Wit" in the trickster sense becomes synonymous with individual freedom and inner personal satisfaction, things of which totalitarian regimes rob their citizenry.

Critical Context

Set in the period immediately prior to the uprising in Beijing's Tiananmen Square, *Griever* deals with China's internal political conflicts. The book reveals that the Chinese acknowledge the need for international trade that will attract Western dollars, yet the nation is mired in an oxcart society in which change, while inevitable, will not be orderly.

Here is a society in which people shoot rats for meat and for the skins to be fashioned into shoes. In sharp contrast to this sort of economy is a boom in Beijing that sees the opening of Maxim's, a restaurant where lunch will cost the equivalent of what an average worker earns in four months.

With considerable irony, Vizenor writes that people are discouraged from drinking distilled spirits when they eat dog meat because to do so is thought to cause hemorrhoids. He goes on to say, however, that this is a small price to pay for the consumption of a devoted pet. Such biting ironies are typical of this book and of Vizenor's other novels, some of which share characters from *Griever*.

It is not easy to compare Vizenor's writing to that of his contemporaries. His approach and style are unique. At times, because of his frequent temporal and geographical shifts, his writing reminds one of J. R. R. Tolkien's or of Lewis Carroll's, although Vizenor is by no means derivative. The fantasy world he constructs reminds one of these two authors, yet Vizenor's work also exudes the mysticism of Native American tradition.

Bibliography

Hochbruck, Wolfgang. "Breaking Away: The Novels of Gerald Vizenor." *World Literature Today* 66 (Spring, 1992): 274-278. Succinct but penetrating. Hochbruck has a comprehensive view of Vizenor's fiction. Shows how Vizenor bolts from literary conventions.

Lowe, John. "Monkey Kings and Mojo: Postmodern Ethnic Humor in Kingston, Reed, and Vizenor." *Melus* 21 (Winter, 1996): 103-126. Lowe attempts to correct errors in definitions of postmodernism by providing comparative readings of works by Ishmael Reed, Gerald Vizenor, and Maxine Hong Kingston. He focuses on the nature, goals, and types of humors used in the three books, as well as general and social functions of postmodern writing.

Martin, Calvin, ed. *The American Indian and the Problem of History*. New York: Oxford University Press, 1987. Demonstrates how revisionist history is at the heart of much Native American writing. Places Vizenor high among those who use history in imaginative and sometimes fanciful ways. One of the more balanced discussions of Vizenor.

Rigal-Cellard, Bernadette. "Vizenor's *Griever*: A Post-Modernist Little Red Book of Cocks, Tricksters, and Colonists." In *New Voices in Native American Literary Crit-*

icism, edited by Arnold Krupat. Washington, D.C.: Smithsonian Institution Press, 1993. This in-depth critical collection focuses on four points: "Griever, the Trickster of the In-Between"; "Socialist China As the Signifier for Mind Colonization"; "Intertextuality and the Pilgrimage Strategy"; and "The Originality of *Griever*: Language and Text."

Vizenor, Gerald. "Head Water: An Interview with Gerald Vizenor." Interview by Larry McCaffrey and Tom Marshall. *Chicago Review* 39 (1993): 50-54. In this revealing interview, Vizenor discusses *Griever* and *The Heirs of Columbus*. He explains his use of the word "survivance" and addresses the idea of the trickster or mind monkey inspired by the Monkey King opera in China.

R. Baird Shuman

GRINGOS

Author: Charles Portis (1933-   )
Type of plot: Adventure
Time of plot: The early 1990's, in the season of Christmas and the New Year
Locale: Mérida, the capital of the state of Yucatán, Mexico
First published: 1991

> *Principal characters:*
> JIMMY BURNS, a freelance teamster, tracer of lost persons, and onetime
>   dealer in illicit Mayan artifacts
> REFUGIO BAUTISTA OSORIO, Jimmy's stalwart friend and Mexican
>   counterpart, a jack-of-all-trades
> RUDY KURLE, an investigator of extraterrestrial visitations
> LOUISE KURLE, Rudy's wife and assistant, a helpful woman with a
>   degree in human dynamics
> DAN, an overage hippie and leader of a dangerous band of outcasts
> DOC RICHARD FLANDIN, a self styled expert on Mayan culture
> FRAU ALMA KOBOLD, the invalid widow of a talented but neglected
>   photographer of Mayan temples

The Novel

Gringos is, as its title suggests, a novel about expatriate Americans in Mexico. It is an adventure story, as Portis's novels sometimes are, and the account of a quest, as Portis's novels almost always are.

The protagonist and narrator is Jimmy Burns, a native of Shreveport, Louisiana, a former Marine military policeman who is both a teamster and a tracer of lost persons. Jimmy resides in a small hotel, the Posada Fausto, in Mérida, in the Yucatán peninsula. Frau Alma Kobold, the wheelchair-ridden, chain-smoking widow of an archaeological photographer, is a fellow resident for whom Jimmy often acts as errand boy. Mérida has a large community of gringos (Americans) who comprise a comic gallery of soldiers of fortune, eccentrics, and misfits.

Jimmy gets what he believes to be a routine job hauling supplies to an archaeological site. While working on his truck in preparation for the trip, he is menaced by a gang of hippies calling themselves the Jumping Jacks. They are led by an aging biker, Dan, whose two lieutenants are toughs with shaved heads and vacant eyes. Other Jumping Jacks are Beany Girl, a tall woman who horrifies Jimmy by urinating in front of everyone, and Red, a girl hardly more than a child. Jimmy later learns that Red is LaJoye Mishell Teeter of Perry, Florida, a runaway for whose return a two thousand dollar reward has been offered. Jimmy faces the hippies down with a shotgun and disables their rattletrap station wagon, but they later escape. During the encounter, Jimmy has learned that the Jumping Jacks are on a quest: They are seeking the inaccessible City of Dawn and a mystical leader known as El Mago.

On his run to the archaeological site, Jimmy meets Rudy Kurle and allows the latter to tag along with him. Jimmy stops to conduct some business with Refugio Bautista Osorio, an old friend with whom he will later team up in a search to which the middle third of the novel is devoted. Rudy is also searching for the City of Dawn, which he believes to be a landing site for visitors from outer space. He takes voluminous notes, and although he is secretive about the information he possesses, he peppers Jimmy with pseudoscientific babble about flying-saucer landings around the world. The archaeological expedition breaks up when its leader, Dr. Henry Ritchie, unexpectedly dies of a fever. Jimmy finds two of Dr. Ritchie's assistants, college students named Gail and Denise, suddenly on his hands. Rudy wanders off down the river and does not come back. At this point, the novel becomes the story of Jimmy's quest for the City of Dawn, where he believes he may find both Rudy Kurle and LaJoye Mishell Teeter.

Doc Richard Flandin has studied Mayan ruins for many years and is writing a book which, he says, will put all the posturing university professors in their place. He announces that he is dying of prostate cancer and will accompany Jimmy and Refugio on their trip downriver as a kind of defiant final gesture. Denise returns to the United States, but Gail joins the new expedition and takes up with Doc Flandin, who immediately replaces the deceased Dr. Ritchie as her affectionate tutor. Ramos, a pugnacious dog, completes the company.

Along the way, the group discovers a shriveled body floating in the river; the corpse is that of a tiny, hairy old man with huge feet. Refugio calls him a *chaneque*, a small woodland creature of mysterious origin. Others in the party think he may be a howler monkey. The expedition discovers that the City of Dawn is Likín, a hilltop ruin across the river in Guatemala, and that hippies and flying-saucer seekers have gathered there from all over North America to await the appearance of El Mago. Jimmy, Refugio, and Ramos cross the river and eventually confront Dan and his two lieutenants atop a Mayan temple in a driving rainstorm. Dan refuses to give up the girl or a Mexican boy he has kidnapped since their previous encounter. In a brief but violent scene, Jimmy shoots Dan to death, and Refugio does the same to the henchmen. Rudy then reappears, unharmed and in high spirits.

The Mexican boy is returned to his relations and LaJoye Mishell Teeter to her father. Doc Flandin no longer speaks of dying. Instead, he returns to work on his book with Gail as his assistant and confidante. Rudy carries the pygmoid corpse away in a trombone case and embarks upon a lecture tour on which he represents the *chaneque* as an unfortunate visitor from the stars. Frau Kobold is dying, and Jimmy learns that she is responsible for the debacle at the City of Dawn. She wrote an anonymous letter to a flying-saucer newsletter prophesying the appearance of El Mago at Likín, which she and her husband had visited and photographed many years earlier. Emmett, an expatriate friend, dies and bequeaths his trailer, the Mobile Star, to Jimmy. Louise Kurle reveals that she is Rudy's sister; Rudy had presented her as his wife because he wished to prevent unwanted advances by the gringos of Mérida. Louise nurses Jimmy through a siege of dengue fever, and they then get married. Finally, Eli

Withering, an old temple-robbing colleague, pays a visit. Freda, his new live-in girl-friend, turns out to be Beany Girl, much cleaned up and made up. Gallantly, Jimmy does not expose her.

The Characters

Charles Portis's protagonists are usually gentle, naïve fellows who drift artlessly through an absurd, often savage world. Since Portis's fictional world is a comic one, the characters' very innocence serves as their shield and as a comfort to the reader. Jimmy Burns, however, resembles Mattie Ross and Rooster Cogburn—the central characters in Portis's second novel, *True Grit* (1968)—far more than he does the author's other protagonists.

Jimmy is self-sufficient, competent (he can repair a clutch and perform other equally esoteric mechanical tasks), resourceful, brave, and loyal. He was a military policeman in the Marine Corps and saw combat in Korea. He is unaffected and approachable. He is extremely tolerant of others, but he does have his own code of conduct. For example, during his first encounter with the Jumping Jacks, he seems less offended by their insults and threats than by Beany Girl's act of immodest urination. There are certain things, he thinks, that no decent woman will do, and that is one of them. Of course, Jimmy has his blind spots and shortcomings. It is so difficult for him to make a commitment to a member of the opposite sex that Louise Kurle, who experiences no such difficulties, finally transfers the matter of marriage from his to her own capable hands.

Although by no means one-dimensional, the other characters—as in Portis's earlier fiction—are generally ruled by some particular obsession or eccentricity. Doc Flandin takes a perverse delight in the neglect with which the academic Mayanists treat his work and theories. Frau Kobold feeds upon her own bitterness and resentment. She and her late husband, Oskar, once appeared in a Fox Movietone Newsreel, but that was many years ago. She dislikes Doc Flandin because he considers himself a scorned outsider while, in her judgment, he lives like a king. Jimmy learns the depth of her bitterness only after her death. For many years, he has been receiving anonymous hate letters. It turns out that despite—or, perhaps, because of—his many kindnesses toward her, Frau Kobold was their author.

Rudy Kurle finds evidence of extraterrestrial visitation all around him, but he is loath to share his notes with any other investigator. His wife, Louise, is a social worker without portfolio; it is simply her nature to help people. Dan, an ex-convict, is a former member of a motorcycle gang and a white supremacist group; he represents the dangers of charisma in a time when emotion is too seldom leavened with thought. Jimmy characterizes Beany Girl and LaJoye Mishell Teeter (Red) as girls who too easily get into cars with strangers.

Refugio Bautista Osorio is the Latin personality, the explicit contrast to all the gringos of the book. He is the revered head of the family and has a fine son, Manolo, who is just approaching manhood. Refugio is a shrewd businessman who delights in haggling with Jimmy. He boasts that his name appears on many leaves of Doc Flandin's book and that he will someday be famous. He fights bravely, and lethally, at Jimmy's side in the battle against the murderous hippies. Thereafter, Refugio will date all occurrences as either before or after the time he and Jimmy killed the "pagans."

Themes and Meanings

Gringos is the story of a mission to free a silly adolescent girl from the influences of an evil, deranged man, partly for pecuniary and partly for humane reasons. The mission concludes in a bloody gun battle. *Gringos* is also a spoof of the flying-saucer mania and the New Age silliness so prevalent in America during the last decades of the twentieth century. The novel is also a perceptive, though understated, commentary on the clash between North American and Latin American cultures. Finally, it is a study, simultaneously wry and sympathetic, of a community composed of outcasts.

All the gringos in the novel have come to Mexico in search of something—wealth, fame, enlightenment, sanctuary from the law or alimony payments or some past disgrace. The quest is the motif around which all of Portis's novels are constructed.

Another consistent element in Portis's novels is their tone of tolerance and undemonstrative compassion. Following the success of *True Grit*, Portis was sometimes compared to Mark Twain because of the subject matter, the setting, and the humor of the book. The comparison is not very apt. While the angry, bitter Twain is a descendant of Juvenal and Jonathan Swift, Portis is from the line of Geoffrey Chaucer, Miguel de Cervantes, and William Shakespeare—writers who could satirize human beings and institutions, yet retain an affection for them. *Gringos* glows with affection for the flotsam and jetsam who congregate at Shep's bar in Mérida. For example, at Emmett's funeral, Harold Bolus sings "Let Me Be Your Salty Dog," a lively bluegrass number. The effect is ludicrously inappropriate, but Harold means well. He thinks, mistakenly, that the song was Emmett's favorite.

Portis's protagonists survive, and sometimes thrive, by means of their common sense, while others who pretend to greater wisdom flop about like a fish on the shore. These characters are nonintellectual, not anti-intellectual. Jimmy, who is also the narrator, never disparages the skewed learning of Doc Flandin and Rudy Kurle, even when they patronize him. He simply chooses to live according to a folk wisdom more appropriate to himself. After Rudy has given a long discourse on flying-saucer landings and their significance, Jimmy declares—to himself, not to Rudy—that he is a geocentrist. He means this spiritually rather than astronomically. He will, to use Voltaire's phrase, cultivate his garden.

It seems proper to invoke the name of Voltaire, since *Gringos* is reminiscent of *Candide* (1759) in several ways. Like the latter, the former is a rambling, episodic comic tale with a picaresque hero. Characters appear, disappear, and reappear, often in another guise. The hero winds up far from his home in Caddo Parish, Louisiana, but he has overcome adversity thanks to his resolve, his common sense, and his innate humanity.

Critical Context

Gringos, said one reviewer at the time of its publication, would be hard to categorize. Would it be found on the bookstore shelves under adventure, humor, or general fiction? *Gringos* is not the first Portis novel to resist classification. *Norwood* (1966) and *The Dog of the South* (1979) are clearly comic novels. The protagonists, Norwood Pratt and Ray Midge, are innocents. Like Don Quixote, each man inhabits a world of his own creation as he conducts his quest. *True Grit*, on the other hand, blurs the generic lines. It has been called a Western, and that designation was no doubt reinforced by the successful film adaptation starring John Wayne. Yet anyone reading *True Grit* immediately realizes that "Western" is too limited a term to describe the book. *Masters of Atlantis* (1985), Portis's fourth and quirkiest novel, has been found shelved under the heading of science fiction. Yet whatever *Masters of Atlantis* is—and that is not easy to say—it is not science fiction.

Portis is a regional writer, in the sense that his novels are either set in the South or feature Southern protagonists (like Jimmy Burns in *Gringos*). He is a master of the dialect of the Arklatex, Jimmy's native soil. His novels, however, have much more than a regional appeal. Portis is not an experimenter in fiction. He uses traditional forms, and although his plots are loosely constructed, his scenes are written with precision and economy. In *Gringos*, he once again proves that he is a major comic writer by displaying the wit, the unpretentious charm, and the affirmative qualities that have won him a loyal readership.

Bibliography

Houston, Robert. "Weirdos in a Strange Land." *The New York Times Book Review* (January 20, 1991): 7, 9. Houston praises *Gringos* as a true depiction of Mexico and its American expatriates and states that the book is driven by Portis's love for his characters and for Mexico. Even though his focus may occasionally blur and his plot wander, Portis always furnishes his reader with delight.

Jones, Malcolm, Jr. "Happy Motoring in Mexico: Charles Portis's Wonderful High-Test Hi-Jinks." *Newsweek* 17 (February 11, 1991): 60-61. Jones remarks on the literary establishment's neglect of Portis's work and the probable reasons for it. He discusses the deft alternation between aimlessness and purposefulness in the narrative. Finally, he asserts that this is the author's most inward-turning book, one in which the comedy rests upon a bedrock of melancholy.

Michaud, Charles. Review of *Gringos*, by Charles Portis. *Library Journal* 116 (January, 1991): 155. The reviewer notes, as have many others, that most of the book's characters are on some kind of quest. The author spoofs these often ridiculous quests but also portrays a world that can turn suddenly deadly. The reviewer concludes that readers who delighted in *True Grit* and *The Dog of the South* will not be disappointed in *Gringos*.

Rosenbaum, Ron. "Our Least-Known Great Novelist." *Esquire* 129 (January, 1998): 30-32. An admiring profile of Portis that discusses his stature in modern American literature, as well as some of his books. Useful as an introduction to Portis's work.

Steinberg, Sybil. Review of *Gringos*, by Charles Portis. *Publishers Weekly* 237 (October 26, 1990): 56. Steinberg concentrates primarily upon identifying the book's characters in this largely unfavorable review. She finds a tiresome sameness to Portis's uprooted Americans. Further, Steinberg argues that the story does not really go anywhere.

Wolfe, Tom. *The New Journalism.* New York: Harper & Row, 1973. In 1960, Portis joined the *New York Herald Tribune*, where he worked with Jimmy Breslin, Dick Schaap, and Wolfe, practitioners of the "new journalism." Portis eventually was named London correspondent, one of the paper's choicest assignments. Wolfe comments upon Portis's days at the newspaper in the early pages of his book.

Patrick Adcock

THE GROUP

Author: Mary McCarthy (1912-1989)
Type of plot: Social chronicle
Time of plot: 1933-1940
Locale: New York City
First published: 1963

Principal characters:
> CATHERINE LEILAND STRONG (KAY), who is married to Harald
> Petersen
> HELENA DAVISON, Kay's former roommate from Cleveland
> MARY PROTHERO (POKEY), "a fat, cheerful New York society girl"
> DOROTHY RENFREW (DOTTIE), a Bostonian descendant of Hawthorne
> ELINOR EASTLAKE (LAKEY), from Lake Forest, Chicago
> ELIZABETH MACAUSLAND (LIBBY), from Pittsfield, Massachusetts
> POLLY ANDREWS, from Stockbridge, Massachusetts
> PRISS HARTSHORN, of Oyster Bay
> NORINE SCHMITTLAP BLAKE, a classmate, not a groupmate, later
> Norine Rogers
> GUS LE ROY, an editor and Polly's lover
> JIM RIDGELEY, a psychiatrist married to Polly
> PUTNAM BLAKE, the first of Norine's two husbands
> MRS. RENFREW, a Vassar mother (class of 1908) who is understanding
> and empathetic
> MRS. DAVISON, a Vassar mother who never went to college
> MR. ANDREWS, Polly's eccentric father

The Novel

The uniqueness of Mary McCarthy's social chronicle *The Group* resides in the inherent irony of the very title of the novel. Unlike her earlier writing, fictional and nonfictional, this novel has no single character or voice through whom the intellectually severe voice of the author is heard. The main character is a composite of nine Vassar graduates of the by now famous class of 1933. Fragments of the author's own attitudes and experiences appear in each of the nine classmates, more so in some than in others, perhaps. The composite voice, then, can be heard as the voice of Vassar College, as it is the ideas instilled in the group by their professors that form a bond among them. That bond marks them as Vassar girls and makes others self-consciously outsiders.

Among the nine graduates, minor groupings exist. The original group consists of Lakey, Helena, Dottie, Pokey, Libby, and Priss. Because eight girls are needed to occupy the South Tower of Main Hall, Polly and Kay are invited by Lakey to join them. Another classmate, but not a groupmate, Norine, provides a dissonant counterpoint to the elitism of the others, and as such she is part of the composite character.

Two other groups function importantly in the novel, one as sympathetic participant in the group's elitism and the other as antagonist to the insiders. The families, especially the mothers, comprise the former; the husbands, lovers, friends, and assorted acquaintances (mostly male) constitute the latter.

The novel consists of fifteen untitled chapters, each a vividly detailed characterization of one of the women in her specific relationship to a situation, a job, a lover, or a husband. What develops in the course of each characterization is threefold: the distinctive physical, emotional, and intellectual nature of the "sister"; the strong Vassar presence in the influences of real-life professors, such as Hallie Flanagan, whose words and ideas remain with the women throughout; and the controversial nature of the times, as left-wing ideas swing adventurous minds from their conservatively Republican backgrounds to the liberally Democratic programs implemented by Franklin D. Roosevelt during the New Deal era. (In fact, Hallie Flanagan headed the Federal Theatre Project of the New Deal.) The Vassar bond not only brings the varied women together on the important occasions of their lives but also justifies the gap between their elitist, idealistic, and cloistered backgrounds and the economic and political realities of the world into which they have graduated. This world and their times are dominated by the economics of the Great Depression and the early events of World War II.

The Vassar bond is so strong that the characters remain at the end of the novel what they are at the beginning, only slightly the better or worse for having had their attitudes tried in the court of the world outside the ivied walls.

As in a musical composition, the motifs are introduced in the first chapter. Variations of these motifs are developed in chapters 2 through 14, and the coda of chapter 15 brings the women together once more for the funeral of the first woman of the group to die, just as in chapter 1 they are assembled for the first wedding. Both the wedding and the funeral are Kay's. All except Norine are present for the wedding. All except Dottie arrive for the funeral. Between these two events (1933 and 1940), McCarthy orchestrates the discordant music of the privileged and adventuresome lives of women who have the intellectual and financial freedom to forge their brave new world. Their failure to do so is most clearly symbolized by Kay, and their success in so doing is realized in the quiet way in which Polly, a hospital laboratory technician, arranges her own life satisfyingly. (Significantly, Polly is there when Kay experiences her life falling apart and needs help.) McCarthy's own criticism of those successes and failures and of her friends and times finds its explicit expression, perhaps, in the cynicism of Norine, who, although a classmate, never becomes a groupmate.

The Characters

The insularity of the members of the group is established immediately when all gather in New York for the wedding of "Kay Leiland Strong, Vassar '33, the first of her class to run around the table at the Class Day dinner," to "Harald [spelled with an "a"] Petersen, Reed '27, in the chapel of St. George's Church, P. E., Karl F. Reiland,

Rector." The girls, most of whom have grown up in the Eighties or on Park Avenue, delight in discovering for the first time various sections of the city such as Murray Hill, MacDougal Alley, Patchin Place, and the Heights section of Brooklyn. As a group, they feel adventuresome, armed with their ideas fresh from Vassar's campus. Kay, who has worked with Hallie Flanagan in dramatic production and has been changed by her course in animal behavior with "old Miss Washburn," is beginning a merchandising career at Macy's. All eight sisters are excited, yet disquieted, by some of the daringly unconventional aspects of her wedding.

In this first chapter, each groupmate is briefly introduced by her reactions to the unconventionalities. "Who would have thunk it?" "What perfect pets they look!" "Not too bad," said another, "Except for the shoes." In all of their excitement and their questioning, however, they "knew they had something to contribute to our emergent America" and were "not afraid of being radical either; they could see the good Roosevelt was doing, despite what Mother and Dad said." Even the most "conservative of them, pushed to the wall, admitted that an honest socialist was entitled to a hearing. The worst fate, they utterly agreed, would be to become like Mother and Dad, stuffy and frightened." As though to underscore this unconventionality, older persons, even Kay's parents, were absent at the wedding.

Slowly Kay is removed from center stage in the novel into the role of simply one of the nine classmates. As their varied lives cross paths, McCarthy documents with heavy detail the "progress" of each. She is ruthlessly clinical, for example, as she describes the manner in which Dottie Renfrew, Bostonian *par excellence*, decides, two nights after Kay's wedding, that the time for sexual initiation has arrived. After the event, described with near-scientific objectivity, Dottie is persuaded by her lover, Dick Brown, to arrange for a diaphragm. She does so, but, embarrassed and devastated by not being able to get in touch with him, she leaves her package under a bench in Washington Square and takes a train to Boston. McCarthy's treatment of this scenario is a mixture of the clinical and the comic: Dottie's thoughts during her initial sexual experience keep flitting affectionately to "Mother, Class of 1908," who would probably understand though she might be startled "that there had been no thought of love on either side," and the comedy is continued when Dottie consults Kay, as Dick has suggested, and both women visit the woman doctor together.

Soon Kay's marriage is observed by the group to be failing, yet Kay refuses to recognize publicly what is so obvious to others—namely, Harald's infidelity. Norine Blake and her politically active but sexually impotent husband attend a party given by Kay and Harald, and it is obvious that Norine satisfies her sexual needs with Harald. Norine eventually divorces Putnam Blake, marries a Jewish banker named Rosenberg (who has changed his name to Rogers), and has her own family. She is as concerned with "meanings" as another group member, Helena, is with "forms," as the reader discovers from the latter's visit to Norine regarding Norine's affair with Harald.

Pokey, perhaps the wealthiest of the group, marries into even greater wealth, settles in Princeton, and flies her plane to Cornell, where she enrolls in veterinary studies. She maintains elements of both her Vassar independence and her family tradition.

Similarly, Priss Hartshorn, who marries a pediatrician and breast-feeds her baby, is not quite sure that she trusts her baby to her Republican husband.

Polly Andrews seems the most balanced of the group. After a serious affair with a married man, an editor who returns to wife and family, she marries Jim Ridgeley and continues working as a laboratory technician. It is she who visits and helps Kay in a mental hospital and who takes in her own recently liberated father when he decides it is time that he and his wife separate.

The most successful careerist of the group is the cool, dispassionate, and ambitious Libby MacAusland, who becomes a literary agent and marries a novelist. The most disquieting unconventional sister, however, is Elinor Eastlake, nicknamed Lakey, who has been living in Europe. Because of the events of World War II, she returns to New York, accompanied by her lesbian lover, a German baroness. Their arrival is another occasion for the group to meet. The account of this particular reunion is cleverly inserted between Kay's funeral service at the church (the same Episcopal church in which she was married) and the cemetery rites.

Both Lakey's arrival and Kay's death, although separated in time, are related to war events. Following her divorce, Kay lives at the Vassar Club and is active in the effort to stop Adolf Hitler before he reaches American shores. As part of that effort, she has been seen leaning out the windows to spot enemy aircraft. One day she leans too far and falls to her death.

Themes and Meanings

In McCarthy's own words, *The Group* is a novel about the "history of the loss of faith in progress." If the novel's uniqueness resides in the close orchestration of nine women into one character, it is no less unique for the documentary tone by which the progressive ideas of the time are captured, especially as these contrast with the conservative backgrounds of wealth from which the women come.

The novel's documentary flavor is heavy in long passages such as those describing a first sexual experience, the implanting of the diaphragm, and theories of breast-feeding. At other times, the McCarthy intellect asserts itself in lectures on the melancholia psychosis that afflicts Polly's father and the political theories debated by two of Polly's housemates: Schneider, a Trostskyite, and Scherbatyef, a Stalinist. Although McCarthy invests her characters with ideas, they are not all her ideas, nor is any one character her clear raisonneur. Rather, it is the Vassar education that provides the women with intellectual views which they do not necessarily understand fully but which they insist on applying to their lives.

The autobiographical nature of much of the novel created a sensation in 1963. McCarthy herself was the first of her group to be married. Like Kay she married a Harold (spelled in the novel with "a") and also spent some time in psychiatric treatment. Like Lakey, she wore her hair in a black knot at the nape of her neck. Like Norine, she has expressed lack of faith in progress. Scholars have identified at least four of the group members as real-life graduates of 1933, as well as recognizable composites of other friends and acquaintances of McCarthy.

Critical Context

Published thirty years after the class of 1933 had been graduated from Vassar, the novel was timely in its objective and intellectually honest discussion of women's issues and problems approached from a feminist point of view. The ideas were not as shocking in 1963 as they would have been to a reader of the 1930's. What caught her 1960's reading public by surprise was the descent to self-indulgent gossip, particularly in the views of members of the Vassar community who were able to identify specific persons and situations from real life. Indeed, in an appearance at Vassar College in the fall of 1985, McCarthy described *The Group* as her least favorite and most embarrassing book.

A versatile writer, McCarthy is a keen observer and intellectual analyst of the people she has known and of the nature of her times. As drama critic for *Partisan Review* and as a general essayist, she has cast a cold and critical eye on the theater, books, writers, and world events. *Mary McCarthy's Theatre Chronicles 1937-1962* (1963) is a collection of reviews, and *The Company She Keeps* (1942) is an edition of character studies reminiscent of a literary genre popular in the seventeenth and eighteenth centuries. In the latter volume, she develops generic characters who take on formulaic stature as she describes the physical qualities, the profession or position in life that each character holds, and the distinctive behavioral patterns of each.

From these essays it is a short step to the novels, which at times seem to consist of character essays unified by sociological backgrounds and events of a particular time or class. A Utopian colony of intellectuals inhabit *The Oasis* (1949), a philosophical tale. *The Groves of Academe* (1952) is about another group of intellectuals in a fictitious college, with evocations of Bard and Sarah Lawrence, colleges at which McCarthy had taught. In *A Charmed Life* (1955), New Leeds is yet another Utopian community (in New England). Social criticism, satire, and irony are dominant tones in her work.

Bibliography

Auchincloss, Louis. *Pioneers and Caretakers: A Study of Nine American Novelists*. Minneapolis: University of Minnesota Press, 1961. Auchincloss regards McCarthy the novelist as a caretaker of American culture. Covers McCarthy's transition from novellas ("a perfect medium for [her]") to longer works such as *The Oasis*. Considers *The Groves of Academe* the apex of her satirical art. A valuable guide to McCarthy.

Brightman, Carol. *Writing Dangerously: Mary McCarthy and Her World*. New York: Clarkson Potter, 1992. Supplements but does not supersede Carol W. Gelderman's earlier biography. Like Gelderman, Brightman was able to interview her subject, and her book reflects not only inside knowledge but (as its subtitle suggests) also a strong grasp of the period in which McCarthy published. Includes a biographical glossary and notes.

Gelderman, Carol W. *Mary McCarthy: A Life*. New York: St. Martin's Press, 1988. Probably the most thorough study available on McCarthy and a must for scholars of her work as well as fans of good biography. Essentially a biography, but includes much valuable criticism of her novels and extracts from her letters and other writings. The material is arranged chronologically and is well organized. No bibliography, but includes extensive notes.

Grumbach, Doris. *The Company She Kept*. New York: Coward, McCann, 1967. A full-length study of McCarthy with special emphasis on her Catholic upbringing. In a personal and accessible style, Grumbach skillfully interweaves biography with criticism of McCarthy's novels, stressing her profoundly feminine approach. Follows McCarthy's development as a writer, including her involvement with the *Partisan Review* circle in the late 1930's, her time in Europe, the elusiveness of critical acclaim for her work, and the popular success of *The Group*.

Stock, Irvin. *Mary McCarthy*. Minneapolis: University of Minnesota Press, 1968. A pamphlet that offers accessible, readable criticism with insight into McCarthy's motives as a writer. Takes the point of view that McCarthy's work is loyal to the life that she lived—that the mind's accomplishments are worth little in the face of life's difficulties. Includes discussion of McCarthy's nonfiction as well as her novels, in particular her controversial piece *Vietnam*. Selected bibliography.

Susan Rusinko

THE GROVES OF ACADEME

Author: Mary McCarthy (1912-1989)
Type of plot: Social satire
Time of plot: The early 1950's
Locale: Jocelyn College, Jocelyn, Pennsylvania
First published: 1952

> *Principal characters:*
> HENRY MULCAHY, a literature instructor at Jocelyn College
> DOMNA REJNEV, a young colleague of Russian background
> MAYNARD HOAR, the college president
> JOHN BENTKOOP, a colleague who supports Mulcahy
> ALMA FORTUNE, a colleague who organizes things
> ARISTIDE PONCY, a member of the French department
> HOWARD FURNESS, the department chairman, who does not trust
> Mulcahy

The Novel

In *The Groves of Academe,* Mary McCarthy presents a typical academic novel in that the events that dominate and determine the lives of the characters gain their importance from their roles in a specific academic culture. In the very first paragraph, literature instructor Henry Mulcahy receives notice that his contract at the fictitious Jocelyn College will not be renewed. The entire plot revolves around his reaction to this termination, ending in revenge when Mulcahy's contract is renewed and the president who tried to fire him is forced to resign.

Mulcahy's methods define academic politics through which people try to win at any cost, with no concern for the truth that an academic institution is supposed to uphold. Mulcahy immediately circulates two lies that are calculated to put pressure on Maynard Hoar to rehire him. He claims that at one time he was a member of the Communist Party, and he claims that his wife Catherine is suffering from a vaguely defined medical problem, which would mean that the pressure of his job change might kill her.

The direct confrontation between the literature professor and the college president draws on the situation that would have prevailed in a small liberal arts college in the early 1950's. This was a situation Mary McCarthy would have experienced firsthand while teaching at Bard College and later at Sarah Lawrence. Before the American Association of University Professors encouraged the establishment of procedures for granting tenure, college presidents had a free hand in governing faculties. Thus, Maynard Hoar can dictate the fate of Henry Mulcahy, and the only way to get him to change his verdict is through internal, psychological pressure.

While the novel shifts among the points of view of various characters, it presents a unified judgment of human nature as it appears in faculty circles. Mulcahy's initial reaction to the firing involves a great deal of self deception, as he convinces himself that Hoar is actually the one at fault. His analysis of other people rests on a set of skewed values; within his circle, only certain schools, experiences, and lifestyles give a person credibility.

The other faculty members share these feelings, which can become simultaneously sources of solidarity and of mutual distrust. When a group gathers to discuss Mulcahy's case, they all feel good about joining his cause. Individual paranoia separates them, however, and they end up spying on one another.

The basis of all judgments involves trivial academic matters, but even these things, when subjected to the scrutiny of campus gossip, are interpreted as statements of academic loyalties. The plot turns not so much on events as on rumors and suppositions. Still, finally, there is a need for action. The faculty group, having taken the case quite out of the hands of Mulcahy, decides that Domna Rejnev and John Bentkoop should make an appeal to Maynard Hoar.

The scene of the two faculty members in the president's office reflects all the hierarchy of academic power. They have had to wait ten days for an appointment only to be seen during a holiday, while others are away. Though they feel they have made a positive appeal, Hoar has clearly manipulated them.

A crucial revelation occurs when Domna Rejnev goes to dinner at Mulcahy's house and learns from his tipsy wife that he has lied. Further revelations come out when a communist poet appears at the departmental poetry conference. At this point, however, Mulcahy's lies have so confused the situation that the president, who has already renewed Mulcahy's appointment, feels he must resign. In the last pages of the novel, Mulcahy, by now feeling quite justified in his own moral superiority, bursts into Hoar's office to accuse him of having investigated Mulcahy's political affiliations by talking with the communist poet. To Hoar, who had made a reputation by standing up for the political freedom of faculty members, exposure would be worse than the loss of his job.

The Characters

In a sense, all of the characters in *The Groves of Academe* are rigidly set in their ways and see themselves as loyal to certain principles. All are in turn flexible, however, as they react to external events and reinterpret principles to suit the occasion.

Henry Mulcahy can launch a pattern of lies when he becomes desperate. He has already accepted his job at Jocelyn as a last resort and has no other prospects for supporting his family. Thus he convinces himself that all methods are justified in striking out against a system that will not reward him or his work.

Domna Rejnev is the most developed character in the work and the most changing, in that her one constant seems to be vacillation. When facing difficulties, she asks herself, "What would Tolstoy say?" and tries to live according to precepts from her literary heroes. Her Russian background makes her especially sensitive to the issues of communism and of any form of political persecution. Mulcahy turns to her first, therefore, as the colleague most likely to sympathize with his position.

Several characters are presented from single perspectives that maximize comic effects. Henry's wife Catherine seems constantly overwhelmed by her responsibilities, whether with Henry as chaperone of a student dance or at home surrounded by their four messy and demanding young children. She usually fills these roles with good humor and supportiveness for her husband. Thus, when she drinks too much and lets Domna know she is not really sick, she makes her influence felt for the first time.

Similarly, the college president, Maynard Hoar, remains straitlaced while running the school and adhering to the liberal views he feels appropriate as part of his position. Only in the last pages of the novel does his control slip, and then what emerges is not a fallible humanity, as in the case of Catherine Mulcahy, but a chink in his armor with which he can no longer survive.

Within Mulcahy's department, Howard Furness and Alma Fortune represent the dangers of relying on academic colleagues for any sort of specific help. Howard Furness, the chairman, exhibits loyalties divided between the faculty and the president. He does not trust Mulcahy because he does not want Mulcahy to make him look bad. Alma Fortune becomes equally unreliable in her need for action. She organizes the group of colleagues who meet to discuss Mulcahy's plight, but outraged at the situation, she abruptly resigns, thus sacrificing whatever further influence she would have had.

Colleagues from other departments also participate in roles defined by their fields. John Bentkoop from the department of comparative religions joins Mulcahy's defense with dogmatic persistence, while Aristide Poncy of the department of French sympathizes but, true to his role as a world traveler, manages to be out of town when it is time to talk to the president. Characters narrowly defined by their professional fields do manage to create activity when events stir up their special interests.

Themes and Meanings

The central message of *The Groves of Academe* lies in the revelation of how far college faculties deviate from the truth when it serves their purposes. Mary McCarthy takes her title from a line from Horace, "to search for truth in the groves of Academus," but her characters not only abandon truth for personal ends but also are engaged in a profession that seems intent on compromising it even as an ideal.

Jocelyn is portrayed as a model of the "progressive" college where as much care is taken of students' emotions as of their intellect. The student who first hears of Mulcahy's problem, Sheila McKay, illustrates a group with little interest in learning but great devotion to faculty gossip. Except for a few scholarship students admitted to keep some pretense of academic quality, most of the students owe their admissions to their parents' bank accounts.

If the students are neither eager nor particularly able to learn, a certain cynicism on the part of the faculty becomes inevitable. They are shown collectively as a group who would rather be elsewhere, preferably Europe or New York. If the learning at Jocelyn has no great significance, the faculty readily define it not in terms of ideas but in the minute structuring of project formats and reading periods. Form overcomes substance.

As ideas may be judged by their form, people may be by their appearances. A form of shabby international chic pervades the campus, and a character's credibility can be undermined by too close an association with, for example, Mulcahy's messy children or Maynard Hoar's contrastingly fussy household. Truth depends on its packaging.

Critical Context

At the same time *The Groves of Academe* appeared, higher education was a center of opposition to Senator Joseph McCarthy's pursuit of communists in positions of power. Maynard Hoar is described as having authored a pamphlet, "The Witch Hunt in Our Universities," which he clearly composed to establish appropriate credentials as a college president, but the title of which aptly evokes the atmosphere of the day.

Domna Rejnev may be an extreme case, but she is not alone in her concern for political persecution. In reaction to government inquiry, college professors banded together in an automatic reaction against any investigation of an individual's personal background, a reaction that, in effect, made it impossible to hold anything against anyone.

The communist poet who appears at the poetry conference that ends the novel continues the general evasion of truth through his use of two names. To maintain anonymity at meetings of the Party, he had been "John Marshall," but he now appears as "Vincent Keogh." Having adopted poetry as his profession, he is, like the faculty, in a field where eccentricity is the norm.

He has nothing to hide, but neither does he have any concern for moral principles or the fates of people around him. When the president asks him what he knows about Mulcahy's alleged communist connections, Keogh's reaction is cavalier. An outsider in the college, he sees events there as having no importance.

For insiders on the faculty, however, perception is all. If the government is seen as wrongly pursuing communists, one must be seen as defending the academy, even if one would rather be elsewhere. Truth, in any case, is only of secondary importance.

Bibliography

Gelderman, Carol. *Mary McCarthy: A Life*. New York: St. Martin's Press, 1988. A chronologically arranged biography. Chapter 11 discusses Mary McCarthy's formative experiences on college faculties. Chapter 13 traces influences in *The Groves of Academe*, setting the novel in the context of the anticommunist investigations of Senator Joseph McCarthy.

Hardy, Willene Schaefer. *Mary McCarthy*. New York: Frederick Ungar, 1981. Chapter 6 analyzes *The Groves of Academe* in detail, with examples of the symbolic value of how characters are portrayed. A generous plot summary follows the machinations and psychological relationships of the characters. The volume contains a chronology of Mary McCarthy's life and bibliography.

McKenzie, Barbara. *Mary McCarthy*. New York: Twayne, 1966. A biography in the Twayne's United States Authors Series, with bibliography. The latter part of chapter 5 situates the novel and summarizes its plot.

Stock, Irvin. *Mary McCarthy*. Minneapolis: University of Minnesota Press, 1968. A
brief biography with bibliography. Pages 24 to 29 focus on *The Groves of Academe*.

Twenty-Four Ways of Looking at Mary McCarthy: The Writer and Her Work, edited
by Eve Stwertka and Margo Viscusi. Westport, Connecticut: Greenwood Press,
1996. A gathering of papers from a conference held in 1993, with references to the
novel throughout. In chapter 10, Timothy F. Waples examines "Political Dilemma
in *The Groves of Academe*."

Dorothy M. Betz

HAWAII

Author: James A. Michener (1907?-1997)
Type of plot: Historical chronicle
Time of plot: 814-1954
Locale: Bora Bora, Hawaii, the United States, the Pacific Ocean, Tahiti, Fiji, Borneo, China, Japan, France, and Italy
First published: 1959

Principal characters:

The Hawaiians
TAMATOA VI, the king of the group of Bora Borans who emigrate to Hawaii
TERERO, his brother
MARAMA, Terero's wife
KEOKI KANAKOA, a Christian trained in the United States, the son of Malama and Kelolo Kanakoa
MALAMA KANAKOA, the ruler of Maui when the missionaries arrive
KELOLO KANAKOA, the brother and husband of Malama
NOELANI KANAKOA, the daughter of Malama and Kelolo; as the future ruler, she marries her brother Keoki and later marries Rafer Hoxworth
KELLY KANAKOA, a descendant of Malama and Kelolo, a beach boy, surfing instructor, and nightclub singer

New Englanders
ABNER HALE, the leader of the group of the first missionaries
JERUSHA BROMLEY HALE, the wife of Abner Hale and a missionary
RAFER HOXWORTH, a sea captain in love with and engaged to Jerusha Bromley before she marries Abner Hale
WHIPPLE HOXWORTH, the grandson of Rafer Hoxworth, known as "Wild Whip"
JOHN WHIPPLE, a doctor and missionary who leaves the church to go into partnership with Retire Janders
MICAH HALE, the son of Abner and Jerusha Hale, who marries Malama Hoxworth, the daughter of Rafer and Noelani Hoxworth

The Chinese
CHAR NYUK TSIN, a matriarch who lives to the age of 106 and founds a dynasty of Chinese businessmen and politicians
KEE MUN KI, Char Nyuk Tsin's husband, who becomes a leper
AFRICA KEE, their son, who becomes a lawyer
HONG KONG KEE, their grandson and one of the "Golden Men"

The Japanese

KAMEJIRO SAKAGAWA, a plantation laborer and later a night-soil
    collector and barbershop owner, who emigrates from Japan
OSHII, a fanatical supporter of the Japanese Empire, who marries
    Kamejiro Sakagawa's daughter, Reiko
GORO SAKAGAWA, Kamejiro Sakagawa's son, a World War II veteran
    and labor organizer
SHIGEO SAKAGAWA, Goro's brother, a World War II veteran, lawyer,
    and politician

The Novel

Hawaii is a multifaceted historical novel with a span of action that moves from 814
and the first immigration of the Bora Borans to the islands through 1954 and the emergence of contemporary Hawaii, soon to become a state. Following a prologue describing the formation of Pacific islands, reefs, and atolls, Michener devotes a section of
the novel to each of the major groups who settled Hawaii.

While it is generally believed that Hawaii was first settled by emigrants from the
other Polynesian islands, Michener's precise details are invented. Tamatoa VI and his
brother Terero are forced to flee Bora Bora by another group who worship a savage
god, Oro, who demands human sacrifices. As his wife, Marama, is thought unable to
bear children, Terero is forced to leave her behind and take a younger wife. Guided
only by the stars and by old songs and legends—"Then we are sailing with a dream for
our guide?" asks Tamatoa—they undergo both adventure and hardship before at last
reaching Hawaii. Though they have abandoned the god Oro, Tamatoa insists upon one
human sacrifice as they build a shrine to Tane. This god is not sufficient protection,
and when the volcano erupts, they are forced to relocate. Terero then sails back to
Bora Bora with a small group of men for the first fire goddess Pele. Terero not only
brings back her stone, but he also brings Marama, who has conceived a child on their
last night together. Through his detailed account of the beliefs of the islanders and
how they influence every detail of their lives, Michener sets the stage for the next section, "From the Farm of Bitterness."

A thousand years have passed, and to Yale College comes Keoki Kanakoa, a descendant of the original settlers of Hawaii. A convert to Christianity, he so eloquently
describes the souls in Hawaii waiting to be saved that Abner Hale and his friend John
Whipple are moved to offer themselves as missionaries. Whipple is accepted immediately: He is a doctor as well as a divinity student, and a handsome, self-possessed
man. Hale is another matter. The Reverend Eliphalet Thorn sees him as "an offensive,
undernourished, sallow-faced little prig, the kind who wrecks any mission to which he
is attached." He has a niece, however, Jerusha Bromley, who has been pining after a
sea captain who promised to return to marry her. Thorn arranges a match between her
and Hale. To Hale's astonishment, she is a beautiful girl, intensely religious, who has
vowed herself to the mission field if her sea captain does not return. Since all the missionaries are required to be married, the brig *Thetis* sets sail with eleven newlywed

couples, four couples to each cabin. Hale, the only one who is not seasick for many weeks, is forced to assume leadership of the group and proves himself to be surprisingly resourceful, resilient, and sympathetic in caring for the sick. He also takes time to study Hawaiian with Keoki. Hale's inflexibility, however, is evident in his manner of preaching to the captain and crew. They encounter another ship in mid-ocean, commanded by Rafer Hoxworth, a young and handsome but rough and brawling man. It is he who is expecting to find Jerusha waiting for him, and, when he discovers that Jerusha is not only married but pregnant, he attacks Hale, leaving him with a permanent limp.

Arriving in Hawaii, the missionaries encounter Malama Kanakoa, the ruler, or Alii Nui, of the island. To his horror, Hale finds that she is married to her brother, and that Keoki Kanakoa is their son. Though he works to convert the islanders, Hale forbids all intimate contact with the "heathen." He is not the only one of the missionaries who is outraged when Abraham Hewlett marries a Hawaiian woman. His first wife died in childbirth; Hale and Hewlett delivered the child themselves, following a medical textbook, rather than accept the aid of the Hawaiian midwives. Hewlett is expelled from the mission; Whipple resigns. Both go into business, Whipple as the partner of Retire Janders, former captain of the *Thetis* and now proprietor of a business on Maui.

Malama is converted, and agrees to new laws for the islands, including forbidding the island girls to swim out to the ships and offer themselves to the sailors. Hale refuses to ordain Keoki Kanakoa as a minister, however, and Keoki, disillusioned, returns to the old gods and marries his sister Noelani. Hale is outraged, even more so when Noelani bears twins. The boy is perfect, but the girl is deformed and not allowed to live. Keoki, unable to live with his religious conflict, refuses any medical aid during a measles epidemic and dies.

Jerusha, who has succeeded in softening some of Hale's inflexible religious views, dies, leaving him with four children. The eldest, Micah, is the most promising and is sent to Yale. Coming back to Hawaii, he travels overland, arriving in San Francisco with a sense of Manifest Destiny and a conviction that Hawaii must become a state. There he encounters Rafer Hoxworth, who has married Noelani. Before the voyage is out, Micah has married their daughter, Malama, and thereafter Hale will have nothing to do with him. Micah leaves the ministry and goes into business with Hoxworth, who settles in Honolulu. So begin the interwoven dynasties of mission families and Hawaiian rulers.

"From the Starving Village" comes Char Nyuk Tsin, escaping the conflict between Punti and Hakka, the hill people, to whom she belongs. Their women are looked down upon because their feet are unbound. She is purchased from a brothel by Kee Mun Ki, a gambler whose uncle has been to the United States and is John Whipple's go-between in arranging for the importation of Chinese labor for the sugar fields. On the voyage, Kee Mun Ki learns to appreciate Char Nyuk Tsin. He marries her, but his "true" wife is the village girl he has married in China. All the Chinese were forced to marry before they left: They were then obligated to send money back to China for the rest of their lives.

Though she bears him five sons, Char Nyuk Tsin is never called by her name, for she is not the official wife. The Kees go to work for the Whipples, and they prosper by a combination of intelligence and hard work, until Kee Mun Ki contracts leprosy. Char Nyuk Tsin goes with him as a *kokua*, a nonleper who voluntarily undergoes the rigors of the leper island, Molokai. There is nothing—no hospital, not even any houses, no food, and no law. Even here the Chinese are ostracized, for it is mistakenly believed that they brought leprosy to Hawaii. After Kee Mun Ki kills the bully who is dominating the colony, because he tries to rape Char Nyuk Tsin, they are respected, and law and order are established. When her husband dies, Char Nyuk Tsin, who has not contracted the disease, is allowed to leave.

She manages to go back to the plot of land that Whipple has given her, and to find her fifth son, whom she sent from the leper colony as soon as he was born. Through incredible work and remarkable intelligence and drive, she manages to educate one son, Africa, who in turn helps the rest of the family. The boys, all named for continents, gradually become established in business, with the aid of Africa, a rising lawyer. Surviving even the bubonic plague and the subsequent burning of Chinatown to prevent the spread of contagion, Char Nyuk Tsin builds a powerful *hui* (the Chinese term for a combination of interlocking family and business interests).

The Japanese laborers are represented by Kamejiro Sakagawa and his friend Oshii. The latter is a fanatical supporter of the Japanese Empire and is representative of the reason that Hawaiians resisted the ascendancy of the Japanese. The Chinese assimilated, though they retained family and financial ties to China; the Japanese supported a government that, it was feared, might eventually take over Hawaii, and this fear was one reason for the push for territorial status and statehood. Nevertheless, Japanese Americans were not treated as harshly after Pearl Harbor as those on the mainland, and many, including Sakagawa's four sons, enlisted in the army in World War II. Two were killed, one at Monte Cassino. Goro Sakagawa returned to become a labor organizer; his brother Shigeo managed an education in the United States and became a lawyer, eventually being elected to the Hawaiian legislature.

Woven through the sections on the Chinese and Japanese is the account of the rise of the great commercial empire dominated by the descendants of the missionaries, notably Hoxworth Hale, Micah Hale's son. The coalition, known as "The Fort," maintains control over the islands' political as well as economic life by gradually admitting powerful outsiders such as Hong Kong Kee to the circle.

The decline of the Hawaiians is shown in the deposition of Queen Lilioukalani. The annexation ceremony is a proud moment for Micah Hale, who has worked all of his life for statehood. For his wife, it is a day of mourning, though she maintains her dignity until she sees the Hawaiian flag ripped up by the crowd for souvenirs, and then she hides her face and weeps. The last Hawaiian shown in depth is Kelly Kanakoa, descendant of Malama and Kelolo, who has become a beach boy, surfing instructor, and nightclub singer.

The Characters

Of the sprawling and complex cast of characters, Abner and Jerusha Hale, Malama and Keoki Kanakoa, Char Nyuk Tsin, and Kamejiro and Shigeo Sakagawa are perhaps the best drawn. As the novel progresses, the characters, particularly those of the dominant political and business group of the missionaries' descendants who tend to have the same family names in various combinations, become sketchy and blurred, necessitating referral to the eight pages of genealogical charts that are provided in an appendix.

Abner Hale is perhaps the most complex individual. In many respects narrow, prejudiced, and unprepossessing, he can at the same time be tender, compassionate, and courageous. Though he is beaten physically, he does not avoid confrontations in defense of his convictions. Developing from a callow and bigoted youth to a young man of moral and physical courage, he wins the honest respect and love of Jerusha. Malama Kanakoa, a majestic woman, well over six feet tall and weighing more than three hundred pounds, is literally as well as figuratively larger than life. Though she wavers between Christianity and the old gods, she accepts many of Hale's teachings and the laws that he proposes, convinced that though accepting them will be at a personal cost to herself, it is best for the welfare of her subjects. Keoki Kanakoa, acclaimed and respected when he recruits missionaries, is deeply distressed to be rejected as a full-fledged minister when the missionaries arrive in Hawaii. Until then, he has been able to reconcile his old faith with his new one. His reversion to the old religion and marriage with his sister is as much an act of desperation as of faith, and he welcomes his early death.

By an irony of history, or a deliberate representation by Michener, or perhaps a bit of both, the Chinese and Japanese immigrants who prosper apply the missionary virtues of hard work, thrift, and good character, not unmixed with shrewd practicality, to enter the world dominated by the missionaries' descendants. Even though Char Nyuk is a woman of unprepossessing appearance, by considerable acuity and determination she survives and prospers, even in the leper colony. Though she has a fair amount of luck, she is not a superwoman, and her rise to eminence is logical. This is not true of many of the other characters, especially "Wild Whip" Hoxworth, a megaversion of the nineteenth century capitalists and entrepreneurs. With an equally avid interest in collecting beautiful women and exotic plants, he imports and establishes pineapple, soon to be the second leading industry of the islands. Kamejiro Sakagawa, though he thinks of himself always as an uprooted Japanese, loyal to the emperor, paradoxically labors all of his life to provide all the advantages of America for his children. Yet on the eve of Pearl Harbor, he still stubbornly refuses to take his children off the list of Japanese citizens. His son Shigeo, constantly in conflict with his father but Japanese enough to respect and obey him, wants desperately to become an American. Through athletic scholarships, the Sakagawas manage to acquire a good education and, in World War II, establish their loyalty as they engage in some of the grimmest battles that occurred during the war.

Michener, though, is at his best characterizing events and groups of peoples. The epic voyage to Hawaii with which the novel opens contains much striking description and, more important, by involving the reader so vividly, conveys a sense of what it must have been like to sail such seas and worship such gods. Counterpointed to the early voyage is the missionaries' voyage a thousand years later, with the climactic attempt to round Cape Horn, and the similar final resort to a combination of faith and seamanship gambled on one decision that will either succeed or prove fatal to all concerned. As vividly done are the scenes of the leper colony, the plague and fire in Chinatown, and above all the account of the Sakagawa brothers during the battle of Monte Cassino, where Michener's war and reporting experience are utilized to their fullest.

Themes and Meanings

Hawaii's main theme is the development of the present-day Hawaiian, the "Golden Men" of the final section: Kelly Kanakoa, Hong Kong Kee, who is one of Char Nyuk Tsin's descendants, Shigeo Sakagawa, and Hoxworth Hale. The latter, both as a representative of the best in the blend of peoples that is Hawaii (he is descended from both missionaries and the Kanakoas) and as the teller of this lengthy tale, is not quite credible, nor is he revealed as the narrator until the final pages. As a ruthlessly reactionary capitalist in many episodes, Hoxworth Hale scarcely seems to have the insight shown in the treatment of labor unrest, the hardships and injustices borne by the immigrants and Hawaiians; nor does he seem likely to have had firsthand accounts of life in early China and Japan. When he travels to other Pacific islands, he points out the ways in which things had been done better in Hawaii, but does not acknowledge anything that had been a mistake.

Almost of equal importance for Michener to the development of the Hawaiian character is the use that people make of the land, though the emphasis is upon growth and development. The first settlers introduced new plants and animals, and subsequent immigrants brought new ideas, new ways of growing or producing goods. The missionaries are appalled at the stripping of sandalwood from the islands, and Abner Hale encourages Malama to stop these practices. Linked to the theme of land use and development is that of thrift, hard work, and willingness to take risks to achieve a goal, traits brought to the islands by the missionaries and reinforced by the Chinese. The Hawaiians' contribution, and a crucial one, is the attitude of *aloha*, a good-natured tolerance of other people, a fondness for children, and a zest for living. These traits enable the more convention- and tradition-conscious Americans, Chinese, Japanese, Filipinos, and many others to intermarry, exchange cultural ideas, and eventually cooperate in business ventures. Michener had planned a section on emigrants from the Philippine Islands, the only major ethnic group not dealt with in the novel, but he abandoned it after he realized that it would make the length of the novel, already more than nine hundred pages, prohibitive.

Critical Context

Michener did not begin writing fiction until he was in his forties. *Tales of the South Pacific* (1947), his first published fiction, was awarded the 1948 Pulitzer Prize in fiction. Michener continued to write fiction about the Pacific for the next twelve years, as well as studies of Japanese art. *Hawaii* is the culmination of his works with a Pacific setting, and it also set the pattern for a subsequent series of novels with a similar scope, theme, and structure, such as *Caravans* (1963), *The Source* (1965), *Centennial* (1974), *Chesapeake* (1978), *The Covenant* (1980), *Space* (1982), *Poland* (1983), and *Texas* (1985).

Hawaii is indeed a historical novel, not a factual record lightly garbed in fiction. Though Michener, with the aid of Clarice B. Taylor, spent a year in research before beginning to write the novel, the reader should be aware that he invents most of his characters and sometimes takes considerable liberties with the facts. Possibly the most flagrant of these liberties is the election with its sweeping victory for the Democrats. In the novel, it takes place in 1954; the actual Democratic landslide did not occur until 1962. Michener, himself an unsuccessful Democratic candidate for a seat in the Pennsylvania House of Representatives in 1962, commented that it was an example of the prescience a writer should have about events. Nevertheless, invented characters and events, including an entire contemporary political structure, work better when set in the distant past rather than in a time that is within recent memory.

The Pulitzer Prize notwithstanding, Michener is not generally regarded as a literary figure of major stature. A. Grove Day, who collaborated with Michener on *Rascals in Paradise* (1957), observes in his critical study of Michener that he is a novelist in the tradition of muckrakers, combining reportorial skills with social conscience. It is this combination that gives his novels, whatever their flaws, a solidity and substance not usually found in lighter popular fiction.

Bibliography
Day, A. Grove. *James Michener.* New York: Twayne, 1964. Day provides a critical and interpretive study of Michener's earlier works with a close reading of his major novels, a solid bibliography and complete notes and references.
Groseclose, David A. *James A. Michener: A Bibliography.* Austin, Tex.: State House Press, 1996. An annotated bibliography of works by and about James Michener from 1923 to 1995. Groseclose has assembled more than 2,500 descriptive entries on all aspects of Michener's life and career.
Hayes, John P. *James A. Michener: A Biography.* Indianapolis: Bobbs-Merrill, 1984. A biography spanning Michener's life through the 1980's. Valuable for background on influences in Michener's development as a writer.
Michener, James. *Literary Reflections: Michener on Michener, Hemingway, Capote, and Others.* Austin, Tex.: State House Press, 1993. Michener reflects on his life as a writer and on his work. He also shares his memories of his era's most influential writers. The collection of essays gives important insights into Michener's views on literature and into his evaluations of his own works.
Roberts, F. X., and C. D. Rhine, comps. *James A. Michener: A Checklist of His Works, With a Selected, Annotated Bibliography.* Westport, Conn.: Greenwood Press,

1995. A comprehensive bibliography of Michener's books and stories and of articles by and about him.

Severson, Marilyn S. *James A. Michener: A Critical Companion.* Westport, Conn.: Greenwood Press, 1996. Severson give an overview of Michener's life and examines the characteristics and themes of his fiction. His major historical novels are discussed and analyzed for plot, structure, and theme.

Shahin, Jim. "The Continuing Saga of James A. Michener." *Saturday Evening Post* 262 (March, 1990): 66-71. An overview of Michener's life and career. A discussion of Michener's research methods and his approach to composition of his historical novels is also presented.

Katharine M. Morsberger

HE WHO SEARCHES

Author: Luisa Valenzuela (1938-   )
Type of plot: Social morality
Time of plot: The 1970's
Locale: Barcelona, Spain; Mexico; and Argentina
First published: Como en la guerra, 1977 (English translation, 1979)

> *Principal characters:*
> PEPE (AZ), whose name is "not determined out of indifference," a
>   psychoanalyst and semiotics professor at the University of
>   Barcelona
> SHE, his patient, an Argentine political exile who works as a cocktail
>   waitress and prostitute and is never named
> SISTER (SHE-SHE), the unnamed sister of the cocktail waitress, a
>   guerrilla leader
> BEATRIZ, the wife of Pepe
> ALFREDO NAVONI, a former lover of the waitress, who is a guerrilla
>   who went underground and forgot her

The Novel

He Who Searches opens with a brief scene in which a man is interrogated and raped with the butt of a gun. This scene ends abruptly, and the novel's first part, entitled "Discovery," begins. The psychoanalyst describes his patient, and the narrative introduces his unusual method of treatment, which includes appearing at her house in various disguises, from postman to transvestite, and having a sexual relationship with her. Their relationship embraces a variety of fantasies, including one in which he is an insurance man. Valenzuela ironically includes in this section questions such as "Against what can she be trying to protect herself?" The reader knows that there is no insurance for a revolutionary in exile. Eventually, the psychoanalyst's wife discovers the affair that her husband is having with his patient.

In the second part, "The Loss," the psychoanalyst spends time with his wife but longs for his patient, who has disappeared. While reading a story in the newspaper about a banderillero in a barroom brawl, he recognizes his patient in an accompanying photograph. He believes that "a trickle of blood" will lead him to her.

In the third part, "The Journey," the psychoanalyst arrives in Mexico, where he participates in a purification ritual and is guided by Nahuatl-speaking Indian women through the mountains. He meets a woman named Maria Sabina, who gives him sacred mushrooms. This passage recalls the Cave of Montesinos, in which Don Quixote experiences self-revelation through an encounter with the heroes of chivalric novels. The narrator explains that the jungle in Mexico is also the jungle in Argentina.

The psychoanalyst experiences the sensation of living the life that his patient has hidden from him, including the words of her former lover, Alfredo Navoni. Here, the psychoanalyst's character merges with hers. He witnesses an all-night vigil for a dead guerrilla. The guerrillas tell him a story in which there is a bizarre ritual of cannibalism, in which a character named Fatty, who likes things from India, is eaten. In the fourth and final part, the psychoanalyst finds himself in the midst of a political uprising in Argentina. When asked why he is there, he explains that he is searching for a woman and for himself, his feminine counterpart. He proceeds past barriers into the fighting. The fighting takes place in a large park. A revolutionary woman gives him an assignment, to place charges. After he plants dynamite in holes in a box of cement, there is an enormous explosion, and he has a vision of his lover in a coffin that shines like a diamond. At this point, the story ends. It is possible, however, that the very first scene in the novel involves the psychoanalyst sometime after he has planted the dynamite, and that he is being interrogated concerning the whereabouts of his patient.

The Characters

Valenzuela's characters both are split and merge into one another: The semiotician refers to himself as "we"; the patient he studies has a twin sister and dreams her lover Alfredo Navoni's dreams as if they were her own. When Pepe travels in the mountains through Mexico, he has access to the knowledge of his patient. His consciousness is no longer distinguishable from hers, even though she is absent.

Pepe, the main character, calls himself a "humble professor of semiotics." He justifies his bizarre behavior to himself and to his jealous wife by claiming that he is merely engaging in a psychoanalytic investigation of his patient. Although he is blind to her political identity, he exploits what he believes to be true regarding her knowledge of his identity: She does not know that he is giving her therapy; she does not know who he is; she does not know that he is the same person every time he sees her, thanks to his disguises. His search ends when he finds her in a vision, dead, and thereby finds himself. This self knowledge is followed by the experience of torture.

Valenzuela shows the reader what the characters cannot see; she guides the reader to the outermost edges of her characters and forces the reader to see them in their sociohistoric environments. Although the characters do not know one another's identities, the reader of the novel does have access to this information.

The revolutionary in exile never identifies herself. She is aware that the psychoanalyst appears regularly in various disguises, although she admits that she does not know who he is and does not ask. She fears that he may be an agent of the army intelligence, Interpol, or the CIA; she carries a weapon just in case he is an intelligence officer.

People in the neighborhood where she lives complain. Her pimp-landlord observes that even though she is a prostitute, she walks down the street "like a virgin pure and clean." He suspects that she has special, witchlike powers and regrets renting her a place. He blames her for the talk of meetings and a strike among the other prostitutes.

The reader is given strange bits of information about the patient. She has a collection of hands. She used to tease adults to buy her toy cars so she could seduce little boys, with their clothes on. She and her twin sister, She-She, were betrayed to the police by Alfredo Navoni. Both were political activists and both were tortured. She fantasizes about murdering the psychoanalyst.

Beatriz is a jealous wife who transcribes and types the notes from the meetings that the psychoanalyst has with his Argentine patient. She agonizes over his absences. Valenzuela describes her as a starving, toothless cat in contrast to the predatory "she" cat.

Alfredo Navoni is a self-serving man who may have betrayed the two sisters to the police. The revolutionary in exile has two of her former lover's dreams, one about a wolf that devours ducks and a dog, and one "Venus in furs" fantasy, a "railroad striptease," in which a woman strips on railroad tracks and then lies down on the tracks. One salient feature of the dreams is that they constitute a binary opposition: One is an active fantasy while the other is passive.

Themes and Meanings

Valenzuela began to treat political themes several years before the publication of *He Who Searches*. As a result of her interest in the secret reality ensconced within people's everyday lives, she began to link her vision of the cosmos, language, and masks to political reality. In *He Who Searches*, masks figure in the hidden identity of "she," and in the multiple identities of the psychoanalyst. Valenzuela has been quoted as saying that the mask that hides in fact reveals. This is a notion shared by poststructuralist critics such as Pierre Macherey, who believes that the text both reveals and conceals, and that the absences are as significant as the presences.

As in *El señor de Tacuru* (1983; *The Lizard's Tail*, 1983), a male character is shown to be blind to his own weaknesses and to treat women as sex objects. Valenzuela is ironic in her use of a semiotics professor, one who should be able to deconstruct social signifiers, as a main character. For all his psychonalytic categories, he is unable to detect the true identity of the waitress. Somehow, political commitment eludes psychonalysis' focus on the individual self. Valenzuela uses feminism to ridicule the excesses of both psychoanalysis and Marxism.

Christian and Indian religious imagery is interwoven with Marxist and feminist references. The eating of Fatty is a grotesque enactment of the ritual of Holy Communion. A link is made between the exemplary life of Jesus and a life of political commitment. The conversion experience of the psychoanalyst, inspired by his love for his elusive patient, results in his decision to engage in a political act and to suffer the consequences of that decision: torture.

There is a discussion of the adoption of invisible fathers. This very ambiguous passage suggests that adopted invisible fathers guide revolutionaries yet appear to abandon them to torture. The imagery here evokes both the martyrdom of Christ and the abandonment of Valenzuela's own generation by the Argentine middle class. Pepe confesses that he will never have the courage to adopt an invisible father, but that he is brave to love his patient. Declaring that he exists because of her, he sets off to find her.

Perhaps the most horrifying aspect of *He Who Searches* is that the psychoanalyst takes it upon himself to cure the patient without either her knowledge or her consent.

This is analogous to the political situation in Argentina, in which the country was "cured" of the disease of subversives. Many of those considered subversives disappeared, some without even knowing why they had been arrested and tortured. Just as the psychoanalyst disguises himself, so the police, during this period, appeared under various pretexts to take away those suspected of being subversives.

Critical Context

Throughout her works, Valenzuela uses feminism and Marxism to interrogate each other. Her familiarity with French poststructuralism is seen in her reference to the work of French psychoanalyst Jacques Lacan. She quotes him: "The signifier [is] destined to designate the overall effects of the signified."

Valenzuela's treatment of characters suggests that she shares with Lacan the notion of the alienated self. Lacan's "mirror phase," in which the child discovers a corporeal unity or form through his or her perception of another human being, accounts for the fascination with the other's image as an anticipation of identification with this image. Considering *He Who Searches*, it can be said that the psychoanalyst searches for himself through his image of his patient. The psychoanalyst is already an adult, but Valenzuela may be somewhat ironic in her treatment of this and other psychoanalytic categories. At a deeper level, she subscribes to the Hegelian and Marxist view that the self cannot be understood except in relation to the other, and she applies this view to the Argentine nation. The family from the country, waiting in line in the political uprising, explains that its members need to be heard and that the people in the city must listen to them. This is a reference to a fundamental division in Argentine society between the urban and the rural populations.

Valenzuela's work cannot be understood apart from the political, social, cultural, and historical context of Argentina, which includes the fact that many Argentines live in exile. The situation of the main character of *He Who Searches*, "she," is a poignant illustration of a character who is forced to deepen her understanding of her own culture in absentia, while living in another country. This situation is not specific to Argentina; it is a metaphor which speaks to all political exiles.

In *Cambio de armas* (1982; *Other Weapons*, 1985), Valenzuela also juxtaposed political issues and the male-female relationship. In *He Who Searches*, it is the psychoanalyst who falls in love with the political exile. In "The Word 'Killer,' " a story in *Other Weapons*, the female character falls in love with a torturer. The woman is fascinated and aroused by his violent past and fears that she loves him *because* he is a killer. In both stories, the identities of male and female characters are inextricably bound. These stories lead one to question the nature of the erotic hold on the desire that links individuals to violence. If Valenzuela could tease these links free and examine them, perhaps she could find a cure. In the meantime, it is clear that she believes that the enemy is within our own fascination with violence. The development of a vaccination will probably have to draw from the very traditions that Valenzuela parodies, psychoanalysis and Marxism. Most certainly, a valuable component in the cure will be feminist analysis.

Bibliography
Bach, Caleb. "Metaphors and Magic Unmask the Soul." *Americas* 47 (January/February, 1995): 22-27. Offers a fascinating look at Valenzuela's life and writing career. Briefly explores some of her themes and examines some of the writers who have influenced her, such as Jorge Luis Borges.
Garfield, Evelyn P. "Luisa Valenzuela." In *Latin American Writers*, edited by Carlos A. Solé and Maria I. Abreau. Vol. 3. New York: Charles Scribner's Sons, 1989. Offers an entry on Valenzuela that covers her life and career. Presents in-depth readings of many of her works, and includes a selected bibliography.
Hoeppner, Edward H. "The Hand That Mirrors Us: Luisa Valenzuela's Re-Writing of Lacan's Theory of Identity." *Latin American Literary Review* 20 (January/June, 1992): 9-17. Hoeppner focuses on the narrator, a professor who is violently tortured and whose violent quest for love parallels his physical suffering. Hoeppner argues that Valenzuela's use of the symbol of the phallus as symbolic of desire is linked to the theories of Jacques Lacan.
Kadir, Djelal. "Focus on Luisa Valenzuela." *World Literature Today* 69 (Autumn, 1995): 668-670. A revealing profile of Valenzuela that covers her tenure as a Puterbaugh Fellow at the University of Oklahoma, the quality and style of her writing, and her focus on human potential and failures. Although this essay does not address any particular work, it offers interesting background information.
Pinto, Magdalena. *Women Writers of Latin America: Intimate Histories*. Austin: University of Texas Press, 1991. A collection of interviews with Latin American women writers, including one with Luisa Valenzuela. Features helpful bibliographic references for further reading and an index.

Emily Hicks

HEARTBREAK TANGO

Author: Manuel Puig (1932-1990)
Type of plot: Psychological realism
Time of plot: Primarily 1937-1939, 1949, and 1968
Locale: Coronel Vallejos, a mythical town in Argentina, and Buenos Aires
First published: Boquitas pintadas, 1969 (English translation, 1973)

>   *Principal characters:*
>   JUAN CARLOS ETCHEPARE, a ladies' man who is suffering from
>   tuberculosis
>   LEONOR SALDÍVAR DE ETCHEPARE, his mother
>   CELINA ETCHEPARE, his sister
>   NELIDA ENRIQUETA FERNÁNDEZ (NENÉ), a young woman who
>   believes that she was in love with Juan Carlos
>   DONATO JOSÉ MASSA, a local auctioneer who marries Nelida
>   FRANCISCO CATALINO PÁEZ, a police officer and a friend of Juan
>   Carlos
>   MARÍA MABEL SÁENZ, a teacher and the daughter of a local official
>   ANTONIA JOSEFA RAMÍREZ (BIG FANNY), a servant in the Sáenz
>   household
>   ELSA DICARLO, a widow who cares for Juan Carlos in his illness

The Novel

Although *Heartbreak Tango* may be classified as a realistic novel for its representation of an ordinary, familiar reality, it is not at all traditional in the development of its narrative. The portrayal of Juan Carlos Etchepare, dead from tuberculosis as the story begins, is effected primarily through his letters and through the testimonies of the other characters of the novel. The interviews, letters, newspaper reports, descriptions of photo albums, objective eyewitness accounts, and stream-of-consciousness passages included in the narrative present Juan Carlos as a childish, lovable, worthless philanderer, as if his personality were the incarnation of the less offensive characteristics of the literary and cultural stereotype of Don Juan.

Ten years after her infatuation with Etchepare, Nené writes letters to his mother, exploring the unfulfilled passion that she feels for him and gradually reconstructing the relationships of the dead man and the people who knew him. The scenario includes Francisco, who tries to emulate the romantic escapades of Juan Carlos but is murdered by Fanny, the young woman whom he impregnates, and Celina Etchepare, who fiercely defends her brother and at the same time tries to live up to his reputation for promiscuous, unbridled sexual freedom. Nené's friend Mabel moves with no hesitation from lover to lover according to her idle whims. All of these characters recall the life of Juan Carlos with much nostalgic distortion and exaggeration of his sexual expertise and disarming charm. The woman who was really devoted to him, the widow Elsa DiCarlo, insists on presenting honestly and directly the true portrait of the unfortunate, unhappy consumptive lover whom she nursed through the last stages of his illness.

The letters from Nené to Leonor, Juan Carlos's mother, form the opening section of the novel, interspersed with objective narrative passages that portray the reactions of the recipient of the letters. Toward the end of the novel, as the letters of reply from Leonor are presented, it becomes obvious that it is not Leonor but her daughter Celina who has been corresponding with Nené, surreptitiously using her mother's name. As an act of vengeance, Celina sends the letters from Nené to Nené's husband, Donato, in hopes of destroying their marriage. The novel ends with the notice of Nené's death twenty years later, after which Donato honors his wife's request that her private collection of letters (which she received thirty years before from Juan Carlos) be burned without being read by anyone.

The Characters

The characters of the novel are developed not through the guidance of the overseeing narrator, as in most traditional realistic novels, but rather through the things that they say about one another and through what they reveal about themselves in their testimonies. The characters are firmly grounded in the popular culture of mid-twentieth century Argentine society, revealing the powerful influence of films and the popular lyrics and music of the tango. The characterization of Juan Carlos Etchepare as the supreme Latin lover is a reflection of the popular stereotypes presented in the films of the period and is juxtaposed to the "truth" of Juan Carlos's experience with the women who have loved him and the men who have envied him.

The portrayal of the desperate, pitiful attempts of these characters to find fulfillment and happiness through love is contrasted to the idealized view of life presented in the mass media. Each of the sixteen episodes of *Heartbreak Tango* is preceded by quotations from films, tango lyrics, or commercial advertisements—quotations that reveal a romanticized view of reality. In an effective mixture of dreadful seriousness and ironic ridiculousness, Big Fanny murders the father of her unborn child, and Bette Davis laments, "I wish I could say I was sorry." Nené romantically mourns the loss of her unrequited love, refusing to admit that she has settled for the kind of life that she has always had: marriage to an unexciting, long-suffering husband who provides her with two children and a secure home. In the midst of all these characters who cannot recognize the disparity between their illusions and the reality of their situation, Elsa DiCarlo and Donato alone accept that their dedication and love have gone astray, spent on shallow partners, Juan Carlos and Nené, who are incapable of true devotion.

Although Puig's techniques of narration are notable for their departure from the realistic literary tradition, his techniques of characterization are very much within that tradition. The characters are portrayed through an exploration of their relationship to the social milieu in which they move and through a presentation of the ways in which they relate to one another. The ironic juxtaposition of the fantasies of popular culture and the realities of life reveals the self-deception and unawareness of most of the characters of *Heartbreak Tango*, and this juxtaposition is effected primarily through "historically" verifiable documents, the fictive representations of texts such as diaries, notes, police reports, letters, film scripts, and song lyrics.

Themes and Meanings

As in his first novel, *La traición de Rita Hayworth* (1968; *Betrayed by Rita Hayworth*, 1971), Puig explores the phenomenon of popular culture and the force of its fantasies in the lives of the people. Jean Harlow loved it when Clark Gable treated her roughly. It was the look in Joan Bennett's eyes that made Edward G. Robinson think of murder. As long as one can smile (and this toothpaste lets one smile), one can be successful. "A woman's lips set the frozen north aflame," but for the modern woman (who uses this lipstick), personality is more important than beauty.

This sentimental view of reality is reflected in the written texts produced by the characters of the novel, the letters and diary entries. The police report of the murder of Francisco Catalino, on the other hand, presents a detailed but unemotional account of the crime, and the gypsy's reading of Juan Carlos' future accurately interprets his vapid, opportunistic hedonism.

The novelistic text, then, is a parody of the stereotypes of popular culture, in that the testimonies of many of the characters who are emotionally involved with Juan Carlos create their own stereotype of him. The truth lurking behind that image emerges from the text as a whole. Just as the objective critic of popular culture can understand the conflict of the ideal vision of life and the reality of experience, the objective narrator and reader can perceive the truth beneath the extremes of sentimentality and depersonalized objectivity evident in the various textual fragments of the novel. Puig's extensive use of elements from popular culture, then, is ironic and displaced, for the view of the world that it promotes works its magic directly on the characters but not on the reader. Rather, those cultural elements work on the reader in an inverse way, revealing the disparity of popular fantasies about the fulfillment of needs and the realities of interpersonal relationships.

The complete title of the novel—*Heartbreak Tango: A Serial*—relates the fictional form to a particular manifestation of popular culture, the novel published in installments in popular magazines. The novel is divided into two parts, each consisting of eight episodes. This arrangement of the narrative is Puig's preferred method of imposing order on a very disordered narrative, a method that he has used in other novels: *Betrayed by Rita Hayworth*, *The Buenos Aires Affair: Novela policial* (1973; *The Buenos Aires Affair: A Detective Novel*, 1976), *El beso de la mujer araña* (1976; *The Kiss of the Spider Woman*, 1979), and *Pubis Angelical* (1979). In *Heartbreak Tango*, more than in the other novels of similar form, the organization of the material in episodes is essential to the parody of the sentimentalization of life in the manifestations of popular culture. While the form of the novel reflects that of serialized fiction, the narrative strategies are drastically altered. In the place of the chronological telling of events, the calculated suspense tactics, and the carefully structured revelation of facts that are typical of the installment novel, Puig resorts to a synchronic narrative in which the death of the main character is told first and the circumstances of his life are re-created

through disparate details scattered throughout the sixteen episodes. The authorial manipulation and deception of the reader characteristic of the serial novel are replaced by
other, more complicated authorial manipulations and deceptions. In this way, the parody of the novelistic form reinforces the parody of the influence of popular culture.

Critical Context

From the beginning of his career as a novelist, Puig has been an international writer
in that his narrative material and his own experience have not been limited to the Hispanic culture of his native Argentina. Puig grew up in a small town, General Villegas,
which is transformed into Coronel Vallejos in *Heartbreak Tango*. He was educated in
Argentina and in Rome, where he studied cinema and worked as a film director, and
he has spent much of his life in European cities and in New York. The titles of his novels indicate both his international experience and the force of North American culture
in South American life. One of his narratives, *Maldición eterna a quien lea estas
páginas* (1980; *An Eternal Curse on the Reader of These Pages*, 1982), was written
first in English, revised in Spanish for publication, and then rewritten in an English
edition that incorporated the Spanish revisions. *Boquitas pintadas* was made into a
film in 1974 (known in English as *Painted Lips*) by the Argentine director Leopoldo
Torre Nilsson, and *The Kiss of the Spider Woman* was filmed in 1985 with an international cast and was directed by Hector Babenco.

The later novels of Puig are more clearly political than *Betrayed by Rita Hayworth*
and *Heartbreak Tango*. Although the political themes seem at times to be directed at
the oppression of Latin American governments, they are in fact an attack on the cultural oppression that pervades Western societies, an oppression characterized by the
rigid definition of sex roles. The prevalence in Puig's novels of references to popular
cultural stereotypes is a critique of the influence of the mass media in reinforcing sexual attitudes. The importance of homosexual characters in the later novels is indicative of Puig's interest in the manifestation of those attitudes in the formal and informal
institutions of society.

Puig's popularity as a novelist is limited somewhat by the narrative devices that
render his novels accessible and attractive only to more sophisticated readers. His
view of the mores and prejudices of society and his implied criticism of its attitudes
toward sexual roles make his novels somewhat controversial, but at the same time
they explain the prominence of his work in the context of the outstanding fiction produced by the important Latin American novelists of the second half of the twentieth
century, such as Carlos Fuentes, Julio Cortázar, Ernesto Sábato, Gabriel García
Márquez, Guillermo Cabrera Infante, Mario Vargas Llosa, and José Donoso.

Bibliography

Bacarisse, Pamela. *The Necessary Dream: A Study of the Novels of Manuel Puig.*
    Totowa, N.J.: Barnes & Noble, 1988. Chapters on the major novels. The introduc-
    tion provides a useful overview of Puig's career and themes. Includes notes and
    bibliography.

Kerr, Lucille. *Suspended Fictions: Reading Novels by Manuel Puig*. Urbana: University of Illinois Press, 1987. Chapters on each of Puig's major novels, exploring the themes of tradition, romance, popular culture, crime, sex, and the design of Puig's career. Contains detailed notes but no bibliography.

Lavers, Norman. *Pop Culture into Art: The Novels of Manuel Puig*. Columbia: University of Missouri Press, 1988. Lavers finds a close relationship between Puig's life and his literary themes. Biography, in this case, helps to explain the author's methods and themes.

Magnarelli, Sharon. *The Lost Rib: Female Characters in the Spanish-American Novel*. Toronto: Associate University Presses, 1985. In "Betrayed by the Cross-Stitch," Maganarelli provides a close reading and feminist analysis of *Betrayed by Rita Hayworth*.

Tittler, Jonathan. *Manuel Puig*. New York: Twayne, 1993. The best introduction to Puig. In addition to providing useful survey of Puig's career in his introduction, Tittler devotes separate chapters to the novels. Chapter seven discusses Puig's theatrical scripts, screenplays, and short stories. Includes detailed notes and an annotated bibliography.

Wheaton, Kathleen. "The Art of Fiction: Manuel Puig." *The Paris Review* 31 (Winter 1989): 129-147. An intensive exploration of Puig's themes and techniques.

Gilbert G. Smith

A HERO AIN'T NOTHIN' BUT A SANDWICH

Author: Alice Childress (1920-1994)
Type of plot: Social realism
Time of plot: The 1960's
Locale: New York City
First published: 1973

Principal characters:
BENJIE JOHNSON, a thirteen-year-old African American boy
ROSE JOHNSON (CRAIG), his mother
BUTLER CRAIG, Rose's boyfriend
JIMMY-LEE POWELL, Benjie's best friend
MRS. RANSOM BELL, Benjie's highly religious grandmother
NIGERIA GREENE, an African American teacher at Benjie's school
BERNARD COHEN, a white teacher at Benjie's school

The Novel

Providing a realistic portrait of a young boy becoming a drug addict in the inner city of New York, *A Hero Ain't Nothin' but a Sandwich* suggests that there are no simple answers to the problems of addiction, poverty, and crime. *A Hero Ain't Nothin' but a Sandwich* is told as a series of brief monologues. Presented in a "documentary" style, the novel depicts each of the main characters telling his or her story in turn. This approach serves both to reinforce the novel's graphic realism and to illustrate the complexity of the problems that it addresses. All the novel's characters are distinct individuals, offering their own explanations for Benjie's problems, justifying their own actions, and, at times, impugning the motives of others. By telling her story in this way, Childress is able to strip away her characters' self-deceptions and balance every plausible accusation against an equally plausible countercharge.

The novel begins with Benjie's description of his neighborhood. It is a dismal place: Poverty and drugs are everywhere; rampant crime makes young and old alike afraid to leave their homes; most families have been torn apart by divorce or death. It is important for the reader to see Benjie's world through this character's own eyes and to develop sympathy for him at the very beginning of the novel. If Childress did not structure the plot in this way, the reader might be tempted to dismiss Benjie as merely a thief and an addict. As the author suggests, however, Benjie's situation is quite complicated. While he is, admittedly, a drug user, he also has a number of admirable qualities that make him a likable character.

In the second monologue, Butler Craig indicates that Benjie's use of drugs is more extensive than Benjie has indicated. Butler mentions that Benjie is now "into stealin" and has sold items belonging to his own family in order to support his habit. Though Butler does not condone Benjie's behavior, he does express genuine affection for the boy.

One by one, all the characters interpret Benjie's problem in terms of their own relationship to him. Jimmy-Lee Powell reflects upon the close friendship that he and Benjie once had; he regrets that Benjie's use of heroin has caused a gulf to form between them. Benjie's grandmother feels that the use of drugs can only be cured through prayer and intense religious faith. Nigeria Greene, one of Benjie's teachers, sees addiction as resulting from the oppression imposed by whites upon all African Americans. Benjie's mother is saddened by her son's inability to speak openly about his problem; at the same time, she reveals her own inability to convey her true feelings to Benjie.

All the characters grasp some part of Benjie's situation, but none of them sees it in its entirety. Childress wants the reader to understand that many factors have caused Benjie to experiment with drugs. While he cannot solve his problems until he admits his own responsibility, the poverty and violence of his neighborhood have also been a major factor in making drugs available to him.

When Benjie arrives at school one day obviously under the influence of drugs, Nigeria Greene and Bernard Cohen set aside their personal differences in order to help the boy. They take Benjie to the principal of the school and arrange for Benjie to enter a drug-treatment program. This quick action brings about a temporary improvement in Benjie's situation. Nevertheless, Benjie still finds it difficult to accept Butler as a replacement for his natural father. He regards Butler as a failure and treats him with contempt. The two of them quarrel, and Benjie again begins to think about buying heroin. Finding no money in the house, he pawns Butler's only overcoat and suit. This theft proves to be the last straw for Butler. He leaves Rose and moves into a different apartment in the same building. This decision deprives Benjie of one of the few male role models from whom he could have learned.

A short while later, Butler suddenly feels that he is not alone in his new apartment. As he looks around, he catches sight of Benjie stealing yet again. Benjie panics and goes to the roof in an attempt to cross over to the next building. When Benjie slips, Butler grabs him and saves his life. This heroic action and the drug-related death of one of his friends lead Benjie to ask for help in solving his problem.

One night when Benjie cannot sleep and is again tempted to buy heroin, he writes "BUTLER IS MY FATHER" over and over on a sheet of paper, waiting for the craving to pass. He places this paper in the pocket of Butler's new suit but, on the following day, attempts to retrieve it. Though Butler never mentions it, he has taken the paper, and Benjie knows that he must have read it. He realizes that Butler is "cool," the hero for whom he had long been hoping.

The novel ends ambiguously, as Butler waits for Benjie to report to his new drug-treatment center. Benjie is late, and the reader is led to wonder whether Benjie has succumbed yet again to the drugs that have almost killed him. Childress herself provides no answers, and readers are left to draw their own conclusions.

The Characters

Benjie Johnson, though only thirteen, is old before his time. Having witnessed intense poverty, he gives the impression of being cynical, hard-hearted and indifferent.

Yet Benjie's attitude serves only to hide more tender feelings. Inside, he longs for someone to look up to and fantasizes about the great things that he would like to do.

Benjie's pride is both his undoing and his potential salvation. The pride of showing off has led Benjie to use drugs in the first place. As Nigeria Greene repeatedly says, however, if African Americans developed a genuine pride in the history of their people, they would not allow others to destroy them through addiction.

Butler Craig proves to be the hero in whom Benjie had long ago ceased to believe. As Butler says late in the novel, true heroes are not the rich; they are ordinary people who work day after day to support their families. Butler is also capable of more traditional forms of heroism: He risks injury in order to save Benjie's life and, in his youth, stood up to a racist when everyone else had been afraid.

Benjie's grandmother, Mrs. Ransom Bell, is one of the most complex characters of the novel. At first appearing to be merely a religious zealot, Mrs. Bell gradually reveals herself to be capable of real tenderness. Mrs. Bell had once been a shake dancer (a performer who shook to a musical accompaniment). Though she now condemns her earlier life as immoral, she still takes pride in her skill. In one of the most joyful scenes in the novel, Benjie and Butler persuade Mrs. Bell to show them the dancing for which she had once been famous.

Nigeria Greene is a black nationalist who, without any sense of irony, wears tailor-made English suits. He is fervent in his desire to teach seventh-graders the part of their history that is missing from the school's textbooks. Though often self-righteous, Mr. Greene (dubbed "Africa" by his students) has excellent intentions and is the first one who acts to save Benjie from addiction.

Bernard Cohen is, on the surface, Nigeria Greene's nemesis. In reality, however, the two teachers are working for the same goals. Mr. Cohen cares about the education of his students and is appalled by the quality of their earlier education. Although he wants his African American students to know their own history, he does not believe that this should be all they learn. He attempts to teach black culture in a larger context, improving the skills that his students will need in order to succeed in the world. Mr. Cohen's sincerity is proven by his unwillingness to be transferred to another school even though he could earn more money there.

Themes and Meanings

While *A Hero Ain't Nothin' but a Sandwich* does not glamorize theft or drug use, it does suggest that Benjie's problems are not entirely of his own making. Benjie's addiction has resulted both from his own poor choices and from the limited options that society has offered him. Childress reserves some of the harshest passages of the novel for the social workers who blame everything that Benjie has done on his "environment" and, in so doing, fail to help him. *A Hero Ain't Nothin' but a Sandwich* suggests that, while a person's problems may indeed be the result of poverty or injustice, it is up to each individual to take responsibility for his or her own life.

The title of the novel reflects Benjie's cynicism and his belief that, in the modern world, heroism is no longer possible. Benjie learns, however, that real heroes are not those who are perfect. The heroes of the modern world are people such as Butler Craig who may be flawed and have troubles of their own. Real heroes are those who are willing to help others even when they themselves have nothing to gain.

In many ways, all of the people who surround Benjie share at least some of this heroism. Mr. Cohen and Mr. Greene overcome their personal differences in an effort to save Benjie from drugs. Benjie's mother risks her own relationship with Butler Craig because of her devotion to her son. Even Jimmie-Lee Powell and the school's principal would help if only they knew what to do. Nevertheless, Childress does not present these characters as stereotypical heroes. Like Benjie, all the characters have their own individual "addictions": For Butler, it is jazz and his "name-brand bottle that can be tasted now and then"; for Mrs. Bell, it is religion; for Mr. Greene, it is politics. The temptation toward addiction, Childress suggests, is universal. The true hero (or perhaps the true adult) does not, however, permit this temptation to destroy what would otherwise be a productive and meaningful life.

Critical Context

Alice Childress is a playwright and director as well as a novelist. In 1956, Childress' play *Trouble in Mind* received an Obie Award as the year's best Off-Broadway production. The author's theatrical experience had an important effect upon *A Hero Ain't Nothin' but a Sandwich*. Rather than telling her story through a mixture of narrative and dialogue, Childress relied upon a series of dramatic vignettes to build her novel layer by layer. Each character's point of view serves to change the reader's perspective toward Benjie and his addiction. Like the audience of a play, the readers of this novel see the action not through the eyes of a single individual but through the collective experience of a large number of characters.

The graphic realism of *A Hero Ain't Nothin' but a Sandwich* surprised many readers when the novel first appeared. Although intended for a teenaged audience, the novel contains obscenities, racial epithets, slang, and explicit references to violence and drug use. Childress' intention was not to shock her readers but to permit them to see the world through Benjie's eyes. While Benjie is only thirteen years old, he lives in constant fear of being murdered, robbed, or raped. He has been exposed to suffering more severe than that known by many adults. It should not be surprising, therefore, that Benjie temporarily succumbs to the troubles that surround him. The challenge facing Benjie is how to escape from a life that seems doomed to failure.

The novel's frequent use of dialect (such as "chile" for "child" and "letrit" for "electricity") and slang (including "skag" for "heroin," "cop" for "steal," and "jive" for "phony") places the work in the same general tradition as Mark Twain's *The Adventures of Huckleberry Finn* (1884) and J. D. Salinger's *The Catcher in the Rye* (1951). Like those novels, *A Hero Ain't Nothin' but a Sandwich* uses nonstandard speech in order to create an atmosphere of realism and to underscore the socioeconomic class of its main characters.

A Hero Ain't Nothin' but a Sandwich also bears similarities to *The Adventures of Huckleberry Finn* and *The Catcher in the Rye* in other ways. Childress herself has noted that *A Hero Ain't Nothin' but a Sandwich* was the first novel since *The Catcher in the Rye* to be banned from high-school libraries in Savannah, Georgia. Moreover, this novel, like its predecessors, is a combination of *Bildungsroman* (a coming-of-age novel) and social commentary. It presents a flawed central character who quickly gains the readers' sympathy and, by the end of the novel, their understanding.

Bibliography
Childress, Alice. "A Candle in a Gale Wind." In *Black Women Writers, 1950-1980: A Critical Evaluation*, edited by Mari Evans. Garden City, N.Y.: Anchor Press/ Doubleday, 1983. An extremely useful discussion by the author herself of her attitudes toward writing and the major factors that influenced her works. Childress mentions that she resists the urge to write about "accomplishers," preferring instead to deal with "those who come in second . . . or not at all." Childress also describes the way in which her work in the theater has influenced characterization in her novels.

Hay, Samuel A. "Alice Childress' Dramatic Structure." In *Black Women Writers, 1950-1980: A Critical Evaluation*, edited by Mari Evans. Garden City, N.Y.: Anchor Press/Doubleday, 1983. Hay describes Childress's process of creating a plot through the presentation of information in succeeding episodes. According to Hay, the plots of Childress's works tend to be rather simple; it is only on the level of characterization and motivation that complexity is achieved.

Jennings, La Vinia D. *Alice Childress*. New York: Twayne, 1995. A biography of Alice Childress. Focuses on her writing career of "more than 40 years in which she examined with honesty and passion the meaning of being black, and especially of being black and female, in a culture where being white and male was what counted."

Killens, John O. "The Literary Genius of Alice Childress." In *Black Women Writers, 1950-1980: A Critical Evaluation*, edited by Mari Evans. Garden City, N.Y.: Anchor Press/Doubleday, 1983. Killens discusses Childress's use of humor and satire as weapons against prejudice. Though Killens focuses primarily on Childress' plays, he uses *A Hero Ain't Nothin' but a Sandwich* as an example of the author's ability to construct "awesomely beautiful and powerful moments" in her works. Killens notes the frequent appearance in Childress's works of the themes of struggle and the need for African Americans to love their own people.

Koppleman, Susan. "Alice Childress: An Appreciation." *Belles Lettres: A Review of Books by Women* 10 (Fall, 1994): 6. A tribute to Childress upon her death. Places *A Hero Ain't Nothin' but a Sandwich* into the context of her other works and praises her work for "its powerful and frank treatment of racial issues, the compassionate but unflinching characterizations she created, and the broad appeal of her work."

Jeffrey L. Buller

HIGH COTTON

Author: Darryl Pinckney (1953-   )
Type of plot: Bildungsroman
Time of plot: The 1960's to the 1980's
Locale: The "Old Country" (the South, especially the Savannah River area),
    Indianapolis, New York City, London, and Paris
First published: 1992

> *Principal characters:*
>> THE UNNAMED NARRATOR, a young, reluctant member of the black elite
>>   in search of his identity
>> THE NARRATOR'S FAMILY, his parents and two sisters
>> GRANDFATHER EUSTACE, an old-style black intellectual whose
>>   influence the narrator cannot escape
>> THE BEIGE STEPGRANDMOTHER, Grandfather Eustace's second wife
>> AUNT CLARA, the narrator's great-aunt, matriarch of Opelika, Alabama
>> HANS HANSEN, the narrator's best friend during high school
>> DJUNA BARNES, an aging writer for whom the narrator does odd jobs
>> MAURICE, the assistant managing editor of a publishing company where
>>   the narrator works
>> THE POWER BITCH, the secretary of the publishing company's
>>   managing editor
>> VIRTEA, head of the publishing company's Black Caucus

The Novel

Narrated in the first person by an unnamed protagonist whose story spans three decades, *High Cotton* seems obviously autobiographical, at least in broad outline. Like the novel's protagonist, Darryl Pinckney is the product of an elite black family. His grandfather was graduated from Brown and Harvard Universities and was a minister. Pinckney too grew up in Indianapolis, was graduated from Columbia University, and worked for a New York publishing house, and he too has puzzled over the nature of black identity in America.

Yet how far the novel's anecdotal details agree with the author's life is another matter. The author was selective, both to be discreet and to make his points—around which he perhaps felt free to embroider and invent, since he presented his work as fiction.

The novel's main story line traces the development of the young protagonist. It begins with his boyhood in Indianapolis during the era of the Civil Rights movement. As a child, the narrator gets mixed messages about his blackness: He is told that he is "just as good as anyone else out there," but he still notices that some people "moved away from you at the movies." For him, one of "the Also Chosen," the future beckons, but still the past oppresses via the "collective power" of numerous older relatives who, heavy with their knowledge, "enlisted the departed" to their cause.

Most prominent among the "old-timers" is Grandfather Eustace, proud that he belongs to the black aristocracy, "a sort of dusky peerage with their degrees, professions, and good marriages among their own kind." Grandfather Eustace is anxious to pass on his proud heritage to the narrator. Looking back, however, the narrator confesses that "I spent much of my life running from him, centripetal fashion, because he was, to me, just a poor old darky."

The narrator and his grandfather, however, agree about the narrator's neighborhood. After one visit with the narrator's family, Grandfather Eustace refuses to return to their rundown house, which he says is "on the wrong side of Indianapolis." The block has biting dogs, disreputable neighbors, and Buzzy, a twelve-year-old bully who throws bottles at passing cars and spouts Black Power slogans. Tormented by Buzzy, the bookish protagonist retreats into Anglophilic fantasies, imagining his home as the British Isles and himself as various British worthies.

Life opens up for the protagonist when his family moves to a predominately white suburb, right across from a country club. His grandfather coaches him on how to survive white classrooms, but happily he suffers "no traumas of any kind." Instead, he becomes popular with his white classmates and teachers, and his best friend, Hans Hansen, is white. He has trouble only with black classmates, who call him "Dr. Thomas" or "Tom."

The protagonist briefly joins the revolutionary Heirs of Malcolm, but he hardly seems committed (in a comic twist, Hans Hansen drives him to the group's meetings in a sports car). He appears to join to satisfy his curiosity and his black critics and to reap "the social satisfactions of being a Black Power advocate in a suburban high school." All in all, the protagonist seems well launched on a predictable life course. Thereafter, he enjoys "the paradise of integration" throughout high school, a trip to London, college at Columbia University, life in New York City, and a trip to Paris.

He seems willing to forget his blackness or to wear it lightly, as convenient—if the world will let him; however, the world does not. Despite his ease with the predominantly white world, it constantly reminds him of his blackness, which it sometimes defines in rude and stereotypical terms—for example, when Djuna Barnes insults him, when taxis do not stop for him, and when white women speed up their walks ahead of him. Other blacks, too, will not let him forget. One of these is his grandfather, who lives on in New York City and eventually dies in an Indianapolis nursing home.

The death of his grandfather compels the narrator to make a pilgrimage to the "Old Country," Georgia. There, along the banks of the Savannah and Ogeechee Rivers, in Augusta, in family graveyards, and in the Thankful Baptist Church, the narrator finally confronts his black heritage. The novel ends with his profound and moving meditation on that heritage, the suffering it has involved, and the meaning of being black in America.

The Characters

High Cotton is replete with interesting characters, some developed only in brief sketches, others at more length. They are described directly, through the eyes of the narrator, who is marvelously observant and witty.

The narrator is characterized indirectly, primarily through his allusive language and wry tone. Otherwise, he is prone to be coy rather than confessional, at least about some aspects of his life. For example, readers learn nothing about his love life; in fact, the word "neuter" might best describe him, since the only principle he seems to represent is opportunism. He seems to have no strong commitments to any values or persons, including himself. Rather, he is in the process of finding himself, undergoing a prolonged adolescence supported by indulgent parents who send him checks even after he is graduated from college.

Once the narrator gets into a confessional mode, however, no one can be harder on himself. He acknowledges that for most of his life he has been "out of it," that his indifference to the "old-timers" and the heritage they represent was "like a camouflage maneuver, a prolongation of the adolescent lament that I wasn't real but everyone else was. . . ." He finally accepts his "responsibility to help my people, to honor the race." In this sense, the whole book is a confession, an expiation, a modern rime of the ancient mariner (now become the black artist as a young man).

Many of the other characters are the protagonist's relatives, particularly the old-timers, who fill in the sense of the black past and are lovable for their crankiness and personality. Each offers his or her record of suffering and response. Among these are Aunt Clara, who practically owns a small Southern town, and Uncle Castor, who found his outlet in jazz. Chief among the old-timers is Grandfather Eustace, who recognizes much of himself in the young narrator. Like the narrator, Grandfather Eustace is a highly intelligent man who endured a long adolescence and several trial careers before he found his calling. Unhappily, in the present Grandfather Eustace is "the emperor of out-of-it."

Via other characters, the narrator surveys contemporary black life, from the Civil Rights and Black Power movements through equal opportunity and affirmative action. He gives a brief but charming portrayal of his parents, who take him to a civil rights march in chapter 1 and in the final chapter gently tweak him for not attending National Association for the Advancement of Colored People (NAACP) conventions. A hilarious segment of the novel satirizes the Black Power movement, represented by Sister Egba and her followers in the Heirs of Malcolm. The publishing house where the narrator works contains another interesting collection of characters, including Big Boss, Little Boss, and the Power Bitch. After pressure from the Black Caucus, the bosses promote Maurice to assistant managing editor, but his new position only turns him into a glorified security guard "obliged to spy on employees." His story demonstrates how equal opportunity and affirmative action have not brought an end to suffering and the need to respond.

Themes and Meanings

As the book's range of characters shows, the meaning of being black in America has both not changed and changed tremendously over the generations. The African American experience has always involved suffering, but the degree and nature of that suffering have varied; hence, responses that once seemed valid eventually grow out of date. Thinking of the old-timers, the narrator realizes that he "would never know what they knew"; in the same way, Grandfather Eustace "considered it good form not to talk to us about the hardships he had witnessed," and his grandfather, in turn, "had thought it wise not to speak too truthfully about his years in bondage." Grandfather Eustace's suffering "from being black at a time when everyone was white" and his fusty idea of a black aristocracy date him as "a terrible snob," while the revolutionary poses and rhetoric of the Heirs of Malcolm render them comic.

In particular, *High Cotton* seems to portray the morning after the Civil Rights movement, critiquing with cold realism both low expectations and high hopes. These mixed messages are suggested by the demonstration that the young narrator attends; to him, it is merely confusing and anticlimactic, a spectacle gawked at by white spectators. Grandfather Eustace calls such marches "'Congo' lines," but then the whole movement occurs without his permission. He is even disappointed that his grandson suffers no traumas in white schools. Apparently some people, both black and white, were surprised by and unprepared for the gains of the Civil Rights movement. On the other hand, in others the movement might have inspired inflated hopes that were subsequently dashed or unrealized.

The narrator seems to critique such hopes, even fantasies, by applying the outrageous term "the Also Chosen" to blacks. Most reviewers took the term (which implicitly juxtaposes blacks with Old Testament Jews, God's "Chosen People") to allude to the "Talented Tenth," W. E. B. Du Bois's term for the best and brightest African Americans. Grandfather Eustace would doubtless agree with such a usage, but the narrator also applies the term to his generation, the first born under the dispensation of the Civil Rights movement: "Perhaps the old-timers were right to insist that we, the Also Chosen, live wholly in the future," he speculates.

The Civil Rights movement was an undeniable high point in African American history, but how does one prepare for the inevitable letdown? The narrator concludes the book with a lament for a vanished time:

> Even now I grieve for what has been betrayed. I see the splendor of the mornings and hear how glad the songs were, back in the days when the Supreme Court was my Lourdes, and am beyond consolation. The spirit didn't lie down and die, but it's been here and gone, been here and gone.

Critical Context

High Cotton is a significant contribution to the discussion of race in America, providing a balance in several ways. For one, the novel calls attention to an often overlooked segment of African American society, a literate black middle class that has been established for generations. For another, it examines black identity as a complex concept that has changed over time and that is fraught with ambiguity. For still another, it stresses the weight of African American history on the present: "The past gets longer and longer," the author notes. Finally, the book injects honesty into a public discussion almost stifled by stereotypes, clichés, ignorance, hypocrisy, and political correctness. Pinckney seems to take delight in opening up the discussion by revealing shibboleths and flinging around "bad" words (he refers to Harlem, for example, as "Valley of the Shines").

In *High Cotton*, his first novel, Pinckney already has a successful voice, a voice that is shocking, erudite, entertaining, and distinctive. Prior to publishing the novel, he developed the voice by writing essays on African American literature for *The New York Review of Books*. So what if his narration in *High Cotton* does resemble a string of essays and anecdotes loosely tied together? This narration too seems to be part of his distinctive style.

Bibliography

Als, Hilton. "Word!" *The Nation* 254 (May 18, 1992): 667-670. Describes Pinckney as a writer who is interested in words rather than in promoting an agenda. In his criticism, Als writes, Pinckney explores black authors as writers "whose blackness, politics and flesh and blood made history through their language." In *High Cotton*, Als claims, language is the key to the narrator's search for identity, since it gives him "the voice needed to write his name in the field of existence."

Bell, Pearl K. "Fiction Chronicle." *Partisan Review* 59 (Spring, 1992): 282-295. Bell praises Pinckney as an "astute and independent-minded critic of black literature" who is not "intimidated by orthodox pieties about race and gender." Similarly, the narrator of *High Cotton* is described as "in search of authenticity but distrustful of enthusiasm and wary of commitment." Thus, the hard-won revelation that he finally experiences is "fiercely honest."

Fein, Esther B. "A Writer, but Not a Black Everyman." *The New York Times*, April 9, 1992, pp. C17, C26. This article, based on an interview with Pinckney, notes parallels between him and the narrator of *High Cotton*. Mostly, however, the article records his desire not to be tagged as representative of any one class, race, or group. Rather, "he wants his book to be testimony not only of his race but of his devotion to literature as well."

Kerr, Nora. "Part of My Story, but Not All." Review of *High Cotton*, by Darryl Pinckney. *The New York Times Book Review* (February 2, 1992): 3. A generally favorable review that focuses on the main character of the novel, who, like Pinckney himself, is a young, middle-class African American from a highly educated family. Notes that Pinckney acknowledges that the book includes many of his own life experiences but denies it is autobiographical.

Pinckney, Darryl. "Darryl Pinckney: An Interview." Interview by Jan Garden Castro. *American Poetry Review* 23 (November-December, 1994): 9-14. Pinckney talks about the writers who have influenced him, among them Fyodor Dostoevski and James Baldwin. He discusses the characters in the novel and credits the unique narrative voice of *High Cotton* to his exposure to other authors' experiments with narration.

Stuart, Andrea. "Invisible Man." *New Statesman and Society* 5 (August 14, 1992): 38. Stuart finds *High Cotton* impressive technically but lacking in human qualities. She asks, "What is a black identity when poverty and deprivation play no part in your equation?" She describes the narrator as a nonentity ("the original invisible man"), dubs the book "a curiously chilly experience," and wonders whether the author "has a heart at all."

White, Edmund. Review of *High Cotton*, by Darryl Pinckney. *The New York Times Book Review* 97 (February 2, 1992): 3. White applauds *High Cotton* as "the considered achievement of a seasoned mind." In particular, he praises Pinckney for writing about race without succumbing to "a puerile 'political correctness' [that] imposes hypocrisy on most writers. . . ." Instead, Pinckney "has dared to treat his theme with excruciating honesty" and "total freedom from restraint."

Harold Branam

HOLY PLACE

Author: Carlos Fuentes (1928-   )
Type of plot: Mythical journey
Time of plot: The early to mid-1960's
Locale: Mexico City and Madonna dei Monte, Italy
First published: Zona sagrada, 1967 (English translation, 1972)

>   *Principal characters:*
>   GUILLERMO NERVO, the protagonist and narrator, the son of a Mexican
>   film star
>   CLAUDIA NERVO, his mother, Mexico's leading screen actress
>   GIANCARLO, Claudia's young lover
>   BELA, Guillermo's sirenlike girlfriend

The Novel

As much about myth, literature, and language as it is about worldly existence, *Holy Place* consists of a series of incompletely connected and suggestive episodes in the troubled life of its narrator, Guillermo Nervo. Nicknamed "Guillermito" (the diminutive shows endearment but also condescension), or simply "Mito" (Spanish for "myth"), Nervo unfolds as a parasitic decadent, a Baudelairian dandy totally dependent on and infatuated with his castrating mother, the protean film star Claudia. Guillermo moves from idolizing her and aspiring to be her lover to trying to arouse her jealously by taking Bela as a lover. A measure of his failure emerges when, after losing Claudia to his rival Giancarlo, he resorts to transvestitism in an attempt to possess his mother by becoming her. In the final chapter, he is transformed into a dog and must watch his maid and her lover desecrate his apartment, a literalizing of his neurotically servile role and an unequivocal announcement of the provisional completion of his fall. "Happily Ever After," as the opening tableau is titled, thus proves to be a doubly misleading indicator, for it both appears out of its conventional place and evokes the contrary of the novel's eventual outcome.

The Characters

Concerned as it is with the eternal repetition and transformation of mythical archetypes through the telling of tales, *Holy Place* offers a little in the way of traditional, mimetic characterization. As Guillermo narrates, his narcissistic and Oedipal complexes are so much in the foreground that one can grant little credence to his portrayal of others. Both secondary characters, Bela and Giancarlo, are patent reductions, she the stereotype of the opportunistic temptress and he of the dark Latin lover. Whether Guillermo sees them as such or wants his reader or listener to think so is never clarified. Although treated at much greater length, moreover, Claudia, too, is nothing more than a glossy veneer. Guillermo tries to read depth and substance into her masks, but to judge by her reported words and actions, she has only the depth of a celluloid image. The aging but still attractive star is more interested in advancing her career and tasting the spoils of her success than in understanding her obviously disturbed son. She is a myth in the sense of commercial media hype. Perhaps her perceived hollowness resides in the fact that, despite her fame as an actress (and despite her incessant role-playing), she is never shown acting professionally. Furthermore, even though Guillermo's demands are unreasonable and even impossible to meet, she proves to be no more adept as a mother than as an actress.

Only Guillermo's desultory and sporadic monologue remains, then, as an object of possible psychoanalytic study. Yet his contrived self-portrayal as a modern, twisted Telemachus and his bizarre final transformation into a canine endanger even the serious application of that approach. His fetishes and obsessions draw the reader's attention, to be sure, but psychoanalysis should excavate the unconscious, and Guillermo's desires come across as already considerably intellectualized. Furthermore, and still more distracting, his status as an essentially cultural and specifically linguistic construct never fully disappears from view. He is to an undetermined extent the Mexican embodiment of Telemachus; Giancarlo is not only his rival but also Telegonus, his double who courts Penelope; Claudia is not only his mother but also Circe, Penelope's mirror image and Ulysses' consort; Ulysses is out of the picture, because the archetypal Mexican father is either unknown or absent; Bela has no direct classical antecedent but functions as her own double, a grotesquely painted mask that represents the very principle of masking. Amid all this duplicity the ultimate nature of Guillermo's identity (or identities) must remain a deliberately open question. Characterization is treated as a question of style; it is a dialogue between a modern text and its forebears. Consequently, the critical consensus with respect to his highly self-conscious and elusive postmodern narrative is that its real protagonist is the very process of change undergone by all its key elements.

Themes and Meanings

The central myth underlying the novel is that of Homer's *Odyssey*, mediated to some degree by James Joyce's *Ulysses* (1922) and Robert Graves's *The Greek Myths* (1955). Because the work posits itself as a figural theory of mythical transmutation, however, the basic story of a son's journey in search of his father is at times hard to recognize. Neither chronological order nor narrative development nor systematic spatial displacement—staples of travels recounted—inhabits the narrative. Instead of sallying in search of his progenitor, Guillermo stays at home (one of the novel's "holy places") and tries to find—when he is not trying to avoid finding—himself. Rather than a progression leading to a triumphant reunion and epiphany, the conclusion to his stationary meanderings embodies entropic madness or suicide. The novel thus emerges as a grave intertext, a generic parody of the weightiest sort.

Although the work is decidedly tragic in modality, *Holy Place*'s major symbols resist any single privileged interpretation, signaling instead a broad repertory of diverse and sometimes self-contradictory meanings. Claudia, for example, is a highly complex concatenation of paradigms, both modern and ancient, Western and indigenous (Meso-American). Fundamentally cast as The Woman, she plays all the archetypal roles given the female through history. She is mother, virgin, prostitute, sorceress; she is the earth, the unconscious, life, and destiny. Her antecedents are Eve, Penelope, Circe, la Llorona (the Weeper), la Chingada (the Raped One, Mexico's legendary founding mother), Cihuacoatl (the patron of women who die in childbirth), and Tlazolteotl (the Aztec goddess of death, fertility, and excrement). In addition to Guillermo's apartment, the novel's title refers to the ballfield, the betting table, the site of Aztec sacrifices, the silver screen, Claudia's womb, and the space of literature itself: venues of ritual and renewal.

The many metamorphoses on the thematic front are reflected stylistically in the shifting narrative modes—autobiographic, epistolary, dramatic—and the novel's eclectic mixture of tones—confessional, colloquial, lyric, supplicatory, and denunciatory. Writing and existence are shown to be everywhere fraught with indeterminacy, relativity, and flux. Rather than a moral judgment (though opinionated, Fuentes is never straightforwardly didactic), Guillermo's failure within the context of *Holy Place* would be the result of his ignorance of how the world and the human mind work. Only fairy tales and Claudia's melodramatic movies progress predictably and end with formulaic felicity. Friedrich Nietzsche's eternal recurrence—latently present throughout the work offers no mandate for Guillermo's fatalistic passivity. It requires instead an arduous exercise of will to harness conflictive vital forces toward an outcome that may still be despairing and will inevitably constitute a repetition. *Holy Place*'s ultimate gesture discloses that when time, progress, truth, individual identity, and the prospect of meaning in life are subjected to such radical and penetrating scrutiny, the significance of a literary work that raises these issues can be no less ambiguous, no more decidable.

Critical Context

Since Fuentes is so prolific, several of his shorter works, such as *Las buenas conciencias* (1959; *The Good Conscience*, 1961) and *Cumpleaños* (1970; birthday), are often overshadowed. Perhaps because it was first published the same year as his vaster and more baroque *Cambio de piel* (1967; *A Change of Skin*, 1968) and lacks the compelling combination of epic sweep and psychological introspection of *La muerte de Artemio Cruz* (1962; *The Death of Artemio Cruz*, 1964) or the monumental historical scope of *Terra Nostra* (1975; English translation, 1976), *Holy Place* has received relatively little critical attention. It is, nevertheless, a solidly representative item in the Fuentes canon. In consonance with his fellow countryman Octavio Paz's landmark volume of essays *El laberinto de la soledad* (1950; *The Labyrinth of Solitude*, 1961), Fuentes continues to probe the Mexican national psyche. The possibility of temporal models beyond that of the simple line, and the pervasive presence of ancient indigenous beliefs and structures in a counterfeit of contemporary Western society, are two more of his most characteristic themes. Noteworthy, too, in *Holy Place* is the introduction of figures and attitudes of contemporary mass culture, especially film, an enduring motif which the author takes up also in *A Change of Skin* and again in his later novel *La cabeza de la hidra* (1978; *The Hydra Head*, 1978) and in the drama

Orquídeas a la luz de la luna (1982; *Orchids in the Moonlight*, 1982). Audacious formal experimentation, such as the use of the second-person narrative point of view, moreover, locates him squarely among the foremost practitioners of the "New Spanish-American Novel." Following the lead of the Argentine Jorge Luis Borges, such writers as Fuentes, Julio Cortázar, Guillermo Cabrera Infante, José Donoso, Gabriel García Márquez, and Mario Vargas Llosa undertook in the 1960's a general revamping of a narrative that was formerly rural in setting, naturalistic in technique, and positivistic in outlook. Working independently but not at cross-purposes, these authors of the Latin American "boom" have shown in varying degrees that play and politics, aesthetics and commitment, form and theme in literature are in no way mutually exclusive.

Fuentes is often accused of excessive erudition and of using his fictions to illustrate esoteric theories rather than to tell a story spontaneously reflective of direct experience. Fuentes himself has offered some of the most convincing responses to such criticism in his compilations of essays *La nueva novela hispano-americana* (1969; the new Spanish-American novel), *Casa con dos puertas* (1970; house with two doors), and *Tiempo mexicano* (1971; Mexican time). Availing himself of knowledge in the fields of anthropology, history, linguistics, philosophy, psychoanalysis, and literature, Fuentes expounds on the authentically baroque character of Latin American reality. Both socialist realism and bourgeois realism, he states, impoverish existence and literature. His writing attempts to restore a lost completeness to the way we conceive of ourselves and the world. By avoiding simplistic and foolishly optimistic notions of society, history, the mind, and its creations, Fuentes aims to project a totalizing and therefore truer image of contemporary mankind. Much to his credit, he does not avoid the most difficult global questions, but tackles them with unrelenting energy, lucidity, and responsibility. In the Latin American tradition it is not unusual to combine the roles of author, critic, and statesman (Fuentes has served as the Mexican ambassador to France, among other positions) in one multifaceted individual. What is rare is to find someone like Fuentes who excels in all these areas. Whereas some readers in the United States have found his occasional grandiloquence and solemnity alien to their tastes, his popularity among Latin Americans, for whom he speaks, and the respect he commands among intellectuals in the Americas and Europe attest the validity of his vision.

Bibliography
Duran, Victor Manuel. *A Marxist Reading of Fuentes, Vargas Llosa, and Puig.* Lanham, Md.: University Press of America, 1994. An interesting study comparing the politics in the writings of these three important Latin American authors. Many of Fuentes's works are examined in detail.
Helmuth, Chalene. *The Postmodern Fuentes.* Lewisburg, Penn.: Bucknell University Press, 1997. A solid overview of Fuentes's work from a postmodernist point of view. Several individual works are discussed, focusing on the issues of identity, national and narrative control, and reconsiderations of the past.

Ibsen, Kristine. *Author, Text and Reader in the Novels of Carlos Fuentes*. New York: Peter Lang, 1993. Although Ibsen does not discuss *Holy Place*, she offers valuable insight into the problem of communication, which remains one of the central preoccupations throughout the work of Fuentes. Her analysis focuses on the means of textualization by which Fuentes activates his reader and how this coincides with his notions of the role of literature in society.

Pollard, Scott. "Canonizing Revision: Literary History and the Postmodern Latin American Writer." *College Literature* 20 (October, 1993): 133-147. Scott analyzes the impact of Latin American narrative on Western literary history after World War II. Focusing on authors Alejo Carpentier, Carlos Fuentes, and Lezama Lima, Scott discusses narratives of conquest and exploration, international modernism, the fashioning of cultural identity, and the primacy of European culture. Offers valuable insight into several of Fuentes's works.

Van Delden, Maarten. *Carlos Fuentes, Mexico, and Modernity*. Nashville, Tenn.: Vanderbilt University Press, 1998. Using Fuentes's writings as a springboard for his discussion, Van Delden presents a comprehensive analysis of Fuentes's intellectual development in the context of modern Mexican political and cultural life. Includes extensive notes and a helpful bibliography.

Jonathan Tittler

HOME TO HARLEM

Author: Claude McKay (1889-1948)
Type of plot: Emotional realism
Time of plot: Immediately following World War I
Locale: Harlem, Pittsburgh
First published: 1928

Principal characters:

JAKE BROWN, the protagonist, an army deserter who has returned to Harlem after two years and is now a longshoreman

FELICE, a prostitute who cares for Jake and for whom he searches throughout Harlem

ZEDDY PLUMMER, a compulsive gambler and "sweetman" who threatens to report Jake to the authorities

SUSY, a possessive, compulsive prostitute who keeps Zeddy

CONGO ROSE, an entertainer at the Congo nightclub, a masochistic prostitute who keeps Jake

RAY, a "book fellah" and railroad waiter who befriends Jake and tries to educate him

AGATHA, a Black Belt beauty parlor assistant who wants to marry Ray

BILLY BIASSE, the operator of a longshoremen's gambling flat and a friend of Jake

The Novel

Home to Harlem opens, appropriately, with Jake working as a stoker aboard a freighter "that stank between sea and sky" en route from Cardiff to New York. He had joined the Army from patriotic motives, but when he was assigned noncombat duties in Brest, he went AWOL—first to Havre and then to London, where he lived with a white woman in the East End until race riots convinced him that his true home was in Harlem. Aboard ship, Jake begins to despise the Arabs who are his fellow stokers: their eating practices, their lack of concern for hygiene, their "thought that a sleeping quarters could also serve as a garbage can" revolts him. Yet he overlooks the racial segregation that dictates that he should be a stoker, with Arabs, rather than a deck-hand, with whites—as he does the hordes of lice—because the boat is "taking him back home—that was all he cared about."

Back in Harlem, Jake visits saloons, restaurants, and a cabaret, where he meets Felice, a prostitute, with whom he spends the night after having agreed to pay her fifty dollars (all that he has), though his initial proposal is only five dollars. In the morning, he is serene and discovers that Felice has put his fifty-dollar bill in his trousers pocket with a note that reads "Just a little gift from a baby girl to a honey boy!" The rest of the novel is an account of events that transpire before Jake and Felice are reunited.

Looking for Felice, Jake meets Zeddy Plummer (who, like Jake, has come from Petersburg, Virginia), "a bad-acting, razor-flashing nigger," a compulsive gambler who is always impecunious, and the sometime lover of Felice during Jake's two years overseas. Zeddy's life is saved by Jake during a fight with an unpaid loan shark, but he subsequently tries to slash Jake and threatens to inform the police (who are rounding up army deserters) of his whereabouts. A gun lent by Billy Biasse assures Jake's safety.

Searching for Felice, Jake visits several nightclubs, including the Congo, "African in spirit and color. No white persons were admitted." Here he attracts Congo Rose, the popular "entertainer," who wants him as her "sweetman"—a role that he deprecates and dislikes. Nevertheless, he moves in with her: "He did not love her, had never felt any deep desire for her. He had gone to live with her simply because she had asked him when he was in a fever mood for a steady mate." One evening, after having seen signs that Rose has had another man during his absence, he makes sexual advances and is rebuffed: He gives her "two savage slaps in her face," which please her and revolt him. He leaves Rose and Harlem and takes a job on the Pennsylvania Railroad as a dining-car waiter. While working on the railroad, Jake encounters Ray, a somewhat bookish and serious-minded waiter who has come to the United States from his native Haiti, has taken courses at Howard University in Washington, D.C., and has been developing an antimaterialist philosophy that stresses black racial self-consciousness, a semipuritanical ethic, and responsible sexual relationships. In the employer-provided bunkhouse in Pittsburgh—which is as bug-infested as the freighter on which Jake had returned from Europe—Ray expatiates on the treatment of blacks in America, at first declines and then takes opium in imitation of Jake, and becomes a close friend of his Harlem companion. Back in Harlem, Ray meets Agatha, a "rich-brown girl with soft, amorous eyes," who wants to marry him. Uncertain of himself, he ships off to Europe as a mess boy.

After a series of visits to Sheba's Palace, the Baltimore, the Congo, and other, less formal, nightclubs, Jake rediscovers Felice. Dancing at the Baltimore, where they had met, and where couples were "thick as maggots in a vat of sweet liquor," they decide to leave Harlem for Chicago ("a mahvelous place foh niggers"), where they will be free of the troubles caused by overcrowding and crime (as they think) and able to start a new life together.

The Characters

As in almost all of his fiction, Claude McKay offers in *Home to Harlem* characters who represent the two polarities that he attempted to bridge: the intellectual and the emotional. Ray (who is Haitian and who attended Howard University before working on the railroad) is clearly a version of McKay himself (a Jamaican who attended Tuskegee Institute and worked on the New York-Pittsburgh route as a railroad employee), and in some respects he is unsatisfactorily drawn. Though almost all first novels are largely autobiographical, few are reliable or effective as autobiographies: They lack critical distance and psychological penetration of motives and actions and so become too straightforwardly narrative. Ray is little more than a voice for McKay's social and political opinions: He almost becomes Jake's close friend, but he never really manages to go beyond being a comrade, an associate. He is didactic, a propagandist for McKay's philosophy of the need for blacks to retain their outgoing, nonhypocritical, emotional, sensual ways, of the need for racial self-confidence through an awareness of the past glories of black civilizations, and of the need to struggle within the existing social framework for the speedy amelioration of the conditions under which they lived.

Ray, however, is not really a role model for Jake or for his race. He is remarkably pessimistic: "Civilization is rotten," he says; he sees World War I as "totally evil"; he regards his Howard University education as essentially "white education" and basically unsuitable for an aspiring writer of social realism. "The more I learn, the less I understand and love life," he tells Agatha on one occasion; and both are described by McKay as "slaves of the civilized tradition." Inexplicably, he cannot accept marriage to her, though he needs her physically and intellectually. His explanation is that he does not want to be "one of the contented hogs in the pigpen of Harlem," but this is specious: He is unable, even with whatever confidence he has in his philosophical position, to accept the challenges that life in Harlem presents—and so he ships out for Europe, a convenient escape. Clearly, then, Ray is an inadequate foil for Jake, who, though lacking in formal education or in any discernible understanding of sociology or politics or economics, decides to tackle the challenges with the support of Felice.

Jake, who has always, in the past, made "rude contacts and swift satisfactions," who is "very American in spirit," and who is described as "a free, coarse thing," represents McKay's ideal American black: He is urban, he is streetwise, yet he is principled; though in need of work, he refuses to become a strikebreaker; he has only disdain for sweetmen; and "gambling did not have a strangle hold upon him any more than dope or desire did." His one motive is to find Felice and reestablish himself with her—to find a haven of peace in which to enjoy life together. While he knows the ways of the fast set in Harlem, he does not succumb to their inducements. Rather, he seeks a permanent association with Felice, with no thought of abusing her physically, economically, or psychologically, as they ride off (via the Lenox Avenue subway) into the Midwest. The "natural" black can cope with the problems of urban life, but the "intellectual" one (Ray) cannot.

The other characters, many of whom are introduced merely to provide cameos of the multifarious inhabitants of Harlem and to illustrate the range of activities by which they scratch out a livelihood, are portrayed with such skill and detail that they remain memorable. Madame Adeline Suarez, who operates a "buffet flat" where liquor, sex, and companionship can be obtained, and which is closed after a vice-squad raid, represents a large group of small-time entrepreneurs who cater to the needs of the community. Zeddy Plummer, the razor-wielding ex-army buddy of Jake who has turned informer and sweetman, gambler and strikebreaker, provides a sharp contrast to Jake: Though they were both reared in Virginia, they have grown apart and represent different attitudes toward life. Zeddy's name suggests that he is at the end of the line (the Jamaican pronunciation of Z being "zed") and that he is a conduit for refuse, dirt, and waste. Billy Biasse (whose name carries suggestions of his prejudices and his interest in prostitution), though less than admirable in his dealings, is nevertheless a realist in telling Jake that Harlem is so dangerous that a man must be armed—and so gives him a gun that saves his life.

The characters, with the exceptions of Ray and Agatha, represent the demimonde; there are none of the professional, middle-class, or hard-working ordinary people of the Black Belt. (The omission became the basis of much of the criticism leveled against the book by the intellectuals of the Harlem Renaissance.) As in much of McKay's fiction, some names are clearly to be taken at the symbolic level: Felice (joy, happiness) and Agatha (goodness, kindness) are two; others are noted above.

Themes and Meanings

Home to Harlem is structured around contrasts between opposing philosophies of life, and it is clear that Ray and his outlook are subordinated to the person and philosophy of Jake. Jake's traits—honesty, versatility, perseverance, optimism—are highlighted, while those of Ray—deliberateness, cynicism, retrospection, pessimism—are downplayed. "Jake was as happy as a kid. . . . But Ray was not happy," the reader is told; in fact, Ray is made "impotent by thought." Jake's fortunes go down and out, downtown to the Pennsylvania Station and out to Pittsburgh. Yet he is irrepressible and positive. He undergoes initiation into the adult black life of Harlem, survives the rites of passage, and departs on a quest for the good life with a good woman in a distant (perhaps unrealistically imagined as Edenic) location.

Jake is a symbol of order, stability, and moderation. He has generally admirable qualities and an unusual intuition for correct decisions and actions. He is willing to forgo employment if it means strikebreaking. He is willing to share a room, but not to live off the earnings of a street girl. He can see that the white world is one of materialism and opportunism, but he does not want to be a part of it: He becomes almost a paragon, yet one with great *joie de vivre*, loyalty, and self-esteem.

The two principal nightclubs, the Baltimore and the Congo, serve as representatives of the two ways of life that McKay contrasted throughout his writing and which he always suggested should be bridged. The Congo is "an amusement place entirely for the unwashed of the Black Belt," but the Baltimore, with which Felice and Jake identify, is more restrained—though not sedate. The Baltimore is for men, the Congo for sweetmen. Whenever he writes about the quick action of the cabarets and entertainment apartments, McKay writes in a staccato style: short sentences, short words, parallel structures.

Every once in a while, McKay allows some social criticism to intrude—even in the context of a rather tranquil situation. When Jake finally finds Felice at the Sheba Palace (where she is in the company of Zeddy), he walks her down Madison Avenue to 130th Street past the Presbyterian church: It is described as a "solid gray-grim mass" where "desperate, frightened, blanch-faced, the ancient sepulchral Respectability held on" and "frowned on the corner like a fortress against the invasion." The sight of the building gives the two "moral courage" to continue their walk in "the most Arcadian atmosphere in all New York." It is only in such ways that McKay broaches the larger social issues of the day, which included segregated living. At times he knew when to use a sledgehammer and when not to. In *Home to Harlem*, the emphasis is on individual struggles against overcrowding, unemployment, and discrimination: The issue of black-white relations is peripheral and impinged on only by implication.

Critical Context

The initial critical reception of *Home to Harlem* was extraordinary. The novel was praised by white critics and condemned by black ones. Most reviewers admired the easy, unforced conversation of the characters, the careful reproduction of the argot and pronunciation of Harlem residents (whether West Indian, African, or American), and the stark and at times revealing presentation of the rigors and terrors of life in the Black Belt. In fact, such was the praise for the novel that it was awarded the medal of the Institute of Arts and Sciences. (The detailed descriptions of Harlem life, people, and places are the more noteworthy when it is recalled that McKay had left the United States in 1922, six years before publication of the book. Distance had not diminished his impressions and had perhaps even sharpened his critical faculties.)

Many critics commented on the novel's social realism, though McKay himself chose to emphasize that his aim was emotional realism—the difference being one of focus on people's feelings rather than on their circumstances. It was this emphasis on emotions (involving, inevitably, sexuality, extramarital relationships, frenetic dancing, drinking, gambling, and similar activities), this romanticizing of blacks who were essentially social outcasts in New York, that accounted for the criticism of the black press.

At one gambling game, Jake is accosted by a "hideous mulattress" who has purple streaks on her face, and he recoils from her sexual advances. Then he generalizes that "a woman could always go farther than a man in coarseness, depravity, and sheer cupidity. Men were ugly and brutal. But beside women they were merely vicious children." Such an observation, undeniably an indictment of black women and the black social structure, was too close to the tenor of Carl Van Vechten's *Nigger Heaven* (1926) to be ignored.

The attack was led by Dr. W. E. B. Du Bois in a celebrated comment in his magazine *Crisis* in June, 1928, when he wrote: "*Home to Harlem* for the most part nauseates me, and after the dirtier parts of its filth I feel distinctly like taking a bath. . . . It looks as though McKay has set out to cater to that prurient demand on the part of the white folk for a portrayal in Negroes of that licentiousness which conventional civilization holds white folk back from enjoying." Alain Locke, the principal philosopher of the Harlem Renaissance, took a similar approach, but both Du Bois and Locke were far removed from the daily struggle for existence that was the lot of those folk about whom McKay had written. They wanted to encourage "uplifting" fiction rather than realistic fiction; they wanted to feature the "Talented Tenth" rather than the deprived and struggling masses.

McKay's achievement has, however, long been recognized. Though there are structural flaws in the novel (after all, it was the author's first), especially in the rather casual introduction of Ray and his equally casual departure, it gave rise to a number of imitations that treated life in the black slums of the cities. In fact, it helped to relocate black fiction from the farm to the city, it showed that fiction could become a vehicle for social and political propaganda, and it suggested that the new black would be one who held fast to the achievements of the black past while adapting to the demands of the modern world.

Bibliography
Cooper, Wayne F. *Claude McKay: Rebel Sojourner in the Harlem Renaissance: A Biography*. Baton Rouge: Louisiana State University Press, 1987. Traces McKay's life from his birth in Jamaica through his years in America and England and his journey to Russia, as well as his eventual conversion to Catholicism. A chapter is devoted to the period in which he wrote *Home to Harlem*.
Draper, James P., ed. *Black Literature Criticism*. 3 vols. Detroit: Gale Research, 1992. Includes an extensive biographical profile of McKay and excerpts from criticism on his works.
Giles, James R. *Claude McKay*. Boston: Twayne, 1976. Giles provides a critical and interpretive study of McKay with a close reading of his major works, a solid bibliography, and complete notes and references.
Hegler, Charles J. "Claude McKay's 'If We Must Die,' *Home to Harlem*, and the Hog Trope." *ANQ* 8 (Summer, 1995): 22-26. Hegler points out that McKay uses the same symbolic figures in his poem "If We Must Die," where he protests the slaughter of penned and ignorant hogs, and in *Home to Harlem*, where his characters become the alienated "hogs" of Chicago, searching but never finding a home.
Roberts, Kimberly. "The Clothes Make the Woman: The Symbolics of Prostitution on Nella Larsen's *Quicksand* and Claude McKay's *Home to Harlem*." *Tulsa Studies in Women's Literature* 16 (Spring, 1997): 107-130. Roberts examines the use of prostitution as a metaphor for the position of African American writers.
Tillery, Tyrone. *Claude McKay: A Black Poet's Struggle for Identity*. Amherst: University of Massachusetts Press, 1992. Tillery's biography is a well-documented and fascinating study of McKay's life. Focuses on McKay's turbulent life and personality and examines his various associations with black radicalism, socialism, and communism and his ultimate rejection of them for the refuge of the Catholic Church.

A. L. McLeod

HOMEBASE

Author: Shawn Wong (1949-   )
Type of plot: Bildungsroman
Time of plot: The 1950's and the 1960's
Locale: Guam and the Western United States
First published: 1979

> *Principal characters:*
> RAINSFORD CHAN, a young fourth-generation Chinese American
> BOBBY CHAN, Rainsford's father, an engineer who dies when Rainsford is seven
> RAINSFORD'S MOTHER, the owner of a flower shop, who dies when Rainsford is fifteen
> RAINSFORD'S GRANDFATHER, the man after whom Rainsford is named
> RAINSFORD'S GREAT-GRANDFATHER, the first immigrant in the family, a man who helped build railroads in the American West
> RAINSFORD'S UNCLE, a medical doctor with whom Rainsford lives after his mother's death
> RAINSFORD'S AUNT, manager and owner of a children's shop
> RAINSFORD'S "DREAM-BRIDE," an important creation of Rainsford's mind

The Novel

Homebase is a novel about fifteen-year-old Rainsford Chan, a fourth-generation Chinese American struggling to establish his identity both as a person and as an American. The central events of his life, and the ones with which the narrative is most concerned, are the deaths of his father (when Rainsford is seven years old) and of his mother (when he is fifteen).

The novel is divided into five chapters, each of which has a generous number of what might be called "speculative flashbacks." Rainsford never knew his grandfather or great-grandfather, and he knew his father only slightly before his death. These "speculative flashbacks," which actually make up most of the work, are founded both in reality and in imagination; Rainsford does have some factual information about his grandfather and great-grandfather in the form of letters, documents, and a few family stories and legends that have come down to him. He enlarges upon these to discover and define meaning for his own existence.

Wong begins the novel by giving the basic facts of Rainsford's present circumstances and family history. The reader learns immediately of several important events in the young narrator's life: Rainsford is fifteen years old, and both of his parents are dead. The narrator is pursuing the lives of his family members, especially those of his grandfather and great-grandfather. He tells us that he cannot speak Chinese, but he remembers his own father teaching him "Home on the Range," buying him Superman T-shirts, and taking him to see World War II films. Although his grandfather and great-grandfather are never given names, they become central to the story, and it is through them and through Rainsford's imagined history of their lives that he comes to terms with his own identity. Much of the opening section is a history, mostly contrived by Rainsford, of his great-grandfather's life while helping to build railroads in Nevada and Wyoming.

In the second chapter, Rainsford writes a letter to his father, who has been dead some eight years. The letter is an attempt by the young teenager to establish a relation with someone not present so that he can go on with his life as a complete individual, with a heritage and self-understanding. The other major event of this chapter is Rainsford's recollection of his father's death; a poignant story is told of the young boy ironing his father's shirts on the night his mother comes home to report his father's death. Readers also learn that two years after his father's death, his mother had taken a lover in order to try to escape some of her own pain from the loss; the attempt is not successful, but it has no negative effects on Rainsford himself.

Rainsford's mother dies when he is fifteen, and the youth goes to live with his uncle, a medical doctor, and his aunt, who runs a children's store. It is important in the third chapter that his relatives treat him well, basically by leaving him alone and providing for him. Rainsford assumes many characteristics of his uncle, such as a taste in clothes and personal habits, and has good experiences in high school. He lives with these relatives for three years.

In the fourth chapter, Rainsford's main activity is to drive around in his car, thinking about himself, his past, and his family members—all now dead except for his aunt and uncle, who function successfully as parents primarily by leaving him alone. On one of these night trips, he sees a passing train and begins to speculate about and to recall his great-grandfather's experiences while working on the railroads in the 1860's. Just as important, however, is his creation of a "dream-bride," a fifteen-year-old girl who will, so he thinks, help him to firmly find himself and become, at last, an American by identity as well as residence.

The grandfather is the main character in the last chapter. Rainsford meets a Navajo Indian who has Chinese blood and is able to inform him of his own name—and, therefore, of his own identity. Rainsford Chan had been named, so he always knew, after a place in California ("Chan" is the Chinese word for California). Rainsford has never been able to find a Rainsford, California, and so has felt that his own identity is incomplete; he has had no knowledge of who or what he actually is. In the last pages of the novel, his search for self is successfully concluded: Rainsford learns that the land itself (that is, America) is his ancestry.

The Characters

Rainsford Chan, the narrator and main character of the novel, reveals the process of his struggle for identity as he lets the reader know his thoughts. His development occurs rather quickly as readers realize, rather instantly, that he is "American" in every way. Only Rainsford himself is unaware of this. Moreover, as he tells of events and episodes in his family history, it is clear that other family members before him have already made the transition. Rainsford's struggle and characterization is understood by the reader not so much through his actions (he does little more than drive around in his car at night, and he seldom engages in conversation) as through his thoughts about the past.

Rainsford's father is dead, and they never knew each other as adults. Fixed only and eternally in memory, the father nevertheless exerts tremendous influence on the youth. "Bobby," which is a mispronunciation of "Daddy" by Rainsford as a toddler, is the only character in the work to have a name (except Rainsford himself). Bobby, it is recalled, had spent much time with Rainsford when he was young; the things the child remembers all reflect the father's overt intention to Americanize his son. Through teaching him American games, songs, and traditions, the father effectually denies the Chinese heritage of the family.

Of all these unnamed, dead characters, Rainsford's grandfather is perhaps of most importance. Again, the reader, like the narrator himself, knows little of the grandfather's actual life. Perhaps the most significant fact is that the grandfather had once returned to China but then returned to the United States. At the end of the work, Rainsford's discovery that he had been named after Angel Island in San Francisco Bay—the place where his grandfather had been processed by immigration officials upon his return to the United States—fixes permanently Rainsford's identity as a person and as an American.

The characterization of Rainsford's great-grandfather, who could not speak English and was subjected to prejudice and discrimination of which Rainsford knows nothing, at least by experience, stands in contrast to Rainsford's own life. Even though the fourth-generation American can speculate about his great-grandfather's life, he has nothing in common with him. Rainsford is a stranger in Chinatown, going there out of curiosity like Americans of other racial groups. Rainsford had grown up drinking milkshakes and eating french fries.

Rainsford's aunt and uncle, childless themselves, become his parents after his mother's death. Like other characters in the novel, they are stationary; however, they are different in that they are alive. Primarily, they serve as role models for young Rainsford, who evidently is on his way to acquiring the usual prerequisites of the American Dream after he comes to peace with himself. As successful Americans themselves, the aunt and uncle, though never denying their Chinese heritage, race, and ancestry, live lives in which these things are functionally not important. They live in an upper-middle-class neighborhood near the beach, drive sports cars, and go jogging, for example.

Rainsford's mother is similarly characterized. She, too, is dead from the beginning of the work, and so never changes. Readers learn that she is very proud of her son and favors him with an extreme amount of attention both at home and at the flower shop she owns and manages after her husband's death. Rainsford takes great delight that when "American" customers order "Oriental" bouquets, it is he, Rainsford, who designs them—and does so with absolutely no knowledge of what they are or might look like.

The final character of any consequence is not only dead but also nonexistent.

Rainsford imagines a "dream-bride," a girl of some fifteen years of age who could somehow make his life complete. He envisions a trip with her in the American Midwest, knowing only that somehow such a creature would establish his own worth as an individual. The "dream-bride," of course, turns out to be America herself.

Themes and Meanings

Rainsford Chan's story is one of finding himself. He must determine his identity and meaning as a person, a man, and an American. Of these three, only the second one (that is, his identity as a man) presents few problems; remarkably, he experiences less of this struggle than a reader might lend plausibility. He is athletic and likes girls, cars, war films, hamburgers, and milkshakes; hence, there is rather an absence of problems.

His struggle to find himself as a person revolves mostly around the fact that his parents are dead. This works in the novel not as a Freudian formula; rather, it serves as a way for the novelist to emphasize that Rainsford's background and heritage—even his parentage—are dead. His realizations are never quite made from an existential context, and yet he does discover and define meaning from within the self.

It is the problem of his identity as an American that is of most concern to the novelist and reader. Slowly, Rainsford learns that he is and always has been American, that the problems surrounding him because of his biological ethnicity are not only irrelevant but nonexistent. Wong emphasizes this most especially in the "speculative flashback" technique he uses in telling the stories of Rainsford's parents, father, grandfather, and great-grandfather. All of their experiences as Chinese stand in direct, perhaps even stark, contrast to those of the young narrator. Rainsford's problems are never their problems; indeed, it often seems that Rainsford's struggle, though valid, meaningful, and beautifully rendered, is something of a luxury, a self-indulgence. This fact does not undercut the severity or the importance of his struggle; rather, it emphasizes the totality of his loss of Chinese identity and role as a mainstream American.

Wong uses several epic conventions in his work. The trip that Rainsford takes with his family from Berkeley to New York and back, as well as the few years in Guam, are reminiscent of the journey made by Odysseus. Too, his call to his forefathers to help him find meaning in life has more in common with prayer to the Muses than it does with traditional Asian worship or reverence for ancestors. Moreover, his car becomes something of a weapon in his internal war. These connections are never overt, but such occurrences make young Rainsford's existence and experiences somewhat akin to those of Odysseus.

Critical Context

Homebase, written at the end of the 1970's, is an important statement about the role of Asian Americans in the United States at the time. The author explains minority "mainstreaming" for such Chinese immigrants, but his message applies just as meaningfully to immigrants of other races and nationalities. Such minority fiction was coming into vogue for the first time during this period, following some rather huge publication successes of the 1960's in which books by minority authors became truly important for the first time. Wong writes of a time when newly arrived immigrants could not survive in America without first giving up their history, heritage, and past. He emphasizes this most centrally in the novel by distinguishing between "Chinese" and "Chinaman." Rainsford Chan is by birth "Chinese"—he becomes a "Chinaman" (and therefore an object of discrimination and prejudice) only when he goes to Chinatown. As ethnic fiction, *Homebase* makes its statement clearly through its title: America, not China, is Rainsford Chan's home base. China can never be more to him than other homelands can be to other Americans, virtually all of whom are descended from immigrants.

Bibliography
Gong, Ted. "Approaching Cultural Change Through Literature: From Chinese to Chinese American." *Amerasia Journal* 7 (Spring, 1980): 73-86. Gong delineates the processes of acculturation common to all Chinese immigrants. A reading of Gong's study validates the credibility of Rainsford Chan's experiences.
Hom, Marlon K. "A Case of Mutual Exclusion: Portrayals by Immigrant and American-Born Chinese of Each Other in Literature." *Amerasia Journal* 10 (Fall/Winter, 1984): 29-45. Hom's article, while discussing works written both in English and in Chinese, elucidates various problems between Chinese and American cultures. Helpful in understanding Rainsford Chan's entrapment in middle territory between the two cultures.
Kazin, Alfred. *A Writer's America: Landscape in Literature*. New York: Alfred A. Knopf, 1988. Two chapters of this book discuss the landscape of the American West, which is central to Rainsford Chan's discovery of self and identity. These include chapter 3, which has information about the lands where Chan's forefathers worked on the American railroad, and chapter 6, which explains the role of California in the American identity, something learned by the main character.
Monaghan, Peter. "Writing Novels, Winning Races." *The Chronicle of Higher Education* 42 (January 26, 1996): A5. A brief profile of Wong covering his career as a writer, college instructor, and part-time drag-race driver for the Chrysler Corporation. Offers interesting insight into Wong's background and motivation for writing.
Spencer, Benjamin T. *Patterns of Nationality*. New York: Burt Franklin, 1981. Part 1 of this text, entitled "The Nature of Nationality," spells out particular changes experienced by various ethnic groups arriving in the United States. The author addresses problems that occur when "continuity" and "change" confront various groups of new arrivals.
Yu, Connie Young. "Rediscovered Voices: Chinese Immigrants and Angel Island." *Amerasia Journal* 4, no. 2 (1977): 123-139. Yu discusses in some length the experiences of Chinese immigrants arriving in the United States to be processed for residency through government officials at Angel Island. Such experiences were lived through by both Rainsford Chan's great-grandfather and grandfather.

Carl Singleton

THE HOME-MAKER

Author: Dorothy Canfield Fisher (1879-1958)
Type of plot: Domestic realism
Time of plot: The early 1920's
Locale: A small town somewhere in New England
First published: 1924

>*Principal characters:*
>> EVA KNAPP, a harried housewife and mother who finds fulfillment as a sales manager
>> LESTER KNAPP, her loving but absentminded husband who becomes the homemaker
>> STEPHEN,
>> HELEN, and
>> HENRY, the Knapp children who mature with the exchange of parental roles

The Novel

Much of the action of *The Home-maker* is intended to illustrate the negative consequences of sexual stereotyping. The Knapps, a seemingly typical white Protestant American family consisting of parents, Lester and Eva, and three bright children, live in a quaint New England town during the early 1920's. Nevertheless, this outwardly contented clan suffers from expectations which both Lester and Eva find impossible to meet.

Throughout, a sympathetic narrator acknowledges the determination of Eva, who, with the tenacity of Sisyphus, endures the drudgery of her mindless household tasks. Eva's perfectionism creates an unhappy and frazzled family: Her youngest son, Stephen, becomes belligerent and disrespectful, while the distraught Helen and Henry try to remain as unobtrusive as possible. Ultimately, even they become victims of mother's endless nagging. Eva's only freedom from homemaking consists of her church and community service. Though her neighbors condescendingly sympathize with the poor Mrs. Knapp at home, they readily adopt her organizational skills and comment on the quality of her volunteerism in the community.

Lester, meanwhile finds an equal measure of discontent in his work as bookkeeper for the Willings Emporium, the local clothing and appliance store. When he fails to receive an expected promotion, given instead to a younger and less experienced employee, he sinks into a state of depression and diminished self-esteem. Finally, having lost his job altogether, he considers suicide as a possible method of escaping from the hell that he thinks all fathers share—the necessity of earning the family's income.

Neither Lester nor Eva considers reversing their roles, but Lester's near fatal fall off a neighbor's roof brings about the novel's unexpected resolution. Paralyzed from the waist down, Lester seems doomed to a life of tedium. Ironically though, he is set free by his infirmity. After the fall—a *felix culpa* to be sure—Lester is able to provide the careful and sensitive guidance that his children desperately need.

While Lester convalesces, Eva assumes the position of breadwinner with a profound sense of energy, enthusiasm, and joy. Within a short time, she is promoted to sales manager.

Fisher ends *The Home-maker* on a disturbing note, inasmuch as it is implied that Lester has really recovered enough to walk, he chooses to remain crippled in order to protect his family's newfound cohesiveness.

The Characters

The thrifty, neat, and energetic Eva Knapp appears to her community as an enduring, virtuous wife and mother. Yet she is far from perfect. Fisher redeems what could be a cliche figure of the harried housewife by vividly describing Eva's frustrations and her compulsive need for order. Fisher suggests that Eva's eczema is related to the despair and tension that she suffers at home; her long dark hair, which she keeps tightly coiled about her head, symbolizes her anxiety.

Eva changes when she begins her career at the Willings Emporium. As new talents emerge—Eva discovers that she has a gift for public relations and for marketing ideas—her obsessions with domestic order relax. Thus, Fisher portrays the emancipated American housewife of the 1920's. Her portrait, however, is fundamentally conservative.

Eva epitomizes the Old Testament definition of the virtuous wife. She sells fine linen and wool in the marketplace. She rises early and works at the store with willing hands. She provides for her children with the fruit of her labor and grows to admire and praise Lester's strengths.

Lester Knapp is a complex character. His virtues are more obscure than Eva's, so the sympathy he evokes requires much more finesse on Fisher's part. Drawn probably from a composite of Fisher's own father and husband, who were both professors, Lester has the idealism and the idiosyncracies characteristic of an academic thwarted by circumstance.

By rendering the opinions of Lester's gossipy neighbors and former boss, the reader understands how the world berates Lester's lack of ambition, his absentmindedness, his tendency to daydream, and his failure as a moneymaker. Lester loves to recite poetry, read novels, and conduct cheerful chats with his children.

It is through Lester's own ability to analyze human nature that the reader comes to admire the quality of his mind. Despite acknowledged limitations, Lester is able to perceive the psychological and intellectual needs of his family. During a long and painful recovery, Lester concentrates on ways that he might stimulate his children's individual development.

The reader can infer from dialogue and precise description the great changes that occur in the Knapp children when father takes over as homemaker. Stephen becomes the inquisitive, loving, and gregarious boy whose potential Lester has recognized. The once vacant-eyed and shy Helen responds enthusiastically to her father's literary sensibilities. Henry, who is finally allowed to keep the dog that he dared not mention to mother, gains confidence by exercising his boyhood prerogatives.

The minor characters, including the Knapp relatives and friends, reinforce and vivify what Fisher's omniscient narrator establishes. The delineation of these numerous characters through dialogue promotes a deeper understanding of the Knapp family in their community setting.

Themes and Meanings

The Home-maker is a novel about freedom. The individual, Fisher suggests, possesses inherent tendencies and gifts which society, by way of sexual stereotyping, can thwart or impede. Fisher's idealism is evident, since the innate talents of the Knapps emerge during adversity. Lester's decency and Eva's dignity enable them to overcome hollow forms of duty in order to fulfill the substance of their obligations as caring parents.

Fisher, in other words, urges readers to distinguish the essential requirements of parenting from the superficial busyness that often takes first place. Frantically scrubbing grease spots while stifling a child's innate capacities, Fisher suggests, is self-defeating. Freedom and harmony come to the Knapp home when each member is able to develop his own nature. In this way, *The Home-maker* redefines homemaking in terms of what is nurtured rather than who is nurturing.

Critical Context

The Home-maker has much in common with the fiction of Willa Cather. Both Cather and Fisher practiced a quiet realism less concerned with external action than with the inner struggles of protagonists thwarted by the needs and desires of others. Written during a decade when prose flourished with the glittering passions of F. Scott Fitzgerald's romances and the incisive satire of Sinclair Lewis, *The Home-maker* has been rediscovered by readers who appreciate Fisher's awareness of sexual stereotyping.

The Home-maker was the third of Fisher's six novels. Less autobiographical than her earlier works, it nevertheless draws substantially on Fisher's experience. The implied New England setting, the idealism of the protagonists, their sense of devotion to children and community all reflect elements of Fisher's own life as an acclaimed children's author, adult fiction writer, scholar, and civic leader. Fisher was later named by Eleanor Roosevelt as one of the ten most influential women in contemporary life.

Fisher was a figure worth emulating, and her works are animated by an indomitable spirit and a belief in the inherent goodness of the individual.

Bibliography

Fisher, Dorothy Canfield. *Keeping Fires Night and Day: Selected Letters of Dorothy Canfield Fisher.* Columbia: University of Missouri Press, 1993. Fisher's collected correspondence sheds considerable light on her life and writings.

Madigan, Mark J. "Dorothy Canfield Fisher: 1879-1958." *Legacy: A Journal of American Women Writers* 9 (1992): 49-58. A revealing examination of Fisher's life and how her experiences influenced her writing.

Price, Alan. "Writing Home from the Front: Edith Wharton and Dorothy Canfield Fisher Present Wartime France to the United States: 1917-1919." *Edith Wharton Newsletter* 5 (Fall, 1988): 1-5, 8. Although this essay does not discuss *The Home-maker*, it does offer an interesting perspective on Fisher's early themes, as well as their development in later works.

Washington, Ida H. *Dorothy Canfield Fisher: A Biography.* Shelburne, Vt.: New England Press, 1982. A perceptive biography of Fisher that also offers insight into her various works.

Teresa Chittenden Frary

THE HOTEL NEW HAMPSHIRE

Author: John Irving (1942-   )
Type of plot: Psychological realism
Time of plot: The 1940's to the late 1970's
Locale: Maine; Dairy, New Hampshire; Vienna; and New York City
First published: 1981

> *Principal characters:*
> JOHN BERRY, the narrator and protagonist
> WINSLOW BERRY, his father
> MARY BATES BERRY, John's mother
> BOB BERRY, John's grandfather
> FRANNY BERRY, John's sister and a successful actress
> FRANK BERRY, John's brother
> LILLY BERRY, John's younger sister and a novelist
> EGG BERRY, John's youngest brother
> FREUD, a Viennese Jew and friend of the family
> CHIPPER DOVE, a preparatory school quarterback and Franny's rapist

The Novel

The Hotel New Hampshire is narrated by John Berry, even though he and his brothers and sisters have not been born, not "even conceived," when the story begins with the meeting of their parents. Consequently, the events in the first part of the book are retold by John from his parents' accounts. In fact, John's own account is more imaginative and titillating than the stories told by his idealistic father and more practical, even prosaic, mother. The events that led to his parents' union shape their children's lives and explain why and how they grow or fail to grow. Even though the novel is about three generations and spans some sixty years, it is a novel about the passage from childhood to adulthood; it does not extend into the children's adult lives.

The title, *The Hotel New Hampshire*, provides structure for John Irving's novel, since there are in fact three Hotel New Hampshires, each corresponding to a particular stage in the development of the Berry children. John's parents meet at the Hotel Arbuthnot, what will become the third and most idealized Hotel New Hampshire. The Maine summer resort hotel where both work is also where they meet Freud ("our Freud," not the "other Freud," the psychiatrist) and his performing bear, State o' Maine; where they encounter Arbuthnot, the hotel's owner, whose appearance in a white dinner jacket serves as a premonition of death (he warns the couple that the world is not safe for bears or Jews); and where they fall in love.

After their marriage, they teach at the Dairy School in New Hampshire, but John's father buys an old school for girls and converts it into the first official Hotel New Hampshire. The first hotel is initially a womblike, protected haven for the children, but death and sorrow (Irving has symbolically named the family dog "Sorrow") threaten. Frank is beaten by the football team, Franny is raped, and Sorrow is put to sleep. Frank, an amateur taxidermist, stuffs Sorrow, thereby ensuring Sorrow's recurrent literal and symbolic appearances. Subsequently, Iowa Bob, who represents stability, dies of a heart attack at the unexpected sight of Sorrow. The first part of the novel ends with the sight of another man in a white dinner jacket and the receipt of a letter from Freud, who has invited the family to Vienna to run a hotel.

The Berry family flies to Vienna in separate planes, but the plane with Mrs. Berry and Egg (and the stuffed Sorrow), crashes, killing them. The second Hotel New Hampshire in Vienna is the antithesis of the first: The home to prostitutes and terrorists, it is hardly a haven. Amid the corruption of Vienna, the children are initiated into the real world: Franny sleeps with Ernst, a terrorist-pornographer who resembles Chipper Dove, the high schooler who raped her, and with Susie, also a rape victim, who dresses in a bear's costume; John sleeps with Fehlgeburt, a terrorist who advises him to leave Vienna, and the troubled John also confesses his long-suppressed love for Franny; and the family thwarts a terrorist plot to blow up the opera house. In the fight, Freud is killed and Mr. Berry is blinded.

Because Lilly has written a successful novel, the family has some money, and they return to the United States. The novel is filmed, and Franny becomes a film star and Frank a successful agent. While in New York, John encounters Chipper Dove, whom he lures into a setup, where Dove is sexually humiliated by John, Franny, and Susie, who dons her bear suit and threatens to rape him. The repressed sexual feelings of John and Franny erupt in a painful orgy of lovemaking, and they conclude that their love is indeed destructive. Lilly, whose second novel fails, jumps to her death from her hotel room.

After Lilly's death, John and his father return to Maine and "run" (John never does admit guests) the third Hotel New Hampshire, which they have purchased from Arbuthnot. Some time later, Susie, again in her bear costume, visits John, and they discover that they love each other. Meanwhile, Franny has married Junior Jones, a black professional football player who had been her friend and protector at the Dairy School. At the end of the novel, Franny and Junior are expecting a child, whom they will turn over to John and Susie to rear. The Hotel New Hampshire becomes the idealized hotel envisioned by Mr. Berry when a family from Arizona stops at the hotel, is welcomed, and Susie again puts on her bear suit, not to escape from life but to entertain children. The dreams of "the best hotel, the perfect family, the resort life" finally seem realized.

The Characters

John Berry, Irving's protagonist-narrator, is the moral center of the novel, the spokesman for Irving, who, like John, was born in 1942. (Incidentally, Mr. Berry's first name is Winslow, which is Irving's middle name.) In the course of the novel, John resolves a host of problems, all of which involve maturation and identity. In fact, the novel is almost a casebook on Freudian psychology (the distinction between the two Freuds blatantly makes the point).

Despite the novel's focus on the five Berry children, the reader actually knows only Franny and John well. Egg (whose name is obviously symbolic of the unformed personality) dies when the family leaves the womblike first Hotel New Hampshire. Lilly, whose physical growth is stunted, also exists primarily as a symbol of arrested development: Her first novel concerns autobiographical events that culminate with the fatal plane crash. Her inability to deal with the death of her mother and with the initiation experiences of Vienna is manifested in her failed second novel, which concerns events after the crash. Although Frank is more fully drawn, he is defined almost exclusively in terms of his homosexuality, which he comes to terms with by the end of the novel.

John's parents also serve largely symbolic roles, a point that Irving makes by referring to them not as Win and Mary but as Mother and Father. The reader knows little about Mother, whose primary function is to die, thereby leaving her children to discover themselves in Vienna. Father, on the other hand, is more fully realized, but he symbolizes the failed father whose illusions (about bears, hotels, and life itself) blind him (first, metaphorically, then, literally) to reality. His weaknesses serve as a foil to John's strength at the end of the novel, when John is his father's "parent."

Freud is also an intriguing blend of real-life caricature and symbolic figure. He was blinded in the Holocaust and therefore represents all the victims of "man's inhumanity to man"; he is also representative of those who not only endure but also thrive in adversity. More important, however, he is a symbolic figure who appears at crucial moments in Mr. Berry's life: When the Berrys meet at the Hotel Arbuthnot, he gives Mr. Berry the bear and extracts three promises from him (the bear motif is thereby established); he invites the Berrys to Vienna after the problems in New Hampshire; and he sacrifices himself in Vienna. His shadowy figure is well suited to a novel which, in its sketchy characterizations and lack of attention to setting, resembles nothing quite so much as a fairy tale (and John himself compares his story to a fairy tale).

Franny is the most fully developed female character in the book, and Irving has suggested that Franny is the "prime mover" in the novel, the one who has, as he put it in an interview, "the most to deal with." Franny must "deal" with her rape, and she does through ritual baths, her realization of her parents' sexuality, her cathartic union with Ernst, her affair with Susie, and her incestuous lovemaking with John. Her sexual problems are resolved in the impending birth of her child. On the other hand, she is also the means by which John resolves his sexual problems. Ronda Ray, the maid; Titsie Tuck, a young debutante; and Fehlgeburt, the terrorist—all are women with whom John has had unsatisfying sexual relationships. It is only after he has purged himself of his feelings for Franny that he and Susie can love each other.

Themes and Meanings

The Hotel New Hampshire concerns maturation, the passage from childhood to adulthood, and it involves coming to terms with one's desires, with the real world, and with the world of illusion. The novel suggests that one must confront one's own desires, the "bears" within one, and must come to terms with the society that does not allow those "bears" to live. (State o' Maine is shot, and Susie is whole only when she renounces her bear suit.) The failure to experience life results in defeat and death (Lilly and Egg), while initiation experiences lead to one's testing one's illusions and accepting life as it is.

In Vienna, the children hear a story about a street clown named the King of Mice, who jumps out a window to his death. On the box containing his pets are the words "Life is serious, but art is fun." While life is serious, Irving suggests that one should pass open windows—that is, one should not escape but live life. Lilly's death (she jumps from an open window) suggests the inability to grow; John, Franny, and Frank avoid open windows in spite of their problems. "Sorrow" does float—the bobbing stuffed dog is the only sign of the plane crash in the ocean—and sorrow indeed appears in the novel in a variety of forms. Two are prostitution and terrorism, both linked to Venice and, through parallels, to each other. At the end of the novel, John and Franny have learned that they can lead productive, rewarding lives despite their problems. In fact, Susie has, like Franny, overcome her rape trauma, and she and John convert the third Hotel New Hampshire into a rape crisis center.

Critical Context

The Hotel New Hampshire, Irving's fifth novel, followed closely on the heels of *The World According to Garp* (1978), an enormous critical and commercial success which received the National Book Award for the best paperback novel of 1979. In many ways, it is of a piece with his first four novels: The symbolic use of bears, trips to Vienna, Maine as haven, the academic community, wrestling—all are featured in *The Hotel New Hampshire*. In fact, the seeds for *The Hotel New Hampshire* are planted by Garp: While in Vienna, Garp writes "The Pension Grillparzer," about his father and a hotel, and near the end of the book Garp plans to publish his novel *My Father's Illusions*.

In other ways, *The Hotel New Hampshire* departs from the earlier novels. Even though *The World According to Garp* impressed many readers as an outrageous novel with outsize, grotesque characters and improbable turns of events, it is essentially a traditional novel in terms of its structure, characters, and use of setting. *The Hotel New Hampshire*, despite its similarity to *The World According to Garp* in subjects and themes, breaks with its predecessors: Irving's use of the fairy tale, myth, and Freudian psychology produces a novel in which the journey is the structure, and the characters and settings are symbolic rather than "real."

At the same time, Irving's novel is readable and accessible to the reading public, and it is his apparent simplicity that has made him a popular novelist as well as a serious one. (Indeed, both *The World According to Garp*, in 1982, and *The Hotel New Hampshire*, in 1984, were made into films.) Rather than being self-consciously arty and intellectual, Irving has chosen to emphasize story. It is true that *The Hotel New Hampshire* is a serious work which rewards a close reading, but Irving, unlike many modern novelists, has not lost sight of the King of Mice's motto: "Life is serious, but art is fun." In his entertaining, admittedly popular novels, Irving treats life seriously indeed.

Bibliography

Campbell, Josie. *John Irving: A Critical Companion*. Westport, Conn.: Greenwood Press, 1998. Offers a brief biography as well as an overview of Irving's fiction. Devotes an entire chapter to *The Hotel New Hampshire*, which includes discussion of plot and character development, thematic issues, and a new critical approach to the novel.

Irving, John. Interview by Suzanne Herel. *Mother Jones* 22 (May-June, 1997): 64-66. Irving discusses his views on religion, censorship, literature, abortion, and wrestling. His thoughts on these topics illuminate the tone and philosophy of his writings.

Reilly, Edward C. *Understanding John Irving*. Columbia: University of South Carolina Press, 1991. Chapter 8 gives a thorough analysis of Irving's characterization and symbolism and a brief summary of critical reviews.

Shostak, Debra. "The Family Romances of John Irving." *Essays in Literature* 21 (Spring, 1994): 129-145. Shostak focuses on several of Irving's novels that can be classified as family romances or self-conscious works that center on fathers, including *The Hotel New Hampshire*. She explores the oedipal conflicts as well as the uncertainties about fatherhood and origin reflected in these novels.

Thomas L. Erskine

THE HOUR OF THE STAR

Author: Clarice Lispector (1925-1977)
Type of plot: Social realism
Time of plot: The 1970's
Locale: Rio de Janeiro, Brazil
First published: A Hora da Estrela, 1977 (English translation, 1986)

> *Principal characters:*
> RODRIGO S. M., the narrator, who struggles to write the story of
>   Macabéa
> MACABÉA, a young girl from the northeast of Brazil who has migrated
>   to Rio de Janeiro, where she works as a typist
> OLÍMPICO DE JESUS MOREIRA CHAVES, Macabéa's boyfriend, a thug
>   from the northeast
> GLÓRIA, Macabéa's office mate
> MADAME CARLOTA, a fortune-teller whom Macabéa visits

The Novel

In *The Hour of the Star,* Clarice Lispector creates a male narrator, Rodrigo S. M., to write the story of a young Brazilian girl who has recently moved to Rio de Janeiro. The narrator has caught sight of this young girl on the street. She is nothing special; the slums of Rio de Janeiro are filled with thousands like her, shopgirls and office workers sharing one-room flats, invisible and superfluous, silent in the clamor of the city.

The first quarter of the book is taken up with Rodrigo's ruminations on why and how he is writing the story of this young girl. He declares that her story must be told by a man, for a woman would feel too much sympathy and end up in tears. The story must be told simply and with humility, for it is about the unremarkable adventures and the shadowy existence of a young girl trying to survive in a hostile city. Rodrigo feels the need to identify with his subject, so he decides to share her condition as closely as possible by wearing threadbare clothes, suffering from lack of sleep, neglecting to shave, giving up sex and football, avoiding human contact, and immersing himself in nothingness. He envisions this identification with his protagonist as a quest for transfiguration and his "ultimate materialization into an object. Perhaps I might even acquire the sweet tones of the flute and become entwined in a creeper vine."

After describing the disastrous physical appearance of the girl, Rodrigo briefly rehearses her early history. She was born, suffering from rickets, in the backwoods of Alagoas, where her parents died of typhoid when she was two years old. Later she was sent to Maceio to live with her maiden aunt. The aunt, determined to keep the girl from becoming a prostitute, enjoyed thrashing her niece at the slightest provocation or no provocation at all. The child never knew exactly why she was being punished. The only education she experienced beyond three years of primary school was a short typing course, which gave her enough confidence to seek a position as a typist in Rio de Janeiro.

At the moment Rodrigo's story intrudes into her life, the girl is about to be fired. Her work is hopeless—full of typing errors and blotched with dirty spots. Yet her polite apology for the trouble she has caused inspires her boss to modify his dismissal into a warning. The girl retreats to the lavatory to try to recover her composure. When she looks into the tarnished mirror, her reflection seems to have disappeared; her connection to even her own existence is as fragile and tenuous as is Rodrigo's commitment to identifying her. It is nearly halfway through the text before he even allows her a name.

One day, the girl garners enough courage to take time off from work. She exults in her freedom: the luxury of having the room to herself, of indulging in a cup of instant coffee borrowed from her landlady. She dances around the room and contemplates herself in the mirror. It is a moment of sheer happiness and contentment. On the next day, the seventh of May, a rainy day, she meets her first boyfriend; they immediately recognize each other as northeasterners, and he asks her to go for a walk. He also inquires her name, and for the first time in the text the girl is identified:

> —Macabéa.
> —Maca — what?
> —Béa, she was forced to repeat.
> —Gosh, it sounds like the name of a disease . . . a skin disease.

Macabéa explains that her name was a result of a vow her mother had made to the Virgin of Sorrows.

Although the meetings of Macabéa and Olímpico are rain-drenched, their relationship is parched. Conversation is strained, for what little Macabéa has to offer is scorned as foolish or nonsensical by Olímpico. She costs him nothing; the only thing he treats her to is a cup of coffee, to which he allows her to add milk if it does not cost extra. The one kindness he has shown her is an offer to get her a job in the metal factory if she is fired. The high point of the relationship occurs one day when Olímpico decides to show off his strength to Macabéa by lifting her above his head with one hand. Macabéa feels that she is flying—until Olímpico's strength gives way, and he drops her into the mud. Not long after, he drops her entirely. Olímpico has become enamored of Macabéa's workmate, Glória.

Maternally sympathetic to Macabéa, Glória recommends a doctor to her when she is feeling unwell and lends her money to consult a fortune-teller who has the power to break bad spells. The doctor diagnoses Macabéa as suffering the preliminary stages of pulmonary tuberculosis, but the words mean nothing to her. He is appalled by her diet of hot dogs and cola and advises her to eat spaghetti whenever possible. Macabéa has never heard of the dish. As for the fortune-teller, Macabéa accepts the loan, asks for time off from her job, and takes a taxi to see Madame Carlota.

The fortune-teller cuts the cards to read Macabéa's fortune and immediately exclaims over the terrible life that Macabéa has led; then she sees a further misfortune—the loss of her job. Turning another card, though, brings a life change. All of Macabéa's misfortunes will be reversed: her boyfriend will return and ask her to marry him, and her employer will change his mind about firing her. A handsome foreigner named Hans will fall madly in love with her and shower her with unimagined luxuries. Macabéa is astounded; she embraces Madame Carlota and kisses her on the cheek. She leaves the fortune-teller's house in a daze. When she steps off the curb, she is struck by a hit-and-run driver in a yellow Mercedes.

The narrator observes Macabéa, who is lying on the pavement bleeding, and wonders about her death. Macabéa gathers herself into a fetal embrace and utters her final words: "As for the future." The narrator lights a cigarette and goes home, remembering that people die.

The Characters

Rodrigo S. M., the self-declared narrator of the novel, is the voice of self-consciousness, in counterpoint to Macabéa's almost total lack of self-consciousness. He observes the oblivion of his protagonist, and by writing her story goads her into a kind of self-knowledge. The question of the narrative voice in this novel is complex, for Clarice Lispector's own voice is also heard. At times, the reader hears her directly; at times, she can be detected behind or through Rodrigo's words; at times, she seems to be speaking through Macabéa; and at times, her silence is as expressive as her voice.

In the naming of Macabéa and Olímpico, Lispector reveals her ironic playfulness. The Maccabees were a family of Jewish patriots and rulers in the second and first centuries B.C. who led the Jewish people in their struggle for freedom against Syrian rule. Their recapture of the Temple in Jerusalem is marked by the Jewish festival of Hanukkah. The triumphs, power, and fame of the Maccabees are in direct contrast to their namesake's poverty, vulnerability, and obscurity. Olímpico, of course, suggests Mount Olympus and the Olympic Games—the classical spirit of Greek competition. Olímpico competes, but he does it furtively and criminally. He is an accomplished petty thief and is proud of his secret murder of a rival.

Lispector seems to have created Macabéa as a primitive alter-ego. Like Lispector, Macabéa comes from the northeast of Brazil, and like Lispector, she is a creature of spirit. Lispector, though, was a highly educated woman of the world, the wife of a diplomat, the recipient of a law degree, a journalist, and a highly regarded writer of experimental fiction. Macabéa is an empty vessel, so devoid of a place in the world that the only fortune that she can experience is the divine bestowal of a fleeting state of grace.

Olímpico embodies masculine worldliness and ambition. He is concerned with "important things," while Macabéa only notices "unimportant things." She is impressionable where he is impervious to anything he does not understand. What he does understand is the power of blood and the life force, which are embodied for him in the figure of Glória.

Glória represents the survivor. While she lacks any higher self-awareness, she has mastered the skills of survival. She knows how to use her sexual charms and is capable of handling a clerical position. While she is not troubled by the finer points of conscience, she is capable of a kind of maternal compassion.

Themes and Meanings

The Hour of the Star begins and ends with passages that prominently feature the word "yes." The "yes" at the beginning of the book is acquiescence to life: "Everything in the world began with a yes. One molecule said yes to another molecule and life was born." The "yes" at the close of the book is an acceptance of death:

> Dear God, only now am I remembering that people die. Does that include me?
> Don't forget, in the meantime, that this is the season for strawberries. Yes.

Yet even this acceptance of death is interrupted with the insistence that one enjoy life for as long as it offers itself. Lispector died of cancer in the same year that *The Hour of the Star* was published. She characterizes death, "my favorite character in this story," as the ultimate encounter with oneself.

Death and rebirth and metamorphoses are intimately linked in this twisted fairy tale of a Cinderella whose only transformation into the princess happens at the moment of her death. Lispector hangs Macabéa's story on the frame of the fairy tale, with a wicked stepmother (the aunt), an uncaring father (the boss), a traitorous stepsister (Glória), a false suitor (Olímpico), and a fairy godmother (Madame Carlota). Yet the prince that Madame Carlota promises is only an illusion—at most, he is the driver of the Mercedes that runs Macabéa down. The storyteller cannot conjure a happy ending for this poor girl from the northeast.

Reality intrudes. On one level, Lispector is exposing the cruelty and difficulties faced by those who have been forced to emigrate from the hinterlands of Brazil into the cities. Northeast Brazil is the poorest region of a country that, though blessed with natural resources, has not been able to devise a system in which wealth can be distributed in any equitable way. Macabéa and Olímpico, products of the impoverished northeast, present the faces of the victim and the violent—both are devoid of any "civilizing" culture. Olímpico will fight his way into a marginally bourgeois existence, probably by marrying Glória and joining her father in the butchery business. Macabéa hungers for bits of knowledge; she collects advertisements and listens to the culture capsules presented on the radio. This knowledge, though, seems only to alienate her even further from the urban pathways of modern Rio de Janeiro. Her instinctual being does not accord with official reality.

Critical Context

The Hour of the Star was the last book that Clarice Lispector published during her lifetime. She wrote it at the same time as she was writing *Um Sopra de Vida* (1978; a breath of life), a confessional novel bordering on lyrical poetry. *The Hour of the Star* is unique among Lispector's novels in that it deals with contemporary social and political problems in Brazil.

Lispector is best known for moving Brazilian fiction away from regional preoccupations. Like her Argentine contemporary Jorge Luis Borges, she was more concerned as a writer with such major twentieth century literary preoccupations as existentialism, the *nouveau roman*, and linguistic experimentation. Her prose is highly imagistic, and her protagonists develop more through their interaction with everyday objects than through the action of the plot. In rhythmically developed epiphanies reminiscent of James Joyce and Virginia Woolf, her characters gradually come to an awareness of the isolation and ephemerality of their individual existences. Lispector is one of the early voices of female consciousness in Latin American literature; her protagonists are generally middle-class urban women attempting to find a place in the contemporary world.

The Hour of the Star shares many of these themes and stylistic qualities with such earlier works as *Laços de Família* (1960; *Family Ties*, 1972) and *Maçã no Escuro* (1961; *The Apple in the Dark*, 1967), but Lispector's focus on the devastating effects of poverty in contemporary Brazil marked the first time that her very real social concerns (as revealed in her newspaper columns and elsewhere) were addressed in her fiction. Lispector's early death, a day before her fifty-second birthday, silenced one of Latin America's most experimental and original voices.

Bibliography
Cixous, Helene. *Reading with Clarice Lispector.* Minneapolis: University of Minnesota Press, 1990. Chapters on *The Stream of Life*, *The Apple in the Dark*, "The Egg and the Chicken," and *The Hour of the Star.* The book includes an introduction by Verena Andermatt Conley, carefully explaining Cixous's critical approach to Lispector. Recommended for advanced students.
Coutinho, Afranio. *An Introduction to Literature in Brazil.* New York: Columbia University Press, 1960. A major Brazilian critic assesses Lispector's achievement, emphasizing her place in Brazilian literature and her powerful metaphorical and atmospheric fiction.
Fitz, Earl F. *Clarice Lispector.* Boston: Twayne, 1985. A useful introduction that includes a chapter of biography, a discussion of Lispector's place in Brazilian literature; a study of her style, structure, and point of view in her novels and short stories; and her nonfiction work. Includes chronology, detailed notes, and a well-annotated bibliography.
Lowe, Elizabeth. *The City in Brazilian Literature.* Rutherford, N.J.: Farleigh Dickinson University Press, 1982. Discusses Lispector as an urban writer, focusing mainly on *A cidade sitiada*, *The Passion According to G. H.*, and *The Stream of Life.*
Peixoto, Marta. *Passionate Fictions: Gender, Narrative, and Violence in Clarice Lispector.* Minneapolis: University of Minnesota Press, 1994. Written with a decidedly feminist bias, *Passionate Fictions* analyzes Lispector's frequently violent sub-

ject matter, juxtaposing it with her strange and original use of language. Special attention is paid to the nexus with Helene Cixous and to the autobiographical elements of *The Stream of Life* and *A via crucis do corpo*.

Jane Anderson Jones

THE HOUSE BEHIND THE CEDARS

Author: Charles Waddell Chesnutt (1858-1932)
Type of plot: Social criticism
Time of plot: The late 1860's, shortly after the end of the Civil War
Locale: Rural towns and plantations in North and South Carolina
First published: 1900

> *Principal characters:*
> RENA WALDEN, the heroine, a very beautiful young woman of mixed race, whose skin is light enough to pass as white
> GEORGE TRYON, her fiancé, an aristocratic white Southerner from North Carolina
> JOHN WARWICK, Rena's brother and Tryon's attorney, a gentleman planter, passing as a white man
> MOLLY WALDEN, Rena's mother, whose relationship with a prominent planter produced Rena and John
> JEFFERSON WAIN, the superintendent of black schools in Sampson County, who has lecherous designs on Rena
> FRANK FOWLER, an honest black laborer, who truly loves Rena for herself

The Novel

The House Behind the Cedars is a novel about deception of self and of others—and of the consequences of such deceptions. When John Warwick (formerly Walden) returns to the town of his birth, Patesville, North Carolina, he sets in motion a tragic chain of events. For several years he has been practicing a great deception; shortly before the beginning of the Civil War, he had moved to South Carolina and begun to pose as a white man. He had assumed the name Warwick, passed the South Carolina bar, and, ironically, had become the lawyer whom his white neighbors preferred over the detested carpetbaggers who flooded the region in the period immediately after the war. With the purchase of a plantation, he had become a Southern aristocrat. None of Warwick's successes would have been possible, had it become known that he was not what he pretended to be—a full-blooded white man.

Warwick returns home to offer the opportunity of a lifetime to his sister, Rena Walden. He asks her to leave the black world of Patesville behind and join him in the white world of his South Carolina plantation. Their mother, Molly Walden, who has lived nearly all of her life in the shadow of white domination, is eager for her daughter to escape a certain future of menial, if not hard, labor. Though she will miss her daughter greatly, she encourages Rena to join John and take advantage of the opportunity to lead a life of gentility and respectability.

Rena Walden becomes Rowena Warwick when she is introduced in her brother's social circles in South Carolina. She is adopted by the local women and becomes an integral part of the society scene. Her beauty is not lost on the young men of the region either; in fact, she becomes the Queen of Love and Beauty when the gentleman who wins a local jousting tournament selects her as the prettiest girl at the event. By virtue of her selection as Queen, she becomes the winner's companion for the ball. George Tryon, her escort, is smitten with her, and the two are soon in love.

While the novel deals with deception, it is also the story of a passion that chafes at the bounds placed on it by cruel and arbitrary standards. Rena deceives herself that her relationship with George can continue with the fact of her mixed blood remaining hidden. When George proposes marriage, she considers the problems that might arise with maintaining the secret over a long period with someone as intimate as a husband. She worries about whether the complexion of their children might not reveal the deception, even if she were otherwise able to keep it from George. Though Rena longs to tell George her true identity, believing in the strength of his love for her, she cannot confide her secret to him, because to do so would be to betray her brother's elaborate web of falsehood. She resolves to test George's love by pointing to a black woman who is nurse to her nephew and asking if he would still love her, were she the nurse. Misunderstanding her meaning, George reassures her, in one of the most tragic cases of failed communication in the novel.

Before the wedding can take place, however, Rena answers the call of her lonely and ailing mother and returns to Patesville. In a strange twist of fate, George is called to Patesville at the same time to take care of some family business. One of his friends calls his attention to a beautiful black woman on the street. It is only then that he learns of Rena's presence in Patesville, and it is through this accident that he learns her secret and she learns the folly of her deception—both of herself and of George.

George rejects her vehemently; he considers himself tainted for having loved a black woman. Rena retreats to the black world of Patesville, a shell of her vivacious former self. In an attempt to give her something for which to live, Molly arranges for Rena's employment as a schoolteacher in the black school of Sampson County. Secretly, her mother hopes for Rena's marriage to the seemingly worldly and influential superintendent, Jefferson Wain. Wain proves to be an evil degenerate, and his forced attentions take a heavy toll on Rena's already damaged ego. The final blow comes when George, who lives near the school and cannot forget the great love of his life, attempts to reestablish contact with Rena. His feelings are still ambiguous and tentative, and Rena, permanently and deeply wounded by the first rejection, avoids his overtures. The combined pressures of Wain and George shatter her fragile health; her road to happiness, built on a foundation of deception, ends in her tragic death.

The Characters

Rena Walden is a character haunted by and forever running from guilt. Chesnutt gives the reader a poignant picture of a woman who is unable to understand and unwilling to accept her position as a second-class citizen. She is tragic; her inability to deal with who she is leads her into a situation that eventually forces her to come to terms with her identity and ultimately results in her death. When she leaves Patesville for the first time, she is running from the guilt inherent in being black in the

Reconstructionist South; she is running to freedom. When she leaves her brother's house to return to Patesville, she is running from the guilt of having abandoned both her mother and her sense of self. Her departure from Patesville a second time, to go to Sampson County, is not only a flight from guilt but also an attempt to atone for her abandonment of black identity. Finally, when she flees Sampson County, Rena is making a last desperate effort to run from the guilt that both Wain and George have come to symbolize for her—the guilt she associates with her own sexuality and desire for happiness.

George Tryon also becomes a fugitive from guilt. As Chesnutt presents him to the reader in the beginning of the novel, he is the quintessential Southern aristocrat; he is gallant, proud, and a strict adherent to a code which categorically forbids intimate relations between the races. Immediately after his discovery of Rena Walden's black heritage, George castigates himself for being so debased that he could fall in love with a "colored woman." His guilt is so severe that he refuses to expose John Warwick's perfidy; he is ashamed to admit that he was duped. Yet his love for Rena reasserts itself, and he must deal with the guilt he feels for having so cruelly snubbed the woman he had intended to marry. George is thus the victim of two conflicting guilts and vacillates between salving the one and the other. By the time he chooses love over the cruel standard of his caste, it is too late for Rena.

The author presents the reader with extremes of good and evil in the characters of Frank Fowler and Jefferson Wain. Fowler is a hardworking black man in Patesville who loves Rena enough to let her go. He recognizes that she has an opportunity to escape the limitations of being black in the postwar South. He wishes her success and even travels to South Carolina to observe her secretly and learn whether she is happy. It is Fowler who recovers her body in the end and returns her for the last time to Patesville. His is an unselfish but hopeless love. Wain's interest in Rena is entirely different. He is a violent man who has already driven one wife away and seeks to replace her with Rena. He has a certain respectability outside his immediate neighborhood as a result of his position and relative wealth. Yet he knows something of Rena's troubles, recognizes her beauty and desirability, and seeks to use her as an object of lechery.

Rena's mother and brother rest between the extremes of Fowler and Wain. They love her and desire the best for her. Nevertheless, they are willing to see her attempt to build a life based on a lie, something to which Frank Fowler would not be a party. John had been passing as white as the only way out of a stifling existence; he had recognized this early and had gone about building a successful life as a white man. Only his sister's agony shows him what he has given up by denying his own identity. Molly, too, sees passing as the way out. Nevertheless, she also sees the pitfalls of that pretense and relinquishes up her daughter with some misgiving. All the characters learn the folly of deception.

Themes and Meanings

As with much of Chesnutt's fiction, the major theme is the color line. The author was a very light-skinned man and found the subject of passing fascinating. Each of the major characters in this novel probes that single theme in some way. John is the successful example; he has crossed the color line without being detected. Though he seems happy in his life in South Carolina, he has made an enormous sacrifice. John Warwick can never publicly acknowledge his own family. In fact, he must conceal their existence and has had very little contact with them since leaving home, until the events in the story take place. Rena is destroyed by her attempt to deny her color. Frank Fowler is too black to pass, but he has little respect for those who refuse to acknowledge their identity. Molly Walden, too, is destroyed by her attempt to see her children into the world beyond the color line. In quite a different way, George Tryon has crossed that line too. He has loved a black woman, and this fact forever alters his way of thinking about color. Wain, also too black to pass, sees in Rena a chance for added prestige—the lighter the skin, the better the quality.

Chesnutt raises and attempts to answer the question of whether there is a correspondence between skin color and human quality. There can be no doubt that George believes such a correspondence to be real. He would never consider marrying a woman with the slightest trace of black blood in her. Even in the end, when he has given in to his love for Rena, he still considers himself to be depraved for loving a black woman. Wain, a thoroughly reprehensible individual, believes that marrying a woman with light skin would enhance his reputation among his fellow blacks. What is surprising is the attitude that Chesnutt gives to his "good" black character, Frank Fowler. Frank is decidedly dark-skinned, and the author leads the reader to believe that Frank considers himself to be unfit for Rena because of the difference in their skin color. Fowler's self-denigration leaves some doubt about the color versus quality question, so fundamental to the novel.

There is no question, however, that the author deplores the tremendous waste inherent in a system that automatically categorizes a large part of its population as something less than fully human. Rena Walden comes to symbolize that waste. She is a beautiful woman. She is sensitive and loving. She maintains a certain dignity to the sad end of her life. Nevertheless, an accident of birth negates these characteristics to a bitterly prejudiced world and condemns her to a severely limited existence. Her ancestry is predominantly white. Why must the merest trace of black blood make her unalterably tainted to a white world? Chesnutt seems to be saying that such need not be the case. Love very nearly triumphs over tragedy in this novel. George is too late to save Rena, but the fact that he allows love to overcome some of his prejudice speaks positively for the possibility of eliminating the waste of racial hatred.

Critical Context

The House Behind the Cedars was Chesnutt's first novel-length work. He had worked with the story for a period of years before it was finally published in 1900. Two volumes of short stories, *The Conjure Woman* (1899) and *The Wife of His Youth and Other Stories of the Color Line* (1899), introduced Chesnutt and his racial themes to the reading public (predominantly white) before the novel appeared. The stories in *The Conjure Woman* had been well received, primarily because Chesnutt had very carefully veiled his criticism on race issues. In *The House Behind the Cedars*, however, Chesnutt was very clear about his condemnation of prejudice among both blacks and whites. Some hailed the book as a courageous blow for equality; others spurned it as inflammatory. Its sales were poor, but Chesnutt continued to write, producing two more novels, *The Marrow of Tradition* (1901) and *The Colonel's Dream* (1905). These, too, were controversial, one dealing with miscegenation and the other with eradicating racial prejudices in a Southern town. Chesnutt neglected his literary career after the popular failure of his three novels.

His story of the love between Rena Walden and George Tryon is a powerful one. Despite a plot that seems predictable and overly contrived at times, even in the face of characterizations that border on being stereotypes, the novel is compelling. Above all, it stands as the statement of a black man, in the midst of a society largely aligned against him, that a world that arbitrarily excludes a portion of its human resource does so to its own detriment.

Bibliography
Andrews, William L. "Charles Waddell Chesnutt: An Essay in Bibliography." *Resources for American Literary Studies* 6 (Spring, 1976): 3-22. A valuable guide to materials concerning Chesnutt.
_____. *The Literary Career of Charles W. Chesnutt*. Baton Rouge: Louisiana State University Press, 1980. A good, full-length study of the full range of Chesnutt's writings.
Chesnutt, Charles Waddell. *"To Be an Author": Letters of Charles W. Chesnutt, 1889-1905*. Edited by Joseph R. McElrath, Jr., and Robert C. Leitz III. Princeton, N.J.: Princeton University Press, 1997. The six-part organization is particularly useful to a student of Chesnutt's fiction and of his career development: "Cable's Protégé in 1889-1891," "A Dream Deferred, 1891-1896," "Page's Protégé in 1897-1899," "The Professional Novelist," "Discontent in 1903-1904," "The Quest Renewed, 1904-1905." Includes a comprehensive introduction and detailed index.
Gayle, Addison. *The Way of the New World: The Black Novel in America*. Garden City, N.Y.: Anchor Press, 1975. Examines Chesnutt's literary and historical significance as one of the first black American novelists.
Keller, Frances Richardson. *An American Crusade: The Life of Charles Waddell Chesnutt*. Provo, Utah: Brigham Young University Press, 1978. The most helpful and important biographical resource on Chesnutt available.
Render, Sylvia Lyons. *Charles W. Chesnutt*. Boston: Twayne, 1980. A part of the Twayne series on American writers, this volume offers an excellent introduction and critical overview of Chesnutt's life and work.

Michael Crane

A HOUSE FOR MR. BISWAS

Author: V. S. Naipaul (1932-   )
Type of plot: Comic realism
Time of plot: The early to mid-twentieth century
Locale: Trinidad
First published: 1961

> *Principal characters:*
> MOHUN BISWAS, a poor man whose ambition is to own his own home
> SHAMA BISWAS, his wife
> ANAND BISWAS, his older son
> SAVI BISWAS, his older daughter
> MRS. TULSI, his mother-in-law
> SETH, Mrs. Tulsi's brother-in-law
> OWAD, Mr. Biswas's nephew

The Novel

A House for Mr. Biswas chronicles the unsettled life and death of Mohun Biswas, who is born into a poor Indian family in rural Trinidad. It is divided into two parts, framed by a prologue and an epilogue.

The last of three sons, Mr. Biswas, as he is referred to throughout, is born with six fingers on each hand at the astrologically inauspicious hour of midnight. This is considered by a Hindu pundit to be a sign of misfortune, and the prediction is confirmed when Mr. Biswas's father drowns trying to rescue his son from a river. Mr. Biswas becomes dependent on his Aunt Tara and lives with his penniless mother in a mud hut. Tara has plans for him to become a pundit, but his mentor lacks patience with the unruly boy. Sent to work at a rum shop owned by the family, Mr. Biswas is beaten after being falsely accused of stealing, and he vows never to return. He gets a job as a sign writer for local shopkeepers.

When he goes to Hanuman House to paint signs for the Tulsis, a landowning Hindu family, he meets Shama, a sixteen-year-old girl. The Tulsis arrange a marriage, which Mr. Biswas is powerless to resist. Moving into Hanuman House, he feels trapped and lost in a house that is full of Tulsi daughters, sons-in-law, and children. He receives no dowry and no job, and he acquires a reputation as clown and troublemaker. After a fight with one of the sons-in-law, he moves to The Chase, a settlement of mud huts in the sugar-cane area, and runs a small, decrepit food shop owned by the Tulsis. After six years of boredom there, while Shama bears him a daughter, Savi, and a son, Anand, he moves to a squalid barracks in Green Vale while working as a suboverseer on the Tulsi land. Still feeling trapped, he dreams of building his own house.

Determined to realize his ambition quickly, Mr. Biswas employs a workman to build a house close to the barracks, even though he cannot afford it. Built with inadequate materials, the house is never completed, but Mr. Biswas nevertheless moves into it, with Anand, while Shama, Savi and two recently born babies live at Hanuman

House. A violent storm ruins the house, which is later burned down by discontented laborers.

In part 2, Mr. Biswas moves to Port of Spain, where he stays at his sister's home and gets a job as a reporter for the *Trinidad Sentinel*. He gains notoriety as a writer of sensational human interest stories. Soon he moves into Mrs. Tulsi's house; she has moved to Port of Spain with her son, Owad. For a while Mr. Biswas flourishes, but his future becomes uncertain once more when Owad goes abroad to study, Mrs. Tulsi returns to Hanuman House, and he is demoted at the *Sentinel*.

Mr. Biswas's next move in his life of wandering is to a Tulsi estate northeast of Port of Spain, where almost the entire Tulsi family is moving. Living there rent-free, he saves money and decides to build again. This time, the house is completed in less than a month but is destroyed by fire as a result of his own foolishness. He moves back to Mrs. Tulsi's Port of Spain house, to which many of the Tulsi family also move.

His son Anand excels at school, but Mr. Biswas considers his own career to be over. He forgets his long-held goal of owning a house. He receives a job offer from the government, however, and as community welfare officer he recovers his enthusiasm for life. In his new position, he acquires some of the accoutrements of success and respectability, although he cannot free himself from his insecurities.

These fears increase when Mrs. Tulsi, now old, ill, and querulous, returns to live in her house. She is followed by Owad, returning in triumph from London. Following a quarrel, Mrs. Tulsi evicts Mr. Biswas from her house. This leads to Mr. Biswas's chance encounter with a solicitor's clerk and his hasty decision to buy the clerk's house. He soon discovers that the house is badly constructed and that he has paid an inflated price for it. Yet before his death five years later, he attains some satisfaction; he finally has a house he can call his own, out of the clutches of the Tulsi family.

The Characters

The novel has a full complement of richly developed characters, from the overbearing Seth to the conniving and later self-pitying Mrs. Tulsi and the pompous W. C. Tuttle, and a host of minor ones, each deftly presented and revealed by the habitual gesture or facial expression, the characteristic pattern of thought and speech. On the whole, it is not a flattering portrait of Indian life in Trinidad. The Tulsi family and others reveal more than their fair share of vanity, snobbishness, bullying, callousness, resignation, pettiness, and knavery.

The central character, Mr. Biswas, emerges as a sympathetic figure in spite of his faults. This is partly because of the adverse circumstances of his life, which he does not accept and continually makes efforts to overcome. Mr. Biswas is always the "little man"; physically weak and small, he is dependent on others economically and socially; he is humiliated by them and cannot win any respect even in the family into which he marries. As a result, he hits back by making them the butt of his scathing humor, which lowers his stock even more. Ironically, the most respect Mr. Biswas receives is from the destitutes and villagers with whom he comes into contact as a result of his work as a journalist. He realizes, though, that there is a huge discrepancy between the way they regard him and what he feels to be the depressing truth of his own precarious existence, and this self-awareness produces some of the most hilarious episodes in the novel.

Mr. Biswas's relationship with his wife Shama is for much of the novel one of contempt and mutual incomprehension. They are bound to each other not through love but necessity; there are periods when, following a quarrel, Shama returns to live at Hanuman House for months at a time. The result of these separations is that Mr. Biswas's children grow up distant from him, although he does eventually succeed in forming a bond with Anand, who refuses to leave his father alone at Green Vale.

Shama herself is long-suffering and has a sarcastic wit of her own, but she cannot comprehend her husband's desire for independence from the Tulsis. She is far more conventional and would have been content to live her life in the time-honored way of the Tulsi women. The passage of time does bring some accommodation, however, and in his final years, Mr. Biswas comes to respect Shama's judgment and her optimism.

Themes and Meanings

The primary theme of the novel is the search for a stable sense of personal identity, symbolized by the house for which Mr. Biswas is continually searching. Until he attains his own house, a firm structure within which he can seek his own destiny, he is a faceless man, adrift on the tides of life. This theme of self-knowledge, or the lack of it, is brought out early in the novel, when Mr. Biswas tries to discover why his food shop is unsuccessful. He studies his face in a mirror and asks Shama who he is, based on his face. She cannot answer, and he says, "I don't look like anything at all. Shopkeeper, lawyer, doctor, labourer, overseer—I don't look like any of them." Mr. Biswas worries frequently about falling into a void, a place where there is no structure, no basis for living. Throughout the novel, inner and outer reality reflect each other. His stark realization that he is not whole, for example, shortly precedes the destruction of his house at Green Vale. It is because of the symbolic value that a house possesses, as the external embodiment of an internal value, that the houses in which Mr. Biswas lives are described in intricate detail throughout the novel.

The theme of a search for identity reveals the influence of William Shakespeare's *King Lear* (c. 1606). The novel's prologue refers to the "unnecessary and unaccommodated" conditions of Mr. Biswas's birth, an echo of Lear's lament for "unaccommodated man"; Mr. Biswas's fear of the void echoes a theme of *King Lear* in which everything seems to be collapsing into "nothing"; and the centrally placed storm scene that destroys Mr. Biswas's house recalls the storm scene in the play. Also, *King Lear* is replete with animal imagery, an indication of the barbaric state of nature into which civilization is falling. In the novel, Hanuman House is named after the monkey-god of Hindu scripture, and Mr. Biswas refers to it in terms of many different animals, at one point calling it "a blasted zoo." With its quarrels, back-bitings, disloyalties, harsh discipline, and clannishness, Hanuman House represents a badly flawed communal life, a devouring swamp from which Mr. Biswas must extricate himself in order to achieve his own selfhood. That he succeeds is indicated by two moments of grace at the close of the novel. The first is when the sweet-smelling flowers of a laburnum tree he had planted fill the house, giving nature's blessing to his troubled enterprise. The second comes when Savi, his daughter, returns at the last minute and saves him from debt, which he interprets as an act of providence.

Critical Context

A House for Mr. Biswas was Naipaul's fourth novel, following *The Mystic Masseur* (1957), *The Suffrage of Elvira* (1958), and *Miguel Street* (1959). All four are set in Trinidad. *A House for Mr. Biswas* is usually considered the finest of these novels and one of the masterpieces of comic writing to appear since World War II.

The model for Mr. Biswas was Naipaul's own father, Seepersad Naipaul, and there are numerous parallels between events in Seepersad's life and that of the fictional Mr. Biswas. For example, Seepersad worked as a sign painter, became a journalist on a Trinidad newspaper, and died of a heart attack at the age of forty-six (as does Mr. Biswas). Some events in the novel draw on Naipaul's own experiences as a child.

Apart from its comic verve and its masterful interweaving of plot, character, and imagery to create a unified work of art, the novel is important because of its authentic portrayal of Indian life in colonial Trinidad, a culture that had hardly been portrayed in earlier literature. The novel also creates a picture of the changes this culture underwent over a fifty-year period and shows how these were linked to wider historical events. However, although it is set firmly in a particular place and time, the importance of the novel rests ultimately on the universality of its theme: the struggle of an ordinary man to carve out a place for himself in the face of the absurdity of life, its unwillingness to bend itself to the demands of human will.

Bibliography

Feroza, Jussawalla, ed. *Conversations with V. S. Naipaul*. Jackson: University Press of Mississippi, 1997. A collection of twenty-two interviews, spanning thirty-six years. Includes revealing comments about the circumstances under which *A House for Mr. Biswas* was written.

Hamner, Robert D. *V. S. Naipaul*. New York: Twayne, 1973. An analysis of the structural framework and techniques of each of Naipaul's first eight novels.

Hughes, Peter. *V. S. Naipaul*. New York: Routledge, 1988. A reading that examines the innovative rather than traditional aspects of Naipaul's novels and discusses how the novels can be illuminated by modern literary theory.

King, Bruce. *V. S. Naipaul*. New York: St. Martin's Press, 1993. Discusses *A House for Mr. Biswas* in terms of Naipaul's recurring themes of the violence and purposelessness of life, the comic manner of the novel notwithstanding.

Theroux, Paul. *V. S. Naipaul: An Introduction to His Work*. New York: Africana, 1972. Organized around Naipaul's themes, this includes chapters on creation, fantasy, marriage and householders, rootlessness and travel, a sense of the past, and freedom.

Bryan Aubrey

THE HOUSE ON THE LAGOON

Author: Rosario Ferré (1942-   )
Type of plot: Realism
Time of plot: 1917 to 1993
Locale: Ponce and San Juan, Puerto Rico
First published: 1995

> *Principal characters:*
> BUENAVENTURA MENDIZABAL, a descendant of Spanish
>   conquistadores; Quintín's father
> QUINTÍN MENDIZABAL, a historian by training; a wealthy importer and
>   the husband of Isabel Monfort
> ISABEL MONFORT, a Vassar College-educated writer
> PETRA AVILÉS, Isabel and Quintín's clairvoyant mulatta maid

The Novel

    The House on the Lagoon is the story of an island immersed in constant struggle on many levels: racial, linguistic, religious, economic, and social. It is about one woman's attempt to understand and redeem her history, and that of all the women in her family, by writing an account of their lives. The accuracy of this account becomes an issue in the plot; however, it is her bravery in attempting the rediscovery that becomes significant. It is also about a husband who is terrified of his wife's laying claim to herself and revealing some embarrassing truths about him and his family. The novel illustrates how the continuing debate of statehood versus independence for the island has shaped every generation born in Puerto Rico in the twentieth century.

    The House on the Lagoon is a semiautobiographical family history spanning approximately one hundred years, from the 1880's to the early 1990's. Most of the action, however, focuses on the Mendizabal family from July 4, 1917, when Puerto Ricans were granted U.S. citizenship, to the day of a hotly contested plebiscite on statehood in 1993, when fictional *independentistas* stage a takeover, kidnapping an important executive.

    This account of the Mendizabals' rise and fall serves as a microcosm of twentieth century Puerto Rican history. Rosario Ferré was an upper-class woman whose father, Luis Ferré, was a governor in Puerto Rico in the late 1960's, founder of the pro-statehood New Progressive Party, and one of the island's wealthiest businessmen. In the novel, she satirizes the milieu she fled to become a writer, refining and exaggerating her mocking spirit into something surreal and devastating. She is less harsh when she writes about provincial life in Ponce, where she was born and reared.

    In the multigenerational tale's foreground is the story of an upper-class Puerto Rican couple, Quintín Mendizabal and his wife, Isabel Monfort, whose political views conflict. Isabel advocates Puerto Rican independence, while Quintín supports close ties with the United States. Their views also clash over the role of women—he believes in traditional women's roles; she advocates feminism. In addition, they disagree about the novel Isabel is writing—a history that includes stories about her family as well as her husband's family.

Ferré interweaves the passions and struggles of these two families with several decades of Puerto Rican history, with conflicts of race, class, and changing relations with Spain and the United States. Isabel is writing a novel within a novel chronicling the two families, descendants of Spanish, Corsican, African, and New England ancestors.

Quintín discovers his wife's manuscript hidden in a bookcase. Beginning with marginal notes and condescending comments, Quintín ultimately writes his own interpretation of events and becomes the novel's second narrator. He corrects glaring anachronisms, protests scandalous portrayals of his as well as his family's behavior, and rewrites the stories from his own perspective. Yet when Isabel's manuscript reveals his ruthless business practices, his complicity in the suicide of one of his brothers, and his harsh treatment of his rebellious sons, he feels threatened and decides to suppress her version of the truth. When all else fails, he resorts to violence when she decides to leave him. Finally, she finds the courage to defend herself and her children at the end of the novel; she hits him with an iron bar and kills him.

Within this dual version of history, Ferré also maps out a geography of the haves and the have-nots on the island, centering the action on the Mendizabal family's San Juan mansion. Upstairs are the Mendizabals, with their materially successful fusion of Spanish conquistador and American capitalist methods, their hot tempers and self-destructive habits. Downstairs are the servants, the wise and patient Avilés family, brought as slaves from Angola in the eighteenth century. The Mendizabal patriarchs meet their match in elderly Petra Avilés, granddaughter of an African-born rebel slave whose owners had cut out his tongue. Threatened with censorship and control by her husband, Isabel finds natural allies in Petra and her family.

The Characters

In *The House on the Lagoon*, stereotypical perceptions of Puerto Ricans as docile, reverential, gregarious, and noncompetitive are challenged. Ferré's male and female characters are at times destructive and self-serving. As Puerto Rico has been oppressed by the ruling majority since colonial times, Puerto Rico has, in turn, oppressed its mulatto population.

On the other hand, Ferré's characters have come under attack from some critics. Although hundreds of characters populate the novel—the author includes a detailed family tree of both Quintín's and Isabel's families—critics have accused Ferré of creating stereotypical, one-dimensional portraits: rich men's wives who dabble in the arts to pass the time; greedy, exploitative businessmen; black characters whose main function is to serve the upper classes. Characters who do take up political or feminist beliefs for the most part abandon these beliefs when they are no longer expedient.

By including a multitude of characters in her novel, Ferré is able to represent the complex mix of Puerto Rican society and to incorporate a wide range of opposing political views, from independence and statehood to support of the island's status quo as a commonwealth, from an open endorsement of Spanish as the official language to the struggle to make English the national language. Thus Ferré chronicles some of Puerto Rico's major political and emotional upheavals in the twentieth century while simultaneously focusing on the diplomatic, cultural, and domestic spheres of existence.

Buenaventura Mendizabal, the Spanish father of Quintín, first settled in Puerto Rico in 1917 and built a modest cottage on the Alamares Lagoon. As a descendant of Francisco Pizarro, he inherits a coat of arms. At first he prospers by illegally importing contraband goods, then founds the highly lucrative Mendizabal and Company shipping business. Mendizabal passes on his flair for business, his forceful personality, and his need for social status to his son, Quintín.

Quintín Mendizabal, trained as a historian at Columbia University in New York City, becomes part of the family business and rules his household with the same firm hand as he does his business. His support for Puerto Rican statehood and his fervent embrace of American culture clash with his wife's views. His rewriting of his family's history, through marginal notes in Isabel's manuscript, and his clash over their son, Willie, born from his liaison with a mulatta, lead to an ultimatum from Isabel. As the island is in the midst of a plebiscite on the issue of independence, Isabel decides that her marriage has been a mistake and leaves Quintín. While escaping the island by boat, Quintín dies when Isabel hits him with an iron bar. The death of Quintín opens a new door of independence for Isabel.

Isabel Monfort, the granddaughter of Corsican immigrants and Quintín's wife of twenty-seven years, believes in liberation for women as well as Puerto Rican independence from the United States. Although she is an imaginative novelist with a Vassar education, she is a weak historian and imbues more fiction than fact into her historical account. When she begins writing the family history, she initially intends the manuscript to celebrate their marriage, weaving their respective stories into a single fabric. Yet from the outset, she hides the manuscript from her husband. When she discovers that her husband has found the manuscript and rewritten many key passages, she is too timid to rebel against his interference. She does, however, summon up the courage to fight for her and her children's independence at the end of the novel. The story centers around Isabel, the narrator and chronicler of events, until Quintín becomes narrator in several chapters.

Petra Avilés, the Mendizabals' mulatta servant, functions as confidant to Isabel. She also serves to underscore the theme of racial inequality in Puerto Rican society. The novel's conclusion affirms the necessity of interracial alliances, both sexual and familial, in the development of a healthy Puerto Rican community.

Themes and Meanings

In *The House on the Lagoon*, the story of how Quintín and Isabel interpret their family's past is as important as the colorful saga Isabel tells. About a third of the way into the novel, Quintín discovers his wife's manuscript, and Ferré occasionally interrupts Isabel's narrative with third-person accounts of Quintín's reactions to the finding of the manuscript and, later, his harsh commentaries on it. This innovative narrative strategy is effective in reinforcing the theme of dual identity and independence, for women as well as for Puerto Rico. The themes in the novel are similar to those of Ferré's earlier fiction: the search for personal, social, and political identity.

What is history—fact, fiction, or a combination of the two—and who gets to write it are key questions raised by the novel. Like her narrator, Isabel, Ferré seems not to believe in facts per se. Rather, she believes that there are versions of the truth and that the official version is often the least accurate. To underscore this point, she gives her story two rival narrators. Evaluating the blurred boundaries between fact and fiction, Ferré also highlights the differences between male and female perspectives on history.

In addition, Ferré examines Puerto Rico's severe economic and racial divisions in evocative terms. In one of her stories, Isabel describes how, when Quintín's sisters were children, they sometimes grew weary of playing with one of the servant's babies. The two girls decided it might be more fun if the baby were white, so they painted her. The lead paint made the infant deathly ill, and she had to be rushed to the hospital. This theme of racial inequality is addressed also in the plight of the mulatto characters in the novel, notably Petra Avilés.

Critical Context

Although it was chosen as a finalist for the 1995 National Book Award, *The House on the Lagoon*, Ferré's first novel in English, sparked controversy among critics for its depiction of Puerto Rican society. Some viewed it as derivative in style and clichéd in characterization and theme; others praised it for its complex structure and mocking spirit.

Although there are some thematic similarities to Ferré's earlier works—the theme of personal, social, and political identity—the style of *The House on the Lagoon* is profoundly different from her previous work. Instead of her typically baroque prose, in *The House on the Lagoon*, Ferré uses language that has been described as accessible and concise. Her prose is simple, and she uses a structure that is relatively straightforward. However, Ferré also fills her narrative with prophecy, sorcery, and black magic, drawing comparisons with Gabriel García Márquez and Isabel Allende.

Ferré received a bachelor's degree in English literature from Manhattanville College, a master's degree from the University of Puerto Rico, and a doctorate in Latin American literature from the University of Maryland. Her career developed mainly in the Spanish-speaking world until the 1990's. In the tradition of Latin American writers such as Maria Luisa Bombal and Manuel Puig, Ferré has not only translated some of her own work into English—a novel, *Maldito amor* (1986; *Sweet Diamond Dust*, 1988) and a collection of short stories, *Papules de Pandora* (1976; *The Youngest Doll*, 1991)—but also written in English. Reflecting Puerto Rico's identity crisis, Ferré's writing is informed by the author's dual identity and perspective. The novel is important as an entertaining introduction to Puerto Rican history and culture.

Bibliography

Friedman, Ellen G. Review of *The House on the Lagoon*, by Rosario Ferré. *Review of Contemporary Fiction* (Spring, 1996): 168. Stresses the weakness and predictability of Ferré's characters and their political views.

Hintz, Suzanne S. *Rosario Ferré: A Search for Identity*. New York: Peter Lang, 1995. The only English-language book-length critical study of Ferré's fiction. Although it does not include discussion of *The House on the Lagoon*, this excellent study analyzes the author's earlier works, which contain political and social themes that appear also in *The House on the Lagoon*. Contains a bibliography of works by and about Ferré.

Publishers Weekly. Review of *The House on the Lagoon*, by Rosario Ferré. (July 3, 1995): 47. Discusses Ferré's novel as semifictional autobiography and a compelling panorama of Puerto Rican history.

Stavans, Ilan. "Serving Two Masters." *The Nation* (November 20, 1995): 640-642. Compares *The House on the Lagoon* to other contemporary Latin American works with similar themes—specifically Puerto Rico's divided self—and techniques.

Genevieve Slomski

HOW THE GARCÍA GIRLS LOST THEIR ACCENTS

Author: Julia Alvarez (1950-   )
Type of plot: Social realism
Time of plot: 1956 to 1989
Locale: The Dominican Republic and the United States, primarily New York City
First published: 1991

> *Principal characters:*
> CARLA, the oldest García girl, who has the most difficulty adjusting
>   initially to her new American environment
> SANDI, the second daughter, who feels the loss of her homeland most
>   dramatically
> YOLANDA (YOYO), the third daughter, a poet and teacher
> SOFIA (FIFI), the youngest and, for a period, the most rebellious of the
>   sisters
> CARLOS GARCÍA, the patriarch of the family and a medical doctor, who
>   must flee with his wife and daughters to America after his
>   involvement in a failed attempt to overthrow General Trujillo
> LAURA GARCÍA, the girls' mother

The Novel

How the García Girls Lost Their Accents is Julia Alvarez's account of the Americanization of an immigrant family. It traces the García family's escape from Rafael Trujillo's political dictatorship to their arrival in America and their assimilation into its culture. It is a story of what the family gains and loses in leaving their country for a new one. While the parents sacrifice money, social status, and family connections, the daughters must pay an even higher price. They lose a defining part of their identity: their country, their culture, and the extended family that could help them to know who they are. Yet they also gain the independence and self-determination that their female Dominican aunts and cousins will never realize.

The novel consists of fifteen loosely connected stories divided into three sections arranged in reverse chronological order. The story thus begins with the most recent past, when the "girls" are all adults in their twenties and thirties, confronting issues every young American woman faces—career, identity, romance, family. The opening chapter finds Yoyo back in the Dominican Republic visiting an extended family and a country that seem hardly familiar to her now. Remaining chapters in this section, dated "1989-1972," provide a portrait of the four adult García girls, now thoroughly American, all of whom have had to determine how their Dominican past would shape their present. The second part, "1970-1960,: details the family's political exile from their homeland to their settlement in America. Readers glimpse Laura's imagination as she sketches new inventions to make American housewives' lives more convenient and see the family awkwardly accommodating themselves to their

American sponsors—a medical doctor and his drunken wife—in a Spanish restaurant with bad food and flamenco dancers. The final section, "1960-1956," recalls their lives as members of the Dominican aristocracy on the island in the 1950's. The depiction of the family's privilege and status emphasizes the sacrifice emigration forced upon the Garcías.

In the Dominican Republic, the García de la Torres are part of a large and powerful aristocratic family. Recruited by the Central Intelligence Agency (CIA) to help overthrow the dictator Trujillo, Carlos and some of his brothers experience a fate similar to that suffered by the Cubans in the Bay of Pigs: murder, betrayal, and exile. The girls remember fondly the family compound filled with countless aunts, uncles, cousins, and servants. Parties, art lessons, and extravagant toys from F.A.O. Schwarz mix with other darker memories. The light-skinned Garcías and de la Torres, traced back to ancestors who were "fair-skinned Conquistadores" and a Swedish great-grandmother, occupy a high place in Dominican society from which their black-skinned Haitian servants are barred. The girls have only a vague awareness of the poverty that reveals itself in the naked peasant children in the marketplace and in the house servants' gratitude toward their mother and father for giving them food and shelter. Trujillo's presence also clouds the past. The family can see his mansion from their own compound, and the children never stray too far in that direction. More frightening, however, are the black Volkswagens (which continue to provoke a fearful reaction even years later on New York City streets) of the Dominican police, cars occupied by faceless men in dark mirrored sunglasses who could turn up at one's door at any moment.

This country—with both the good and bad memories—has been lost to the García girls. When they lose their accents, they lose that part of themselves. By most measures, the four daughters are successful: a psychologist, a graduate student, a college teacher, and a mother and wife of a very successful researcher. The three oldest possess professional status in their own right. The youngest finds happiness in her husband and children. Even their immigrant parents have adjusted to their lives in the new country: Carlos establishes a good medical practice and gains respect from colleagues and the community; Laura's imagination and practicality give her daughters strength and serve her husband well. However, Alvarez's novel complicates the immigrant's story with ambivalence: The price of the American Dream is high.

The Characters

Near the beginning of the novel, Alvarez describes the pragmatic way Mami deals with her four daughters in their new American life. She assigns each of them their own color—pink, pastel blue, yellow, and white. She then buys the same outfit in the four designated colors, thereby treating each girl equally while acknowledging in a minimal way her individuality. Carla the psychologist would later write a paper on her mother's system, claiming that "the color system had weakened the four girls' identity differentiation abilities and made them forever unclear about personality boundaries."

Carla's diagnosis describes Alvarez's characterization technique in the novel. While each of the four García daughters has a distinctive personality, each also shares a good deal with her sisters. To understand one, the reader must understand them all. Together, the girls represent the complexity of the immigrant girl's experience in America. The Garcías' story has multiple narrative perspectives, as stories shift from first- to third-person perspective. All the characters contribute to the narrative. Taken together, Alvarez has created characters embodying the individual, social, and political dimensions of becoming an American.

Being the oldest, Carla is shaped for the longest time by Dominican culture. In seventh grade when the family emigrates, she suffers from the blond Irish boys who call her names and mock her mispronunciation of English words. Adolescence and alienation make her bicultural status insufferable. For Carla's sake and then the others', their parents send the girls to a fashionable Boston boarding school, where they count among their classmates the daughters of America's most prestigious families. In such a crucible, Carla not only loses her accent but also becomes thoroughly American. As an adult, she becomes a psychologist whose advice, according to her sisters, always takes the form of aphorisms of self-improvement. She has learned the Horatio Alger lesson well.

Sandi experiences a deep-seated emptiness that manifests itself first in an eating disorder and a compulsion to keep lists of books she must read, methodically checking off each one as she devours them until finally she collapses into madness. The void Sandi is clearly trying to fill is foreshadowed. When instructed to choose only one toy to bring with her to America, Sandi is incapable to making such a choice. Among the numerous expensive toys she possesses, none is worthy of such a special designation. No toy can satisfy her. Similarly, nothing she does as an adult can fill the emptiness Sandi feels.

Yolanda is the novel's narrative center. Her judgments and sensibilities clearly dominate. In returning her to the Dominican Republic, Alvarez also creates a character who reconciles her present American self to the part rooted in the island. Yolanda, a failed poet, wife, and lover, settles for life as a schoolteacher, daughter, and sister. Having emerged from a nervous breakdown after her marriage ends, on the island once more, she realizes, "This is what she has been missing all these years without really knowing that she has been missing it. Standing here in the quiet, she believes she has never felt at home in the States, never." Yet she will not stay and cannot deny her connection to America. She embodies the immigrant ambivalence.

Fifi, the youngest, is a contradiction. As punishment, her parents send her back to the island for a year. Dominican values, they reason, will straighten her out. On the family's Christmas visit, the sisters are horrified. Fifi—hair, makeup, and clothes all exactly like her cousins'—is engaged to a chauvinistic cousin who physically and mentally abuses her. The older García girls slyly reclaim their sister, only to lose her again when her father shamefully disowns her. She drops out of college, runs away to marry her German boyfriend, gives birth first to a son and then a daughter, and in the process reconciles to her father. Ironically, it is Fifi who becomes the good Dominican daughter—and gives Carlos the male heir he has long awaited.

Themes and Meanings

How the García Girls Lost Their Accents explores the personal, social, and political dimensions of the immigrant experience. Julia Alvarez spent her first ten years in the Dominican Republic in circumstances similar to those of her characters. She, too, emigrated to American and spent time "losing her accent." Like Yolanda, Alvarez is a writer, poet, and teacher. This is a work of fiction, not an autobiography; however, Alvarez uses her personal knowledge of the immigrant experience to inform her novel. That politics force displacement is a major theme in the book. While America may be the land of opportunity for some, it proves to be a land of limited opportunity for others. For Carlos, professional and social status pale in comparison to what he possessed in his former life, though he gains freedom from political tyranny. Mrs. García exchanges her opulent home, servants, and the reputation that comes with being a de la Torre for her discovery and assertion of her intelligence and independence.

Biculturalism is another of the author's major concerns. Alvarez explores the difficulty her characters have reconciling the two very different cultures that shape their lives. For the García girls, the social liberation of the 1960's and 1970's—women's rights, sexual freedom, drugs, and self-exploration—contradicts the strict behavior prescribed by Latin culture. In their attempts to be good Dominican girls—chaste, respectful of their elders, and obedient to all male relatives—they draw attention to their difference. In adopting more and more American values, they sacrifice an important part of their identity. Assimilation exacts a high personal and social price.

Critical Context

How the García Girls Lost Their Accents, Julia Alvarez's first full-length novel, is part of an important and growing body of work by contemporary Latina writers such as Cuban American Cristina García and Puerto Rican Esmeralda Santiago, especially given the unique Caribbean perspective they bring to American literature. Major writers such as Rudolfo Anaya, Tomás Rivera, and Nicholas Mohr figure importantly in the most recent stage of development in the Latino tradition, one strengthened by contemporary writers Julia Alvarez, Sandra Cisneros, Ana Castillo, Oscar Hijuelos, Gary Soto, Victor Villasenor, Helen Maria Viramontes, and many others.

In her novel, Alvarez makes two major contributions to American literature. First, in her use of multiple narrators and her experimentation with chronology, she joins other postmodern American writers such as Louise Erdrich and Maxine Hong Kingston who find new ways to construct a novel and tell a story. Second, Alvarez expresses a new voice among the many voices that constitute the American literary tradition, from an island where few voices have yet been heard.

Bibliography

Alvarez, Julia. "Emerging from the Chrysalis: Julia Alvarez on Her Work." Interview by Anne Sawyer. *La Prensa de Minnesota* 4 (November 10, 1994): 5-6. Alvarez talks about being a Latina writer and about others who have influenced her work.

Milanes, Cecilia Rodriguez. Review of *How the García Girls Lost Their Accents*, by Julia Alvarez. *Women's Review of Books* 8 (July, 1991): 39. Milanes judges the book as noteworthy despite its flaws.

Miller, Susan. "Caught Between Two Cultures." *Newsweek* 119, no. 16 (April 20, 1992): 78-79. Provides a discussion of the growing number of Latino and Latina writers finding a reading public.

Rifkind, Donna. Review of *How the García Girls Lost Their Accents*, by Julia Alvarez. *The New York Times Book Review*, October 6, 1991, p. 14. Sees the book's strengths in its description of island life.

Starcevic, Elizabeth. "Talking About Language: *How the García Girls Lost Their Accents*." *American Book Review* 14 (August-September, 1992): 15. Focuses upon the centrality of language in the book.

Stavans, Ilan. "Daughters of Invention: *How the García Girls Lost Their Accents*." *Commonweal* 119 (April 10, 1992): 23-25. Points to the cultural ambivalence at the novel's center.

Laura Weiss Zlogar

HURRY HOME

Author: John Edgar Wideman (1941-   )
Type of plot: Stream of consciousness
Time of plot: The middle and late 1960's, during the wave of school integrations and equal opportunity legislation
Locale: Washington, D.C., Europe (particularly Spain and France), and the waters off Africa
First published: 1970

> *Principal characters:*
> CECIL OTIS BRAITHWAITE, the protagonist, a black law school graduate turned janitor and barber
> ESTHER BROWN BRAITHWAITE, his devoted wife
> CHARLES WEBB, a guilt-ridden writer fancying Cecil as his son
> ALBERT, an American expatriate, mercenary, and drifter, Cecil's drinking buddy in Spain

The Novel

As *Hurry Home* begins, Cecil Otis Braithwaite, the janitor of an apartment complex, dreamily crushes a Carnation milk can and drops it five flights into Dantesque murk. Staring deep into the darkness, he recalls "how they run movies backward, how the can could leap up from the floor, return to his hand and unfold there, a flower opening." This thought suggests the novel's structure: As in one convoluted instant replay, all the characters relate events that occurred months and years earlier, dovetailing past and present through letters, diaries, dialogues, and random thoughts.

The novel's mainstays are Cecil's stream-of-consciousness reminiscences. He has supported his law studies through earnings from janitoring, a scholarship in his final year, and his girlfriend Esther Brown's hard work. His relationship with Esther has been soured by the stillborn birth of their son Simon, which he finally attributes to Esther's being "just too tired to carry him any longer." Nevertheless, he marries her on his graduation day, ostensibly to provide a comfortable life in return for her love and loyalty. Anguished that he cannot return her affection, he deserts her that same night.

Cecil then drifts for three years, mainly on the European continent. He haunts museums, old parks, and libraries as if the past can imbue him with purpose and fearlessness. Often he seesaws to the other extreme, carousing in bars and initiating liaisons with whores, compensating for his losses by plumbing the present all he can.

Unifying Cecil's rovings are significant events that occur during April. This month of spring and Easter—with its contradictory evocations of both hope and despair, forgiveness and bitterness, rebirth and death—embodies Cecil's confusion about his roots. During one April he declares himself "a stranger" to the European past. In another he skims the African coast by boat, hoping to find "where it all came from," a past he truly shares, in its vast lands echoing with kings' boasts and slaves' wails— but this search, too, fizzles. Never setting foot on Africa's soil, Cecil only glances at its shores.

Despite its blossoms and buds, spring itself, Cecil observes, often bears "false, cruel omens not of summer and life but of that unrequited yearning in men's souls that leaves them shivering on street corners in thin clothes at the mercy of sudden arctic winds." Thus, April moments emphasize Cecil's angst because the very season is so uncertain, so reminiscent of and revertible to the dying that has preceded it. While spring blooms in Spain, for example, his own longings are underscored by his encounters with Charles Webb, a man estranged from his son, and Albert, a Hemingway type in Webb's employ who has likewise abandoned his wife. Fittingly, then, another spring finds Cecil back in Washington, processing men's hair in Constance's Beauty, his promising legal career never undertaken.

As if to mock Cecil's fruitless desires, the novel itself, flashing backwards in time from the hairdresser's, ends in the same dark building where it began. In the opening scene it is morning and Cecil is outside his apartment. Here it is midnight as Cecil enters his home for the first time since his nuptials. To emphasize his unproductiveness, nothing seems changed; even the gloom is familiar. In fact, he and Esther end in the same poses they had assumed on their wedding night—she spread-eagled on the bed, he humped and staring blankly in a chair, both dreaming separate dreams.

The Characters

Cecil's initials, when reversed (B.O.C.), recall the name of the Dutch painter Hieronymus Bosch, whose work Cecil admires in the Prado. Indeed, Cecil imagines himself with the damned figures in Bosch's *Garden of Earthly Delights*, reveling in "greediness and absurdity rather than an orderly, calm progress toward salvation." His instability results from his anxiousness to find a heritage. He is at once an upwardly mobile black fast becoming isolated from the neighborhood where he grew up, a son of Africa severed from the motherland, and an American vaguely aware of a European birthright. Wideman thus sets him in a Prufrockan world pressed by time's passage and unanswered questions, inhabited by people as catlike and ragged-claw red as the images in T. S. Eliot's famous poem.

Esther differs from Cecil in that she is grounded unwaveringly by her belief in God. Yet she is a sick saint whose self-negation is repulsive instead of awe-inspiring. She views her troubled marriage as a divine mission: Cecil is the saint while she is the unsteady sinner being tested for her patience and humility. She has married Cecil knowing that he does not love her, hoping that real union will soon come to pass. She bears his scorn and physical abuse as if the blows were thunderclaps from the hand of God Himself. In this way Wideman succeeds in depicting her as a reversal of the biblical Esther who saved the Jews from annihilation by the Persians. Esther Brown is a martyr without the vengeance and action of Esther the Queen. With typically succinct, yet loaded, description, Wideman portrays her as a sad lump in blue corduroy, a victim of sick headaches.

Wideman's skill, particularly in *Hurry Home*, is his use of other characters to illuminate Cecil's turmoil. Charles Webb, a white man remorseful because he has never acknowledged his half-black, bastard son, holds many attractions for Cecil. While his surname implies that he, too, is trapped in emotional entanglements, he tantalizes rootless Cecil because he possesses a tangible, European past, a "continent of archives and documents." Further, his discomfort at being an affluent white among poor Spaniards mirrors Cecil's own alienation as the only black in his law class. Perhaps to show again the deceptive path to stability which Cecil rejects, he dresses in blue corduroy like Esther, applying the same myopic zeal to finding his son that she does to enduring her spouse.

Similarly, Albert is an unlikely companion for Cecil who proves to have more in common at second glance. Halfheartedly searching for Webb's son, flabby Albert seems not to care whether he has a heritage or not. He is referring to material objects when he says, "I'm not the sort to keep things," but he could be indicating his transient lifestyle as well. Of Dutch ancestry like Bosch, he portrays a chaotic world of fear and violence with words instead of paints. Once he is drunk enough, though, he laments the demise of days when there were revolutions and brawny, self-serving men to orchestrate them. He says of younger men, "No background, no roots. Saucy and fresh, ready to throw mud, smear disdain. Tear everything down." Likewise, he clings, leechlike, to Webb, urging Cecil to forsake the man so that he can remain on the payroll. He does value the past—albeit a personal, bloody, mercenary one—and herein lies his appeal to Cecil.

Themes and Meanings

An important theme in this novel is cultural displacement. In this sense the title *Hurry Home* is ironic because the protagonist has no past to which he can return. He has been severed from his African heritage, from the birthright of the conquering Moors as well as that of the terrified tribes who survived the Middle Passage. Doubly displaced, he knows that he can never assimilate fully into the white world of his classmates. Yet he simultaneously represents all people seeking traditions in a throwaway world; he investigates moorings in Europe as well as Africa, family, religion, careerism, the imagination, even sex.

To underscore this theme, Wideman bombards the novel with phrases in French, Spanish, German, Italian, and Latin as well as allusions, to name a few, to the Bible and the Koran, James Joyce and T. S. Eliot, and William Shakespeare and anonymous ghetto wits. This technique, coupled with the stream-of-consciousness style, brilliantly renders Cecil as a man picking through the legacies of many civilizations for a shard he recognizes as his own. In particular, his frustration at interpreting the meanings of paintings manifests his cultural thirst. When he resorts to hairdressing, he describes himself as an artist without a tradition. He proclaims himself to be a "ripplemaker, coiffeur supreme. Creator of an art that has no past or future, no tradition to be sustained or transmitted infinitesmally modified to generations un born."

As if to mitigate the novel's uncertainly, concomitant with this theme of cultural displacement is the emphasis that suffering is inescapable. "Nothing good comes without sacrifice," Cecil observes, and he and the other characters disclose tales of betrayal, separation, and numbness. While Easter symbolism recalls Christ's suffering on Calvary, the cave-like rooms and red objects riddling the novel's landscape suggest a kind of hell. In this context the "soft, sucking earth," the "thick tailed, heavy muzzled grey dog," and the falling, swirling leaves that Cecil once dreams about resemble closely the muddy banks, guard dog Cerberus, and tumbling, jumbled damned of Dante's *Inferno* (c. 1320). Such images question whether the characters' sufferings, like Christ's, have come to any good. They further emphasize the theme of rootlessness because these particular sinners to whom Wideman alludes were condemned for always being indecisive, and prohibited from entering either heaven or hell.

Critical Context

Hurry Home, Wideman's second novel, received from critics the favorable comments that had greeted his first major work, *A Glance Away* (1967). Though both treat black families and share themes, *Hurry Home* employs a more experimental style. In fact, many of its reviewers did not know what to make of Wideman's allusory technique, declaring it to be either stronger than his insights or alternately overwhelming and obscure. Also, its muted racial theme has been disconcerting to readers who have expected an intense exploration of black Americans, given the dramatic Civil Rights movement that antedated it.

This novel is the gymnasium of Wideman's canon, where he flexes his linguistic techniques in preparation for more controlled, integrated works like *The Lynchers* (1973) and the Homewood Trilogy (1981-1983). He has since received the Faulkner Award for one of the Homewood books, *Sent for You Yesterday* (1983), from PEN (the International Association of Poets, Playwrights, Editors, Essayists, and Novelists). Even if *Hurry Home* stands as a minor work next to these luminaries, it is proof of Wideman's potential to create rich, memorable fiction.

Bibliography

Draper, James P., ed. *Black Literature Criticism, Vol. 3*. Detroit: Gale Research, 1992. Provides a biographical profile, as well as excerpts from criticism of many of Wideman's works.

Mbalia, Doreatha Drummond. *John Edgar Wideman: Reclaiming the African Personality*. Selinsgrove, Pa.: Susquehanna University Press, 1995. Mbalia examines a number of Wideman's works while exploring themes such as the African personality in Wideman's writings, the way Wideman portrays women, and the place of the intellectual in the community.

Mumia, Abu-Jamal. "The Fictive Realism of John Edgar Wideman." *Black Scholar* 28 (Spring, 1998): 75-79. Examines the intellectual, social, and racial contexts of Wideman's writings. Discusses the influence of the black liberation movement on Wideman as well as on the family. Concludes that Wideman's novels "speak to that pervasive sense of estrangement, and the restorative power of the family" and calls Wideman's work "a literature of love."

Wideman, John Edgar. "Home: An Interview with John Edgar Wideman." Interview by Jessica Lustig. *African American Review* 26 (Fall, 1992): 453-457. Explores the influence of Homewood, Pennsylvania in Wideman's writings. Wideman talks about the quality of life there, the effect urban renewal can have on a close neighborhood, and the incorporation of the memories of other places he has lived into his portrayal of Homewood. A good resource for background information.

Wideman, John Edgar, and Bonnie Tusmith. *Conversations with John Edgar Wideman*. Jackson: University of Mississippi Press, 1998. This collection of interviews by various people, including Ishmael Reed, Kay Bonetti, and Gene Shalit, presents an in-depth portrait of Wideman. Wideman's discussion of his works is informative and revealing.

Barbara McCaskill

I NEVER PROMISED YOU A ROSE GARDEN

Author: Hannah Green (Joanne Greenberg; 1932-   )
Type of plot: Psychological
Time of plot: The twentieth century
Locale: An American mental hospital
First published: 1964

> *Principal characters:*
> DEBORAH BLAU, the protagonist, a sixteen-year-old girl suffering from
>   schizophrenia
> DR. CLARA FRIED, a prominent psychiatrist
> JACOB BLAU, Deborah's father
> ESTHER BLAU, Deborah's mother

The Novel

This novel provides an inside look at schizophrenia and the experience of mental hospital patients, as well as a glimpse of the emotional cost to the family of a mentally ill child. Jacob and Esther Blau commit their sixteen-year-old daughter, Deborah, to the care of a well-known psychiatrist, Dr. Clara Fried, after the girl has attempted suicide. Three years of slow, almost imperceptible progress with occasional backslides into Ward D, the last refuge for the violent and the lost, must pass before Deborah finally chooses reality over the private world that she calls the Kingdom of Yr.

As Deborah gradually reveals more of her past and her imaginary world to the skillful and sensitive Dr. Fried, the roots of her illness come to light, yet they are never entirely clear. This lingering uncertainty actually lends plausibility to the story, for it avoids oversimplification.

Deborah's problems apparently started when she was five years old, with two traumatic events: a very painful operation for a tumor and the birth of a baby sister. She had presumably been caught by her parents just as she was about to murder the new baby by dropping it out the window. Her parents had pretended to ignore the episode, beginning the sustained "lie" that she could be a worthwhile person. The therapy is quite advanced before Dr. Fried demonstrates that the murder scene was entirely imaginary, a projection of a child's momentary death wish for the new rival. Deborah at last realizes that her parents had not been covering up the dreadful truth about her attempted murder all those years. They had not even known about it.

The terror and pain of the operation apparently got mixed up with Deborah's need for punishment for her sin. Even years later, the pain of the no-longer-existent tumor returned to torment her, part of the nightmare elements that sometimes intruded into the fantasy world initially devised to protect her from reality.

The conviction of her own hatefulness was deepened by a bad experience in a summer camp in which she was the only Jew. Her ordeal confirmed the bitterness displayed by her grandfather, a clubfooted immigrant from Latvia, who had suffered the full brunt of European anti-Semitism. She gradually withdrew from companions her own age, always managing to do something dreadful which she could never afterward remember but which effectively drove away whatever friends she might have had.

As Deborah struggles with her alienation from ordinary mortals, she gradually regains a limited power of relatedness to her doctor and to one or another of her fellow patients. Dr. Fried's absence for several weeks, though she had carefully prepared her patient for it, seems to Deborah to be evidence of renewed betrayal and rejection, and Deborah ends up in the violent ward. She witnesses, as well, the sadistic beating of a fellow patient by an attendant, ironically a religious zealot who is serving alternative duty as a conscientious objector.

In spite of these setbacks, which bring on a pattern of self-torture—she secretly burns herself with cigarettes—Deborah finally ventures from the hospital to a special school for those seeking a high school diploma by examination. When she passes that hurdle with a score that is high enough for her to qualify for college, she suffers her last descent into the emotional Pit, which requires restraint on Ward D. There she again encounters the self-created gods that rule her psychic life, and she makes her decision known to them—her choice of the "other" world on the outside.

There is no unrealistic implication that Deborah's emotional problems are entirely at an end; as Dr. Fried once warned her, "I never promised you a rose garden." The mental patient, like the Jew in a narrowly Christian community, suffers a social stigma which may be hard to overcome. Yet the doctor has made it clear that sanity must be deliberately chosen by the patient. When that happens, a new world and a new life can open.

The Characters

Aside from Deborah herself, there is little depth of characterization in this novel. Dr. Fried acts only in her role as a wise therapist, though the reader learns that she, too, is a Jew who has had personal experience of the Nazi Holocaust. Therefore, she has a special understanding of the old immigrant Jew, Deborah's grandfather, who conveyed to his small granddaughter the bitterness and defiance he had learned in the old country.

Deborah's father, mother, and sister receive some attention, though not enough for the reader to be entirely certain of their motivations. Suzy, Deborah's sister, is understandably pained and confused that her older sister, off "at school" someplace, seems to dominate her parents' attention. She is relieved when at last they tell her the truth, for then she understands and sympathizes with their anxiety.

Jacob Blau has some importance in Deborah's psychic history. Deborah reveals that he had warned her obsessively about boys and men. Jacob, though meaning well, seems to have limited self-understanding; one suspects some unconscious incestuous impulses in his compulsive protection of his favorite daughter from the evil designs of men. The mother, meanwhile, finds herself in the uncomfortable position of keeping the peace between the rigid father and the independent child. Mrs. Blau lies to Jacob at first about the psychiatrist's carefully guarded reports, lest he impulsively take their daughter out of the hospital.

Deborah herself is an unusually intelligent, creative girl, gifted in drawing and in languages. Most of her creativity, however, is devoted to her own inner world of Yr, which has a well-developed language of its own. Several "gods," both male and female, inhabit this world, initially delightful creatures who offer her companionship when she feels lonely and desolate. There is a Censor, who effectively blots out uncomfortable knowledge, but also the Collect, who curses and criticizes her unmercifully, apparently representing all the negative judgments which she has collected through the years. As her illness deepens, what began as escape becomes a nightmare world where her delightful dream companions can engender pain and terror. Her intelligence and creativity, then, are not unmixed blessings, yet without these gifts, she might never have come to understand her illness well enough to withdraw from it.

Themes and Meanings

This novel does not romanticize mental illness, but neither does it show the mental hospital as an unrelieved chamber of horrors. Even Ward D, frightening as it may be with its potentially violent patients and its physical, sometimes painful, restraints, is a kind of sanctuary where at last the pretense of sanity may be dropped. For those who have struggled for years to keep their difference from other people a dark secret, this may come as a welcome relief.

Such patients enjoy a certain honesty and directness of expression not allowed to sane people, especially doctors. They know that they are "crazy" and despise feeble euphemisms. There seems to be some unstated code among the patients that allows them to tolerate one another's irrational behavior without interference or condemnation.

Moreover, the story suggests that psychosis itself may be a temporarily viable way of coping with the world in a situation of special emotional stress. Unfortunately, the "solution" may itself become a trap, shutting out the joy which the real world offers. Nevertheless, Dr. Fried never tries to destroy Deborah's private world; rather, she carefully nurtures her free will and insists on her power to explore the nature of her problems and ultimately transcend them.

Although Deborah's Kingdom of Yr may be intended as a set of archetypal forms patterned on Freudian or Jungian psychology, such an interpretation is not part of the analysis. It seems closer to the kind of serial daydream in which many an imaginative youngster indulges. It picks up and combines random clues and images, erecting its own symbol system which is internally consistent, even "grammatical." The flame-haired Anterrabae (anti-world?), whom Deborah calls the Falling God, is often a friend and comforter, though potentially cruel. Later in the analysis, Deborah recognizes him as patterned after an illustration of the falling archangel Lucifer that she saw in one of her grandfather's books. It is inherently difficult, thus, to distinguish psychological archetypes, such as the Jungian Shadow, from literary ones such as the primordial metaphysical rebel.

The author may be suggesting that some kinds of insanity may be akin to the creative impulses inherent in the writer's craft, only out of control. The aim is not to eradicate the dream, even in its more frightening guises, but to bring it under the control of the will. To express it truly is to shed light on the human psyche and its ability to create mythology out of its secret emotional life.

Joanne Greenberg (who published the novel under the pseudonym Hannah Green) is one of many writers who have explored the connection between mental instability and literary creativity. The poet Robert Graves suffered from severe neurasthenia, complete with hallucinations and nightmares, after World War I but refused analysis for fear of destroying the sources of his poetry. Writers such as Sylvia Plath, Theodore Roethke, and Virginia Woolf have converted their personal experience of neurosis or psychosis into literary art. If doing so is part of Greenberg's purpose, however, she is not so successful as those named.

Nevertheless, Greenberg does speak out of personal experience with mental illness and psychotherapy, experience which lends authenticity to her re-creation of life in a mental hospital. From 1948 through 1951, she was treated by the famous psychoanalyst Frieda Fromm-Reichmann for schizophrenia. She had planned to write a book with her analyst, but the doctor died in 1957. Greenberg wrote *I Never Promised You a Rose Garden* five years later. Not until she discovered that there was another writer named Hannah Green did she admit authorship to this novel.

Critical Context

Insanity is a recurring theme in modern culture. Sometimes it is used in a Gothic setting simply for its macabre fascination for those who enjoy the thrill of the irrational and unpredictable. Occasionally, as in Ken Kesey's *One Flew over the Cuckoo's Nest* (1962) and Joseph Heller's *Catch-22* (1955) or the French comedic film *King of Hearts* (1966), insanity is a tool for satire, an almost benevolent alternative to a reality of greater cruelty and irrationality. Such works are sometimes guilty of romanticizing mental illness, underplaying the pain and fear which may attend it. While religious bigotry is a minor theme in Greenberg's novel, however, social criticism is not a major purpose.

Some novels, such as the well-known studies of multiple personality, are fictionalized case studies. Although *I Never Promised You a Rose Garden* certainly has an affinity for the case study approach, most of the time it avoids the objective observer's perception in favor of the patient's point of view. It is most successful when the reader sees through the eyes and mind of the patient, not through the analyst's mind.

Joanne Greenberg has published several novels and a number of short stories, most of them concerned with themes of isolation and loneliness. *I Never Promised You a Rose Garden* is by far her best-known work. A best-seller which has been reprinted many times and is still widely read, it was made into a film in 1979. This novel was her second, sandwiched between a historical novel exploring a massacre of Jews in 1190, *The King's Persons* (1963), and a case history approach to the professional life of a social worker, *The Monday Voices* (1965). In other works she has explored the problems of physically or psychologically wounded people who have special problems in communicating. *Founder's Praise* (1977) deals again with racial bigotry and how it creates hatred and dissension in a religious sect, far from the purpose of its founder. Greenberg shows that many of the barriers between people are self-created out of private fears and misunderstandings.

Bibliography

Green, Hannah. Interview by Susan Koppelman. *Belle Lettres: A Review of Books by Women* 8 (Summer, 1993): 32-36. Focuses on the career of Joanne Greenberg (Hannah Green). Greenberg discusses the publication of *I Never Promised You a Rose Garden* and talks about her life not as an orthodox Jew but as a "paradoxical" one. Provides useful background for any study of Green's work.

Lewis, Janette S. "Joanne Greenberg." In *American Women Writers*, 1980, edited by Lina Mainiero. Profiles the life and career of Greenberg.

Rubin, Stephen E. "Conversations with the Author of *I Never Promised You a Rose Garden*." *The Psychoanalytic Review* 59 (1972/1973): 201-216. Rubin presents a psychological interpretation of Green's fictionalized account of her schizophrenia.

Yivisaker, Miriam. Review of *I Never Promised You a Rose Garden*, by Hannah Green. *Library Journal*. 89 (February 15, 1964): 881. A laudatory contemporary review.

Katherine Snipes

I, THE SUPREME

Author: Augusto Roa Bastos (1917-   )
Type of plot: Historical
Time of plot: 1800-1840
Locale: Asunción, Paraguay
First published: Yo, el Supremo, 1974 (English translation, 1986)

Principal characters:

JOSÉ GASPAR RODRÍGUEZ DE FRANCIA (DR. FRANCIA), the champion of Paraguayan independence from Spain and the new country's first dictator

POLICARPO PATIÑO, the dictator's naïve confidential secretary

JUAN PARISH ROBERTSON, an English adventurer and representative of British interests in the region

PILAR THE BLACK, the dictator's trusted personal valet and general servant

GENERAL MANUEL BELGRANO, an Argentine general sent first to annex Paraguay by force, then to negotiate an alliance through diplomacy

ANTONIO MANUEL CORREIA DA CAMARA, a Brazilian envoy sent to negotiate an alliance

BERNARDO VELAZCO, the colonial governor of the province of Paraguay, enemy and detractor of Francia

SULTAN, the dictator's republican dog, both companion and critic

The Novel

I, the Supreme offers a fictionalized account of the key events and motives behind the nineteenth century dictatorship of Gaspar Rodríguez de Francia (also known as Dr. Francia), who governed in Paraguay from 1814 until his death in 1840. In the novel, Augusto Roa Bastos presents a revision of the accepted interpretations of this period in history, analyzing not only the lingering effects on Paraguay but also the traditional notions of historical writing as the repository of objective truth.

Although *I, the Supreme* is considered a novel, it exhibits few of the traditional characteristics of the genre. There is, in fact, no sense of logical continuity that could constitute a plot, and no single voice that could be considered to narrate events. Indeed, the book is essentially a juxtaposition of different, and frequently contradictory, conversations, monologues, myths, journal entries, circulars, letters, historical documents, footnotes, and anonymous commentaries, all brought together by an unidentified, ostensibly impartial "compiler." This compiler, who replaces both the traditional narrator and the concept of the author, selects, orders, and presents the diverse fragments that comprise *I, the Supreme*. While the novel is predominantly fictional, many of the incorporated texts are taken from authentic historical sources, the value and veracity of which the reader is forced to judge as the novel unfolds.

Besides rejecting the traditional notions of narrator and narrative plot, the novel also eliminates the concept of chronological time. Past, present, and future all merge into a sense of permanent timelessness. The fictional dictator discusses his death and burial as if it were already past, and he argues with historians not yet born and texts not yet written. At other times, two events occurring at vastly different times are telescoped into one moment and presented as simultaneous. This eternal present is emphasized by the insertion of a variety of both European and native Paraguayan myths into historical events as if they were part of the reality being narrated. As a result, the novel offers no progression but rather functions within the timeless dimension of myth.

Insofar as the events of *I, the Supreme* can be said to be located in space and time, the majority of the text is set in the dictator's office and personal quarters in the national palace during the last few months of his life. The novel begins with the appearance on the door of the main cathedral in Asunción of a lampooned dictatorial decree condemning the dictator to death, dismemberment, and oblivion. The outraged Francia, now isolated, ill, and both politically and physically powerless, defends himself and his policies against the judgment of posterity. The rest of the novel consists of this defense before the judge, represented by the reader. Francia's only companion in this enterprise is his naïve personal secretary, Policarpo Patiño, who serves primarily as a scribe taking dictation and as an audience for the dictator's lengthy ramblings and self-justifications. The central action of the text revolves around their extended discussions and arguments on a variety of topics, ranging from real and imagined events to philosophy, writing, and language. A large portion of this dialogue is devoted to the dictation of a "Perpetual Circular," in which Francia recounts his version of events and his ideas on the nation and power. The dialogue and dictation are continuously interrupted by excerpts from the dictator's personal diary, which provide a more intimate self-analysis and critique. Interspersed with this, the reader frequently encounters documents written by the dictator's contemporaries and by future historians; these documents serve as points of departure for further debate between the dictator, his secretary, and his conscience. In this way, all the major events in the novel are narrated, either by the two main characters or by the different historians and historical documents quoted.

Eventually, as the fictional Francia approaches death and the novel becomes increasingly fragmented, the voices of denunciation become stronger and more heavily judgmental. Conversely, the dictator's defense gradually disintegrates until it joins with the detractors and emerges as a self-condemnation. The novel ends abruptly in incoherence, in the middle of a sentence, which corresponds presumably to Francia's physical demise. The "compiler" does provide a curious postmortem to the novel, however, in the form of an appendix of documents that attempt to pinpoint the final resting place of the dictator's bones. The results of the scientific investigation, like those of the novel itself, are inconclusive and only serve to underscore the unsatisfactory nature of any written text. The reader is left with a sense of incompletion and the awareness that the issues presented are left unresolved. In this way, *I, the Supreme* is deliberately open-ended so that the debate can continue in the reader's mind.

The Characters

Gaspar Rodríguez de Francia (Dr. Francia) is clearly the central figure of *I, the Supreme*. He is merely a voice in the text, an essence rather than concrete presence; he is never described physically. This essence, however, is extremely ambiguous, since it is formed from the different points of view in the novel. Ultimately, he emerges as a lonely, impotent, isolated, sick old man on his deathbed, raging to hang onto the power he formerly possessed and to justify his actions for posterity. The only power left to him is that of speech, and he attempts to use it to manipulate the reader's attitudes in the novel. Unfortunately, he becomes trapped in his own contradictions and dies frustrated and unredeemed by history.

Policarpo Patiño is the dictator's naïve personal secretary and constant companion. Like Francia, he is a disembodied voice in the text, portrayed as ignorant, simple-minded, extremely credulous, and superstitious. He serves as a kind of Sancho Panza to the dictator's philosophical Don Quixote, a foil for his constant ramblings, self-justifications, and desire to "dictate."

Juan Parish Robertson is a fictionalized reconstruction of a historical character. Presented through the dictator's eyes, he represents everything that is negative about British colonialism, specifically the desire to make a fortune at the expense of the inferior colonials. An entrepreneurial adventurer, he is portrayed as weak and hypocritical, and he eventually betrays the dictator who had befriended him and his brother, Roberto. Upon their return to England, the two brothers write a scathing attack on their former benefactor, disguised as an account of their voyage and entitled *Letters from Paraguay*. The inclusion of excerpts in the text serves in the construction of the dictator's ambiguity.

Pilar the Black is the dictator's trusted personal valet, general servant, and food taster. He eventually betrays his master and is put to death for treason. Curiously, there are two vastly different versions of his betrayal given: In one, he attempts to usurp Francia's identity and power; in the other, he steals from the government stores to provide money for his Indian mistress. Neither account is verified, and the conclusion is left to the reader. His presence and subsequent torture and death serve to contradict the dictator's self-image as benevolent despot.

General Manuel Belgrano, the Argentine general who attacked Paraguay in an attempt to annex it, appears as an illusory dream character. Viewed as an honest and idealistic man who withdrew his troops when he realized that the Paraguayans did not want to be "liberated," he later becomes a friend of the dictator when he comes to negotiate an alliance between their two countries.

Antonio Manuel Correia da Camara is presented as a hypocritical, self-serving, and deceitful Brazilian envoy sent to trick Francia into ceding Paraguayan border territory. Like Belgrano, he is presented as if in a dream, and it is never made clear whether his presence is real or imagined.

Bernardo Velazco is the royalist governor of Paraguay prior to its independence from Spain. One of Francia's principal enemies, he is strongly against the formation of a republican state and liberal ideals. He appears in the text through both the dictator's narration and excerpts of his letters. Nicknamed "Bel-Asshole," he is portrayed as hypocritical and untrustworthy.

Sultan is the dictator's remarkable dog, who appears at the end of the novel as an accusatory alter-ego, revealing the dictator's essential contradictions and self-deceptions as he slips into death.

Themes and Meanings

I, the Supreme offers a complex interweaving of several themes equally important to the comprehension of the novel. The text is a reexamination of the nineteenth century dictatorship of the historical Francia, a figure of primary importance whose ambiguous presence continues to haunt Paraguay more than a century and a half after his death. Revered as the "Karai Guasu" ("great white father") and hated as the instigator of the infamous Paraguayan Reign of Terror, Francia still lives in the imagination of the nation. Roa Bastos challenges these images through the juxtaposition of documentary "fact" and novelistic "fiction," in what he himself calls a "transhistory" or an analysis of the validity of the historical interpretations of that period. This means that he does not attempt to rewrite history so much as to demonstrate the shortcomings of historiography (the historians' task to write the "truth" of history) as a scientific process. The fictional Francia continually argues in self-defense against his historians, revealing their political and emotional biases. This theme is directly embodied in the split of the character into "I" and "HE," an important opposition that permeates the novel. The "I" represents the dictator as human being, while the "HE" symbolizes the image of Francia that has been perpetuated in history books.

Since much of the novel deals with the historical dictatorship of Francia, there emerges a second theme that is also very important: the theme of absolute power. One of the major criticisms that historians have leveled at the "founding father" of Paraguay is that he became obsessed with the notion of power and set himself up as the supreme and perpetual dictator, the absolute controlling authority, of the newly formed republic. *I, the Supreme* deals directly with this issue; the incorporated documents and characters debate the concepts of democratic versus despotic governments as well as the origins, and dangers, of power itself. In particular, Roa Bastos plays the dictator's ideals of democracy against the reality that was achieved under his rule, revealing his inconsistencies and ultimate self-betrayal.

The historical background of the novel also serves as a point of departure for the author's examination of the boundaries between reality and fiction, another major theme in the text. The constant debate between authentic and fictional documents, as well as between real and imagined events, demonstrates to the reader that reality is difficult to identify and define. In fact, *I, the Supreme* questions the very notion of what constitutes truth and reality, and whether such things as absolute truth or absolute reality exist. The argument between historical reality and the limitations of historical interpretation exposes at the same time the fact that any written text will, of necessity, be fiction, since it is a product of the biases, preconceptions, and even ignorance of the author.

This leads to the central theme of the novel: the impossibility of language to communicate reality. As the dictator examines his life and argues with his historical interpretations, he realizes that any attempt to convey meaning through words (either written or oral) is doomed to failure, since there is always a gap between the event and the account, as between any object and the word used to express that object. As *I, the Supreme* draws to a close, there is an increasing sense of frustration as Francia's speech becomes disjointed and incoherent and, in the middle of a sentence, finally ceases altogether. Since language is fundamentally unreliable, only silence can remain.

Critical Context

I, the Supreme is Roa Bastos's second novel and his most widely acclaimed work. The author spent much of his life writing short stories and screenplays as well as an earlier novel, *Hijo de hombre* (1960; *Son of Man*, 1965), but this work clearly represents his artistic maturity.

Although it is contemporary to the major works of the Latin American "Boom" era of the 1960's and 1970's, it is not usually analyzed within that context. Instead, it is generally included within the tradition of the "dictator novel" that began in the 1930's with the publication of *Tirano Banderas* (1926; *The Tyrant*, 1929) by the Spanish author Ramón del Valle-Inclán and *El señor presidente* (1946, *The President*, 1963) by the Guatemalan author Miguel Ángel Asturias. This genre focuses on the social, political, and even psychological consequences of dictatorship and its mechanisms for maintaining power, a phenomenon that, unfortunately, has been prevalent in Latin America since the wars of independence at the beginning of the nineteenth century.

Many critics have considered *I, the Supreme* to be the culmination of this genre, along with two other novels in the same category that were published almost simultaneously: *El recurso del método* (1974; *Reasons of State*, 1976) by Alejo Carpentier and *El otoño del patriarca* (1975; *The Autumn of the Patriarch*, 1975) by Gabriel García Márquez. All three novels reject the traditional technique of portraying the dictator as an almost mythical, dehumanized monster constructed by an external point of view and look instead at the internal conflicts of the dictator as a human being. Roa Bastos's creation presents the most radical departure from earlier models. While García Márquez and Carpentier generate a composite or hybrid image of the dictator based on characteristics of actual historical figures from different eras and areas, *I, the Supreme* does exactly the reverse: It begins with one single historical figure (Francia) and presents him through a series of fragmented and contradictory perspectives.

In many ways, this work could be considered a precursor of the postmodern novel in Latin America. Roa Bastos's experimentations with literary techniques (fragmentation of both space and time; elimination of narrative voice, global structure, and plot; incongruous juxtaposition of a variety of texts and textual styles) work continually to challenge and deconstruct the reader's assumptions and expectations, not only with regard to the book's subject, the historical dictator, but even in terms of the written text itself and the borders between fiction and reality.

In the years since the publication of *I, the Supreme*, Roa Bastos has also established himself as an essayist on a broad range of topics, from his own writing techniques to the sociopolitical and linguistic realities of modern Paraguay. His third novel, *Vigilia del Almirante* (1992; the vigil of the admiral) continues his exploration of the realm of historical revisionism with a reconstruction of Christopher Columbus's voyage in 1492 and affirms Roa Bastos's place in the Latin American literary canon.

Bibliography
Bach, Caleb. "Augusto Roa Bastos: Outwitting Reality." *Americas* 48 (November-December, 1996): 44-49. Discusses Rao Bastos's background and writing career. Offers an in-depth examination of *I, the Supreme* along with illuminating comments by Roa Bastos about the book.
Balderston, Daniel. "The Making of a Precursor: Carlyle in *Yo, el Supremo*." *Symposium* 44 (Fall, 1990): 155-164. Examines the use of Thomas Carlyle's 1843 essay on Doctor Francia as an intertext in Roa Bastos's novel. Also discusses the theory that the modern writer creates his precursors, the relationship between literature and history, and the relationship between language and reality.
Da Rosa, Doris C. "*Yo, el Supremo* and Augusto Roa Bastos's Search for the Future of Paraguay." *Discurso Literario* 1 (Spring, 1984): 169-176. Examines the novel as a historical revision of Francia's regime but not as an unqualified justification. Maintains that the historical perspective of the text reflects contemporary circumstances and problems of Paraguay. Offers the conclusion that the nationalist pursuits of the nineteenth century dictator portrayed in *I, the Supreme* provide a model for modern Paraguayan nationalists.
Martin, Gerald. "*Yo, el Supremo*: The Dictator and His Script." *Forum for Modern Language Studies* 15 (April, 1979): 169-183. In this Marxist analysis of the novel, Martin argues that Roa Bastos both reexamines the historical reality of Francia and projects an implied critique of the Latin American "New Novel." Asserts that Roa Bastos exposes writing as a hopelessly one-dimensional form of power that is inadequate to the communication of meaning. Concludes that the novel offers a unique interpenetration of literary and political ideologies, "fusing 'literary revolution' with 'revolutionary literature.'"
Ugalde, Sharon K. "Binarisms in *Yo, el Supremo*." *Hispanic Journal* 2 (Fall, 1980): 69-77. An excellent analysis of the polar oppositions and contradictions that form the structural and thematic basis of the novel. Examines in particular the mythological polarities and concludes that Roa Bastos deliberately rejects resolution of contradictions.
Weldt-Basson, Helene C. *Augusto Roa Bastos' "I the Supreme": A Dialogic Perspective.* Columbia: University of Missouri Press, 1993. One of the finest studies available in English on Roa Bastos's novel. Explores in depth Roa Bastos's thoughts on Francia and supplies two extensive chapters on the historical and nonhistorical intertexts.

D. Jan Mennell

I, TITUBA, BLACK WITCH OF SALEM

Author: Maryse Condé (1937-   )
Type of plot: Historical realism
Time of plot: The seventeenth and eighteenth centuries
Locale: Barbados and Salem, Massachusetts
First published: Moi, Tituba, Sorcière . . . Noire de Salem, 1986 (English translation, 1992)

> *Principal characters:*
>
> TITUBA, a black Barbadian slave, conjure woman, and revolutionary
> MAMA YAYA, Tituba's teacher and spirit guide
> ABENA, Tituba's mother and spirit guide
> JOHN INDIAN, Tituba's husband
> SAMUEL PARRIS, the Salem village minister, the owner of Tituba and
>   John Indian
> HESTER PRYNNE, Tituba's cellmate in Ipswich jail
> BENIAMIN COHEN D'AZEVEDO, a Jewish merchant, Tituba's owner and
>   lover
> CHRISTOPHER, a Barbadian revolutionary and Tituba's lover
> IPHIGENE, a young revolutionary and Tituba's foster son

The Novel

I, Tituba, Black Witch of Salem is a fictionalized portrait of a historical figure who was a main participant in the notorious Salem witch trials of 1692. The novel is divided into three parts. The first section traces Tituba's childhood as a slave in Barbados as well as her voyage across the sea to seventeenth century New England. The second section recounts Tituba's adventures in Massachusetts, including her experiences as an accused witch in Salem Village. The last section tells of Tituba's return to a much-changed Barbados and her execution as a revolutionary. The story is told by Tituba herself, lending an immediacy and power to the narrative.

The main themes of the novel, the violence of slavery and the oppression of women by men, are established in the opening sentence as Tituba recounts the circumstances that surround her conception. She says simply, "Abena, my mother was raped by an English sailor on the deck of *Christ the King* one day in the year 16**." This savage incident foreshadows other events in Tituba's life in which she is treated cruelly by both white and black men.

After Abena arrives in Barbados, she becomes the house slave of a plantation owner. When he discovers that she is pregnant, he banishes her from the house to the fields. When Tituba is seven, she witnesses the attempted rape of her mother by the master. Abena defends herself and stabs him. Although the master does not die, Abena is hanged for attacking a white man.

After Abena's death, Tituba is adopted by Mama Yaya, a natural healer who teaches Tituba her art. Tituba becomes proficient in using spells and herbs for healing.

When Tituba is fourteen, Mama Yaya dies, and Tituba lives in the forest. However, Tituba is not alone. Mama Yaya and Abena act as her spirit guides and offer her solace and advice.

Tituba eventually ventures into the surrounding towns and meets John Indian. Smitten with the smooth-talking slave, she marries him. When he is sold to Puritan minister Samuel Parris, Tituba is part of the deal. She and John sail with Parris and his family to New England, where Parris obtains a pastorate in Salem Village.

Tituba and John are regarded with contempt by the villagers, and Tituba feels alienated and homesick. Her familiar spirits, Mama Yaya and Abena, cannot communicate with her because they are forbidden to cross the sea. Nevertheless, Tituba practices her healing art and is in demand by the villagers. Although she helps cure their diseases, the people regard Tituba with a mixture of awe and suspicion. When several village girls experience strange fits, they accuse Tituba and two more women of bewitching them. Soon, the girls charge others with consorting with the devil. John Indian advises Tituba to admit to the charge to avoid the death penalty. Tituba acts on his advice and is jailed in Ipswich. Afraid for his own life, John abandons Tituba.

While incarcerated, Tituba meets Hester Prynne, the main character in Nathaniel Hawthorne's 1850 novel *The Scarlet Letter.* Condé portrays Hester as a seventeenth century feminist who is angered by the fact that she is jailed—and pregnant—while her partner in "crime" is free. Unlike the Hawthorne heroine, who comes out of prison and resumes life doomed to wear the scarlet "A," Condé's Hester commits suicide as a protest against her humiliating fate. After the witch hysteria subsides, Tituba is freed from prison and sold to Benjamin Cohen d'Azevedo, a rich Jewish merchant and widower with children. Tituba and Benjamin, both outsiders in a Christian society, find a common bond in their isolation. They become lovers, and their affection for one another surmounts the slave/master relationship. When Benjamin's children die in a suspicious fire, he decides to move to Rhode Island, where religious tolerance is practiced. Before he leaves, he frees Tituba and arranges for her passage to Barbados.

Soon after her return to her homeland, Tituba meets Christopher, a fugitive slave who is the leader of a revolutionary group. She becomes pregnant by him, but after they have a falling out, Tituba returns to the cabin where she lived as a teenager. Her reputation as a healer grows, and one day several slaves bring her Iphigene, a boy who is near death as a result of a severe whipping. Tituba nurses him back to health and treats him like a son. Iphigene is also part of the revolutionary movement, and he asks Tituba's help in mounting an insurrection. Christopher, though, discovers their plans and betrays them to the planters, who ask English troops to crush the revolt. Tituba and Iphigene are hanged for their crime. Tituba is reunited with Abena and Mama Yaya in the spirit world where she continues to influence her people as they fight for their freedom.

The Characters

Although *I, Tituba* is partly based on actual people connected with the Salem witch trials, Condé had little historical information about Tituba's life in Barbados, and she possessed a limited number of facts concerning the role Tituba played during the witch hysteria. Condé invents characters such as Mama Yaya, Abena, and Benjamin to give Tituba a history of her own. Condé's characters are often deliberately exaggerated or overdrawn, and her use of parody emphasizes the novel's central themes.

The reader is immediately drawn to Tituba's humanity and warmth. She is loving, compassionate, and gentle. She uses her healing power for the good of the communities where she lives, not for her own gain. Her sense of ethics is apparent when one Puritan woman secretly asks her to cast a spell on one of her neighbors, a request Tituba refuses. When she is tried for witchcraft, Tituba is naturally resentful and angry, but she does not take revenge. She declines to point her finger at innocent people, even though the court pressures her to do so. Her loving nature is also expressed through her passionate sexuality and appreciation for life. However, her love for others is both a strength and a weakness. Mama Yaya and Abena warn her that she loves men too much. Her relationships with John Indian and Christopher end in abandonment and betrayal. Yet she holds no grudges and readily forgives. In many ways, Tituba is a mock-epic heroine. She is almost too good, and her extreme goodness diminishes the people who, because of race, gender, or social class, believe that they are her superiors.

The appearance of Hester Prynne is another example of Condé's use of parody. At first, it is puzzling to find the main character of Hawthorne's *The Scarlet Letter* in another author's novel. The fact that Hester engages in modern-day feminist discourse is even more jarring and subverts the historical basis for the story. Condé portrays Hester as a woman who, like Tituba, loved a man too much. Pregnant by a clergyman and incarcerated for her adultery, Hester criticizes her lover, who walks free while she languishes in prison. Hester is the victim of a patriarchal culture. She protests her situation and cheats the system by taking her own life and that of her unborn child.

Samuel Parris is a historical figure whose part in the Salem witch trials has been amply documented. His tenure as Salem's village pastor was marked by controversy. The witch hysteria began in his house when his daughter and niece experienced unexplained seizures. While Condé bases her portrayal of Parris on actual events, her characterization of him is exaggerated and goes beyond historical fact. He is more Puritan than the most dedicated Puritans. Tituba says of Parris, "However fanatical and dour were those who shared his convictions, they were not as frightening as this tall, irate silhouette with his words of reprimand and warning." Although a minister, Parris is the very antithesis of Christian love. He also verbally mistreats his wife and daughter. Condé's portrayal of Parris is a reflection of the repression nonwhite people suffered under colonial rule as well as a commentary on the domination of women by men.

Themes and Meanings

The twin themes of racism and sexism resonate throughout *I, Tituba, Black Witch of Salem*. As a black female slave living under colonial rule, Tituba is a nonperson, rendered invisible by her race, gender, and social status. The actual records of the Salem witch trials, written by white males, offer limited information about the historical Tituba, demonstrating how unimportant the officials of Salem considered her. Condé's revisionist novel gives Tituba a voice, an identity, and a profession of which she is proud. She practices her calling as a conjure woman with dignity, compassion, and empathy, and her power is respected among her own people in Barbados. However, the Puritan view of witchcraft reveals an ingrained racism and sexism within white colonial culture. The Puritans believe black to be the color of Satan. By implication, Tituba's skin color links her to the devil. The fact that Tituba's native religion focuses on the mysteries of herbal healing and is matriarchal in nature also presents a threat to the patriarchal Puritan society. Tituba is feared because of her power, and yet some in the Puritan community hypocritically ask her to weave spells that will harm their neighbors.

Another theme running through the novel is the enduring power of love, which Condé ties to the feminine principle. Tituba, Abena, Mama Yaya, and Hester form a transcendent spiritual community of women around which the novel revolves. Although the male culture (both black and white) may gain dominance over women and wreak havoc in society, Tituba and her spirit guides subvert masculine cruelty on an emotional and spiritual level—-a level that men cannot experience because they are too blinded by their own violence. Yet Condé also sees hope in the "feminine" principles of love and compassion, believing that, when practiced, they can bring about social change.

Critical Context

Maryse Condé's fourth novel, *I, Tituba, Black Witch of Salem*, was the winner of France's prestigious Grand Prix Literaire del la Femme in 1986. It was the first French-language novel to link the histories of Africa, the Caribbean, and the United States. The novel also parallels Condé's own literary quest to discover what it means to be a Caribbean woman. A native of Guadeloupe, she moved to the Ivory Coast as a young woman. Her first three novels, *Hérémakhonon* (1976; English translation, 1982), *Une Saison à Rihata* (1981; *A Season in Rihata*, 1988), and *Ségou* (1984; *Segu*, 1987), are set in Africa. Condé also lived in Paris, where she taught West Indian literature at the Sorbonne. When Condé moved back to Guadeloupe, she began to come to terms with her own Caribbean identity, which finds its expression in the character of Tituba. Her later novels, *La Vie scélérate* (1987; *Tree of Life*, 1992), *Traversée de la mangrove* (1990; *Crossing the Mangrove*, 1995), and *Les Derniers Rois mages* (1992; the last magi), are all set in Guadeloupe.

A staunch supporter of independence from France for Guadeloupe, Martinique, and French Guiana, Condé is politically active. She has been a member of Union pour la liberation de la Guadeloupe, a coalition working for Guadeloupe's independence, and was a candidate for the regional council in 1992. Her political involvement parallels her literary commitment to represent a Caribbean identity to the international community.

Bibliography

Arnold, A. James. "The Novelist as Critic." *World Literature Today* 67, no. 4 (Autumn, 1993): 711-717. Discusses *I, Tituba* within the context of the triangle trade and the racism of Puritanism.

Bernstein, Lisa A. "Demythifying the Witch's Identity as Social Critique in Maryse Condé's *I, Tituba, Black Witch of Salem*." *Social Identities* 3 (February, 1997): 77-89. An astute exploration of the voices of women writers in Caribbean literature.

Dukats, Mara L. "The Hybrid Terrain of Literary Imagination: Maryse Condé's Black Witch of Salem, Nathaniel Hawthorne's Hester Prynne, and Aime Cesaire's Heroic Poetic Voice." *College Literature* 22, no. 1 (February, 1995): 51-61. Discusses the issue of "voicelessness" as it relates to the shaping of identity in the works of Nathaniel Hawthorne, Aime Cesaire, and Condé.

_____. "A Narrative of Violated Maternity: *Moi, Tituba, Sorcière . . . Noire de Salem*." *World Literature Today* 67, no. 4 (Autumn, 1993): 745-750. Explores the feminist theme of the violated slave mother and relates it to colonization.

Manzor-Coats, Lillian. "Of Witches and Other Things: Maryse Condé's Challenges to Feminist Discourse." *World Literature Today* 67, no. 4 (Autumn, 1993): 737-744. Connects the black woman as "witch" to angry contemporary women and feminism.

Mudimbe-Boyi, Elisabeth. "Giving a Voice to Tituba: The Death of the Author?" *World Literature Today* 67, no. 4 (Autumn, 1993): 751-756. Parallels reconstruction of Tituba's history to that of Caribbean history.

Pegge A. Bochynski

IF BEALE STREET COULD TALK

Author: James Baldwin (1924-1987)
Type of plot: Realism
Time of plot: The 1950's
Locale: New York City and San Juan, Puerto Rico
First published: 1974

Principal characters:

> CLEMENTINE RIVERS (TISH), the narrator and protagonist
> ALONZO HUNT (FONNY), her jailed boyfriend and the father of her
>   unborn child
> ERNESTINE RIVERS (SIS), Tish's sister
> SHARON RIVERS, the mother of Tish and Sis
> JOSEPH RIVERS (JOE), the father of Tish and Sis
> FRANK HUNT, Fonny's father
> ALICE HUNT, Fonny's mother

The Novel

In the opening scene of the novel, nineteen-year-old Clementine Rivers (Tish), sitting with phone in hand on one side of a solid glass barrier, tells twenty-two-year-old Alonzo Hunt (Fonny), who is in jail, and on the other side of the glass wall, that she is pregnant with his child. That she is unmarried does not bother Tish. She knows that she and Fonny had planned to marry, and had Fonny not been falsely accused of raping a Puerto Rican woman, they would have been wed.

The novel is divided into two parts. Part 1, "Troubled About My Soul," constitutes about 90 percent of the book; the remaining 10 percent is part 2, "Zion." The novel begins when Tish is in her third month of pregnancy and ends as the birth of the child is imminent. Between these momentous events is the tale of the efforts of the families of Tish and Fonny to get him released from prison and to ensure the well-being of the first grandchild.

After telling Fonny that he is about to become a father, Tish goes home, where she tells her mother, Sharon Rivers, who relays the information to her husband, Joe, and her daughter Ernestine (Sis). Mrs. Rivers makes this moment into a joyous occasion, showing the support and love of this family for Tish, Fonny, and the child-to-be-born.

When the Hunts are told of the impending birth, Frank, Fonny's father, is ready to celebrate. In contrast to Frank Hunt's reaction is the response of his wife, Alice, who accuses Tish of destroying her son. Worse, she says, "The Holy Ghost will cause that child to shrivel in your womb. But my son will be forgiven. *My* prayers will save him." This curse comes from a Holy Roller who is a self-righteous parent.

Sis has found a white lawyer for Fonny. The family is not always certain that he can be trusted, but he is the only hope they have. Hayward, the attorney, does believe in Fonny's innocence. He knows that Bell, the prosecuting officer, is a racist and a liar who needs a victim. It is obvious that the wheels of justice will turn against Fonny unless Hayward can demolish the state's case before a jury.

Although postponement of the case keeps Fonny incarcerated, the final paragraph of the novel provides some hope that one day Fonny will be free. Presumably the world into which this child is born will be a safer one than the one in which Fonny has grown up.

The Characters

Tish Rivers as narrator provides an account of the day-to-day events that move the plot forward, and she also provides the background information that gives credence to the evaluations that she makes of the people around her. Baldwin, writing from the female point of view, appears to understand the female psyche and has made Tish into a believable human being. That the vocabulary and the philosophy are sometimes those of James Baldwin does not make Tish less of a woman; instead, she appears at times to have wisdom beyond her age and education, to be fifty rather than nineteen.

The unborn child is the catalyst for the novel. Without the reactions to this expected birth, the gentleness and love of family life could not be told as effectively.

Fonny, the sculptor, is a sensitive young adult, secure in the knowledge of Tish's love and in his ability to sculpt. His interactions with his friend Danny, when they meet by chance after Danny's having been in prison, emphasize the positive aspects of friendship. Fonny's asking Joe for Tish's hand in marriage also adds to the portrait of a youth who is forthright in his dealings with people. Yet Tish does relate that Fonny quit vocational school only after stealing woodworking tools, breaking into the school, and stealing most of the wood from the shop. As far as Tish is concerned, these acts are justifiable because the educators are teaching the students to be slaves.

In the Rivers family, there seems to be ample love among the family members. Sis has two jobs. From one, she has the contacts that enable her to find an attorney for Fonny. She steals from the other employer to make life more comfortable for members of her family and also to help raise money to pay Fonny's lawyer. Sis is the one who gives Mrs. Hunt a tongue-lashing for cursing Tish and the child: Sis's loyalty to family cannot be doubted.

In addition to her daily support, Sharon goes to Puerto Rico to see the woman who has falsely accused Fonny. At the suggestion of Hayward, Sharon attempts to get this woman to admit that she really could not see her attacker and could not possibly identify him. Sharon hates to fly, and she is a novice at what she tries to do, but she does make the trip. Her husband, too, makes an effort that shows his support. Joe is willing to steal to raise money for bail. The love for Tish and Fonny is obviously a motivating force, although the morality is questionable.

In the Hunt family, the relationships are not as harmonious as in the Rivers family. Frank and Alice appear not to be in love, even though, as Frank says, they once were. Frank loves his son and his son loves him. That Frank will do anything for Fonny is shown when he steals in an attempt to help his son and is caught and fired from his job. Humiliated, he commits suicide.

Mrs. Hunt, although professing devotion to God, indicates through her actions that self-love is the primary force in her life. Her relationship with her son lacks warmth. Her daughters, Adrienne and Sheila, appear to do her bidding, but they are not wholly committed to pleasing their mother. Mrs. Hunt is really a hypocritical simpleton who loves herself, her fine clothes, and her view of her position in the Church. As a professed representative of the organized Church, she represents a destructive force in Christianity. She may know the Second Commandment, but she does not practice it. She, like her daughters, is light-skinned, in contrast to the members of the Rivers family and to the men in her own family, thus pointing to another reason why Alice Hunt feels superior.

Themes and Meanings

The major themes in *If Beale Street Could Talk* involve various kinds of love. There is the love of Tish and Fonny, that of man and woman. Baldwin uses Tish's parents to emphasize parental love: It is in relation to Tish that their devotion as parents can be observed. Sharon Rivers, when she learns that her daughter is pregnant, immediately shows concern not only for Tish but also for the unborn child. Her husband, too, is supportive of the unwed daughter, and each parent is determined that life for this child will be better than it has been for them. Human love, according to Baldwin, is the central force in the universe. It is love that brings the family together, and it is love that enables the family to function and survive. It is also love that will build a better world for the children. Lest anyone mistake this basic premise, Baldwin also shows the effects of the absence of love.

Other major themes are evident in the portrayal of life in prison and the system of justice. Fonny is punished for refusing to be raped; jails obviously are not safe places. Fonny's being falsely accused is one thing, but the slowness with which the case moves forward with no guarantee of a fair resolution is further evidence of injustice. That he is at the mercy of the justice system becomes clear as Sis tells Tish, "We have to disprove the state's case. There's no point in saying that we have to make *them* prove it, because, as far as they're concerned, the accusation is the proof. . . ."

Critical Context

Highly praised as a spokesperson for blacks, James Baldwin writes essays, short stories, and novels that are forceful, powerful, and brilliant. He has also received recognition as a competent dramatist.

If Beale Street Could Talk, Baldwin's first novel with a female narrator, takes its title from the lyrics of "Beale Street Blues," by W. C. Handy. Baldwin has used the blues thematically or as counterpoint in such works as the short story "Sonny's Blues" and the drama *Blues for Mister Charlie* (1964).

If Beale Street Could Talk is based on Baldwin's experiences while he was attempting to aid a jailed friend. The injustices that he observes are some of the same injustices on which he expounds in some of his provocative essays in *Nobody Knows My Name: More Notes of a Native Son* (1961), a volume which, along with his novel *Go Tell It on the Mountain* (1953), clearly established him as an artist of the first rank.

In *Go Tell It on the Mountain*, his first novel, Baldwin attacks the organized Church, and this attack is continued in *If Beale Street Could Talk*, where Baldwin portrays the Christians as less caring and less loving than those outside the Church.

Baldwin also uses many of the themes of this novel in *Tell Me How Long the Train's Been Gone* (1968), a longer, more rambling novel than *If Beale Street Could Talk*. The tautness of the latter strengthens Baldwin's premises and makes the novel a very powerful work. Of *If Beale Street Could Talk*, Joyce Carol Oates writes: "[It] is a moving, painful story. It is so vividly human and so obviously based upon reality, that it strikes us as timeless. . . ."

Bibliography

Campbell, James. *Talking at the Gates: A Life of James Baldwin*. New York: Viking, 1991. A good narrative biography, with detailed notes and bibliography.

Kinnamon, Keneth, ed. *James Baldwin*. Englewood Cliffs, N.J.: Prentice-Hall, 1974. A part of the Twentieth Century Views series, this collection contains some important appraisals of Baldwin's work and career by Langston Hughes, Eldridge Cleaver, and Sherley Anne Williams, among others.

Macebuh, Stanley. *James Baldwin: A Critical Study*. New York: Third Press, 1973. A good presentation of the social and historical background of Baldwin's work.

Standley, Fred L., and Nancy V. Burt, eds. *Critical Essays on James Baldwin*. Boston: G. K. Hall, 1988. A collection of contemporary reviews and essays covering Baldwin's entire career.

Sylvander, Carolyn Wedin. *James Baldwin*. New York: Frederick Ungar, 1980. A study that examines in particular the links between Baldwin's works and his life.

Troupe, Quincy, ed. *James Baldwin: The Legacy*. New York: Simon and Schuster, 1989. Equally divided between memoirs of the writer and discussions of his work. Includes a very useful bibliography.

Weatherby, W. J. *James Baldwin: Artist on Fire*. New York: Donald I. Fine, 1989. An important biography written by one of Baldwin's friends. Weatherby is, at times, too close to his subject to be objective.

Virginia A. Duck

IF HE HOLLERS LET HIM GO

Author: Chester Himes (1909-1984)
Type of plot: Social criticism
Time of plot: The 1940's, during World War II
Locale: Los Angeles, California
First published: 1945

> *Principal characters:*
> ROBERT JONES, the protagonist, a black foreman in a shipyard
> ALICE HARRISON, his fiancé, a social worker, daughter of a physician
> MADGE PERKINS, a white, female shipyard worker

The Novel

Bob Jones, a tense, intelligent, sensitive, black shipyard worker, is anxious to succeed in his position as leaderman at Atlas Shipyard; he yearns to be "just a simple Joe," distinguished by neither color nor ambition. Caught in a world filled with unleashed hatred and tensions intensified by war, Bob is so haunted by his nightmarish existence that he lives in constant terror. Fear and panic dominate his entire world to such an extent that he cannot distinguish his terrifying nightmares from reality.

As an assistant foreman in a predominately white, hostile environment, Bob desires acceptance and respect, but he and his black crew receive little cooperation from their white coworkers and supervisors. He is agonizingly aware of the problems he must deal with in order to keep his position, one that is vital to his self-image, the affirmation of his manhood; at the same time, he sees the precariousness of his situation as the sole black leaderman in a racially charged atmosphere. This tremendous strain produces such private anguish and intense fears that Bob Jones exists on the borderline between murderous impulses and total collapse.

As the indignities and humiliations steadily increase, Bob is driven compulsively to fantasies of violence—his only means to restore his sense of manhood—but he is psychologically incapable of carrying them out. When Madge Perkins, a white coworker, insults him and refuses to work for "niggers," he loses his temper and calls her a "cracker bitch"; for this act he is demoted and loses his draft deferment. During a dice game, Johnny Stoddard, a white worker, beats him. Bob plots the murder of Stoddard and stalks him, and although he cannot act out this violent fantasy, he derives a measure of satisfaction from it, for it is clear that Stoddard fears him. Continuing his pursuit of Madge, whom he wishes to humiliate but to whom he is simultaneously attracted, Bob discovers that she is also attracted to him; he tries to seduce her but panics and flees when she urges him to rape her.

Bob is caught in a growing despair. He is consistently emasculated in all his relationships. His torturous relationship with Alice Harrison, his fiancé, is fraught with deception, misunderstandings, and violence. Alice's compromising attitude, numerous demands, and ultimatums are equally threatening to his masculinity. Bob knows that the kind of accommodation in which she and her wealthy parents believe and to which they have adjusted will not work for him. Thus, he harbors a deep resentment of their smug, complacent attitudes and of his helplessness.

This inability to act stains Bob's entire existence with a sense of imminent destruction. He finally realizes that as a black man he cannot beat the system. He tries to compromise by accepting Alice's terms, but the instruments of his defeat are still in motion. In the course of his rounds at the shipyard, Bob discovers that his work crew rejects him in favor of his white replacement, Tebbels. Still trying to put his troubles behind him, Bob finds himself locked into a room with Madge, who tries to seduce him but, upon discovery by the company executives, screams rape. He is framed on a trumped-up charge of rape by Madge, is severely beaten by white workers, and is jailed. At his arraignment, the president of Atlas Shipyard, though well aware of Bob's innocence, berates him for being a disgrace to his race and company. Although the rape charges are dismissed to quell racial tensions at the plant, Judge Muran forces Bob into the army anyway on the condition that he promise to stay away from white women.

The Characters

The central character, Bob Jones, is an educated black man who seeks success in a cruel, unjust, racist world, a world that defines him as a "nigger." Bob is an idealist trapped in a world that negates idealism. In his pursuit of the American Dream, he learns that black men are blocked from every direction and that his visions of success can be achieved only if he accepts himself as defined by society, a nigger. Refusing to accept that identity, Bob strikes back and is progressively destroyed. Yet at the same time, pressures force him to respond by acting in the way society expects. Bob becomes violent, an act of self-assertion that, for him, is the only way he can regain a sense of manhood. For his violence, he is defeated at every step. Bob Jones's difficulty rests in his unexplainable desire for Madge, one mingled with hatred and repulsion, and in his ambivalence toward his own race. His terror stems from his powerlessness, his inability to find an appropriate stance from which to fight. Thus Bob is trapped, in part, by his own weakness. The redeeming feature and one that makes him a memorable character is his anger. Poised and generally self-confident, Bob willingly moves into battle; although the pressures are deadly, he remains resilient. He is forced to enlist in the army; although the American Dream excludes him, the concluding sentence affirms his strength: "I'm still here."

Alice Harrison, Bob's fiancé, is beautiful, wealthy, and highly respected in her career, but she is a victim. Although she has all the trappings of success, she is a frustrated, confused woman. Indeed, despite the Harrisons' professional status—Alice's father is a physician—they are forced repeatedly to compromise their dignity and self-respect in order to survive. Dr. Harrison has been refused service at a downtown restaurant, and Alice is called a coon by a white policeman. The Harrisons must depend upon the white powers of the community to maintain their precarious position.

As a result, they are incapable of responding naturally and with understanding to the problems of fellow blacks. These self-destructive attitudes destroy Alice's possibilities for freedom and a sense of worth, and they result in her disturbing problem of sexual identification and her flight from racial identification.

In focusing on Madge Perkins, a worn-out peroxide blonde from Texas, and Bob Jones, Himes presents in a series of alternating and contrasting scenes, the pressures of a racist society that drive both to destruction. Both characters are victims of oppression and are consumed by fear, anger, and hatred of themselves and of society.

Madge is a frustrated, fearful, and lonely woman. Her outcast state is revealed at the plant—"there's a whole lot of stinkers like her in the yard" (Don tells Bob)—and in her meager existence at the run-down hotel Mohave. Madge's husband has run off with another woman, and she is now a defeated, angry woman. Still Madge delights in game playing. As a victim who is acutely aware of her isolation from mainstream white society, she is dangerous. With her special powers as a white woman, she takes revenge by expertly inflicting pain and humiliation on her black victim. Whenever Bob and Madge meet at the plant, she plays the game of a frightened, wide-eyed innocent and "backed away from one as if she was scared stiff, as if she was a naked virgin and I was King Kong." When she is alone with Bob, however, she is attracted to him. Madge's inferior status compels her to seek association with Bob as a panacea while still smugly feeling superior to blacks. This element of self-destruction makes her a pathetic character.

Themes and Meanings

Fear is the principal theme of the novel. From the first page—the nightmare sequence that structures the book, the war-effort atmosphere, and the accumulation of indignities—to the last page, Chester Himes reinforces this main idea: the psychological terrors of the black man trapped in a racist society and the brutalizing effects of those terrors will destroy him. Bob Jones is a victim of America's double standards. What he wants to be is an effective leaderman and to live peacefully. He has been brought up to believe that every man in America can achieve these goals, but he cannot. Bob is blocked in every aspect of his life and is offered no chance to assert his identity. The nightmares through which he suffers each night are not different from the nightmare he suffers each day. His terrors stem from his lack of an identity and of a structure to shape and define his life. Bob's only recourse is self-directed rage, for he will not seek accommodation with white society. Without a sense of purpose and a sense of understanding and support, Bob sees only the threat of continued failure. As he seeks to obliterate his pain and finds only helplessness, Bob Jones is reduced to a mechanical existence. For him there is no available bridge between black and white worlds. There is nothing to obviate the terror.

Critical Context

When Chester Himes's first novel, *If He Hollers Let Him Go*, was published in 1945, it received only brief attention. Although the novel was considered the outstanding book on a black theme published that year, it was rejected as the winner of the twenty-five-thousand-dollar Doubleday Doran-George Washington Carver Memorial Award. Himes did, however, receive a fellowship from the Julius Rosenwald Foundation, but from that point on, a bitter battle started between Himes and the publishing industry and continued until it became one of the major factors that caused him to expatriate from the United States.

The novel received mixed reviews, although many were positive. Many critics, however, compared the novel to Richard Wright's *Native Son* (1940) and found it lacking in power, depth, and subtlety. These critical objections were to follow him throughout his later novels written in America: objections to the melodramatic turns of plot, the bitter tone, the uneven behavior of the protagonist, and the general unpleasantness of the narrative.

Himes's vision in this first novel results in a severe indictment of American society, and this vision placed him firmly in the mainstream of African American literature. Although he is generally categorized as one of the Wright School of Urban Realists, descendants of the early literary naturalists, Chester Himes possesses a wider range and depth than the protest genre allowed.

Bibliography

Fabre, Michael, and Robert E. Skinner, eds. *Conversations with Chester Himes*. Jackson: University Press of Mississippi, 1995. A collection of interviews given by Himes. A revealing portrait of Himes's background, personality, and evolution as a writer.

Fabre, Michael, Robert E. Skinner, and Lester Sullivan, comps. *Chester Himes: An Annotated Primary and Secondary Bibliography*. Westport, Conn.: Greenwood Press, 1992. A comprehensive bibliography of Himes's novels, short fiction, periodical publications, and nonfiction. A chronology of his life and career is also included.

Himes, Chester. *The Quality of Hurt: The Early Years*. New York: Paragon House, 1990. Himes chronicles his life from 1901 to 1954. He reveals how each of his works came into being and discusses the critical responses to his writing. When he wrote *If He Hollers Let Him Go*, he was criticized for being too narrow in his theme.

_____. *My Life of Absurdity: The Later Years: The Autobiography of Chester Himes*. New York: Paragon House, 1990. Himes continues his reflections on his life and writing from 1954 to 1972. His autobiography is a valuable resource for forming a complete picture of Himes's career within the cultural and political context of his times.

Margolies, Edward, and Michael Fabre. *The Several Lives of Chester Himes*. Jackson: University Press of Mississippi, 1997. A thorough biography by Margolies and Fabre, who knew Himes. Chronicles Himes's life and career from his turbulent youth in the south to his expatriation to Europe, where he found personal and artistic freedom.

Muller, Gilbert H. *Chester Himes*. Boston: Twayne, 1989. Muller provides a critical and interpretive study of Himes, with a close reading of his major works, a solid bibliography, and complete notes and references.

Jacquelyn L. Jackson

IN THE BEAUTY OF THE LILIES

Author: John Updike (1932-   )
Type of plot: Family
Time of plot: 1910 to 1990
Locale: Paterson, New Jersey; Basingstoke, Delaware; Hollywood, California; and Lower Branch, Colorado
First published: 1996

> *Principal characters:*
> CLARENCE WILMOT, a Presbyterian minister-turned-encyclopedia-salesman in Paterson
> THEODORE "TEDDY" WILMOT, Clarence's son, a postman in a small Delaware town
> ESTHER "ESSIE" WILMOT, Teddy's daughter, an actress who takes the screen name Alma DeMott
> CLARK DeMOTT, Esther's son, called "Esau" by members of the Colorado cult he joins

The Novel

In the Beauty of the Lilies is divided into four sections of roughly similar lengths, each named for one of the novel's central characters. The third-person narrator of each section has a limited point of view: that is, the narrator knows the thoughts and feelings of the character for whom the section is named.

The "Clarence" chapter begins in 1910 in Paterson, New Jersey. Mary Pickford, the famous actress, is starring in a film being made nearby. It is a warm day, and Pickford faints on the set. At the same moment, a few miles away, Reverend Clarence Wilmot, a socially secure Presbyterian minister, feels "the last particles of his faith leave him . . . a visceral surrender, a set of dark sparkling bubbles escaping upward." Clarence finds himself unable to serve a God in whom he no longer believes. Facing social humiliation and risking the loss of means to support his family, Clarence resigns his ministry. Three years later, the economy of Paterson stymied by labor unrest, Clarence ekes out a living peddling *The Popular Encyclopedia* door-to-door. In seriously reduced circumstances, Clarence finds comfort where he can: at the movies.

The "Teddy" chapter concerns Clarence's youngest son, named for President Theodore Roosevelt. Teddy, however, lacks Roosevelt's virility, his can-do spirit; he is quite happy staying out of harm's way. After Clarence's death, Teddy, his mother, and his sister are taken in by relatives in Basingstoke, an isolated northern Delaware town. Teddy, just graduated from high school, sees the move as a step down. The locals are "rubes." Furthermore, there is the problem of what he should "do." The son of an educated man, it would not do for Teddy to work in the local bottle-cap factory, and when he announces that he does not want to "sell anything, and I don't want to teach anything . . . and I don't want to *make* anything," the situation looks bleak. Eventually he finds a job in a drugstore, falls in love with Emily Sifford, and winds up working as a postman—a happy niche for Teddy. He marries the physically lame Emily and, at the chapter's end, walks in on her as she is bent over the crib admiring the physical perfection of their baby girl, Esther. If Teddy's life is not a picture of domestic bliss, it is nevertheless one of harmony.

Esther, whose family calls her "Essie," remains a beauty. The third chapter, dedicated to her story, opens with the portrait of a girl full of her own good fortune: "The joy of being herself flooded seven-year-old Essie's skin; it felt so tight she wanted to scream or laugh out loud." Her childhood experiences with the magic of cinema seal her fate: Life, for Essie, will be glamorous. Essie's triumph as second-runner-up in the 1947 Miss Delaware Peach contest leads to photo opportunities. These lead to a long career as a movie star that requires her to shed her name and become "Alma DeMott." Alma's acting career is full of valleys and peaks, but "among the many roles that Alma undertook, motherhood proved one of the few for which she was clearly miscast." Her son Clark, born in 1959, is a trial for Alma, and the news in 1987 that he has joined a Colorado cult comes as a relief.

The novel's final chapter is Clark's. The son of Alma and a scriptwriter to whom she was briefly married, Clark has a troubled childhood and adolescence. He lands a job with his great-uncle, Jared, who runs a ski resort in Colorado. There he meets Hannah, with whom he plans to go home for a sexual encounter. Her home turns out to be a commune the members of which belong to a cult, the Temple of True and Actual Faith; its leader, Jesse Smith, believes himself an incarnation of God. Clark joins, finding for the first time a meaningful life in rural Colorado, among Jesse's misfit cultists. Here Clark is given the name Esau. Things begin to disintegrate when one member shoots at a school bus; federal and state agents, after a lengthy standoff, fire tear gas into the compound. Rather than surrender, Jesse masterminds a mass suicide plan. He and his followers set fire to the Temple and begin distributing poison to other believers and their children. Esau undergoes an epiphany, which he experiences as "a flock of sparkling dark immaterial bubbles" descending into his body, and immediately knows that Jesse must die. In a heroic act, he shoots Jesse. The novel ends with television news anchors showing clips of the story to a transfixed America.

The Characters

One of John Updike's strengths is his ability to create fully rounded characters who also symbolize larger ideas. The symbolism, however, never overshadows character development, and most readers will not feel as if Updike is using his characters to pursue purely didactic aims. The characters in this novel are fully rounded, but they also represent their eras in American history, particularly as regards the prevailing religious tenor of the times.

Clarence's loss of faith is partially the result of pressures created by his times; by 1910, it becomes difficult for an educated person to reconcile religious faith with rapid scientific advances and social changes. Charles Darwin's theories of evolution have made traditional religious accounts of the origin of human beings appear doubt-

ful. Karl Marx's economic and social theories have argued that religion has historically been used to oppress the working class. Telegraph wires quickly bring news of
famines, natural disasters, and armies poised to attack. Clarence finds it difficult to
reconcile the idea of a loving God with so much human suffering. The final blow to
Clarence's faith is the rapid proliferation of American popular culture, specifically the
developing film industry. As the religious stories and heroes of the past are replaced
by inexpensively procured narratives and larger-than-life heroes whose magic is so
intoxicatingly present, religious faith for Clarence, as for American society generally,
undergoes trauma.

Clarence's loss of faith, rooted in history, shapes the identity of his descendants.
Teddy, in reaction to his father's emotional and intellectual upheaval, chooses a life of
nonconfrontation with the world and God. The house in which Teddy and Emily live
symbolizes nicely Teddy's strategy for dealing with the world: "He liked the way the
house seemed to hide, to hang back, between its two imposing neighbors." Teddy, like
his father, lacks faith, but Teddy's lack of faith stems from loyalty to Clarence rather
than any intellectual or emotional crisis. This is not to say that Teddy is untouched by
history. Born in the early years of the century, Teddy is too young for World War I, too
old for World War II, and as a postman who lucked into a government position before
the stock market crash in 1929, mostly insulated from the Great Depression.

Essie, however, is not be satisfied with a life of noninvolvement. As if to make up
for her father's desire to get through life making little trouble, Essie opts for a life in
the limelight. Her career as an actress takes her far from Basingstoke and straight into
Hollywood, the popular culture capital of America. She also signals a return, in the
novel, to religious faith; her faith, however, is not the inward-looking, intellectual
Presbyterianism of her paternal forebears, but something worn lightly, a faith tem-
pered by her mother's Methodism. Essie never wrestles with her religious faith. For
her, faith is instinctive: "She had trouble understanding how people could doubt
God's existence: He was so clearly there, next to her, interwoven with her, a palpable
pressure, as vital as the sensations in her skin, as dependable as her reflection in the
mirror." Faith—like sex, fame, and money—comes easily to Essie. Born in 1930, she
is too young to be adversely affected by the Depression, and she comes of age during
the unreflective, sunnily optimistic post-World War II economic boom.

Her energy seems admirable, especially in contrast with the lassitude of her lovable
but ineffectual father; nevertheless, her son Clark reacts against the shallowness and
heartlessness in her character. A child of rootless California who never knows his father and whose religious training is minimal, young Clark is a drifter attracted to the
easy highs of drugs and gorgings of American popular culture. A lost soul, he
searches for meaning in life and finds it within the Temple of the True and Actual
Faith, with its charismatic father-figure leader Jesse. Clark, a true member of his generation, suffers from a sense of meaninglessness in the radically fragmented American culture of the 1980's and attaches himself, although with some sense of postmodern irony, to whatever source of meaning he can find.

Themes and Meanings

Updike takes his title from the second verse of "Battle-Hymn of the Republic": "In the beauty of the lilies Christ was born across the sea,/ With a glory in his bosom that transfigures you and me:/ As he died to make men holy, let us die to make men free,/ While God is marching on." Are these lyrics, reprinted in the novel's epigraph, to be taken as a stirring tribute to the idealistic impulses of soldiers who died for the preservation of the American freedoms and the American way of life? Or are they a horrifying reminder of the quasi-religious patriotic propaganda for which naïve youth have been sacrificed in war? The tension this question raises points to a central question in the novel, most concretely formulated through Updike's treatment of Clark: Is this novel, and indeed is the American religious experience in the twentieth century, the story of faith tragically perverted—is this primarily a story of the tragedy of the deaths at the Temple compound? Or is this the story of faith regained, the story of a young man who, in the end, heroically remembers the faith of his forebears and prevents an even greater catastrophe when he shoots and kills Jesse? Furthermore, is American popular culture, specifically the Hollywood film industry, hopelessly degraded, or is it a genuine expression of the human imagination, America's great contribution to the world of art? Are the more optimistic and the more pessimistic readings of this novel simultaneously possible? It is easy to say that Updike allows readers to make up their own minds. It would be more accurate to remark how Updike points to the paradoxes at the heart of the American experience.

Critical Context

Throughout his prolific career, especially in *A Month of Sundays* (1975), *Roger's Version* (1986), and *S.* (1988), Updike has revisited issues surrounding America's Puritan, Protestant heritage posed over a century earlier by Nathaniel Hawthorne. If Hawthorne recognized the human suffering that Puritanism wrought as a defining characteristic of the American experience, Updike too sees the history of religious faith in America as inextricably interwoven with the nation's destiny. The Hawthorne parallels in this novel are unmistakable, and the reader will note Updike's use of the name Esther, echoing Hester from *The Scarlet Letter* (1850), and also that Clarence's middle name is Arthur, recalling Arthur Dimmesdale from the same novel.

The literary context of this novel is no more important than the historical. In the spring of 1993, in Waco, Texas, federal authorities stormed the compound of the Branch Davidians, a religious sect led by David Koresh. The deaths of members and their children touched a nerve in America's conscience. Updike echoes the events in Waco in the novel's final chapter, leading the reader to wonder to what degree a kind of Puritanical religious intolerance might have been responsible for the tragedy in Waco. In a nation under a constitution guaranteeing religious freedom, but in a nation suspicious of religious heterodoxy, the possibility for such terrifying events, in which the government, the charismatic cult leader, and the culture itself share blame, looms omnipresent.

Bibliography
Bloom, Harold, ed. *John Updike: Modern Critical Views*. New York: Chelsea House, 1987. A wide-ranging assortment of essays by important critics assessing various aspects of Updike's work.
Greiner, Donald J. *Adultery in the American Novel: Updike, James, and Hawthorne*. Columbia: University of South Carolina Press, 1985. Explores the Updike-Hawthorne connection in regard to the theme of adultery.
Plath, James, ed. *Conversations with John Updike*. Jackson: University of Mississippi Press, 1994. Updike discusses various concerns raised by his work.
Schiff, James A. *John Updike Revisited*. New York: Twayne, 1998. A brief, readable survey of Updike's work.
Wood, Ralph C. "Into the Void: Updike's Sloth and America's Religion." *The Christian Century* (April 24, 1996): 452-457. A major review of *In the Beauty of the Lilies* exploring Updike's religious vision.

Douglas Branch

IN THE BEGINNING

Author: Chaim Potok (1929-)
Type of plot: Impressionistic memoir
Time of plot: Primarily the 1920's to the 1940's
Locale: New York City
First published: 1975

> *Principal characters:*
> DAVID LURIE, the narrator
> MAX LURIE, his father
> RUTH LURIE, his mother
> ALEX LURIE, his younger brother
> SAUL, his cousin
> SHMUEL BADER, a successful businessman and David's private Bible
> teacher
> RAV TUVYA SHARFMAN, David's yeshiva instructor

The Novel

In the Beginning is a journey into the heart of an Orthodox Jewish family, Polish immigrants who have settled in the Bronx. It is the reminiscence of David Lurie, now a teacher, then a young boy struggling to piece together the meaning of his life in the midst of dark and troubling visions. When the novel opens, David is approaching six years of age; at its close, he is setting off for graduate study at the University of Chicago.

David is a sickly child, his frequent fevers the result of an undiagnosed deviated septum sustained in a fall with his mother, who was bringing him home from the hospital after his birth. Mishaps continue to plague his early childhood, and one day he accidentally runs over the hand of Eddie Kulanski, one of the neighborhood boys, with his tricycle. Eddie, a violently anti-Semitic bully, uses the incident as a pretext to threaten and torment David, who thus experiences at first hand the reality of the irrational hatred that even then was preparing the way for the Holocaust. Throughout his childhood, David is haunted by his impotence against the goyim in his neighborhood and those in Poland whose pogroms had so angered his father, Max Lurie. In fever dreams, David imagines the Golem of Prague, a kind of Frankenstein's monster, able to subdue all those who persecute the Jews.

David's earliest memories involve meetings of the Am Kedoshim (Holy Nation) Society, founded by his father. Successful in real estate, Max Lurie is working with fellow Jews to bring relatives and friends to the United States to escape the bloodshed in Poland. Max is no passive victim; in his homeland he had organized the Lemburg Jews to defend themselves, and when he saw that the situation there was hopeless, he led a group which emigrated to the United States.

David's early life centers on Shabbat, Sabbath observances. David is a prodigy, asking uncomfortable questions about adult life and catching the "whispers and sighs and glances and the often barely discernible gestures that are the real message carriers in our noisy world." Soon he begins studies at the yeshiva with his older cousin Saul, and soon his father is confronted with the stock-market crash.

Max Lurie's business fails during the Depression, the Am Kedoshim Society is bankrupt, and Max plunges into deep despair. Eventually the Luries move to smaller quarters, and Max begins to develop a new trade of watch repair. David remembers his frail mother, writing letters to her family remaining in Poland, nursing her husband, reading to David in German, fearful.

David studies Torah, the first five books of Moses, with Mr. Shmuel Bader.

> I had never been taught Bible that way in school. For my teacher, the words of the Bible . . . were simply there. Our task was to understand, to memorize, and to give back what we had learned. When Mr. Bader was done with that page it quivered and resonated with life.

Max Lurie's new business prospers, and the family moves to a larger apartment house. In the midst of dark rumors of Jewish deaths in Adolf Hitler's Germany, David's time is occupied with intense study of the strange books given to him by a superstitious neighbor, Mrs. Horowitz, now long dead. The books, which belonged to her father, are in German; they are works of biblical criticism that study not a seamless Torah with one (divine) author but rather a collection of writings from many sources.

After completing his undergraduate work at the yeshiva, David chooses secular Bible study at the University of Chicago. His younger brother, Alex, explores modern novels and the works of Sigmund Freud. The grief of David's father, who fears that his sons are becoming traitors to Orthodoxy, is put into perspective in the novel's visionary conclusion, which takes place years later, on a visit to the site of the Bergen-Belsen death camp. There, David has an imaginary conversation with the spirit of his namesake, Max's brother, killed in a pogrom. They are joined by the spirit of David's father, also dead now, and father and son are reassured that there has been neither failure nor betrayal: From the goyim, Jews must draw culture to enrich the roots of Orthodoxy. It is not rage, says the ghost, but a deep penetration of that evil culture that will in the end transform it.

The Characters

The characters are drawn with broad strokes, as befits a story much of which is recounted from the point of view of a boy. Although first-person narrator David Lurie is a mature young man by the time the book ends, the bulk of the narrative centers on his boyhood and adolescence, and Potok frequently exploits the dramatic irony occasioned by youthful lack of knowledge.

To the young David, his father, Max Lurie, is a larger-than-life figure, a pillar of strength—at least until the Crash of 1929, which ruins him. Even this loss, however, does not permanently break his spirit. A revisionist Orthodox Jew, he fought against the Red Cossacks who invaded Poland in 1920. When his brother David died in a pogrom, Max married David's widow, Ruth, in accordance with the Law of Moses. Max is a resourceful provider for his family, burdened always with the belief that the tradition must be preserved. Despite fits of anger at the pogroms and at his son David's choice of studies, Max tries to recognize that there is another way besides rage:

> You want to fight the goyim with words? All right. Good. Fight them with words. My little brother would not have been troubled too much to see you reading German books if you were thinking to use them as weapons. I will fight them with guns.

David is a counterpoint to his father's strength. A brilliant, precocious youth, David is hounded by childhood accidents and recurring illnesses, bullied by bigger, stronger boys, haunted by extraordinarily vivid nightmares. Yet David is less an individual and more a means for the author to exemplify the confrontation of Orthodox Judaism with anti-Semitism and secular culture. He is an ideal. He is simply too good—seemingly free, for example, of sexual desire. It is through him that Potok presents a reconciliation of the demands of Orthodoxy with those of modern gentile culture.

Aiding in that task are Mr. Bader and Rav Sharfman. Shmuel Bader's mysterious business in Europe often keeps him away from tutoring David, yet his intellectual influence is profound on the boy. At an early point, Bader tells David that he does not hate goyim, because he was fortunate to be in the United States during World War I. Yet Bader feels guilty of his good fortune and does what he can to help Max in the Am Kedoshim Society. Bader seems worldly-wise, yet he remains a practicing Jew.

The raspy-voiced Rav Sharfman encourages David to study the Bible texts. He "deliberately sought to make room for the intellectually brave to chart their own lives." He tells David that it is not a crime to argue against the revered Jewish commentators.

David's mother, Ruth Lurie, uses words in a different way. She is superstitious and often repeats a charm that was used by Mrs. Horowitz to ensure David's health. She is protective of her two children when Max is angry at them, yet she takes a kind of dark joy in their inquisitiveness. David's character is much like that of her dead husband. Ruth suffers much—Max's breakdown after the Crash, her parents' refusal to resettle in America, the growing tension between Orthodoxy and David's awakening mind—and she is often withdrawn.

If David represents Potok's spiritual quest, Alex is the author's aesthetic side. Alex is enthralled with English novels and wants to become a teacher of English literature. Alex is moved to tears by *Oliver Twist*. Potok, during his own high school days, devoured the works of not only Charles Dickens but also William Faulkner and Ernest Hemingway.

David's cousin Saul is a friend and ally until it is clear that David will be pursuing secular studies. Saul reminds David that it is the Torah of Moses he will be studying and writing about. To deny that authorship is to deny the Torah and Orthodoxy itself. In their early years, Saul had been an older and wiser guide for David, but now, like Vergil guiding Dante, here was a new world, a new way of seeing things, that Saul could not enter.

Themes and Meanings

In the Beginning is a dramatization of a closed religious and cultural system in tension with a secular world that threatens to swallow it up. Potok fashions his resolution using principles inherent in Orthodoxy itself, argumentation and consolidation. Two conflicting rabbinical arguments are reconciled by yet a third argument, which is then challenged by a new generation. Orthodoxy is not simply the latest argument but rather the entire rabbinical tradition. Potok's most riveting scenes are those where David confronts not only his instructors but also the rabbinical commentators on points of Scripture. Thus, though David is driven to seek answers outside his tradition, those answers may well someday provide fresh streams for Jewish Orthodoxy itself.

There are many beginnings in the book: the start of David's life, the new lives of Jewish émigrés, a new intellectual adventure for David. There are parallels to the Book of Beginnings, Genesis, in David's literal fall from his mother's arms, his infatuation with the zoo and with accounts of the Flood, and his comprehension of the power of words. Though all beginnings may be hard, the hardest one of all is to make one's own beginning.

Critical Context

In the Beginning was Potok's fourth novel; in it, he sought to recapture his earliest memories and define his struggle against his strict Orthodox upbringing (which he has called essentially Hasidic without the outward trappings). All of Potok's novels are efforts to portray the lives of people precious to him, and in the present work, an air of kindliness, of sympathy, is pervasive. At the same time, however, the novel reflects Potok's traumatic break with the subculture in which he was reared—a break he made in 1950, when, for his rabbinical studies, he opted for Conservative Judaism, with its openness to secular, historical study of biblical texts.

With his third novel, *My Name Is Asher Lev* (1972), Potok had mastered his craft, moving beyond the stylistic infelicities that marred his enormously successful first novel, *The Chosen* (1967), and its sequel, *The Promise* (1969). *In the Beginning* marked a further advance in craftmanship. A best-seller, like its predecessors, it was also by far his most complex book to date.

While it is undeniable that Potok has grown as a novelist, it is also true that there is a remarkable consistency to his work; this is both a strength and a weakness. Like *My Name Is Asher Lev* and a later novel, *Davita's Harp* (1985), *In the Beginning* centers on the childhood and adolescence of a gifted, precocious first-person narrator; like those two works and *The Book of Lights* (1981), a third-person narrative based on Potok's experiences as an army chaplain in Korea, *In the Beginning* is structured poetically, built around a pattern of recurring images. Finally, like all of Potok's novels, *In the Beginning* deals with what he has called "the problem of faith in a secular world."

Bibliography

Hock, Zarina Manawwar. "Authority and Multiculturalism: Reflections by Chaim Potok." *Language Arts* 72 (April, 1995): 4. Hock discusses Potok's use of multicultural themes to expose attitudes toward social issues. She demonstrates how his fiction reflects the battle between traditional and new sources of conduct.

Potok, Chaim. "The Invisible Map of Meaning: A Writer's Confrontations." *Tri-Quarterly* 84 (Spring, 1992): 17-45. Potok discusses the major theme that runs throughout his works, that of cultural conflict and the influence this conflict has on the direction of an individual life. Potok describes his first encounter with mainstream Western literature and shows how this experience shaped his subsequent writing, including *In the Beginning*.

_____. *Wanderings: Chaim Potok's History of the Jews*. New York: Fawcett Books, 1990. Potok's compelling history of the Jews recreates historical events and explores the many facets of Jewish life through the ages. Although this work does not address Potok's fiction, it does provide insight into Potok's ethnic heritage which has a direct bearing on his writing.

Walden, Daniel, ed. *The World of Chaim Potok*. Albany: State University of New York Press, 1985. This rich resource on the writing of Chaim Potok features critical essays, as well as reviews and a bibliographic essay. It does not directly discuss *In the Beginning* but provides valuable insight into Potok's fiction that can be extended to the entire body of his work.

Dan Barnett

IN THE HEART OF THE VALLEY OF LOVE

Author: Cynthia Kadohata (1956-   )
Type of plot: Science fiction
Time of plot: 2052
Locale: Southern California
First published: 1992

>   *Principal characters:*
>   FRANCIE, the narrator and protagonist of the novel, a nineteen-year-old
>   Japanese American
>   AUNTIE ANNIE, Francie's aunt, who takes care of her niece after her
>   parents die
>   ROHN JEFFERSON, a boyfriend of Auntie Annie who disappears
>   abruptly after his arrest
>   MARK TRANG, a student at a Los Angeles community college who
>   becomes Francie's boyfriend
>   JEWEL, a student at the college who is in her late thirties
>   HANK and EMMY, Jewel's parents
>   MATT BURROUGHS, a fellow student of Francie, Mark, and Jewel who
>   is accused of murder
>   CARL, a tattooist and a friend of Mark

The Novel

In the Heart of the Valley of Love is set in a future Southern California of the mid-twenty-first century. It centers on the experiences of Francie, a young Japanese American girl of that time, and her family and friends. The story is told in the first person and is divided into sixteen short chapters.

In the Heart of the Valley of Love begins with the narrator and protagonist, Francie, driving through the Mojave Desert in the company of her Auntie Annie, who has taken care of her since the death of her parents. With them is Annie's boyfriend, Rohn. On their way to the desert, they had been stopped by a highway patrolman, but Rohn had bribed the officer to let them go. Despite this incident, the three people in the car are having a good time as they speed eastward. In the scarcity of this projected twenty-first century, such necessities of life as water are jealously hoarded and dearly priced. When Rohn is offered an opportunity by an enigmatic man named Max the Magician to buy some water, he agrees with alacrity. The entire water purchase, though, is a trick played by the authorities, with Max as either tool or dupe. Rohn is arrested and carted off to an unknown locale. Even though Auntie Annie is far senior to her in years, Francie feels a responsibility to take care of her aunt in the wake of Rohn's disappearance. Having weathered many travails during her life, Francie sees herself as supremely adaptable.

Francie reflects on the death of her parents. They had known that they were dying and had been understandably bitter. This bitterness, however, was laced with bursts of sincere optimism. The memory of her parents' courage lends Francie the strength to persevere even after the upsetting episode of Rohn's kidnapping.

Francie enrolls in a local two-year college that serves primarily the underprivileged classes. Here, she develops a circle of friends for the first time since she had moved to California from Chicago in her early teenage years. Among these is Mark Trang, a fellow student who becomes her boyfriend, and Jewel, an older woman who becomes the unofficial leader of the group. Jewel is involved in an abusive relationship with a real-estate agent named Teddy. When Teddy is arrested, Jewel, accompanied by Francie, bails him out.

Francie works part-time in a law office, but her primary efforts are concentrated upon school, especially her work on the school newspaper. She realizes that, because of the class stratification in twenty-first century America, she will never be permitted to be a member of the social elite, who are isolated in heavily garrisoned "richtowns." She is nevertheless determined to make the best of her life. Her relationship with Mark deepens as they realize that they share many experiences, beliefs, and values. Mark and Francie go together to visit Jewel's parents, Hank and Emmy. Hank recounts a time in his long-ago childhood, in the year 2000, when he had walked with his father to a secluded arroyo unblemished by the overpopulation and technology rampant even then in the region. He wonders why his father had taken him there.

Mark and Francie go to be tattooed by Carl, a friend of Mark. For the couple, it is a kind of ceremony, a ritual of self-affirmation against the prescriptive norms of society. They become involved in trying to help Matt Burroughs, a fellow student accused of murder. They attend a rally on his behalf, and Francie becomes close to Matt's mother, Madeline, after interviewing her for the school paper. Matt, however, betrays all of his supporters by skipping bail; he may also have killed his mother. Francie and Mark also become involved in trying to expose a school administrator, James Goodman, who is soliciting prostitutes from among the students. When Goodman kills himself, however, they decide not to publish the evidence they have.

Rohn has not returned, but Auntie Annie still holds out hope. Francie agrees, especially because the riots that overtake Los Angeles after the June primaries mean that petty criminals such as Rohn are no longer such a major concern. Jewel is still tantalized by the secret of her grandfather's arroyo, and Mark and Francie accompany her on an expedition there. Their excavations yield a box that reveals that Jewel's grandfather had once loved a woman name Maria, though he had not left his wife for her. Jewel takes the rings that had belonged to her grandfather and Maria; she writes her own name on a piece of paper and puts it in the box as a substitute. Mark and Francie follow suit, writing not only their own names but those of all of their friends and relatives. Not only have they gotten in touch with the past, they have staked their own place in history as they prepare for their future.

The Characters

Francie, the heroine and narrator of the book, is a nineteen-year-old Japanese American woman. The story is told through the prism of her first-person awareness and recounts the development of her social and cultural attitudes. In using a young narrator to describe a strange future universe, Kadohata gains the advantage of being able to have her character assume the novelties of the future rather than convey them to the reader in a didactic manner. Francie spent her childhood in Chicago but moved to Los Angeles in her early teenage years. Her parents died prematurely, leaving her in the care of her Auntie Annie. At first confused by the complexities of adult life and by the bleak circumstances of her own life, Francie matures in the course of the novel. In contrast to the older women in the book, Auntie Annie and Jewel, Francie does not let the obstacles posed by the persistent misogyny of her society stand in her way. Through her work on the school newspaper, her romance with Mark, and her other friendships and loyalties, she develops a strength that enables her to face courageously the difficult social problems that exert so much pressure upon her.

Auntie Annie, Francie's aunt, is desolated by the disappearance of Rohn. Somewhat hapless and vulnerable at times, she nevertheless is a stabilizing influence on her niece.

Rohn Jefferson, Annie's boyfriend, gets on the wrong side of the law simply by trying to provide for his family. His arrest reflects the social turmoil and dislocation that pervade the novel.

Mark Trang, Francie's boyfriend, is her principal ally in navigating the intricacies of the depressing world of Los Angeles in 2052. Humorous, independent, and determined, he helps Francie to elucidate her own values, thus assisting in making them clear to the reader as well.

Jewel, an older woman and fellow student of Mark and Francie, possesses a maturity and a set of life experiences that aid Mark and Francie in establishing their adult identities. A good influence on others, she is less fortunate in her own personal life, which is dominated by her seemingly permanent relationship with the bullying Teddy.

Hank and Emmy, Jewel's parents, present the distant past—in other words, the late twentieth century. The arroyo mentioned by Hank to his daughter provides the scene for the inspiring denouement of the book.

Matt Burroughs, a young man accused of murder, betrays those who trust him. He shows that even though the Los Angeles of 2052 is an unjust society, not all those deemed criminals are basically innocent men like Rohn; for some, the punishment is merited by the crime. There is still personal evil as well as a broader social corruption.

Carl, Mark's tattooist friend, is a kind of unofficial priest. His tattooing of Francie and Mark becomes a ceremonial, metaphoric acknowledgment of their commitment to each other.

Themes and Meanings

In the Heart of the Valley of Love uses science-fiction conventions and a future setting to discuss concerns very much of the time of its writing. In the recessionary 1990's, California, long the utopian embodiment of the American Dream, was afflicted with an unfamiliar sense of limitation and despair. Kadohata's California of sixty years hence is an extrapolation of the trends perceived as dominating the California of the author's present. The scarcity of resources, the sharp division between the privileged inhabitants from the "richtowns" and the benighted urban proletariat, and the potential of authoritarian solutions to problems of social unrest are but the most prominent of the cultural factors operating in the world of *In the Heart of the Valley of Love*. A good primer on the sociology behind Kadohata's world, especially in the division between a technologically advanced elite and an underprivileged lower class, is Mike Davis's *City of Quartz* (1990), a meditation on the economics and culture of the Los Angeles of the author's day.

Kadohata is one of a number of writers interested in a future Southern California setting. The most visible of these manifestations is in the "cyberpunk" school of science fiction, which tends to emphasize the depersonalizing effects of hegemonic corporate and media power while stressing that the future will not lead to the kind of radical or redemptive transformation traditionally heralded by science fiction. Kadohata's hypothetical Southern California, though, is sharply different from that of cyberpunk. Kadohata's female protagonist is quite a change from cyberpunk's typical hardboiled male heroes. Cyperpunk has also been accused of stressing degrading and obvious caricatures of Asian and Asian American people. Both Francie and Mark are Asian American, and both are pictured affirmatively, as visionaries who will help to change their society for the better.

This sense of affirmation is not exclusively ethnic in stripe. Like the characters in Kim Stanley Robinson's *The Gold Coast* (1988), Kadohata's protagonists are in search of some sort of moral center upon which they can premise their young lives so they will not end in the despair of previous generations. The scene at the secluded arroyo, even though in dramatic terms it is more significant to Jewel than to the two main characters, is crucial in this respect. Here, Francie and Mark make a kind of covenant with their own future, storing their own just-established identities in the receptacle that for so long had symbolized a dead man's long-lost love. In inscribing themselves onto the past, they are carving out an identity for themselves in eternity.

Kadohata recognizes the perils that the future may hold, but she does not yield to cynicism or despair. In this, she echoes the convictions set forth in Carolyn See's courageous and transformative novels *Golden Days* (1987) and *Making History* (1991). Kadohata, like See, stares into a terrifying future and views it as full of hope.

Critical Context

Cynthia Kadohata's first novel, *The Floating World*, was published to broad acclaim in 1989. That novel was an autobiographical work tracing the experiences of a young Japanese American girl growing up in the America of the 1950's. Although the title is taken from a famous Japanese art style of the eighteenth and nineteenth centuries, the novel is thoroughly American in setting and orientation. Many of the motifs and details—the long, exhilarating drives through desert terrain, the observant sensibility of a young girl who acts as the narrator—will be familiar to readers of *In the Heart of the Valley of Love*. Whereas *The Floating World* is set in the past and appeals to the nostalgia in readers, however, Kadohata's second novel is set many decades in the future and appeals to readers' sense of speculation and wonder.

Ethnic writers in America are often expected to restrict their subject matter and themes. Portrayal of established minority communities is common; less frequent is a searching look at how those communities might be transformed and catalyzed by the America of the future. Kadohata's turn to science fiction marks her as a writer not content simply to write according to conventional formulae that will automatically garner her good reviews. Kadohata aims for a more genuine imaginative freedom; it is this imaginative willpower that makes her one of America's most promising writers.

Bibliography

Blackford, Staige D. Review of *In the Heart of the Valley of Love*, by Cynthia Kadohata. *Virginia Quarterly Review* 69 (January, 1993): SS21. Discusses the social and chronological setting of the novel, laying particular emphasis on the depiction of scarcity and poverty in the future Southern California.

Kadohata, Cynthia. Interview by Lisa See and Sybil Steinberg. *Publishers Weekly* 239 (August 3, 1992): 48-49. Kadohata talks about both *The Floating World* and *In the Heart of the Valley of Love*. She also discusses her personal and educational background, the artistic controversies and conundrums she has not been able to sidestep, and the source of her inspiration.

Li, Cherry W. Review of *In the Heart of the Valley of Love*, by Cynthia Kadohata. *Library Journal* 117 (June 15, 1992): 102. Centers on Kadohata's depiction of an engaging young Asian American heroine. Also discusses Kadohata's panoramic vision of a future society.

Quick, Barbara. Review of *In the Heart of the Valley of Love*, by Cynthia Kadohata. *The New York Times Book Review*, August 30, 1992, p. 14. Assesses Kadohata's skill in creating a convincing representation of a dystopian future and of the characters who populate the novel's fictional world.

Nicholas Birns

IN THE SKIN OF A LION

Author: Michael Ondaatje (1943-   )
Type of plot: Family
Time of plot: c. 1908 to 1938
Locale: Ontario, Canada
First published: 1987

> *Principal characters:*
> PATRICK LEWIS, a farmboy who moves to the city and becomes
>   involved in radical politics
> ROWLAND HARRIS, the commissioner of public works for metropolitan
>   Toronto
> AMBROSE SMALL, a millionaire businessman, the subject of a massive
>   manhunt
> CLARA DICKENS, his lover, a radio actress
> ALICE GULL, Clara's best friend, a former nun, later an anarchist
> HANA GULL, her daughter
> DAVID CARAVAGGIO, a thief, Patrick's cellmate in prison
> NICHOLAS TEMELCOFF, a Greek immigrant

The Novel

According to a brief prefatory note, *In the Skin of a Lion* is told by a man driving at night from Toronto to a town in rural Ontario. He is weary and worried, and his narrative swerves from one scene to another very much as his car swerves through the moonlit night. Yet he has a good listener, a girl of sixteen.

Patrick Lewis grows up on a farm in eastern Ontario. His father, Hazen Lewis, teaches him how to work with dynamite, blasting mines and breaking up logjams. After his father dies in a mining accident, Patrick goes to Toronto to find work. He becomes a detective or "searcher" whose job is to locate a missing millionaire named Ambrose Small. When he finds Small's former mistress, she seduces him. They live together, and he comes to love her deeply, but she always says she will leave one day to rejoin Small. One day, she sets out on a train journey from which she never returns.

Meanwhile in Toronto, a young nun is knocked off a new bridge during a freak construction accident. Miraculously, she is caught by a daring worker from Macedonia who saves her life. She has never been so close to a man before, and she decides she will not return to the nunnery. She meets a Finnish immigrant with revolutionary ideas and becomes pregnant by him. A gifted actress and accomplished speaker, she takes part in political rallies and espouses the cause of anarchy: opposition to any exercise of power over the working people. Her lover, Cato, is murdered before their daughter is born.

These are the events recounted in book 1, though some details appear only in the novel's third and last book. The former nun is Alice Gull. Her rescuer is Nicholas Temelcoff, an immigrant who soon after marries and opens a bakery. Her best friend is Clara Dickens, an actress who becomes involved first with Ambrose Small and then with the "searcher." Alice meets Patrick through Clara and looks him up in the city after Clara has disappeared.

In book 2, Patrick is a construction laborer, helping to dig a tunnel for the city's new waterworks. Though attracted to Alice, he is still obsessed with Clara. He tracks her (and her still missing millionaire) to their hiding place. Because he is no longer interested in the reward, and because Clara is no longer interested in him, he returns to Alice. He loves her and her daughter, Hana, but his life is shattered when Alice takes the wrong satchel one day and carries a load of explosives to the site of her accident years earlier. Unable to forget her and her radical ideas, he burns down a lakeside resort and blows up the dock. He is arrested and serves five years in prison. Again, some details are supplied only in book 3.

In prison, Patrick meets David Caravaggio, a former bridge worker who has turned to theft. He learns Caravaggio's story and begins to plot his revenge on the powers that Alice fought. After his release, he plots a bombing at the city's new water-filtration plant. Injured in the daring underwater approach, he is confronted by the commissioner of public works, and they talk late into the night about the city, their dreams, and the people with the real power. Exhausted, Patrick falls asleep, while the commissioner calls the police to defuse the bomb but lets the bomber go free. As Patrick is recovering at home, Alice's daughter, Hana, awakens him to say that Clara has called. After hearing that Ambrose has died, he agrees to meet Clara and begins the six-hour drive with Hana.

The Characters

The story covers thirty years in the life of Patrick Lewis, from childhood to the attempted bombing in 1938. It takes only six hours to narrate, about as long as the novel takes to read. The narrative is confusing, ostensibly because Patrick is tired but also because Ondaatje deliberately throws the reader off balance. He offers the novelist's equivalent of a filmmaker's extreme close up. He provides much sensory information, as Patrick works with his hands, but little generalization. This forces the reader to reconstruct the action and re-create the plot.

Patrick is the main character, and five of the novel's seven chapters are told from his point of view. Of the remaining chapters, one is told from several points of view, including Alice's, and the other from Caravaggio's point of view. The novel's narrator knows what Patrick knows by the time he takes Hana on the night drive. Yet the narrator knows more, including what Patrick will later read in the Riverside Library in Toronto and what Ondaatje will learn as he does research for the novel. The story is Patrick's, and it becomes Hana's, but the words are Ondaatje's.

Patrick is also the most fully realized character. When there is dialogue, he is usually taking part. By contrast, most of other characters are two-dimensional, painted with a few simple strokes of the brush. Patrick's father, Hazen, is a farmworker who seeks a better career in explosives and is hoist with his own petard. Ambrose Small is a "jackal." Rowland Harris, the commissioner of public works, is a visionary who turns out to have humble origins. Temelcoff is a daredevil who dreams of owning a bakery. Hana is a good child on the brink of adulthood.

All these characters belong to their time and place. They serve to make "Upper America" what it became by World War II. If there is some irony in the minor characters' stories, if they are somehow living in the wrong time and place, that is part of the conundrum of existence as Patrick reflects on it.

Themes and Meanings

In an interview while he was writing the novel, Ondaatje said he disliked "political theses" and needed "to be affected emotionally or in a sensual way" before a story took hold. In Patrick Lewis he created an old Ontario boy, with an Irish first name and a Welsh surname, whose work brought him together with tarrers and tanners, whose heart made him open to radical ideas, and whose experience with explosives made him valuable to the radicals. The closest Patrick gets to the real money and power is when he tracks down Small and nearly blows up Harris.

Ondaatje does not sit in judgment on his character, nor does he ask readers to do so. Small is seen sitting in meditation toward the end of his life, as though looking for something better than his capitalistic ventures could produce; Harris is seen dreaming of a city that was never built, much as Hana dreams of favorite places in the city. Patrick is often seen under water, whether trying to rescue a cow or destroy a city project. The most morally ambiguous character is Caravaggio, a house painter who prefers to rob houses. Caravaggio has the last name of a famous Renaissance artist who insisted on painting people as he saw them, warts and all, and who tried to keep his amoral lifestyle private. Ondaatje's Caravaggio has the anonymity that a novelist might well admire.

Ondaatje takes his title from the ancient Sumerian creation epic. The epic hero Gilgamesh promises to mourn the death of his best friend by wandering the earth "in the skin of a lion." As Patrick tries to make sense of his memories, he recalls a story Alice once told him: a group of actresses took turns improvising parts of a story, each one putting on an animal pelt to signal that she was going to play her role. Patrick too takes on a role as he tries to revenge Alice's death. Perhaps anyone who seeks revenge must do so.

Critical Context

Ondaatje's first novel, *Running in the Family* (1982), tells the story of Ondaatje's origins in Ceylon (modern-day Sri Lanka). It shows how a young person is formed by the stories he or she hears, especially when family members are dead or absent. (Ondaatje's parents divorced when he was a small child.) *In the Skin of a Lion* shows the same interest in a family's traditions, its "hand-me-downs." Patrick is not Hana's biological father or even, perhaps, her legal stepfather; one learns only that he loved her mother and wanted to spend his life with them. Caravaggio is not "family" in any proper sense, only a former jailmate of Hana's guardian. They are, however, representative of Toronto's ethnic diversity.

Like many Torontonians, Ondaatje drove into town on a freeway built along a river that runs into Lake Ontario. Like other drivers, he admired the Bloor Street Viaduct, which he drove under as he crossed the city's main east-west artery. He liked the design and wondered about the people who built the city's infrastructure. Like his "searcher," Patrick, he went to public libraries. He read about Small, the theatrical impresario who financed the viaduct, and about Harris, who supervised its construction. He found an account of Temelcoff, who worked on the project and who was still alive in the 1980's.

After the first draft, he despised Small, whom he calls a "jackal," and was bored by Harris. He wanted to know more about the men who actually built the bridge. It seemed to him that the official history of Canada was in danger of becoming racist because it was erasing the contributions of its immigrant population.

The novel won many awards in Canada, where Ondaatje was already known as a poet and filmmaker. It won a nomination for the prestigious Booker Prize in England, awarded to the best novel of the year. Ondaatje finally won the prize for *The English Patient* (1992); although that novel is set in bombed-out Italy in 1945 and tells the story of a man who had never been to Canada, it has a close link to this one. The patient tells his story to Hana, who remains a fine listener and is now a caring nurse. They are visited by Caravaggio, who tells of new exploits. It takes a careful reader to make sense of their stories, but the extraordinary detail and emotional charge make the effort worthwhile.

Bibliography

Barbour, Douglas. *Michael Ondaatje*. New York: Twayne, 1993. A comprehensive account of the author's life and works, both poetry and fiction.

Cooke, John. *The Influence of Painting on Five Canadian Writers: Alice Munro, Hugh Hood, Timothy Findley, Margaret Atwood, and Michael Ondaatje*. Lewiston, N.Y.: Edwin Mellen Press, 1996. An interesting look at the visual arts' effect on Ondaatje and other prominent Canadian authors.

Jewinski, Ed. *Michael Ondaatje: Express Yourself Beautifully*. Canadian Biography Series. Toronto: ECW Press, 1994. Follows Ondaatje's odyssey from his arrival in Canada in 1962 to his Booker Prize for *The English Patient* thirty years later. A beautifully written story and a pleasure to read.

Siemerling, Winfried. *Discoveries of the Other: Alterity in the Work of Leonard Cohen, Hubert Aquin, Michael Ondaatje, and Nicole Brossard*. Toronto: University of Toronto Press, 1994. Includes a chapter on identity issues in Ondaatje's work and a section on oral history in *In the Skin of a Lion*.

Solecki, Sam, ed. *Spider Blues: Essays on Michael Ondaatje*. Montreal: Véhicule Press, 1985. Published before *In the Skin of a Lion*, this collection includes many fine essays on Ondaatje's early work. Especially pertinent are Linda Hutcheon's essay on *Running in the Family* and the editor's interview with Ondaatje.

Thomas Willard

IN THE TIME OF THE BUTTERFLIES

Author: Julia Alvarez (1950-   )
Type of plot: Historical realism
Time of plot: 1928 to 1994
Locale: The Dominican Republic
First published: 1994

> *Principal characters:*
> DEDÉ MIRABAL, surviving sister of the Butterflies
> MINERVA MIRABAL, the most passionately political of the four sisters
> PATRIA MIRABAL, the most religious and eldest of the sisters
> MARÍA TERESA (MATE), the youngest of the sisters

The Novel

In the Time of the Butterflies is the fictional story of four real persons, the Mirabal sisters of the Dominican Republic. In 1960, three of the sisters, members of the underground movement opposing the regime of the dictator Rafael Trujillo, were ambushed on a lonely mountain road and assassinated. Alvarez's novel, made up of three sections and an epilogue, intersperses chapters for each sister. All except Dedé's are first-person narrations; Dedé does narrate the epilogue, however.

Section 1 of the novel ("1928 to 1946") opens in 1994 with a woman interviewing Dedé about her martyred sisters. The section then describes how youthful Minerva, María Teresa, and Patria awoke to political awareness. Minerva learned of the dictator's brutality from her schoolmate Sinita, whose family lost all of its men to Trujillo. Minerva educates young María Teresa (Mate). Patria begins to quest on her faith in God and Trujillo as a young wife plunged into a religious crisis after a stillbirth. Minerva is the first to act on her political convictions. Won over to Sinita's hatred of Trujillo, she performs in a play covertly celebrating pre-Trujillo freedom. Near its end, Sinita, playing Liberty, suddenly walks up to Trujillo with her toy bow and aims an imaginary arrow at him. She is quickly subdued, and the tense moment passes, but Minerva has come to Trujillo's notice.

Section 2, "1948 to 1959," covers the years of the Mirabals' resistance activity. Minerva meets activist Virgilio (Lío) Morales and continues in his path when he is forced to flee the country. One day, she discovers her father's mistress and four illegitimate daughters living in poverty. She also finds letters from Lío that her father has kept from her. Shortly thereafter, Trujillo summons her to attend a dance; when he tries to hold her vulgarly close, she slaps him. Her family quickly whisks her away, but she leaves behind her purse, containing Lío's letters. Her father is soon detained for interrogation, and the experience breaks his health. Over the next months, Mate joins Minerva in the underground; both marry fellow revolutionaries and have daughters. Eventually, Patria's son Nelson yearns to join too, and Patria is herself converted when she witnesses a massacre of young rebels by Trujillo forces.

Section 3 relates events leading up to the death of the three sisters, now known nationwide as "The Butterflies." Trujillo attacks the underground, and Minerva, Mate, the three husbands, and Nelson are arrested. Mate and Minerva keep up the spirit of resistance in their crowded cell, and a solidarity grows between the political and non-political prisoners there. Mate is eventually subjected to electric shock torture. Meanwhile, though, the political tide has begun to turn. The Organization of American States comes to investigate prison conditions, and Mate manages to slip their representative a statement by her cellmates. Soon afterward, Trujillo releases the Butterflies. When Minerva tries to track down information on the state of the underground, she learns that they have become national symbols of resistance. In fact, Trujillo claims his biggest problems are the church and the Mirabal sisters. Before long, Minerva's and Mate's husbands are moved to a remote prison. On November 25, 1960, the two wives and Patria set out with Rufino, their driver, to visit the men, despite Dedé's warning that it is dangerous for them to travel together. They make it to the prison safely, but midway home the narrative breaks off abruptly. In the epilogue, Dedé recalls that for weeks afterward, people brought her information about her sisters' last hours. They were strangled and clubbed, then returned to the Jeep and pushed off the cliffside. Dedé, enmeshed in grief, barely noted events of the next few years: Trujillo's assassination, the murderers' trial, the country's first free elections in thirty one years, a coup followed by civil war, and finally peace. The Mirabal sisters, meanwhile, become legends, and Dedé the conservator of their memory.

Alvarez's postscript explains that her father was a member of the same resistance movement as the Mirabals and fled the Dominican Republic shortly before their deaths. Alvarez grew up hearing about the sisters and decided to write their story. When she began researching their lives, however, she uncovered a wealth of legends and anecdotes about them, but few verifiable facts. She thus turned to fiction to discover who they were. She began this project to answer the question, "What gave them that special courage?" She ends by noting that the anniversary of their deaths, November 25, is now, appropriately, the International Day Against Violence Toward Women.

The Characters

Alvarez uses each of the four Mirabal sisters to demonstrate different routes to resistance against political oppression. Minerva, the next to youngest and the most passionately political of the sisters, is the most intellectually savvy. She understands that Trujillo's oppression is part of a larger issue of patriarchy. Prevented for years from attending law school, then denied a license to practice once she earns her degree, she knows firsthand the restrictions on women in Trujillo's dictatorship. She also understands that her own father exercises a similar authority, able to approve or withhold education for his daughters and covertly keeping his second family of daughters in poverty. She responds with passionate, often dramatic, acts. Mate, the youngest, becomes Minerva's disciple, but not her duplicate. Mate is a romantic, drawn to resistance work by the adventure. She follows her heart, not her head, and fully commits to the underground when she falls in love with a young revolutionary. Patria, the eldest, is devout and devoted to her family. She begins to question her loyalty to Trujillo as the result of a religious crisis brought on by a stillbirth early in her marriage. Her grief leads her to question everything in which she once had faith, including God and Trujillo, but she does not join Minerva and Mate in their resistance work until years later. When her son Nelson begins to become involved, she expresses her tacit support of his cause by naming her new child after two Cuban freedom fighters. Her real conversion comes, however, when she witnesses a massacre of young rebels. A youth who is about the age that her stillborn son would have been is shot right before her. She has an epiphany: These rebels are her sons. She joins the movement as the third Butterfly.

Dedé's role, in some ways, is the most complicated. The second oldest, she is the most domestic and the most opposed to resistance activities. Her loyalty to her sisters never wavers, though, and her silence about what she knows of their involvement in the underground makes her somewhat complicitous in their work. She blames her reluctance to join the resistance on her husband, who orders her to have nothing to do with the movement and refuses to let Patria bury boxes of weapons on his property. Gradually, though, she comes to realize that she has used her husband's authority as a way to hide her own lack of courage. Toward the end of the story, Dedé begins to consider joining her sisters in their cause, but she does not find the courage before they are killed. After the deaths of Minerva, Patria, and Mate, Dedé becomes identified to both herself and to Dominicans as the surviving sister. In this role she lives out the rest of her life, telling and retelling the story of her sisters, keeping the memory of their courageous example alive. As preserver of their legacy, she finds a kind of redemption.

Themes and Meanings

Alvarez's most pervasive theme is that heroism exists side by side with the mundane, that extraordinary courage can be a part of ordinary life. To emphasize this, she intertwines the story of the sisters' political lives with stories of their courtships, motherhood, and concerns about daily trivia. On the day of their deaths, she has them gleefully splurge on new purses; one of their last acts is to make a stop for beer and lemonade.

In Dedé, she also explores themes of personal memory versus public remembrance and of the obligations of the living to the memory of the dead. After Trujillo's regime, Dedé sacrifices her personal identity to become the living repository of her sisters' memory. For thirty-four years, she faithfully attends events honoring the Butterflies and answers endless questions about them. She says she does this to return hope to her people by helping them to make sense of their past. Her life as their representative also seems to redeem her former noninvolvement. At times, Dedé yearns for the day when she can be her own self again. Even her career, she knows, she owes to her sisters, for many want to own life insurance sold to them by the sole surviving Mirabal sister. Yet she knows the value of keeping the memory of her sisters' heroism alive, and she is not ready to set aside her duty.

Dedé also is still trying to manage her personal grief over the loss of her sisters. She plays back memories of their lives together. These memories honor Patria, Minerva, and María Teresa not only as patriots and martyrs but also as sisters, daughters, wives, and mothers. As the story ends, Minerva's daughter Minou arrives to visit her aunt, and she tells Dedé that Fela, the Mirabals' elderly servant who claims to be in contact with the sisters' spirits, was unable to talk to the martyrs today. Dedé knows this is because the sisters were with her all afternoon, but she tells Minou that the sisters would not come because they have finally achieved peace. Readers know that it is Dedé who needs and is seeking peace.

Alvarez portrays all four Mirabals as ordinary young girls and women, not as the larger-than-life heroes of Dominican lore. Her choice makes their courage and political resistance seem possible for anyone, without diminishing its remarkable nature, and the Mirabals emerge as inspiring and forceful role models.

Critical Context

In the Time of the Butterflies is Alvarez's second novel. Her first, *How the García Girls Lost Their Accents* (1991), chronicles the experiences of four sisters who leave the Dominican Republic for life in the United States; her third novel, *Yo!* (1997), continues the story of Yolanda, one of the García girls. Selected a Best Book of 1991 by *Library Journal* and winner of the 1991 PEN Oakland/Josephine Miles Book Award for its contribution to multicultural literature, *How the García Girls Lost Their Accents* focuses on the four sisters' responses to U.S. culture. Yet Dominican life is always in the background, and sections of the novel are set on the island. These depict ordinary family life punctuated with fears that come from living in a police state. *In the Time of the Butterflies* continues this depiction of the impact oppressive regimes have on families and citizens. Here, however, the story shows how ordinary citizens can become politically aware and active. Therefore, although specifically about the Mirabal sisters, it is in a larger sense a story about the rise of grassroots resistance. The novel can also be viewed as part of a transnational feminist movement in literature. Alvarez's works add to a growing body of literature by Latina writers that simultaneously addresses gender and cultural issues. Among other concerns, Alvarez depicts the Latina woman's construction of gender identity.

Bibliography

Bergman, Susan, ed. *Martyrs: Contemporary Writers on Modern Lives of Faith*. San Francisco: Harper, 1996. One chapter of this collection is "Chasing the Butterflies. The Mirabals: Dominican Republic, 1960," Alvarez's description of the path that led her to write about the Mirabal sisters.

Corpi, Lucha, ed. *Máscaras*. Berkeley: Third Woman Press, 1997. Included in this volume is Alvarez's essay "An Unlikely Beginning for a Writer," in which she describes her struggles to adjust to the English language and to perceive herself as a writer.

Cudjoe, Selwyn. *Resistance and Caribbean Literature*. Athens: Ohio University

Press, 1980. This study of Alvarez's predecessors helps map out one literary tradition to which she belongs.

Ghosh, Bishnupriya, and Brinda Bose, eds. *Interventions: Feminist Dialogues on Third World Women's Literature and Film.* New York: Garland, 1997. Although it does not discuss *In the Time of the Butterflies* specifically, this collection of essays provides international perspective for Alvarez's work.

Grace McEntee

IN WATERMELON SUGAR

Author: Richard Brautigan (1935-1984)
Type of plot: Surrealistic
Time of plot: Simultaneously no time and all times
Locale: Simultaneously no place and every place
First published: 1968

> *Principal characters:*
>> THE NARRATOR, an unnamed protagonist who is writing the first book
>> to be written in thirty-one years in the community known as
>> iDEATH
>> MARGARET, the narrator's previous girlfriend
>> PAULINE, the narrator's present girlfriend
>> CHARLEY, the leader of the community
>> INBOIL, Charley's brother

The Novel

In Watermelon Sugar is difficult to discuss in the language of ordinary rational discourse. For example, one cannot speak of time and space separately. If the novel is set in the present or in the distant past, then it must be operating in some remote civilization, perhaps someplace else in the galaxy or on some world of spun sugar and dreams. If the novel is set in the distant future, then it is possible that it takes place on earth, perhaps after a holocaust of such terrible dimensions that the historical past has become an alien memory. More likely, time and place are to be accepted as a combination of all possibilities, forming a montage in the mind such that boundaries between present, past, and future, the concrete and the abstract, and the denotative and connotative remain malleable, in constant and fluid motion, transitory and ephemeral. The name of the community where the action is set is a case in point. It is unclear whether one should pronounce iDEATH emphasizing "death" or emphasizing "idea." Only the mind can create the montage that enables a reader to hear both sounds at the same time.

In iDEATH, the historical memory extends back only one hundred and seventy-one years. The remnants of a civilization, apparently very similar to the real world, are relegated to "The Forgotten Works," which "go on and on and on and on and on and on and on and on." The people of the community have no idea how old "The Forgotten Works" are, but they reach into distances that the people will not travel. A sign above the gate to "The Forgotten Works" warns the curious: "Be careful. You might get lost."

The narrator heeds the warning, but Margaret does not. As spokesman for the village, the narrator is not only the chronicler of a society that proceeds day by day as words follow one after another, not necessarily related in terms of cause and effect of fixed meaning, but also a poet-seer through whose eyes "reality" is reflected and through whose subconscious meaning is provoked. For, despite the fact that the narrator insists that he lives a gentle and satisfying life, he is restless, troubled, and insecure. Margaret's forays into "The Forgotten Works" serve to pique her continuing curiosity but, for the narrator, are the stuff of which nightmares are made. Chapter titles, rather than the narrator, make the point: "Margaret," "Margaret Again," six times repeated until finally "Margaret Again, Again, Again, Again, Again."

The action that takes place concerning the narrator and Margaret and that leads to her suicide is the most conventional of the levels of narration in the novel. At this level, a reader can discern a movement from exposition to complication to climax and denouement, with Margaret's funeral being the last piece of action. On another level, the story of inBOIL takes on greater importance. The narrator dreams the history of inBOIL and his gang and the "terrible things that happened just a few short months ago." If the entire action of the novel is considered to be a dream vision, then inBOIL's story is a dream within a dream, a kind of parenthetical expression, but one having central significance.

Other structural patterns can be discerned: a rising movement, for example, that never comes to climax or denouement. At the end of the novel, one must remember that the musicians are poised to begin, and all is ready to be done (and done again as life is done) in watermelon sugar. On the other hand, a deeper structure, revealed to the reader but unknown to the narrator, moves with continual falling action, so that anticipation merges with despair, and the sense of continuing renewal becomes a conviction of ultimate end.

Through a process of deduction, a reader can determine three time sequences operating in the novel: a distant past of which "The Forgotten Works" are emblematic (the narrator's twenty-eight-year life when he lived with his parents in a shack by the river, listened with Margaret to inBOIL's stories, watched the tigers kill and eat his parents, participated in the tiger hunt, joined the commune of iDEATH, and established an intimate relationship with Margaret); the recent past (the breaking up of the liaison between Margaret and the narrator and what happened to inBOIL); and the three days that make up the present time of the novel, during which period the narrator and Pauline establish their relationship and Margaret kills herself. Margaret's funeral takes place on Thursday, the black and soundless day. The action begins on Tuesday, the gold day, and proceeds through Wednesday, the gray day.

Part of the magical effect of the novel derives from the descriptions of iDEATH. As is suggested above, the sun on different days is different in color. The watermelons, too, are different in color, depending on the day. Seeds gathered from a blue watermelon, for example, picked on a blue day (Saturday), and then planted on a blue day make blue watermelons. (The stars, however, are always one color—red.)

The watermelons are processed to make watermelon sugar, which in turn is spun out to make everything in the community. The weather is always temperate. There are many waterways, creeks and rivers, some only inches wide. The houses are a delightful combination of indoors and outdoors. Statues of vegetables adorn the community. Lighted bridges decorate the night. The dead are buried in glass coffins placed at the bottoms of rivers, and the coffins glow at night because fox fire is put in the tombs. Such is the world of *In Watermelon Sugar*, passing strange and full of quirky charm.

The Characters

Much of the sense of disparity in the novel results from the incongruity inherent in the person of the narrator, who insists that everything in iDEATH is exactly as it should be—the people gentle, pleasant, and tolerant. Despite the narrator's insistence that iDEATH is a stable Utopia, however, many of the things that happen are fraught with pain and violence. Balancing the easygoing and vegetarian people with their light chores and flower-filled parades are the man-eating tigers, the burning of the mutilated corpses of inBOIL and his gang, Margaret's suicide, and the emptiness felt by the narrator but never named.

Indeed, the narrator never really names anything, even himself. In chapter 3, the narrator invites the reader to do the naming: "My name depends on you. Just call me whatever is in your mind." Though the narrator clearly plays the role of poet-seer, he came upon his vocation by accident. He was not good at anything else, though he had tried several occupations. It is Charley who suggests that the narrator write a book. Margaret's excursions into "The Forgotten Works" disturb the narrator so greatly that he cannot cope with his feelings for her. Nor is the narrator's restlessness assuaged by his liaison with Pauline. He remains an insomniac and nightwalker throughout the novel. Thor's day is his favorite—black, silent, and long.

Margaret is the only character in the novel who exhibits what one would normally call the signs of an active and curious mind. Her visits to "The Forgotten Works" and her continuing conversations with inBOIL, however, cause the community to isolate her and the narrator to shun her. Only Pauline seems to wonder how Margaret is re-sponding to the loss of a long-standing relationship with the narrator and her alien-ation from the community. The narrator expresses no interest and refuses to discuss the matter beyond saying that everything will be alright. Yet Margaret's desolation and hurt are apparent. She returns to the narrator's shack, knocking at his door with a persistence that bothers him; she walks past Pauline without responding to her greet-ing. Only Margaret seems shocked and pained by the death of inBOIL and his gang, and only she seems to understand its significance. Her suicide, which she accom-plishes by hanging herself from an apple tree, clearly results from a sense of profound despair over the community's inability to recognize what inBOIL was trying to say by means of his immolation and over the community's and the narrator's total rejection of her.

InBOIL and Charley, the community's acknowledged leader, are Janus-like coun-terparts, Charley having accepted the bland and docile as the only acceptable reality, and inBOIL insisting on the reality of pain and loss. When inBOIL and his men come to confront Charley and the iDEATH community, inBOIL insists that he is going to show Charley what is really going on. Without the tigers, inBOIL says, there can be no iDEATH. InBOIL accuses Charley and his group of living "like a bunch of clucks."

Then inBOIL and his men slowly and deliberately cut off their thumbs, their noses, and their ears, systematically removing their sense organs and thus illustrating the deprivation of the iDEATH community.

Other characters in *In Watermelon Sugar*, particularly Pauline, play significant roles. Pauline seemingly accepts without question her role in the community, especially after her liaison with the narrator: Apparently, she stops her nightwalking and sleeps well, and she appears content taking her turn in the kitchen. Charley, who knows "about everthing there is," has been the unquestioned leader of the community for a long time. All the members of the commune, including Fred, who is a fine craftsman, Al, who takes turns in the kitchen with Pauline, old Chuck, who lights the lanterns, and the young girl who picks strawberries play a contributing role, each according to his or her own special interests and needs.

Themes and Meanings

Critics have argued both sides of the question as to whether iDEATH is Heaven or Hell. Only a few have recognized the paradoxical nature of Brautigan's statement. Rational discourse in the Western world establishes absolutes, insists on a categorical difference between Heaven and Hell, up and down, fiction and fact, love and hate. Yet Brautigan appears to be trying to mesh the opposites, suggesting that rather than being antithetical, opposites are identical. The world is Janus-like. IDEATH is both idea (creation) and death. Life is not simply passive or violent; life and death are not contraries. Each partakes of the other. It is the separation of the two that is unnatural. In terms of the novel, watermelon sugar is also polyurethane foam.

Apparent polarities thus form the base of *In Watermelon Sugar*; in this respect, the novel recalls the Surrealists' *point sublime*, where contraries are identified, where the "yes" and the "no" merge. It is not necessary to limit time and space as people are accustomed to doing. Time and space are one. Past and future yield to the simultaneous. In dreams, one understands that which one's culture and language have in the past made difficult to apprehend. Thus, Brautigan's effort to get above or beyond the language of rational discourse and to eschew ordinary novelistic techniques, where time and linear plots carry the story line, is closely tied to the meaning of *In Watermelon Sugar*. Form and content are also one.

Critical Context

In Watermelon Sugar was one of three early works—the others were *A Confederate General from Big Sur* (1964) and *Trout Fishing in America* (1967)—which established Brautigan as one of the most popular writers of the 1960's. His books were particularly popular on college campuses; photographs of the author showed a rangy figure with shoulder-length hair, granny glasses, and a walrus mustache—the quintessential San Francisco writer. At the same time, he was recognized by some critics as a writer whose works could stand on their own merit; Guy Davenport, reviewing Brautigan's early novels in *The Hudson Review*, described him as "one of the most gifted innovators in our literature."

In the decade and a half between the appearance of *In Watermelon Sugar* and his death by suicide in 1984, Brautigan published many more books, but none of them enjoyed the success of his early works. His identification with the counterculture worked against him; from the beginning, many hostile critics had rejected his work as cute and ephemeral, and it became fashionable to dismiss him as a phenomenon of the 1960's, no longer of interest.

In time, Richard Brautigan will find a permanent place in American literature. Whatever the vicissitudes of critical opinion (his later works are only beginning to receive an objective critical reading), it is certain that *In Watermelon Sugar* will be numbered among the lasting works of the 1960's—a book which captures as few others do the spirit of that extraordinary moment in American history.

Bibliography

Abbott, Keith. *Downstream from "Trout Fishing in America": A Memoir of Richard Brautigan*. Santa Barbara, Calif.: Capra Press, 1989. A personal account of Brautigan from a longtime friend. Some of the book is Abbott's own memoirs, but it also contains interesting anecdotes and insights into Brautigan's life and work. Chapter 8, "Shadows and Marble," presents critical commentary on Brautigan's novels, in particular *Trout Fishing in America*.

Bradbury, Malcolm. *The Modern American Novel*. Oxford, England: Oxford University Press, 1983. Chapter 7, "Postmoderns and Others: The 1960s and 1970s," cites Brautigan, placing him in the genre of writers who "celebrated the hippie youth spirit." Bradbury gives succinct but insightful critical commentary on Brautigan's novels. He sees Brautigan as much more than a hippie writer, whose spirit of "imaginative discovery" has spawned a number of literary successors.

Chenetier, Marc. *Richard Brautigan*. London: Methuen, 1983. Assesses Brautigan's writing in the context of the 1960's, and traces the development of his art beyond the confines of a cult figure. An appreciative study that analyzes Brautigan in the light of his poetics.

Kaylor, Noel Harold, ed. *Creative and Critical Approaches to the Short Story*. Lewiston: The Edwin Mellen Press, 1997. See Farhat Iftekharuddin's essay, "The New Aesthetics in Brautigan's *Revenge of the Lawn: Stories 1962-1970*." Although this essay deals primarily with Brautigan's short stories, Iftekharuddin's discussion of literary innovation and his treatment of other Brautigan critics make this an important contribution to an understanding of the longer fiction as well.

Wanless, James, and Christine Kolodziej. "Richard Brautigan: A Working Checklist." *Critique: Studies in Modern Fiction* 16, no. 1 (1974): 41-52. A compilation of secondary material on Brautigan, complete through 1973. Lists novels (including their serial form), poetry, short stories, and uncollected pieces, as well as reviews and critical commentary on individual works. A valuable resource for the Brautigan scholar.

Mary Rohrberger

INDEPENDENCE DAY

Author: Richard Ford (1944-   )
Type of plot: Character study
Time of plot: 1988
Locale: Haddam, New Jersey
First published: 1995

> *Principal characters:*
> FRANK BASCOMBE, real-estate agent, a 44-year-old divorcée with two
>   children
> PAUL BASCOMBE, Frank's emotionally troubled fifteen-year-old son
> ANN DYKSTRA, Frank's ex-wife, a former professional golfer
> SALLY CALDWELL, marketing director, Frank's girlfriend
> IRV ORNSTEIN, a designer of flight simulators, Frank's half-brother

The Novel

Independence Day is the first-person narrative of Frank Bascombe, a sportswriter turned real-estate agent. The novel continues the odyssey of self-discovery on which Frank embarked in Ford's 1986 novel, *The Sportswriter. Independence Day* recounts a Fourth-of-July weekend in which Frank attempts to juggle work, relationships with family and friends, and a trip to the Baseball Hall of Fame in Cooperstown, New York, that he hopes will be therapeutic for his emotionally disturbed teenage son, Paul.

The novel's events unfold primarily at different points along the highways that separate Frank's home in Haddam, New Jersey, from Deep River, Connecticut, where Paul lives, and Cooperstown. This circuitous route mirrors the course of the narrative, which moves back and forth in time as Frank attempts to relate memories of the past to his current situation. Once a promising young fiction writer, Frank lost his bearings following the death of his young son from Reye's syndrome. The trauma of this loss led to the breakup of his marriage to Ann Dykstra and his gradual drift into sports journalism, an occupation that allowed him to make a living while avoiding coming to grips with his profound emotional crisis. This "bad season" ended with Frank quitting his job and taking brief sojourns in Florida and Paris before returning to Haddam "aquiver with possibility and purpose." Selling real estate comes naturally to him because he is "not one bit preoccupied with how things *used to be*" and because intimacy has begun to matter less to him. Frank is upbeat and optimistic about his community, where he serves as an exemplary landlord for two houses he maintains in Haddam's black neighborhood, and he is persuasive in his real-estate dealings. He is very positive about his upcoming trip with Paul, and he plans to instruct his son with ideas gleaned from the Declaration of Independence and Ralph Waldo Emerson.

Nevertheless, a mood of apprehension colors the novel's events. Frank's casual romantic relationship with Sally Caldwell is coming to an end, owing to his unwillingness to make a sincere emotional commitment, and his relationship with Ann, who has custody of their two children and is remarried to a man whom Frank detests, has grown strained. Property values are falling, and Haddam is not as safe as it used to be. Frank was mugged recently in town, and he is haunted by the murder of a fellow agent with whom he was once intimately involved. One of Frank's tenants is a hostile former black militant who forces Frank to pick up the rent personally. The last such visit ended in a confrontation with the police over a misunderstanding, one of two such incidents in the book. Frank discovers that a business partner keeps a shotgun for protection at his roadside food stand, and he finds that a murder has just been committed at a highway motel at which he stops for the night. The experience of two of Frank's clients, Joe and Phyllis Markham, crystallize the tensions within the story. Recently moved from Vermont, where they enjoyed successful careers and a splendid home, they are disappointed to find that Haddam's homes fail to live up to their high expectations. With each discouraging house viewing, Joe grows surlier and his relationship with Frank more contentious, aggravated by Joe's worsening manic depression and Phyllis's chronic health problems.

Frank's trip with Paul proves more difficult than he expected. The obvious affection between father and son is mitigated by Paul's belligerence, which has gotten him into trouble with the law and estranged him from his mother and stepfather. Frank believes that Paul feels "compelled to figure out life and how to live it far too early," but his efforts to distract Paul with trips to the basketball and baseball halls of fame and the simple character-building pleasures of normal adolescence prove futile. Events come to a head in Cooperstown when Frank, upset over Paul's indifference and a number of personal and professional setbacks on the trip, challenges Paul to prove his mettle in a batting cage set up outside the baseball museum. Paul, perhaps intentionally, leans into a fast pitch and sustains a serious eye injury that requires emergency hospitalization. In the ensuing chaos, Frank is consoled by his half-brother Irv, who coincidentally is also visiting Cooperstown. Conversations with Irv at the hospital force Frank to acknowledge the self-deception on which his optimism is founded and his still unfulfilled need for emotional and spiritual healing. The novel ends on a bittersweet note, with Frank wiser and more self-aware, facing with hope an uncertain future in which Paul, Sally, and Ann will almost certainly play major roles.

The Characters

A number of characters play key roles in *Independence Day*, and reader perceptions of them are shaped primarily by Frank Bascombe's point of view, which dominates the novel. To that extent, the perceptions Frank conveys of others are as much an index to his own character as to their individual identities.

Frank is a complex and enigmatic person. He loves his two children and stills feels strong emotions for his ex-wife even though they have grown estranged from each other. The ordeal of his past—which includes the death of his son, the break up of his family, and the aimless drift of his professional life—seems to have endowed him with wisdom and understanding that others in his life lack. He invites reader sympathy and beguiles with his calm, assuring manner as he smoothly conducts business and navigates the obstacles his awkward family situation puts before him. Yet Frank's behavior sometimes contradicts the principles of self-reliance and independence that he promotes. He mildly embellishes the truth about his personal life to the Markhams as part of his tactics to sell them a house that he believes will be right for them. Moreover, he is not completely honest with himself about his feelings. Although he professes to be aloof from the emotions that troubled his past, he is bitter about Ann's remarriage and unable to accept the exclusion from her life this suggests. In one of the novel's most poignant moments, Frank chances upon a used copy of his one published book at the inn at which he and Paul stay in Cooperstown. He casually dismisses his discovery, and its reminder of life with Ann, until he reads a caustic inscription someone has written in it and is overcome with painful memories of their divorce. The scene subtly confirms that Frank is not in control of his emotions or as free from the ghosts of his past as he professes to be.

Paul Bascombe is in many ways the spitting image of his father. He is articulate, sensitive, and likeable despite his outbursts. Superficially, his problems can be understood as adolescent growing pains aggravated by anger and upset with his broken family. Yet Paul is also a surrogate for his father, on whom Frank projects his own emotional turmoil. Paul still clings to memories of his family's happier past and is unable to forget the death of his brother Ralph or the family's pet dog. His tantrums embody the same overpowering, unexpressed emotions with which his father grapples. Paul, like Frank, needs to establish "independence from whatever holds him captive: memory, history, bad events he struggles with, can't control, but feels he should." The climactic moment in the batting cage, when Paul angrily rises to Frank's challenge and allows himself to be struck by a high-speed pitch, symbolizes how poorly father and son are faring in their mutual struggle for independence.

Ann and Sally are the women in Frank's life. Although neither plays a major role in the events of the novel, each establishes a significant presence through her relationship with Frank. Ann is a loving mother who has put her past behind her in a way that Frank has not. However, her inability to control her son suggests that the course she has taken is possibly more beneficial to her than to her family. Sally is an admirably tolerant woman with whom Frank could have a more fulfilling relationship if only he could shake free of his memories of Ann and make a stronger emotional commitment. Frank's ambivalence toward her sums up the dilemma of other characters in the novel, who cling to illusions of the past and miss out on the opportunities of the moment.

Themes and Meanings

Independence Day is a penetrating study of the psychological and social forces that mold individual character. In particular, it offers an insightful look at how ordinary individuals adapt to disillusionment and disappointment in their lives.

Early in the novel, Frank Bascombe describes himself as living in what he calls

the Existence Period, the high-wire act of normalcy, the part that comes *after* the big struggle which led to the big blow-up, the time in life when whatever was going to affect us 'later' actually affects us, a period when we go along more or less self-directed and happy, though we might not choose to mention or even remember it later were we to tell the story of our lives, so steeped is such a time in the small dramas and minor adjustments of spending quality time simply with ourselves.

Frank, though, has yet to accept the compromises that distinguish the Existence Period, and this precipitates a kind of midlife crisis. He is shackled by memories to a past that was more stable and full of promise, and this hinders his ability to establish fulfilling relationships with family and friends in the present.

Frank's situation is mirrored in the experiences of other characters in the novel. His son, Paul, longs for a past free of the tragic losses that have dismantled the Bascombe family. His efforts to monitor the ups and downs of life and bring them under control have overwhelmed his fifteen-year-old coping strategies. Joe and Phyllis Markham likewise cling to an outdated version of the American Dream. Their discouragement with the real-estate listings Frank shows them is a commentary on the gap between hopes and realities in contemporary middle America.

Ford uses the Independence Day weekend as unifying metaphor in the novel. All the characters seek an independence from the past that will allow it continuance with, rather than control of, their present.

Critical Context

A central issue of *Independence Day*—"staying the course, holding the line, riding the cyclical nature of things"—is a recurrent concern of most of Ford's novel-length fiction. Frank's efforts to survive and adjust to life's ups and downs are prefigured in the personal dramas of experience and the wisdom it imparts from which *A Piece of My Heart* (1976), *The Ultimate Good Luck* (1981), and *The Sportswriter* (1986) are built. The novel also represents a culmination of the first-person narrative techniques that Ford perfected in his collection of short fiction *Rock Springs* (1987).

Independence Day won the Pulitzer Prize in fiction in 1997. The novel typifies a trend in contemporary fiction of locating in the quiet struggles of ordinary lives the substance of powerful drama. Set on the Fourth-of-July weekend and laced with references to current events, modern history, and American literature, the novel universalizes the moments of its protagonist's personal life. Frank Bascombe's evolution over the course of the two novels in which he has been featured—*Independence Day* and *The Sportswriter*—put him in the same class as John Updike's Rabbit Angstrom and Philip Roth's Nathan Zuckerman: a series character whose growth and development over time serves as a touchstone for exploring fundamental aspects of contemporary American experience.

Bibliography

Ford, Richard. "The Art of Fiction CXLVII." *Paris Review* 38, no. 140 (Fall, 1996). Lengthy interview in which Ford discusses the craft of writing and offers personal observations on all of his work.

Hardwick, Elizabeth. "Reckless People." *The New York Review of Books* 42, no. 13 (August 10, 1995). Review essay of *Independence Day* that discusses Ford's use of the first-person narrative in the context of his other fiction.

Hobson, Fred. *The Southern Writer in the Postmodern World*. Athens: University of Georgia Press, 1991. Contains the chapter "Richard Ford and Josephine Humphreys: Walker Percy in New Jersey and Charleston," which provides a basic overview of Ford's fiction.

Lee, Don. "About Richard Ford." *Ploughshares* 22, no. 2-3 (Fall, 1996). Excellent overview of Ford's work, written shortly after the publication of *Independence Day*.

Schroth, Raymond A. "America's Moral Landscape in the Fiction of Richard Ford." *Christian Century* 106, no. 7 (March 1, 1989). A study of Ford's writing as a commentary on contemporary American experience.

Stefan Dziemianowicz

INDIAN AFFAIRS

Author: Larry Woiwode (1941-   )
Type of plot: Psychological realism
Time of plot: 1971
Locale: Northern Michigan
First published: 1992

>   *Principal characters:*
>   CHRISTOFER VAN EENANAM, a part Native American Indian graduate
>   student of English who is writing his dissertation on the poetry of
>   Theodore Roethke
>   ELLEN STROHE VAN EENANAM, Chris's wife of seven years
>   BEAUCHAMP NAGOOSA, Chris's Indian friend, a poet and a petty thief
>   GAYLIN, a young Indian from the local village, an arsonist

The Novel

Indian Affairs describes the internal and external events experienced by Chris and Ellen Van Eenanam as they live under primitive conditions in her grandparents' hunting lodge in the wilderness of northern Michigan during a freezing winter in 1971. The novel is subtitled *Book Two: The Native Son*, identifying the work as the second volume of a planned trilogy by Woiwode. The first part, *What I'm Going to Do, I Think, Book One: The Boy*, published in 1969, tells the story of Chris and Ellen's courtship, marriage, and honeymoon at the same hunting lodge in Michigan. Much of the background of the characters in *Indian Affairs* is provided, and although the second volume may be read independently of the first, familiarity with *What I'm Going to Do, I Think* greatly enhances the reading of *Indian Affairs*.

By the end of the first novel, Chris has decided that in order to provide financially for his wife and their expected child, he will not return to the graduate school where he has been studying mathematics. The child, however, arrives prematurely and dies shortly after birth. *Indian Affairs* opens with the couple returning to the hunting lodge in the dead of winter; six years have passed since the action of *What I'm Going to Do, I Think*. Chris has returned to graduate school, this time to study English literature, and plans to finish his dissertation on the poetry of Theodore Roethke. Ellen intends to write a personal journal that explores her feelings about the death of their child and their continuing childlessness.

Shortly after their arrival, Chris and Ellen learn of a fire that has burned down a shack in a small Indian village nearby. This is the first in a series of mysterious fires—apparently the work of an arsonist—that occur throughout the novel. Along with this mystery, Ellen and Chris have another: a prowler, possibly a peeping Tom, has been stalking about outside their cabin at night. A gang of young Indian toughs has repeatedly been threatening Chris because he has refused to buy them the liquor that are too young to buy for themselves. Ellen is lured to secret "women's lib" meetings, held at the local library, by an oddly interested stranger.

As the plot relies on these events for its forward movement, the internal lives of the two main characters, and especially of Chris, are explored. Chris speculates philosophically on the nature of life, death, and of nature itself, inspired by the poetry of Roethke. Chris's friend Beauchamp Nagoosa has provided him with peyote, a hallucinogenic substance, with which both Chris and Ellen experiment. Chris's encounters with the local Indians, his studies of the historical and persistent injustices suffered by Native Americans, and his exploration of their current ways of life lead him to come to embrace his own Native American heritage. His final thought in the novel, a line from Roethke, is *"I'll be an Indian."*

Ellen, brought up by her grandparents from a very young age after her own parents were killed in a mysterious "accident," comes to understand that her beloved Christian Scientist grandparents are extremely prejudiced anti-Semites and that her father was most likely Jewish. She believes that this conflict may have driven her parents to suicide and that, most likely, the automobile "accident" was actually a deliberate and calculated act. By the novel's end, Ellen has, like Chris, realized that she must come to terms with her family history and her ethnic heritage.

The climax of the novel is reached after the mysteries of the prowler and the arsonist are solved and after Chris has achieved a tentative truce with the local roughnecks. He has finished his dissertation, and Ellen has completed her journal. She is pregnant. On the day they are to leave for New York to begin a new life, they stop to attend the funeral of Jimmy Jones, a local Indian who was killed in the most recent house fire. Because Jimmy is a war veteran, an incongruous color guard from the American Legion attends the funeral and honors the deceased with a twenty-one-gun salute. The genuine terror of the Indians at the sound of the gunshots, the sight of men, women, and children falling to the ground as they must have done at Wounded Knee, evokes images of Judgment Day and so horrifies and moves Chris that he feels a sudden sense of conviction that settles his life: the absolute surety of the resurrection of the dead, of the life of the world to come. This, finally, is the only way that justice may be truly had for all.

The Characters

Christofer Van Eenanam is a hero alienated from the world—even, it seems, from his own wife. The final pages of *What I'm Going to Do, I Think* strongly suggest that the character is leaning toward suicide; there is a distinct emptiness in Chris Van Eenanam's soul at the end of the first novel. By the time *Indian Affairs* opens, six years later, Chris has given up working for the "Establishment" in a brokerage firm, a period of his life that now is a source of embarrassment to him. His choice of English literature over mathematics as a field of study further reflects this change in his temperament. He feels the need to understand himself, to explore his heritage, and to find some deeper meaning to his life. Woiwode's often disjointed plot line and the obscurity of Chris's reasoning help to render his sense of confusion and of aimlessness throughout the novel.

Woiwode renders the conflicts in his main character's life in a number of ways. Almost immediately, the uneasy relations between Chris and his wife are dramatized. Chris has apparently been drinking more than Ellen would like, and she disapproves of his buying liquor for underage locals. Chris's thoughts ramble widely, now focused on cutting down a tree, now following a train of thought that leads to a childhood memory. From the beginning, Chris is established as a complex, confused, self-centered young man.

It is not until the final pages of the novel that Chris begins to feel a sense of self, as the threads of all of his experiences and interests come together. Finally, he feels that he has found some meaning in his life. He is reconciled with his now-pregnant wife and with his Indian heritage, which he finally acknowledges publicly and has come to accept. He also finds spiritual satisfaction, not in the doctrines of any established religion but in the certainty of the resurrection of the dead. Belief in this fundamentally Christian doctrine, whether or not it is arrived at through association with the Christian church, Woiwode suggests, is the only way in which the great evils and injustices of the world may be reconciled with the belief in a loving God.

Ellen, Chris's wife, is seemingly as self-centered as her husband at the novel's opening. She is still obsessed with her childlessness, and she appears to resent Chris for this reason. She is unable to break the emotional stranglehold that her grandparents—particularly her grandmother—have over her. Ellen's disenchantment with Chris reaches a climax with the discovery that the mysterious prowler, Peggy, is one of Chris's former lovers who seems to have a kind of "fatal attraction" for him.

Beauchamp Nagoosa is a Native American who is a poet and a thief. He is by turns sympathetic and nonsympathetic. At times a poet in love with nature, indignant at the exploitation of the Native American by whites, he exploits that same history to justify his own stealing and "squatting" in a house that does not belong to him. He eagerly takes the teenaged daughter of a neighborhood prostitute into his bed. Beau demonstrates both the best and the worst traits of modern American Indians.

Gaylin, a young man from the village, takes on the role of temporary son to Chris. Chris acts as Gaylin's "guide" when the boy first experiences the effects of peyote. Chris teaches Gaylin to build a teepee in the traditional manner, an episode that turns out to be as much an initiation rite for Chris as it is for the boy. These experiences compel Chris to rediscover and accept his own Native American heritage.

Themes and Meanings

Woiwode is a Christian author, and despite the book's Native American themes, the ultimate consolation for the main characters in the novel is also a fundamental Christian belief, the very foundation of Christianity: the resurrection of the dead. This belief is the only hope for one who needs to keep faith with a benevolent God. It is with this act of faith that Chris accepts both his heritage and his destiny.

In the meandering plot of the novel, the senseless and violent acts of the teenage Indians, the arson of Gaylin, and the deaths and injuries sustained by this violence can in no way be morally justified. The irrational hatred of the implied anti-Semitism of

Ellen's grandparents, a hatred that seemingly is so strong that it drove her parents to suicide, is especially ironic as it comes from a supposedly devout Christian Scientist couple. The willingness of the book's Native Americans to exploit their own customs and religion for profit belies their indignant protestations of having been ravaged by whites. For Woiwode, it seems, this senseless perpetuation of injustice can never be understood in this life. The only hope for true understanding is in the afterlife.

Family dynamics are also explored in the novel. The pain experienced by the death of a child and the rift that such an event can create in a marriage becomes clear as the issue continually arises but is never discussed by Chris and Ellen. It is a seemingly unresolvable pain. Chris's inability to break away from his family history is clear with his final reconciliation to his heritage. The emotional stranglehold that parents are capable of inflicting upon their children is seen in the Strohes' relations with Ellen. Woiwode never overtly praises or condemns his characters, however; he merely renders them in action and dramatizes the consequences.

The theme of death predominates in the novel. The death of Chris and Ellen's first-born son precedes the events of the novel. The death of Ellen's parents is still something with which she must come to terms even twenty years after the event. Thoughts of Chris's dead mother arise briefly throughout the novel. The death of Ellen's grandfather seems imminent. Ellen feels that the revelation of the mysterious Peggy has caused her to feel the death of the person she believed Chris to be. Jimmy Jones is killed in a fire set by one of his kinsmen. The climax of the novel occurs at his funeral, during which the images of the massacre at Wounded Knee are evoked. All of these deaths, including that of Beau's dog, are devastating to the survivors and are senseless.

Yet there is also hope. Ellen is once again pregnant. If the Chris she had known is dead for her, her husband now lives in a different way, a more positive way. Ultimately, moreover, the dead of all ages will live again on Judgment Day.

Critical Context

Woiwode's first novel, *What I'm Going to Do, I Think*, published in 1969, was an enormous critical success for which he received a William Faulkner Award and an American Library Association Award. He was also awarded Guggenheim Fellowships in 1971 and 1972. Woiwode went on to publish other successful works, including the novels *Beyond the Bedroom Wall* (1975) and *Born Brothers* (1988) and the collection *The Neumiller Stories* (1989). He has also published a volume of poetry, *Even Tide* (1977).

Although twenty-three years have elapsed between *What I'm Going to Do, I Think* and its sequel, *Indian Affairs*, the two novels are intimately related. Many of the characters, themes, and story lines of the second volume appeared in the first. *Indian Affairs*, although more complex, is also more obscure than its predecessor, a literary trait of Woiwode's that has been alternately praised and criticized. For this reason, the book has received mixed reviews, and a reading of *What I'm Going to Do, I Think* may be necessary for a complete understanding of *Indian Affairs*.

Bibliography

Nelson, Shirley. "Stewards of the Imagination: Ron Hansen, Larry Woiwode, and Sue Miller." *Christian Century* 112 (January 25, 1995): 82-85. Nelson interviews Hansen, Woiwode, and Miller, focusing on the role of religion in their works and on readers' reactions to their novels.

Woiwode, Larry. "Homeplace, Heaven, or Hell." *Renascence* 44 (Fall, 1991): 3-16. Woiwode explores the positive aspects of writing within a specific, detailed regional landscape and how such specifics are inherently universal. The author also gives a personal account of the circumstances surrounding his decision to move his family to North Dakota and provides some insight into his religious beliefs. Sheds some light on Woiwode's Christian ethics and thus on the philosophical meanderings of *Indian Affairs*.

_____. "An Interview with Larry Woiwode." Interview by Ed Block, Jr. *Renascence* 44, no. 1 (Fall, 1991): 17-30. Woiwode discusses the circumstances of his conversion experience. He also declares the central importance of the family as an expression of values in his work and discusses his use of fragmentation to encourage a sense of struggle within the reader. Includes a brief reference to *Indian Affairs*: "It's a comedy."

_____. "The Reforming of a Novelist." Interview by Timothy Jones. *Christianity Today* 36, no. 12 (October 26, 1992): 86-88. Jones gives a brief background on Woiwode and *Indian Affairs* before the interview proper. Woiwode answers questions regarding his own Christianity and the role of faith in his fiction.

_____. "What I'm Going to Do, I Think." *Library Journal* 94 (February 1, 1969): 579. The author gives a brief summary of his background. He cites Leo Tolstoy as the single greatest influence on his writing and states that his intention in writing is not to be deliberately obscure but "to tell the truth as clearly as I can."

_____. "Where the Buffalo Roam: An Interview with Larry Woiwode." Interview by Rick Watson. *North Dakota Quarterly* 63 (Fall, 1996): 154-166. A revealing interview about Woidwode's homecoming and its effect on his writing.

Diane M. Almeida

THE INDIAN LAWYER

Author: James Welch (1940-   )
Type of plot: Suspense
Time of plot: 1989
Locale: Western Montana
First published: 1990

> *Principal characters:*
> SYLVESTER YELLOW CALF, the "Indian lawyer," once a star athlete on the reservation, now a city attorney
> JACK HARWOOD, an intelligent but desperate inmate whose parole Sylvester denies
> PATTI ANN HARWOOD, Jack's wife, an innocent and loving woman caught in her husband's schemes
> LENA OLD HORN, Sylvester's high-school guidance counselor, who inspires him to succeed

The Novel

Set in the cell blocks of a state prison and the back rooms of state politics, *The Indian Lawyer* depicts one man's effort to survive the penal system and another's search for the best way to represent the interests of Native Americans and others whom the political system neglects. The novel contains sixteen chapters that move freely between the main characters' points of view. The plot progresses chronologically, but it is interrupted by reminiscences that take characters back to such pivotal moments in their pasts as Sylvester's basketball championships and Jack's courtship of Patti Ann.

The book begins with Jack Harwood's parole hearing. Jack is serving a long sentence for armed robbery and is beginning to crack under the pressure of incarceration. Sylvester is a board member, and Jack is drawn to him because he is a Blackfeet. Jack has had problems with the Indian inmates who rule the violent prison. Insufficiently repentant and a onetime escapee, Jack is denied release. That afternoon, visiting with Patti Ann, Jack asks his wife to dig up information on Sylvester.

Back in Helena after the parole hearings, Sylvester, with his girlfriend Shelley, attends a party at Buster Harrington's mansion. Buster, the founder of a law firm that is ready to make Sylvester a partner if he will agree to run for Congress, has arranged for a meeting with Fabares, a Democratic Party official. Sylvester is encouraged by his discussion with Fabares and tells Shelley that he is seriously considering becoming a candidate.

Patti Ann contacts Sylvester at his office. She is lonely from the years without Jack and has been traumatized by a series of miscarriages and a hysterectomy, but her vitality is restored in Sylvester's presence. She manages to interest him in her phony story of a contested will, and Sylvester promises to investigate the situation. Jack phones Patti Ann and instructs her to see Sylvester socially, to intensify her relationship with the lawyer. Awakened by Sylvester, but fantasizing about adopting a child and rearing a family with a freed Jack, Patti Ann agrees.

When a meeting with Sylvester in a restaurant bar leads to her bedroom, Patti Ann knows she should feel guilty, but she does not. She is revived by their intimacy, but Sylvester is bothered. He does not know why he would risk shaking up his life at such an important juncture or why he is letting his relationship with Shelley deteriorate. He drives to Browning, to the Blackfeet reservation where he grew up. He visits Lena Old Horn, hoping that she will encourage his political ambitions. Somewhat reluctantly, Lena tells Sylvester, her former student, that she has faith in him.

Strengthened by his trip home, Sylvester returns to Helena and tells Buster that he will run. As the campaign begins to take shape, Jack Harwood's plans also unfold. Although Jack wanted Patti Ann to sleep with Sylvester, the fact that she did enrages him. His plot is no longer merely for the purpose of escape. When he thinks of his tormentors in the prison, Jack realizes that he seeks revenge against Sylvester in particular and against Indians in general. After receiving sinister phone calls, Patti Ann knows that Jack's contacts on the outside are working to blackmail Sylvester into granting Jack's freedom. The affair with Patti Ann is a breach of legal ethics, a political disaster. When Jack's contacts, Woody Peters and Robert Fitzgerald, decide to cut Jack out of the plan and make Sylvester pay for their silence, Sylvester's political ambitions, his entire career, and Patti Ann's safety are threatened.

Patti Ann and Sylvester are able to run Peters and Fitzgerald off, but Sylvester is afraid the former convicts will make trouble for him down the road. He decides not to run for Congress and risk a future humiliation. Buster and Shelley tell Sylvester that his chance will come again, and Buster quickly withdraws Sylvester's candidacy. Shelley walks out after hearing of Sylvester's affair. Sylvester helps Patti Ann by arranging a safe way for Jack to serve out his sentence and work toward parole. Buster tells Sylvester to take time off and travel to Europe. Instead, he goes to a Sioux reservation in North Dakota, where he helps the tribe with a water-rights dispute. Sylvester remains immersed in his work for the Sioux until he is called back to Browning for his grandfather's funeral. The novel ends as Lena Old Horn watches Sylvester play basketball in a spring snowstorm. Lena knows that, playing all by himself, Sylvester is challenging the only person who ever stood in his way.

The Characters

Sylvester is the central focus of *The Indian Lawyer.* The other characters in the novel exist primarily as foils; they illuminate aspects of Sylvester through their interaction with him.

Sylvester is a man of both physical and intellectual prowess who is accustomed to achieving his goals. From the basketball court to the courtroom, Sylvester's victories have been of heroic proportion. He is never sure whether he competes for his own glory or for the sake of the tribe and race he always represents but from which his success has made him feel detached. This distance between Sylvester and his people creates a sense of loneliness that is the hero's tragic flaw. Giving way to the temptations of Patti Ann is a mistake that costs Sylvester his biggest game, the congressional election. His defeat strengthens him, however, and the novel suggests that the Indian lawyer has regained his sense of cultural mission by joining the Sioux's legal battle.

Jack Harwood is not a typical convict. He is more intelligent and compassionate than his fellow inmates. His fascination with the concepts of crime and punishment, not a truly criminal nature, seems to have led him to prison. Subject to the harshness of incarceration, Jack gradually loses his strength and assuredness until he is reduced to the role of a cornered animal. Flashbacks to better times, to the days when he was able to protect himself from prison predators—or, better still, to his happiness with Patti Ann—contrast with the vulnerable, desperate state of mind in which Jack now finds himself. Through this comparison, the novel depicts how easy it is for an individual to fall from grace, a descent Sylvester narrowly escapes.

Patti Ann illustrates the process by which an individual reawakens to the world. A small-town girl before her first marriage, Patti Ann is quickly overwhelmed by the pressures of adulthood. After twice miscarrying and being abandoned by her husband, Patti Ann is rescued by Jack's love. When Jack is sent to prison, Patti Ann slips into limbo, waiting for the happiness she remembers to return. Her affair with Sylvester tests Patti Ann's innocence, but she endures, helping Sylvester to bluff his way out of the blackmail plot and committing herself to wait for her husband's expected release. The novel hints that Patti Ann will be able to reclaim her former happiness with Jack.

Significantly, it is through the wearied perspective of Lena Old Horn that Sylvester is last shown. Lena knows that she will always be a Crow in Blackfeet country, a member of a strange tribe. Like Lena, Sylvester will always be an outsider, an Indian in the courtroom and a lawyer in Indian country. Lena's inability to conquer the loneliness of the outsider suggests to the reader that Sylvester's battle with alienation is far from over.

Themes and Meanings

The Indian Lawyer focuses on the issue of assimilation, the merging of once-separate cultural groups. As a boy playing basketball with other members of his tribe, Sylvester displays exceptional athletic ability that allows him to envision a life beyond the boundaries of the Blackfeet reservation. When a sports journalist writes a column exhorting Sylvester to become an inspiration to his people by rising above the "degradation" so often associated with reservation life, his teammates react with resentment and distance themselves from the group's new star. This is the first suggestion in the novel that by moving toward his goals in mainstream society, Sylvester will have to sever, or at least weaken, his cultural roots.

A basketball scholarship to the University of Montana leads Sylvester to law school, but time spent learning courtroom procedure is time spent forgetting Blackfeet history and ritual. Welch makes sure the reader knows, even if Sylvester does not, that a grandson who learns his tribal history from textbooks instead of taking time to listen to the elders speak is a source of secret shame for Mary Bird. The most profound symbol of Sylvester's neglect is the war medicine, a hide pouch with secret contents, worn by his great-great-grandfather. Mary had presented the pouch to Sylvester before he left for college. Instead of cherishing the relic, which represents the strength and nobility of his ancestors, Sylvester leaves it behind, hidden in a bookcase. Later, as Sylvester prepares to announce his candidacy, his grandmother again places the war medicine where Sylvester can see it. This time, he accepts the link to his cultural heritage. While in possession of the pouch, Sylvester begins to understand that a congressional campaign backed by Buster's wealth and the Democratic Party machine may be a step too far removed from the people he wants to help. The war medicine takes Sylvester not to Congress but to the Sioux reservation. For once, the Indian lawyer balances his heritage with his future as he tries to make sense of his own cultural identity.

In poignant contrast to Sylvester's attempt to adjust to life outside his ancestral home stands Jack Harwood's struggle to adapt to the demands of an existence on the inside of prison. Welch reverses the reader's cultural assumptions concerning identities that represent power and influence and those that are assumed to stand for disenfranchisement. Furthermore, the white Jack Harwood becomes a racial minority in the predominantly Indian prison population. This irony demonstrates the considerable influence of circumstance, of capricious fate, over the lives of individuals. Harwood must learn a set of "con-codes" for behavior, without which survival is almost impossible. At first, Jack learns his lesson so well that he is able to teach new inmates the ropes. He is unable to alter his inmate façade even long enough to win his freedom at a parole hearing. Soon, like Sylvester, Jack begins to crack under the pressure of an alien environment. The way in which Sylvester and Jack escape the dangerous tangle in which they have become involved focuses attention on the presence of women in the novel.

In *The Indian Lawyer*, men receive invaluable aid and comfort from women. Without the contributions of his grandmother, Lena Old Horn, and Shelley, Sylvester would not be in a position to contemplate running for Congress. Even though she seems to trap Sylvester and betray Jack, Patti Ann's nearly angelic support eventually saves both men from the violence that threatens them. This aspect of the novel suggests a belief in the ultimate importance of the affection and trust to be gained from the union of man and woman, from primary human relationships.

Critical Context

James Welch grew up in Montana. He attended reservation schools and has taught English literature and Indian studies at the University of Washington. Many of Welch's life experiences are reflected in *The Indian Lawyer*; he sat for years on the Montana State Board of Pardons, and the portrait of Sylvester Yellow Calf, a Native American man who achieves what other members of his tribe have not been able to, is particularly poignant in relation to the author's life.

In his third novel, *Fools Crow* (1986), Welch continued to explore themes of success and responsibility. The hero of that moving historical novel asks, "what good is your own power when the people are suffering. . . . ?" In *The Indian Lawyer*, Welch gives Sylvester the insight to arrive at, and begin answering, the same difficult question. The importance of the character of the Indian lawyer, the new warrior, to the body of Welch's work is clear from Sylvester's name. "Yellow Calf" is the name of the protagonist's revered grandfather, a redemptive figure in Welch's first novel, *Winter in the Blood* (1974). A moving passage in *Fools Crow* describes a yellow calf that embodies all the beliefs cherished by a dying warrior who wants to take the animal's name for his grandson. By bestowing the name on the hero of *The Indian Lawyer*, Welch creates a symbol of the ancient beliefs in an empowering modern form.

Bibliography
Hoagland, Edward. "Getting off the Reservation." Review of *The Indian Lawyer*, by James Welch. *The New York Times Book Review*, November 25, 1990, p. 7. Hoagland is one of the few critics who finds the novel to be as accomplished as Welch's previous works. He praises the novel's construction and character development. Particular attention is paid to the uplifting aspects of the book's conclusion.
Larson, Sidner J. "The Outsider in James Welch's *The Indian Lawyer*." *American Indian Quarterly* 18 (Fall, 1994): 495-506. Larson's study of *The Indian Lawyer* examines the transformation from insider to outsider within the context of the Blackfeet Indian tribe. Analysis of the main characters highlights the tension between these two opposing groups and is enhanced by the comments and observations of literary experts.
McFarland, Ron. "'The End' in James Welch's Novels." *American Indian Quarterly* 17 (Summer, 1993). Explores the significance and implications of four Welch novels, including *The Indian Lawyer*.
Saul, Darin. "Intercultural Identity in James Welch's *Fool's Crow* and *The Indian Lawyer*." *American Indian Quarterly* 19 (Fall, 1995). Saul's instructive essay examines the cultural similarities and differences between Welch's *Fool's Crow* and *The Indian Lawyer*. He focuses on the nineteenth century cultural upheaval when the Blackfeet lost much of their population to sickness and white attacks. He then looks at the struggles of Sylvester Yellow Calf in *The Indian Lawyer* and concludes that individual autonomy and hope for the future are possible for Native Americans.
Seals, David. "Blackfeet Barrister." *The Nation* 251 (November 26, 1990): 648. Seals, himself a Native American author, places Welch's novel within the context of other recent works of Native American fiction, sometimes finding fault with the book's sophisticated construction. Seals wonders if the novel's discussion of assimilation is provocative enough, suggesting that there are many Native Americans in law firms. He goes on to assess literature's capacity to reflect a culture's value system.

Nick David Smart

INFANTE'S INFERNO

Author: Guillermo Cabrera Infante (1929-   )
Type of plot: Fictional autobiography
Time of plot: The 1940's
Locale: Havana, Cuba
First published: La Habana para un infante difunto, 1979 (English translation, 1984)

> *Principal characters:*
> THE NARRATOR, a sex-crazed cineast
> ZOILA, his mother, the head of the family
> JULIET ESTÉVEZ, a liberated woman who is the narrator's first lover
> HONEY HAWTHORNE, a lustful ballerina
> MARGARITA DEL CAMPO (VIOLETA DEL VALLE), a one-breasted beauty
>   who entraps the narrator in a consuming passion

The Novel

Cabrera Infante's inferno centers on women or, rather, on their ultimate inaccessibility even when attainable. The twelve-year-old narrator, an Alexander Portnoy *avant la lettre,* dreams about love and cerebrates about sex in a rumpled, one-room tenement apartment. His father, one of the founders of the clandestine Cuban Communist Party, has recently moved the family to Havana and there started to work in the newly created party newspaper, *Hoy.* It is 1941, and the spindly adolescent has the impression that he has died and gone to heaven. He is mesmerized by the trolley cars, dazzled by the lights and by the equally luminous characters who people the tenement building, veritable walking novels who enact the human comedy a mere step from his door. Life can well imitate art because art is so much better than life (at least in the hero's mind) that it need not fear the competition. One art form, especially, has thrilled the narrator ever since a friend of the family took the narrator and his brother to see a double feature one memorable Sunday. From then on, films become the only lasting passion that he will know. They are made even better because, in the womblike darkness of seedy and not-so-seedy theaters, the films become amalgamated with erotic experience: "In the pitch-black theaters, platonic caves before the screen, the pursuit of sex interfered with my passion for films, the contact of flesh awakening me from my movie dreams." Watching and feeling his way simultaneously, the hero fulfills the screen dreams that whet his appetite: picking up women in the dark, rubbing elbows, and squeezing thighs.

Time passes, but the heart is a lonely hunter. One passion leads to another, and all that remains of these afternoon loves are memories. The tactile memories become literature (as in *Infante's Inferno* itself); the visual memories are churned out as film criticism when, not surprisingly, the narrator becomes the film critic for a well-known Cuban weekly, *Carteles.* Age can barely keep pace with the hero's ever-mounting lust (even if he seldom gets the many women for whom he pines). His cronies' attempts to initiate him (in a brothel) turn out to be "sour gropes," a complete failure. It is not until he meets a generous, liberated woman—Juliet Estevez—that he shifts his scrimmages from the dark theater to the clear light of the bedroom. The love affair with Juliet is a turning point in the novel. When it is over, the narrator continues his love hunt, but in the instances described thereafter, the liaisons evolve far beyond the casual squeeze in the dark that typifies relationships during the first part of the novel. He marries, but this alliance is portrayed as an event that is peripheral to the action (which is, after all, about pursuit and not about fulfillment). One such pursuit, the relationship with the actress Margarita del Campo ("Daisy of the Field"), is, in fact, the culminating adventure in the narrator's eventful life.

The last section of the novel describes in frenzied detail their tempestuous encounters during one hot Havana summer. In the end, they part ways: Margarita (who works for Venezuelan television) invites the narrator to leave everything and return to Caracas with her, but he refuses, steeling himself against the love that they both feel. The impossibility of sustaining love becomes more explicit in this episode than ever before in the novel. It is clear that quests in *Infante's Inferno* are always frustratingly unfinished, and one cannot help seeing the novel as a tragicomic meditation on the incompleteness of human experience. As the narrator discovers, "the tree of knowledge of good and evil, because it is forbidden, won't let you attain any knowledge and they'll kick you out of the garden if you insist on tasting its fruit."

It is impossible not to feel the hero's profound dissatisfaction, to get a sense that he will never obtain what he covets from an ever-disappointing reality. Yet if facts are frustrating, fiction is an exhilarating experience (as the novel makes amply evident). The power of the imagination channeled through art allows the protagonist to transcend the commonplace and transform it into a lasting experience. This transformation is the substance of the long epilogue, an oneiric journey into one last movie house. The narrator enters a theater in hot pursuit of an alluring blonde who seems to give him the eye from the ticket booth. He sits next to her, and their conversation promptly evolves into a fanciful dialogue suggesting, in every way, a return *in utero*. Transported from the theater to a soft cave where the color varies "from deep purple to pale pink and the floor was first grainy and then striated," the narrator finds a mysterious "book about books," which contains fragments from a ship's log, tales of seamen in hot pursuit of a huge, waterspouting creature which may well be "a projection of the mind, a monster of the id in a forbidden land."

Suddenly the cave begins to heave and toss, the narrator falls, and his body begins to move along the floor, now flooded with a mudlike, red substance. He fears that he is going "to be thrown out, expelled, rejected. . . ." The book concludes with a vivid description of the experience of birth culminating with the hero's pivotal observation, "Here's where I came in."

The Characters

Infante's Inferno is composed like a film, in a series of vignettes, readily comparable to stills or to cinematic portraits. Read as a series of character portraits rather than as a series of events, these vignettes give the illusion of flow, of motion across time and space. They are further harnessed together, since all the portraits are shot by the same camera, which is the narrator's eye. He is twelve years old when the action starts and in his thirties when it ends, but since the narrative (ostensibly autobiographical) is presented from an adult perspective, the boy has many of the perceptions of the grown man and all the foreknowledge that only hindsight can provide. He is lustful, hilarious, perpetually unsatisfied, a body hunter in the dark jungle of theaters. As he grows older, he trades the classroom for the school of life, careening through Havana in hot pursuit of skirts. Most women escape him; they are described in fleeting, if memorable, vignettes. At least three of them accept his overtures, however, and their character portraits are the longest and most developed in the book. The first is Juliet Estévez, the girl who provides the narrator's sexual initiation. An ardent devotee of art and a body worshiper, Juliet is both liberated and liberating, a free spirit whose deepest physical pleasure comes from making love to the accompaniment of Claude Debussy's *La Mer*. The next woman to fall for the hero's fanciful line is Honey Hawthorne, a lustful ballerina whose strong penchant for fiction (her ostensible virginity; her hair color) is equaled only by a fiery penchant for making love. Yet neither character is as charismatic as the passionate, complex, two-named and one-breasted Margarita del Campo, a green-eyed Amazon who makes Tom Jones's most lubricous adventures pale by comparison. Besides her prowess in bed, Margarita offers the narrator a companionship that goes far beyond the sundry brief encounters which fill the pages of *Infante's Inferno*. In the end, however, the hero turns cad and turns away from her. Momentarily doubled up with grief, he is swiftly consoled by Margarita's sister.

In the epilogue, the hero goes back to his first love (from which he has never strayed very far): films. It is here that he finds contentment and a sense of fulfillment. It is here, in this dark womb, that he mimics a return to the soft and pliable "caves" (both reminiscent of Plato's construct and allusive to maternity and birth) before concluding with a last quip, as affirmative of life as Molly Bloom's "yes" at the end of James Joyce's *Ulysses*.

Themes and Meanings

The three fundamental themes of *Infante's Inferno* are remembrance, the transformational powers of the imagination, and the hardships of love—or, rather, of lust. More than a creation, the novel is a re-creation which takes full advantage of the disadvantages of the transient, forgettable nature of things past in order to create the fiction: "Perhaps she never had a permanent or straight hair," argues the narrator while referring to one of his many idols, "but I have to be faithful to my memory even though I may betray me." Faithful to it, at least, he always is.

The entire action takes place in a deceptive present which looks forward to a future while actually taking place in the past. The mature narrator looks over his shoulder to the child he no longer is (the title in Spanish is literally "Havana for a dead infant," an allusion to the irretrievability of youth—the author's patronymic means "infant"—as well as to Maurice Ravel's musical composition *Pavane for a Dead Infant*). Because all action harks back to the past, life in this novel is a primal screen of sorts, filled with sex and films and signifying the—perhaps illusory, undoubtedly elusive—quality of life. To underscore this quality, Cabrera Infante turns to his real-life passion for film, both in his search for form (the novel is a series of vignettes or still compositions) and as a metaphor of the ephemeral: Films, like life, are made up of fleeting images.

For this reason, action in *Infante's Inferno* is often described from the viewpoint of a camera: "What she had created," observes the hero about Margarita, "was an image almost shot in black and white: a scene taken unwittingly from the visual repertoire of both Von Sternberg and Orson Welles." Life is so much like pictures, in fact, that characters often flow from the make-believe of one medium to the make-believe of another. As one of them notes, "We were so damn close—not to each other but to the screen. So near, in fact, that sometimes we were projected onto the sheet and straight into the picture."

The fiction is also a transformation of all the flotsam and jetsam that culture has accumulated in the narrator's mind, a witty collage of quotes ("I say si again and again si"), name games ("Van Goghnorrhea"), parodied titles ("Créme et châtiment"; "How Green Was My Valli Then"), and puns of every conceivable origin ("her face, that immaculate complexion"). This transformational grammar casts more than a shadow of a doubt on the verisimilitude of all souvenirs alluded to in the novel.

Cabrera Infante makes amply clear that all fiction is made up of half-lies and transformed truths ("I said that art was a lie to which the artist gave an appearance of truth"), a fact which helps distinguish him from the narrator despite their many similarities. The author may be telling his life story, but because it is remembered, this story is transformed; because it is written down, it is altered, transmuted into art.

As fleeting as memories is sex, the life force which permeates *Infante's Inferno*. The narrator knows many women, but all relationships in the novel are portrayed as ephemeral. Men and women communicate—with their bodies, at least—but such communication, the author seems to be saying, endures only as volatile souvenirs ("the missing mammory") for which he thanks the many women in his life in the manifesto which is this novel.

Critical Context

Infante's Inferno is undoubtedly the finest work written by Cabrera Infante since his ground-breaking *Tres tristes tigres* (1967; *Three Trapped Tigers*, 1971). Erotic tableaux are central to the development and understanding of this novel as a whole, but they must be seen as vehicles or motives for reflection: on the nature of relationships, on the incompleteness of human experience, and, not least important, on man's (and woman's) artful penchant for fantasy. Like Georges Bataille and William Burroughs, Cabrera Infante portrays sex as a form of expenditure, as the most primal form of expression. This does not mean, in any way, that his erotic fiction should be seen as pornography; he makes evident that the body is in every way the mirror of the soul, the most tangible evidence of being. By depicting the coming together of man and woman and the profound loneliness of both, he has chosen to ponder essential questions, ontological in nature, from a philosophical perspective but with the acerbic wit typical of Menippean satire.

Eroticism as the raw core of human experience is essential to understanding *Infante's Inferno*, but the reader must keep foremost in mind that sex in this novel is always remembered—lived in the past and re-created in the present. For this reason, *Infante's Inferno* is also a witty meditation on that most Proustian of preoccupations: the act of remembrance. Yet, whereas the French novelist believed that an accurate, untainted retrieval of the past was possible through the senses, Cabrera Infante makes clear that to remember is to re-create, a notion that he develops with relish as an inquiry into the role of the artist (transformer of facts) and the relationship between life and art.

The fact that Cabrera Infante is, as he himself states, "the only British author writing in Spanish," adds yet another nuance to this art of transformations. The excellent translation from the Spanish by Suzanne Jill Levine was done in collaboration with the author. It is in most ways the same canvas, but painted with a different brush or, at least, with a change of varnish. Naturally, many of the puns and even proper nouns have had to be altered and, in some instances, completely recast. The further addition and transformation of sentences makes *Infante's Inferno* more a brilliant transcription than a translation, a phenomenon as rare in the history of fiction as the novels of Vladimir Nabokov.

Bibliography

Cabrera Infante, Guillermo. "Wit and Wile with Guillermo Cabrera Infante." Interview by Suzanne Jill Levine. *Americas* 47 (July-August, 1995): 24-29. In this interview, the Cuban-born author discusses his career and the influences that have shaped it. He talks about his Cuban and British roots, his love of puns, and his interest in film and music. A good source of background information.

Rogers, Michael, et al. "Classic Returns" *Library Journal* 123 (September 1, 1998): 224. Offers brief reviews of reprinted books, including *Infante's Inferno*.

Souza, Raymond D. *Guillermo Cabrera Infante: Two Islands, Many Worlds*. Austin: University of Texas, 1996. An informative and lively biography of one of the most prominent contemporary Cuban writers. Souza's work offers intriguing insight into Cabrera Infante's family history as well as his literary career.

Steinberg, Sybil, and Jonathan Bing. "Notes." *Publishers Weekly* 245 (June 15, 1998): 44-45. This article reviews several books, including *Infante's Inferno*. Although the review of Cabrera Infante's book is brief, it provides valuable insight into the novel.

Vargas Llosa, Mario. "Touchstone." *The Nation* 266 (May 11, 1998): 56-57. Vargas Llosa offers a tribute to Cabrera Infante, commenting that "from the typewriter of this harassed man . . . instead of insults there poured a stream of belly laughs, puns, brilliant nonsense and fantastic tricks of rhetorical illusion."

René Prieto

THE INNOCENT

Author: Richard E. Kim (Kim Eun Kook, 1932-   )
Type of plot: War
Time of plot: 1953
Locale: South Korea
First published: 1968

Principal characters:

> MAJOR LEE, a young officer in the South Korean army, a brilliant military strategist philosophically opposed to any but the most unavoidable violence
>
> COLONEL MIN, a revolutionary of great integrity and courage who grimly accepts responsibility for bloodshed as the price demanded by justice
>
> COLONEL MCKAY, an American CIA officer who keeps largely in the background but abets Colonel Min's coup efforts
>
> GENERAL MAH, head of Armed Forces Intelligence, the Presidential Brigade, and the Metropolitan Police of Seoul

The Novel

The Innocent takes its title from the almost paradoxical reluctance to take human life of Major Lee, an army officer who is masterminding the overthrow of his own government. Major Lee's respect for law, order, and human life pits him in an allegorical struggle with Colonel Min, the military leader of the coup to which the novel builds up. The conflict between the two officers dominates the story, which is narrated by Lee himself. Lee's idealism is understandable for someone so obviously dedicated to his country, but his innocence often appears to be sheer naïveté in a military genius. Colonel Min is Lee's antagonist, but Min is not a bad man; he is, in fact, an exceptionally good one, although he is at times given to an unconvincing Byronic brooding over the metaphysical conundrums of guilt, fate, and necessity.

Given these narrative weaknesses, *The Innocent* reads best, perhaps, as a version of the medieval psychomachia, a battle of allegorical abstractions. Major Lee thus becomes Colonel Min's conscience, and the real conflict becomes the painful tug of opposed impulses in the psyche of a good man of whom history makes difficult demands for action. At crucial moments, Min acts to preserve Lee's innocence by doing the dirty work himself—even sending Lee to Japan under virtual house arrest while the coup is being fought—and he seems to admire Lee's pure-mindedness, even though he finds it ineffectual.

As for the long, drawn-out buildup to the coup itself (which finally comes to pass three-fourths of the way through this almost four-hundred-page work), it consists not so much of action scenes as of long conversations in which the major characters, who are not always sharply differentiated, explain to one another various events from the past or analyze the motives of their fellow officers. Despite the potential for boredom in this narrative procedure, the intricacy of the intrigues actually holds it all together. The coup itself is never described at first hand but is summarized in a lengthy news dispatch that effectively catches the tone and style of such reports.

The Innocent is told in retrospect by Major Lee, and it opens in 1953, shortly after the end of the Korean War, with a dialogue between Major Lee and Reverend Koh, an army chaplain and an old friend of Lee's from the recent war. Lee is about to leave for an officers' course at Fort Benning, Georgia, and Reverend Koh has come to bid him a good voyage and ask him why, with a good university teaching career ahead of him, Major Lee has chosen to stay in the army. The scene establishes Lee's patriotism and idealism—ironically revealing the chaplain to be the more cynical of the two—and sets the tone for Lee's behavior throughout the novel.

Lee's reminiscences then reveal that several years have passed, during which he has completed his tour at Fort Benning, studied at the Command and General Staff College at Fort Leavenworth in Kansas, and served as a military attaché in Southeast Asia and Europe. With this exposition out of the way, the novel proper opens in chapter 2 on August 18 of an unidentified year, "four days before the coup." Major Lee has just been ordered home from Turkey and assigned to the Joint Chiefs of Staff in Seoul, where he has apparently just planned the impending coup.

The coup has been hatched among a small group of general officers led by Lieutenant General Hyun. A command group of nine officers carries out the actual planning and execution under Colonel Min, special assistant to General Hyun. Before the coup can actually take place, various political problems with renegade general officers must be overcome. The jockeying for position with these corrupt dissidents leads to an extended and truly engrossing scene: a night-time showdown between a large force led by Colonel Min (abetted by Colonel McKay, the Central Intelligence Agency operative) and the treacherous Major General Mah, head of Armed Forces Intelligence, who wants to cut a deal to save himself from a post-coup court-martial and probable execution.

The dramatic—and well-told—confrontation with General Mah occurs halfway through the novel. With Mah out of the way, Min senses that the way is clear for the coup, and he orders Major Lee back to Japan, under supervision by the Central Intelligence Agency (CIA). Min's motive is apparently to remove Lee from the scene of bloodshed and preserve by force the major's idealism and innocence. The coup, although bloody, succeeds except for the machinations of the vicious General Ham, who takes a group of hostages.

Ham thinks he has the CIA's support, and, indeed, Colonel McKay does not want to see a civil war break out. He brings Lee back to Seoul to negotiate peacefully. Yet McKay also wants Colonel Min to give him, for intelligence purposes, two officers who have turned out to be Communist infiltrators from North Korea, and so McKay and Min agree on a swap: Min can have Ham if McKay can have the two officers. The hostages are murdered by rebels in Ham's group, however, leaving Ham with no trump card, and he dies when his plane is shelled as he tries to leave the scene of a parley with Min.

The coup is complete, then, but in a bloody finale, Min is assassinated in his automobile, and the peacemaker Lee kills the last assassin with a grenade. These events spell the end of Major Lee's idealism. The novel ends as it began: with Lee, now a civilian, engaged in an earnest farewell dialogue with Chaplain Koh before leaving his country for what may be forever.

The Characters

Only two characters in *The Innocent* demand any consideration: the narrator, Major Lee, and Colonel Min. Lee is by temperament and training more of an academic than a military officer, but love of his country impels him to take up a military career after the Korean War ends. Lee met Colonel Min during their teaching days together at a university in Seoul. After the war, a year before the coup, both Lee and Min were in Paris, where Min conceived of the plans for the coup in a sidewalk café. Their relationship thus has a long history.

The idealist Lee is haunted by a story about Min that he is told by a young officer from Min's village. Min is rumored to have shot and killed a North Korean officer in cold blood in the time immediately following World War II. The true story turns out to have been that Min had been in Manchuria with Korean units fighting with Communist Chinese forces, and that these Korean forces had become the vital cadre of the new North Korean army. Min, however, simply left his unit and went home, only to have a North Korean major come and take him under arrest to a nearby Russian garrison. The North Korean major was an intensely patriotic Communist who wanted Min to come back and work with the Korean Communists.

What happened at the Russian garrison became the basis for the rumor of Min's brutality. In the presence of the Russian commander, a major, and a Russian lieutenant, the North Korean major had given Min a cruel lashing with a whip. The North Korean major, already in a frenzy, became infuriated by the Russian officers' laughter at the abuse of Min and had suddenly grabbed the Russian major by the neck and strangled him. Min, meanwhile, had whipped and shot the Russian lieutenant. Min and the North Korean had then driven away to Min's village, and Min left the major in the jeep while he roused friends. When Min returned to the jeep, however, he found the major apparently dead from his own pistol.

Later, after the coup, Colonel McKay explains to Lee that the North Korean major did not die from his wound after all but was taken to a Russian hospital to recover. The Russians naturally thought that the two dead Russians and the wounded North Korean were Min's doing, and Min thus gained his reputation as a ruthless killer. Major Lee learns all this about his friend with great relief.

Themes and Meanings

The tension of the relationship between Colonel Min and his conscience, Major Lee, holds the narrative together. Colonel Min carries his reputation and his responsibilities with much solemnity. He has, of course, killed other men when the situation demanded it, and he is weighed down by the cruelties inflicted by war. In his brooding, Byronic moments, he sits in his quarters in the dark, listening to somber music. His long friendship with the idealistic Lee makes Lee his natural conscience. At one point after the coup, Min actually tells Lee: "There are many things we have to do together, do you understand? I suppose I can afford to have one prosecutor and one judge all put together in you?" Lee parries, "I am not your prosecutor and your judge!" Min, however, insists, "Ah, but you are, yes, you are!"

The strain of their complementarity sometimes becomes extremely difficult for both men. After the coup, when they are trying to put down General Ham's rebellion, Min loses patience with Lee and tells him, in effect, to shut up. Min then lectures Lee: "If I always listened to your voice, Major, I would never, never get anything done in this maddening world! This world, do you understand, this world full of idiots like me in flesh and blood—not pale lifeless saints like you!" After Min has finally had to kill Ham and his men, Lee arouses Min's extreme anger by calling him a murderer, and Min erupts by blistering Lee's "tear-jerking, mushy, holier-than-thou self-righteousness and melodrama" and sneering at his "pure heart," his "clean conscience," and his precious "innocence."

With the bloody denouement, in which Min dies and Lee blows a man to bits with a grenade, Lee's long and exhausting apprenticeship to an absurd world ends with him completely disillusioned. When he says goodbye to Chaplain Koh, he is a changed man, and he cannot put much faith in such traditional pieties as the chaplain's insistence that "Colonel Min did not die in vain." Min states his existential philosophy when he tells Lee, "There is nothing out there in the heavens, Major. Remember? We have only ourselves." This bleak credo is perhaps the main theme of the novel.

Critical Context

In *The Innocent*, Richard E. Kim writes of a world he knows well. He was born in Hamhung, Korea, in 1932, and during the Korean War he served as liaison officer to the U.S. Army and as an aide-de-camp in the Korean military. After the war, he took graduate degrees from Middlebury College, the State University of Iowa, and Harvard University.

Kim's first novel was *The Martyred* (1964), a philosophical speculation on goodness and truth set in Seoul shortly after the North Korean invasion. The martyrs of the title are twelve Christian missionaries shot to death in Pyongyang by Communists. Two other missionaries are spared, however, and their good fortune becomes the subject of speculation and the basis of a probing examination of moral and spiritual issues that foreshadows the theme of *The Innocent*.

In *Lost Names* (1970), Kim re-creates, in the words of his subtitle, "Scenes from a Korean Boyhood." These seven scenes are set during World War II in a Korea that is occupied by the Japanese, and the "lost names" are names that Koreans have to give up and replace with officially registered Japanese names. The Kims' new name becomes Iwamoto, or "rock foundation." These seven essays recover movingly a period and place little thought of by most Westerners and do much to illuminate the sensibility behind Kim's two philosophical novels.

Bibliography
Clark, Colin. Review of *The Innocent*, by Richard E. Kim. *Library Journal* 93 (October 1, 1968): 3578. Clark is critical of the novel's lack of action, background, and development. He describes the book's conversations as "stilted" and the characters as "a faceless pack of colonels and generals."

Gropman, Donald. Review of *The Innocent*, by Richard E. Kim. *The Christian Science Monitor*, October 31, 1968, p. 13. Judges Colonel Min to be more believable than Major Lee in a novel that fails to convince the reader that its characters could be real people.

Kim, Richard. *Lost Names: Scenes from a Korean Boyhood*. New York: Praeger, 1970. Recalling that the Japanese invaders forced Koreans to abandon their own names when the Japanese occupied the country from 1932 to 1945, Kim paints seven vivid scenes from his boyhood. Although this book does not deal with Kim's fiction, it does provide insight into his background and the reasons behind the drawing of certain themes.

Nichols, Christopher. "The Tough and the Tender." *National Review* 21 (February 25, 1969): 183-184. The longest and most flattering review of "Mr. Kim's vivid, timely and courageous rendering of his native land's ordeals." Nicholas responds pugnaciously to a negative review in *The New York Times*, lauding the "basic Christian theme" that animates *The Innocent* as well as its "secular insights."

O'Brien, R. E. Review of *The Innocent*, by Richard E. Kim. *Best Sellers* 28 (October 15, 1968): 288. Praises everything about the novel: its insights and suspense, its artistically handled theme, and its excellent dialogue.

Simpson, H. A. Review of *The Innocent*, by Richard E. Kim. *Saturday Review* 51 (November 23, 1968): 66. Complains about the long stretches of dialogue that do not advance the plot, but judges *The Innocent* a "worthy successor" to *The Martyred*, if not ultimately as good as the earlier novel.

Frank Day

THE INVENTION OF MOREL

Author: Adolfo Bioy Casares (1914-1999)
Type of plot: Science fiction
Time of plot: The twentieth century
Locale: An unidentified island
First published: La invención de Morel, 1940 (English translation, 1964)

> *Principal characters:*
> THE NARRATOR, who tells the story in the form of a diary
> MOREL, a man who leads a group of people to the island
> FAUSTINE, a woman in the group with whom the narrator falls in love
> THE EDITOR, who annotates the manuscript of the narrator's diary

The Novel

The text of this short novel is presented as a diary of an unnamed narrator, a fugitive from justice, living on an island that he assumes is in the Ellice archipelago. The narrator has found the island with the help of a rug seller in Calcutta who told him about a group of people who came to the island in 1925, built several buildings, and then disappeared. The island is known to be the focal point of a mysterious disease that attacks the body and works inward, its victims losing fingernails and hair and, finally, skin.

After a period of time spent alone on the island, exploring the museum, church, swimming pool, and mill built by the group in 1925, the narrator suddenly sees a group of people dancing and singing. He observes the group unnoticed for several days and becomes fascinated by Faustine, a beautiful woman who sits for long periods of time admiring the sunset. When he finally musters the courage to reveal himself to the woman, he finds that she pretends not to see him. As he becomes more open about his presence on the island, he realizes that he is invisible to all of the people and that they seem to be repeating at certain intervals their exact actions and words, as if they were acting parts in a play.

As the narrator eavesdrops on a meeting of the group, he hears Morel explain to the group that he has invented a machine which photographs the people through a complex process of recording their senses completely. The machine is then capable of projecting the sights, smells, sounds, tastes, and touch of the objects photographed, so that the images seem to be real. One entire week of their experience has been recorded and will be played forever through a kind of projector powered by the tides, so that the members of the group achieve immortality, forever re-created and forever repeating the actions of that week.

Once the narrator understands the nature of the mysterious images that he has seen on the island, he goes down into the basement of the museum, where the machine invented by Morel is contained. When he tries to leave, he finds that he is imprisoned. As he breaks an escape hole in the wall, it immediately repairs itself to the state of its existence when it was photographed. He must wait until the tides recede and the machine stops projecting the wall.

Desperately in love with Faustine, the narrator decides to try to inject himself into the photographed drama so that he may be with her forever. He observes the images until he has memorized every word and every movement, then sets the sensory receptors of the machine to record the images as he steps into the scenario. He plays to the images as if he were an actor in the scenes that they are playing. In this way, he becomes a part of their drama, so that no observer will suspect that his part has been added later.

Toward the end of the novelistic text, the narrator senses that he is dying and begins to recall his life in Venezuela. He desperately clings to the hope that he will survive and find that Faustine is a living person rather than merely a photographed image, and that they may love each other in a real, eternal existence. Then he awaits his death, at which time his soul will pass over to the image that duplicates and preserves his sensorial experience.

The Characters

Because of the unusual premise on which *The Invention of Morel* is based, the only fully developed character in the novel is the narrator. All the others are only shadowy images of a prior reality. Of the people that the narrator discovers on the island, the only one who is treated thoroughly enough to have what could be called a characterization is Morel, who becomes the narrator of his own document, the text of the speech that he delivers to the members of the group that he has brought to the island.

Because Faustine is only a sensorial image, the narrator's attempts to interact with her are futile, for her actions are predetermined by the circumstances of her creation as an image. Her actions and her responses are all immutable and have no relationship to the narrative time of the novel. Thus, the only possibility for interaction between the narrator and Faustine is an artificial one. The narrator memorizes her actions, her words, and her reactions so that he may inject himself into the predetermined story as if he were a part of that unchangeable plot, as if her reactions were in response to his presence.

All the characters of the plot created by Morel's invention are immutable and unresponsive to the narrator. The text of the novel, then, presents a set of personages whose characterizations are predetermined and one character—the narrator—whose attempts to understand the nature of the reality in which he finds himself form the plot of the novel. His final solution—creating from himself another immutable character in the plot of the story eternally reproduced by the machine—is a process of altering the aesthetic object, the novel of the projected images within the novel, so that the narrator becomes a part of that aesthetic object.

Themes and Meanings

Primarily because of the way in which Bioy Casares contains within the text of his novel both the adventure story, with its emphasis on plot, and the plotless, formless, psychological novel, *The Invention of Morel* has been considered extraordinarily inventive and original. Bioy Casares develops a psychological study of the narrator's fascination for Faustine first in terms of the narrator's belief that she is a mysterious, elusive woman and then in terms of his knowledge that she exists on another temporal plane. The problem established by the novel, that of two different kinds of reality—one, the sensorial experience of the narrator, and the other, the projected record of the sensorial experience of Faustine—is a fantastic one that the narrator proceeds to solve in a rational manner. If it is true, as Morel contends, that the soul passes over to the recorded complex of sensorial experiences when the original photographed object ceases to exist, the narrator can effect his inclusion in Faustine's world by photographing himself as he interacts with the images.

The Invention of Morel poses the essential questions of ontology, for it deals with the very nature of human existence. It also is allegorical, in that the questions posed are equally valid in the ontology of the artistic or literary creation. The images are fictitious inventions, formulated by an exact reproduction of all the senses. When the narrator approaches the problem of the two distinct planes of reality, he is in fact inquiring into the dichotomy between the real, historical experience and the fictional. The narrator, as reader of the "novel" created by Morel, "writes" himself into Morel's creation, hoping that future readers will be deceived into believing that his reality is as fictional—or as real—as is Faustine's.

The theme of literary creation is further developed by the presence of the editorial emendations. The implied presence of the editor as the final compiler of the material creates a work that incorporates several stages of manuscript activity in the final work—the part of Morel's manuscript which he read to the group and which is reported in the narrator's diary, the sections of Morel's manuscript which he did not read and which are interpolated by the editor, the diary manuscript of the narrator, the marginal notes made by the narrator after finishing the diary, and the editor's own footnotes.

The mystery of the photographed copy of reality, with its endless variations—what if the machine photographed itself at work, or what if it photographed the tides?—reveals the ambiguous, complex nature of the duplication of experience that is artistic creation. Even the title of the novel suggests this ambiguity, for the "invention" is not only the invented machine, but also the replica of Morel created by the machine.

Critical Context

The prologue to *The Invention of Morel* is written by another Argentine, Jorge Luis Borges, the writer with whom Adolfo Bioy Casares has most in common. Borges quotes sthe Spanish essayist José Ortega y Gasset, who discusses, in *La deshumanización del arte* (1925; *The Dehumanization of Art*, 1956), the impossibility of inventing an adventure story that would appeal to the contemporary British reading public, and the predominance of the plotless, formless "psychological" novel in current fiction. Borges offers the short novel of Bioy Casares, *The Invention of Morel*, as proof that Ortega y Gasset was wrong. He might have offered his own work, which consists of many stories that fit the description that Borges gives of *The Invention of Morel*, a "perfect" work of "reasoned imagination" which employs allegory, the exaggerations of satire, and, sometimes, simple verbal incoherence.

Borges and Bioy Casares have had a long career of collaboration on such novels as *Seis problemas para Don Isidro Parodi* (1942; *Six Problems for Don Isidro Parodi*, 1981) and *Crónicas de Bustos Domecq* (1967; *Chronicles of Bustos Domecq*, 1976). Their partnership began in 1940 with the publication of *Antología de la literatura fantástica* (anthology of fantastic literature), edited by Bioy Casares, his wife, Silvina Ocampo, and Borges. Bioy Casares and Borges also collaborated on an anthology of the detective stories of writers such as Edgar Allan Poe, Robert Louis Stevenson, Sir Arthur Conan Doyle, Jack London, and Ellery Queen, and on film scripts for Hugo Santiago's *Invasione* (1969; *Invasion*) and *Les Autres* (1974; *The Others*).

The Invention of Morel, which is modeled after the novel by H. G. Wells, *The Island of Doctor Moreau* (1896), was not well received by the public when it was first published, but it was read and admired by many young writers, including Julio Cortázar, Juan José Arreola, and Alejo Carpentier. Bioy Casares's postulation of the ontology of human existence and of artistic creation places him in the role of precursor to later Latin American fiction writers who have dealt with the same problem. In particular, Cortázar has portrayed the interdependence of the real and the fictional in stories such as "Continuidad de los parques" ("Continuity of Parks") and "Las babas del diablo" ("Blow-up").

In the second half of the twentieth century, this particular type of fiction, of which *The Invention of Morel* is a flawless example, has been labeled "metafiction"—the self-conscious fictional work that, within itself, deals with the processes by which fictional literature is created. Bioy Casares has had a significant influence in the development of the Magical Realism of writers such as Gabriel García Márquez, whose *Cien años de soledad* (1967; *One Hundred Years of Solitude*, 1970) initiated international appreciation of Hispanic writers.

Bibliography
Bach, Caleb. "The Inventions of Adolfo Bioy Casares." *Americas* 45 (November-December, 1993): 14-19. Bach provides a comprehensive overview of Bioy Casares's works. Bioy Casares's early years as law student and his collaboration with Borges and Ocampo are detailed.
Camurati, Mireya. "Adolfo Bioy Casares." In *Latin American Writers*, edited by Carlos A. Solé and Maria I. Abreu. Vol 3. New York: Charles Scribner's Sons, 1989. An essay on the life and career of Bioy Casares. Includes analysis of his works and a bibliography.
Coleman, Alexander. "Fantastic Argentine." *New Criterion* 13 (October, 1994): 65-70. Coleman profiles Bioy Casares and focuses on his fictional works. Includes an analysis of *The Invention of Morel*.
Levine, Susan J. "Science Versus the Library in *The Island of Dr. Moreau*, *La invención de Morel* (*The Invention of Morel*), and *Plan de evasion* (*A Plan for Es-*

cape)." *Latin American Literary Review* XVIII (Spring-Summer, 1981): 17-26. Levine relates Wells's *The Island of Dr. Moreau* with Bioy Casares's *The Invention of Morel* and *A Plan for Escape*.

Snook, Margaret L. "The Narrator as Creator and Critic in *The Invention of Morel*." *Latin American Literary Review* XIV (1979): 45-51. An analysis of the narrative voice in Bioy Casares's novel.

Gilbert G. Smith

THE IRON HEEL

Author: Jack London (1876-1916)
Type of work: Science fiction
Time of work: 1918 to 2832
Locale: The United States, principally San Francisco and Chicago
First published: 1908

>   *Principal characters:*
>   AVIS EVERHARD, the daughter of a university professor and wife of
>   Ernest Everhard; a proselyte from capitalism to socialism, she is
>   both narrator and actor in the political scene
>   ERNEST EVERHARD, a blacksmith turned intellectual revolutionary
>   JOHN CUNNINGHAM, Avis's father, a professor of physics at a state
>   university
>   BISHOP MOREHOUSE, an Episcopal clergyman who neglects to practice
>   the Christian values he preaches
>   ANTHONY MEREDITH, a social historian who discovers Avis's
>   manuscript and edits it for publication
>   ANNA ROYLSTON, the "Red Virgin," a friend of Avis and the heroine of
>   the battle in the Chicago commune

The Novel

   The Iron Heel is supposedly taken from a fragmentary manuscript written in the early twentieth century by Avis Everhard, the militant socialist widow of the socialist leader Ernest Everhard, whose militancy results in his execution by an American fascistic organization called "the Iron Heel," the militant arm of the great corporate monopolies. The monopolies suppress an uprising of socialist workers who have organized a Chicago commune and rule the United States until 2232, when socialist power eventually triumphs. Avis had hidden her manuscript away in 1932, and it is not found for seven hundred years, when it is discovered by historian Anthony Meredith. He edits the manuscript and supplies the political history of the United States up to his own time. When the story begins, poverty is rife in big cities in the East such as New York City and Boston, where thousands of people live either in cellars or in flimsy, overcrowded tenements. Unemployment is common, with millions of people out of work. Wages are exceedingly low, and woman and child labor are ruthlessly exploited. The "robber barons" of the age keep consolidating their holdings into "trusts," or virtual monopolies. A small army of the rich exploits the large army of the poor.

   When several socialists are elected to Congress, they are not allowed to take office. Fearful of a general strike, the Iron Heel of the oligarchy creates "favored unions"; explodes a bomb in the House of Representatives; employs "Black Hundreds" (counterrevolutionaries such as those employed by the czarist government in the Russian Revolution) to wreck the socialist presses; and hires mercenary soldiers whose mission is to take over the central government.

Meanwhile, Avis has infiltrated the Iron Heel's intelligence agency as a "mole," or double agent. She is then caught in the bloody massacre of "the people of the abyss," the socialist mob of the Chicago commune, and she nearly loses her life. Eventually the fascists triumph and take over the government of the United States. They rule for three hundred years, or until the year 2237.

The memoir Avis began writing in 1932 marks a time when the American socialists have started a counterrevolution against the fascist oligarchy. However, fearing for her own life she hides her memoir, and it is not recovered for seven hundred years. Meanwhile, the American socialists have defeated the fascists and have established the utopia of the Brotherhood of Man. The socialist historian Anthony Meredith has discovered Avis's memoir, the "Everhard manuscript," and has edited, annotated, and published it in the year 2632.

Among the revelations of Meredith is that just before World War I, the American oligarchy wanted war with Germany for "a dozen reasons," mainly because such a war "would reshuffle the international cards" and no doubt put the Americans in full possession of the world market. Hence, on December 4, 1912, a German fleet attacked the American navy at Honolulu, sinking three American cruisers and a cutter and bombarding the city. The next day, both Germany and the United States declare war on each other. However, in the meantime, cables are passing back and forth across the Atlantic between the German and the American socialists, both bodies finally favoring a general strike against both governments to stop the war. In the end, the strike aborted the war altogether.

The Characters

The character Ernest Everhard is undoubtedly London's own alter ego, who writes and lectures to well-to-do bourgeois groups who support industrial capitalism. Ernest takes pleasure in taunting his audience. When he tells a group that the proletariat will one day in the future triumph over them, one indigent bourgeois rises to his feet and snarls at Ernest: "We will grind you revolutionists down under our heel, and we shall walk upon your faces."

Ernest's wife, whom he has converted to socialism, is the daughter of a university professor and a distinguished scientist. Although politically naïve, Avis is the narrator of the fragment that is the "Everhard manuscript"; Ernest has been killed, executed by the fascist organization known as the Iron Heel. He is conceived of as a Nietzschean "blond beast" and in terms of Social Darwinism; that is, he is a working-class prodigy who is also a "natural aristocrat." He sees his mission in life as to spread the gospel of socialism and to convince those attached to capitalism of the desirability of a socialist society. (Despite London's desire to give the character of Ernest Everhard a Nietzschean coloring, this blacksmith proletarian intellectual seems likely modeled on or suggested by the New England world-peace evangelist Elihu Burritt (1810-1879), known in his day as "the Learned Blacksmith."

Themes and Meanings

After London's novel *White Fang* (1905) proved popular with the public, he decided he could risk writing a novel he had long dreamed of undertaking: a socialist novel, "a la Wells, out of the idea of wage-slaves, ruled by industrial oligarchies." After some three centuries, the fascistic oligarchies are overcome by the proletariat under the aegis of "The Brotherhood of Man." The novel thus reflects London's wish to be the evangelist of socialism.

Yet London's book is not only a Marxist proletarian novel but also a futurology that purports to predict the future of the United States. Indeed, Robert E. Spiller has called London's novel "a terrifying forecast of Fascism and its evils." London's prescient description of World War I, and the resemblance between the attack on the American fleet in Honolulu and the World War II attack by the Japanese on the U.S. fleet at Pearl Harbor, are most interesting.

Much of the novel, though, is founded on the recent history of the United States. The novel opens in Chicago, where there had been serious labor problems after the fire of 1871, which destroyed much of the city. In 1886, the Haymarket Square Riot occurred in Chicago when, amid labor's drive for an eight-hour day, a demonstration by anarchists was staged in the square, where about 1,500 people were gathered. When police attempted to disperse the crowd, a bomb was exploded, killing eleven persons and injuring more than a hundred. In 1894, the Pullman strike stopped all rail traffic between Chicago and the West until President Grover Cleveland sent in cavalry and field artillery, under the pretext of protecting the U.S. mail, to break the strike.

London's novel is thus grounded in the class distinctions, violence, poverty, and labor strife of late nineteenth and early twentieth century America. The welfare of the masses was dependent on the owners and managers of the trusts, which were controlled by a handful of the nation's wealthiest families, such as the Vanderbilts, Harrimans, Carnegies, Morgans, and Rockefellers. *The Iron Heel* is a cautionary tale of the even darker future to which the author believed such naked capitalism would lead.

Critical Context

London wrote *The Iron Heel* based on his own experiences and his wide reading. His formal education was minimal; nevertheless, he read such serious authors as Ernest Haeckel, Charles Darwin, Herbert Spencer, Frederick Nietzsche, and Karl Marx, from whose works he derived his own philosophy. When he wished to insert in *The Iron Heel* historical incidents such as the Paris Commune of 1871 and the Russian Revolution of 1905, he researched them. Finally, he took certain ideas from contemporary popular fiction, notably Edward Bellamy's *Looking Backward, 2000-1887* (1888), Ignatius Donnelly's *Caesar's Column* (1891), and H. G. Wells's *When the Sleeper Wakes* (1899).

The Iron Heel ought not to be judged in terms of realism, because it shapes itself into a heroic romance endowed with the contradiction of a Marxist dialectic, an apocalyptic vision of Christianity, and the pains of martyrdom of Social Darwinism.

Critic Charles N. Watson, Jr., rightly judges *The Iron Heel* to be a "minor revolutionary classic" instead of a major one. It is, Watson argues, a novel "that London seems to have written too much out of his heart, too little out of his head." Watson keenly points out one of the novel's most serious flaws: that of the double characterization of Avis. Watson says boldly that London asks his reader "to accept the existence of two Avises simultaneously—the fluttering young woman of the love adventure and the hardened revolutionary of the political drama." In the long view nevertheless, *The Iron Heel* offers a reader an imaginative prediction of some of the most important events of the century. Indeed, that expert on the Russian Revolutions of 1905 and 1917, Leon Trotsky, rendered *The Iron Heel* high praise as a work of imagination.

Bibliography

Beauchamp, Gorman. "Jack London's Utopian Dystopia and Dystopian Utopia." In *America as Utopia*, edited by Kenneth Roemer. New York: Burt Franklin, 1981. Argues that *The Iron Heel* is London's "most noteworthy and sustained fictive future."

Cassuto, Leonard, and Earle Labor, eds. *Reading Jack London*, with an afterword by Earle Labor. Stanford, California: Stanford University Press, 1996. Throws new insights on London's fiction.

Johneton, Carolyn. *Jack London: An American Radical?* Westport, Conn.: Greenwood Press, 1984. A good treatment of London's leftist leanings.

Labor, Earle, and Jeane Campbell Reesman. *Jack London*. Rev. ed. New York: Twayne, 1944. A good general survey of London's work.

Littel, Katherine M. "The Nietzschean and the Individualist." *Jack London's Newsletter* 15 (May-August, 1982): 76-91. A good discussion of traits evident at different stages of London's career.

Portelli, Alessandro. "Jack London's Missing Revolution: Notes on *The Iron Heel*." *Science Fiction Studies* 27 (July, 1982): 81. Alleges that some important themes are significant by virtue of their absence in the novel.

Watson, Charles N., Jr. *The Novels of Jack London: A Reappraisal*. Madison: University of Wisconsin Press, 1983. The chapter on *The Iron Heel* is an outstanding critical assessment of London's novel.

Richard P. Benton

ISLANDS IN THE STREAM

Author: Ernest Hemingway (1899-1961)
Type of plot: Adventure romance
Time of plot: The late 1930's and early 1940's
Locale: Bimini, Cuba
First published: 1970

> *Principal characters:*
> THOMAS HUDSON, a successful American painter
> TOM, his son by a first marriage
> TOM'S MOTHER, a film actress
> DAVID and
> ANDREW, younger sons by a second marriage
> ROGER DAVIS, a writer and Thomas Hudson's friend
> HONEST LIL, a Havana prostitute
> HENRY and
> WILLIE, two of the crew on Hudson's boat

The Novel

Islands in the Stream was assembled from Hemingway's manuscripts by his widow and his publisher ten years after his death, and although the book has a certain unfinished quality, it contains most of the Hemingway ingredients. Like much of his fiction, *Islands in the Stream* is strongly autobiographical, but this last novel carries even more of the fears and fantasies of this major American writer.

The novel is divided into three separate books, held together mainly by the character of Thomas Hudson. Part 1, "Bimini," is the longest and most successful of the three. Little happens: Hudson, a painter "respected both in Europe and in his own country," works; his three sons from two earlier marriages (his third wife never appears) arrive for a summer vacation; they all swim and fish. The descriptions are often rich, the scenes humorous, and the focus is on feelings, particularly on Hudson's largely unexpressed love for his sons: "He had been able to replace almost everything except the children with work and the steady working life he had built on the island."

In the longest scene, Hudson's middle son, David, battles a huge broadbill for hours, only to lose him at the last moment. (In several significant ways, the scene resembles the fight between Santiago and the giant marlin in *The Old Man and the Sea*, 1952.) In another scene, the boys play drunkards in a local waterfront bar, to the dismay of a group of American tourists. Yet one of the group turns out to be Audrey, an old friend of Hudson and of Roger Davis, and in the end Audrey and Davis leave the island together, and then so do the boys. The ending of book 1 is abrupt and shocking; Hudson gets a telegram: "Your sons David and Andrew killed with their mother in motor accident near Biarritz."

Part 2, "Cuba," takes place a few years later on the farm or *finca* where Hudson is living (although his wife is absent). It is during World War II, and Hudson is no longer painting; instead, he has armed his fishing boat (as Hemingway himself did at this time), and he and his crew hunt German U-boats off the Cuban coast. Yet much of the action of part 2 takes place in a Havana bar, where Hudson has gone on a break from his patrol duties. Something is bothering him: "He could feel it all coming up; everything he had not thought about; all the grief he had put away and walled out and never even thought of on the trip nor all this morning." As the reader finally learns, Hudson's son Tom has been killed in air action over Europe. Instead of talking about it, Hudson has long and rambling conversations with various bar patrons, including Honest Lil, until Tom's mother unexpectedly turns up, and the two of them drive to the *finca*, make love—and then Hudson tells her that their son is dead (but not the true details of his death). The agony of this scene is relieved only when Hudson is called back for patrol duty. "Your boy you lose," he tells himself. "Love you lose. Honor has been gone for a long time. Duty you do."

In part 3, "At Sea," Hudson and his ragtag crew hunt down and kill the survivors of a sunken German submarine, on some uninhabited section of the Cuban coast, but not before Hudson himself is mortally wounded. "We didn't do so good, did we?" Hudson concludes.

The three parts of the novel are not tightly interconnected; each could stand as a separate work, except that the action is so minimal in each. The focus of the whole novel is on Thomas Hudson and what will happen to him under the horrible circumstances of losing all three of his sons. Slim as the action is (and the fishing scene in part 1 and the hunt in part 3 are probably the best), there are some good descriptions, especially in the "Bimini" section, of painting, fishing, and drinking (in few modern novels is there so much alcohol consumed), and readers can still hear the clear Hemingway voice: "When Thomas Hudson woke there was a light east breeze blowing and out across the flats the sand was bone white under the blue sky and the small high clouds that were traveling with the wind made dark moving patches on the green water." The last two parts of the novel, unfortunately, lean toward melodrama and sentimentality.

The Characters

The only complete character in *Islands in the Stream* is Thomas Hudson—although readers never learn very much about him either. All the other characters are either reflections of Hudson (his sons, Roger Davis) or antagonists (women and some of his crew, such as Willie). Hudson stands in the direct line of Hemingway heroes, from Jake Barnes in *The Sun Also Rises* (1926) through Frederic Henry in *A Farewell to Arms* (1929) to Robert Jordan in *For Whom the Bell Tolls* (1940). All of these characters have lost something crucial and stand in imminent danger of losing much more. There is a tension in all of them, both because the surface of life may explode at any moment (as it does in the end for Thomas Hudson) and because the characters themselves are often in the process of repressing thoughts and feelings (as Thomas Hudson does throughout the last two parts).

In part 1, Hudson has built a secure life through work: "He knew he must keep working now or he would lose the security he had built for himself with work." In parts 2 and 3, he holds to the concept of "duty" to keep himself intact: "Duty is a wonderful thing. I do not know what I would have done without duty since young Tom died." Yet there is always the danger that he may come apart or give in to drink. By the end of part 3, Hudson can barely cover up "all the hollownesses in him."

Thomas Hudson resembles Hemingway even more than the author's earlier heroes did, and it is easy to understand why the book was unfinished at his death: It is too close to Hemingway's own experiences—and to his fears and fantasies. (When George C. Scott played Hudson in the film version of the novel, he resembled the grizzled, older Hemingway.) Readers who know the details of Hemingway's life will find many parallels in the novel: the children from previous marriages, the early artistic life in Paris (Hudson and young Tom reminisce about Pablo Picasso, Ezra Pound, and others they knew in the 1920's), the fishing off Florida, the *finca* in Cuba, and the search for German submarines (although Hemingway, in the refitted "Pilar," never actually encountered one). Unfortunately, these materials of Hemingway's own life have not been sufficiently transformed into the stuff of fiction, and much of the novel reads as barely disguised autobiography and/or as romantic melodrama.

Other characters are nominal. Roger Davis seems Hudson's alter ego, a writer who has been "misusing his talent" and has sold out to Hollywood, and who may not be able "to write straight and simple and good now." Hudson's sons are rich and precocious and talk like characters out of the short stories of J. D. Salinger. "'You're damn right I was a friend of Mr. Joyce,' young Tom said. 'He was one of the best friends I ever had.'" The characterization of women is best summed up by "Tom's mother," who has no other name, and "beat-up Honest Lil," the Havana whore-with-the-heart-of-gold.

Themes and Meanings

In spite of its incompletion and limitations, *Islands in the Stream* contains variations on most of the Hemingway themes. Primary here is the initiation theme that is central to so much of Hemingway. In nearly every Hemingway work—from the young Nick Adams in the stories of *In Our Time* (1924) to the old fisherman Santiago in *The Old Man and the Sea*—the typical protagonist is being tested in a world where the rules no longer work, and where justice and fairness are absent. It is essentially a man's world—which is why the sporting activities and metaphors work so well. (David becomes a man when he wins and then loses the giant fish—and acts bravely throughout the battle.) Yet the Hemingway images (of the bull or boxing ring, and here of deep-sea fishing) also capture the world that Hemingway's heroes inhabit: a world of random and brutal violence, where death may be sudden and arbitrary. As Thomas Hudson says early in this novel, "truly, there is something about every day to frighten you." Into such a world, the most important qualities a character can carry are courage, toughness, and a stoic calm. In *Islands in the Stream*, Thomas Hudson stands up in spite of all the blows life deals him and, in the end, loses his life in the battle to help save his country—even though by then he does not "care anything about anything." What saves Hudson, Hemingway wants the reader to believe, is his concept of "duty," first to his work and then, when he can no longer paint, to the war. The trick is not to give up, and certainly not to sell out one's talent, as Roger Davis may have done. "Any form of real betrayal can be final," Hudson thinks late in the novel. "Dishonesty can be final. Selling out is final."

This initiation story recurs in a great number of American novels, from Mark Twain's *The Adventures of Huckleberry Finn* (1884) through F. Scott Fitzgerald's *The Great Gatsby* (1925) to J. D. Salinger's *The Catcher in the Rye* (1951), but usually it involves a younger protagonist moving from innocence to experience and learning how crooked are the paths of the world. The theme was first used by Hemingway in short stories (such as "Indian Camp" and "In Another Country") and novels written more than a quarter century before *Islands in the Stream*, and in those early works, the account of a young man's initiation into adulthood seems fresher and more succinct. Although Hemingway used the same idea with some success in *The Old Man and the Sea*, in *Islands in the Stream* readers may reasonably expect that Thomas Hudson should have learned life's lessons by his age and be better prepared to operate in the Hemingway world of death and violence. The theme, in short, seems old and overworked.

Furthermore, the initiation in *Islands in the Stream* is achieved at the expense of others. No one can argue that Hemingway ever described women well or sympathetically (except for certain asexual characters such as Pilar in *For Whom the Bell Tolls*), and the depictions of women in this novel are particularly offensive. Most of them are "bitches," if not worse, and a typical description is "a plain girl with thickish ankles and not very good legs," a description that sounds like it is of a horse. Hudson seems happiest, as in book 2, when he is alone with his cat, reading letters from his absent wife. "'She's a bitch, Boise,' he told the cat and opened another letter."

It is as if the courage and heroism here can be achieved only at the expense of weaker others—mainly women. Thomas Hudson must keep proving his manhood, his "duty," again and again—but there is always some "bitch" waiting to sabotage this action. Or, like "Tom's mother" and Honest Lil, women are brief respites in the great storm that is life, where essentially only men, alone or in groups (as in part 3), can test their manliness on the high seas. The distrust of women in earlier Hemingway seems blatant and self-destructive here. Hemingway is painting a world where, as in book 3, a man will surely end up alone.

Critical Context

According to Carlos Baker, Hemingway's official biographer, *Islands in the Stream* was part of the big "sea" book on which Hemingway was working in the last decades of his life. Part 4 of this larger work was actually broken off and published separately in 1952 as *The Old Man and the Sea* (and honored, indirectly, in Hemingway's Nobel Prize of 1954). The remaining three parts were published as *Islands in the Stream* after Mary Hemingway and Charles Scribner, Jr., "made some cuts in the manuscript," as Hemingway's widow writes in a prefatory note, but "added nothing to it."

Islands in the Stream adds little if anything to Hemingway's international reputation, which had actually been established by 1930 with his first two novels (*The Sun Also Rises* and *A Farewell to Arms*) and the early brilliant stories (collected in *In Our Time* and *Men Without Women*, 1927). After 1930, Hemingway's output was spotty and uneven, and he never regained the power and intensity of those early works. Still, *Islands in the Stream* is no great disappointment for lovers of Hemingway, and flashes of the novel carry the old Hemingway spirit and style.

The main problem with the prose of *Islands in the Stream* is that Hemingway editorializes too much. The lean, spare, objective Hemingway style appears less frequently (only in the "Bimini" section is the writing consistently strong); there are stretches of overblown exposition and description. The Hemingway "iceberg" theory (according to which the writer spells out as little as possible, allowing that which is unsaid, which lies beneath the surface of the story, to carry the weight of meaning) no longer operates.

Hemingway was best as an action writer of dramatic situations, but even these always bordered on the sentimental and the melodramatic. In *Islands in the Stream*, sadly, the sentimentality tends to take over, and the best passages are echoes of a younger writer who is no longer present.

Bibliography

Benson, Jackson J., ed. *New Critical Approaches to the Short Stories of Ernest Hemingway.* Durham, N.C.: Duke University Press, 1990. Section 1 covers critical approaches to Hemingway's most important long fiction; section 2 concentrates on story techniques and themes; section 3 focuses on critical interpretations of the most important stories; section 4 provides an overview of Hemingway criticism; section 5 contains a comprehensive checklist of Hemingway short fiction criticism from 1975 to 1989.

Bloom, Harold, ed. *Ernest Hemingway: Modern Critical Views.* New York: Chelsea House, 1985. After an introduction that considers Hemingway in relation to later criticism and to earlier American writers, includes articles by a variety of critics who treat topics such as Hemingway's style, unifying devices, and visual techniques.

Lynn, Kenneth S. *Hemingway.* New York: Simon and Schuster, 1987. A shrewd, critical look at Hemingway's life and art, relying somewhat controversially on psychological theory.

Mellow, James R. *Hemingway: A Life Without Consequences.* Boston: Houghton Mifflin, 1992. A well-informed, sensitive handling of the life and work by a seasoned biographer.

Meyers, Jeffrey. *Hemingway: A Biography.* New York: Harper & Row, 1985. Meyers is especially good at explaining the biographical sources of Hemingway's fiction.

Reynolds, Michael. *The Young Hemingway.* Oxford, England: Blackwell, 1986. The first volume of a painstaking biography devoted to the evolution of Hemingway's life and writing. Includes chronology and notes.

_____. *Hemingway: The Paris Years*. Vol. 2. Oxford, England: Blackwell, 1989. Includes chronology and maps.

_____. *Hemingway: The American Homecoming*. Vol. 3. Oxford, England: Blackwell, 1992. Includes chronology, maps, and notes.

_____. *Hemingway: The 1930s*. Oxford, England: Blackwell, 1997. Vol. 4 of Reynolds's biography.

David Peck

JAILBIRD

Author: Kurt Vonnegut (1922-   )
Type of plot: Antinovel
Time of plot: 1977
Locale: Cleveland; Cambridge, Massachusetts; New York City; and rural Georgia
First published: 1979

    Principal characters:
        WALTER F. STARBUCK, the protagonist and narrator, a minor
            government employee
        RUTH, his wife
        ALEXANDER HAMILTON MCCONE, an eccentric millionaire who sends
            Starbuck to Harvard
        LELAND CLEWES, a friend of Starbuck who is accidentally ruined by
            him
        MARY KATHLEEN O'LOONEY, a bag lady, the secret head of the
            RAMJAC Corporation, and Starbuck's former lover; she is really
            Mrs. Jack Graham

The Novel

    After a rambling autobiographical prologue relating the quasi-historical backgrounds of some of the characters, *Jailbird* presents the memoir of one Walter F. Starbuck, recently released from jail after serving time for a minor role in the Watergate conspiracy. The novel relates the events of Starbuck's first two days of freedom, during which he goes to New York City and encounters two people from his past: Leland Clewes, whom he accidentally ruined in the 1940's by testifying that Clewes was a former Communist, and Mary Kathleen O'Looney, now a bag lady but formerly his lover and coworker during his own days as a Communist in the 1930's. Starbuck's narrative is full of flashbacks, and by the time he encounters Clewes and Mary Kathleen, he has related his entire history in a somewhat jumbled fashion.

    Starbuck, the son of European immigrants, is sent to Harvard by Alexander Hamilton McCone, his parents' employer and a stammering recluse. McCone has avoided the world ever since he witnessed the massacre of his father's striking factory employees. McCone wants Starbuck to become a gentleman, but, instead, as a college student Starbuck becomes a union sympathizer, the editor of *The Bay State Progressive*, and the lover of Mary Kathleen O'Looney. In the 1940's, Starbuck gives up his radical affiliations to begin working in a series of bureaucratic government positions. In 1949, he tells a congressional committee, in reply to a question by Congressman Richard M. Nixon, that Leland Clewes was at one time a Communist, thus unwittingly ruining Clewes, who had never before been publicly associated with Communism.

    Several years later, no one will give Starbuck a job because of this betrayal, and his wife must support him. When Nixon becomes president, however, he appoints

Starbuck as his special adviser on youth affairs, a completely meaningless job. Starbuck, however, allows a trunk full of money to be hidden in his White House office and hence becomes a Watergate conspirator.

Despite the fact that he is a Harvard man, Starbuck believes that his life is a failure. Upon his release from prison, he fears that he will become a bum, unable to find a job. Yet Mary Kathleen, with her gigantic basketball shoes and six shopping bags, turns out to be Mrs. Jack Graham, the reclusive majority stockholder of RAMJAC, the largest, most powerful conglomerate in the Western world. Mary Kathleen runs the corporation by sending her officials instructions signed with her fingerprints. Convinced that someone is trying to kill her and cut off her hands in order to take control of RAMJAC, she hides on the streets of New York in her disguise. Finding Starbuck again and hearing his story convinces her that kind people do still exist. She arranges for Starbuck and all those people who have been kind to him during his two days of freedom to be made RAMJAC vice presidents, but then she is hit by a taxi. When Starbuck finds her dying, he finally realizes her true identity. He hides her will, which bequeaths RAMJAC to the American people, and spends two years as a rich and influential businessman in the entertainment industry. As the novel ends, however, he is about to become a jailbird once more for unlawfully concealing a will. RAMJAC's various divisions are being sold, with the profits going to the federal government.

The Characters

Walter F. Starbuck is an antihero, a minor, inconsequential figure caught up and manipulated by greater forces. While on the outskirts of great movements—the union strikes of the 1930's, the Nuremberg Trials, the McCarthy era, Watergate—he never plays an active or important role. He ruefully acknowledges near the end of his memoirs, "The human condition in an exploding universe would not have been altered one iota if, rather than live as I have, I had done nothing but carry a rubber ice-cream cone from closet to closet for sixty years." Starbuck always is a loser, a perpetual jailbird, even in a moral sense. He admits,

> The most embarrassing thing to me about this autobiography, surely, is its unbroken chain of proofs that I was never a serious man. I have been in a lot of trouble over the years, but that was all accidental. Never have I risked my life, or even my comfort, in the service of mankind. Shame on me.

Yet in his self-critical, wry, and humorous narration, Starbuck creates a sense of empathy in the reader. This man is a bumbler, but he is an entertaining, likable, and somewhat poignant bumbler.

Because the novel is his autobiography, Starbuck is the most fully developed character. Vonnegut is not interested in psychological realism in *Jailbird*. Most of the characters remain satiric caricatures of corrupt lawyers, unemployed Ph.D.'s, and hard-hearted businessmen. Cleverly drawn with vivid, idiosyncratic detail (one man has a french-fried hand), Vonnegut's characters are more like comic-strip figures than real people. Starbuck's minimum-security federal prison in Georgia is populated by

Harvard men and Watergate criminals. His guard, Clyde Carter, is a third cousin of President Jimmy Carter and looks exactly like him. Clyde spends his extra time taking correspondence courses in bartending and locksmithing until he is made a RAMJAC vice president. Another prisoner, Emil Larkin, was President Nixon's hatchet man. Vonnegut describes him as "a big man, goggle-eyed and liver-lipped, who had been a middle linebacker for Michigan State at one time. He was a disbarred lawyer now, and he prayed all day long to what he believed to be Jesus Christ." Vonnegut excels in such small, barbed parodies.

The other major characters are also depicted through idiosyncracies and remain types rather than fully developed personalities. The ironic juxtapositions of the plot serve to establish these characters: Leland Clewes marries Starbuck's Harvard girl-friend, Sarah; Mary Kathleen's mother died of radium poisoning from a factory run by Sarah's family; the ardent socialist Mary Kathleen is the major stockholder in one of the most powerful conglomerates. Vonnegut further stereotypes his characters by their names: Alexander Hamilton McCone is a millionaire, Mary Kathleen O'Looney is a bit crazy, and Starbuck recalls the well-meaning but powerless first mate who is overwhelmed by Ahab in Herman Melville's *Moby Dick* (1851). Leland Clewes's bland identity is suggested by the appearance of another character named Cleveland Lawes. The significant names, the stereotyped detail and caricature, and the fabulous twists of the plot suggest that all the characters are, in a sense, jailbirds in terms of be-ing trapped and manipulated by seemingly meaningless forces.

A final kind of characterization which further adds to this theme is Vonnegut's use of historical figures as varied as Nicola Sacco and Bartolomeo Vanzetti, Richard M. Nixon, and Robert Redford. In the tradition of John Dos Passos's *U.S.A.* (1937-1938) and E. L. Doctorow's *Ragtime* (1975), Vonnegut's novel asserts that larger historical movements are always lived and experienced by actual little people.

Themes and Meanings

Jailbird is one prolonged black joke about a society that has rejected Jesus Christ's Sermon on the Mount for a new gospel of acquisition. It unrelentingly satirizes the power-hungry and money-hungry elite of American society. The running joke about the incompetencies of Harvard men emphasizes this point. Throughout Starbuck's own undistinguished career, he is controlled by rich people, from McCone's first at-tempts to mold him to Mary Kathleen's last act of philanthropy. Starbuck's plight, along with that of the other major characters, emphasizes what happens to the little people in a capitalistic system.

An important focus of the novel is on the historical account of Sacco and Vanzetti, two labor leaders in the 1920's who were executed on suspect murder charges despite massive public protests. *Jailbird*'s epigraph comes from Sacco's last letter to his thirteen-year-old son: "Help the weak ones that cry for help, help the prosecuted and the victim, because they are your better friends." As young agitators in the 1930's, Mary Kathleen and Starbuck hear Sacco and Vanzetti's story told by Kenneth Whis-tler, a dynamic union organizer, at a labor rally. Whistler's vivid account and vision of a socialist utopia lies behind Mary Kathleen's attempt to rescue the American people from their economy by leaving them RAMJAC.

Yet Starbuck finds, unsettlingly, that few people in 1977 have even heard of Sacco and Vanzetti. He reflects, "When I was a young man, I expected the story of Sacco and Vanzetti to be retold as often and as movingly, to be as irresistible, as the story of Jesus Christ some day." The story of Sacco and Vanzetti provides a historical basis for the themes of the cruel and unjust treatment of the masses by the American economic and political systems, and of the well-meaning but ineffective attempts to change those systems. These motifs are echoed in the story of the Cuyahoga Massacre at the McCone family factory, the radium-poisoning disaster that killed Mary Kathleen's mother, the Communist activity of young Harvard students in the 1930's, and the crimes of the Watergate era.

Mary Kathleen's plan for "a peaceful economic revolution" provides the central irony of the novel. To accomplish this revolution, she gives the American people the epitome of the capitalistic system, RAMJAC, whose motto is "acquire, acquire, acquire." Her scheme makes little impact. As Starbuck explains, the businesses owned by RAMJAC were

> rigged only to make profits, were as indifferent to the needs of the people as, say, thunderstorms. Mary Kathleen might as well have left one-fifth of the weather to the people. The businesses of RAMJAC, by their very nature, were as unaffected by the joys and tragedies of human beings as the rain that fell on the night that Madeiros and Sacco and Vanzetti died in an electric chair.

Starbuck concludes: "The economy is a thoughtless weather system—and nothing more. Some joke on the people, to give them such a thing." The government only sells RAMJAC's divisions and puts the money into maintaining its own bureaucracy. As corrupt and uncaring as was industry in the early part of the century, government is the force that swallows up people in the 1970's.

Critical Context

Vonnegut's novels are protest literature, full of black humor and satire employed to provide a moral commentary on the evils of twentieth century life. His early works, such as *Player Piano* (1952) and *Cat's Cradle* (1963), earned for him an enthusiastic cult following, but he emerged as one of the most influential and provocative leaders of the black-humor literary movement of the 1960's with his apocalyptic *Slaughterhouse-Five* (1969). These early works often employed science fiction in order to depict bleakly humanity's self-destructive nature.

In the 1970's, Vonnegut's work began focusing more on American social and political history. *Jailbird* represents his response to the Watergate era as well as important earlier events in American history, but it continues in the parodic, black-humor tradition. Some critics believe that Vonnegut's work in the 1970's, and in *Jailbird* in particular, represents a diminishment of his early creativity. Nevertheless, much of the social and political satire in *Jailbird* is very effective. Also, Vonnegut seems, for the first time, to be suggesting some moral alternatives to the evils that he depicts. The emphasis on the Sermon on the Mount, on kindness and courtesy, on the giving and caring natures of Sarah Wyatt and Mary Kathleen, shows the values that Vonnegut would have replace the impersonal and greedy capitalism that he condemns. His books since *Jailbird*, especially *Deadeye Dick* (1982) and *Galápagos* (1985), continue to offer in small ways some optimistic alternatives to the corrupt systems that humanity has created.

Bibliography

Boon, Kevin A. *Chaos Theory and the Interpretation of Literary Texts: The Case of Kurt Vonnegut*. Lewiston, N.Y.: Edwin Mellen Press, 1997. Extending the scientific theory of chaos to literary criticism, Boon uses words and phrases such as "strange attractors," "fractals," and the "micro/macro connection" to describe certain aspects of Vonnegut's prose. A somewhat offbeat but neveretheless astute analysis of Vonnegut's work.

Broer, Lawrence. *Sanity Plea: Schizophrenia in the Novels of Kurt Vonnegut*. Ann Arbor, Mich.: UMI Research Press, 1989. Broer offers an in-depth analysis of individual novels by Vonnegut, including *Jailbird*. His study gives the reader a unique perspective on the common themes that run throughout Vonnegut's work.

Mustazza, Leonard, ed. *The Critical Response to Kurt Vonnegut*. Westport, Conn.: Greenwood Press, 1994. Critical essays present a detailed study of Vonnegut's various works, including *Jailbird*. A biographical introduction and a selected bibliography make this a valuable resource.

Reed, Peter J., and Mark Leeds, eds. *The Vonnegut Chronicles*. Westport, Conn.: Greenwood Press, 1996. Presenting a series of interviews and critical essays on Vonnegut's writing, this volume offers a broad variety of opinions and observations from scholars and journalists. A good source of information that helps the reader see more clearly the unique characteristics of individual novels against the wider context of Vonnegut's work.

Vonnegut, Kurt, Jr. *Fates Worse than Death: An Autobiographical Collage*. New York: G.P. Putnam's Sons, 1991. A revealing look at Vonnegut's life. This collection of Vonnegut's essays examines both the personal issues and social events that shaped his distinctive writing style as well as his view of modern culture. Vonnegut offers a rare glimpse of his heart in this intimate self-portrait.

Susan VanZanten Gallagher

THE JAILING OF CECELIA CAPTURE

Author: Janet Campbell Hale (1947-   )
Type of plot: Psychological realism
Time of plot: 1980
Locale: Berkeley, California; Spokane and Tacoma, Washington; and reservations
    in Idaho and Washington
First published: 1985

> *Principal characters:*
>   CECELIA CAPTURE WELLES, a thirty-year-old Indian woman in her
>   second year of law school
>   MARY THERESA CAPTURE, her mother
>   WILL EAGLE CAPTURE, her father
>   BRIAN (BUD) DONAHUE, her first lover and the father of her son
>   NATHAN WELLES, her husband, a teacher in Spokane

The Novel

Drawn from the author's experiences of growing up as a Native American in a white-dominated society, *The Jailing of Cecelia Capture* consists of the reflections of the title character, who is spending a weekend in jail after her arrest for drunk driving. She scans her entire life, discovering that in many ways she has been repeatedly imprisoned by her society and culture.

The novel begins in jail. Cecelia's immediate fears center on the compulsory mugshots: They will make her look ugly, because she could not fix her face and hair. She recognizes that only a woman would care about this, and only in a culture that disproportionately glorified female attractiveness. In a cell with a white prostitute and a black thug, Cecelia realizes that, like them, she has spent her life trying to attract men. She bypasses the chance to call her husband for help, reassured that she will be released as soon as she sobers up.

Gradually, she pieces the past day, her birthday, together. As usual, she had forced herself through the deadening routine of law school, alleviating the pain with a rare thermos of wine to celebrate the day. The alcohol brings little relief; only the pressures of professional school keep at bay the emptiness of her life. She lives in a shabby apartment with few pleasantries; her husband—by now a husband in name only—and children are hundreds of miles and several months away; she has no transportation in the rainy winter of San Francisco Bay; her life consists of unrelieved study; she feels overweight and unattractive. Her most recent effort at romance lasted one night with a nameless man. At school, she has to confront a lover whom she reluctantly left after learning he already had a permanent relationship. Yet the wine at least gets her through the day.

After school, she makes the rounds to celebrate. She toys with a man who tries to pick her up. The experience reminds her of a game she plays with her husband in which they act like strangers who discover each other in bars. Remembering Nathan, she recalls what their marriage has become. That thought drives her in tears out of the bar. Her car is stopped before she gets home.

While waiting in her cell to be interviewed, Cecelia recollects her childhood on various reservations. She had been the last surviving child of an Indian father and a white mother. Her mother had belittled her because she was darker and coarser-haired than her older sisters; her mother's whole side of the family shunned their Indian relations. She insisted that the girl's dreams were ridiculous; like all women, Cecelia could rely only on her looks to make her way. Cecelia's father, however, was exceptional among his race because of his education, and he drove this last daughter to become an example of success. Because he had failed at that himself, having dropped out of college before fighting in World War II, he now spent every evening getting drunk. Cecelia grew up desperate to escape the squalor of a reservation life made worse by an alcoholic father and a physically and emotionally crippled mother.

Cecelia is stunned to learn that she is not being released because of an old charge of welfare fraud. After she had fled her home at the age of sixteen for the Summer of Love in 1967 San Francisco, she had met a gentle college-age man at one of the park "events" of the period. Under the influence of drugs, alcohol, and the spirit of the time, she had taken him as her first lover. After a single weekend, he had disclosed that he had been drafted; his ship was leaving for Vietnam immediately. She was bearing his child when he died there. In the early years of single motherhood, she was caught working while on welfare, and she skipped town before repaying the entire assessment. Later, she completed college and met her present husband.

Now she has to call him. On the day he bails her out, they agree to divorce. Before the hearing, Cecelia buys a gun; she will kill herself rather than return to jail. Her case, however, is dismissed because of time limitations. The novel ends when she drops the bullets at the grave of Bud, her first lover.

The Characters

The novel has essentially only one character, Cecelia herself. Although the book is narrated in the third person, Cecelia is the only character presented internally as well as externally; hers is the only consciousness readers enter. All other characters—including those with direct bearing on the action—appear only as they affect her. This close-up technique highlights and heightens Cecelia's persona, enabling the reader to identify easily with her, to experience events through her. Because the novel is an exercise in ethnic consciousness-raising, this succeeds: Readers certainly learn the problems in development faced by Native American women. Yet the approach also reduces the status of all other characters and possible points of view.

Cecelia is complex enough and her situation difficult enough to deserve central staging in a work devoted to her. Simply describing that situation illustrates the complexity and difficulty. She is a thirty-year-old, reservation-reared, codependent Native American woman in her second year of law school. She thus exemplifies at least six levels of social and cultural dislocation, six barriers to her chosen goal.

Reared in segregation, she begins with the burdens of inferior education and inadequate role models, conditioned to accept secondary, or even tertiary, status. With an alcoholic father and disabled mother, she has grown up assuming that such deficiencies are normal. Membership in an ethnic minority reinforces many of these patterns, as does being female; both compound the prejudice she encounters trying to overcome them. She is an older student; even her Ph.D.-pursuing husband skips her university graduation, apparently because he finds something distasteful about her failure to graduate until the age of twenty-six.

Furthermore, she has dropped out of both high school and law school; she has a history of failure. Moreover, she has two school-age children, the older already in academic and social trouble, supposedly because of his absentee mother. Moreover, this is only a partial list of her problems. Looming over all is the fact that the program of study she is pursuing involves a partial betrayal of her heritage. She is becoming expert in the legal system that justified the brutal depredation of her ancestors, and she is running the risk that she may use her education to turn her back on her people. Her own personal history seems likely to trip her up, if not trap her completely. Her story begins with a drinking bout, merely the last of a long series, and she fails to find a single stable love relationship by the age of thirty. If life were a baseball game, she would have struck out before ever getting to the plate.

Yet all this serves only to spotlight her saving quality: Cecelia Capture simply will not quit. She is indomitable, a pillar of resolution. What makes this more remarkable is that she clearly does not enjoy what she is doing. Law school is drudgery for her; she suffers it only because it alone will get her what she wants. The discipline is so uncongenial that her only effective recitation occurs when she has drunk enough wine to anesthetize her normal tensions. Her classmates find her aloof and disconnected, and she has no close relations with any of them. She hates being separated from her children, especially because she knows her absence is hurting them. Exactly what motivates her is not clear. She does what she does partly to fulfill her father's ambitions, but more to overcome the limitations imposed on her by family, race, and culture. She simply will not be stopped.

Themes and Meanings

The Jailing of Cecelia Capture is an apologia, an explanation and justification of the central character. Its objective is to illustrate how and why Cecelia came to be the way she is, in herself and in relation to her culture. Since her major quality is perseverance, the novel seems at times almost like a promotional manual for that trait. Cecelia's life is a progressive and continuing overcoming; her motto might well be, "That won't stop me."

This focus, however, is not as transparent as it seems in summary, primarily because the novel establishes starkly just how formidable the obstacles facing her are. The example of her father is constantly before her. He had been, after all, a respected elder of the tribe, often a member of the tribal council before he was impeached for drinking in office; he had volunteered for service during World War II, at a time when

Indians were not American citizens and had to give up their native names to enter the Armed Forces; and he had a career as a prizefighter. Yet he did not live up to his own father's measure; Eagle Capture had served as tribal judge, designing the legal norms that gained status for the tribal government under the laws of the country. Will was educated at the white high school, entirely so that he could gain the college degree expected of his father's son. Even though his football skills earned him a college scholarship, however, he proved unable to keep up academically, and his decline into alcoholism seemed inevitable. Now, however, he was expecting his daughter to succeed where he, a male, had failed.

The book emphasizes that the problems multiply for each new generation, if only because the expectation of personal defeat becomes the norm. Cecelia's parents fell short of their parents' achievements. The loveless, abusive, codependent life they lead forms part of the context of Cecelia's consciousness; in fact, one major episode relates her attempt to break herself and her mother free of her father's abuse. This attempt fails. Her family is too snared in traps of their own fashioning to accept liberation. Yet the failure teaches Cecelia that the limitations of her parents and siblings are not necessary, and certainly not inescapable. It also teaches her the cost of liberation: Realizing herself will be possible only at the sacrifice of her family and others who demand her subordination. Having come so far, against such odds, can she now accept less?

Critical Context

The Jailing of Cecelia Capture is possibly more important as a cultural document than as a novel. Published in 1985, long after the energies of the radical American Indian Movement of the 1960's and 1970's had largely burned out, the book demonstrates that self-realization and cultural integrity for Native Americans remain possible even under the jurisdiction of the United States. The novel shows that a person can work for her people while giving up only—or mainly—the limitations they confuse with their culture—and also shows how lonely such a passage can become.

The book is hard-eyed and uncompromising. Its depiction of common reservation life pulls few punches: The majority appear alienated from the ways of the past, which require too much effort to sustain, and mired in the unnourishing bread and pompous circuses of American commercial culture. The tribes seem caught in a world compounded of the dregs of two societies, able to function in neither. Cecelia gains only credit for turning her back on the shabby mobile-home and junked-car surroundings of her parents and siblings, but the urban American Dream, on close inspection, seems hardly congenial. Upward mobility into material culture is not Cecelia's ambition, but it is about all she is offered. None of the men she meets is capable of recognizing her for herself. Her most positive encounter is with another Indian, who offends her by referring to her as a squaw with an education. Eventually, she discovers that even her Ivy League-educated *Mayflower*-descended husband has chosen her not for what she is but for what she represents to him—the victim of the crimes of his ancestors. Yet it is precisely her self, her embattled self, that she finally discovers as worth preserving from assaults from two cultures leagued together to deprive her.

Bibliography

Bataille, Gretchen M., and Kathleen M. Sands. *American Indian Women: A Guide to Research*. New York: Garland, 1991. This standard reference work lists all of Hale's publications in books to 1991 and directs students to relevant studies of her culture and background.

Berner, Robert L. Review of *The Jailing of Cecelia Capture*, by Janet Campbell Hale, and *Last Fall*, by Bruce Stolbov. *American Indian Quarterly* 14 (Spring, 1990): 214-215. Explores the differing ways both novels treat the concept of tribal identity in relation to "modern individualism." A brief but incisive examination of Hale's novel.

Bruchac, Joseph, ed. *Songs from This Earth on Turtle's Back: Contemporary American Indian Poetry*. Greenfield Center, N.Y.: Greenfield Review Press, 1983. Bruchac collects several poems by Hale, including some that connect with the world of Cecelia Capture.

Hale, Janet Campbell. *Bloodlines: Odyssey of a Native Daughter*. New York: Random House, 1993. This is not a strict autobiography but rather a collection of semi-autobiographical essays that shed light on Hale's personal and tribal background. In many, she touches on connections between her actual experiences and the fictional ones of Cecelia Capture and reflects on the situation of the Native American caught between cultures. She also illuminates many tribal customs and traditions, particularly those concerning women.

Wiget, Andrew O. "Native American Literature: A Bibliographic Survey of American Indian Literary Traditions." *Choice* 23 (June, 1986): 1503-1512. Contains little direct information about either Hale or the novel, but does place both in the burgeoning context of Native American literature. A useful forging of lineages.

Wolitzer, Meg. Review of *The Jailing of Cecelia Capture*, by Janet Campbell Hale. *The New York Times Book Review* 90 (April 7, 1985): 14. Wolitzer summarizes the plot neatly, focusing on the series of repressions suffered by Cecelia from unhappy childhood to parental programming to loveless marriage.

James Livingston

JAPANESE BY SPRING

Author: Ishmael Reed (1938-   )
Type of plot: Satire
Time of plot: The 1990's
Locale: The fictitious Jack London College in Oakland, California
First published: 1993

> *Principal characters:*
> BENJAMIN "CHAPPIE" PUTTBUTT, a black conservative, son of career
>   Air Force officers, professor of "Humanity" at Jack London College
> ISHMAEL REED, the author himself, who appears as a character in the
>   novel
> DR. YAMATO, Puttbutt's Japanese instructor, who later becomes
>   president of Jack London College
> JACK ONLY, the billionaire patron of a conservative think tank opposed
>   to multiculturalism
> DR. CRABTREE, a conservative English professor who opposes
>   multiculturalism (and Puttbutt's tenure) but later has a change of
>   heart
> ROBERT BASS, JR., a student at Jack London College who edits the
>   racist newspaper that lampoons Puttbutt
> ROBERT HURT, the dean of Jack London College, who defends
>   multiculturalism
> BRIGHT STOOL, the president of Jack London College, fired when a
>   Japanese group buys the college
> MARSHA MARX, the chair of the women's studies department at Jack
>   London College

The Novel

A satiric interpretation of Ishmael Reed's America in the early 1990's, *Japanese by Spring* is the story of a typical (though fictitious) California college in the final years of the George Bush administration. *Japanese by Spring* is written in three parts of unequal length, and concludes with an epilogue. Part 2 could be considered merely a brief interlude (at ten pages, it is half the length of the epilogue), except that it advances the plot sharply and is a focal point of the action in the novel.

The story begins with a brief biography and character sketch of the protagonist, Benjamin "Chappie" Puttbutt. The son of two African American career Air Force officers, Puttbutt was sent to the Air Force Academy in the 1960's. There, Puttbutt went through a rebellious black consciousness stage, but he took a conservative turn after a tragic love affair with the wife of his Japanese professor. Unnerved by the experience, Puttbutt becomes a pacifist and ends up teaching English at Jack London College.

As the novel opens, a decision is pending on whether or not Puttbutt will be granted tenure. The tenure decision dominates the entire first section of the novel. Puttbutt does everything he can to appear to be a team player: When black students are lynched on campus, Puttbutt tells the press that the students deserved their beatings because of their excessive demands. Yet there are signs of trouble for Puttbutt.

The first sign is in the classroom. Some of the more bigoted white students, notably Robert Bass, Jr., the son of a local industrialist who contributes heavily to the college, openly ridicule him in class.

Puttbutt tries to be conciliatory on all fronts: Many liberal professors (especially the dean of "Humanity," Robert Hurt) are outraged at the blatant racism of the attack on Puttbutt, but the college president, Bright Stool, quiets demands for Bass's expulsion. The chair of the African studies department, Dr. Charles Obi, who should be most sensitive to attacks on a black professor, asks Puttbutt not to rock the boat. Puttbutt himself defends Bass's racist cartoons and remarks as protected forms of free speech.

Other threats to Puttbutt's security as a black conservative scholar arise from his past. His father, still an active-duty general, warns him that his grandfather, the only Puttbutt who did not serve in the military, and who in fact sympathized with the Japanese in World War II, may be trying to contact him. Grandfather Puttbutt in fact kidnaps his grandson with a gang of Japanese toughs and outlines a seemingly paranoid plan to side with the Japanese in an upcoming global economic conflict. Just as he is told that he may be on the losing side, Puttbutt returns to campus to receive the crushing blow that ends the first section: His tenure has been denied.

The pace of the plot quickens precipitously in part 2: Still reeling from his denial of tenure, Puttbutt learns that Bass's father, angry over the threatened suspension of his son, has pulled his financial backing from the college, and his corporate friends follow suit. Japanese investors buy the college and institute radical changes, including hiring a new president and naming Puttbutt vice president. Part 2 ends melodramatically with the revelation that the new president is Puttbutt's former Japanese tutor, Dr. Yamato.

For the first few chapters of part 3, Puttbutt enjoys his reversal of fates: People who once held authority over him are now under his authority. Robert Bass, Jr., apologizes to Puttbutt and becomes his household servant. Angry mobs who threaten Puttbutt are beaten back by Ninja warriors. Yet revenge is not sweet for Puttbutt, who grows increasingly uneasy.

At this point, Ishmael Reed himself becomes a character in the novel, reversing the point of view from Puttbutt's Western cultural chauvinism to Reed's embrace of multiculturalism. After Reed's point of view is established, he meets Puttbutt in the faculty club at Jack London College. Returning to his office, Puttbutt finds the college's name changed: Instead of being named for Jack London, who is presented in the novel as anti-Asian, the school is now named for Hideki Tojo, the prime minister of Japan during World War II.

As the changes come more and more rapidly, Puttbutt becomes more and more opposed to the new administration. They institute new intelligence tests for students, with questions weighted toward Japanese culture. Japanese American students are expelled for having become too Westernized. When Reed protests, he is fired.

Organizing a faculty protest, the pacifist Puttbutt faces his first battle since leaving the Air Force Academy, but his father intrudes, bringing armed troops to subdue President Yamato. Yamato is arrested (the charge is not specified) but is soon free, showing up in Puttbutt's house and telling him about an impending struggle for control of the United States. The novel ends with an epilogue describing the country in 1992 from Reed's point of view.

The Characters

Benjamin "Chappie" Puttbutt represents a departure in characterization for Reed, whose protagonists are usually close to his own point of view. Puttbutt is very nearly Reed's opposite in many areas: a conservative from a military family, opposed to multiculturalism, defending Western cultural values. Reed builds up readers' sympathy for Puttbutt by making him the underdog but then undermines that sympathy when Puttbutt gains power. Puttbutt's pacifism, which arises partly from chafing at the role his parents have chosen for him and partly from shock at his lover's suicide while he is at the Air Force Academy, is shown to be mere capitulation to whoever is in power. The most subtly drawn of the characters in the novel, Puttbutt changes during the course of the book, learning how to rise above cultural parochialism. Nevertheless, the story leaves him just at the point of discovery of his limitations: His future is left open to question.

Ishmael Reed, the author appearing as a character in the novel, serves as a foil to Puttbutt—or vice versa. Their opposition is not antagonistic: Both are African American men of letters, both have been attacked by feminist groups, both are studying difficult foreign languages. Yet the differences are telling, and crucial to the plot: Reed has staked his career on a multicultural philosophy that Puttbutt has opposed as a threat to Western cultural values.

Dr. Yamato, who is first seen simply as Puttbutt's Japanese instructor, is something of a mystery. His diatribes on the cultural supremacy of Japan are disturbing for Puttbutt, who sees them as cultural chauvinism and bigotry—though he does not see, as the reader does, that they closely mirror Puttbutt's own claims for Western cultural supremacy. When Yamato becomes president of Jack London College, his contempt for Western culture becomes more overt.

Jack Only, a mysterious billionaire, is now so old and decrepit that his black chauffeur has to carry him around. Reed describes Only as "a giant, craggy-faced cucumber with flippers where legs and arms should have been." He speaks through an electronic box. Only's misshapen form represents the moral shrivelling resulting from his bigotry. His name suggests the exclusivity of his cultural ideal. Only believes that civilization is threatened by multiculturalism, and he pays his think tank to prove it. When Reed demonstrates that multiculturalism can be big business, however, Only listens. His love of money overcomes his aversion to minorities.

Robert Hurt, the dean of "Humanity" at Jack London College, is a passionate de-fender of liberal causes. This puts him in an ambiguous position when Puttbutt is attacked by Robert Bass, Jr., in the racist student paper *Koons and Kikes*. On one hand, Hurt cannot tolerate a racial slur against a black faculty member; on the other hand, the target of the slur, Puttbutt, believes that the attack is justified by white frustration.

Dr. Crabtree is a professor of English literature who secretly opposed Puttbutt's tenure. A champion of the "classics," Crabtree snubs Puttbutt until the tables turn and Puttbutt becomes his superior; then he curries favor, but to no avail. Puttbutt condemns him to teach "Freshman Yoruba." Yet Crabtree learns from the experience, and changes: By learning the African language, he begins to appreciate another culture, and the scales fall from his eyes. Reed's surprisingly sympathetic portrait of a white bigot suggests that Crabtree's bigotry was only ignorance, not blind hatred.

Robert Bass, Jr., becomes another redeemed bigot in the course of the novel. The leader of student ridicule of Puttbutt, his humiliation and punishment result not in greater hatred toward the black professor but in the discovery that, like Crabtree's, his bigotry was simply lack of understanding.

Themes and Meanings

Japanese by Spring is a satire on contemporary American attitudes toward cultural diversity, especially on college campuses. The title comes from the name of a language instruction book that promises the protagonist quick mastery of Japanese. The book, which soon becomes abbreviated to "J.B. Spring," and finally just "J.B.S.," is a symbol of the consumer attitude to other cultures that many characters in the novel exhibit. The main character, Benjamin Puttbutt, for example, seems to be studying Japanese simply to make himself more marketable.

Reed makes the satire much more amiable than some of his earlier novels by making the villain cultural elitism itself rather than any one character. The enemies of cultural diversity are not evil, merely crippled by various forms of chauvinism, from which many characters recover. It is not only the defenders of the white status quo who are carriers of this disease: The Japanese educators who take over the college end the elevation of Western culture in the curriculum, but they threaten to replace it with an equally narrow, Japan-centered vision of the world. The African studies department is run by an "Afrocentrist" who believes that Africa is the source of all good and that African culture is morally superior to any other.

Stylistically, Reed continues a trend in his novels toward realism, though there is a touch of his earlier fantasy style in making the character Jack Only "a giant cucumber with flippers." Characterization is muted in the novel, as is usual with satire and with Reed's fiction in general. Characters tend to be readily recognized types, probably drawn from Reed's own experience as a college professor in Berkeley, California. There are several touches that echo Reed's own experience: He, too, was involved in a bitter and public battle over tenure at the University of California at Berkeley. He, too, has come under fire by enemies of diversity in all camps, European, African, and Asian. Yet the major intent of the book is not autobiographical, despite the fact that the character "Ishmael Reed" plays an important role in it.

Another aspect of realism in the novel is the presence—sometimes oppressive—of names and events from the real world. At times, passages can read like a 1992 newsmagazine, dropping names in the news such as Anita Hill, Rodney King, and Dan Quayle. Often, the names seem mere attempts to lend legitimacy to whatever claim the narrator is making, in the manner of an authoritative footnote. There are about thirty fictional characters in *Japanese by Spring*, most of them minor; there are more than a hundred real people mentioned and quoted, most of them contemporary, and most mentioned only once. This obsessive referencing to the world outside the novel at times threatens to destroy the illusion of Jack London College, which may be Reed's intention.

It can be argued that multiculturalism itself is the novel's protagonist, for though Chappie Puttbutt is the point-of-view character, he is not the moral center. He is a ghost of what Ishmael Reed might have become under other circumstances. The fictive symbiosis of the characters of Reed and Puttbutt, in fact, is a major point of interest in the novel. Both are African American academic intellectuals, Reed a pro-multicultural poet and novelist, Puttbutt an anti-multicultural literary critic. Though Reed is held in the background for the first half of the novel, he is first seen in scenes that parallel Puttbutt's: struggling to learn a difficult tonal language (in Reed's case Yoruba, in Puttbutt's Japanese). Despite the fact that Puttbutt is Reed's opposite in many political and cultural issues, he is shown as victimized by some of the same forces that oppose Reed. Reed takes great pains to make his reader sympathize with a protagonist who is nearly the opposite of himself.

Critical Context

Chappie Puttbutt represents a new development in characterization for Reed. Protagonists such as the Loop Garoo Kid in *Yellow Back Radio Broke-Down* (1969), PaPa La Bas in *Mumbo Jumbo* (1972), and Raven Quickskill in *Flight to Canada* (1976), while not autobiographical characters, represent Reed's point of view: The values of these characters are the values of their respective novels. Beginning with the character of Ian Ball in *Reckless Eyeballing* (1986), however, Reed began to develop characters who did not completely embody the point of view of the novel or the novelist. Like Puttbutt, Ball had adjusted his beliefs to fit those of the people who could most help his career.

Perhaps one reason for an avoidance of what Reed elsewhere calls a "Neo-Hoodoo," or Africa-conscious, protagonist is that characters such as PaPa La Bas or Loop Garoo, steeped in African tradition, might upset Reed's carefully crafted cultural balance in the novel. Reed's earlier Neo-Hoodoo aesthetic championed African art forms as they appeared in African American works. The aesthetic of *Japanese by Spring* is subtly different: It champions *all* cultures, never one at the expense of another. While it is possible to celebrate African elements in American art and letters without becoming Afrocentric—in fact, elsewhere Reed has done so—it would be easy for an audience to misread such celebration as cultural chauvinism, which would be contrary to the spirit of *Japanese by Spring*.

In turning away from the biting satire and wild fantasy of his earlier period, Reed is also turning away from much that gave his fiction its power. A devil's advocate for this novel might say that its satire is more subtle, more sophisticated, and therefore represents a sharpening of Reed's powers. To critics such as Gerald Early in *The New York Times*, however, this mellowing is merely a blunting of Reed's rapier. Evidence for the former view, and perhaps a reason for it, may be found in the epilogue to the novel, which is written from Reed's own point of view.

The epilogue is as broad in focus as the whole novel. In essence, it is a picture of the multicultural America of the twenty-first century, imaged in the California Reed saw in 1992. The epilogue centers, however, around a single plot element, a specific ritual of an African church in Oakland, California, on June 7, 1992. The ritual involves the resurrection of a god of the Yoruba people with whom Reed says, African Americans have lost touch. Reed's fiction in the 1960's and 1970's demonstrated the influence of the African Vodun ("voodoo" or "hoodoo") religion on American popular culture; *Japanese by Spring* notes the importance of recovering another "lost" religion.

This time, however, there is a difference: Reed is presented as an impartial observer at the ritual, not as a partisan in the struggle between African gods and Iahweh. In fact, it is in the context of the ritual that Reed experiences a change of heart toward the African Methodist Episcopal Zion Church of his stepfather. He realized that this African American church, founded forty years before American slaves were freed, preserved many of the Nigerian religious practices in a different form.

This change of heart affects the whole tone of Reed's satire in *Japanese by Spring*, but it does not in any way lessen the intensity of his denunciation of injustice in his culture. It only makes it less shrill. There are no villains in *Japanese by Spring*, at least, none who cannot be redeemed by learning to appreciate other cultures. Reed continues to challenge the way readers see themselves and others, and *Japanese by Spring* does so in a more subtle way than do his other novels, but no less effectively.

Bibliography

Dick, Bruce, ed. *The Critical Response to Ishmael Reed*. Westport, Conn.: Greenwood Press, 1999. Focusing on Reed's nine published novels, this volume features a wide range of critical opinion concerning Reed's writings, including *Japanese by Spring*. A detailed introduction surveys the response to Reed's works, a chronology lists the major events in his life and career, and a bibliography suggests books for further reading.

Hume, Kathryn. "Ishmael Reed and the Problematics of Control." *PMLA* 108 (May, 1993): 506-518. This essay's academic jargon may pose a problem for some readers, but it is valuable as a cogent summary of many attacks, largely feminist, on Reed's fiction. Viewing the theme of power and control as one of Reed's major contributions to contemporary fiction, Hume demonstrates that Reed's use of the theme reveals as much about him as it does about America. Reed's frequent use of grotesque violence is explained as a function of the theme of control.

Kato, Tsunehiko. Review of *Japanese by Spring*, by Ishmael Reed. *MELUS* 18 (Winter, 1993): 125-127. Explores Reed's satirical tone in *Japanese by Spring*, which is targeted toward "reactionary elements that have clout over power structures." Although Reed fights against Eurocentrism in the novel and supports multiculturalism, Kato takes him to task for overlooking the many accomplishments of black scholars and feminists.

Playhell, Benjamin. "The Gospel According to Ishmael." *World & I* 8 (August, 1993): 320-327. Playhell argues that Reed's novel takes to task nearly all deeply held beliefs stemming from the multicultural movement, including radical feminist and African American ideological views.

Singh, Amritjit, and Bruce Dick, eds. *Conversations with Ishmael Reed*. Jackson: University of Mississippi, 1995. Interviews with Reed that cover his life, career, and reasons for writing. Reed discusses several of his works in detail.

John R. Holmes

JASMINE

Author: Bharati Mukherjee (1940-   )
Type of plot: Bildungsroman
Time of plot: 1965-1989
Locale: India, New York City, and Iowa
First published: 1989

Principal characters:

JASMINE, the protagonist and narrator, a young Hindu woman from India who illegally enters the United States

PRAKASH VIJH, Jasmine's husband, killed by a Sikh fanatic's bomb in India

LILLIAN GORDON, an elderly Quaker woman who teaches Jasmine how to act American

DEVINDER VADHERA, Prakash's former Indian professor, now living in New York

KATE GORDON-FELDSTEIN, Lillian's daughter, who introduces Jasmine to Taylor and Wylie Hayes

TAYLOR HAYES, a Columbia University professor, Jasmine's first American employer and lover

WYLIE HAYES, Taylor's professional wife

DUFF, the adoptive daughter of Taylor and Wylie Hayes

BUD RIPPLEMEYER, an Iowa banker with whom Jasmine lives as his common-law wife

DU THIEN, a Vietnamese refugee boy adopted by Bud and Jasmine

DARREL LUTZ, a young Iowa farmer in love with Jasmine

The Novel

Jasmine is a novel of emigration and assimilation, both on physical and psychological levels. In this novel, Bharati Mukherjee fictionalizes the process of Americanization by tracing a young Indian woman's experiences of trauma and triumph in her attempt to forge a new identity for herself.

The story is told from the first-person point of view by the female protagonist, who undergoes multiple identity transformations in her quest for self-empowerment and happiness. Mukherjee uses the cinematic techniques of flashback and cross-cutting to fuse Jasmine's past and present. The novel is steeped in violence.

The book begins with the twenty-four-year-old narrator, Jane Ripplemeyer, living as the common-law wife of Bud Ripplemeyer, a fifty-four-year-old invalid banker in Baden, Elsa County, Iowa. Through flashbacks, she recalls her story from childhood in Hasnapur, a village in Jullundhar District, Punjab, India, where she was born as Jyoti, the unwanted fifth daughter in a poor, displaced Hindu family. When she was seven, an astrologer predicted that she was doomed to widowhood and exile. Determined to fight her destiny, Jyoti begins to empower herself through learning English, for "to want English was to want more than you had been given at birth, it was to want the world."

Her first notable transformation begins when, at fourteen, she marries Prakash Vijh, an engineering student and a modern city man who does not believe in the subservient role of the Indian wife. "To break off the past," Prakash renames her "Jasmine" and gradually molds her to become a new woman, untrapped by the traditional beliefs of a feudal society. He implants the American Dream in her mind, and both plan to leave for America to begin a new life. When Prakash falls victim to a Sikh extremist's bomb, she decides to emigrate to the United States to fulfill her husband's dream.

Her American odyssey accelerates the process of her metamorphosis. Upon her arrival in Florida, when she is brutally raped by a monstrous skipper, she symbolically turns into the goddess Kali to slaughter her assailant. She also burns her husband's suit outside her motel, as if to burn her Jyoti-Jasmine self and her Indian past. With help from a kindly mentor, Lillian Gordon, she reinvents herself into her first American identity, "Jazzy in a T-shirt, tight cords, and running shoes."

After her initiation into the American way of life, Jasmine moves on to New York. She lives temporarily with the family of her late husband's professor, Devinder Vadhera, but she feels stifled by the pseudo-Indian cultural environment in the Vadhera household. To distance herself further from India and everything Indian, she seeks the help of Lillian's daughter, Kate, to secure the job of a live-in "day mommy" for Duff, the adoptive daughter of a Columbia University couple, Taylor and Wylie Hayes.

In her emancipating position as the couple's au pair, Jasmine starts living the American Dream. She falls in love with Taylor and his world of ease and comfort. Taylor accepts her without sanitizing her foreignness and gives her a new identity, "Jase," a woman who lives for today and becomes aware of the plasticity and fluidity of American culture. Her happiness, however, ends when, by a strange quirk of fate, she happens to spot her husband's killer in a New York park. To escape her past, she flees New York and ends up in rural Iowa, to be reincarnated as "Jane Ripplemeyer."

Even in Elsa County, however, fates seem to be intertwined. She and Bud adopt Du Thein, a Vietnamese refugee boy who constantly reminds her of her own past. She thinks of Du as the son that she and Prakash might have had, but she is carrying Bud's child. When Bud is shot and crippled by a distraught farmer, she refuses to marry him, because she hopes to save him from what she believes is her destiny. She also resists Darrel Lutz, her tormented lover, who wants to run away with her. When Du leaves for California to be with his sister's family, however, she realizes that she will not be far behind. Darrel's suicide reaffirms that Iowa is closing in on her. She feels totally isolated as Jane Ripplemeyer and hopes that Taylor will come to her rescue.

When Taylor and Duff finally track her down, she walks out on her life with Bud and is headed toward California, "greedy with wants and reckless from hope," to set up "an unorthodox family" with Taylor, Duff, and Du.

The Characters

Jasmine is a complex, resourceful, and dynamic character who undergoes dramatic changes throughout the novel. A young, daring woman from India, she represents Bharati Mukherjee's concept of "the new breed" of Americans from non-European countries who are imperceptibly changing the face of America. Endowed by nature with good looks and a good mind, she uses them both to her fullest advantage to seek happiness and self-fulfillment. With her remarkable willpower, she fights an undesirable fate as she resists the hold of a feudal and patriarchal family. Her marriage to Prakash allows her to break the mold of the traditional female role in Indian society and strengthens her hopes for a bright future. When Prakash decides to go to school in America, she sees this as a possible way to subvert the fate predicted by the astrologer. Even her husband's death does not deter her from realizing her American Dream. Her arduous voyage to America shows her stubborn will to survive and her determination to re-create her destiny. She goes through several rebirths to become all-American. Her adaptability and readiness to reinvent herself aid her assimilation into American society.

Prakash Vijh, Jyoti's husband, impresses the reader with his modern outlook and revolutionary ideas. He liberates Jyoti from her feudal past and transforms her into a new kind of modern woman, capable of independent thought. He renames her Jasmine and stirs her mind with new possibilities. Jyoti rightly thinks of him as her Pygmalion.

Lillian Gordon, an old white Quaker woman who provides sanctuary to refugees and illegal aliens, represents the best in the American spirit of compassion, tolerance, and philanthropy. She facilitates Jasmine's assimilation into mainstream America.

Professor Devinder Vadhera, an Indian expatriate living in New York, embodies the conflict between assimilation and cultural preservation. As Prakash's former teacher, he serves as Jasmine's American connection. Yet Jasmine rejects the stifling aloofness of his Indian world to merge into the great American melting pot.

Kate Gordon-Feldstein, Lillian's daughter and the author of a book on migrant workers, is the first person to applaud Jasmine's expression of will. By helping her to find a job with the Hayeses, Kate opens up new possibilities for Jasmine to fulfill her dream.

Taylor Hayes, an academic who falls in love with Jasmine and calls her "Jase," teaches her how to take charge of her life and harmonize her Hindu concept of destiny with her American expression of will. Most important, he does not fear her foreignness and accepts her as she is. Under Taylor's loving tutelage, as Jasmine puts it, "I bloomed from a diffident alien with forged documents into adventurous Jase." It is Taylor who eventually leads her to "the promise of America."

Bud Ripplemeyer, the disabled banker, offers Jasmine a haven of economic security and the prospect of motherhood, but he cannot offer her "adventure, risk, transformation," for which she craves. Though he wins Jasmine's deep affection and admiration, he fails to satisfy her emotional needs.

Du Thien, the Vietnamese boy adopted by Bud and Jasmine, plays an important part in Jasmine's emotional life. He constantly reminds her that she is living in exile among strangers. She regards Du as the son she and Prakash might have had.

Themes and Meanings

Primarily an immigrant narrative, *Jasmine* explores the process of Americanization and brings out the conflict between assimilation and cultural preservation. It is a poignant story of survival, expediency, compromises, losses, and adjustments involved in the process of acculturation to American life. As Jasmine says in the novel, "There are no harmless, compassionate ways to remake oneself. We murder who we were so we can rebirth ourselves in the images of dreams."

The process of rebirth, even in a metaphoric sense, has been extremely painful for both Jasmine and Du. Both have confronted death closely, endured severe hardships, suffered horrible indignities, and survived. Jasmine calls her own transformation "genetic," whereas Du's was "hyphenated." In her desire for assimilation into mainstream America, Jasmine immolates her Jyoti-Jasmine self to burn her Hindu past. To accomplish her genetic transformation, she conceives a child by a white American from the heartland and feels potent in her pregnancy, as if she is "cocooning a cosmos."

Du, on the other hand, has retained his identity as a Vietnamese American. A survivor and an adapter, he learns to camouflage himself within the expectations of others, but he instinctively resists the idea of the American melting pot. Although it seems that he is fast becoming all-American, he keeps his language and ethnic heritage alive by secretly keeping in touch with the Vietnamese community. Like Jasmine, he too experiences three lives—one in Saigon, the other in a refugee camp, and the third as Yogi Ripplemeyer—but he never severs his connection completely from his roots. Du's character exemplifies that in a multicultural society one does not have to erase one's ethnic identity entirely to become an "American."

The novel also portrays the problems of immigrants who arrive in the United States with dreams of wealth and success but find it difficult to adjust to the new environment and ethos. Mukherjee probes such troubles through the character of Professor Devinder Vadhera, once a scientist in India, now working as an importer of human hair in Flushing, New York. He does not like his job, but he needs to work to support his wife and old parents. To adapt to his new environment, he undergoes a name change and becomes a diminutive "Dave." He lives in a ghetto, always feels stressed, and complains that America is killing him. He regards Flushing as a neighborhood in Jullundhar and encloses himself in "the fortress of Punjabiness," artificially created in his home environment. According to the narrator, Vadhera "had sealed his heart when he'd left home. His real life was in an unlivable land across oceans. He was a ghost, hanging on."

The novel obviously moves from Vadhera's cultural isolation to Jasmine's intense longing for assimilation. Since the novel focuses on the physical, emotional, and intellectual growth of the female protagonist and her quest for self-determination and identity, it can also be viewed as a *Bildungsroman*, or rite-of-passage novel.

Critical Context

Acclaimed as brilliantly written and superbly crafted, *Jasmine* grew out of a short story of the same title in *The Middleman and Other Stories* (1988), which won Mukherjee the prestigious National Book Critics Circle Award. In *Jasmine*, the author successfully employs a number of narrative strategies, such as the use of a first-person point of view (unlike the omniscient perspective of her previous novels), singular and plural narrative voices, flashbacks, introspective asides, and cross-cutting, which allow the reader to roam in time, within a chapter, even within a paragraph, from one continent to another. Mukherjee also experiments with the form of the novel by creating a female *Bildungsroman* in the picaresque mode.

Thematically, *Jasmine* is central to Mukherjee's mission as a writer. "My material," as she has stated, "is the rapid and dramatic transformation of the United States since the early 1970s. . . . My duty is to give voice to continents, but also to redefine the nature of *American* and what makes an American." *Jasmine* is basically a story of transformation. Like Mukherjee's first two novels, *The Tiger's Daughter* (1972) and *Wife* (1975), and her first collection of short stories, *Darkness* (1985), it deals primarily with the South Asian immigrant experience. Whereas these earlier works dramatize cultural disorientation and alienation, however, *Jasmine* celebrates the process of assimilation and Americanization prefigured in *The Middleman and Other Stories*. Her novel *The Holder of the World* (1993) traverses the continents.

In addition to her novels and two collections of short fiction, Mukherjee has written a travel memoir, *Days and Nights in Calcutta* (1977; coauthored with her husband Clark Blaise); a documentary, *The Sorrow and the Terror: The Haunting Legacy of the Air India Tragedy* (1987, in collaboration with Blaise); a political treatise, *Kautilya's Concept of Diplomacy* (1976), and a number of essays, articles, and reviews. Her work has appeared in several newspapers, magazines, and anthologies. Her immigrant narratives, chronicling the saga of "new Americans," are contributing to the literature of American multiculturalism and have won for her a distinctive place among first-generation North American writers of Indian origin.

Bibliography

Boire, Gary. "Eyre and Anglos." Review of *Jasmine*, by Bharati Mukherjee. *Canadian Literature* 132 (Spring, 1992): 160-161. In this highly suggestive review, Boire views *Jasmine* as "the paradigmatic 'postcolonial' narrative." He points out that young Jyoti's abandonment of novels by Charles Dickens and Charlotte Brontë because she found them too difficult to read, is significant because it symbolizes the author's "own need to 'rewrite' past literary and political wrongs" by rejecting well-known icons of the British Empire.

Chua, C. L. "Passages from India: Migrating to America in the Fiction of V. S. Naipaul and Bharati Mukherjee." In *Reworlding: The Literature of the Indian Diaspora*, edited by Emmanuel S. Nelson. Westport, Conn.: Greenwood Press, 1992. Chua offers a perceptive analysis of *Jasmine*, stressing "survival and reincarnation" as the book's integral themes. He also points out apparent similarities between *Jas-*

mine and *Jane Eyre* (1847). The concluding section traces Mukherjee's evolution as an artist.

Faymonville, Carmen. "Mukherjee's *Jasmine.*" *The Explicator* 56 (Fall, 1997): 53-54. Faymonville discusses the burden of the Old World responsibilities and cultural ties that represent the potential of American-style individualism and female liberation. The narrative depicts Jasmine as a pioneer who will eventually become a true American.

Kaye-Kantrowitz, Melanie. "In the New New World." Review of *Jasmine*, by Bharati Mukherjee. *The Women's Review of Books* 7 (April, 1990): 8-9. Calls the novel "a witty, dazzling fairy tale disguised by naturalism." Kaye-Kantrowitz demonstrates, with textual evidence, the novel's three themes: identity, hovering mortality, and "the contrast between the escapee/immigrant vision of America and the vision of the protected American."

Koening, Rhoda. "Passage from India." *New York* 22 (September 25, 1989): 132. Tracing the protagonist's passage from her native village to the city and thence to America, Koening shows how "first with love, then with courage and cunning," Jasmine "creates her destiny."

Kristen, Carter-Sanborn. "'We Murder Who We Were:' *Jasmine* and the Violence of Identity." *American Literature* 66 (September, 1994): 573-593. Kristen explores the similarities between Charles Dickens's *Great Expectations* (1860-1861), Charlotte Brontë's *Jane Eyre*, and Mukherjee's *Jasmine*. She concludes that Mukherjee's novel is similar to those of Dickens and Brontë and that it offers a colonial perspective on gender and feminist issues.

Leard, Abha Prakash. "Mukherjee's *Jasmine.*" *The Explicator* 55 (Winter, 1997): 114-117. Leard argues that Mukherjee gives Jyoti, the Hindu teenage widow, more than one name during the course of the story to portray the ability of a woman to experience multiple selves during her lifetime. She also asserts that the body merely serves as a vehicle for the inner self's journey toward a higher plane.

Ruppel, F. Timothy. "'Reinventing Ourselves a Million Times': Narrative, Desire, Identity, and Bharati Mukherjee's *Jasmine.*" *College Literature* 22 (February, 1995): 181-190. Ruppel explores the problems of enforced identity in Mukherjee's novel. Ruppel argues that Mukherjee uses her novel to reinvent the Indian drama by portraying the emergence of an immigrant family's success.

Schaumburger, Nancy Engbretsen. "Chaos and Miracles." Review of *Jasmine*, by Bharati Mukherjee. *Belles Lettres: A Review of Books by Women* 5 (Summer, 1989): 29. Gives a summary of the novel, highlighting the young heroine's different identities, which "the various circumstances and men in her life have bestowed upon her."

Chaman L. Sahni

JAVA HEAD

Author: Joseph Hergesheimer (1880-1954)
Type of plot: Historical
Time of plot: The 1840's
Locale: Salem, Massachusetts
First published: 1919

> *Principal characters:*
> JEREMY AMMIDON, the senior partner in a family shipping firm
> GERRIT AMMIDON, his son, the master of the *Nautilus*
> WILLIAM AMMIDON, his other son, an active partner in the firm
> RHODA AMMIDON, William's wife, an insightful woman
> TAOU YUEN, Gerrit's wife, the daughter of a Manchu nobleman
> NETTIE VOLLAR, Barzil Dunsack's illegitimate granddaughter
> EDWARD DUNSACK, Barzil's evil son, an opium addict

The Novel

Java Head is a historical novel, set in the 1840's, about Salem, Massachusetts, shipowners who had grown wealthy from trade with the Far East, especially China. The novel consists of ten chapters, reflecting the viewpoints of nine different characters. As a result of these changing perspectives, *Java Head* is a complex novel based on a fairly simple plotline.

At the beginning of *Java Head*, the primary concern of the wealthy Ammidon family is that Gerrit Ammidon's ship, the *Nautilus*, is months overdue. There are, however, tensions within the family—some of them trivial, like the squabbling between Laurel and her prissy sister Camilla; others more serious, like the frequent confrontations between the elderly Jeremy Ammidon, who spent most of his life at sea, and his son William Ammidon, whose only experience is in the countinghouse of the family firm. William's wife Rhoda rebukes her husband for arguing with Jeremy about replacing their ships with the speedier clippers and about the profits to be derived from the opium trade. Either suggestion sends Jeremy into such a fury that Rhoda fears for his health. However, she sees no harm in the flirtation between her oldest daughter, Sidsall, and a middle-aged family friend, Roger Brevard.

The Ammidons are also troubled about the bad feeling between their family and that of another former ship captain, Barzil Dunsack. Jeremy has had nothing to do with his old friend since Dunsack refused to let Gerrit continue seeing Nettie Vollar, Barzil's illegitimate granddaughter. Hearing that Barzil is ill, Jeremy pays him a visit in hopes of mending their friendship, but the meeting ends in another quarrel. Rhoda sympathizes with Nettie, who loathes Salem society, which has always snubbed her, and clearly has strong feelings for Gerrit.

The Ammidons are all relieved when they hear that the *Nautilus* is on her way into port. However, when Gerrit arrives at his home accompanied by a Chinese wife, they do not conceal their disapproval. Even after Gerrit explains that Taou Yuen is the aristocratic daughter of a Manchu nobleman whose life would have been sacrificed had he not married her, Rhoda suggests that he has only postponed tragedy, for his wife will never be accepted anywhere in America.

Having left China in disgrace, Barzil Dunsack's son Edward has also returned to Salem, bringing with him a chest filled with opium for the habit he cannot or will not break. When Edward sees Gerrit's beautiful, aristocratic Chinese wife, his old jealousy of the ship captain becomes an obsession, and he decides somehow to use Nettie to break up the marriage so that he can acquire Taou Yuen for himself. However, recognizing Edward for what he is, Taou Yuen contemptuously rejects his advances. After Barzil, Nettie, and her mother Kate see Edward in an opium-induced stupor, they, too, realize that he is a lost soul.

By accident, Jeremy learns that William and his brother-in-law have committed the firm to everything Jeremy despises, and the shock kills him. When Taou Yuen goes into mourning in the Chinese fashion, Gerrit is obviously repelled by her ugliness. Meanwhile, he has been drawn into closer contact with Nettie, and they declare their love for each other. Sensitive to the change in Gerrit, Taou Yuen goes to see Nettie, who has been injured and is bedridden. For a moment, Taou Yuen considers killing her. When Edward enters, locking the door behind him, Taou Yuen realizes her own danger. Aware that no one will hear her call for help, Taou Yuen escapes from Edward by swallowing a lethal dose of opium. Roger arrives too late to save her life.

After Taou Yuen's funeral, Gerrit and Nettie are married and leave on the *Nautilus*. Learning that Sidsall is to be sent to school in Switzerland, Roger approaches her parents with a request for her hand. However, when they express their disapproval, his courage leaves him, and he backs down, losing Sidsall's respect and his only chance at love.

The Characters

In *Java Head*, by using limited omniscience, the author explores the viewpoints of nine different characters, some of them major, others primarily observers.

Jeremy Ammidon is one of the most fully realized characters. He is a man of principle, as proven by his opposition to the opium trade, but he has unwisely given over the conduct of the business to his son William and his son-in-law. Jeremy is too plainspoken for Salem, which thrives on indirection and subterfuge. Jeremy's outspokenness alienates his old friend Barzil Dunsack and drives William to conceal the firm's activities from his father in order to avoid confrontations.

Gerrit Ammidon is also happier at sea than on land. However, though Gerrit calls himself a simple man, he has a habit of introspection. He knows that what he feels for Taou Yuen is primarily admiration and that he is drawn to Nettie because she seems to need him more than his wife does. However, Gerrit is blind to Taou Yuen's love for him and to Edward's designs upon her. His hasty marriage to Nettie suggests that he does not understand how much his neglect and infidelity contributed to Taou Yuen's tragic end.

Taou Yuen is a somewhat shadowy figure, defined primarily by such externals as her clothing, her cosmetics, and her religious practices, which reflect her adherence to tradition. Unfortunately, she is so self-disciplined that she cannot confide in Gerrit and so uncompromising that she sees her thoughts about killing her rival as a loss of integrity so appalling that she does not deserve to live.

Nettie Vollar views herself as a victim, rejected by Salem society and by the man she loves. By emphasizing her need for him, she wins Gerrit away from his wife.

Edward Dunsack also considers himself a victim, justifying his evil deeds by his supposed ill-treatment by the world. Taou Yuen's scorn and his own addiction propel him into insanity.

William Ammidon is a foil to Jeremy and Gerrit. Though he is a good family man and a prominent citizen of Salem, he has no principles where business is concerned. However, he loves his father and is devastated when he sees that his underhandedness caused Jeremy's death.

Rhoda Ammidon's gift for empathy makes her the peacemaker within the family. The author uses Rhoda to foreshadow coming events, as when she warns William about upsetting his father and tells Gerrit that Taou Yuen will never find happiness with him.

Themes and Meanings

Java Head is an indictment of the evils Hergesheimer sees in his own society, evils that he believes can be traced to changes that occurred in the previous century. Once, he suggests, people cherished honor, integrity, and independence. When they abandoned those values, as William does in *Java Head*, Americans doomed themselves and their descendants to meaningless lives.

The author illustrates this conflict between tradition and change, principle and profit, by dividing his major characters into two groups. For Jeremy and Gerrit, tradition and principle are both important. They disapprove of the new clipper ships as much as they do of opium. Taou Yuen, too, represents tradition and principle. Even though it would have made her life easier had she attempted to adopt American ways, Taou Yuen clings to old customs because they represent more profound values and reinforce her own integrity.

By contrast, William Ammidon welcomes change, hopes for profit, and refuses to let tradition or principle get in his way. Although William is not malicious like Edward, there are marked similarities between them. Both act in their own self-interest, ignoring the consequences to others; both are willing to conceal the truth in order to attain their goals; and both are involved with opium, which clearly symbolizes the poisonous effects of greed.

In *Java Head*, life at sea represents tradition and integrity; life on land, the new corruption. At sea, as in the early years of the Republic, the dangers are external. As Jeremy's stories show, storms can usually be survived if one has skill, courage, a good ship, and a little luck. On land, however, hypocrisy reigns, as is evident when Taou Yuen attends church with the Ammidons and is politely made to feel like an outsider, unworthy to live in Salem.

While right and wrong are clearly differentiated in *Java Head*, there are also hints of determinism. Jeremy's temper is so much a part of his nature that it is not clear he could control it, any more than Gerrit could become more perceptive, Taou Yuen less reserved, or Edward less malicious. Since Roger Brevard is one of the most civilized characters in the book and obviously one of the most sympathetic, it is significant that even he cannot take charge of his own life. The fact that his defeat ends the book suggests that Hergesheimer sees events as proceeding inevitably from flaws in character.

Critical Context

With *Java Head*, his sixth volume of fiction and his fourth novel, Joseph Hergesheimer consolidated the reputation that had been established in 1917 with *The Three Black Pennys*. Hergesheimer continued to publish fiction until 1934, but these two early novels, along with *Cytherea* (1922), were his most popular. Many critics call *Java Head* his best work. It demonstrated the capacity for painstaking research that enabled him to re-create a past era so effectively. Critics praised Hergesheimer's finely wrought style, so unlike that of the realists and naturalists who dominated the literary scene at the time he was writing. There were objections to what some saw as a neglect of characterization and plot in favor of what the author admitted was his primary interest, theme. However, though the resolution of Gerrit's problems in *Java Head* was both melodramatic and implausible, there was much to admire not only in the author's style and his use of detail but also in the way he employed various narrative voices and managed complex thematic patterns.

Although Hergesheimer's early historical novels and his later fiction set in his own time continued to have a wide readership, it eventually became evident that, despite the fact he shared their pessimism, he was too different from the angry young realists and naturalists to maintain his position in the literary world. After *The Foolscap Rose* (1934), Hergesheimer virtually abandoned his craft. The paucity of critical study of Hergesheimer indicates how greatly his reputation has declined over time. Though occasionally a critic will praise his style or find his aestheticism of interest, Hergesheimer is now thought of primarily not as the serious artist he was but as someone who produced fiction for casual reading.

Bibliography

Cabell, James Branch. *Joseph Hergesheimer: An Essay in Interpretation*. Chicago: The Bookfellows, 1921. An important monograph in which one of Hergesheimer's contemporaries comments on the early books. Cabell notes that the author's most sympathetic characters, including several of those in *Java Head*, attempt to preserve beauty and order but always fail in their efforts.

Clark, Emily. *Ingénue Among the Lions: The Letters of Emily Clark to Joseph Hergesheimer*, edited by Gerald Langford. Austin: University of Texas Press, 1965. Lively, informal letters from the editor of *The Reviewer* reveal much about Hergesheimer, his fiction, and the stellar literary circle of which he was a part. Helpful index.

Gimmestad, Victor E. *Joseph Hergesheimer*. Boston: Twayne, 1984. An excellent introduction to the author's work. Includes chronology and bibliography. Chapter 4 analyzes the thematic development of *Java Head*, describes its reception at publication, and summarizes later critical opinion, which agreed that the novel is more effective pictorially than dramatically.

Jones, Llewellyn. *Joseph Hergesheimer: The Man and His Books*. New York: Alfred A. Knopf, 1920. Perceptive comments on the early works suggest reasons the author became so popular.

Martin, Ronald E. *The Fiction of Joseph Hergesheimer*. Philadelphia: University of Pennsylvania Press, 1965. A thorough scholarly study, focusing especially on technique and theme. *Java Head* is compared to two other novels, *The Three Black Pennys* (1917) and *Cytherea* (1922). According to Martin, although *Java Head* excels in its evocation of a past era as well as in characterization and technique, the plot is flawed, and the conclusion seems contrived.

Rosemary M. Canfield Reisman

JAZZ

Author: Toni Morrison (Chloe Anthony Wofford, 1931-   )
Type of plot: Social realism
Time of plot: The 1920's, with flashbacks reaching back to 1873
Locale: Harlem, New York, and rural Virginia
First published: 1992

>
> *Principal characters:*
>> JOE TRACE, an amiable fifty-three-year-old salesman of beauty products
>> VIOLET TRACE, Joe's wife, an emotionally volatile fifty-year-old
>>   hairdresser
>> DORCAS, Joe's mistress, an impressionable eighteen-year-old orphan
>> ALICE MANFRED, Dorcas's aunt and Violet's confidante, a dignified
>>   fifty-nine-year-old widow
>> ROSE DEAR, Violet's mother, a suicide
>> TRUE BELLE, Violet's grandmother, maidservant to Vera Louise Gray
>> VERA LOUISE GRAY, an eccentric white woman, mother of Golden Gray
>> GOLDEN GRAY, Vera's blond, light-skinned mulatto son
>> HUNTER'S HUNTER (HENRY LESTORY), the father of Golden Gray and
>>   hunting mentor of Joe Trace
>> WILD, Joe's mother, a feral woman who lives in the woods
>> FELICE, Dorcas's friend, a seventeen-year-old girl

The Novel

Jazz, Toni Morrison's sixth novel, is a lyrical, multifaceted narrative that explores the Harlem lives and back-country roots of a number of African American characters in the years from 1873 to 1926. In keeping with the loose, improvisational nature of the music that gives the book its title, *Jazz* is composed of ten untitled, unnumbered chapters. The principal first-person narrator is an unnamed omniscient observer with a distinctly subjective personality who knows Harlem and the main characters well. The novel also includes first-person passages narrated by Joe, Violet, Dorcas, and Felice, that give the reader a rich and sometimes conflicting range of perspectives on the characters and action.

The main events of the novel take place in the six months or so from fall 1925 to spring 1926. The locale is Harlem, site of the 1920's Harlem Renaissance, a legendary period of African American creativity in fiction and poetry. Morrison's emphasis, however, is on jazz, the distinctively urban African American music that reached an early peak in this period. Her novel begins *in medias res* in January, 1926, with an anecdote that seems the novelistic equivalent of such blues ballads as "Frankie and Johnny." Joe Trace, a married man in his fifties, has a "deepdown, spooky love" for eighteen-year-old Dorcas, but when their three-month-old affair goes awry, he shoots her at a party. (The reader later learns that Joe is never arrested for this murder because no one will admit to witnessing the crime.) Joe's wife, Alice, then takes a strange revenge by bursting in on Dorcas's funeral and trying to slash the dead girl's face.

Playing off this sensational opening anecdote, Morrison's mercurial narrative ranges in many directions, much as a jazz musician might improvise on the opening statement of a melody. In a vividly sensuous style, the author brings to life both the excitement of Jazz Age Harlem and the racism, violence, and unresolved mysteries of the places its citizens had left behind—the rural South and the cities of the Midwest.

The early chapters focus on the midlife crises of Violet and Joe that lead to their desperate actions. As Violet reaches the age of fifty, she begins to feel more keenly the lack of a child in their marriage. Her despair causes her to withdraw into silence and to bouts of insane behavior, including an impetuous attempt to steal another woman's baby. Joe, on the other hand, yearns to regain the excitement that he and Violet had when they "train-danced" into Harlem in 1906. Once he has gained Dorcas as his mistress, however, he finds that it is not the excitement of youth that he needs so much as someone to whom he can talk.

In later chapters, Morrison explores the troubled family pasts of Violet and Joe through an intricately interwoven series of flashbacks set in fictional Vesper County, Virginia. Violet is left to endure the memories of her father's abandonment of his family when she was a young girl, of her family's eviction from their home by whites when she was twelve, and of her mother True Belle's suicide when Violet was sixteen. Joe, also an orphan, is haunted by the memory of his search for his mother, Wild, a feral woman who lived in the woods. Though he learns how to stalk from tracking expert Hunter's Hunter, Joe is never able to catch a glimpse of his mother. In a related subplot that reaches back even earlier, Golden Gray, a young mulatto, travels from Baltimore, where he lives with his white mother Vera Louise Gray, to Vesper County in search of his black father, Hunter's Hunter. En route, Golden Gray rescues Wild when she knocks herself unconscious against a tree, and Golden and Hunter help the feral woman to deliver a baby (Joe Trace).

Like Violet and Joe, Dorcas is also suffering from the loss of her parents, both of whom were killed in the East St. Louis riots of 1917. Harlem transforms Dorcas from a sorrowful nine-year-old into a reckless flapper enraptured with Harlem's flashy styles and uninhibited attitudes. Yet Dorcas allows herself to be drawn into an affair with Joe partly because he serves as a father figure.

In contrast with Violet, Joe, and Dorcas, who let their emotions and their haunted pasts propel them into destructive or self-destructive behavior, is Alice Manfred, Dorcas's dignified aunt. Early in the novel, Alice tries unsuccessfully to prevent her niece from losing herself in Harlem's immoral sensuality. Later, Alice generously befriends Violet (the violator of her niece's funeral) and helps Violet to gain an old-fashioned but stabilizing sense of herself.

Toward the end of the novel, Joe and Violet move closer to each other by embracing a quiet domestic existence. Even Felice, the teenaged best friend of Dorcas who shared her appetite for Harlem's frenzied nightlife, seems to find the happiness that her name denotes by gradually accepting a cozy role as Joe and Violet's surrogate daughter.

The Characters

Joe Trace, a middle-aged salesman, gains the reader's sympathy despite his seemingly perfidious acts that begin the novel. A charming, avuncular man, trusted in his community, Joe nevertheless takes an eighteen-year-old girl as his mistress. He drifts into this unsavory behavior because of his wife's emotional withdrawal and his own midlife melancholy, but also because he sees Dorcas as a needy, vulnerable girl whom he wants, in his own odd way, to protect. The reader feels sorry for Joe in the flashback passages when he is tracking Wild, his inaccessible mother; despite his grimmer purpose, Joe's tracking of Dorcas, when he has lost control of their relationship and of himself, retains some of that pathos from earlier in his life.

Violet Trace is a fifty-year-old hairdresser who is hardworking but subject to spells of emotional derangement. The reader's attitude toward Violet shifts from shock over her desperate violence at Dorcas's funeral to sympathy when one learns of the traumas of Violet's past, particularly her mother's suicide. Ironically, after striking out in hate against Dorcas's corpse, Violet then becomes preoccupied with the life of the dead teenager. Fortunately, Violet finds Alice Manfred to be the kind of caring maternal figure that Violet has missed having in her life, and with Alice's help, Violet regains her emotional balance.

Dorcas, the catalyst for the most violent acts in the novel, is viewed differently by different characters. The narrator presents her as an emotionally damaged adolescent who chases the thrills of Harlem to escape her painful past, while on a deeper level she actually wants to die. Alice sees Dorcas as the defenseless victim of an older man's seduction; Violet sees her as the beautiful daughter she wishes she could have had. To her best friend Felice, Dorcas seems an unscrupulous, less-than- attractive girl who habitually uses people, while Joe is struck by her softness, beauty, and neediness.

Alice Manfred serves as the moral pivot of the novel. A maternal figure who embodies an old-fashioned sense of morality, she fails to keep Dorcas from succumbing to Harlem's temptations; after Dorcas's funeral, however, Alice helps Violet to regain control of herself as a "lady." This change in Violet revives her marriage with Joe, and they in turn serve as stabilizing parental figures in the life of Felice.

Though they are not characters in the conventional sense, two other important personalities in the novel should be noted: the City and the narrator. Curiously, in *Jazz* Morrison almost never uses the word "Harlem." Instead, throughout the novel she refers to this section of New York as "the City," a place of mythic power that exerts strong influences on its inhabitants. For example, Joe's decision to take a mistress seems as much an aspect of his love for the City as an attraction for a particular woman. Joe begins his affair with Dorcas in October, a time of special beauty in the City's weather; and the main action moves from this golden October, through the cold January of Dorcas's murder and Joe and Violet's despair, to the "sweetheart weather" of early spring, when life begins to blossom in the City and for Joe and Violet once again.

Morrison's first-person narrator undergoes curious changes in her views of the characters, the City, and even of the plot and of herself. At first, she speaks with a confident voice that ranges from a gossipy, sensationalistic view of the characters' perversities to a lyrical celebration of her love for the City. Early on, she also raises the suspense level of the plot by stating that there will be another shooting later when Felice arrives at the home of Joe and Violet. Yet a strange irony of the novel is that as Violet, Joe, and Felice become more stable in the final chapters, the narrator seems to become emotionally unhinged. The foreshadowed ending is changed so that no second shooting occurs, and the narrator proclaims herself unreliable and helpless.

Themes and Meanings

Toni Morrison has stated that the overarching purpose of her novels is to show readers "how to survive in a world where we are all of us, in some measure, victims of something." She begins *Jazz* with an anecdote in which Dorcas seems to be the clear victim of the actions of Joe and then Violet. By the end of the novel, however, Morrison has shown how all the characters are victims, for all are scarred by their pasts— often by the racism, dispossession, and violence that are the heritage of slavery. Most of the characters are thus preoccupied with a search for self that involves working out the complex family patterns that haunt them. Some characters, such as Joe and Golden Gray, conduct an actual search to find a parent. On a less conscious level, most of the characters—including Joe, Violet, Dorcas, Alice, and Felice—are searching for people who will fill the gaps left by the relatives they have, in one way or another, lost. For example, as a result of her mother's suicide, Violet loses both her mother and her desire to become a mother; yet she comes to find in Alice and in Dorcas (and then Felice) both the mother and the daughter that she longs to have in her life.

Even the narrator is the victim of her own illusions and mistaken projections. She finds that she must partially give up the romantic view of the City, presented early in the novel, as a place of ideal liberation where people are inspired to become "their stronger, riskier selves." As the novel proceeds, the narrator must also consider the havoc that the City's passions wreak in the characters' lives, and she must admit that the old-fashioned values of Alice Manfred and the quiet domesticity embraced by Joe, Violet, and Felice at the end ultimately lead to a richer kind of happiness. Thus the narrator learns that the characters have outgrown the need for violence and that the shooting scene involving Joe, Violet, and Felice that she foreshadowed at the beginning of the novel no longer fits the way that the characters have evolved.

Ultimately, the great achievement of *Jazz* is that Morrison goes beyond the mere illustration of how her characters are victims who survive; she dramatizes how they move beyond their victimization and grow in moral stature. When Violet is in the depths of her despair, Alice advises her, "You got anything left to you to love, anything at all, do it." In their various ways, Joe, Violet, Felice, and the narrator all eventually absorb this all-important lesson: They learn to give and to receive a mature kind of love.

Critical Context

In 1987, Toni Morrison achieved a decisive plateau in her career with her fifth novel, *Beloved*, a Pulitzer Prize-winning best-seller that solidified her position as the leading African American novelist of her generation. With *Jazz*, on the other hand, Morrison dared to risk her established position by writing a novel that is less masterful and confident, more exploratory and tentative.

One measure of Morrison's adventurousness in *Jazz* is her choice of setting. She begins the novel not in the rural and small-town settings that have been her recognized forte, but rather in 1920's Harlem; she uses the novel to explore her ambivalence toward that legendary time and place. On the one hand, Morrison enjoys celebrating Harlem and its jazz as a metaphor for the exhilarating liberation felt by blacks who moved to Northern cities after World War I, when it seemed as if racism and war might be things of the past. On the other hand, she is also honest enough to recognize that the excitement and sensuality of the City lured people away from the kinds of love and maturity that could truly heal them.

Jazz is also audacious in the lengths to which Morrison is willing to go to make her narrator fallible. Rather than excising the early passage that mistakenly foreshadows a second shooting, Morrison chooses to leave the passage in and to dramatize the feelings of anxious inadequacy that this dissonance in the plot brings up in the narrator. In this way, Morrison provides the narrator with the same opportunity that the characters have enjoyed: the chance to realize her mistakes and to renew and reinvent herself on a stronger footing.

Though *Jazz* seems at times less in control than Morrison's other novels, its adventurousness and inventiveness are exhilarating, and its many stories, characters, and perspectives are richly imagined and frequently moving. Ultimately, *Jazz* shows Toni Morrison to be a great American writer who is not content to let her past successes become formulas for her future works. In 1993, her achievements were recognized with the Nobel Prize in Literature.

Bibliography

Hulbert, Ann. "Romance and Race." Review of *Jazz*, by Toni Morrison. *The New Republic* 206 (May 18, 1992): 43-48. Hulbert criticizes *Jazz* as a failed experiment in self-conscious improvisation. She argues that Morrison's characters are flat and her descriptions clichéd. According to Hulbert, although Morrison intends to avoid romanticizing blackness, she instead ends up sentimentalizing family domesticity.

Jones, Carolyn M. "Traces and Cracks: Identity and Narrative in Toni Morrison's *Jazz*." *African American Review* 31 (Fall, 1997): 481-495. Jones discusses *Jazz* in relation to its precursor, *Beloved*, tracing the theme of healing and reconstructing "cracked" black identity through love. She compares the formation of identity to the improvisation of jazz and concludes that *Jazz* represents both the ongoing construction of personal identity and the formation of community.

Kubitschek, Missy D. *Toni Morrison: A Critical Companion*. Westport, Conn.: Greenwood Press, 1998. Discusses Morrison's writing in traditions of African

American, modernist, and postmodernist American writers. Chapters focus on individual novels, including *Jazz*, and feature sections on plot and character development, narrative structure, thematic issues, and critical approaches. Ideal for students and general readers.

Leonard, John. "Her Soul's High Song." *The Nation* 254 (May 25, 1992): 706-718. This discussion of *Jazz* in relation to Morrison's other novels finds her dominant theme to be "identity-making" in a black culture of broken families and failed dreams. Leonard admires *Jazz*'s wealth of characters, its exploration of their Southern roots, and its witty use of a self-conscious narrator. According to Leonard, Morrison is "the best writer working in America."

Mbalia, Doreatha D. "Women Who Run with Wild: The Need for Sisterhoods in *Jazz*." *Modern American Fiction* 39 (Fall/Winter, 1993): 623-646. Mbalia offers a plot and character analysis of *Jazz* while discussing the theme of shared unity of African people as a defense against the racial oppression of blacks. She explores the analogy of jazz music with narrative form and the merger of form and content in Morrison's novel.

Pereira, Mali W. "Periodizing Toni Morrison's Work from *The Bluest Eye* to *Jazz*: The Importance of *Tar Baby*." *MELUS* 22 (Fall, 1997): 71-82. Focuses on *Tar Baby* as a transitional novel connecting Morrison's earlier work with her later books. Offers an in-depth analysis of *Jazz*, showing how the novel compares with and comments on *The Bluest Eye*.

Rodrigues, Eusebio, L. "Experiencing *Jazz*." *Modern American Fiction* 39 (Fall/Winter, 1993): 733-754. Rodrigues presents a literary analysis of *Jazz*, focusing on the music symbolism of the novel. He interprets jazz as an analogy for black experience and its literary construction and discusses the literary devices of punctuation and rhythmic use of words.

Terry L. Andrews

JEWS WITHOUT MONEY

Author: Michael Gold (Irwin Granich; 1893-1967)
Type of plot: Autobiographical
Time of plot: The early twentieth century
Locale: New York City
First published: 1930

> *Principal characters:*
> MIKE GOLD, the protagonist and narrator
> KATIE GOLD, his mother
> HERMAN GOLD, his father
> ESTHER GOLD, his sister
> REB SAMUEL ASHKENAZI, his neighbor

The Novel

Jews Without Money is based on its author's own childhood. It re-creates the Jewish immigrant Lower East Side in Manhattan in which he lived, and it provides insight into the life of first- and second-generation Jewish Americans around the turn of the twentieth century.

As the central character and narrator, Mike grows; he learns more and more about the struggles that his parents and their neighbors undergo to earn a living. Mike's father had been a housepainter, but he is disabled by a fall and by lead poisoning. At one point in the book, Mike finds him trying to earn money selling half-rotten bananas. Mike's mother is the central figure in the family; she supports them by working in a cafeteria. After and before work, she takes care of her husband and children. On a terribly snowy winter day, Mike's younger sister, Esther, goes out into the streets to collect wood for the stove; she is run over by a truck and dies. A lawyer comes to their home and says that if the mother and father will sign a paper, he will get them a thousand dollars from Adams Express, the company that operated the truck, as damages. Herman wants to sign the lawyer's paper, but Katie throws him out of the house. It is, she says, "blood money."

Repeatedly, Mike learns how terrible life is for people in America without money, especially Jews. They need to cope not only with poverty but also with anti-Semitism. Because six-year-old Mike uses a dirty word, his teacher washes out his mouth with soap. The teacher also calls him "Little Kike." Herman and Katie are furious because the soap the teacher uses is not kosher. When a politician sends them a Thanksgiving meal, Katie asks Mike to tell her the story of Thanksgiving. After he narrates the tale of the Pilgrims, his mother decides that Thanksgiving is "an American holiday . . . and not for Jews." The family cannot even eat the beautiful, fat turkey because it is not kosher. When Herman seems to be doing well in the housepainting business and thinks he will begin to earn more money, he falls from a ladder and cannot work. After Esther dies, the mother also is unable to work. When the family is nearly starving, a man from the United Charities visits them and asks all kinds of personal questions, including whether Herman beats Katie. Herman throws the man out of the house. Mike concludes that "starvation was kinder" than organized charity.

Mike keeps hearing from those around him that the Messiah will come and lead the Jews to the Promised Land. He asks his neighbor, Reb Samuel, a very religious man, about the Messiah. Reb Samuel, who teaches Mike about Judaism, describes a "pale, young and peaceful" Messiah, but Mike prefers one who looks like Buffalo Bill and "could annihilate our enemies."

At age twelve, Mike quits school to go to work. He finds a variety of unpleasant, sometimes hellish jobs and discovers anti-Semitism in employment. Even some businesses owned by Jews, he discovers, refuse to hire Jews. One night, he hears a man on a soapbox declare that a world movement is coming to end poverty. Listening to him, Mike learns about the workers' revolution, which he calls "the true Messiah." The revolution, he says, forced him to think, struggle, and live. The book then ends with the words, "O great Beginning!"

The Characters

The characters in *Jews Without Money* contribute to the growth of Mike. He runs wild in the slums of the Lower East Side, playing with his "Gang of Little Yids." He describes the bums, horse drivers, prostitutes, and workers who live in his neighborhood. His father becomes a figure of despair. For Herman, nothing goes right. All of his get-rich-quick schemes go awry. Cruelly conscious of the need for money in America, he bitterly rejects the New World in which he suffers so much, at one point uttering, "A curse on Columbus! A curse on America, the thief!"

The most admirable character in the book is Katie. Many critics see the book as being primarily in praise of Gold's own mother, on whom Katie is based. Several years after the book appeared, Gold himself called Katie the book's heroine. She shows kindness to all, even the prostitutes who live near their apartment. When she works in the cafeteria, the other workers come to her with their problems. She remains gentle and concerned with doing the right thing, even though life for her is a constant round of work. The one time Mike sees her truly happy is when the family goes to Bronx Park and Katie takes the children to gather mushrooms in the woods. She accepts hardship and tragedy with dignity and grace. Only the death of her daughter Esther is too much for her. After Esther dies, Katie is defeated.

Many of Mike's neighbors are highly religious. Mike theorizes that the more persecuted a minority is, the more religious its members become. Yet beneath the religion, Mike sees hypocrisy in many, especially in the fat Chassidic rabbi imported from Europe at great cost to his relatively poor congregation. When the Chassids celebrate the coming of the rabbi, Mike sees the rabbi stuffing himself and thinks the rabbi will eat all the food at the celebration before the children get a chance to eat anything. He mentions that possibility to Reb Samuel, who sends Mike home without having eaten any of the feast; but, Mike says, Reb Samuel should have listened to the wisdom of the little child. After a while, the rabbi accepts a better paying job at a wealthy congregation. The rabbi's leaving crushes Reb Samuel. Reb Samuel, a truly pious, gentle man, cannot understand America and the effect it has on people.

Themes and Meanings

When Mike Gold wrote *Jews Without Money*, he was an active member of the Communist Party. Although critics disagree on whether the book is thesis ridden, they agree that it was designed to be a tale of the making of a radical. In the book, the ideas Mike hears about the coming of the Messiah easily lead to ideas connected with the coming of a secular Messiah, the workers' revolution.

Yet *Jews Without Money* is not simply a piece of propaganda about the evils of capitalism. It is also a sensitive treatment of the life of a child in an immigrant neighborhood in the slums of New York City. The book has been the center of much debate about its origins. Some critics claim that it simply flowed from Gold's pen, illustrating his theories that proletarian or workers' art should flow from the heart and not involve artwork. Others point to the changes Gold made between the material he originally published in magazine articles that he later worked into the novel and the book itself to show that the novel is really a work of art, carefully revised and shaped, and not thinly disguised, straight autobiography.

A major theme of the book is the unfairness of the American capitalist system that leads people to dream of financial success but prevents them from achieving it. The hard-heartedness of the capitalist system is best symbolized by the Adams Express truck that kills Esther and the lawyer who tries to make money from her death. The only character who is really happy in America is Harry the Pimp. The honest workers, however, "eat the bread of sorrow and shame in America." The book paints for the most part a bleak picture of Jewish immigrant life at the turn of the twentieth century in America—a picture that will remain bleak, the book's ending implies, until the workers' revolution occurs.

Critical Context

Jews Without Money is, Gold felt, an example of the proletarian novel, the novel by a member of the working class and about members of the working class. In this kind of novel, truth is supposed to be more important than art. Yet Gold was a professional writer and editor and seems to have expended much energy on making the book an artistic success. In part as a result, many communist reviewers attacked the book, pointing out that Herman is a would-be capitalist (he was partners in a suspender shop and is bitter because it failed; he feels his cousin cheated him out of the shop while Herman was on his honeymoon). Thus, the communist reviewers argued, the novel is not a proletarian work at all. Gold defended it, arguing that Herman is an example of the way capitalism destroys workers. As several critics indicate, the book fits Gold's definition of proletarian realism, the novel by the worker about the things a worker knows best.

Jews Without Money proved very popular. It became a best seller and was reissued many times in several languages, including Esperanto. It produced enough money for

Gold to buy a home in the country. In spite of his income from the book, however, Gold remained a loyal member of the Communist Party until his death. Throughout the 1930's, he helped to edit the *New Masses*, a communist periodical, and into the 1940's he wrote a daily column entitled "Change the World" for the *Daily Worker*, a New York-based communist newspaper. In 1935, an edition of *Jews Without Money* appeared with a short introduction by Gold. In it, he wrote that Adolf Hitler should read the book and discover that all Jews are not rich capitalists. Thus even after the book's publication, Gold, perhaps naïvely, believed that his book could serve additional propagandistic purposes.

Bibliography
Bloom, James D. *Left Letters: The Culture Wars of Mike Gold and Joseph Freeman.* New York: Columbia University Press, 1992. Places *Jews Without Money* in the context of the debate over proletarian art and in the context of Gold's and Freeman's efforts as spokespersons for radical literature.
Fiedler, Leslie A. *To the Gentiles.* New York: Stein and Day, 1972. A largely negative treatment of Gold and *Jews Without Money* in the context of Jewish American literature.
Guttmann, Allen. *The Jewish Writer in America: Assimilation and the Crisis of Identity.* New York: Oxford University Press, 1971. Sees Gold's book as communicating the spirit of the ghetto but lacking a plot in any usual sense of the term.
Klein, Marcus. *Foreigners: The Making of American Literature, 1900-1940.* Chicago: University of Chicago Press, 1981. Treats Gold as a central character in the making of modern American literature. Gives a very sympathetic reading of *Jews Without Money*.
Sherman, Bernard. *The Invention of the Jew: Jewish-American Education Novels, 1916-1964.* New York: Thomas Yoseloff, 1969. Treats *Jews Without Money* as a Marxist education novel as well as a representation of a simplistic view of life.

Richard Tuerk

JOHNNY GOT HIS GUN

Author: Dalton Trumbo (1905-1976)
Type of plot: War
Time of plot: The first two decades of the twentieth century
Locale: Shale City, Colorado; Los Angeles, California; and a hospital room in an
   unknown country
First published: 1939

>   *Principal characters:*
>   JOE BONHAM, a bomb blast survivor, horribly disfigured
>   COREEN, Bonham's girlfriend before his departure to war
>   BILL HARPER, Bonham's childhood friend
>   NURSE, a faceless figure who comes to understand Bonham's attempts
>   to communicate
>   JOSÉ, a Puerto Rican who works with Bonham in a Los Angeles bakery

The Novel

   Johnny Got His Gun is a modified stream-of-consciousness narrative occurring in
the mind of a soldier whose arms, legs, ears, eyes, nose, and mouth have been blown
away in a bomb blast during World War I. Written by Hollywood screenwriter Dalton
Trumbo, the novel is told using cinematic techniques, particularly in book 1, "The
Dead," which is a fusion of flashbacks and soliloquies in the mind of Joe Bonham.

   Awakening in a hospital bed, Bonham first remembers the announcement of his father's death. Recalling sensory images of his youth, Bonham slowly realizes the extent of his injuries, and he has flashbacks of the night before he left for war, when he
made love to his girlfriend, Coreen. In a montage of sounds, Joe recalls his parting
words with Coreen, which were mixed with phrases from political speeches and the
lyrics from the song from which the book draws its title. This description captures the
excitement of the moment and the flavor of the times and also establishes the political
backdrop against which Bonham eventually rebels.

   As he realizes each loss from his body, Bonham remembers a youthful incident that
emphasizes the loss. Each flashback is told in the third person. Joe's present circumstances are related in the first person as he explores the sensations within his body.
Unable to communicate, move, or sense the outside world beyond his limited perceptions, Bonham reviews times with past friends and family, including his attempt to escape a broken love affair by working on a section gang in the desert. He recalls the betrayal of his best friend, Bill Harper, who had stolen Bonham's first girlfriend.
Bonham remembers a fishing trip with Harper and his father and describes scenes of
his mother's cooking.

   In between these memories, signaled by fade-outs in the narrative, Bonham's mind
moves through varying psychological states as he explores the extent and ramifica-
tions of his wounds. Describing his world in short, simple sentences, he first sees him-

self as returning to the womb, entirely dependent on the feeding tube in his stomach. His inner battles include the inability to distinguish between dreams and reality. He struggles to control his dreams to avoid insanity. He measures his loss first in physical terms, then realizes that he is a prisoner of his mind and must be able to respect his own thoughts. His narrative breaks into fragmentary sentences when he discovers that he is losing his sense of time. Bonham begins to measure his life by the warmth of the morning sun and the visits of the nurses who change his bandages and bathe him.

Book 1 is largely set in the past. Book 2, "The Living," records Bonham's thoughts as he begins to consider himself dead, with the mind of a living man. After exhausting all of his youthful memories, Bonham late in the narrative begins relating his war experiences, noting that it was in September, 1918, that he was hit by an exploding shell in his foxhole. He believes that four years have gone by, and he now has a sense of place and knows what is happening in his room. His thoughts turn from memories to imagination, as he pictures the making and movements of the bomb that hit him. He has a nightmare of Jesus Christ in Arizona where, at a poker game reminiscent of the Last Supper, Jesus announces that Joe will lose his limbs and face in a bomb blast.

In the book's most moving and eventful section, Bonham discovers that he can communicate by tapping his head in Morse code on his pillow, but none of his nurses seems to understand his motions. He believes he is beginning to go insane, unable to escape the trap of his own thoughts, becoming the ultimate prisoner unable to respect his own thinking. His surreal dreams include becoming a Carthaginian slave during the Roman Empire. He comes to believe that he is the symbol of every one who has been enslaved or imprisoned.

A new nurse begins tracing letters on Bonham's chest, and he realizes that she is telling him "Merry Christmas." He finally gets her to understand his Morse code tapping, and someone replies by asking him "What do you want?" He is surprised because he can now communicate, and he reflects before giving his answer. Bonham replies that he wishes to go on tour as an educational exhibit—a tangible statement that "This is War." His contact with the world turns to conflict when he receives the answer to his query, "This would be against regulations." He tries to communicate but is drugged to keep him from asking questions. His last thought before becoming lost in the drugged fog is "Why?" With this abandonment, Bonham loses hope and succumbs to rage. The book concludes with a lecture on the future. Bonham sees himself as a harbinger of things to come and as one who must be silenced so future wars will have their soldiers.

The Characters

Dalton Trumbo's third novel was both innovative and difficult to write. The entire book is set in the mind of one character who can recall people from his past in vivid detail but is unable to describe visitors to his hospital room except through the sensation of touch. As Bonham himself realizes, he is more a symbol than a man, but Trumbo successfully uses a range of human experiences to make Bonham believable, fully developed, and able to grow despite his extraordinary circumstances.

Joe Bonham is not simply an "everyman" but is drawn from Trumbo's own experiences. The character was named after Trumbo's father, Orus Bonham Trumbo, and Bonhams's youthful memories of Shale City, Colorado, and Los Angeles were based on Trumbo's years in Grand Junction, Colorado, and his nine years as a night worker in a Los Angeles bakery. Trumbo uses these settings to establish Bonham's essentially innocent past, and the flashbacks not only tell what life was like in a small town but also reveal what it was like to be Joe Bonham before the war. One important passage in the bakery focuses on José, an honorable Puerto Rican, whose attempts to lose his job are more than an anecdote to help flesh out Bonham's education. José is a strong, solitary loner whose strength prefigures Bonham's own forced exile as a silent, solitary hero. Other characters also act as contrasts between past and present. For example, Coreen's repeated pleas for Joe not to leave foreshadow his doom.

Bill Harper, his childhood friend who betrays him by stealing his girlfriend, is a character who establishes Bonham's youth as largely that of an average American boy. In the juxtapositions of past and present, he also represents the life Joe can no longer live. Harper symbolizes the people whom Bonham does not want to see him in his diminished condition. Instead of being comforted by his family and girlfriend, he is surrounded by hands that touch him in pity or revulsion.

In one pivotal scene, faceless men surround Bonham, and one of them kisses him on the forehead and lays a medal on his chest. Joe is repulsed by the act but aware that he cannot communicate his disgust to the officials, who can offer him nothing of substance. This limited interaction with humanity both reinforces Bonham's separation from humankind and demonstrates how human he remains.

Themes and Meanings

Trumbo uses Joe Bonham to personify and capture the horror of war by emphasizing what is lost on the battlefield. He continually reinforces the theme of loss in Bonham's life, from the loss of time to Bonham's ultimate inability to have the power for self-destruction. By emphasizing the sensory images of his past life, largely drawn with sound and smell imagery, Trumbo demonstrates the loss from the wounds that dehumanize and isolate Bonham. Bonham's isolation is the ultimate loss.

Trumbo also uses sensory details to underline his political themes. Mixing images in sound collages, Trumbo mocks patriotism and points to the youthfulness of soldiers. Visual images are ironic parodies of propaganda. For example, when the first airplanes are introduced as machines of peace, love, and understanding, they ultimately become instruments of war.

Trumbo's antiwar messages are often overt in the narrative, as when the novelist lists other war atrocities in Joe's memory to demonstrate he is not unique. After Bonham realizes that he is among the dead, he breaks into didactic statements on war, commenting that abstractions such as liberty, democracy, and honor are concepts not worthy of a man's life. If a corpse were asked to choose between honor and life, Joe asserts, it would choose life. He says no one can speak for the dead or sanctify the dead. He is angered when a medal is placed on his chest. There is no principle larger than life, and no man is a coward for refusing to fight. These principles, all spoken with Bonham's voice, are often awkwardly inserted into the narrative, and these passages are a weakness in the novel.

Sternly stated in the novel's closing passages is the theme that war will not end, despite the strong indictment of Bonham's story. Historical images, from Bonham's youth to his surreal dreams as a Carthaginian slave, clearly place Bonham in a stream of warriors of the past and present. His sermon on the future reinforces Trumbo's theme that Bonham, while an individual in a unique position, is but one war story in a never-ending series of atrocities.

Critical Context

Johnny Got His Gun was first published two days before the outbreak of World War II in Europe and was quickly serialized in the communist newspaper *The Daily Worker*. It was immediately popular with critics and the public and was embraced by the American Civil Liberties Union and right-wing pacifists. Trumbo elected not to reprint the book until after the war was over despite its winning of the National Book Award in 1939 and the American Book Sellers Award in 1940. He wrote that there are occasions when the individual voice must give way to a greater good, in this case the defeat of fascism. He was not pleased by many of the supporters of his book whom he considered subversive.

In 1949, Trumbo became a symbol of individual freedom when the House Committee on Un-American Activities headed by Senator Joseph McCarthy blacklisted him. As the most prominent member of the "Hollywood Ten," moviemakers who refused to cooperate with the committee, Trumbo was cited for contempt of Congress and served a one-year prison sentence. As a result, when *Johnny Got His Gun* was reprinted in 1970, the author was known as a courageous spokesman for individual rights, lending the novel a new credibility during the Vietnam War. Actor Donald Sutherland read passages from the book at antiwar demonstrations, and disabled veterans found the novel particularly affecting. Quadriplegic Vietnam veteran Ron Kovic cited the novel as having influenced his own *Born on the Fourth of July* (1976), a book later made into a motion picture.

In 1972, Trumbo directed the film version of his novel; although the film received lackluster response in the United States, it earned eight international awards and drew comparison with other powerful cinematic statements on war such as *Paths of Glory* (1957) and *Catch-22* (1970).

Bibliography

Cooke, Bruce. *Dalton Trumbo*. New York: Charles Scribner's Sons, 1977. Describing Trumbo's life and career, Cooke provides useful insights into the composition and response to the novel and film version.

Kovic, Ron. Introduction to *Johnny Got His Gun*, by Dalton Trumbo. New York: Citadel Press, 1991. In this twelve-page response to Trumbo's novel, Kovic points to

the importance of the book to the veterans of the Vietnam War, particularly those
with extreme injuries.

Trumbo, Dalton. *Additional Dialogue: Letters of Dalton Trumbo, 1942-1962*. New
York: M. Evans, 1970. Though it makes little mention of *Johnny Got His Gun*, this
collection illuminates Trumbo's thoughts and friendships in the post-World War II
years.

Wesley Britton

JOURNEY TO THE SKY

Author: Jamake Highwater (1942-   )
Type of plot: Fictionalized biography/travelogue
Time of plot: From 1839 to 1840
Locale: Central America and southern Mexico
First published: 1978

Principal characters:

JOHN LLOYD STEPHENS, "Meester Estebans," an American lawyer, diplomat, explorer, and travel writer

FREDERICK CATHERWOOD, Stephens's exploring partner, an English architect and artist

COLONEL ARCHIBALD MACDONALD, the British administrator of Belize

PATRICK WALKER and

LIEUTENANT JOHN CADDY, British explorers, the rivals of Stephens and Catherwood

AUGUSTIN, the faithful servant hired by Stephens and Catherwood

THE MULETEER, the quarrelsome head mule driver hired by Stephens and Catherwood

DON GREGORIO, a rich landowner and the petty dictator of the village of Copan

DON JOSÉ MARIA ASEBEDO, the owner of the site of the Copan ruins

FRANCISCO MORAZAN, the leader of liberal forces fighting in Central America

RAFAEL CARRERA, the leader of conservative forces fighting in Central America

HENRY PAWLING, an American adventurer who joins the expedition in Mexico

The Novel

The subtitle of *Journey to the Sky* accurately describes the book: "A Novel About the True Adventures of Two Men in Search of the Lost Maya Kingdom." The two men are John Lloyd Stephens and Frederick Catherwood, pioneering nineteenth century explorers of the Maya ruins whose writings and drawings, respectively, provided the basis for Highwater's fictionalized account. Stephens, a disaffected lawyer from a rich New York family, met Catherwood in London, became his friend, and persuaded the British architect to move his business and family to New York. Later, when Stephens decided to go exploring for the Maya, his friend happily signed on as artist. *Journey to the Sky*, a combination of novel, biography, travelogue, and cultural analysis, concentrates on Stephens and Catherwood's first expedition.

The two board the *Mary Ann* in New York on October 3, 1839, and, after a month-long voyage culminating in a horrendous tropical storm, arrive in Belize.

There the British colonial administrator, Colonel Archibald MacDonald, entertains them royally, since Stephens is traveling officially as a United States diplomat, appointed by President Martin Van Buren. Behind Stephens's back, the conniving Briton not only has his eyes on additional American territory but also sends out a rival archaeological expedition, led by Patrick Walker and Lieutenant John Caddy. The stop in Belize, however, has one positive result: Stephens and Catherwood hire Augustin, who proves to be a resourceful and faithful servant despite his cutthroat appearance.

From Belize, Stephens and Catherwood sail to Izabal, Guatemala, to begin their overland expedition. Hiring mules and mule drivers, they cross infamous Mico Mountain, the narrow trail a quagmire fed by frequent heavy rains. Once they are into the wild interior, the head muleteer starts disputing decisions and demanding renegotiation of his contract. Rising early, he and the mule train leave behind Stephens, Catherwood, and Augustin, who, short on supplies, chase the mule train for days. Luckily, they find hospitable villages along the way, but in one village they are captured by a drunken mob. Eventually someone appears who can read their diplomatic credentials, so the mob decides not to shoot them. When they finally catch up with the mule train, the muleteer promises to make amends by leading them to Copan, a large Maya ruin just over the border in Honduras. After circling through the mountains, the muleteer obviously lost, they actually do stumble upon Copan, now a humble Indian village ruled by a dictatorial landowner, Don Gregorio. Don Gregorio takes an instant dislike to Stephens and Catherwood, and the delighted muleteer joins forces with him.

Luckily again, the nearby Maya ruins are owned not by Don Gregorio but by Don José Maria Asebedo, who considers them useless. Though fearing to buck Don Gregorio, Don José finally sells the ruins to Stephens, the foolish Yankee, for fifty dollars. Now, in recovering the monumental Copan ruins, Stephens and Catherwood have to contend only with the jungle, the rain, the mud, the insects, and the heat and humidity. After some of the underbrush is cleared, Catherwood stays on at Copan to make his drawings while Stephens goes off to fulfill his diplomatic mission.

The political tangle in the Central American Federation is as dense as the jungle around Copan: A civil war is taking place. When, after much difficulty, Stephens arrives in Guatemala City, the capital, there is no government in charge to receive him. The capital waits in fear and trembling for Rafael Carrera's advancing Indian forces, noted for their ignorance and atrocities. Carrera's conservative rebels fight in defense of religion against the liberal president, Francisco Morazan, who tried to restrict the church's power. Carrera enters Guatemala City and grants Stephens an audience, but as of yet the twenty-three-year-old illiterate half-breed holds no official capacity. So, even though overcome with malaria, Stephens takes ship for El Salvador in search of Morazan. Unable to find him there, Stephens sails on to Costa Rica, then travels back through Nicaragua and El Salvador to Guatemala. He finally presents his credentials to Morazan, Central America's best hope, just before the decisive battle, which Morazan loses.

The final phase of Stephens and Catherwood's trip is the worst—a grueling journey of several hundred miles from Guatemala City across another mountain range to Palenque, a Maya center in southern Mexico. Henry Pawling, a well-armed American adventurer, joins the expedition as general manager; his help, it turns out, is sorely needed. Stephens suffers from malaria all the way, and at Palenque both he and Catherwood come down with niguas, little parasites that burrow under the toenails and lay their eggs, which then hatch and cause painful swelling and jungle rot. Jungle rot and mold creep throughout the camp as the rainy season descends. Yet the spectacular ruins at Palenque are worth all the trouble, even if Walker and Caddy have already been there and gone (news that they were horribly slaughtered by hostile Indians proves incorrect).

In an epilogue, Highwater wraps up the trip and summarizes Stephens and Catherwood's second expedition (to the Yucatan Peninsula) and subsequent careers. As might be expected, both men continue to live rather adventurous lives, becoming business speculators in high stakes, traveling about the Continent, and dying with their boots on within about ten years of their search for the Maya.

The Characters

Although Stephens and Catherwood are the main characters of *Journey to the Sky*, they are not the most interesting. As archaeologists, they are gifted amateurs, nineteenth century gentlemen who have a yen to traipse through the jungle but who say things like "Shocking, shocking!" Instead of worrying about snakes and bandits, they worry about getting their clothes muddy or not getting their meals on time. One reward of the novel is to see them devoured by mosquitoes and *niguas* while their Indian servants remain untouched.

Stephens and Catherwood, however, are adaptable. By the end of the novel, they have begun to dress and smell like their mule drivers, though they still do not repel mosquitoes. Yet their adaptation only fits them to exercise their sense of Manifest Destiny with greater assurance. They investigate the Palenque ruins despite a Mexican ban on archaeologists; indeed, Stephens plans to buy the Palenque ruins and transport them to New York City. His plans never succeed, though at one time he is willing to marry a local girl to qualify as a purchaser. One thing to his and Catherwood's credit is their intense interest in the Maya, for whose civilization they helped develop a new appreciation.

More interesting than the explorers are the local people, mostly descendants of the Maya. These people are extraordinarily gentle and hospitable, easily impressed by the strangers, especially when Stephens dons his diplomatic regalia. Yet they also have an extraordinarily vicious side, which comes out when they gain a little power. Prime examples are the tantrum-throwing muleteer and the sullen Don Gregorio. In addition, Stephens and Catherwood meet a succession of petty officials—various *alcaldes* and army officers—who exercise their authority like great dictators. This psychology of alternating humility and haughtiness (not to mention cruelty) seems to arise from the entrenched pattern of peon-aristocrat relations, which provides only two models.

The two leaders in the civil war both represent unsuccessful efforts to overcome the entrenched social pattern, with tragic consequences for Central America. Francisco Morazan, the enlightened liberal, wants to change the social order but loses. Rafael Carrera leads the upsurging peasant masses, who discover their power in numbers but who, in their ignorance, exercise power like their old masters and are manipulated by the priests. The result is perpetuation of the old order under worse forms. Carrera remains the illiterate, conservative, and brutal dictator of Guatemala for twenty-five years.

Themes and Meanings

The main theme of *Journey to the Sky* is the civilization achieved by Indians in the Americas. Jamake Highwater, an American Indian of Blackfeet-Cherokee heritage, is particularly concerned to counter the view of Indians as savages who obstructed the advance of civilization, a view perhaps still current in the popular imagination. During the time of Stephens and Catherwood, the period of Manifest Destiny, such a view justified white policies of conquest, sometimes in combination with missionary efforts. Stephens and Catherwood hold such views until they come upon the Maya ruins. The ruins are monumental evidence of a highly advanced Indian civilization, circa A.D. 300-900, in one of the most intractable regions of the world. It is the old Maya, not Stephens and Catherwood, who are the heroes of *Journey to the Sky*; Stephens and Catherwood, nineteenth century gentlemen, representatives of Manifest Destiny, are merely the proper people to acknowledge Maya achievements.

The Maya achievements stand out, in *Journey to the Sky*, in contrast with the state of affairs reached under Spanish rule. Descendants of the Maya live in squalid villages next to the fabulous ruins and are too ignorant even to understand the value of the ruins. Central America is in political chaos, and Rafael Carrera emerges as the natural leader of the Indian masses. What happened, the reader asks, to the great Maya?

The Spanish cannot be entirely blamed for the state of affairs, since the Maya civilization fell long before the Spanish appeared. Much about the Maya remains a mystery, including their hieroglyphic writing and the causes of their downfall. It could be that the Maya civilization contained the elements of its own undoing. Highwater is curiously quiet, for example, about the practice of human sacrifice among the later Maya. The Maya theocracy also apparently originated the pattern of peon-aristocrat relations which the Spanish reinstituted with Christian symbols. One theory is that the Maya civilization fell because of a peasant revolt. If so, the roots of chaos and decline in Central America go far back.

Critical Context

Journey to the Sky is entertaining reading, but its factual basis gives it something of a textbook tone. So, too, do the occasional sections of cultural analysis. In its instructive purpose and theme, *Journey to the Sky* is related to *The Primal Mind: Vision and Reality in Indian America* (1981), Highwater's fullest statement on Indian culture.

Although his novel *Anpao: An American Indian Odyssey* (1977) won the 1978 Newbery Honor Award, Highwater is really better at cultural analysis than at fiction. He has written numerous expositions of American Indian art, music, dance, and ritual. Dealing with the high point of Indian achievement, *Journey to the Sky* is an important part of Highwater's overall expression of the Indian point of view.

Bibliography

Highwater, Jamake. *Shadow Show: An Autobiographical Insinuation.* New York: Alfred van der Marck, 1986. Highwater discusses the cultural conflicts of his American Indian characters, which also have a personal resonance for him. In *Shadow Show*, he describes the jet-set circles among which he lives at the same time he is writing his works on American Indian culture.

Kirkpatrick, D. L., ed. "Jamake Highwater." In *Twentieth Century Children's Writers.* 3d ed. Chicago: St. James Press, 1989. An entry on Highwater draws on personal comments from several autobiographical sources.

Shirley, Carl R. "Jamake Highwater." In *Dictionary of Literary Biography Yearbook, 1985.* Detroit: Gale Research, 1986. Provides a comprehensive biography of Highwater that includes commentary on his writings.

Harold Branam

JUBIABÁ

Author: Jorge Amado (1912-   )
Type of plot: Political romance
Time of plot: The 1920's and 1930's
Locale: The seaport city of Salvador, in the state of Bahia, Brazil, and neighboring areas
First published: 1935 (English translation, 1984)

> *Principal characters:*
> ANTÔNIO BALDUÍNO (BALDO), the black protagonist, a street-gang leader, song composer, fighter, and labor leader
> JUBIABÁ, an old voodoo priest of the *candomblé* or *macumba* sect
> OLD LUÍSA, Antônio's aunt, who reared him
> ZE CAMARÃO, a storyteller, singer, *capoeira* fighter, and Antônio's teacher
> AMELIA, a white cook who beats young Antônio
> VIRIATO, a dwarf
> GORDO, Antônio's best friend, highly religious
> LUIGI, Antônio's trainer, later a part owner of a circus
> JOANA, one of Antônio's lovers
> MARIA DOS REIS, another of Antônio's lovers
> ROSENDA ROSEDÁ, a circus-ballet performer, another of Antônio's lovers
> LINDINALVA PEREIRA, a rich white girl, later a poor prostitute, whom Antônio loves
> GUSTAVINHO, Lindinalva's illegitimate son
> GUSTAVO BARREIRA, Gustavinho's father, an ambitious lawyer

The Novel

Although *Jubiabá* is named for an old voodoo priest, the novel relates the romantic, adventurous life of Antônio Balduíno, a black hero of the Bahian masses. The loose, episodic story begins with Antônio's childhood and continues through his mid-twenties. An ABC ballad at the end tells of his death at the hands of a treacherous murderer. Antônio thus realizes his lifelong ambition to become the subject of an ABC ballad.

The novel opens on a brief boxing match, showing Antônio, the Bahian heavy-weight champion, beating the Central European Champion, a blond German, to the delight of the partisan Bahian crowd. Chapter 2 quickly switches back to Antônio's childhood. As an eight-year-old, he lives with his old aunt, Luísa, and roams Capa-Negro Hill with his playmates, whom he leads into mischief. He does not attend school, but he imbibes a rich folklore from the poor people around him, especially Zé Camarão and old Jubiabá. For example, Jubiabá explains that Capa-Negro Hill got its name from a cruel white master who castrated slaves for not reproducing. Jubiabá also tells about Zumbi dos Palmares, a slave who ran away and led a warlike confederation of other runaways. Zumbi dos Palmares becomes Antônio's hero.

When his aunt goes crazy (and eventually dies), the twelve-year-old Antônio is adopted by a well-to-do white family, the Pereiras, who live on Zumbi dos Palmares Street. The Pereiras give him some schooling and light servant's duties and make him a companion of Lindinalva, their daughter. Yet Amelia, the white cook, beats him constantly and, when he is fifteen, accuses him of looking at Lindinalva's legs. Punished severely, Antônio runs away. He completes his growing up on the seafront streets of Salvador, where he leads a gang of intimidating young "beggars" and sleeps with girls on the nearby sand dunes. After two years, the police break up his gang by arresting the members and beating them.

Antônio returns to Capa-Negro Hill, where he learns *capoeira* fighting and guitar playing from Zé Camarão. He earns his livelihood by composing and selling an occasional samba, which invariably makes the Bahian hit parade, but he spends most of his time attending parties, festivals, and Jubiabá's wild *macumba* sessions and making love to Joana, Maria dos Reis, and other eager girls. His life takes an especially exciting turn when, discovered and trained by Luigi, he becomes a professional boxer. Known as Baldo the Negro, he demolishes all competition. He appears to be bound for Rio de Janeiro and North America, but then he learns of Lindinalva's engagement on the day of a big bout, gets drunk, and is knocked out by Miguez the Peruvian.

Antônio now begins a two year period of wandering. Ashamed and in disgrace, he sails on the *Homeless Traveler* up the Paraguaçu River to the tobacco country, where he and his pal Gordo work in the tobacco fields. Without women, he becomes so desperate that he lusts after a twelve-year-old girl at her mother's wake, even though the bloated corpse eyes him accusingly. He eventually gets into a knife fight with the boss, Zequinha. Thinking that he has killed Zequinha (who lives but wants revenge), Antônio flees and evades a massive manhunt. Hopping a train, he winds up in Feira de Santana, where he again meets Luigi, now part owner of a near-bankrupt circus. Antônio joins the circus, fighting challengers or the bear and falling in love with Rosenda Rosedá, the sexy black ballerina. When the circus fails, he, Rosenda, and the bear return to Salvador.

In Salvador, the bear goes to Gordo, and Antônio and Rosenda eventually split up. Again Antônio hears of Lindinalva, whose fortunes have meanwhile plummeted. Her father died bankrupt, and her fiancé left her pregnant. So, after the baby was born, Lindinalva turned to prostitution. The changes in her name marked her decline: Lindinalva, Linda, Freckles. Now, physically spent, she is dying, and on her deathbed she evokes a promise from Antônio to help Amelia care for little Gustavinho. Antônio goes to work as a stevedore, just in time to become involved in a bitter strike. Ironically, the workers' negotiator is the lawyer Gustavo Barreira, Gustavinho's father, who sells out to the owners. The workers reject Barreira's watered-down deal, however, as well as Barreira himself; the strike continues, spreads to other workers throughout the city, and becomes violent. With Antônio as one of their leaders, the workers hold out and triumph totally, winning all of their demands, including a 100 percent raise.

The Characters

There is a large cast of colorful characters in *Jubiabá*, but most of them exist only to fill out the cast or to add color. Amado's concept of character in *Jubiabá* is strictly ad hoc—whatever serves the purpose of the moment, usually some need of the rambling plot or diffuse theme. Poor, working-class characters make brief appearances, providing varied exhibits of how the working class is ground down. Some of these characters also allow for momentary diversions, often sentimental or titillating. For example, Ricardo the tobacco worker shows the plight of womanless men: He lies in his bunk, fantasizes about a picture of a nude actress on the wall, and masturbates. Then, in a bit of overdone irony, he accidentally blows off his hands with a bomb.

Like Ricardo, several other characters seem to be walking sideshows (some are actually in the circus, such as the Snake-Man). At least one of these serves a higher function, Viriato the dwarf, a member of Antônio's street gang. After the gang is broken up, Viriato becomes so despondent that he drowns himself; when his corpse is pulled from the harbor, crabs can be heard rattling around inside his abdominal cavity. In the novel, Viriato's gruesome death comes to represent one important alternative, "the road home" which Antônio sometimes contemplates and which other working-class characters take.

Some characters exist mainly to satisfy the needs of Antônio. Antônio needs a teacher, so Zé Camarão is invented. Antônio needs a street gang, so the gang is invented. Antônio needs lovers, so Joana, Maria dos Reis, and countless nameless girls are invented. Exceptions here are Lindinalva Pereira and Rosenda Rosedá, whose characters are somewhat more developed, but even they do not escape a stereotyped treatment. Rosenda is sexy and sassy, while Lindinalva is pretty and pathetic. The young women, incidentally, tend to satisfy not only Antônio's needs but also the most demanding macho expectations. Rosenda's breasts are said to fill a room, and Maria dos Reis gets so excited at a *macumba* session that she falls to the floor foaming at both the mouth and genitals.

Even Jubiabá, despite having the novel named after him, exists primarily through his relationship to Antônio. The old priest is interesting in himself, but his marvelous voodoo skills—which can cure diseases, bring back straying lovers, and wreak revenge—are taken for granted. More important, Jubiabá represents the old spirit of freedom and cultural continuity with the African past. He implants this spirit in young Antônio and intermittently reinforces it: The mysterious priest has time off from his voodoo miracles and *macumba* sessions to show up at the Pereiras, dressed in his Sunday best and out of character, to take young Antônio on instructive visits to old Luísa. Nor does it matter, near the novel's end, that Jubiabá does not understand labor unions and strikes: It remains for his protégé, Antônio, to translate the old spirit of freedom into modern terms.

Despite his macho shallowness—his fighting and loving, relieved by an occasional samba—Antônio's character is even more inconsistent than old Jubiabá's. Antônio, a man who uses women and who lusts after a twelve-year-old girl at her mother's funeral, is presented as a hero. (Supposedly, this lecher was not guilty of looking at Lindinalva's legs.) Supposedly, too, he thinks only of Lindinalva when he loves the other women, and, after not seeing her for years, he immediately becomes her willing slave. This good-time Charlie, who has always eschewed work and responsibilities, is thus converted into a man of commitment: He takes on little Gustavinho (with the help of "kind-hearted" Amelia who had beaten him when he was a child) and the aspirations of the working class.

Themes and Meanings

Antônio's conversion from good-time Charlie to man of commitment embodies the two main themes of *Jubiabá*, which, like Antônio's two phases, seem somewhat inconsistent. On the one hand, Amado celebrates the local color of Bahia, particularly its Afro-Brazilian culture. He refers to local history and waxes poetic about the city of Salvador, its environs, and the sea. He incorporates bits of local folklore songs, superstitions, stories. The richest of this local culture seems to belong to the poor blacks who inhabit Capa-Negro Hill. They enjoy a sense of community, are fun-loving, and have a priest who wields the powers of African voodoo. All of these elements are combined in their religion, whose insistent drums roll out over the town below.

On the other hand, Amado pursues a political theme, championing the downtrodden poor (who include those happy blacks on Capa-Negro Hill). Beautiful Bahia, it seems, is rife with social injustice. Examples of victims abound, from assorted individuals to Antônio's street gang to the tobacco workers to prostitutes to the dockworkers. Their plight is represented most poignantly by the near-bankrupt circus, whose performers go on display and risk their lives daily but rarely earn enough to make ends meet. If the poor worker's life is a crazy circus, there is always a way out—Viriato the Dwarf's way. Yet a better way, Amado suggests, is to fight back—to go on strike, shut down the city, and take power into one's own hands. Why should the circus's hungry lion cry, when it can eat its trainer?

The slumbering power of the poor is symbolized by the drums rolling out over the city, by the fervor of the *macumba* sessions, and, most of all, by the rippling muscles of Baldo the Negro. His fighting spirit is inherited from Africa and handed on to him by Jubiabá. For a long time, Antônio expends his energy in aimless loving and fighting, in boxing matches and circus acts. Yet even he eventually becomes aware of the lack of purpose in his life. In the end, he learns to love the suffering poor and to direct his fighting spirit at their oppressors.

Critical Context

Any critical estimate of *Jubiabá*—its rambling plot, its inconsistent characters and themes, its uneven style, its gross excesses—must take into account that Amado wrote it during his early twenties: It is a fervent young man's novel. For all its logical disunity and lack of restraint, *Jubiabá* has a powerful unity of feeling, as Amado announces his loyalties to Bahia, to Afro-Brazilian culture, and to leftist politics. This emotional unity makes *Jubiabá* perhaps the best of Amado's early propagandistic works, certainly a representative example.

Amado's early work long remained untranslated into English; therefore, for readers of English familiar only with his mature work—particularly such comic, sexy bestsellers as *Gabriela, cravo e canela* (1958; *Gabriela, Clove and Cinnamon*, 1962), *Dona Flor e seus dois maridos* (1966; *Dona Flor and Her Two Husbands*, 1969), and *Tiêta do Agreste* (1977; *Tieta, the Goat Girl*, 1979)—his early propagandistic phase may come as a surprise. Yet, as a formative novel, *Jubiabá* forecasts much of the later Amado. Although he toned down his politics (after repeated clashes with censors, jail terms, and exiles), no one can deny Amado's continuing interest in local color and sex; nor, if his techniques have become more refined, can he be accused of developing inhibitions or restraint. With his political sympathies, his panorama of local color and characters, and his lack of restraint (whether sentimental or sexual), Amado might be called the twentieth century Brazilian Charles Dickens.

Bibliography
Chamberlain, Bobby J. *Jorge Amado*. Boston: Twayne, 1990. Useful, informative, and readable, this critical analysis of Amado's work covers all periods of the novelist's output while focusing on a few of the author's most important works. A biographical chapter is included, along with an extensive bibliography.
Hinchberger, Bill. "Jorge Amado Writes from Heart, Home." *Variety* 366 (March 31, 1997): 56. Hinchberger explores the inspirations that shape Amado's work, the filming of Amado's novels, and Amado's reaction to the critical acclaim he has received. Offers interesting insight into the influences that shaped Amado's work.
Robitaille, L. B. "These Men of Letters Speak for the Powerless." *World Press Review* 38 (December, 1991): 26-27. An intriguing profile of Amado, covering his political activity, his life in Paris, and his feelings for his native Brazil. Presents background that sheds considerable light on his writings.

Harold Branam

JUBILEE

Author: Margaret Walker (1915-   )
Type of plot: Historical realism
Time of plot: The 1840's through the 1860's
Locale: Dawson, Georgia, and Abbeville, Troy, Luverne, and Greenville, in
    south-central Alabama
First published: 1966

> *Principal characters:*
>> VYRY, the protagonist, a slave of the Dutton family and the daughter of
>> her master, John Morris Dutton
>> RANDALL WARE, a free black man who is Vyry's husband in a slave
>> ceremony
>> INNIS BROWN, Vyry's husband after emancipation
>> JOHN MORRIS DUTTON, the master of the plantation, Vyry's father by a
>> slave
>> SALINA (BIG MISSY) DUTTON, John Dutton's wife
>> LILLIAN DUTTON, the daughter of John and Salina
>> JOHNNY DUTTON, the son of John and Salina
>> ED GRIMES, the overseer of the Dutton plantation

The Novel

Jubilee follows the protagonist, Vyry, from the age of two, when her twenty-nine-year-old mother dies after having borne fifteen children, many of them to the master of the plantation, through the Civil War and Emancipation, finally leaving her in her own home at Greenville, Alabama, with the knowledge that her children will be educated. The novel is unified by the central character Vyry, who comes to represent all of the thwarted aspirations of the slaves; by the continuing associations of the principal characters who survive into the Reconstruction period; and by the theme of freedom, embodied in the hopeful spiritual from which comes the title of the book.

Jubilee is divided into three equal sections. In the first, the orphaned child becomes accustomed to the loss of those whom she loves: of Mammy Sukey, who had mothered her in infancy and who dies of a "plague" brought by a new slave; of Aunt Sally, the slave cook, sold because of rumors of poisonings on other plantations. Later, this pattern of loss is continued when Vyry's husband, Randall Ware, a free black man, and therefore suspect, flees North, begging Vyry to leave their two children and escape with him. Because she insists on taking her children Jim and Minna, Vyry is caught, and the section ends with her being beaten almost to the point of death.

The second section involves suffering and loss both for blacks and for whites. John Morris Dutton dies of gangrene after an accident, his promise to free the slaves either unkept by him or unheeded by Salina Dutton. Both Johnny Dutton, the young heir, and Lillian Dutton's young husband die of wounds received on the battlefield. As the

Yankees approach, Salina dies of a stroke, and after the house is ransacked, Lillian's already precarious sanity is lost forever. After she and her children are turned over to relatives, Vyry and her new husband, Innis Brown, leave the plantation to find a place of their own. Having heard that Randall Ware has died, Vyry feels free to build a new future.

In the third section of the book, Vyry and Innis wander through Alabama, settling first on swampy, malarial land which they must leave, then on a tenant farm where they are in effect enslaved again, later outside a hilly town from which they are driven by the Ku Klux Klan, and finally at Greenville, Alabama, where they find a permanent refuge. In the final section of the novel, Vyry must choose between the bitter, militant Randall Ware, who has at last found her, and Innis Brown, who, though poor and un-educated, finds himself inspired by Vyry's spiritual leadership. When Vyry reveals the scars of her whipping and asserts her Christian forgiveness of those who whipped her and of all whites who abused her, Ware and Brown are both awed by her depth of character and accept her primacy as a true mother of her race.

The Characters

Because Margaret Walker wishes to make the novel about her real great-grandmother Vyry a realistic picture of two decades in the South, she chooses in *Jubilee* to write as an omniscient author, venturing onto the Confederate battlefields and into the minds of the slave owners and tracing the adventures of Vyry's husband, Randall Ware, when he has been assumed to be dead. Yet all the characters in *Jubilee* and all the events are important to Vyry, who is Walker's admirable heroine. During slave days, Vyry is intelligent enough to survive. She learns to work hard and to avoid confrontations, particularly with Salina Dutton, who hates this slave-born offspring of her own husband even more because Vyry resembles Salina's daughter Lillian. She learns to be skeptical of the easy promises of her white father and of the courting gestures of her admirers. As one by one her protectors vanish from her life, Vyry must depend on her own strength. During the later days of the war and the Occupation, it is Vyry's leadership and her practical good sense which enable the surviving whites and the remaining blacks on the plantation to cope with the dangers of disease and starvation. Above all, through her living Christianity Vyry subdues hatred and bitterness, and because of a typical charitable act, she gains for her family a home and a place in the community.

Vyry's two husbands are very different from each other. Randall Ware, the free black, is well educated and intelligent but consumed by his hatred of whites and of the white Christian God. The stable and hardworking Innis Brown lacks Vyry's faith in education, which he sees as denying him the field help which he needs. His whipping of Vyry's oldest boy, Jim, Randall Ware's son, comes very close to breaking up the marriage; it is only after Innis sees Vyry's scars that he finally understands why his own violent actions so repel her.

The aristocratic Duttons see themselves as the leaders of the plantation gentry. What his wife and the slaves see as careless irresponsibility, John Morris Dutton thinks of as ambition for leadership in a larger sphere, perhaps state office. Despite Dutton's insistence on the concept of honor, Vyry finds that his promises mean nothing and that he is only infrequently interested in her welfare. To her plea for freedom, his answer is laughter and a patronizing explanation of how much better off she is as a slave. His daughter Lillian shares his good nature but also his weakness. Although she likes little Vyry, her playmate, she is willing to obey her mother's orders to shun her. After the death of her husband and the destruction of the plantation, she loses her mind, perhaps from a blow on the head, but perhaps as much from weakness of character. It is Vyry who must then care for all of the children, Lillian's as well as her own.

No one would accuse Salina Dutton (Big Missy) of weakness. Soon after her marriage, she discovers that she does not like sex or childbearing. She also discovers that her husband is indolent and ineffectual, and that therefore she must run the plantation. With the overseer Ed Grimes, she does so. She is cruel but efficient, and she is able to make a profit. During the war, as loss follows loss, she remains steadfast, sacrificing all of her funds for the Confederate cause. Only a massive stroke can destroy her, ironically, as the Yankee guns boom nearer and nearer to the plantation.

Johnny Dutton believes that he is like his mother, whose strength he admires. Perhaps he would have returned after the war to run the plantation according to her principles. He is shown, however, as a West Pointer who yearns for adventure, not for the duties and the dullness of life on a plantation. Despite his respect for his mother, he may well have inherited his father's irresponsibility without his good nature.

Whether the descendant of slave owners or the descendant of slaves is writing an antebellum novel, the least-sympathetic character is likely to be the landless, harsh overseer. In this novel, Ed Grimes is used by Big Missy and feared by the slaves, on whom he inflicts the cruel punishments that she decrees and others of his own contrivance. Yet Margaret Walker reveals Grimes's own feelings of social inferiority, his resentment of the Duttons, and his discontent with his own lot. It is out of this bitterness that Grimes becomes a Klan leader after the war. As with Big Missy, Walker explores the motivations of Grimes, proving that even an unsympathetic character merits understanding.

Themes and Meanings

Through her own family history, Margaret Walker seeks in *Jubilee* to show plantation life and the early days of freedom through the eyes of the blacks. Although she refuses to divide good from evil on the basis of skin color, she does create a dual world, in which slave owners assume that only foolish or insane slaves could be unhappy, while slaves, pretending to be contented, yearn and plot for freedom. When the Yankees, their longed-for redeemers, do come, the former slaves are disillusioned to find that the Northern deliverers are as unconcerned about the future of the blacks as are their desperate former masters. At this point the theme of the first part of the book, the human longing for freedom, is redefined. Having been freed from slavery under the law, blacks are threatened with economic slavery as tenants or as menials: Furthermore, the threat of violence as effectively stifles their freedom of expression as it did in slave days. After emancipation, blacks must fight for education as the only way out of the new slavery. As Vyry insists in the last pages of the book, however, the will to achieve must come not from bitterness but from spiritual strength, based in the same sense of God's immanence that sustained the slaves in their secret religious meetings in the woods.

Critical Context

Although most of Margaret Walker's work has been in the form of poetry, her novel *Jubilee* is important both because of its carefully researched re-creation of two decades of black history and because of Walker's insistence on transcending the level of propaganda, with stereotyped characters and bitter invective, to which any mistreated people may descend. Surprised to hear Big Missy called monstrous, Walker denied the charge. Given Salina's sexual ignorance, her husband's demands, and the living evidence of his invasions of the slave quarters, Salina reacts, not virtuously, says Walker, but understandably. Like her great-grandmother, Margaret Walker draws her strength from compassionate understanding.

Also like her great-grandmother, Walker sees hope for the future in a dynamic, spiritual Christianity. Commenting on the materialism of white society, Walker has suggested that the great gift of blacks to white America can be their spirituality, which sustains them now as it always has in times of trial and challenge.

Bibliography

Alexander, Margaret Walker. "The Fusion of Ideas: An Interview with Margaret Walker Alexander." Interview by Maryemma Graham. *African American Review* 27 (Summer, 1993): 279-286. Although the focus of the interview is on Walker's *This Is My Century*, the exchange offers useful insights as Walker discusses her lengthy career, the Civil Rights movement, and her approaches to literature.

Baraka, Amiri. "Margaret Walker Alexander." *Nation* 268 (January 4, 1999): 32-33. A tribute to Walker and an appreciation of her contributions to the Civil Rights movement as well as an assessment of her works.

Carmichael, Jacqueline M. *Trumpeting a Fiery Sound: History and Folklore in Margaret Walker's "Jubilee."* Athens: University of Georgia Press, 1998. Carmichael presents a thorough analysis of Walker's historicist approach and the use of folk motifs in the novel.

Debo, Annette. "Margaret Walker." In *Contemporary African American Novelists: A Bio-Bibliographical Critical Sourcebook*, edited by Emmanuel S. Nelson. Westport, Conn.: Greenwood Press, 1999. Debo provides a biographical and critical assessment of Walker's works as well as a primary and secondary bibliography for further study.

Draper, James P., ed. *Black Literature Criticism*. 3 vols. Detroit: Gale Research, 1992. Includes an extensive biographical profile of Walker and excerpts from criticism on her works.

Walker, Margaret. *How I Wrote "Jubilee" and Other Essays on Life and Literature.* Edited by Maryemma Graham. New York: Feminist Press at City University of New York, 1990. Walker gives a detailed account of the creative process of shaping her novel. Also included are other illuminating essays by Walker on black women writers and the black aesthetic.

Ward, Jerry W., Jr. "Black South Literature: Before Day Annotations." *African American Review* 27 (Summer, 1993): 315-326. Ward presents a useful bibliography of criticism on Walker's works. He comments on *Jubilee* and discusses its adaptation as an opera in 1977.

Rosemary M. Canfield Reisman

JUST ABOVE MY HEAD

Author: James Baldwin (1924-1987)
Type of plot: Ethnic realism
Time of plot: The 1940's to the 1970's
Locale: New York City; Birmingham, Alabama; Paris; and London
First published: 1979

> *Principal characters:*
> HALL MONTANA, the narrator
> ARTHUR MONTANA, a gospel singer, Hall's brother
> JULIA MILLER, a child evangelist
> JIMMY MILLER, Julia's brother, Arthur's accompanist and lover
> JOEL MILLER, Julia and Jimmy's father and Julia's incestuous lover
> CRUNCH, a member of the Trumpets of Zion musical group
> GUY LAZAR, Arthur's lover in Paris

The Novel

Just Above My Head is divided into five books. The first opens when Hall Montana receives word that his younger brother, thirty-nine-year-old Arthur Montana, a renowned gospel singer, has died, presumably of a heart attack, in the basement men's room in a restaurant in London. Hall, who is forty-six when Arthur dies, has great difficulty reconciling himself to the death of his brother, an active homosexual. It is he, through reflective and extended flashbacks, who relates the story of his brother's life. In doing so, Hall also reveals how his younger brother helped him to gain insights into love and the meaning of life. At the beginning of book 5 of the novel, Hall Montana calls his story "a love song to my brother." It is the younger brother who teaches the older, who causes him to gain new perceptions.

Hall and Arthur Montana have known the Millers since the thirteen-year-old Arthur met eleven-year-old Julia in a Pentecostal church in which he was singing and she was preaching. Both Julia and her brother, Jimmy, children of Joel and Amy Miller, are precocious. Julia has been a child evangelist with a large following from the time she was nine years old. Jimmy, two years younger than his sister, is a good musician. Amy Miller dies shortly after the Millers and the Montanas meet, and her widower, Joel, soon seduces Julia, who has a continuing affair with her father.

Still in his teens, Arthur joins the Trumpets of Zion, a gospel singing quartet, and tours with them. He rooms with Crunch, another member of the group, on tour, and the two soon fall into a love affair. Arthur struggles with guilt about his homosexuality but is confirmed in his lifestyle. When the quartet disbands after touring the South, Arthur continues to tour on his own.

Meanwhile, Julia, at fourteen, has given up preaching and for the next few years is enmeshed in her incestuous affair with Joel. Then Crunch, having been drafted to serve in Korea, passes through New York and has a fleeting affair with Julia, who finds herself pregnant by him. When her father discovers this, he beats Julia severely and the fetus is aborted.

The scene now shifts to five years later. Hall, who had also been drafted to serve in Korea, is now thirty. He is out of the service and is living and working in San Francisco. On a trip to New York, he looks up Julia, now a comely model, and the two fall in love. Jimmy is living with Julia, and he and Arthur meet each other again. Julia and Hall continue their affair for some time. Hall wants to marry Julia, but she instead decides to go to Abidjan in West Africa, where she has an affair with an African chieftain.

A forlorn Hall leaves New York and joins Arthur, who is on a singing tour of the South with his former Trumpets of Zion cohort, Peanuts. Racial strife is at its height at this time, and in the course of their Southern tour, Peanuts disappears, never to be found. Presumably he is a victim of the racial unrest that was rife in the 1960's.

Hall returns to New York, where he joins the staff of a black magazine, marries a woman named Ruth, and fathers two children, Tony and Odessa. Meanwhile, Arthur goes to Paris, where he meets a French businessman named Guy Lazar, who helps Arthur live with his guilt about his homosexuality and come to grips with his inmost racial conflicts.

Again the time shifts many years ahead. Hall is at home alone, while his wife and children have gone to the theater. He is reflecting on Arthur's death when Jimmy comes by. Jimmy and Arthur had fallen into a serious affair after Arthur's return from Paris, and the affair had lasted for fourteen years. Jimmy had been Arthur's most sensitive accompanist, and the two had always had a great affinity for each other.

It is revealed that Arthur had gone alone to London on what proved to be his last trip because he and Jimmy had had a lover's quarrel. Jimmy struggles with his guilt about having quarreled with Arthur and about not having reconciled before Arthur's death, but he has coped with his guilt by going to all the places where he and Arthur had performed and playing alone. Although Hall himself is not homosexual, he has come to understand and honor Arthur, to accept his need to love men. The book ends on a note of resignation. Hall has a dream in which he and Julia, and Jimmy and Arthur, are on the porch of a house sheltered from the rain, harmonious and protected.

The time frame of *Just Above My Head* is not always easy to follow, despite the pains that James Baldwin took to keep it consistent. Book 1 begins with Arthur's death and moves back to give the recent history of the Montana family. Book 2 begins two years after Arthur's death, and it presents background material about the Montanas and the Millers. It also gives details about Julia's evangelistic preaching and of Arthur's association with the Trumpets of Zion. It tells of Hall's and Crunch's being drafted to serve in Korea.

Book 3 begins five years after Hall's return from Korea and continues through Julia's leaving for Africa and Hall's joining Arthur and Peanuts on their Southern tour. Book 4 focuses on Arthur's prolonged stay in Paris and on his affair with Guy Lazar. Finally, book 5 brings the reader back to Hall's house on a Sunday afternoon in winter two years after Arthur's death and fills in many of the details of the intervening fourteen years.

The Characters

The only fully realized character in *Just Above My Head* is Hall Montana. As the narrator, he is present in every scene. Although he is seven years Arthur's senior, he learns much from Arthur. Indeed, through Arthur, his whole philosophy of life is changed drastically. Arthur helps Hall to understand how a man can love another man, and Hall comes to accept this phenomenon without moral judgment, as merely an alternative form of loving.

Julia, one of the novel's more compelling characters, is, nevertheless, quite stereotypical. A somewhat offensive prodigy who preaches until she is fourteen, Julia ultimately becomes deeply disturbed by her incestuous relationship with her father: "Every thrust of her father's penis seemed to take away the life that it had given, thrust anguish deeper into her, into a place too deep for the sex of any man to reach." Julia is too sexually distorted to think of marriage, although she is capable of leading a life that is fulfilling in other ways. Her way of loving is as far from conventional as Arthur's is, although it is on the surface somewhat less noticeable to society as being divergent.

Although the book's narrative is generated by Arthur's death, Arthur in many ways remains a secondary character. He lives with conflict generated, on the one hand, from his guilt about being homosexual and, on the other hand, from the racial situation that becomes progressively tense during the course of his life. He is a reasonably well-adjusted person despite his conflicts. The suggestion that Guy Lazar in a few nights of love is able to eradicate most of Arthur's conflicts, however, seems naïve.

Jimmy is a relatively flat character, overshadowed in the book by the more enticing Julia and by Hall and Arthur. Talented and reasonably secure, Jimmy is able to cope with his guilt over being homosexual and over having the quarrel with Arthur that caused him to go to London. He has regrets, but these regrets do not keep him from going on, from forming a productive life for himself.

In *Just Above My Head*, Baldwin presents a large number of characters, but most of them are unrealized. The reader never comes to know Hall's wife or his children, for example, nor are such characters as Crunch and Peanuts developed to the point that they are more than apparitions. This lack of development is not really a handicap in the novel, however, because Hall's development is so well handled. The other characters essentially contribute to that development but, aside from Julia, do not develop significantly themselves.

Themes and Meanings

Just Above My Head is largely an exploration of types of human love, although the book contains a strong subtheme that involves racial conflict. Eldridge Cleaver had attacked Baldwin in *Soul on Ice* (1968) for abandoning racial matters in some of his earlier books in favor of concentrating on homosexual themes. *Just Above My Head* was presumably an answer to Cleaver's attack. Although Baldwin was unwilling to abandon his homosexual theme totally in favor of writing about racial matters, he sought to merge the two concerns in this book.

The novel is also very much concerned with music and with the effects that gospel music has on the lives of black people. The individual books begin with lyrics from gospel songs, and elements of these lyrics permeate the novel both in direct quotation and in the rhythms and vernacular of Baldwin's own writing.

Indeed, the novel's concerns go beyond music and also explore some aspects of evangelism, focusing on the not uncommon phenomenon of the child evangelist, presumably divinely inspired to go forth and do the Lord's work. The interweaving of this evangelism with sexual love, particularly incestuous sexual love between a pubescent evangelist and her father, offers a provocative theme to explore.

Critical Context

Just Above My Head was published following a period when much literary attention had been focused on two of its major concerns, homosexuality and racial conflict. Twenty-three years earlier, Baldwin had written *Giovanni's Room* (1956), which was one of many postwar homosexual works, including Gore Vidal's *The City and the Pillar* (1948), Truman Capote's *Other Voices, Other Rooms* (1948), Alberto Moravia's *Two Adolescents* (1948), James Barr's *Quatrefoil* (1950), Arthur A. Peters's *Finistère* (1951), Tennessee Williams's *Cat on a Hot Tin Roof* (1955), and Edward Albee's *The Zoo Story* (1959). Baldwin's presentation of the homosexual theme of *Just Above My Head* would have been quite revolutionary in the late 1940's or early 1950's, but by the late 1970's, when the book appeared, the theme had come to be quite easily accepted.

Also, the racial anger which had spilled over into many of the books of the Black Revolution, and which Baldwin had addressed to some extent in *Notes of a Native Son* (1955), had been considerably dissipated by 1979. The festering fury evident in the contributions that make up *Black Fire* (1968), which LeRoi Jones (Amiri Baraka) and Larry Neal edited, and the militant anger seen in such LeRoi Jones plays as *The Baptism* (1964), *Dutchman* (1964), *The Slave* (1964) and *The Toilet* (1964) are not present in *Just Above My Head*. Racial rage, such as that expressed by Malcolm X in *The Autobiography of Malcolm X* (1965), is also not present in the Baldwin novel or in any of the significant literature of the last years of the 1970's, largely because social conditions affecting blacks had begun to change and racial pride had begun in most quarters to replace racial anger. *Just Above My Head* is more a statement of sorrow about racial inequalities than one of rage.

Bibliography

Campbell, James. *Talking at the Gates: A Life of James Baldwin.* New York: Viking, 1991. A good narrative biography, with detailed notes and bibliography.

Kinnamon, Keneth, ed. *James Baldwin.* Englewood Cliffs, N.J.: Prentice-Hall, 1974. A part of the Twentieth Century Views series, this collection contains some important appraisals of Baldwin's work and career by Langston Hughes, Eldridge Cleaver, and Sherley Anne Williams, among others.

Macebuh, Stanley. *James Baldwin: A Critical Study.* New York: Third Press, 1973. A good presentation of the social and historical background of Baldwin's work.

Standley, Fred L., and Nancy V. Burt, eds. *Critical Essays on James Baldwin*. Boston: G. K. Hall, 1988. A collection of contemporary reviews and essays covering Baldwin's entire career.

Sylvander, Carolyn Wedin. *James Baldwin*. New York: Frederick Ungar, 1980. A study that examines in particular the links between Baldwin's works and his life.

Troupe, Quincy, ed. *James Baldwin: The Legacy*. New York: Simon and Schuster, 1989. Equally divided between memoirs of the writer and discussions of his work. Includes a very useful bibliography.

Weatherby, W. J. *James Baldwin: Artist on Fire*. New York: Donald I. Fine, 1989. An important biography written by one of Baldwin's friends. Weatherby is, at times, too close to his subject to be objective.

R. Baird Shuman

KAMOURASKA

Author: Anne Hébert (1916-   )
Type of plot: Stream of consciousness
Time of plot: 1820-1860
Locale: Quebec Province, Canada
*First published:*1970 (English translation, 1973)

> *Principal characters:*
> ELISABETH D'AULNIÈRES, first the wife of Antoine Tassy and then of
>   Jérôme Rolland
> DR. GEORGE NELSON, a handsome physician and Elisabeth's lover
> ANTOINE TASSY, the squire of Kamouraska and the debauched and
>   abusive husband of Elisabeth
> AURÉLIE CARON, an adolescent companion and later maid to Elisabeth
> JÉRÔME ROLLAND, a solid member of the upper middle-class,
>   Elisabeth's second husband
> ADÉLAIDE,
> LUCE-GERTRUDE, and
> ANGÉLIQUE LANOUETTE, maiden aunts of Elisabeth
> MME CAROLINE TASSY, Antoine's indulgent but domineering mother

The Novel

Kamouraska presents the psychological drama of Elisabeth d'Aulnières in a series a flashbacks spanning some forty years. As Hébert herself states on the copyright page, she based her novel of passion and murder on real people and historical events of the 1830's in Sorel and Kamouraska, in the Quebec Province of French Canada.

As she nurses Jérôme Rolland, her dying husband, the first-person narrator-heroine reveals her mysterious past during a horrifying night of alternating insomnia and drug-induced sleep. Her story jumps back and forth from September, 1840, when she was formally accused of complicity in the murder of Antoine Tassy, her first husband, and her subsequent trial and brief imprisonment; she remembers with resentment and even hatred how her still-unnamed lover safely escaped across the Canadian American frontier to Burlington, Vermont, leaving her alone to face police and prosecutors and the finger-pointing people of her hometown. That is why it became essential to remarry quickly so as to recover her honor as an honest woman. Despite Elisabeth's eighteen years of selfless devotion, if not love, and eight children, Rolland, now on his deathbed, not only is afraid that she might poison him but also seeks to elicit her confession of sin.

At other times, Mme Rolland relives her childhood and adolescence with her socially correct widowed mother and spinster aunts, when she would rebel against their straitlaced upbringing by chasing after the Sorel boys in the company of her sexually precocious contemporary Aurélie Caron. Terrorized by demons and nightmares, Elisabeth imagines in her fevered mind Tassy's violent death at the hand of Dr. George Nelson, who had been her lover, and she visualizes the blood on the snow outside her in-laws' Kamouraska estate, not unlike the blood-red rose she had been embroidering when Dr. Nelson called on her after an illness.

Next in Elisabeth's surging memories, Aurélie testifies at the murder trial of the affair between the doctor and her mistress, which the aunts swear never took place. Yet juxtaposed with these angry denials is Elisabeth's shocking conduct with George, which she justifies by showing how increasingly abusive and debauched Tassy was becoming to her. That Nelson and Tassy had been schoolmates and rivals only adds to the piquancy of the situation.

However, George too carries psychological scars, since his father sent him to Canada to be educated in a Catholic school, where he is a foreigner and is constantly reminded that as a Protestant he will never enter Heaven. Through his good, selfless work as a physician, he hopes finally to be accepted by his community, but to no avail.

In going back and forth in her mind between her present home in Quebec City and Sorel, where she had returned after her humiliation at Antoine's hands, she finds passion, even salvation, in her lover's arms until she encourages him to consider murdering her husband. First, both bribe Aurélie to poison Tassy, thereby preserving their alibi and innocence. When the maid fails in her attempt, the only recourse left is for the lover to do the deed himself. After a two-hundred-mile trip through snow and cold, Nelson shoots Tassy dead and then bludgeons him, splattering blood on the pure snow, his clothes, hands, sleigh, and coverlet.

The pace of events then accelerates as Elisabeth follows in her mind her lover's rapid progress and escape to the United States, which refused to extradite him, leading to the dismissal of the charges against him. She waits to hear from him, but his letter is not delivered until many years later. To protect the Tassy and d'Aulnières names, both families conspire to save her from the death penalty; only Aurélie is jailed for her attempted poisoning.

At the time of the story's narration, Kamouraska has burned to the ground, all its inhabitants have died or are dying, and George Nelson has disappeared somewhere in America. A mysterious figure is watching and following Elisabeth; it may be Aurélie as Elisabeth's conscience. Elisabeth has only her memory and the constant reminder of her crime as she cries, alone, at the novel's end.

The Characters

In re-creating the circumstances of a historical murder, Hébert concentrates on depths of personality rather than development, portraying characters whose origins are in the Romantic literature of their time and place. Elisabeth has three identities. To her mother and aunts, she is "la Petite" ("the Little One"), to be protected from a nasty world. At sixteen, torn between sexual desire and a need for virtue, she becomes the wife of Antoine Tassy. Battered by a husband she does not love, she nevertheless willingly accepts sexual abuse. Her subsequent adultery and manipulation of her lover to murder Tassy are her acts of defiance against the laws of marriage and society. Finally, as Mme Rolland, she seeks to escape criminal responsibility through self-deceit and duplicity. Acting in bad faith, she distorts the past to accommodate her present, as she had earlier blamed her maid and her lover for her own lack of moral strength. With her second husband dying, she finds herself alone, living behind a mask of wifely innocence, deprived of the salutary and cathartic effects of punishment.

An American living in Canada, George Nelson is an outsider and, as a Protestant, lost and cursed. Doomed in his quest for acceptance, he vainly tries to find a redeeming love with Elisabeth by fulfilling her wish to rid themselves of Tassy. Following a mad ride, tortured by the enormity and horror of his deed, he tells his apprentice that "that damned woman" has ruined him.

Antoine Tassy, Elisabeth's depraved and abusive husband, finds in drink and sex an escape from his failures. Immature and full of contradictions, he is dominated by a cold and unfeeling mother who tolerates and even encourages his depravity, the better to control him and reign as the grand lady of Kamouraska. Often threatening to kill himself, his wife, or both together, he is much too weak-willed actually to do anything.

As the sexually aware companion and maid to Elisabeth, Aurélie Caron witnesses her escapades and becomes the confidante of her unhappiness. Moreover, because of her reputation as a sorceress, Aurélie is endowed with extraordinary influence. She encourages her young employer to pursue Nelson and goes so far as to accept beautiful clothes for trying to poison Tassy. At the murder trial, she testifies against Elisabeth but is viciously attacked by the three aunts as a lying and spiteful slut. For her conduct, she goes to jail for two years, while Elisabeth has her case dismissed after a few weeks of imprisonment.

The other characters, while contributing to the reader's understanding of the main protagonists, have a limited psychology. Jérôme Rolland indirectly forces his wife to confront her past and assume her guilt, while the well-meaning Lanouette sisters, fearing scandal above all, defend their niece at the risk of losing their own souls.

Themes and Meanings

"Murderous love. Treacherous love. Deadly love. Love. Love. The only living thing in the world. The madness of love." In the first pages, Elisabeth states one of the overriding themes of her life, as her search for a sentimentality found in girlish stories and sexual gratification can only be destructive to her and to George and Antoine. Despite an unblemished, though loveless, second marriage, she realizes the dark truths at the center of her story: Blighted love is a form of bondage, death provides a terrible freedom, and murder injures the survivors and culprit as well as the victim.

Kamouraska also points out the tragic aspects of one woman's rebellion against her traditionally subjugated role in society and her victimization in a harsh land. Dissatisfied with the standards of behavior imposed by her widowed mother and maiden aunts, unable to compete against men, and yet questing for an identity and a virtue that would affirm her presence in the world, she can only use her beauty and virginity as bartering chips in her struggle between the subterranean world of her femininity and the world of daily existence.

In addition, fate in its various representations is another ruling force that afffects the central characters, female and male. They believe that they are haunted by an ancient curse; they think that they have inherited from Adam a nature so sinful that there is no hope for them. Elisabeth is driven by a sexual frenzy she cannot control; the self-destructive Tassy, a product of his physical and family environment, must find rest in death, either by suicide or murder; George is a cursed alien who is forever destined to remain an outsider.

A mostly unchanging nature testifies further to this sense of fatalism; the impersonal, perhaps infernal, power of the natural world adds to the depiction of doomed relationships as well. In the end, for Hébert, the protagonists' haunting sense of guilt, unrelieved by expiation, sullies and destroys them.

Critical Context

Violence has been a pronounced characteristic of Canadian writing, seemingly born out of the inevitable clash between two orders of reality—a confining and strictured society and the need for expression of unbridled, passionate love. Hébert examines how people react in such a situation, often questioning the role of women by treating conflicts of instinct and repression. An early example in her fiction, "Le Torrent" (from a 1950 collection, *Le Torrent*, published in English as *The Torrent* in 1973), presents themes and techniques that reappear in *Kamouraska*. Similarly, violence and even murder were issues for Hébert in radio and stage plays that she wrote in the 1950's and 1960's. Most important is her first novel, *Les Chambres de bois* (1958; *The Silent Rooms*, 1974), in which the heroine, whose unsuccessful quest for happiness is told not in a conventional, sequential chronology but through a series of fitfully narrated scenes, already embodies several of Elisabeth's desires and frustrations.

Among Hébert's later works, two stand out in particular. One, *Les Fous de Bassan* (1982; *In the Shadow of the Wind*, 1983), is a fascinating Faulknerian investigation of a rape and murder told from the viewpoint of six different narrators. The other, a 1989 play, *La Cage* ("the cage"), tells of the murder of the heroine's husband as the inevitable result of an impossible love affair.

Exquisite control of tone, delicate human insight, and above all compassion are qualities that distinguish Hébert's work, communicated through her quasi-poetic use of fragmented, verbless sentences, shattered syntax, and modified stream-of-consciousness technique. By relating a situation through Elisabeth's dual vision, Hébert makes event and memory immediate to the reader through a fascinating use of levels of truth evoked by fictional manipulations of reality as well as of the interior and exterior dimensions of consciousness. Finally, by drawing the past into the present and analyzing how the relationship between truth and reality bears on self-concepts and identity, *Kamouraska* reveals in their infinite variety the truer though oftentimes hidden natures of humankind.

Bibliography

Boak, Denis "*Kamouraska, Kamouraska!*" *Essays in French Literature* 14 (1977): 69-104. An excellent overview of important motifs in the novel, focusing on the themes of witchcraft, absence, and love.

Knight, Kelton W. *Anne Hébert: In Search of the First Garden*. New York: Lang, 1998. A thorough examination of how Hébert uses memory to reconstruct the past and thus explain her characters' present moral dilemmas.

McPherson, Karen S. *Incriminations: Guilty Women/Telling Stories*. Princeton, N.J.: Princeton University Press, 1994. This comparative study of the process and language of incrimination looks at crime, culpability, and survival in modern novels by women, including *Kamouraska*.

Northey, Margot. *The Haunted Wilderness: The Gothic and Grotesque in Canadian Fiction*. Toronto: University of Toronto Press, 1976. The chapter on *Kamouraska*, though brief, is an insightful analysis of Hébert's particular kind of psychological gothic.

Russell, Delbert W. *Anne Hébert*. Boston: Twayne, 1983. A good starting point to and survey of Hébert's life and works to the early 1980's. Useful bibliography, mostly of French-language sources.

Shek, Ben-Z. *French-Canadian and Québécois Novels*. Toronto: Oxford University Press, 1991. A short but highly readable introduction to a rich body of fiction, including *Kamouraska*.

Pierre L. Horn

KATE VAIDEN

Author: Reynolds Price (1933-   )
Type of plot: Psychological realism
Time of plot: 1937 to 1984
Locale: North Carolina and Virginia
First published: 1986

> *Principal characters:*
> KATE VAIDEN, a fifty-seven-year-old woman suffering from cervical
>   cancer
> FRANCES VAIDEN, Kate's mother
> DAN VAIDEN, Kate's father, who murders his wife, then commits
>   suicide
> CAROLINE, Frances Vaiden's sister, who rears Kate
> HOLT PORTER, Caroline's husband
> SWIFT PORTER, Holt and Caroline's son
> WALTER PORTER, Holt and Caroline's son
> GASTON STEGALL, Kate's first love
> DOUGLAS LEE, a boy who impregnates Kate when they are both in their
>   teens

The Novel

Kate Vaiden's protagonist is an aging woman trying to exorcise the demons of her past. She needs to recount the events of her troubled life to the son she abandoned more than forty years ago, when he was four months old, to win his forgiveness. In piecing together her story, Kate discovers much about herself and reveals an impressive inner strength.

In 1984, Kate Vaiden is recovering from cancer surgery. Her life-threatening cervical carcinoma causes her to reflect upon her life and makes her determined to find the son she, as a frightened, unmarried, ashamed seventeen-year-old in a small Southern town, left in the care of her aunt, Caroline Porter. Kate lives near Macon, North Carolina, where her son is reared, but she has suspended all contact with her family there.

From age eleven, Kate's life is melodramatic. Price, however, succeeds in raising the story above its surface sensationalism by focusing on universal truths that direct Kate's life. The only child of Dan and Frances Vaiden, Kate was reared by her Aunt Caroline, Frances's sister.

Early in the novel, Kate has come with her mother from Greensboro, where they live, to Macon, the small town near the Virginia border where Frances was reared, for the funeral of cousin Taswell Porter, recently killed in a motorcycle accident. Frances's husband, however, has refused to attend the funeral, and he is enraged when his wife insists on going. Kate learns late in her life that her father suspected Frances of having an affair with her cousin, Swift Porter, who would surely attend the funeral.

The day after Taswell's burial, Swift asks Frances to go with him to check the grave. Dan Vaiden, smoldering with jealousy, has come to Macon and is stalking his wife. He follows her when she goes into the woods with Swift and, confronting her, fires his revolver, wounding her fatally before turning the gun on himself.

Kate, orphaned at age eleven, is overcome by sorrow, confusion, and guilt. She thinks that if she had accompanied her father when he went to look for her mother, as he asked her to, the deaths might have been avoided. She is too innocent to realize that if she had done so, she too might be dead. The events of this memorable day fester in Kate's troubled mind and color her existence. Price, who in several of his other works has been intensely concerned with how the sins of the fathers are visited upon their children, clearly demonstrates that after the events Dan precipitated, Kate must bear a crushing burden from which she will never be free.

As a result of Kate's early life, she has never been able to trust people. The shattering blow of her parents' deaths heightens her distrust and makes her distant. When she is thirteen, however, Kate has an affair with a sixteen-year-old neighbor, Gaston Stegall. She grows to love Gaston. Just when Kate has begun to find some stability in a relationship, Gaston, now eighteen, joins the Marines. When he is killed during a training exercise, Kate becomes more withdrawn and suspicious than ever. Kate's mother once made her a penny-show garden with a slogan, "People will leave you," that seems prophetic for Kate. If the people she loves do not run away, death will snatch them from her.

Shortly after Gaston's death, Kate is impregnated by Douglas Lee, a youth whom her cousin Walter has rescued from an orphanage and taken to Norfolk to live with him. Walter uses Douglas sexually; Douglas, defiant and retaliatory, impregnates Kate. Rejecting Walter's suggestion that all of them live together in Norfolk after she bears the child, Kate sets out for Raleigh with Douglas.

Fearing, however, that living with Douglas will not work out, she bolts when the train stops in Macon, returning to Aunt Caroline, who sees her through her pregnancy. Kate then tracks down Douglas Lee, now a chauffeur to Whitfield Eller, a blind piano tuner in Raleigh. Soon, Eller is brutally attacked by an unidentified intruder—most likely Douglas, who disappears. Kate takes Douglas's place chauffeuring Eller, who begins to have romantic inclinations toward Kate. Later, Douglas is found dead by his own hand in Eller's bathtub.

Kate goes to Greensboro. She finishes high school by correspondence and works for the next forty years, never communicating with her family. As the novel closes, Kate has established contact with her son, now past forty, who has inherited Walter Porter's house in Norfolk, where he lives and serves in the Navy. Kate is preparing to meet him and tell him her story. The novel ends before they meet. One thing, however, is clear: Kate Vaiden is facing realities that she could not face from the time her parents' violent deaths robbed her of her childlike innocence and confirmed her inherent distrust of people.

The Characters

Kate Vaiden recounts her first-person narrative partly as a means of dealing with her tortured past and partly as a rehearsal of what she will tell her long-lost son, Lee. Price presents Kate as a woman who fears intimacy, who runs from commitment. The people young Kate admits into her life and emotions die: her parents, Gaston Stegall, and Douglas Lee. In her convoluted way, she feels guilt for these deaths. Life for her is easier if she strikes out on her own and shrinks from intimacy, because intimacy— even platonic closeness—threatens her. People are drawn to Kate, but as a part of her self-protective mechanism, she eventually must shun them.

Aunt Caroline Porter is extremely interesting. She is a saintly woman but nobody's fool. She always steps into the breach when she is needed. She rears the orphaned Kate, she sees Kate through her pregnancy, and she ultimately rears Kate's child. On the surface, she seems self-sacrificing, but underlying her actions is deep-seated guilt. Caroline has some inkling that Kate's parents are dead because of her son Swift's romantic involvement with Frances. This is why she insists that Swift break the news of the murder-suicide to Kate. She also realizes that the intentions of her son Walter are not entirely pure when he takes Douglas Lee from the orphanage to live with him. Her good deeds can be viewed as an expiation for her son's bad deeds. Readers learn more about Caroline Porter from what she does than from what she says.

Douglas Lee has a temper, but readers see little of it. He once cut Walter's hand with a knife and, almost certainly, he has beaten Whitfield Eller, the blind piano tuner, although he is never directly accused of the attack. Douglas seethes with internalized anger. He seduces Kate to retaliate for the sexual liberties Walter takes with him. Douglas's suicide is aimed directly at hurting three people: Kate, Walter Porter, and Whitfield Eller.

Gaston Stegall is a sympathetic character who joins the Marines to serve his country in time of war. He never sees active duty; during a training exercise, he unaccountably stands up in the line of fire and is killed. His death is officially labeled a training accident but can legitimately be called a suicide. Price offers no overt motivation for Gaston's brash act; the episode, however, certainly helps the author to build his characterization of Kate Vaiden, because her reaction to Gaston's suicide leads ultimately to her pregnancy and her forty-year absence from Macon.

Holt Porter, Caroline's husband, although a minor character, plays a definite part in building the milieu in which *Kate Vaiden* takes place. Caroline runs the household and makes the decisions. Holt goes along with them, although they certainly cost him both money and the freedom that many people crave in later life. Holt is not exactly the henpecked husband, but he is compliant and dutiful, never complaining, never running from responsibilities that really should never have fallen to him.

Themes and Meanings

In her critical biography of Reynolds Price, Constance Rooke suggests that Price's work is characterized by two conflicting problems, which very much influence his themes and his resolution of those themes. According to Rooke, Price wrestles with the paradox of how one can live a solitary existence without longing for the company of others. People who escape their solitary situations, ironically, quickly realize that they have sacrificed much of their individuality and personal autonomy.

Kate Vaiden is a striking example of Rooke's contention, reached three years before the publication of *Kate Vaiden*. Kate wants, even seeks, love. Every time she allows her heart to become involved with someone else, however, that person leaves her, not infrequently through the most permanent departure of all—death. By the time Kate is eighteen, she loses the four people who mean the most to her.

Rather than jeopardize her emotions again. Kate allows relationships to progress just to the point that they might stand a chance of permanence; then she withdraws. Whitfield Eller begins to think romantically of Kate, but after Douglas kills himself, she takes Eller to the Great Smoky Mountains and leaves him with his aunt.

Kate has a romance with a veteran returned from World War II. Shortly before they are to marry, she tells him her whole life story, which causes him to flee. After she returns to Raleigh as a legal secretary, Kate ceases to pursue romance or to allow it to enter her life.

In much of his writing, particularly in such novels as *The Surface of the Earth* (1975), *The Source of Light* (1981), *Good Hearts* (1988), and *The Tongues of Angels* (1990), Price is obsessed with death and with how it affects the living. He is fascinated as well with the biblical notion that the sins of the fathers are visited upon their children, a theme that cries out from almost every page of *Kate Vaiden*.

Using the cohesive family as a base, Price makes Kate's separation from it more pitiful than would be a relative's separation from a family less steeped in Southern familial tradition. Caroline is the glue that holds the family together, but death, disappointment, and guilt are the forces Price uses to unglue Kate from her family for forty years.

Kate, however, cannot overcome the family ties in which Price so strongly believes. As the novel ends, she is on the brink of forging a new beginning with her son. She has already made her peace with Swift, whose sexual aggressiveness led to her parents' death and to her leaving Macon (because of Swift's advances to her) for Norfolk, where she stayed with her cousin Walter and his ward, Douglas Lee.

Critical Context

Reynolds Price published thirteen books before *Kate Vaiden* appeared. Five of these were novels, including his much-heralded *A Long and Happy Life* (1962). He had produced as well two collections of short fiction, two of poetry, a translation of thirty stories from the Bible, two plays, and a collection of essays.

He finished the first third of *Kate Vaiden* the day before he had surgery for a spinal cancer that nearly killed him, the aftermath of which left him without the use of his legs. In an effort to control the incredible pain he was enduring, Price underwent a course of hypnotism that was aimed at helping him control his pain through posthypnotic suggestion.

The result of this treatment was that Price was put in touch with vivid memories of his early life, going back as far as the first few months of his existence. The result was an outpouring of writing, including his autobiography, *Clear Pictures: First Loves, First Guides* (1989). *Kate Vaiden* assumed a new shape following Price's hypnotism and, upon publication, became both his greatest commercial success and a notable artistic triumph, winning the National Book Critics Circle Award in fiction.

In *Kate Vaiden*, Price connects with many of the feminist concerns of the 1980's, although he does so without overt intention: that is, he did not set out to write a feminist tract. Rather, his picaresque narrative, his occasional use of epistolary technique in the revelation of plot, and his graceful use of flashbacks all result in a book that was precisely right for its time.

Bibliography
Dewey, Joseph. "A Time to Bolt: Suicide, Androgyny, and the Dislocation of the Self in Reynold Price's *Kate Vaiden*." *The Mississippi Quarterly* 45 (Winter, 1991): 9-28. Dewey argues that Price's portrait of Vaiden as a viable female character succeeds because of her disassociation from the limits of gender. He contends that Vaiden emulates male behavior in order to distance herself from her understanding of the female as passive, thereby transcending gender so that the author's male voice speaks through Vaiden while not making her into a male.
Price, Reynolds. *Learning a Trade: A Craftsman's Notebooks, 1955-1997.* Durham, N.C.: Duke University Press, 1998. Price's notebooks offer a rare glimpse of the sometimes tortuous, often glorious creative process that a writer is compelled to engage in if he or she is serious about the craft. Price shares the observations and feelings that led to the writing of *Kate Vaiden* and some of his other novels.
_____. "Narrative Hunger and Silent Witness: An Interview with Reynolds Price." Interview by Susan Ketchin. *The Georgia Review* 47 (Fall, 1993): 522-542. This interview focuses on Price's religious beliefs and how his convictions influence his writing. Although he is sometimes regarded as a Christian writer, he tries to convey a nonjudgmental vision of the world and thus believes that the label is inappropriate.
Schiff, James A., ed. *Critical Essays on Reynolds Price.* New York: G. K. Hall, 1998. This outstanding collection of critical essays from major literary figures and scholars, reviews, and previously unpublished material offers an in-depth view of Price's work. Includes pieces on *Kate Vaiden*.
_____. *Understanding Reynolds Price.* Columbia: University of South Carolina Press, 1996. Schiff offers an astute critical analysis of Price's essays, memoirs, poetry, drama, and biblical interpretations. An excellent source for understanding the whole spectrum of Price's work, Schiff's book features essays on individual novels, including *Kate Vaiden*.

R. Baird Shuman

THE KEEPERS OF THE HOUSE

Author: Shirley Ann Grau (1929-   )
Type of plot: Mythic chronicle
Time of plot: The 1960's, with frequent references to earlier generations and times
Locale: Mississippi and its environs
First published: 1964

> *Principal characters:*
> ABIGAIL HOWLAND TOLLIVER, the protagonist, a Southern woman who
>   tries to understand and integrate the pieces of her life and heritage
> WILLIAM HOWLAND, her grandfather and surrogate father
> MARGARET HOWLAND, his mulatto mistress and second wife
> ROBERT,
> NINA, and
> CHRISSY, William and Margaret's quadroon children
> JOHN TOLLIVER, Abigail's husband

The Novel

The Keepers of the House is a compelling narrative about three generations of the Howland family and their relationships to their house and community. The story exists on several levels. On one level, it is a historical account that attempts to explain why a group of Southern men set fire to the Howland barn, threatening not only the house but also its keepers. Looked at another way, the novel is a mythic romance that recounts a love story enacted in a fallen Eden, corrupted before the players come onstage. Still another level focuses on a woman who must learn how to manage threatening forces in a way that will not destroy both the attackers and the attacked in a modern apocalypse, when, as prophesied in Ecclesiastes 12:7, the dust will "return to the earth as it was and the spirit shall return unto God who gave it." Grau uses lines from Ecclesiastes 12:3-5 as prologue to her novel, and from these lines she takes the novel's title.

The story is told in four sections and an epilogue. Abigail narrates all the sections, though two, which carry the names of William and Margaret, respectively, focus more on these characters than on Abigail. As narrator, Abigail is gifted with omniscience, entering at will into the minds of the other characters and explaining that her memory goes back before her birth, the people of past generations being like ghosts constantly surrounding her, even at times talking with her. As keeper of the Howland house, she feels the pressure of generations: "It is as if their lives left a weaving of invisible threads in the air of this house, of this town, of this county."

William's section chronicles the generations of Howlands. The first William Howland passed through Mississippi on his way to fight alongside Andrew Jackson but returned to settle down. This William was murdered by marauding Indians but left six children to avenge his death. A William Howland was killed in the Civil War, but another took his place as keeper of the house. The present William Howland is a peaceful man, enjoying the bright moon and the scents and sensations of the earth more than he does the hunt. Widowed at an early age, he remains unmarried until he meets Margaret.

Margaret's genesis in Mississippi also begins with Andrew Jackson, who freed the slaves who fought along with him. Her people, the Freejacks, came to the area, kept apart from other blacks, and intermarried with Choctaws, taking on many Indian customs. Margaret's mother was impregnated by a white man who was passing through the community and who kept on going, but Margaret shows no outward signs of white blood, and her first memories are of having buttermilk smeared on her face, having her hair dampened, and being placed outside by her mother to bleach in the sunshine.

After William and Margaret meet, she lives with him for thirty years until his death, and she bears him three children: Robert, Nina, and Chrissy, all of whom are sent away to school as soon as they are old enough. The townspeople accept the liaison between William and Margaret as long as no attempt is made to legitimize their relationship.

Howland's daughter by his first wife is named Abigail, and she comes home after ten years of marriage, bringing her own daughter, also named Abigail. It is this second Abigail, William's granddaughter, who tells the story. She grows up with Margaret as surrogate mother, William as surrogate father, and Robert, Nina, and Chrissy as surrogate brother and sisters. (For outsiders, however, a strict legitimacy with regard to the separation of the races is maintained—when a white doctor is called to care for Robert, Abigail is put to bed and the doctor is told that she is ill.)

Abigail's growth and maturation bring Grau's narrative into contemporary times. In grammar school at the time of Pearl Harbor, Abigail listens as the president declares war. She attends college during the postwar years and marries John Tolliver, a young man with an overriding ambition to run for elective office. At the same time, each in his or her own season, Margaret's children grow up angry that they have had to be sent away, and they are made more furious by John Tolliver's public alignment with racist doctrines and policies.

When William dies, Margaret leaves the Howland house, and Abigail and John take over as keepers of the estate, but John leaves when it is made public that William and Margaret had married and legitimized the three children. The announcement moves the townspeople to fury, and they attempt to destroy the Howland house as they believe the Howlands have destroyed the customs and mores of the community. Continuing the line of vengeance, Abigail strikes back by setting fire to the townspeople's cars and trucks and thus saving her own house. Yet her anger and bitterness remain. She threatens to bring down the entire house of the South and of her part-black but light-skinned brother and sisters. She knows, however, that the action that she takes is not the way of her grandfather, and she knows that to continue to fight her neighbors will cause her own destruction as well.

The Characters

Abigail is the most difficult of the characters to understand because the entire action of the novel is played through her consciousness. Consequently, a reader has the task of clarifying Abigail's role in the drama as the narrator clarifies the roles of William and Margaret and brings them to life out of her own memories. Adding to the complexity of the character of Abigail is her growth from childhood innocence, to naïve adolescence, to unthinking young adulthood, and finally to an adult awareness of the presence of evil in her community and in herself. Whether Abigail will go on to destroy the community is unclear at the end of the novel, though the novel's end circles back to its beginning, a November evening in which, with pristine clarity, the stripped trees, bleached grass, drought-shrunken river, and granite outcroppings mirror the condition of Abigail's soul.

Though William and Margaret have historic roles to play in the chronicle of the South, they are also presented as mythic characters endowed with mysterious attributes and living in their own supernal world. Both are more comfortable in natural surroundings than in society. Both pit their strength against the natural world while willingly aligning themselves with it. Before he meets Margaret, William spends three days in a swamp in a kind of cleansing ritual. Margaret appears to have inherited some of the magic of her great-grandmother, whose hand carries the jagged scar of ceremonial magic. Margaret converses with her dead great-grandmother, and, in the woods, she often sees ghost faces and figures, sometimes friendly and sometimes hostile. She reads signs that signal William's approach.

In the liaison between Margaret and William, Grau makes a strong tie with the mythic figures of Alberta and Stanley Albert Thompson, who are protagonists of Grau's short story "The Black Prince." William appears to Margaret out of nowhere in the same way that Stanley Albert appears to Alberta. William finds himself calling Margaret "Alberta." Since Stanley Albert is a supernatural being, Alberta's children simply "come to her" without a father in a way similar to Margaret's children, whose father is not recognized by society.

The meeting of Margaret and William in the woods takes on an aura of magic, and this magic clings to them throughout the novel. They seem an Adam and Eve in an Eden given to them for a short spell, an Eden that is theirs only if they shut all others out and keep it for their own exclusive use. Thus Margaret sends her children away one by one without what would be, given the conditions of the ownership, false sentimentality. And thus Margaret leaves the Howland house as soon as William dies. After four years, she returns to their original meeting place and there, apparently, takes her own life.

Themes and Meanings

Through the structure of her novel, Grau places emphasis on birthing and dying, on seasonal changes, on cyclic expansions and contractions as they occur through successive generations. In this emphasis, the novel echoes Ecclesiastes 1:4, "One generation passeth away, and another generation cometh: but the earth abideth forever."

"They come in their season," William says of two spiders who return to the same bush year after year. "Our children grow old and elbow us into the grave," William thinks before he meets Margaret to begin life anew.

Clearly Abigail gets no real satisfaction from her attempts to destroy her neighbors in order to avenge their attacks on her. At the end of the novel, she describes her own "sob-wracked echoing world" into which she feels locked, and, crying, she slips off her chair and huddles "fetus-like against the cold unyielding boards." The reader may recall Ecclesiastes 1:14, "I have seen all the works that are done under the sun; and behold, all is vanity and vexation of spirit." It remains to be seen, for Grau's chronicle cannot say, whether Abigail has learned from her experience what Ecclesiastes proclaims in 1:18, "For in much wisdom is much grief; and he that increaseth knowledge increaseth sorrow."

Critical Context

The Keepers of the House, which won the Pulitzer Prize in 1965, was Shirley Ann Grau's third novel. Her first novel, *The Hard Blue Sky* (1958), received critical acclaim, as did her second, *The House on Coliseum Street* (1961). Since the publication of *The Keepers of the House*, Grau has published two more novels—*The Condor Passes* (1971) and *Evidence of Love* (1977). Grau is author also of three collections of short stories: *The Black Prince and Other Stories* (1955), *The Wind Shifting West* (1973), and *Nine Women* (1986).

Grau's work has been difficult for critics to categorize since her themes and styles shift from novel to novel, and she resists being classified as a "Southern" writer. Whether "Southern" or not, her work clearly belongs in the modernist mode. The surfaces of her works are slick; critics often overlook the works' underpinnings and complexities and thus misread and misinterpret. There is evidence, however, of continuing and growing interest in Grau's fiction. On the basis of the excellence of her output, Grau should be recognized as a major contemporary author.

Bibliography

Berland, Alwyn. "The Fiction of Shirley Ann Grau." *Critique: Studies in Modern Fiction* 6 (Summer, 1963): 78-84. A dated but interesting perspective.

Kissel, Susan S. *Moving On: The Heroines of Shirley Ann Grau, Anne Tyler, and Gail Godwin*. Bowling Green, Ohio: Bowling Green State University Press, 1996. This critical analysis of Grau, Tyler, and Godwin reveals how the work of Kate Chopin, Carson McCullers, Flannery O'Connor, and other southern women writers has influenced each author. Also discusses the tendencies in Grau's work to carry on the tradition of the father.

Martin, Linda Wagner. "Shirley Ann Grau's Wise Fictions." In *Southern Women Writers: The New Generation*. Tuscaloosa: University of Alabama Press, 1990. A useful overview of Grau's work.

Pearson, Ann. "Shirley Ann Grau: Nature Is the Vision." *Critique: Studies in Modern Fiction* 17 (1975): 47-58. An interesting thematic study.

Schlueter, Paul. *Shirley Ann Grau*. Boston: Twayne, 1981. Schlueter provides a critical and interpretive study of Grau, with a close reading of her major works, a solid
   bibliography, and complete notes and references.

Mary Rohrberger

THE KILLER ANGELS

Author: Michael Shaara (1929-1988)
Type of plot: War
Time of plot: June 29, 1863-July 4, 1863
Locale: Gettysburg, Pennsylvania, and environs
First published: 1974

> *Principal characters:*
> ROBERT E. LEE, the revered commander of the Confederate Army of
>   Northern Virginia
> JAMES LONGSTREET, a Confederate corps commander, trusted by Lee
>   despite their disagreements about tactics
> LEWIS ARMISTEAD, a Confederate brigadier, deeply troubled by having
>   to fight against his old friend Winfield Hancock
> JOHN BUFORD, a veteran cavalryman, the first Union commander at
>   Gettysburg
> JOSHUA LAWRENCE CHAMBERLAIN, the commander of the Twentieth
>   Maine Infantry, the Union regiment on the extreme left during the
>   crucial second day's battle

The Novel

The Killer Angels tells of the Battle of Gettysburg, the turning point of the Civil War. The novel has four parts: the armies' convergence on Gettysburg; the first day of fighting, when Confederates push the Union forces back but fail to drive them from superior defensive positions; the second day, when the Confederates attempt to surprise and overwhelm the Union left; and the third day, highlighted by Pickett's Charge against the Union center. On June 29, Robert E. Lee's invading army is widely divided, living off the wealth of Pennsylvania. No one with the main bodies of the army knows where its cavalry is, or—since the cavalry is responsible for intelligence on the march—where the Union forces are. The pragmatic James Longstreet gets some information from a spy. Lee has an aristocrat's distaste for information acquired thus, but he prudently decides to concentrate his army, and the roads dictate concentration at Gettysburg. In the meantime, Lee instructs A. P. Hill, commanding his leading corps, to avoid a general engagement.

In Gettysburg, Buford, with two brigades of Union cavalry, knows that Hill's troops are coming. Buford likes the high ground south of Gettysburg, which would make a fine defensive position. Much further south, the young commander of the Twentieth Maine Infantry, former professor of rhetoric Joshua Lawrence Chamberlain, takes charge of mutinous soldiers from another Maine regiment. Chamberlain, suffering the aftereffects of sunstroke, does not feel well. Neither do several other principals in the coming battle, including Lee, who suffers from heart disease.

On July 1, Buford's troops confront Hill's corps northwest of town. Thinking he faces only local militia, Hill presses on; the struggle intensifies, and Union reinforce-ments appear. Then a second Confederate corps arrives and assaults the Union right flank. The Union infantry's commander, John Reynolds, is killed, and under the new assault, the Union troops flee. They reform south of town, on the ground that Buford had admired. Lee wants to drive the shaken Union troops from their position, but his subordinates cannot mount an attack before nightfall. Later, Lee and Longstreet dis-cuss the situation; Longstreet, convinced of the tactical advantages accruing to a de-fender, advises that Lee maneuver to find a strong defensive position, but Lee wants to fight the enemy where he is. Chamberlain's regiment, including the mutineers, is among the Union forces still headed for Gettysburg.

The next morning, Longstreet again unsuccessfully urges Lee to fight defensively. Instead, Lee decides that Longstreet's troops should attack the Union left, taking it by surprise if possible. Meanwhile, Union troops continue to deploy. Longstreet's assault is delayed as his men countermarch to avoid observation. The Confederates discover Union troops in unexpected positions, but Longstreet does not adjust his movement to the new situation, and the attack begins according to Lee's orders.

As it does, Chamberlain's regiment occupies a position on a rocky hill on the ex-treme Union left. Chamberlain must hold this position, or the whole army will be jeopardized. In desperate fighting, Chamberlain improvises brilliantly and success-fully. Intense fighting also occurs to his right. Repeatedly, Confederate troops almost break the Union lines, but they ultimately withdraw with heavy casualties. After nightfall, the Union commander, General Meade, considers withdrawal but is dis-suaded by his corps commanders. Many Confederates celebrate their near victory, but Longstreet, weighing its cost, again urges disengagement and maneuver. Lee prom-ises to consider Longstreet's proposal.

On the morning of July 3, against Longstreet's continuing advice, Lee decides to at-tack the Union center with Pickett's division of Longstreet's corps. Pickett rejoices, believing that with this attack, his troops will win the war. Far less sanguine, Longstreet can only hold his tongue. Meanwhile, Chamberlain's surviving troops move to a position behind the Union center—"the safest place in the Union army," they are told. Pickett's attack is preceded by a prolonged, intense artillery exchange, and Chamberlain hugs the ground as shells burst around him. When Confederate am-munition runs low, thousands of attacking troops step off in exact array, as if on pa-rade. Chamberlain, recognizing their deadly intent, nevertheless perceives their beauty. As they approach the Union lines, their ranks are decimated by cannon fire and musketry. Armistead with a handful of followers reaches the Union lines. Mortally wounded, he sends his friend General Hancock an apology for the attack, in which Hancock, too, has been wounded.

The remnants of the attackers, including Pickett, return to their own lines. Long-street hears Lee telling these survivors, "It is all my fault." Anticipating a possible counterattack, Lee orders, "General Pickett, I want you to reform your division." Pickett, pointing into the smoke, replies, "General Lee, I have no division." The battle is over. In the aftermath, Longstreet tells Lee that he thinks the Confederacy cannot now win the war, and Lee replies that they will continue to fight because that is what soldiers do. The next day is the Fourth of July.

The Characters

Shaara uses multiple points of view. Most of the characters who are his centers of consciousness are Confederates, although if the novel has an individual hero, it is Chamberlain. Ultimately, however, the novel's focus is collective, and the story's closing reference to the Fourth of July underscores Shaara's understanding, like Abraham Lincoln's, that what happened at Gettysburg was a pivotal experience in the life of the nation.

Many historical figures at Gettysburg are presented only as flat characters in the novel. A character so flat that he is almost transparent, General Meade, the commander of the Union Army, hardly appears at all. Another example is the English observer Freemantle, who is always presented as awkward-looking and utterly uncomprehending. One simple memory of Hancock figures frequently in Armistead's thoughts, and Hancock himself appears later in a brilliant cameo, sitting elegantly astride his horse, reassuring his troops in the midst of the artillery barrage that has Chamberlain lying flat on the ground.

The novel's central characters are more fully developed. Shaara graphically and realistically describes the sensations of Lee's heart disease and implies that Lee's respect and affection for Longstreet have roots in his own physical weakness as well as in his appreciation of Longstreet's solid merit. Lee's aristocratic ethic shows in his distaste for Longstreet's spy and his insistence that his troops treat Pennsylvania's civilians properly, regardless of past Union behavior in Virginia. His sensitivity shows in his restrained reproach of his delinquent cavalry commander, Jeb Stuart. Deeply committed to command, Lee wants to repeat the success of Chancellorsville, where he gambled against great odds, attacked, and won. With another victory, Lee might win the war. He does not understand that his problem at Gettysburg is not that he has lost his trusted right hand, Stonewall Jackson, who was killed at Chancellorsville, but that not all the Union commanders that he faces can be counted on to be as inept as his opponent at Chancellorsville was.

Longstreet has been controversial in the history and mythology of Gettysburg, recognized by some modern commentators as a tactical genius far in advance of his time but blamed by many of his contemporaries for uncooperativeness with Lee at Gettysburg and disloyalty to Lee's memory after the war. Shaara's portrait is strongly sympathetic. Longstreet remembers not Chancellorsville (where he did not fight) but Fredericksburg, where his well positioned troops cut down attacking Yankees in great numbers. The events of Gettysburg prove him right about the superiority of defensive tactics, but the vindication comes at a price Longstreet can hardly bear: the blood of many of his men; defeat in a battle that need not have been lost; loss of any prospect for victory in the war; and loss of his respect, if not his affection, for Lee.

Chamberlain's character is even more fully realized than Longstreet's. Younger, less experienced, and closer to his men than the other major characters, Chamberlain is just as focused as they on the responsibilities of command. When challenged, he improvises brilliantly, first with the mutineers and then in the desperate fight on the Union left. After this fight, he remembers plugging a hole in the line with his younger brother Tom; he begins to recognize his true, hard soldier's vocation—a vocation not unlike Lee's.

Themes and Meanings

Readers should not regard "historical fiction" as a contradiction in terms. An imaginative extension of experience, fiction must be plausible to the extent that it cannot be documented. History, limited to what can be documented, is nevertheless subjective—not fact "as it actually happened" but an inevitably selective interpretation of the past from the perspective of the present. Historical fiction attempts to present a plausible and currently relevant imaginative representation of the past consistent with the documented record.

Unlike Stephen Crane in *The Red Badge of Courage* (1895), Shaara chooses in *The Killer Angels* to present clearly the essential strategies and salient events of the battle he recounts. Early in the novel, particularly, Shaara's exposition sometimes results in rather wooden dialogue. However, Shaara's novel is both less and more than merely another history of a widely studied battle. Shaara has changed some nineteenth century language to avoid any impression of quaintness that might compromise the immediacy of his narrative. If style is the man, these changes in language are misrepresentations, but they help readers to imagine actually being Lee, Longstreet, Armistead, or Chamberlain. Shaara's presentations of these individuals' responses to the problems confronting them and his sometimes vividly impressionistic descriptions of what they perceived often succeed, much as Crane's novel succeeded.

Even while appreciating *The Killer Angel*'s successful re-creation of the past, the reader should also appreciate its relationship to the era from which it stems. Just as *The Red Badge of Courage*'s story of a vulnerable individual trying to cope with the confusions and threats of combat reflects Crane's perception of his own era's powerful but faceless pressures on ordinary people, so *The Killer Angels* reflects concerns of the 1970's. The civil rights struggle prompts an interpretation of the Civil War as a conflict about slavery rather than one about constitutional law; the U.S. Vietnam experience prompts an interpretation of war emphasizing chance and coincidence, the miscarriage of plans, and the unpredictable ends that often await good and capable soldiers. This understanding of war is the novel's main message.

Critical Context

Shaara wrote many short stories before his first novel, *The Broken Place* (1968), which presents the experiences of a Korean War veteran. *The Killer Angels* is Shaara's masterpiece. More artistically written and more deeply meaningful than most Civil War romances, *The Killer Angels* won a Pulitzer Prize for Shaara and later served as the basis for the epic 1993 film *Gettysburg*. After Shaara's death, his son Jeff found the manuscript of a baseball novel in his father's papers and published it posthumously as *For Love of the Game* (1991). Jeff Shaara went on to write two companion novels to *The Killer Angels*: *Gods and Generals* (1996), which begins the trilogy, and *The Last Full Measure* (1998), which concludes it.

Bibliography
Coddington, Edwin B. *The Gettysburg Campaign: A Study in Command*. New York: Scribner's, 1968. A thorough, insightful, and judicious account of the battle.
Connelly, Thomas Lawrence. *The Marble Man: Robert E. Lee and His Image in American Society*. New York: Alfred A. Knopf, 1977. Psychohistory intended to counter the hagiography attached to Lee's memory.
Freeman, Douglas Southall. *R. E. Lee: A Biography*. 4 vols. New York: Scribner's, 1934-1935. The classic biography of Lee, supplemented but not replaced by works such as Connelly's.
Luvas, Jay, and Harold W. Nelson, eds. *The U.S. Army War College Guide to the Battle of Gettysburg*. Carlisle, Pa.: South Mountain Press, 1987. A collection of excerpts from the battle reports by unit commanders.
Piston, William Garrett. *Lee's Tarnished Lieutenant: James Longstreet and His Place in Southern History*. Athens: University of Georgia Press, 1989. A balanced, generally convincing attempt to rehabilitate Longstreet's reputation.
Trulock, Alice Rains. *In the Hands of Providence: Joshua Lawrence Chamberlain and the American Civil War*. Chapel Hill: University of North Carolina Press, 1992. Based on letters and other family papers as well as Chamberlain's own published writings.

David W. Cole

THE KING

Author: Donald Barthelme (1931-1989)
Type of plot: Alternative history
Time of plot: The early 1940's
Locale: Great Britain
First published: 1990

> *Principal characters:*
>> KING ARTHUR, the legendary British leader, who is pictured as still
>>> living in 1940
>> GUINEVERE, the queen, his wife
>> LAUNCELOT DU LAC, the queen's lover and chief general of King
>>> Arthur
>> LORD HAW HAW, a German radio propagandist
>> SIR KAY, Arthur's aide
>> SIR ROGER DE IBADAN, the Black Knight, a visiting knight from Africa
>> VARLEY, Guinevere's maid
>> LYONESSE, the queen of Gore
>> LIEUTENANT EDWARD, a former plasterer, Lyonesse's lover
>> MORDRED, Arthur's bastard son, a traitor
>> THE BROWN KNIGHT, a knight from Scotland
>> THE YELLOW KNIGHT, Sir Colgrevaunce of Gore
>> THE RED KNIGHT, Sir Ironside of the Red Lands, a Communist
>> THE BLUE KNIGHT, a man searching for the Grail, the ultimate weapon

The Novel

The King is an attempt to fit the Arthurian tales of Sir Thomas Malory to the situation during the Battle of Britain. In a series of small, unnumbered chapters, Donald Barthelme delineates, in an almost offhand, oral style, the concerns of Arthur, Guinevere, Lancelot, and many minor characters.

The first chapter, written in a parody of the medieval Malory's convoluted style, describes Launcelot riding about furiously in a state of wild and random action. It becomes clear that this story will be something different, however, when Guinevere is shown in the next chapter sitting with her maid listening to Lord Haw Haw, a historical English traitor who broadcasts propaganda for the Germans in World War II.

The story, what there is of one, is told as a series of conversations by an ever-widening number of characters who discuss the Battle of Britain, worry that the war is not going well, and intersperse their comments with talk of love affairs and politics. The main plot is the attempt of Arthur and the few knights to deal with World War II, especially the Battle of Britain. They endure two radio harassments: Lord Haw Haw, the legendary English traitor trying to convince the English to surrender, seems to concentrate his satire on Queen Guinevere, continually harping on her infidelities to

Arthur and her frivolous lifestyle. Readers wonder how he seems to know every one of her deviant actions. The other radio annoyance is known only as Ezra, an obvious reference to Ezra Pound, the famous American poet who made pro-Axis broadcasts. He harps on anti-Semitic propaganda, blaming World War II on the Jews. The characters all seem to listen carefully to these men and then ignore them.

Side plots erupt. The lady Lyonesse, Queen of Gore (wherever that is), falls in love with a medical officer, a Lieutenant Edward, who in civilian life is a plasterer. Sir Roger de Ibadan, the Black Knight from Dahomey, tells tales of his native land, with its evil king and its love of sculpture. He in his turn falls hopelessly in love with a ruthless highwaywoman named Clarice. A quasi-communist crusade is preached by a homeless beggar named Walter the Penniless; another communist, the Red Knight, advocates the overthrow of Arthur, whom he derides as an anachronism. The Blue Knight, on the other hand, has a solution for the war: The Holy Grail. It is a bomb, he says, a blue bomb made of cobalt that is bigger than all the other bombs of the world and will successfully end the war.

In the spring, Guinevere decides to leave the government in the hands of Mordred, whom everyone knows is no good. The young Mordred immediately has dreams of power and plots to overthrow Arthur. Arthur is in military headquarters with Sir Kay, lamenting the loss of Tobruk to General Rommel and having trouble reconciling his plans with the interference of Sir Winston.

Sir Kay, worried about the outcome of the war, wants to look at the prophecies of Merlin, which only Arthur is supposed to see. Arthur, after much cajoling, allows Sir Kay a brief look at the next few years of the prophecy. All readers of Malory's original story know that Arthur's reign is supposed to end in an immense battle with Mordred in which almost everyone, including Arthur and Mordred, is killed. The battle is indeed held, and Mordred is indeed killed, along with almost all the others involved, but Arthur is not. Kay, surprised, asks Arthur about his; Arthur explains that he did not like the prophecy the way it was, so he rewrote it.

The war seems to recede into the distance, even though there is mention that it ends much as the real war did, through the intervention of rather unsympathetic Americans. The King and Queen go back to playing their mythic roles, and the book ends as it began, with an adventure of Sir Launcelot told in the language of Malory.

The Characters

King Arthur, the legendary leader of Great Britain, is a somewhat shadowy character. He leaves politics to "Winston" and the propaganda machines and interests himself in the military. He vaguely feels that his kingly role has outlived its usefulness and feels keenly the loss of the old, romantic Round Table.

Guinevere plays the part of the bored and spoiled queen, a characterization Barthelme appropriated from Malory. Like all the characters, she is not rounded out, because the purpose of the novel is not the characterization but the reaction of the characters to the situation. Guinevere seems to accept the accusations of Lord Haw Haw, the radio traitor, that she is "dallying" with Sir Launcelot, even though during the period of the book she is sleeping with the Brown Knight and not with Launcelot. She feels weary and bored and perhaps understands that the romantic role of queens is dead. She does insist, however, that "all myths come from queens."

Sir Launcelot du Lac is a sort of noncharacter. The book opens with his fighting, and his character seems to be defined by his first jousting with and then befriending a strange knight. The book ends with his dream of "the softness of Guinevere." He is concerned only with Malory's two principal themes, fighting and love.

Sir Kay is King Arthur's aide-de-camp and is primarily a sounding board for Arthur's discussions of war and kingship. He worries about Merlin's prophecies because, although he has never read them, he knows that there is an upcoming battle with Mordred.

Sir Roger de Ibadan, the Black Knight, is a visitor from the African country of Dahomey, where "white people are regarded as freaks of nature." There seems to be little prejudice here, however; Launcelot invites him to join "our side." Sir Roger is a vaguely passionate fellow who falls "tragically" in love with the female thief, Clarice, to whom he is second only to her thieving in importance.

Lyonesse is the Queen of Gore and is the wife of King Unthank. She claims that her husband does not love her and treats her badly, so she seeks comfort in the arms of Lieutenant Edward. She seems to stand for the dislocation of people and the dissolution of families that inevitably occur in wartime.

Lieutenant Edward is the soldier freed from the bonds of duty and family, footloose and confused. In civilian life, he was a plasterer, and he feels quite ashamed of his common upbringing, especially after he falls in love with the queen of Gore.

Less developed characters include the Red Knight, a communist who spouts the party line about parasitic nobles stealing money from the people; the Blue Knight, who urges Arthur to seek the Grail, an atomic bomb; the Brown Knight, a Scotsman with bad taste who sleeps with Queen Guinevere; and a crusading fanatic named Walter the Penniless who lashes out in a sermon at the "Pomp and Orgulity" of Arthur and his knights.

Themes and Meanings

The King is a delicate attempt to communicate the fragile relationship between romance and reality. By combining the romantic tale of Arthur and his knights with a horrible twentieth century reality, the Battle of Britain, Barthelme slowly draws out the consequences of the relationship.

Arthur is a no-nonsense romantic, if there is such a thing. He understands that against the propaganda machines and manipulativeness of modern politics, not much can be done, but he seems to continue on anyway, with a romantic sense of duty. Guinevere and Launcelot try to keep up the good old days of athletic combat and "Maying"; they sigh a lot because these activities are no longer appreciated.

In short, all the knightly characters pursue a life of love and beauty in the face of a world that holds their pursuits of no account. The Brown Knight even apologizes for wearing brown armor on a black horse, for in the world of knighthood, bad taste is a no-no. Barthelme is neither satirizing nor endorsing the "lifestyle" (if anything so tenuous could be so called) of the Arthurian characters. Yet the world they are fighting—represented by Lord Haw Haw, the Germans (who are "insane"), and even Sir Winston—are dull by comparison.

Other forces impinge on their world: The Blue Knight wants to achieve the Grail, which his cobalt blue armor helps to identify as the big bomb. This, he says, will win the conflict and utterly destroy the enemy, making England safe for knighthood. Then there is the communist, the Red Knight, who has the party line down pat. He wants to overthrow the government (such a wisp of a government as it is) and give the power to the working man. Since the only working man in the book is the former plasterer Lieutenant Edward, who is wooing the aristocratic Queen of Gore, his message seems vaguely vacant.

Is there then a specific positive theme of the novel? The peculiar ending perhaps gives a clue. Arthur, having shown Sir Merlin's prophecy to Sir Kay, rewrites the prophecy so that he wins, creating a happy ending. Launcelot, disgusted by the slaughter of the last battle in which Mordred is defeated, rides off by himself despite Guinevere's pleas. Arthur and Guinevere then have a conversation about their roles, which they affirm as romantic foci of the human dream: peace, family, and justice. The book ends with Launcelot dreaming, under a tree, of the beauty of Guinevere; she "enters the dream in her own person," bringing a bottle of wine to drink with Launcelot "under an apple tree." This is the story of Eden, the great tragic, romantic love story of humanity, the continuing attempt of fragile, rather comic people to achieve peace and justice, joy and beauty, and their continual and tragic failure.

Critical Context

Barthelme identified his primary influence as Samuel Beckett. From the beginning of his career, however, he has been identified as a postmodernist, one who has absorbed the techniques of Ernest Hemingway, William Faulkner, D. H. Lawrence, and James Joyce and gone "beyond" them. His writing technique seems to be that of the collage, a form borrowed perhaps from modernist painters. In his use of this form, Barthelme joins literary allusions, attitudes, and clichés, often of a romantic nature, in a sort of upside-down way to modern moral and social problems. His method demonstrates, in an inappropriateness of the fit, how badly such romantic formulae illuminate the modern world.

The King seems to be a mellower version of this constant practice. The merging of a romantic Camelot with the Battle of Britain creates a strange, inappropriate world. The romantic clichés seem inadequate, and the more modern situation seems banal and not to the point.

The tone of the novel is less harsh than in many of Barthelme's earlier stories; the author seems to be saying that this is certainly not the way to run the world, but that he cannot think of another way. Such a tone is perhaps more in tune with more optimistic postmoderns such as Frederick Turner. There is, for example, a sense of affirmation in

Guinevere's assertion that queens are myth-makers, and Arthur almost accepts the fact that a mythic structure shapes his life.

The novel's impact has been small. Barthelme's popularity has never been overwhelming; in fact, he has often been accused of elitism, of appealing only to the well-read and culturally chic. In the wake of his death, his works have been removed from some anthologies in favor of works by such writers as Raymond Carver, James Allen McPherson, and Bobbie Ann Mason. Such a practice indicates that the editors of anthologies, at least, believe Barthelme to have been no more than a minor writer.

Bibliography

Couturier, Maurice, and Regis Durand. *Donald Barthelme*. London: Methuen, 1982. A brief (eighty-page) but illuminating consideration of the use of language in Barthelme's fiction, with an eye to situating this use among that of other postmodern authors. Specific works are considered only in fragmentary excerpts.

Gordon, Lois. *Donald Barthelme*. Boston: Twayne, 1981. The most accessible and complete overview of Barthelme's fiction up to 1981. Its 223 pages begin with a biographical sketch and, besides analyses of the first two novels and most of the short-story collections, include a selected bibliography.

Klinkowitz, Jerome. "Donald Barthelme." In *The New Fiction: Interviews with Innovative American Writers*, edited by Joe David Bellamy. Urbana: University of Illinois Press, 1974. One of the most informative, standard sources for biographical information regarding Barthelme's life.

_____. *Donald Barthelme*. Durham, N.C.: Duke University Press, 1991. Klinkowitz writes about all of Barthelme's major novels, but he argues for the "centrality" of *The Dead Father*. Includes a useful bibliography.

Stengel, Wayne B. *The Shape of Art in the Short Stories of Donald Barthelme*. Baton Rouge: Louisiana State University Press, 1985. This longer (227-page) scholarly work is a readable consideration of Barthelme's short stories, examined under typal rubrics. Despite the lack of overt consideration of the novels, the work is useful in situating the longer works in their larger context.

Trachtenberg, Stanley. *Understanding Donald Barthelme*. Columbia: University of South Carolina Press, 1990. A basic guide to Barthelme's body of work, including brief discussions of his biography and major work. Includes excellent annotated bibliography.

Robert W. Peckham

THE KINGDOM OF THIS WORLD

Author: Alejo Carpentier (1904-1980)
Type of plot: Magical Realism
Time of plot: 1750 to after 1830
Locale: Haiti, Cuba, and Italy
First published: El reino de este mundo, 1949 (English translation, 1957)

> *Principal characters:*
> TI NOËL, the protagonist, a house slave and rebel
> MONSIEUR LENORMAND DE MEZY, his master and a plantation owner
> MACKANDAL, a fugitive slave, rebel, and Ti Noël's spiritual father
> PAULINE BONAPARTE, the wife of General Leclerc and a symbol of
> decadent European culture
> SOLIMAN, Pauline's masseur, who abandons his African past, works for
> Henri Christophe, and accompanies Christophe's wife and daughters
> to Rome
> HENRI CHRISTOPHE, a black ruler who governs the northern part of
> Haiti as would a European monarch

The Novel

Mixing history and fiction, *The Kingdom of This World* recounts the transition of Haiti from slavery to emancipation and from colony to republic. The change occurs through the use of African religion. The novel begins by establishing a difference between black African culture and white European culture. Although these two systems take on different forms throughout the novel and history, they remain antagonistic toward each other. One is dynamic, the other static. Mackandal, Bouckman, and Ti Noël represent the liberating spirit of African religion and culture, while Monsieur Lenormand de Mezy, Monsieur Blancheland, General Leclerc, Rochambeau, Henri Christophe, and the Mulatto Republicans represent the oppressive force of European culture. The two groups offer conflicting interpretations of history; the novel supports the African perspective.

Mackandal initiates the struggle against slave owners. After losing an arm in a sugar mill accident, he studies poisonous plants as a means of fighting the whites. Drawing on his knowledge of African lore, he transforms himself into an animal or an insect to elude his pursuers. When Mackandal is captured and burned at the stake, the whites who are present witness his death, but the blacks see him transformed into an insect, and they watch as he escapes. This important passage illustrates clearly the difference between the European and African worldview.

Bouckman and Ti Noël follow in Mackandal's tradition and continue to fight for the liberation of blacks: Bouckman plays a prominent role during emancipation and Ti Noël during the struggle against Henri Christophe and the Mulatto Republicans. To Ti Noël, Mackandal is a spiritual father of sorts and a link with the African past.

After the success of the Haitian Revolution, in which the French are ousted from the island, Henri Christophe rules the northern part of Haiti. The ruthless Christophe betras his own people and continues to oppress them; with his reign, oppression transcends racial designation. Like Mackandal and Bouckman before him, using a knowledge of voodoo, Ti Noël joins the struggle against the enslavement of the Haitian people.

The novel ends by proposing that the cycle of oppression and liberation is ongoing, perhaps endless. Recognizing this cyclic pattern in human history, disillusioned with the prospects for meaningful change, Ti Noël transforms himself and escapes into the animal and insect worlds. He soon discovers, however, that their world, although superficially harmonious, is not any different from the human one. Having gained a greater understanding of his life and destiny through African religion, Ti Noël continues the fight against oppression and for liberation.

The Characters

The characters in the novel participate in and contribute to a historical process. They are divided into two groups, one supporting European culture, the other African. Although there is no protagonist in the traditional sense, Ti Noël comes closest to fulfilling that role, if only because the novel opens and closes with his presence and spans his life. A Haitian-born slave, Ti Noël has no direct ties with mother Africa, but he learns about voodoo from Mackandal. From this perspective, the novel is not only a description of history but of Ti Noël's development as a major rebel figure.

After Bouckman's rebellion and the extermination of blacks, Monsieur Lenormand de Mezy rescues Ti Noël and a few other slaves and, as did many Frenchmen in history, escapes to Cuba. While the exiled Frenchmen preserve and promote their own European culture, Ti Noël realizes that voodoo has a common ground with African religions in Cuba. Eventually, he buys his freedom and returns to Haiti, only to discover that the former master chef, Christophe, who had joined the colonial forces, is now the ruler of the Plain du Nord. Christophe lives like a white ruler, constructing the palace of Sans Souci, modeled after Versailles, and the fortress of the Citadel, which Ti Noël and others are forced to build.

Unlike Mackandal, Bouckman, and Ti Noël, Christophe and Soliman abandon their African origin and accept European culture. They uphold values best represented by the sensual Pauline Bonaparte; Soliman, who becomes Pauline Bonaparte's masseur and religious adviser, serves as a link between Pauline and Christophe. When the plague claims Leclerc's life, Pauline survives her husband by accepting voodoo. Once Pauline returns to France, however, Soliman, who has been contaminated by white culture, works for Christophe, and upon the ruler's death, Soliman accompanies Christophe's wife and daughters to Rome, claiming to be his nephew. The African gods punish both Christophe and Soliman for rejecting their religion and destiny; both meet with tragic deaths.

Themes and Meanings

The Kingdom of This World relates history and fiction; events in the novel have been documented with precision. In its historical investigation, the novel discloses a cyclical structure: If there are movements of oppression, there will be others of rebellion; if there are movements of rebellion, there will be others of oppression. Indeed, the cycles documented in the novel continue into contemporary Haitian history. When Carpentier arrived in Haiti in 1943, Élie Lescot was president. Popular reaction against his corrupt government led to the election of Dumarsais Estimé in 1946, but Estimé's benevolent government was soon followed by the dictatorships of François "Papa Doc" Duvalier and his son, Jean-Claude. If the structure proposed by Carpentier were to hold true, one could foresee the defeat of Jean-Claude Duvalier in favor of a popular government, but also the defeat of that government and the imposition of another ruthless one.

The Kingdom of This World offers profound insight into the problems regarding the founding of the first black nation and the first country to receive independence in Latin America and the Caribbean. The racial and cultural tensions depicted in the novel were indeed present from the moment Africans were brought to the New World. These tensions, however, became more intense during the time of the novel, toward the end of the eighteenth century, mainly because of the development of the sugar industry. The Haitian Revolution brought the black struggle to a climax but not to an end. With Christophe and other black and mulatto rulers, the racial confrontation between whites and blacks evolved into a struggle between those who accept and those who reject African religion.

Thus, the black struggle is not only political but also religious. A religious interpretation, which the novel strongly suggests, highlights a broader strategy in which man is but a mere participant. During the night of the Solemn Pact, Bouckman, in his final admonition, reveals the following: "The white men's God orders the crime. Our gods demand vengeance from us. They will guide our arms and give us help. Destroy the image of the white man's God who thirsts for our tears; let us listen to the cry of freedom within ourselves." In the end, the historical, cultural, and religious themes of the novel complement one another.

Critical Context

In the prologue to the original edition of *The Kingdom of This World*, Carpentier discusses what he calls "Marvelous Realism," anticipating the vogue for the closely related term Magic Realism, which has been widely used to describe the style that brought the Latin American novel to international prominence in the 1960's and 1970's. Only a style that embraces the marvelous, the magical, he suggests, is capable of doing justice to the reality of America, the New World. In the novel itself, although not in the prologue, Carpentier emphasizes the African component in the heterogenous culture of the Americas, linking Marvelous Realism to African traditions.

In *The Kingdom of This World*, Carpentier continued the exploration of black history begun in such early works as *Ecue-Yamba-O! Historia Afro-Cubana* (1933) and

"El milagro de Anaquille" (1927), a scenario for a ballet. Of Carpentier's works with a black theme, *The Kingdom of This World* is clearly his best. Within the context of Cuban literature, his concern with blacks and the theme of slavery is not isolated. *The Kingdom of This World* is part of a continuum which can be traced from the antislavery narratives of the 1830's to the literature of the Cuban Revolution. By writing about the lives of an important but marginal segment of Western society, Carpentier brings the history of blacks to the foreground of literature.

Although many critics regard *El siglo de las luces* (1962; *Explosion in a Cathedral*, 1963) as Carpentier's greatest literary accomplishment, Carpentier himself continued to believe in the historical significance of *The Kingdom of This World*, citing the importance of Mackandal, Bouckman, and the Haitian Revolution for an understanding of Caribbean history and culture. Yet there is no need to choose one novel over the other; indeed, they are best read together: *Explosion in a Cathedral* is set during the Haitian transition from colony to republic—that is, from 1789 to 1809—and many of the themes developed in that novel are already present in *The Kingdom of This World*.

Bibliography

Echevarria, Roberto González. *Alejo Carpentier: The Pilgrim at Home*. Ithaca, N.Y.: Cornell University Press, 1977. Explores what seems like a radical disjunction between Carpentier's fiction and nonfiction. Echevarria finds unity, however, in certain recurring themes, which he illuminates by discussing Carpentier's debt to writers such as José Ortega y Gasset and Oswald Spengler. The novelist's penchant for dialectical structures and for allegory is also explored. Includes a bibliography and index.

Harss, Luis, and Barbara Dohmann. *Into the Mainstream*. New York: Harper & Row, 1966. Includes a chapter often cited as a succinct introduction to Carpentier's work up to the early 1960's.

Janney, Frank. *Alejo Carpentier and His Early Works*. London: Tamesis, 1981. An introductory survey that is still useful.

Kilmer-Tchalekian, Mary. "Ambiguity in *El siglo de las luces.*" *Latin American Literary Review* 4 (1976): 47-57. An especially valuable discussion of Carpentier's narrative technique and handling of point of view.

King, Lloyd. *Alejo Carpentier, Caribbean Writer*. St. Augustine, Fla.: University of the West Indies Press, 1977. Often cited for its perceptive introduction to Carpentier's work.

Shaw, Donald L. *Alejo Carpentier*. Boston: Twayne, 1985. Chapters on Carpentier's apprenticeship, his discovery of the "marvelous real," his handling of time and circularity, his fiction about the Antilles, his explorations of politics, and his last works. Includes chronology, notes, and annotated bibliography.

Souza, Raymond D. *Major Cuban Novelists: Innovation and Tradition*. Columbia: University of Missouri Press, 1976. Should be read in conjunction with Harss and Dohmann.

William Luis

THE KITCHEN GOD'S WIFE

Author: Amy Tan (1952-   )
Type of plot: Family
Time of plot: The 1980's (in the United States) and the 1920's to the 1940's (in China)
Locale: Northern California and China, particularly Shanghai
First published: 1991

> *Principal characters:*
> JIANG WEILI (WINNIE), a woman who seeks a deeper understanding with her daughter by telling her about the past
> WEN FU, Weili's first husband, who turns out to be a liar, gambler, coward, and womanizer
> JIMMIE LOUIS, Weili's second husband, who brings her to the United States, out of Wen Fu's clutches
> PEARL, Weili's American-born daughter, who conceals her life-threatening illness from her mother
> HULAN (HELEN), Weili's best friend in China, who runs a flower shop with her in California
> PEANUT, a relative with whom Weili is reared who eventually shows her how to escape her despotic husband

The Novel

The Kitchen God's Wife is about a mother and daughter who have mutually reinforcing secrets. Their inability to communicate is based partially on their different backgrounds. The mother was reared in China and emigrated to California later in life, while her daughter was born and reared in the United States. In the beginning, the story is told by the daughter, Pearl, who has informed everyone but her mother that she has multiple sclerosis. Pearl is afraid that her mother, Winnie, will get overexcited by the news. Pearl feels especially guilty about covering up the information because she believes that her mother would never hide anything from her.

Most of the story, however, is given in the voice of the mother, whose Chinese name is Jiang Weili (in Chinese, the family name is given first). Out of an unrealistic fear of her former husband Wen Fu's reappearance—especially unrealistic since he is in China and she in California—Weili has never told her daughter anything but generalities about her first marriage. Now that Wen Fu has died, she tells her story, in the process revealing certain long-veiled circumstances of Pearl's nativity.

When Weili is six years old, her mother deserts the family, bringing shame on the house. Weili is sent to live in her uncle's residence so that she will not be a constant reminder of her mother's betrayal. In her new home, she plays second fiddle to her uncle's children, which is particularly galling in relation to Peanut, the daughter, who is Weili's junior by a year. Thus, Weili jumps at the chance to marry Wen Fu, a local boy who begins by romancing Peanut but who switches matrimonial targets when he learns that Weili is from the richer branch of the family.

At the time of the couple's marriage, China is in a skirmishing war with Japan, and the newlyweds pack off to live at the Chinese Air Force Academy, where Wen Fu is a pilot. As she lives with him, Weili comes to understand her husband's perversity. With his friends, he is quick-witted, generous, brash, and gutsy. To his wife, he is cruel, spiteful, and overdemanding sexually. Moreover, he is a coward who turns tail whenever the other fighter pilots fly into combat. Perhaps as a compensation for his increasingly ill-concealed derelictions of duty, he plays the bully with his wife. He takes possession of some of her personal savings and wastes them, and he begins to flaunt his extramarital affairs, to the point of moving his mistresses into the house. These actions do not merely personally affront Weili; since the couple must share their housing with another married couple, they also cause her to lose face.

The rapid deterioration of their marriage takes place against the backdrop of China's collapsing defense against a Japanese invasion. Wen Fu's air force unit repeatedly relocates, moving deeper into China's interior as the Japanese blitzkrieg continues. Meanwhile, new personal disasters harden the marriage partners' hearts against each other. Wen Fu loses an eye in a jeep mishap and so loses both his looks and the status of being a pilot. Weili loses the last vestiges of feeling for her spouse when he prevents a doctor from seeing their daughter, who is struck by a sudden sickness and dies. For Weili, aside from her children, the only bright spots during the war years are her deepening friendship with a fellow pilot's wife, Hulan, and an enchanting meeting with a Chinese American translator, Jimmie Louis.

Back in Shanghai after the war, two encounters persuade Weili to leave her marriage. She finds Peanut, who has left her husband and set up a house for runaway wives, and meets Jimmie Louis again and falls in love with him. She does escape her husband and, after a series of misadventures that include being thrown in jail on trumped-up charges preferred by Wen Fu, joins Jimmie in California as his wife. On the day before she leaves for America, however, Weili is surprised and raped by Wen Fu. Pearl is born about nine months later, and the question of her father's identity is left open.

Now, however, after years of doubt, Weili is convinced that Jimmie Louis, who has died, is Pearl's true father, a fact that Weili tells her daughter as she brings her narrative to a close. Overwhelmed by her mother's history and by her courage in revealing it, Pearl reciprocates by informing her mother of her own sickness. The novel ends with a flow of trust between mother and daughter. Each has been brought abreast of the other's heartaches, the mother's found in an unhappy past and the daughter's in a struggling, uncertain future.

The Characters

Jiang Weili (Winnie), who tells most of the story, is a woman who, it is said, combines weakness and strength. Plucked out of her home and placed in her uncle's house when her mother deserts the family, she grows up taught to defer to her uncle's children. Yet her first years with her mother, who spoiled her, have given her an ineradicable sense of self-worth. When Weili makes a poor marriage to Wen Fu, she at first acts docilely, putting up with his abuse. Her repression of her better instincts in this relationship acts as one of the book's sharper critiques of the man-as-master ideology of old China. Later, Weili revolts and escapes her first marriage. At the time of the story's telling, it is her past that separates her from her daughter; Weili does not want to reveal her history, which would show her weaknesses. Eventually, however, Weili unburdens herself and draws her daughter to her in the process.

Wen Fu, Weili's first husband, is the villain of the piece. He seems to have little but the most superficial qualities, such as surface good humor and bravado, to recommend him. At bottom, he is a domestic tyrant, gambler, and womanizer. Although Tan makes him unsympathetic, she does allow the reader to glimpse some of the bases for his cruelty. He is obsessed with his status as a "war hero," yet he is not a hero but a drunken coward; his self-esteem is therefore rooted in self-deception. His character can be taken as symbolic of the Chinese military as a whole, since his shallow bluster reproduces the widely proclaimed but largely illusory effectiveness of their war effort. In the end, Wen Fu loses out to both Weili, who escapes his power, and to his own greed, since he wrecks his house looking for an imaginary hidden fortune.

Pearl, Weili's daughter, is a foil to her mother. Although she is a well-developed character who constantly mediates between the demands of her mother (who Pearl thinks is too meticulous in observing family conventions) and her American husband (who she thinks is too nonchalant in regard to Chinese culture), Pearl is not as well-rounded as her mother. What Pearl is afraid to tell her mother acts as a minor counterpoint to her mother's more resonant secret, Weili's whole unrevealed youth. After her mother tells all, Pearl is enabled to divulge what is in her own heart, leading to a richer understanding of both her mother and the family history.

Hulan (Helen) is, with Weili, the co-owner of a flower shop in California. She meets Weili while their husbands work together in the Chinese air force. The outspoken, bossy Hulan is a conservative counselor to Weili, telling her to try to endure her husband. Finally, she comes to adopt Weili's more progressive views on marriage, although she continues to lecture her on right living.

Jimmie Louis, Weili's second husband, is a Chinese American who meets and falls in love with her when he is working in China. He is romantic and loyal, but he is ineffectual in dealing with the Byzantine complexities of the Shanghai bureaucracy. He helps Weili to get away from Wen Fu, but he has to leave her when he is called back to America. Once they are reunited, they have a few years of marital bliss before his untimely death from cancer.

Themes and Meanings

The Kitchen God's Wife is structured around two interrelated dichotomies: between China and the United States and between mother and daughter. At first, it would seem that China has little to offer Weili and other immigrant women except nostalgic memories of its food and landscapes. As wives in prerevolutionary China, women have little voice in running their families; if they have made bad marriages, they must put up with husbands who may be sadistic or uninterested. Divorce initiated by a woman is unthinkable. Women are often forced into bad marriages, because as daughters they have limited say in whom they will marry and little chance to get to know their prospective partners. Moreover, people in wartime China have to put up with extreme political instability. As the story unfolds, for example, Weili and her husband must keep relocating as Japanese troops keep occupying new parts of the country.

Life in the United States, where women have more equality with men and political conditions are generally calm, seems like paradise compared to existence in China. Yet there is a definite critical undertone to Tan's discussion of the American environment.

Pearl is something of an epitome of American life, with her petty trials and triumphs, her bickering with her husband and children, and her mostly picayune concerns. Yet she seems to be living on a small scale. Her mother's life journey of catastrophe, heartache, violence, and passion in China has tested her to the utmost and bonded her friends to her with ties forged in adversity. In the United States, in contrast, most potentials remain unrealized. Women have security and formal equality but little chance to develop their independence, as Weili has, through resistance to authority and oppressive customs.

The difference in each woman's upbringing leads to an unspoken rupture in their familial connection. Each conceals a secret because each believes the other does not really recognize the true mortar of culture. For Weili, this mortar is the complex configuration of established deference patterns that should guide interfamilial relations. Her daughter's lack of openly displayed grief at her father's funeral—a display that should have been made whether the girl felt grief or not—symbolizes Pearl's lack of appreciation for custom. How, Weili thinks, can her daughter understand the choices her mother made in her life if she does not honor these traditions?

Meanwhile, Pearl thinks her mother cannot comprehend the emotional shadings that govern American life. Although Pearl was devastated by her father's death, she could not express her feelings at the funeral, and her mother's demand for tears seemed to violate her emotional integrity. Pearl thus anticipates that if she tells her mother about her illness, her mother will make a scene—that is, respond in an emotionally inauthentic manner.

Each sees the other as lacking in sensitivity to either cultural or emotional nuance. It is the mother, the more daring, who saves the situation by telling her story. In a way, she trumps her daughter by revealing that, while steering meticulously through the protocols of Chinese tradition, she has had as rich and adventurous of an emotional life as Pearl has. What Weili basically establishes by her tale, however, is that custom and emotion can fruitfully work together. To approach each other, the two women have suspended disbelief about the values of Chinese and American principles and have become willing to see that each has something to offer a harmoniously integrated life.

Critical Context

The Kitchen God's Wife was Tan's second novel. Her first, *The Joy Luck Club* (1989), brought her success and critical acclaim; Tan, however, did not attempt to re-create her earlier triumph by rewriting her first book. Her second novel departs substantially from the first in structure, in the weight given to the different claims of China and the United States, and in approach.

The Joy Luck Club is told by eight narrators—four mothers and four daughters, all friends—whose stories jump around in time and space, leaving the reader to sort out their chronologies and relationships. In contrast, *The Kitchen God's Wife* has the relatively simpler structure of a tale within a tale. Further, the first novel gives equal attention to the lives of the American daughters and Chinese mothers, while the second work concentrates on Weili in China.

The most important departure in the second book is that Tan has exchanged her earlier Magical Realism for a realistic tone. Magical Realism, first associated with Latin American writers, is a style that remains realistic but constantly skims near the edge of fantasy. It dwells on plausible but unusual events involving pageantry, humor, and hints of folklore. In the United States, Magical Realism has been associated with African American women writers such as Toni Morrison. More to the point, however, it was the chosen style of Tan's most prominent Chinese American literary predecessor, Maxine Hong Kingston, who in books such as *The Woman Warrior* (1977) captured the history of Chinese immigrants in a fabulist style.

The Joy Luck Club blends Magical Realist passages about old China with less extravagant narrative strands describing San Francisco's Chinatown. *The Kitchen God's Wife*, on the other hand, though set largely in China, opts for a thoroughgoing realism. The times themselves are often extraordinary, but Tan avoids her earlier dreamlike tone and settles on a sober, steady, fearless examination of circumstances. In truth, the most notable remaining touch of Magical Realism in the second book occurs in the recounted legend of the Kitchen God that gives the book its title.

Feminism finds strong spokeswomen in all of Tan's major characters, especially those who come from China. These women are (or grow to be) spirited, assertive, and decisive. The American-born heroines of Tan's novels aspire to these same qualities, although their dual heritage often undermines their self-assertion by plaguing them with ambivalence.

Tan's books also touch on issues of ethnic pride and multiculturalism. Advocates of multiculturalism seek to highlight the intrinsic value of each immigrant ethnic culture rather than to see each as merely a contributor to the larger U.S. culture. Within this general framework, Tan takes a moderate position, pointing immigrants and their children neither toward Americanization nor toward a complete return to ethnic roots. Rather, she describes characters who struggle to integrate the psychic demands of two worlds.

Bibliography

Huntley, E. D. *Amy Tan: A Critical Companion*. Westport, Conn.: Greenwood Press, 1998. This first book-length study of Tan's work focuses on the mother/daughter relationship in *The Joy Luck Club*, *The Kitchen God's Wife*, and *The Hundred Se-cret Senses*. A short biographical chapter plus individual chapters exploring each novel in-depth make this ideal for students of Tan's novels.

Kim, Elaine H. *Asian-American Literature: An Introduction to the Writings and Their Context*. Philadelphia: Temple University Press, 1982. Although the book does not discuss Tan's work, it is a useful guide for those who want more background on the tradition from which she springs. It focuses on the interwoven immigrant experi-ences of the Japanese and the Chinese in the United States. It details both the ste-reotypes of Orientals in American literature and early attempts by Asian Ameri-cans to combat them.

Tan, Amy. "Angst and the Second Novel." *Publishers Weekly* 238 (April 5, 1991): 4-7. In this essay, Tan dissects the problems facing an author who has to live up to a huge first-novel success. Cautioning other writers about publishing a second book, she warns that critics are harder on a second effort. She also discusses the generally useless advice she received when writing a second novel and details her false starts as she worked on *The Kitchen God's Wife*.

_____. "Double Face." In *Home to Stay: Asian-American Woman's Fiction*, ed-ited by Sylvia Watanabe and Carol Bruchac. Greenfield Center, N.Y.: Greenfield Review Press, 1990. This anthology includes a selection by Tan taken from *The Joy Luck Club*. The excerpt is prefaced by a statement by Tan that tells about her own extraordinary life, which was more unconventional than that of her characters. The anthology also has generous selections from other Chinese American female writ-ers whose work can be read to locate Tan's work within a developing tradition.

Young, Pamela. "Mother with a Past." *Maclean's* 104 (July 15, 1991): 47. This discus-sion of *The Kitchen God's Wife* focuses on Tan's problems writing a follow-up book to her first spectacular success. Tan made false starts, such as beginning and abandoning books on the San Francisco earthquake and on immortality. Young compliments Tan on her second book, which, the critic argues, shows incredible deftness at switching styles to capture different types of scenes.

James Feast

LaBRAVA

Author: Elmore Leonard (1925-   )
Type of plot: Detective and mystery
Time of plot: The 1980's
Locale: South Miami Beach, Florida
First published: 1983

> *Principal characters:*
> JOE LABRAVA, a freelance photographer of the Miami Beach street
>   scene, formerly a Secret Service agent and Internal Revenue Service
>   investigator
> MAURICE ZOLA, an elderly hotel owner-manager who was a
>   photographer years ago
> JEAN SHAW, a former motion-picture star, Zola's friend and business
>   associate
> RICHARD NOBLES, a sociopathic he-man, thief, and private security
>   guard
> CUNDO REY, a Cuban expatriate, nightclub go-go dancer, and car thief

The Novel

LaBrava, Elmore Leonard's tenth crime novel, takes place in the 1980's in South
Miami Beach, Florida, a resort that is a decadent remnant of its Art Deco heyday. Into
this seedy milieu the author places a varied group of characters, including such grotesques as a hustler who preys upon women and a psychopathic Cuban refugee who is
a go-go dancer and car thief. Joe LaBrava, the title character, an erstwhile Secret Service man who guarded former First Lady Bess Truman, is a freelance photographer in
his late thirties who prowls the streets with camera in hand.

Through his friendship with hotelman Maurice Zola, LaBrava finally meets Jean
Shaw, a fiftyish former film star with whom he recalls having fallen in love when he
was twelve years old. When she is brought drunk to a county crisis center one night,
LaBrava takes Zola there to get her released. Richard Nobles, a private security guard
and all-around thug who comes there for the same purpose, challenges LaBrava, but
the physically imposing hulk is no match for the photographer, who flattens him. After a quarter of a century, LaBrava is still smitten with Shaw, and they become sexually involved. Unclear, however, is whether he is attracted to the woman or to her film
images, which he vividly recalls from childhood. Adding intriguing complexity to
Leonard's carefully woven plot and characterizations is the fact that Shaw herself often confuses film fiction with real life, seemingly reenacting old screenplays in actual
situations.

By winning the battle over Shaw, LaBrava earns Nobles's enmity. The sociopath
starts tailing the photographer and eventually decides to kill him with his crony Rey's
assistance. (Rey already has killed Nobles's vengeance-seeking uncle, who believed

his nephew's false testimony led to a son's lengthy prison term.) LaBrava, meanwhile, also stalks Nobles, unnerving his prey by surreptitiously taking pictures of him, which he uses to forestall an attempt by Nobles and Rey to shake down local merchants. Paralleling this petty extortion scheme, which amounts to a few hundred dollars per store, is a much more ambitious plan. Nobles also has been preying upon Jean Shaw after she had encouraged his attention. Her attitude toward him is ambivalent, but they soon become partners in crime, although she may be setting him up for a big fall. This lack of certainty about Shaw's motives and the ambiguous morality that is central to her character is an aspect of the illusion-versus-reality motif that Leonard develops throughout the novel. All of this adds depth and resonance to the novel, qualities not often present in crime fiction.

In the main story line, Shaw receives a crudely typed extortion note threatening her with death unless she follows subsequent instructions demanding the payment of $600,000. Since she barely has enough income on which to live, such a sum is far beyond her means to raise, so she looks to Zola. The police are certain that Nobles is a key player in the scheme and believe that, since he is an inveterate bumbler, their task of catching him in a self-incriminating act should be simple. Leonard, though, has laid the groundwork for necessary complications: the odd relationship between Nobles and Shaw, the focus upon her motion-picture career, and her tendency to infuse much of her conversation with lines from old films. In any event, LaBrava and the others realize, Nobles is neither orchestrator nor dupe, but rather accomplice and front man in a scam too complex for him to have concocted. Jean Shaw is the brains behind the alleged extortion, but rather than a product of her imagination, it is primarily a reworking of a plot from *Obituary*, a film in which she starred with Tyrone Power.

Leonard is full of surprises in *LaBrava*, not the least of which is his conclusion. Though Jean, it finally is clear, has double-crossed and tried to swindle Maurice, the two are going to get married. Maurice promises, "I'm gonna take good care of her," which is precisely what he has been doing for years. Evidently putting her celluloid past wholly behind her and ready at last to embrace real life, Jean tells LaBrava, "It's not the movies, Joe." This statement can also explain the relevance of numerous minor characters and subplots that flesh out the novel. Inherently interesting, they do more than merely increase the number of perilous scenes, for just as Joe LaBrava's photography eschews illusion in favor of raw realism, the minor players and incidents focus attention upon and enhance the reality that ultimately becomes the controlling force in the main characters' lives.

The Characters

Maurice Zola describes Joe LaBrava as "one of those quiet guys, you never know what he's gonna do next." As a photographer, according to Zola, LaBrava "shoots barefaced fact. He's got the feel and he makes *you* feel it." The skills emerge from his keen understanding of people, because his eye, like the lens of his camera, penetrates to the essence of those he meets. These qualities, as well as his ubiquitous picture-taking, help him to solve the crimes that occur. LaBrava also inspires confidence and trust in people, such as canny Maurice Zola (who confides, "I'm going to tell you a secret I never told anybody around here") and worldly-wise women like cosmetic salesperson Franny Kaufman and actress Jean Shaw. Although he lives in Zola's Della Robbia Hotel and becomes deeply involved (sexually and otherwise) with its residents, LaBrava remains an outsider, fundamentally detached, and thus can credibly function as the moral center and conscience of the novel. He is a touchstone by which others are measured.

Maurice Zola, about eighty years old, has had several careers before settling upon hotel ownership and management. A onetime bookmaker and railroadman, in the 1930's he was a photographer for the Farm Security Administration, "documenting the face of America during the Depression." Part of the south Florida scene for half a century, he has experienced it all: women, scams, good times and bad. He has made a lot of money and lost some of it, but he still has plenty left. Given all he has been through, he retains a surprising amount of trust for people and looks out for the well-being of those he admires, especially LaBrava and Jean Shaw. Maurice's knowledge of the milieu, his patience, and his sound common sense are vital to the former's efforts and help to rein in the latter.

Jean Shaw, the onetime actress, who portrayed beautiful but dangerous seductresses (in the manner of Bette Davis, Mary Astor, and Veronica Lake), continues to live in a make-believe world, watching her old films and luring young men. Her motives for bringing to life an old film extortion plot are not fully clear but probably have as much to do with her obsession with reliving past cinematic glories as with her need for money. She may also be attracted to the scheme by the realization that Maurice, her devoted protector, could and would provide the payoff. Seen as vulnerable through much of the novel, she does kill Nobles in a coldly deliberate manner, but mitigating the shock is the fact that it is a precise replay of a scene from her film *Obituary*.

The real villains of the piece, Richard Nobles and Cundo Rey, are stereotypical hustlers, partners in crime but untrusting of and disloyal to each other. Though they possess the requisite fearlessness and determination of thugs, ineptness and lack of vision inhibit their dreams of grandeur. Big and muscular Nobles, in his mid-thirties, is a fellow LaBrava "knew by sight, smell and instinct" who "pumped his muscles and tested his strength when he wasn't picking his teeth." A brute who preys on women and boasts of having eaten a snake and an eagle, he has had a varied career and once acted as an informer against his cousin for the federal Drug Enforcement Agency. Cundo Rey, his sidekick, is a bisexual murderer whose criminality makes him a willing accomplice in just about anything, as long as money is to be made. One of his guiding principles is that anger is good if one can "use it right away" and "let it pick you up and carry you." Ironically, he rarely exhibits the emotion, and the maxim more appropriately describes Nobles. Significantly, both men are undone by the same nemesis, LaBrava, who personifies calmness. In his climactic battle of wits and pistols with LaBrava, Cundo is dead moments after boasting, "I say to St. Barbara I believe this is my day."

Themes and Meanings

The novel develops according to a standard Leonard pattern: An ordinary, fundamentally good man gets caught up in a crime but eventually prevails over those who are greedy, evil, and amorally ambitious. What distinguishes Joe LaBrava is that when challenged, he cannot remain the dropout he had become and is impelled to involvement by a strong social conscience, romantic nature, loyalty to a friend, and innate curiosity. At the end, though, he is still merely a solitary freelance photographer, someone who has been in a peck of trouble but has emerged basically unchanged, although disillusioned, by his experiences.

LaBrava is a fast-paced narrative with noteworthy verisimilitude, a result of Leonard's keen ear for spoken language and his grimly realistic settings, whether a hotel inhabited by old widows or a county crisis center filled with alcoholics and assorted psychotics. Counterpointing and in contrast with this realism is the pervasive illusion theme, centered around the nostalgia enveloping Jean Shaw, whose words and actions are so intertwined with the film lines she spoke and roles she played years ago that there is no discernible boundary between make-believe and reality. Leonard suggests, though, that everyone needs illusions to survive, whether one is an aging film star or simply an ordinary old lady using Franny Kaufman's Bio-Energetic Breast Cream. Even levelheaded Joe LaBrava has been sustained for twenty-five years by cinematic illusion, his childhood love for a film actress whose name he could not even remember.

In addition to the security that their illusions provide, perhaps as escape from the dismal reality surrounding them, these people need one another. Even the villains, Nobles and Rey, almost always operate as a team. Zola and Shaw long ago forged an odd yet useful symbiotic relationship. Although LaBrava at the end is as much a loner as at the start, his vocation keeps him amid people, even if he is separated from them by a camera lens, and he is quick to form close, if usually temporary, relationships. When he agrees to be best man at the Zola-Shaw wedding, he gives the couple a smile and thinks to himself, "Why not?" This slight suggestion of wistfulness coupled with ambivalence is appropriate, given all that has transpired and the questions that remain about Shaw. Zola must be speaking for the author on the last page of the novel when he stops speculation about the mystery by saying that "you always got a few loose ends. Who needs to know everything?" Using film language to reinforce Zola's statement, Shaw ends the discussion by agreeing, "It's a wrap."

Critical Context

Elmore Leonard was a successful writer of Western fiction in the 1950's and early 1960's, producing five novels and many stories, including *Hombre* (1961), which the Western Writers of America named one of the twenty-five best Westerns of all time and which was made into a film starring Paul Newman. Thinking the market for Westerns was diminishing, Leonard turned to crime fiction, but numerous publishers rejected his first such novel, *The Big Bounce*, before it finally came out as a paperback original in 1969. Though he averaged a crime novel a year during the 1970's,

Leonard did not become a popular and critical success until *Stick* (1983) and *LaBrava*, the latter of which won the Mystery Writers of America Edgar Allan Poe Award in 1984. Widely praised, it secured his reputation as one of the major American crime writers, though he has said, "I think that I'm really writing novels, not mysteries, but I don't want to sound pretentious."

Leonard's crime fiction stands apart from much else in the genre: His characters are less stereotypical and more substantive; he does not have a recurring detective who confronts cases in a predictable manner; and his locales and casts change considerably from book to book (though the Detroit area is the setting of a number of his novels, and *LaBrava* is the fourth set in the Miami Beach area). Partly by avoiding adherence to formula writing, he has advanced beyond the genre author label into the mainstream of American fiction.

One of his major influences is Ernest Hemingway, and Leonard has acknowledged that a close reading of Hemingway's *For Whom the Bell Tolls* (1940) focused his attention on the importance of dialogue and narrative point of view. Leonard has recalled being especially struck by how Hemingway "told so much just in the way a character talked." Yet Leonard says that he differs from Hemingway in important respects, claiming to see more absurdity, to like people more, and to be more tolerant. In terms of attitude (sardonic humor, for example), Leonard can be compared to contemporaries such as Mark Harris and Kurt Vonnegut, Jr., both of whom he has praised; he also has spoken of the influence on his work of George V. Higgins's *The Friends of Eddie Coyle* (1972), primarily for its use of dialogue and monologues as means of increasing realism, and of John O'Hara and John Steinbeck. He has disclaimed being influenced by the leaders of the "hard-boiled" school of American crime fiction—Raymond Chandler, Dashiell Hammett, and Ross Macdonald—but his depictions of urban realism and physical violence and his pervasive morality link him unmistakably to the hard-boiled genre.

Bibliography

Geherin, David. *Elmore Leonard*. New York: Continuum, 1989. The first full-length study of Leonard. Starts with a short biography and then summarizes and analyzes the novels and some stories. The last chapter, "Why Is Elmore Leonard So Good?", makes a good case for Leonard as a major American writer, and the bibliography is a useful research tool.

Hynes, Joseph. "'High Noon in Detroit:' Elmore Leonard's Career." *Journal of Popular Culture* 25 (Winter, 1991): 181-186. Hynes examines several books by Leonard, demonstrating that Leonard's works are superior to mainstream mystery stories. Although Leonard is well regarded by his colleagues, some critics have awarded him a lower rating than he deserves.

Leonard, Elmore. "A Conversation with . . . Elmore Leonard." Interview by Lewis Burke Frumkes. *The Writer* 110 (November, 1997): 22-24. Leonard discusses the writing process, revealing that he does not plot a novel before he begins to write. He also prefers to write from the point of view of various characters and makes use of dialogue to advance the story. Although it does not discuss *LaBrava* directly, this is a useful interview that offers interesting insight into Leonard's thought processes as he writes.

Millner, Cork. "Elmore Leonard: The Best Ear in the Business." *Writer's Digest* 77 (June, 1997): 30-32. Millner points out that Leonard is a master at capturing the sound or voice of his characters. Millner discusses other aspects of technique, including developing an ear for dialogue.

Prescott, P. S. "Making a Killing." *Newsweek* 105 (April 22, 1985): 62-64. Focusing upon Leonard's belated emergence as a widely recognized popular writer, this article also provides a useful review of his themes.

Reed, J. D. "A Dickens from Detroit." *Time* 123 (May 28, 1984): 84-85. Discusses *LaBrava* and then considers themes and techniques.

Shah, Diane K. "For Elmore Leonard, Crime Pays." *Rolling Stone* (February 28, 1985): 33-34. A useful biographical as well as critical piece. Includes an interview with the author in which he is characteristically frank.

Yagoda, Ben. "Elmore Leonard's Rogues' Gallery." *The New York Times Magazine*, December 30, 1984, p. 20. A well-informed and in depth review of Leonard's career and literary production. Yagoda's emphasis is on Leonard's crime fiction.

Gerald H. Strauss

LADY ORACLE

Author: Margaret Atwood (1939-   )
Type of plot: Satire
Time of plot: The late 1940's to the 1970's
Locale: Toronto, Canada; Terremoto, Italy; London, England
First published: 1976

> *Principal characters:*
>> JOAN DELACOURT FOSTER, the narrator, an author of romance novels
>> FRAN DELACOURT, Joan's middle-class, social-climbing mother
>> AUNT LOU, Joan's aunt, who opens the world of fantasy for Joan
>> ARTHUR FOSTER, Joan's idealistic husband, who fights for "almost lost" causes
>> THE ROYAL PORCUPINE, an eccentric artist who preserves road-killed animals
>> PAUL, the Polish Count, a political refugee who writes romance novels

The Novel

Lady Oracle is a five-part narrative in which Joan Foster, the first-person narrator, tells the story of her life. Spanning the time period from the early 1940's through the mid-1970's, Joan's story describes her growing up in Toronto, becoming an author of gothic romances, marrying, and faking her suicide to escape the complicated turmoil of her life.

The first narrative begins immediately following Joan's phony suicide. Planning her "death" very carefully, she aims for a neatness and simplicity in it that would counter the spreading tendency of her life. Yet having fled to Terremoto, Italy, the very place where she and her husband, Arthur, had vacationed the previous year, Joan begins to regret going there. Her attempts at disguise are ineffectual, and her romances (written under an assumed name) are not going well. Overcome with nostalgia, she is forced to admit that, rather than beginning a new life, she has brought the past with her.

In the second narrative, Joan describes her childhood in Toronto. She recounts the misery of being a fat child and the discomfiture her obesity caused her beauty-obsessed mother and her Brownie companions. One of their pranks, tying Joan up on a bridge over a Toronto ravine where she is eventually rescued by the same man who had earlier exposed himself to her, causes her anxieties about identity. Further confusion ensues about her mother, who holds Joan responsible for the incident. Other painful episodes erode her self-image, and, to accommodate perceived expectations of her, Joan begins to explore and sustain various identities.

The third narrative reveals Joan living in a Toronto rooming house following an attack by her mother. Using the name of her aunt, Louisa K. Delacourt, who has left her two thousand dollars on condition that she lose one hundred pounds, she begins to write gothic romances. Joan achieves a new shape and determines that she needs to construct a past to accompany it. Traveling to London, England, she meets Paul, the Polish Count, who becomes her first lover because she mistakes the offer to share his apartment as a gesture of friendship. Later, when she meets Arthur, she falsifies her past, neglecting to tell him of her childhood obesity, the facts of her earlier relationship, or her authorship of gothic romances. When her mother dies accidentally, Joan goes home to Toronto and is shocked to find that her father has already given away her mother's clothes. Searching for clues about her mother's life before she was born, Joan locates a photograph album containing a picture of her father and another young man with their heads cut out. Joan begins to understand her mother's anger resulting from her entrapment in the role of making her family her career.

The fourth narrative tells of Arthur's coming to Toronto to find Joan and of their marriage. Unknown to Arthur, Joan continues writing romances, mainly as a defense against the complexity of his nature. Joan seeks stability in writing fantasy and maintaining the identities of both Joan Foster, wife of Arthur, and Louisa K. Delacourt, writer of popular romances. A foray into automatic writing produces *Lady Oracle*, a book of quasi-mystical poems that propels her into becoming an overnight literary cult figure. Her notoriety initiates an affair with a bizarre avant-garde artist named The Royal Porcupine and also incites Fraser Buchanan to discover her various identities and blackmail her. Joan's inability to cope with the tangle of her life or manage her separate identities prompts her staged suicide and her journey abroad for yet another life.

The fifth section brings the reader full circle. In Terremoto, Joan learns that in Toronto, two friends who aided her in her "suicide" have been arrested for murder. She determines to go back and rescue them. She strikes a reporter with a bottle, knocking him unconscious. While nursing him back to health, she makes the first step toward her real new life—telling the truth about her life to him, vowing to give up romance writing, and facing Arthur with the truth.

The Characters

The characters of Atwood's novel function not only as individuals but also as a means of exploration of new identities for Joan. Joan searches for her self in the characters she creates in her romance novels—in that they are all versions of herself—and in the "escapes" she precipitates from her various relationships. Her identity confusion, which centers on two images of herself—a ballerina and a circus fat lady—is played out through her writing of fantasies. As narrator of *Lady Oracle*, Joan describes the significant people in her life in terms of restrictions that mass-produced fantasies place on women. She registers certain cultural attitudes regarding femininity within the descriptions of herself and other characters in the novel.

Joan's mother, Fran Delacourt, is perceived by Joan as a mother-monster, an evil queen presiding over Joan's tormented childhood. Fran is disgusted with Joan's obesity and seeks constantly to change her into someone else. Her efforts to ascribe to Joan the girlhood ideal of femininity strikes Joan as so loathsome that Fran seems transformed by her three-way mirror into a three-headed monster. Joan hates not only her mother but also the mother within herself. After Fran's death, Joan's image of her cold, menacing mother continues to suffocate and cause her to fear engulfment by her mother. Toward the novel's end, Joan witnesses another spectral visitation of her mother's image and begins to understand that her mother, for good or ill, is part of her own personality.

Although Aunt Lou appears to Joan as cuddly and loving (the opposite of her mother), it is she who begins many of the fictions Joan never outgrows. Aunt Lou signs her name to pamphlets she does not write, conceals facts about her life from Joan, and leaves Joan inheritance money that will free her from her mother and start her on a new life.

Paul, the Polish Count, is a strange and mysterious author of romance novels who regales Joan with accounts of his heroic escape from Poland. Assigned a fictional role as gothic hero by Joan, he fails to fulfil her erotic fantasy in his unromantic pajamas. Paul, whom Joan suspects of having a secret, sinister life, has "two selves," which indicates Joan's fear of the man she looks to for rescue.

Arthur Foster also follows the romantic pattern begun by Paul. Melancholy and idealistic Arthur appears to be aloof, covering his real romantic nature with feigned indifference. Although his "Byronic" looks remind Joan of the hero of her current novel, once married to Joan, he soon becomes ordinary and therefore "multidimensional and complicated like everyone else."

The Royal Porcupine, with whom Joan has an affair when the romance in her marriage fades, seems in part the perfect romantic hero. A bizarre, avant-garde artist whose works include the bodies of road-killed animals, he wears a cape, dresses in absurd costumes, and waltzes in his apartment clad only in a lace tablecloth. When the Royal Porcupine, alias Chuck Brewer, commercial designer, confesses to Joan that he would like to lead a normal life, their affair is doomed.

Themes and Meanings

A parody of the gothic romance, *Lady Oracle* establishes Joan Foster as an escape artist intent on evading reality and commitment by "writing" her own world. Modeling her life on a romance plot, Joan attempts to dramatize the romantic myth given to women in an unromantic world. As Joan moves through self-deluding fictions into a realm of fairy tales and myth and a mirrorlike world of identities that ultimately produce entrapment, Atwood debunks the romantic ideal through her comic descriptions of mundane married life. Unable to accept the multiplicity and complexity of human beings, and therefore the reality of her own identity, Joan enacts feminine roles in her relationships with men. Fictional constructs in popular romances for women bind and confine women in their roles and also in the roles they place upon men. After Joan loses weight and becomes attractive to men, she embarks on a course through which Atwood deliberately exposes the seductive but repressive power of mass-culture romance fictions.

However, Atwood makes her point most emphatically through Joan's "professional" fantasy life—her romance-in-progress that evolves throughout *Lady Oracle*.

In *Stalked by Love*, the heroine, Charlotte, is haunted by anxieties and fears that, though mocked by Joan, are, at the same time, Joan's fears. At first, following the conventional pattern of gothic romance, Joan depicts Charlotte as good and innocent and Felicia as the angry, bad, destructive wife. As Atwood's narrative moves deeper into Joan's psyche, the reality of Joan's life and the fantasy of the novel-in-progress begin to coalesce as Joan and Felicia become one. Joan identifies with Felicia, who, drawn into the maze of the gothic text, meets four women who claim to be her, paralleling the multiple identities of Joan's multiple selves. Felicia seeks her husband, Redmond, who appears to offer freedom but conceals a terrorizing domination, representing a composite of all the men in Joan's life. To be "stalked by love" is to be trapped in the ideology of the romance plot. Women who seek rescue and fulfilment seek entrapment in the dominance of men, and it is to escape this that Joan becomes and "escape artist" by creating her own plot. Through Joan, the artist, Atwood also challenges cultural myths about female artists, specifically those that assert that women must sacrifice the traditional satisfaction of being women, or must automatically become self-destructive women authors.

Critical Context

Margaret Atwood's third novel, *Lady Oracle* continues her woman-centered approach, specifically her elaboration of the effects of romance fantasies upon women. An astute observer of culture, Atwood believes that popular fiction successfully connects with the reality of women's lives and thereby perpetuates ideologies that limit their self-definition and self-fulfillment. The energies of *Lady Oracle* toward enumerating women's needs in a male-defined society follow themes that had begun years earlier in her prose and poetry. Her first major collection of poetry, *The Circle Game* (1966), although demonstrating a more private voice, contains images of repression and attempted escape with special aversion to patterns of myths that bind human beings. *The Animals in That Country* (1968) suggests the Canadian search for identity in the face of false perceptions encouraged about Canada, particularly among Americans. *The Journals of Susannah Moodie* (1970), a modern-day look at the mid-nineteenth century settler in Canada, continues a preoccupation with a search for identity amid repressive circumstances. Furthering the emphasis on the submerged side of life, Atwood published *Procedures for Underground* in the same year.

Atwood's prose craft is an outgrowth of her early apprenticeship. *The Edible Woman* (1969) describes a movement away from romantic connections, and in *Surfacing* (1971), Atwood angrily rejects masculinist culture and idealizes femininity. Following *Lady Oracle*, *Life Before Man* (1979) contests the socially accepted myths of romantic love and marital harmony. *Bodily Harm* (1981) and *The Handmaid's Tale* (1985) lay bare the misogyny, or hatred of women, inherent in a patriarchal culture, whereas *Cat's Eye* (1988) and *The Robber Bride* (1993) reject the idea of women's superiority, focusing on the power politics of women's relationships and exposing them as potentially exploitative and oppressive. Atwood's books sound a cautionary voice about the damaging effects of society's repressive forces.

Bibliography

Bouson, J. Brooks. *Brutal Choreographies: Oppositional Strategies and Narrative Design in the Novels of Margaret Atwood*. Amherst: University of Massachusetts Press, 1993. A chronological discussion of Atwood's novels, emphasizing the psychological and political concerns in each.

Hutcheon, Linda. "From Poetic to Narrative Structures." In *Margaret Atwood: Language, Text, and System*, edited by Sherrill E. Grace and Lorraine Weir. Vancouver: University of British Columbia Press, 1985. Brief but informative discussion of the life/art opposition in *Lady Oracle*.

Rigney, Barbara Hill. *Margaret Atwood*. Totowa, N.J.: Barnes & Noble, 1987. Contains a chaper on *Lady Oracle* that depicts Joan Foster as one who escapes reality and lives only in her art.

Rosenberg, Jerome H. *Margaret Atwood*. Boston: Twayne, 1984. Comprehensive study of Atwood's works and development of her craft.

Vincent, Sybil Korff. "The Mirror and the Cameo: Margaret Atwood's Comic/Gothic Novel, *Lady Oracle*." In *The Female Gothic*, edited by Juliann E. Fleenor. Montreal: Eden Press, 1983. Explores *Lady Oracle* as an example of a new subgenre, the Comic/Gothic.

Mary Hurd

THE LAND OF PLENTY

Author: Robert Cantwell (1908-1978)
Type of plot: Social realism
Time of plot: The early 1930's
Locale: A small mill town in western Washington State
First published: 1934

Principal characters:

>HAGEN, an electrician and natural leader of the night shift at the veneer
>   factory
>JOHNNY, his son, recently hired at the plant
>CARL BELCHER, the night foreman
>MACMAHON, the manager of the plant
>WINTERS, another experienced worker
>WALT CONNOR, a contemporary of Johnny's
>ELLEN and
>MARIE TURNER, sisters working at the plant
>ROSE MACMAHON, the manager's daughter

The Novel

The Land of Plenty is divided into two parts and covers a few tense days in a strike at a veneer plant in western Washington. While little time passes in the novel, Robert Cantwell manages to convey fully both the socioeconomic forces and the psychological tensions in this workplace.

Part 1, "Power and Light," covers less than an hour, but it is a gripping depiction of the confused actions in that brief time. The first chapter opens, "Suddenly the lights went out." A failure at the power house away from the plant is the cause, but the factory is now in darkness, both literally and figuratively. Carl, the night foreman, who should be in charge, is paralyzed by the darkness and by his unfamiliarity with the plant. Meanwhile, a hoist man has been hurt when the power shut down and a huge log crushed him, and part of the drama of part 1 comes from the reader's knowledge that this worker lies injured somewhere in the darkness.

While Carl is wandering around in the dark, Hagen, the real leader of the night shift, is advising other workers what to do, trying to send messages to Carl, and working to save life and property. Yet the tensions between management and workers are terrible, and every action is preceded by a calculation of how it will affect job security. These tensions make the decisions of part 1 doubly difficult: whether to "pull the fires" in the furnaces, for example, or to break into the locked factory office to call the power house.

As the characters wander in the dark, Cantwell slowly reveals their situations. The date is July 3, the day before a national holiday, but there is hardly a festive mood. It is early in the Depression of the 1930's, and the economic troubles of the country are apparent in the Northwest as well. Fifty men have been fired since Carl arrived, and there have been two paycuts. These economic woes have been compounded by personal problems. Ed Winters, the halfbreed who is Johnny's crew boss, has a wife dying of cancer in the hospital; Marie Turner, on the line this night, is still sick from the abortion she had a few days before.

In the one chapter of part 1 that leaves the darkness of the factory, Cantwell depicts the tensions in Rose MacMahon's house as her parents fight over money. The only thing that saves the situation is the power failure, and Rose is enlisted to drive her father to the plant to see what is wrong. Once he is there, the action of the novel, in the last four chapters, accelerates. Winters hits Carl and grabs his flashlight to help save the hoist man. He then commandeers Rose's car and drives it over the tideflats to use the headlights to illuminate the rescue scene. Carl, meanwhile, wandering in the plant, falls through the floor and runs into MacMahon in the mud below the factory; the two managers argue economics as they struggle in the muck.

The hoist man is finally freed and sent to the hospital, but in his frustration at the whole situation, Carl fires Winters and then Hagen. The workers convince MacMahon to rescind the firings and now realize their power; in the last lines of part 1, Cantwell writes, "They were proud; they were excited. . . . They had their first sure knowledge of their strength."

Part 2, "The Education of a Worker," develops the consequences of this dark night. It is the Fourth of July, the hoist man has died, and different characters meet and talk about what will happen. When they arrive for work the next day, Johnny and his father discover that management has laid off twenty workers, including Hagen and Winters, and the night shift walks out, calls out the day shift, and the strike begins. Yet the strikers soon realize that they are facing not only the owners but also the combined forces of management, the police, and the press.

A picket line is set up, and everything moves smoothly until a rainstorm hits and the strikers break for the shelter of the factory. Once inside, they mingle with the scabs who have taken over their jobs, and the police have trouble maintaining order. One of the strikers cuts the power, the police shoot a scab by mistake, and the strikers take over the plant. The die has been cast, and the forces in this tragedy are now arrayed against each other in the driving rain. Digby, the plant's owner, shows up at MacMahon's house to direct the actions against the strikers. More strikers sneak into the factory; in the last dramatic moments, fights break out in the rain, Ellen Turner is clubbed by the police, and Hagen is shot. Johnny escapes across the tideflats, and the novel ends as he sits in the brush with two other workers, "listening and waiting for the darkness to come like a friend and set them free."

The Characters

Each of the twenty-three chapters in *The Land of Plenty* is titled with a character's name. Six chapters are Johnny Hagen's, five revolve around Walt Connor, three Carl Belcher, two each for Hagen and Winters, and one each for Marie, Ellen, and "The Light Man" who is trying to collect money from Hagen on his electricity bill. In this way, Cantwell is able to describe both action and motivation from different perspectives; in fact, in what is a daring move, the first chapter of *The Land of Plenty* is narrated from the consciousness of Carl Belcher, who of course becomes one of the leading villains in the story. Cantwell's method works well; instead of feeling that the odds have been stacked in this class war, readers view Depression situations from the perspectives of all the different characters, strikers and managers alike.

While the major action in the novel is carried by the more experienced characters such as Hagen, Winters, and Carl, the title of part 2—"The Education of a Worker"—shows that the novel is really about the next generation, Johnny and Walt, and these two characters have nearly half the chapters in the book, all but four in part 2. The parallels between the two young men are clear, for both have had to forgo plans for college to return to work. Yet while Johnny learns over the course of the novel that "the workingman hasn't got a chance," Walt goes over to management. It is his education as well as Johnny's, however, for he learns in the end just how corrupt the owners are.

The focus in the novel is not exclusively on character, for Cantwell uses character to drive the dramatic action, and part of his attention is on the conditions of these people. Given this stress, it is amazing how full drawn many of the characters are. Only a few characters—such as the owner Digby, who blames imaginary communists for the strike and urges managers to bribe city officials—come across as two-dimensional. In short, there is a psychological accuracy to the novel that matches the socioeconomic truths Cantwell is revealing. This is a strike novel, but it works because readers care about all the characters and how they are trapped, both in the world of the veneer factory and in the Depression.

The novel is also successful because its style is clean and not overloaded with literary devices. Even the symbolism of the novel is underplayed: The story begins and remains much in darkness, which clearly represents the condition of all the characters as well as the failure of capitalism itself. Similarly, the setting is a door factory, and yet there are few exits or escapes for any of the characters. The managers fall through holes in the floor and wander lost in the muck; the strikers must run free of the factory to save themselves.

Themes and Meanings

The Land of Plenty is a strike novel, a subgenre of the proletarian novel of the 1930's, a social realist literary form that tells a story from the perspective of working-class people. Cantwell shows not only the economic situations of these people but also how the strikers learn to gain their own power. The irresolute conclusion, however, reveals that there is no guarantee that such strike actions will result in triumph. It would be a few years before sit-down strikes in Akron, Ohio, and Flint, Michigan, would show workers what they could do when they took over plants.

The novel also succeeds because it captures the complexity of the strike situation and shows what drives managers as well as workers—the naturalistic forces that play upon all the characters. As Hagen's son-in-law Bill, who has just lost his job in Texas, asks:

What the hell has happened to everything? You read in the paper things have never been so good; there's never been so much prosperity; the God-damned stock market is booming; and then you find out you can't get work, everybody's losing his job, or their wages are being cut.

This is "Puzzled America," as the writer Sherwood Anderson described it in 1935, and both managers and workers are in the dark about what is happening to them. The novel is a tragedy in which the characters must play out their parts in a deterministic, nightmare Depression world.

Critical Context

The Land of Plenty was one of the best proletarian novels that was produced during the Depression, especially in the first half of the 1930's, as writers responded to worsening socioeconomic conditions and described these conditions for the poor and unemployed. The leftward literary movement, which would culminate in novels like John Steinbeck's *The Grapes of Wrath* (1939) and Richard Wright's *Native Son* (1940), also saw dozens of novels such as Cantwell's and plays such as Clifford Odets's *Waiting for Lefty* (1936), social realist works that depicted working conditions from the perspective of the laboring classes and envisioned workers finding the strength to overcome the forces of capitalism that exploited them.

Cantwell produced one earlier novel, *Laugh and Lie Down* (1931), and wrote a number of short stories, but, like many 1930's writers, he drifted away from his early social realism and actually ended his career in the 1960's as one of the first editors of *Sports Illustrated*. Still, his novel stands as a landmark in an important literary movement in America, sparked by Marxist literary criticism but truly fueled by the conditions under which people in the Depression were forced to live. In 1932, when one out of every four workers was unemployed, even the blindest of American writers recognized emerging social realist subjects. Robert Cantwell was one of dozens of writers who responded to these Depression conditions and produced lasting literary works. More than half a century later, it is hard to name a novel that describes working conditions and strikes with the accuracy and drama of *The Land of Plenty*.

Bibliography

Conroy, Jack. "Robert Cantwell's *Land of Plenty*." In *Proletarian Writers of the Thirties*, edited by Harry T. Moore. Carbondale: Southern Illinois University Press, 1968. A proletarian novelist himself (*The Disinherited*, 1933), Conroy gives a positive reading of Cantwell's novel thirty-five years later.

Denning, Michael. *The Cultural Front: The Laboring of American Culture in the Twentieth Century*. London: Verso, 1996. Denning only deals with *The Land of Plenty* in passing, but his study is the best account of the radical literary culture of the 1930's.

Moore, Harry T. Preface to the *The Land of Plenty*, by Robert Cantwell. Carbondale: Southern Illinois University Press, 1962. Moore's preface to this reissue of *The*

Land of Plenty gives the broad biographical background to Cantwell's novel.

Rideout, Walter B. *The Radical Novel in the United States, 1900-1954*. Cambridge, Mass.: Harvard University Press, 1956. This early study is still the best overview of the proletarian novel of the 1930's. Includes an excellent four-page analysis of *The Land of Plenty*.

David Peck

LAST EXIT TO BROOKLYN

Author: Hubert Selby, Jr. (1928-   )
Type of plot: Social realism
Time of plot: The 1950's
Locale: The Red Hook area of Brooklyn, New York
First published: 1964

> *Principal characters:*
> VINNIE, a local gang leader
> GEORGETTE, a local transvestite who loves Vinnie
> TRALALA, a prostitute
> HARRY BLACK, a union steward
> MARY BLACK, Harry's wife
> GINGER and
> ALBERTA, homosexuals whom Harry meets
> MIKE and
> IRENE KELLY, occupants of a housing project
> ADA, a widow in the housing project
> LUCY and
> JOHNNY, a married couple in the housing project
> ABRAHAM WASHINGTON, an inhabitant of the housing project

The Novel

Last Exit to Brooklyn consists of five parts and a coda. There is a central episode about a labor strike that involves the novel's characters either directly or as peripheral onlookers. The elapsed time of the novel is several months, though no definite time markers appear in the story.

There is a single omniscient narrator who describes each scene with an unflinching eye while recounting the horrors of the brutal environment of Brooklyn's Red Hook area, which includes a military base, a manufacturing plant, and a public housing project as the focal points upon which the novel turns. Central to the action and serving as a rallying point is a diner where a group of young men make obscene comments about other patrons, including Georgette, a transvestite. Georgette loves the gang leader, Vinnie, who appears to ignore Georgette, yet the impression the author gives is that Vinnie, despite his outwardly heterosexual appearance, has had a past sexual relationship with Georgette. The scene moves to the street, where Georgette is stabbed by one of Vinnie's gang immediately after the gang has brutally beaten three soldiers, almost killing one. When the police arrive, the gang lies about the attack. Vinnie and Alex take Georgette home, where he is confronted by his violent brother, Arthur, who hates Georgette's sexual ambiguity. Georgette escapes from his home, brother, and overly protective mother to the home of a fellow transvestite named Goldie. Several effeminate transvestites have gathered at Goldie's apartment to take drugs, drink, and plot how to lure Vinnie and his gang in for a sexual encounter. Their success in this endeavor ends the first and second sections, "Another Day Another Dollar" and "The Queen Is Dead."

Section 3, "And Baby Makes Three," recounts rapidly the marriage of Tommy and Suzy and the introduction of Spook, whose only goal in life is to own a motorcycle to establish himself in the motorcycle culture that surrounds them all. Section four, "Tralala," shows Tralala, a prostitute, becoming addicted to alcohol and sex. After a series of casual relationships, she becomes more degraded, until she takes on a series of men in the gutted remains of a car. The section ends with Tralala left for dead in the car.

"The Strike" traces the brutal relationship between Harry Black and his wife, Mary, with whom he has violent sex. Harry then goes to work as a lathe operator at a manufacturing plant. Harry has some limited power as the shop steward; as the result of a fight over union rules, a strike is declared. Harry becomes the picket-line overseer and spends his days drinking in the union office. While he is drinking one day, Ginger, a male homosexual, comes in with some of the striking workers. Ginger's exotic nature attracts Harry, who soon becomes a regular at Mary's, a local homosexual bar. At Mary's bar, Harry meets Alberta, a male homosexual, and they start a relationship. As Harry falls more deeply in love with Alberta, the strike comes to an end, and Harry is deprived of the extra money he received as strike boss, so Alberta leaves him. On his way home, Harry molests a young boy in a vacant lot, after which he is beaten by Vinnie, Joey, and Sal who rescue the boy.

The final section, "Landsend," is the coda to the novel and is a series of vignettes beginning with Mike and Irene Kelly. All the couples, such as Mike and Irene, and the single people, such as Ada, lead a double life. There is the life that other people see, and then there is the life that the characters actually live. For example, on the surface Mike and Irene are a normal married couple, but the reader discovers that their marriage is violent and abusive. Ada is a lonely widow; however, the woman's chorus (a group of project women who gossip about the other inhabitants) say that she is old, decrepit, and crazy as she sits in the warmth of the spring sun remembering her dead husband and son. Lucy and Johnny seem to be a nice young family with well-adjusted children. However, Lucy is a compulsive cleaner, and her husband is a student who obsesses about his studies. The very moral Lucy goes to bed with Abraham Washington, the local lady's man, who is married to the alcoholic Nancy. This coda picks up all the brutality that has played in the novel and repeats, it bringing the book to an end.

Themes and Meanings

Last Exit to Brooklyn is a violent, realistic, and brutal novel that captures the animalistic world of 1950's Brooklyn. The novel displays a gangland underbelly and reflects the grinding poverty, financial and moral, of Brooklyn's Red Hook. Some critics believe that the novel mirrors the characters and situations that its author knew before he left New York for California.

The novel is a recollection of a time when the world should have been basking in the peace following World War II yet was preparing for the Korean War. Its main theme is anxiety brought on by the location. The novel shows the anxiety about being a man and rebelling against being a man. The novel also shows the anxiety about being a woman and mother during the time and coping with husbands and boyfriends who are unsure of their own personas. It is no surprise that the character of Vinnie is drawn in such a stereotype of gang masculinity that he has no other outlet than to beat soldiers who pass by the diner because he cannot be one of them, with their socially acceptable appearance of manhood. Instead, Vinnie is a predator who laughs as Georgette is stabbed yet flirts with him in the security of Goldie's apartment when everyone is high on drugs and alcohol. Similarly, in the final section, Lucy is obsessive with her cleaning and in the end sleeps with Abe as an act of defiance against the role society has forced upon her. All the characters are stereotypes of their sexual or societal roles and suffer from great anxiety as a result.

Anxiety is carried into the workplace with the extended middle section, "The Strike." Harry Black can have sex with his wife only if he literally attacks her in bed; she responds in a violent manner to his attempts at lovemaking. Harry's outlet from anxiety is found in the arms of Alberta, his homosexual lover. The molestation at the chapter's end clearly reflects society's disapproval delivered at the hands of its cruelest and ironic messengers: Vinnie and his gang.

The concern with anxiety is presented effectively using some techniques of experimental fiction. For example, the author makes no attempt to punctuate the text, and in dialogue where the couple is yelling at each other, full capital letters are used to display emotion. What will also strike the careful reader is the novel's organization and tempo, which mimic the musical form of a sonata. First, in its "allegro" section, the novel moves through a brief section of seventy-nine pages in which the theme of anxiety is quickly introduced; the second section, like an adagio, develops that theme more slowly with "And Baby Makes Three" and "Tralala." The third, scherzo, section, occupied by "The Strike," rapidly develops the anxiety that Harry feels about his manhood and work. The coda, "Landsend," recapitulates the violence, anxiety, and brutality that play through the preceding movements.

Critical Context

Last Exit to Brooklyn was Selby's first novel and was very controversial because of its frank depiction of homosexuality, wife and child abuse, drug abuse, street violence, and language. There was an obscenity trial in England over the novel upon its release there; an R-rated movie version was released in 1989.

The book's author takes his cues from his life experiences. Selby continued writing on the violent topics in *Last Exit to Brooklyn* in *The Room* (1971), which is about a small-time criminal in a holding cell. Selby's third novel, *The Demon* (1976), is about Harry White, who leads a life of escalating crime ending in murder. His fourth novel, *Requiem for a Dream* (1978), describes the downward spiral of four addicts. His 1986 *Song of the Silent Snow* is a collection of fifteen short stories about the character

Harry, who is portrayed differently in each story. Selby also made a spoken-word recording, *Live in Europe 1989*, with Henry Rollins, a performance artist with whom Selby toured Europe; the recording contains selections from *Last Exit to Brooklyn*.

Selby expresses the rage and outspoken criticism common to much of the other literature of the Beat generation. Such Beat artists as Allen Ginsberg and Jack Kerouac, who made their names in the 1950's, thus stand as precursors to Selby.

Bibliography

Gontarski, S. E. "*Last Exit to Brooklyn*: An Interview with Hubert Selby." *The Review of Contemporary Fiction* 10, no. 3 (Fall, 1990): 5. A frank interview with the author about his first novel.

Hicks, Chris. "Turkey!" *Deseret News* (October 5, 1990): 1. An unfavorable review of the 1989 movie version of *Last Exit to Brooklyn*; an interesting perspective on the novel.

Selby, Herbert, Jr. "Examining the Disease: An Interview with Hubert Selby, Jr." Interview by Allan Vorda. *The Literary Review* 35, no. 2 (Winter, 1992): 288. Selby explains the themes that he explores in his novels.

Dennis L. Weeks

THE LAST GENTLEMAN

Author: Walker Percy (1916-1990)
Type of plot: Comic realism
Time of plot: The mid-1960's
Locale: New York City, the South, and the Southwest
First published: 1966

> *Principal characters:*
> WILLISTON (WILL) BIBB BARRETT, the protagonist, a humidification
>   engineer at Macy's and a former Princeton student from the South
> CHANDLER VAUGHT, a self-made Alabamian, owner of the world's
>   second largest Chevrolet dealership
> KITTY, Vaught's daughter, with whom Will falls in love
> SUTTER, Kitty's older brother, an assistant coroner
> VALENTINE (VAL), Kitty's sister, who has joined a Catholic order to
>   care for poor black children
> JAMIE, Kitty's younger brother
> RITA, Sutter's former wife

The Novel

After five fruitless years in psychoanalysis, Will Barrett decides to become an observer rather than the observed. He is twenty-five years old and subject to frequent fugue states; his only gift is "the knack of divining persons and situations." One day in Central Park he spots Kitty Vaught through his newly purchased telescope. Suddenly in love, he tracks Kitty to a New York hospital where she and her family are tending to Jamie Vaught, her younger brother. The Vaughts take to Will because he adapts to each of them in the manner of the perfect gentleman: To Chandler Vaught, he is the kind of Southern boy an older man befriends; to Mrs. Vaught, he is all courtesy and lightness; to Jamie, he is a fellow technician.

Will's ability to communicate with Jamie leads first Mr. Vaught, then Rita Vaught, to hire Will to accompany the family as they take Jamie back home. Later, after missed connections, Will strikes out for the South in search of the Vaughts. He spots the family's Trav-L-Aire parked at a motel on the outskirts of Williamsburg, Virginia. Rita tells Will to take Jamie in Ulysses (her name for the Trav-L-Aire) and find their destiny, but Will does not want to stray far from Kitty, whose kisses he finds are nevertheless "too dutiful and athletic," as if she were auditioning for the part of a proper Southern girl.

Will lives for a time with the Vaughts in their mansion in Atlanta, which overlooks a golf course. Valentine Vaught, Kitty's sister, enters Will's life, having sought him out to explain that Jamie's salvation may well be up to him and that he must see to it that Jamie is baptized into the Faith. Ironically, moments later Will is face-to-face with Sutter Vaught, who is pleading for help for his own maladies. Will senses in Sutter something beyond mere possibility, mere courteous existence;

Sutter in his unbridled life knows more than anyone else.

One day Jamie disappears. He has gone off with Sutter, and Will must take the Trav-L-Aire and bring the poor boy home. There follows a series of misadventures that take Will through his hometown of Ithaca, Mississippi, and eventually to New Mexico, guided by a map which Sutter has left in his apartment. Along with the map, Will finds a steno notebook in which Sutter has entered autopsy reports mingled with journal-like passages and ironic, highly personal philosophical reflections, many of which center on the peculiar power of sexuality in "post-Christian" America. Will takes the notebook with him on his journey and reads from it periodically; thus, at intervals, the narrative includes excerpts from this strange diary—a venerable device which allows Percy to explore novelistically some of the notions that have continued to preoccupy him in such (largely) nonfictional works as *Lost in the Cosmos: The Last Self-Help Book* (1983).

Sutter is now working at a guest ranch in Santa Fe and has put Jamie in the hospital. Jamie is dying of pulmonary edema, yet in the midst of Jamie's frequent dizziness his friendship with Will deepens. Sutter is an outsider, thankful for Will's ministrations. In the final passages of Sutter's notebook, Will learns of Sutter's suicide attempt a year ago, while in the midst of severe depression at the prospect of Jamie's unpleasant death. Will is astonished for the first time in his life when he realizes that Sutter again intends to take his own life.

Just before his death, Jamie murmurs the words of faith, coached by the hospital chaplain brought by Will. Moments later, as Sutter leaves for the ranch, Will confronts him, imploring him not to leave. Sutter laughs and heads off in his Edsel. Will runs after the car, yelling for Sutter to wait, and the car slowly stops. For the engineer, pure possibility has given way to determined choice, and he will bear it.

The Characters

Williston Bibb Barrett is handsome, friendly, and intelligent, but unremarkable. His courtesy reflects not a studied culture but the natural adaptability of a person who is pure possibility. Will makes "the highest possible scores on psychological aptitude tests, especially in the area of problem-solving and goal-seeking. The trouble was he couldn't think what to do between tests." Will is subject to fugue states that blot out his recent past, yet inklings return in his frequent déjà vus.

The omniscient narrator of the novel rarely refers to Will by name; instead, he is called "the courteous engineer" or "the sentient engineer," an ironic mixing of Will's gentlemanly nature and keen insight with his inability to engineer his own life. Until the end of the book, his life course is basically determined by others.

Sutter Vaught made high grades at Harvard Medical School, but at age thirty-four he does not practice medicine; instead, he writes pathology reports as an assistant coroner. Sutter's medical insurance was cancelled after he put a depressed patient in the terminal ward of the hospital (where the patient became quite cheerful) and then sent him home to his family and garden after the patient suffered what was to be a fatal heart attack.

Sutter does not fit the boundaries of courtesy; in his notebooks he extols the virtues of lewdness. He rails against so-called Christian America for its outward decorum but covert lewdness (as seen in soap operas and in the theater). As overtly lewd, Sutter calls himself the only sincere American. Will needs Sutter as a kind of shock treatment to the soul.

Kitty Vaught is twenty-one and pretty, but her life is a performance. After years of ballet lessons she is still not a dancer. Though she accepts Will's marriage proposal, in their failed sexual encounter, which occurs one evening in Central Park, she is still very much a child trying to act the proper role. Will becomes a father figure as well as courteous suitor.

Kitty finds life as a Southern girl in her parents' home simply boring. Rita Vaught's seeming devotion to the Zuni Indians and her love of poetry excite Kitty. Rita basks in Kitty's adoration though it drives Rita and Sutter further apart. Rita calls Sutter selfish; she is most unpleasantly meddlesome, domineering, and patronizing.

Val is devoted to the children of poverty. Her faith takes even her by surprise. She tells Will that she is mean, a hater, hoping her enemies fry in Hell. In the outlandishness of her faith, she is self-deprecating. Yet she believes what the Church teaches, and she is especially concerned for Jamie, her sixteen-year-old brother.

Jamie is a catalyst for the others. Their lives revolve around his illness. Chandler Vaught is the Old South. Self-made, uncomprehending of Sutter's strange actions, he is happy to give Kitty in marriage to Will. After all, Will can talk to Jamie; Mr. Vaught has a dealership to run.

Themes and Meanings

Sutter's notebook contains some key observations. If man is a wayfarer, he never stops anywhere long enough to hear that there is hope that conquers despair, salvation that conquers death. Will's amnesia is not a symptom but the human condition: Man struggles to make the world anew at every moment; because he is ill-fitted for this Godlike task, it is not ennobling but pitiable. Sutter's solution involves extremes of emotion and choice, as if they could somehow exalt a man to the stature necessary to reconstruct the world. For Will it is different; Sutter is wrong in his extremes: "God and not-God, getting under women's dresses and blowing your brains out. Whereas and in fact my problem is how to live from one ordinary minute to the next on a Wednesday afternoon."

The Last Gentleman is Will's journey from pure possibility to actuality, from telescopic observer and wayfarer in a Trav-L-Aire named Ulysses, to comforter of a dying friend and agent of salvation for a living one. Will has in some sense become a preserver of continuity.

Walker Percy takes ample opportunity to observe the passing scene. He wryly comments that though the North has never lost a war, Northerners have become solitary and withdrawn, as if ravaged by war. In sharp contrast, the South is invincibly happy. Will feels most homeless when he is among those who appear to be completely at home: "The happiness of the South drove him wild with despair."

Percy presents no simple solution to the plague of homelessness. If Will is to reenter the South and marry Kitty, he wants Sutter with him. Perhaps Will is still a wayfarer, yet in *The Last Gentleman* he has stayed around just long enough to hear something of the honest truth.

Critical Context

The Last Gentleman was Percy's second novel and was nominated for a National Book Award—a prize which his first novel, *The Moviegoer* (1961), won in 1962. Percy's life experiences are mirrored in his works. An Alabamian and an avid film buff, he contracted tuberculosis while performing autopsies. During his long convalescence, Percy began constructing his novels. His stories trace the journeys of people whose selves have been "lost in the cosmos" and how those selves might reenter the world. A life of pure possibility, comprehending all choices, is not the way. Rather, an existential choice must be made to put the self in relationship with other selves. That is where transcendence is discovered. Will Barrett appears again, this time middleaged, in *The Second Coming* (1980), and he reflects on the visage of an old priest: "Could it be that the Lord is here, masquerading behind this simple silly holy face?"

Bibliography

Allen, William Rodney. *Walker Percy: A Southern Wayfarer.* Jackson: University Press of Mississippi, 1986. Allen reads Percy as a distinctly American, particularly Southern writer, claiming that the formative event in Percy's life was his father's suicide, not his reading of existentialist writers or conversion to Roman Catholicism. Allen's readings of individual novels emphasize the presence of weak fathers and rejection of the southern stoic heritage on the part of Percy's protagonists.

Coles, Robert. *Walker Percy: An American Search.* Boston: Little, Brown, 1978. An early but always intelligent and certainly sensitive reading of Percy's essays and novels by a leading psychiatrist whose main contention is that Percy's work speaks directly to modern humanity. In Coles's words, Percy "has balanced a contemporary Christian existentialism with the pragmatism and empiricism of an American physician."

Desmond, John F. *At the Crossroads: Ethical and Religious Themes in the Writings of Walker Percy.* Troy, N.Y.: Whitston, 1997. Chapters on Percy and T. S. Eliot; on Percy's treatment of suicide; on Percy and Flannery O'Connor; on his treatment of myth, history, and religion; and his philosophical debt to pragmatism and Charles Sanders Peirce. A useful, accessible introduction to Percy's background in theology and philosophy.

Hardy, John Edward. *The Fiction of Walker Percy.* Urbana: University of Illinois Press, 1987. The originality of this book, comprising an introduction and six chapters (one for each of the novels, including *The Thanatos Syndrome*), derives from Hardy's choosing to read the novels in terms of internal formal matters rather than (as is usually the case) Percy's essays, existentialism, Catholicism, or southern background. Hardy sees Percy as a novelist, not a prophet.

Lawson, Lewis A. *Following Percy: Essays on Walker Percy's Work*. Troy, N.Y.: Whitston, 1988. Collects essays originally published between 1969 and 1984 by one of Percy's most dedicated, prolific, and knowledgeable commentators. Discussions of *The Moviegoer* and *Lancelot* predominate.

Percy, Walker. *Conversations with Walker Percy*, edited by Lewis A. Lawson and Victor A. Kramer. Jackson: University Press of Mississippi, 1985. This indispensable volume collects all the most important interviews with Percy, including one (with the editors) previously unpublished. The volume is especially important for biographical background, influences, discussion of writing habits, and the author's comments on individual works through *Lost in the Cosmos*.

Quinlan, Kieran. *Walker Percy: The Last Catholic Novelist*. Baton Rouge: Louisiana State University Press, 1996. Chapters on Percy as novelist and philosopher, existentialist, explorer of modern science. Recommended for the advanced student who has already read Desmond. Includes notes and bibliography.

Tharpe, Jac. *Walker Percy*. Boston: Twayne, 1983. Reading Percy as a Roman Catholic novelist concerned chiefly with eschatological matters, Tharpe divides his study into ten chapters: "Biography, Background, and Influences," "Theory of Art," "Christendom," "Techniques," one chapter on each of the five novels through *The Second Coming*, and conclusion. The annotated secondary bibliography is especially good.

_____, ed. *Walker Percy: Art and Ethics*. Jackson: University Press of Mississippi, 1980. Ten essays by diverse hands, plus a bibliography. The essays focus on settings, existential sources, Martin Heidegger, Percy's theory of language, the semiotician Charles Sanders Peirce, Percy's politics, and *Lancelot* (in terms of his essays, Roman Catholicism, medieval sources, and semiotics).

Dan Barnett

THE LAST HURRAH

Author: Edwin O'Connor (1918-1968)
Type of plot: Political
Time of plot: The 1950's
Locale: A large New England city
First published: 1956

> *Principal characters:*
> FRANK SKEFFINGTON, the mayor, a former governor
> FRANK SKEFFINGTON, JR., Skeffington's weak son
> ADAM CAULFIELD, a newspaper cartoonist and Skeffington's nephew
> MAEVE CAULFIELD, Adam's wife
> ROGER SUGRUE, Adam's father-in-law
> AMOS FORCE, a newspaper publisher and bitter enemy of Skeffington
> SAM WEINBERG and
> JOHN GORMAN, Skeffington's chief advisers
> DITTO BOLAND, one of Skeffington's hangers-on
> THE CARDINAL, a high Catholic church official and old enemy of
> Skeffington
> KEVIN MCCLUSKEY, a political neophyte and Skeffington's mayoral
> opponent

The Novel

The Last Hurrah is divided into four parts and fourteen chapters. The first three parts relate the tale of Frank Skeffington, former governor of an eastern state and now mayor of a large unidentified city, clearly meant to be Boston, and his campaign for reelection. The fourth section relates the election's aftermath. Many commentators believe that O'Connor modeled Skeffington on James Michael Curley, several times mayor of Boston, onetime governor of Massachusetts, and the paradigm of the second-generation immigrant politician and big-city political boss. O'Connor's Skeffington was apparently close enough to the real Curley for the latter to sue for invasion of privacy when *The Last Hurrah* was turned into a movie of the same name.

The story of what proves to be Frank Skeffington's last political campaign is told in the third person. Now in his seventies, Skeffington has been mayor long enough to engender considerable popular support among many members of the various ethnic groups that make up the city's population, not least among his fellow Irish Americans. He has also made many enemies, partly because he represented those first- and second-generation immigrants who displaced the earlier establishment, partly because as a successful politician he had frequently and blatantly rewarded his friends by providing jobs, awarding city contracts, and conducting other marginally legal activities, and partly over personal rivalries and animosities, often long-standing.

To Skeffington, a widower, his only child, Frank Skeffington, Jr., is a failure. Somehow, the latter became a lawyer and, with his father's support, obtained an adequate position, but in reality he is superficial, lacking in perception as well as ability, preferring nightclubs and dancing to anything more substantial. Rejecting his son, Skeffington instead approaches his nephew, Adam Caulfield, and asks if he would like to observe the impending reelection campaign for mayor. Never close to his uncle before, and knowing his wife, Maeve, influenced by her bigoted father, objects to Skeffington and all his deeds, Adam, who has lost his own parents in an automobile accident, is somewhat reluctant; nevertheless, he agrees, becoming a witness to a passing age in American politics. An old-style political boss, Skeffington has achieved his successes by taking care of the immigrant and working-class voters, primarily through personal contacts. His door is open every morning to anyone who needed a few dollars, a job, help with the law, or whatever was necessary to survive in urban America. His evenings are spent at various ethnic and immigrant social gatherings, at a church, a wake, or a Columbus Day dinner. Politics means organization, down to the ward and precinct levels, and Skeffington's organization is superb; in the past, that was sufficient. However, Skeffington's longstanding enemies, notably newspaper publisher Amos Force, are determined defeat him, and have hand-picked a nonentity, Kevin McCluskey, as their candidate of choice. McCluskey seems perfect; he has no record that can be attacked, his family is telegenic, and he is malleable. The only element McCluskey lacks is an equally telegenic dog, so the McCluskey campaign rents an Irish setter for the duration.

Until the end, Skeffington and his long-serving advisers assume that victory is theirs, but defeat is total and overwhelming. It is not necessarily caused by overconfidence: rather, the old-style political bosses such as Skeffington have been overtaken by a new generation of voters, products of a new era and of Franklin Roosevelt's New Deal programs who no longer need the Skeffingtons to survive. As these new voters move away from their immigrant roots, Skeffington becomes largely a figure from the past.

The final section details Skeffington's final hurrah. The evening after his electoral defeat, Skeffington suffers a heart attack. His final days are spent in remembering his past, seeing his close supporters for the last time, and keeping up their spirits by telling them that he is planning to run for governor once again. In the absence and incompetence of the junior Skeffington, Adam serves as the surrogate son, and the relation between the two becomes closer than ever. Adam's wife, Maeve, appears at Skeffington's death bed along with her father, who comments sneeringly that he is confident that if Skeffington had it to do over again, he would do it differently. From his bed Skeffington replies, "The hell I would!" His last words are addressed to Adam: "'See you around,' he whispered." After the funeral, which brings together many of Skeffington's admirers and not a few of his opponents, Adam makes a last pilgrimage to Skeffington's home, and there in his mind's eye he can see the long lines of supplicants which daily formed outside his uncle's door.

The Characters

In *The Last Hurrah*, Edwin O'Connor creates characters who are recognizable archetypes of big-city ethnic politics. Frank Skeffington is the last in a long line of urban bosses such as New York's William Marcy "Boss" Tweed. Although the author denied using Boston's Joseph Michael Curley as his inspiration for Skeffington, others, and Curley, thought differently. Skeffington is more than merely a stock character. He and his campaign for reelection are not only the story of *The Last Hurrah* but also a recessional for a changing America. Skeffington is portrayed as a corrupt opportunist, manipulating the needs of various immigrant groups in order to achieve and maintain political power. Yet he also represents a sense of nostalgia for a time that is passing into history and memory, and Skeffington himself exhibits increasingly nostalgic feelings in his relationship with Adam. There is much humor in the novel, which leavens the nostalgic elements, but Skeffington himself is not a figure of fun. Rather, with his sure confidence in imminent victory followed by overwhelming defeat, Skeffington is almost a figure from Greek tragedy.

Adam Caulfield is the other crucial character. In addition to his role as Skeffington's relation, he also serves as the objective observer, and although the narrative is in the third person, it is most often through Adam's eyes that Skeffington, both the person and the politician, is viewed. In comparison to Skeffington and his major opponents, Adam represents a younger and more apolitical generation, and he is more of an outsider than a political participant. However, Adam's involvement with his uncle's campaign also results in increasing admiration for the old man, and by the time of Skeffington's final illness and death, Adam has come to feel a deep love and respect for him.

The rest of the characters are more two-dimensional. Ditto Boland is the stock political hanger-on, the comic relief, while John Gorman and Sam Weinberg, the former Irish and the latter Jewish, are, with their ethnic connections, Skeffington's two chief advisers. Amos Force and others represent the old Anglo political establishment that has frequently succumbed to Skeffington's machine in past decades; Maeve and her father, Roger Sugrue, are predictable figures, as is Frank, Jr., the weak son, dwarfed by the accomplishments and personality of his powerful father. Still, if at times superficial and predictable, the characters are sufficiently developed to carry Skeffington's story to its denouement.

Themes and Meanings

O'Connor's *The Last Hurrah* is a political novel, but a novel that says as much about the past as the present of the 1950's when it was written. The author uses the story of Frank Skeffington to connect the America of the late nineteenth century and its immigrant flavor with mid-twentieth century America, an America moving to the suburbs, an America increasingly influenced by Madison Avenue's seductive advertisements, an America wherein television is transforming not only politics but also all aspects of life. In Skeffington, O'Connor has created one of the great larger-than-life fictional politicians in American letters, but even before his shocking defeat, the reader has become aware that Skeffington belongs to an earlier time, a quickly vanishing America. Skeffington's past successes in mastering the old-style politics give him a sense of hubris, and like Oedipus, he fails to listen for his Tireseis; he sees McCluskey's lack of accomplishment and his made-for-television family image as liabilities. Instead, they represent the new politics of O'Connor's own day.

O'Connor is also writing of his own Irish-American background, with its older roots in Ireland and its newer roots in America's big cities. There, alongside New York's Tammany Hall and Skeffington's front door, the new Irish immigrants' other solace was the Roman Catholic Church. The town hall and the bishop's palace, however, were not always mutually supporting, and in *The Last Hurrah*, the cardinal is a bitter enemy of Skeffington. The novel is also a family saga and a generational love story. Skeffington has "lost" his son. Frank, Jr., is superficial, and his relationship with his father is a mixture of misunderstanding, ignorance, and fear. Adam in turn has lost his parents. The two, never close before, come together during Skeffington's last campaign, his last hurrah, and by Skeffington's death, he has become in essence Adam's surrogate father.

Finally, *The Last Hurrah* is a wonderfully humorous novel, filled with comic characters such as Ditto Boland, who attempts, unsuccessfully, to ape Skeffington's every manner (thus his nickname). O'Connor includes a wonderful depiction of an Irish wake, which most of the mourners attend for political reasons as well as the food and drink and only incidentally, and with Skeffington's prodding, to honor the deceased and comfort his widow. An often acute study of politics, past and present, the novel is filled with many satiric moments and offbeat characters.

Critical Context

O'Connor wrote several other acclaimed novels, but none achieved the popularity of *The Last Hurrah*, in part because of his magnificent creation of Frank Skeffington and in part because it became a popular movie starring Spencer Tracy. He wrote about a vanishing America during the time of the Cold War, the threat of nuclear obliteration, the possibility of a third world war, and the anticommunist crusade of Senator Joseph McCarthy, another Irish American politician. Readers were not only captivated by the accurate historical portrayal of the urban boss in fiction but also comforted and reassured by the nostalgia of recognition that O'Connor brought to his story.

There have been relatively few satisfactory political novels in American fiction that have endured much beyond their initial publication. Henry Adam's *Democracy* (1880) satirically pilloried the politics of the Gilded Age in the late nineteenth century, Robert Penn Warren wrote fictionally of Louisiana's Huey Long, the Kingfish, in *All the King's Men* (1946), and Allen Drury's *Advise and Consent* (1959) was highly praised as a knowledgeable novel of Washington politics. *The Last Hurrah* well deserves its place in that select company.

Bibliography

Blotner, Joseph. *The American Political Novel, 1900-1960*. Austin: University of Texas Press, 1966. The author analyzes *The Last Hurrah* in the context of a chapter on "The Boss" in American politics.

Milne, Gordon. *The American Political Novel*. Norman: University of Oklahoma Press, 1966. Includes an extensive commentary about O'Connor's novel in a chapter that also discusses *All the King's Men* and *Advise and Consent*.

Rank, Hugh. *Edwin O'Connor*. Boston: Twayne, 1974. The only full length study of O'Connor and his writings. Includes a long and satisfactory discussion of *The Last Hurrah*.

Schlesinger, Arthur M., Jr. Introduction to *The Best and the Last of Edwin O'Connor*, by Edwin O'Connor. Boston: Little, Brown, 1980. One of America's most eminent political historians comments insightfully on O'Connor and his novels.

Eugene Larson

THE LAST PICTURE SHOW

Author: Larry McMurtry (1936-   )
Type of plot: Comic realism
Time of plot: The mid-1950's
Locale: Primarily the fictional West Texas town of Thalia
First published: 1966

>   *Principal characters:*
>   SONNY CRAWFORD, the main character, a sometime high school athlete
>   DUANE MOORE, another athlete, his friend
>   SAM THE LION, the elderly proprietor of the pool hall, "picture show,"
>   and café
>   HERMAN POPPER, the high school football coach
>   RUTH POPPER, Herman's wife and Sonny's lover
>   JACY FARROW, a rich, fickle young woman, alternately involved with
>   Sonny and Duane, among others
>   LOIS FARROW, Jacy's mother
>   GENEVIEVE, a waitress at the café
>   BILLY, Sonny's mentally retarded friend and Sam's ward

The Novel

   The Last Picture Show is a frank, vivid, and at times broadly satiric portrayal of rural Texas in transition. At the time of the action, both Sonny Crawford and his friend Duane Moore are prematurely emancipated high school seniors, living together in a rooming house and supporting themselves through part-time jobs, though each boy has one living parent. Most of their free time, such as it is, is spent in one or another of the establishments owned by an elderly patriarch known as Sam the Lion— the pool hall, movie house ("picture show"), or café. On weekends, the boys inconveniently share Sonny's old pickup truck for their dates, Duane with the rich, alluring Jacy Farrow and Sonny with the plainer, foul-tempered Charlene Duggs. As the girls' names would imply, McMurtry leaves little doubt that life in a town such as Thalia is never far removed from the barnyard, an impression underscored by the name and occupation of Sonny's initial employer, a bottled- gas dealer named Frank Fartley. The true action of the novel begins early when Sonny, somewhat to his own surprise, decides that he really does not like Charlene and impulsively breaks up with her on the first anniversary of their steady dating. Thereafter, the novel traces the steep contours of Sonny's "sentimental education" against the temporal backdrop of irreversible changes occurring in the town of Thalia.

   Once he has broken up with Charlene, Sonny is known to be "available"—not only to other women but also to experience in general. Soon thereafter, he falls into an unlikely liaison with Ruth Popper, the shy, neglected wife of the high school football coach. Ruth is both able and willing to teach Sonny about more than sex and love, but the difference in their ages continues to loom between them. Duane, meanwhile, remains attached to Jacy Farrow, little suspecting that Jacy plans to drop him as soon as she has made the right connections, with a moneyed, high-living, nude-bathing young crowd in nearby Wichita Falls. It is Jacy's mobility—and volatility—that will keep both Sonny and Duane off-balance, precipitating the novel's principal crises.

Life in Thalia, meanwhile, keeps changing in response to progress elsewhere. Curmudgeonly, avuncular Sam the Lion dies while Sonny and Duane are in Mexico on an impulsive weekend trip; although Sam has left a detailed will, leaving the pool hall to Sonny and his other properties to suitably responsible parties, it is clear that little of Thalia will in fact survive him; the closing of the movie house for want of customers, occurring near the end of the novel, serves also as the source of its title, announcing the theme of irrevocable change as clearly as Thomas Wolfe's *You Can't Go Home Again* (1940). Sonny's retarded friend Billy, an orphan adopted by Sam who becomes Sonny's eventual charge, will be run down and killed by a truck not long after the closing of the "picture show" that he considered his home, further underscoring the author's stated point.

As noted above, however, it is the alluring, fickle Jacy Farrow whose impulsive yet oddly premeditated behavior will force the action toward its unresolved conclusions. The only child of a restless, sensual mother and a father grown rich through a rare (for Thalia) combination of hard work and good luck, Jacy perceives the outward effect of her charms before she perceives her own inner needs. She initially took up with Duane, it appears, because he played football and because he was there; it does not take her long, however, to figure out that Duane will probably always be as poor as he is now. Always a manipulative opportunist with her parents, Jacy soon turns those same skills on her many male admirers; once she has decided to "dump" Duane, she tricks him into seducing her so that she can use the acquired experience to her profit in Wichita Falls, having first gained entrance to the social life there through a boy to whom she consistently denies her favors. When her carefully planned scheme falls through, Jacy then turns her attentions upon Sonny Crawford, despite her awareness of Sonny's affair with Ruth Popper and of Duane's departure from Thalia not long after her initial rejection of him. Duane, returning to town with news that Sonny has been seeing Jacy, provokes his former friend into a fight that leaves Sonny blind in one eye. Jacy, quick as ever to perceive a possible advantage, soon hatches yet another scheme, that of eloping with Sonny in full confidence that her parents will pursue the couple and have the marriage annulled. Duane, it seems, enlisted in the army during Sonny's hospitalization, and Jacy sees little but boredom ahead during the rest of the summer until she starts college.

Just as Jacy had foreseen and hoped, the Farrows intercept the newly married couple with some help from the Oklahoma state police. Lois Farrow, alone with Sonny in Jacy's car, suggests a brief stopover during which she encourages Sonny to make love to her, advising him that he would have been far better off to stay with Ruth Popper but expressing doubts that Ruth would ever take him back. In the novel's final scene, occurring just after Billy's death, Ruth Popper does in fact take Sonny back despite her own strong misgivings and her certainty that history can only repeat itself.

The Characters

As elsewhere in McMurtry's fiction, the strongest and most powerful characters in *The Last Picture Show* are to be found among the women. Ruth Popper, although less assertive than some of McMurtry's other featured female characters, is perhaps the best delineated and most memorable of the lot, notable for her generally repressed complexities of thought and feeling. It is she who in fact, however hesitantly, initiates the liaison with Sonny, although she allows him to take the lead whenever he shows the inclination. Also revealing of Ruth's character are the scenes with her husband, Herman, a "man's man" who may well be a repressed homosexual and who is utterly critical of Ruth's attempts to be other than totally passive in their own conjugal life. Significantly, Sonny and Ruth first meet when Coach Popper asks the young athlete to take his "hypochondriac" wife to the doctor. Soon thereafter, Ruth undergoes successful breast surgery, yet Popper never seems to care about the outcome. In the novel's final scene, Ruth quite credibly vents her pent-up wrath and frustration at Sonny before agreeing to go on.

Compared to Ruth, the other female characters of *The Last Picture Show* are somewhat closer to stereotype, yet in a number of cases McMurtry's particular skill at portraying strong, assertive women is very much in evidence. Genevieve, the principal waitress at the café, serves as Sonny's confidante during this critical period of his life; although aware of Sonny's attraction to her, Genevieve is careful to define the terms of their friendship, remaining faithful to her husband, who is recuperating from injuries sustained in the oil fields. Lois Farrow, Jacy's mother, intensely sensual and no doubt a borderline alcoholic, freely admits to Jacy that she has "scared" and badgered her husband, Gene, into his phenomenal material successes, adding that he has never pleased her but that he has found a million dollars while attempting to do so. Jacy, fittingly less self-aware than her mother yet surely no less treacherous, is portrayed in the very process of discovering both her powers and her needs. If, at first glance, Jacy seems the stereotype of the indulged rich girl, McMurtry spends just enough time and attention on developing her character to show that she is developing into the kind of complex, headstrong woman that he portrays so well in such later novels as *Moving On* (1970) and *Cadillac Jack* (1982): If less than fully "liberated" as a result of their sustained need for male foils or audiences, such women are nevertheless self-contained, representing a later stage of evolution than the males, who, at their own peril, inevitably admire them.

Sonny and Duane, the principal male characters of *The Last Picture Show*, are caught and portrayed at an age which perhaps lends itself most readily to stereotype, an age characterized mainly by sexual needs and curiosity. Of the two, it is Sonny who is more fully particularized, notable for his abiding friendship toward the retarded orphan Billy and his occasional sensitivity to Ruth Popper's needs. Like most Mc-

Murtry males, however, Sonny, too, is putty in the hands of women, utterly unable to spot or understand blatant subterfuges such as Jacy's. The other male characters, including Billy and Coach Popper, run dangerously close to stereotype, as do a number of the minor female characters. Given the tone of the novel, however, it is altogether possible that McMurtry has chosen stereotype in order to underscore the relative lack of individuality among the inhabitants of towns such as Thalia.

Themes and Meanings

Immediately after the *The Last Picture Show*, with the trilogy comprising *Moving On, All My Friends Are Going to Be Strangers* (1972), and *Terms of Endearment* (1975), McMurtry drew considerable notice for developing the "urban Western," a new convention portraying the instability of human relationships in an increasingly urbanized, motorized American West. *The Last Picture Show* represents a transition in that direction from the rural, wide-open-spaces setting and focus of McMurtry's earliest novels. Even in a small town such as Thalia, suggests McMurtry, life is crowded and in a constant state of flux; only the internal-combustion engine, mounted in a car or pickup truck, offers any hope of escape, and, more often than not, that hope turns out to have been an illusion. *The Last Picture Show* presages McMurtry's later work also through its generally bleak portrayal of modern marriage, in which happiness or even compatibility are in like manner illusory: Of those couples seen at closest range, the Farrows are hopelessly out of phase with each other, and the Poppers' marriage is a disaster; similarly, the mendacious foundation of Jacy's brief marriage to Sonny would seem to leave little hope for either of them in the future. Sonny, meanwhile, is left with little more than the fleeting consolation of his adulterous attachment to Ruth Popper.

If *The Last Picture Show* marks a transition between McMurtry's rural novels and his urban ones, its title also insists upon the fact of transition itself as an inevitable feature of contemporary life. During the course of the novel, civilization, such as it is, is moving away from towns such as Thalia in the general direction of the cities, such as Houston, that loom large in McMurtry's later fiction: Not surprisingly, those cities will be largely populated by deracinated misfits from the country, as well as from small towns such as Thalia.

Critical Context

Strongly identified with his native state, McMurtry is among the most eminent regional novelists of his generation, with a considerable nationwide audience and following. Curiously, however, he is perhaps better known for the films adapted from certain of his novels than for the novels themselves: *Horseman, Pass By* (1961) was later filmed as *Hud* (1963), *Leaving Cheyenne* (1963) as *Lovin' Molly* (1974). *The Last Picture Show* was the second of his novels to be filmed; *Terms of Endearment* would follow in 1983. McMurtry, himself a student and critic of the cinema, can hardly be displeased with the trend, although his novels are generally deserving of more critical attention than they have received.

McMurtry's first two novels, *Horseman, Pass By* and *Leaving Cheyenne*, featured a rural setting with strong ties to the Old West. With *The Last Picture Show*, McMurtry turned his attention to small-town life, proceeding thereafter to examine such cities as Houston in *Moving On*, *All My Friends Are Going to Be Strangers*, and *Terms of Endearment*. Those three loosely connected novels, generally grouped together as McMurtry's "urban trilogy," demonstrated the author's increasing skill at social satire, at times approaching the novel of manners. Featuring generally the same cast of recurring or overlapping characters, the "urban trilogy" established McMurtry as the creator and prime practitioner of the urban Western, which stresses the effects of technological and social change as rural Westerners, uprooted from the land, drift toward the cities in search of a better life.

After the "urban trilogy," McMurtry carried his penchant for social satire outward from Texas into such locales as Hollywood (*Somebody's Darling*, 1978), Washington, D.C. (*Cadillac Jack*), and Las Vegas (*The Desert Rose*, 1983). With *Lonesome Dove* (1985), McMurtry returned his attention to Texas and to the Old West, telling the epic tale of a cattle drive across the prairie in the late 1870's. *The Last Picture Show* may thus be seen as a transitional work in McMurtry's varied literary canon, announcing his considerable talent for social satire while retaining the strong rural consciousness of his two earlier novels. Notable for its strong sense of time and place and for occasional flashes of black humor recalling the writings of the Beat Generation, *The Last Picture Show*, despite occasional flaws in viewpoint and narration, remains worthy of consideration among McMurtry's greater accomplishments.

Bibliography
Busby, Mark, and Tom Pilkington. *Larry McMurtry and the West: An Ambivalent Relationship*. Denton: University of North Texas Press, 1995. Offers a comprehensive overview of McMurtry's fiction, including insights on the film version of *The Last Picture Show*. Also includes bibliographical references and an index.
Cawelti, John G. "What Rough Beast—New Westerns?" *ANQ* 9 (Summer, 1996): 4-15. Cawelti addresses the revival of the Western in print, film, and on television. He notes that the new genre reflects the loss of the mythic West of the past and shows how the contemporary Western, instead of glorifying the American spirit, now criticizes America's shortcomings. Offers a brief assessment of *The Last Picture Show*.
Crawford, Iain. "Intertextuality in Larry McMurtry's *The Last Picture Show*." *Journal of Popular Culture* 27 (Summer, 1993): 43-52. Crawford explores what he sees as the major themes of *The Last Picture Show*: the popular fiction of the 1940's; the movies, including Westerns; and the mainstream literature and television of the 1950's. He particularly focuses on the common theme of the consequences of living in the moral vacuum of contemporary society.
Jones, Roger Walton. *Larry McMurtry and the Victorian Novel*. College Station: Texas A & M University Press, 1994. Jones explores McMurtry's lifelong love of

Victorian authors and explores three Victorian themes that are prominent in all of McMurtry's fiction: the individual's importance in society, the conflict between society and nature, and the search for a coherent spirituality in an age that does not believe in God. He particularly focuses on *The Last Picture Show*.

David B. Parsell

THE LAST VOYAGE OF SOMEBODY THE SAILOR

Author: John Barth (1930-   )
Type of plot: Metafiction
Time of plot: The ninth and twentieth centuries
Locale: Ninth century Baghdad and twentieth century Maryland
First published: 1991

> *Principal characters:*
> SIMON BEHLER, a twentieth century journalist who later becomes
>   Somebody the Sailor
> BIJOU, Simon's twin sister, who died at birth yet lives on in his mind
> JANE PRICE, Simon's first wife
> SINDBAD THE SAILOR, the famous maritime hero of the *Arabian Nights*
> JAYDA, Sindbad's former concubine
> KUZIA FAKAN, Sindbad's current concubine
> YASMIN, Sindbad's daughter, eventually the wife of Somebody

The Novel

In *The Last Voyage of Somebody the Sailor,* Scheherazade, the heroine of the medieval Arabic short-story collection *The Thousand and One Nights* (ca. 900) and her sister Dunyazade have now grown old. Their husbands and even their children have died. They wonder if their fabulous story is finally coming to an end. Meanwhile, at a lavish banquet, the mysterious Somebody the Sailor is telling the people of Baghdad about his many voyages. He is matched in this storytelling feat by Baghdad's most famous hero, Sindbad the Sailor.

In another dimension, Somebody was once Simon Behler, an American journalist. Simon Behler is a young boy in Maryland in the 1930's. Simon is a typical young boy with parents, an elder brother, and cousins, but he also had a female twin, Bijou, who died as both of them were coming out of the womb. Simon always feels that he experiences the absent Bijou's feelings as well as his own. The most memorable adventure of Simon's boyhood is going up in a small plane with the aviator Howard Garton. Simon sees his entire community from above and begins to perceive it as but one in a number of possible worlds. This adventure has its emotional parallel when Simon is fourteen, when he conducts a passionate affair with Daisy Moore, a slightly older girl with a family history of madness (her mother is periodically hospitalized in an insane asylum). Daisy initiates him sexually with humor and tenderness, and he faces teenage ethical dilemmas such as whether to tell the druggist for whom he works that he stole a can of floor polish from the store in order to help his family. The curtain falls on childhood innocence as Simon's older brother, Joe Junior, is reported missing while fighting in World War II

Sindbad the Sailor is perplexed by the mysterious Somebody, whose modern-day American origins are even more mysterious to him as Sindbad's mythical Arabic origins are to the modern reader. Yet Sindbad is a congenial host nevertheless. Somebody becomes immersed in the domestic milieu of Sindbad's household. He flirts with Sindbad's daughter, Yasmin, and becomes friendly with his former concubine, Jayda. Jayda has had many experiences since her birth in Cairo, many of them sexual in nature, and Simon finds her as entertaining a storyteller as he is himself. The entire household is entertained by the story of Sindbad's early voyages. These include stories of flying carpets as well as magical birds such as rocs and distinctly unmagical ones such as vultures, who put Sindbad through a terrible ordeal in which he loses some fingers.

Joe Junior was in fact not killed in the war, and he and his wife accompany the adult Simon and his wife, Jane Price, on a cruise to the British Virgin Islands. Simon (who now spells his last name "Baylor") has become a successful and famous autobiographical journalist, but he has been unfaithful in his marriage, having had brief affairs with two younger women, Teri from Teaneck and Teresa Aginelli. When Simon's watch is water-damaged and Jane does not particularly care, Simon realizes that his marriage has stumbled. He goes on shore in order to buy a new watch, only to find he is suddenly in a new dimension, more like an Arab marketplace than anything to be found in the Caribbean. With the help of a kindly Arab merchant, he escapes any danger, but his sense of what is real and what is imaginary is totally muddled.

In Baghdad, Somebody and Yasmin have fallen in love. In order to win Yasmin's hand, Somebody at first has to accompany Sindbad on his voyages, then has to take his place entirely as the great sailor declines into degeneracy and ill temper.

Divorced from Jane and with his head still filled with Arabian dreams, Simon encounters Julie Moore, Daisy's younger sister, in Spain. Daisy, like her mother, is now in an insane asylum. Simon falls in love with Julie, and they decide to take a voyage to the Far East together. On the way, though, a storm strikes their ships, and Simon finds himself cast fully into the world of Sindbad, in which he is only "Somebody the Sailor."

Accused by the caliph of Baghdad of financial skullduggery and of mistreating his family, Sindbad is punished and, along with Jayda, exiled. Having proved his mettle, Somebody marries Yasmin. His personal happiness achieved, Simon imaginatively returns to his beginnings, the marshes of Maryland. He realizes that Daisy and Yasmin are both aspects of his lost twin Bijou, his ultimate female complement. Nothing is ever lost, as there are always more tales to be told. Scheherazade need not fear; the circle of storytelling will continue.

The Characters

Simon Behler is at once a realistic protagonist and the fulcrum of Barth's narrative. Like many a novelistic hero, Simon grows up, develops, and forges his own identity. Yet his experience is not narrowly biographical. It encompasses reams of stories, old and new, stretching in space from his boyhood home to the other side of the world and also back into the mythical recesses of time. Simon loses his identity when he is translated to the Arabian Nights world, becoming only "Somebody." Yet this loss of his self's former solidity is an eventual boon for Simon, as he merges with Sindbad, taking advantage of the permeability of character emblematic of fantasies and fairy tales. At the book's end, Simon is both a better "hero" than Sindbad ever was and also more truly himself than he could ever be in the real world with the narrowly constructed, biographical identity he had there.

Though never a full-fledged character, Bijou radiantly projects the principle of love in the book. As Simon's lost twin, she is the other side of his self, its complementary pole. His early relationship with Daisy brings him closer to his primal kinship with Bijou, though in adult life he becomes separated from that unity in his loveless marriage to Jane. Julie and Yasmin are two sides of the same character, the realistic and fantastic versions of the woman who at once ends Simon's voyage and brings him back to its beginnings.

Some of the women characters in the Arab segments do not fully emerge as individuals. Kuzia Fakan, for example, does little more than intrigue and provide sexual pleasure. Yasmin is a more rounded character, though, and Jayda has her own series of stories in which she is the heroine and all the other characters are bit players.

Barth's interest in storytelling means that he is not as interested in character as more realistic novelists. However, the novel's characters both move the reader and provide the conceptual framework for the novel's faith in storytelling.

Themes and Meanings

At first, Barth may seem simply to be reusing old material. The *Arabian Nights* stories are a major theme in his *Chimera* (1972), and themes of voyaging, storytelling, and love are dominant in *The Tidewater Tales* (1987). Yet *The Last Voyage of Somebody the Sailor* adds a new, biographical note to Barth's ongoing body of fiction. The various "voyages" of Simon/Somebody are a story not so much of somebody's life but of their imagination. Simon at first seeks self-discovery along a conventionally realistic axis, but he finds true satisfaction only when he is immersed into the world of storytelling.

Storytelling is not something that people typically do for pleasure, to while away the time, or even for exclusively aesthetic purposes. Storytelling, for Barth, is a way to bind together the myriad episodes of life, to give life meaning. By recounting his life, Simon ends up creating it, as the stories he tells Yasmin end up being the foundation of their love. Not that the Arabian Nights world is unilaterally superior to our own; Sindbad has lived in that world all his life, but he ends up being seen as a blowhard and a reprobate. Perhaps Somebody can function better in the fantasy world because, being from outside it, he can regard it with a broader perspective.

Interestingly, despite the wholly mythical nature of his Arabian Nights world, Barth takes pains to describe Islamic culture in factually correct terms. The geography, the various accent marks used in the character names, and the representation of Islam are all scrupulous. It is partially because he has secured this base of empirical fact that Barth's imagination can rove so freely.

Critical Context

Barth is usually characterized as a metafictionist, an author who writes fiction about fiction and is unapologetic about its fictional nature, not fiction depicting allegedly real persons or events. This is partially true of *The Last Voyage of Somebody the Sailor*, yet the many episodes that are conventionally realistic should not be discounted. Simon's memories of growing up in Maryland are rendered in an affectionately realistic style similar to nonfiction reminiscences such as Sidney Offit's *Memoir of the Bookie's Son* (1995). Simon's first two "voyages" are as realistic as anything Barth ever wrote, perhaps more realistic than his actual autobiography, *Once upon a Time* (1994).

Barth playfully comments on the impossibility of totally distinguishing fantasy and realism when he depicts the Arabs' reaction to Somebody's first two voyages. Ibn al-Hamra objects to Somebody's second voyage, the Daisy Moore story, by claiming that it forsakes the ground of "traditional realism," which he then defines as having to do with rocs, genies, and magic carpets. Of course, in Ibn al-Hamra's world, these things are taken as the norm, whereas such workaday objects as cars and automobiles are so flagrantly eccentric that for him they should not be allowed within the canons of serious literature. Readers may laugh at ibn al-Hamra and complacently conclude that his world is fictional, but the novel then provokes them to wonder whether their own existence is fictional as well. Ibn al-Hamra is the mirror image of a modern reader who might find the story of Simon's boyhood more "realistic" than Sindbad's voyages. Realism, Barth implies, is a function of expectations; if readers suspend those expectations, they will see that fantasy is at least as viable a medium for storytelling as the mode termed "realism."

Barth has been accused by critics of being self-indulgent in his flamboyant adventures. His self-conscious retellings of myth are sometimes criticized as evading American realities of the twentieth century, just as Ibn al-Hamra sees Somebody's outrageous stories as neglecting the thematic realities of fantastic Baghdad. Barth's juxtaposition of fantasy and realism turns the tables on these critics, revealing them as constrained by expectations that, unlike Somebody's voyages, are merely of their own time.

Bibliography

Barth, Johm. "Conversation with Prime Maximalist John Barth." Interview by Bin Ramke and Donald Revell. *Bloomsbury Review*, 1991. This interview with Barth reveals some of the autobiographical bases of the novel's narrative.

Bowen, Zack R. *A Reader's Guide to John Barth*. Westport, Conn.: Greenwood Press, 1994. An accessibly written general overview; concentrates on the inverse relationship between Sindbad and Simon/Somebody.

Kirk, James. *Organicism as Reenchantment: Whitehead, Prigogine, and Barth*. New York: Peter Lang, 1993. Comments on Barth's mystique of storytelling as well as its formal relation to modern science.

Lindsay, Alan. *Death in the Funhouse: John Barth and Poststructuralist Aesthetics*.

New York: Peter Lang, 1995. Sometimes complicated but rewarding insights on the complexity of Barth's vision.

Tobin, Patricia. *John Barth and the Anxiety of Continuance*. Philadelphia: University of Pennsylvania Press, 1992. Emphasizes the affirmative quality of the novel, seeing the modern-day Simon as replenishing the legend of the storied Sinbad.

Nicholas Birns

LAUGHING BOY

Author: Oliver La Farge (1901-1963)
Type of plot: Regional romance
Time of plot: 1915
Locale: Arizona and New Mexico
First published: 1929

> *Principal characters:*
> LAUGHING BOY, the protagonist, a young Navajo
> SLIM GIRL, his wife
> JESTING SQUAW'S SON, his best friend
> TWO BOWS, his father
> RED MAN, the antagonist, a jealous Navajo

The Novel

Laughing Boy is both a love story and a narrative of cultural and individual conflict. Set in 1915 on the Navajo Reservation of the Southwest before the first automobile arrived, the novel depicts an unspoiled way of life. An omniscient narrator recounts the action in a straightforward, linear manner, though considerable foreshadowing of events occurs.

Attending a ceremonial dance at Tsé Lani, a Navajo village on the southern edge of the reservation, Laughing Boy meets and falls in love with Slim Girl, a beautiful young Navajo who has been reared in Anglo society near the reservation. From Red Man, one of her admirers, he wins a wrestling match but acquires an enemy at the same time. Against the advice of his uncle and others who have heard of her past, he marries Slim Girl, and they move into her adobe hut outside Los Palos, a town near the reservation. While Slim Girl learns weaving and Navajo customs, Laughing Boy continues his life much as it had been on the reservation, tending his horses and sheep and crafting fine jewelry.

Slim Girl goes into town periodically, explaining to Laughing Boy that she is working for a missionary's wife. In reality, she is meeting an American rancher whose mistress she has been for some time. She does this in order to save the money he gives her for eventual resettlement on the reservation, her major objective in life. When she and Laughing Boy travel far into the reservation to attend a ceremonial dance, his relatives recognize the progress she has made in learning the Navajo way of life and many of them accept her, despite the unfavorable stories they have heard about her.

One day, by chance, Laughing Boy discovers the infidelity of Slim Girl, and, enraged and aggrieved by the deception, wounds both her and the American with arrows. She returns home with him, and through a long account of her past, convinces him that she took money from the American only to further their plans. Laughing Boy understands and forgives. They gather their belongings and set out for the spot on the reservation where they have planned to live.

Along the way, they are seen by Red Man, who, in his jealousy and anger, sets an ambush for them. His aim is for Laughing Boy, but his bullet strikes Slim Girl, mortally wounding her. Laughing Boy provides a Navajo funeral for her, and, after four days of grieving, returns sadly to his people, having promised her that he will not avenge her death.

The Characters

Laughing Boy, ceremonially named "Sings Before Spears," represents the young, talented, and exuberant Navajo from the reservation—a "blanket Indian" who speaks no English. Skilled in jewelry-making and at home on horseback, he finds fulfillment in creating beautiful works and in tending his animals. Yet he is competitive as well, even aggressive at times. He enjoys contests, gambling, and occasional unfriendly encounters with traditional Navajo enemies, the Ute and the Hopi. For the most part, he follows the Navajo way, the trail of beauty; he takes part in traditional dances, rituals, and ceremonies, finding significance in the Navajo religion.

Slim Girl, "Came With War," the heroine, enables the author to overcome the taciturnity and reserve of the Indian character and bridge the two conflicting cultures. A Navajo whose grandmother was an Apache, she attended an Indian school where she learned English and adopted the values of American culture. Her life with a missionary family ended abruptly and unhappily, however, when she became pregnant by a cowboy who refused to marry her. Cared for by local prostitutes, she became one of them after bearing a stillborn child. She disliked her existence and American ways and longed to return to the reservation, to follow the Navajo way, of which she knew little. Her interest in Laughing Boy, originating because she sees him as affording her a way back, grows into love. From him she learns the Navajo culture—everything from the pattern of daily life to ceremonies and religious beliefs. The reader learns these matters at the same time.

Slim Girl is adaptable, intelligent, energetic, and cheerful, an extroverted young woman whose knowledge of the world exceeds that of the other characters. She attempts to make the best of life, to reach the goal she has set for herself, and to build a secure and happy life with her husband.

Two Bows, Laughing Boy's father, represents a kind of model to his son, in whom he takes pride. Though not agreeing with all of his son's choices, Two Bows is both understanding and supportive, holding attitudes that reflect his own sense of self-worth and dignity. Having taught Laughing Boy the art of making jewelry, he generously praises his son's work. He is tolerant, indulgent, and proud of his son, yet taciturn and reserved.

Jesting Squaw's Son, a close friend of Laughing Boy, shares his exuberance, high spirits, and competitive nature. At one point, deeply troubled, he tells Laughing Boy how he had come to love a girl of his own clan and had been disappointed, for this was a taboo among Navajos. At first shocked by the story, Laughing Boy gives his friend understanding and sympathy. The episode may indicate an effort to make romantic love more prominent in the novel. Except for the love of the two main characters, it hardly appears as a theme.

Red Man, a treacherous, vengeful Navajo, is little more than a stock character, the introverted villain. A shadowy and furtive figure, he loses a wrestling match with Laughing Boy and his hopes of winning Slim Girl; thereafter, he seeks revenge.

Themes and Meanings

Laughing Boy has been called an idyll, an adolescent novel, and a love story. It is primarily the story of young love, idealistic though flawed and ill-fated, somewhat resembling the love theme in novels such as W. H. Hudson's *Green Mansions* (1904) and Robert Nathan's *Portrait of Jennie* (1940). The love of Laughing Boy and Slim Girl survives the crisis of infidelity and grows stronger and more secure until Slim Girl's death. The story leaves a poignant regret for what might have been, for La Farge has successfully created the illusion that love will last. The reader believes that Slim Girl would have adjusted to life on the reservation and, as she hoped, would have remained beautiful, unlike most Navajo women, who grow old too soon.

The love theme, the youthful characters, and the rather exotic setting make the novel appealing to young readers, as does the discreet handling of the sexual love theme. Until he meets Slim Girl, Laughing Boy does not know what a kiss is. La Farge permits his major characters a romantic love drawn from American culture, not from that of the Navajo. In his preface to the 1963 edition of the novel, he expresses satisfaction that the work is widely read by young people.

In the same preface, the author notes that the novel seeks to defend no special position regarding American Indians but to depict their culture and traditions. Yet there can be little doubt that La Farge, a trained and experienced anthropologist, seeks to celebrate a culture that he regards as passing out of existence. In the novel, Indians who remain on the reservation retain a dignity and a nobility of spirit that those who leave quickly lose. Ill-equipped for the competition they face, Americanized Indians often succumb to despair and disintegration of character.

La Farge translates Navajo chants, describes ceremonial dances, and attempts to clarify for the reader Navajo religious values. He explains what the Navajo regard as sacred—for example, the dwellings of the Anasazi and various natural phenomena on the reservation. He explores their taboos and customs: not looking at one's mother-in-law, ensuring that the entrance to a hogan is in the right place, following the proper ritual for burial, and selecting a mate from outside the clan. The novel suggests that its author consciously attempted to make the Navajo way of life, the "beautiful trail," not merely understandable but also aesthetically pleasing.

Critical Context

The novel, La Farge's first, won for him the Pulitzer Prize in 1929 and brought him instant acclaim. His work following the book includes numerous other titles devoted to Indians of the Southwest, but none is so well-known or so sympathetic to Indian culture. Still widely read, particularly by adolescent readers, the book is not among those that influenced the development of the novel as a form. Its originality is limited to its treatment of the subject—the culture and character of the Navajo Indian. Because of the author's choice to commemorate the culture of an important Southwestern Indian tribe, the work holds a secure place in the history of regional fiction.

Bibliography
Dennis, Philip A. "Oliver La Farge, Writer and Anthropologist." In *Literature and Anthropology*, edited by Philip Dennis and Wendell Aycock. Lubbock: Texas Tech University Press, 1989. Profiles La Farge as both a writer and an anthropologist, detailing how each discipline complemented the other.
Gillis, Everett A. "Oliver La Farge." In *A Literary History of the American West*. Western Literature Association. Fort Worth: Texas Christian University Press, 1987. Gillis traces the career of La Farge as a southwestern writer.
Hecht, Robert A. *Oliver La Farge and the American Indian: A Biography*. Metuchen, N.J.: Scarecrow Press, 1991. A thorough biography that focuses on La Farge's depiction of the Indian world, its social conditions, and La Farge's role in it as an authority on American Indian culture.
Krefft, James H. "A Possible Source for Faulkner's Indians: Oliver La Farge's *Laughing Boy*." *Tulane Studies in English* 23 (1978): 187-192. Speculates that William Faulkner's portrayal of Indian characters was influenced by La Farge's *Laughing Boy*.
La Farge, Oliver. *Yellow Sun, Bright Sky: The Indian Country Stories of Oliver La Farge*. Edited by David L. Caffey. Albuquerque: University of New Mexico Press, 1988. A collection of short stories spanning from 1927 to La Farge's death. The collection reflects La Farge's change from a pessimistic to more positive viewpoint regarding the survival of Native American cultures. Caffey's introduction presents a useful biographical sketch of La Farge.
McNickle, D'Arcy. *Indian Man: A Life of Oliver La Farge*. Bloomington: Indiana University Press, 1971. A critical biography that was nominated for a National Book Award.
Pearce, Thomas M. *Oliver La Farge*. New York: Twayne, 1972. Pearce provides a critical and interpretive study of La Farge, with a close reading of his major works, a solid bibliography, and complete notes and references.

Stanley Archer

LAWD TODAY

Author: Richard Wright (1908-1960)
Type of plot: Contemporary black tragedy
Time of plot: The 1930's, sometime during the Great Depression
Locale: Chicago
First published: 1963

Principal characters:

     JAKE JACKSON, the protagonist and antihero, a black postal worker in
        Chicago
     LIL, his wife and the victim of his abuse
     AL,
     BOB, and
     SLIM, his fellow postal workers and pals

The Novel

    Lawd Today opens with Jake Jackson rising out of bed, apparently after a night on the town. The day in question is Lincoln's birthday, and throughout the day, no matter where Jake goes, radios haunt him with words from that president's speeches and statements about the Great Emancipator—as though to remind Jake that he is the victim of another kind of slavery. Jake is caught in a web that entangles his soul. It will take much more than a presidential proclamation to set his spirit free.

    From the beginning, Richard Wright lets the reader know that Jake, although caught in circumstances beyond his control, is an unsavory individual, one neither to be admired nor empathized with. Jake begins his day by physically and verbally abusing his wife, Lil: In response to Lil's brief conversation with the milkman, Jake falls into a jealous rage. The reader later learns that Jake married Lil only because the couple thought that she was pregnant. Jake's resentment at being "tricked" into marriage has grown into a rage that he frequently and violently vents on his wife. Lil, though far from being an aggressive individual, forewarns Jake that his time for this kind of behavior is running out: "This is the last time you going to do this to me." In the book's final scene, Lil lives up to her promise and violently subdues Jake in his drunken assault on her by slashing him with a piece of broken glass—a symbolic emasculation.

    After Jake's morning encounter with his wife, the novel takes the reader on a journey with Jake as he goes through the drudgery of his life. He stops by a local numbers operation with the unrealistic dream of increasing his meager pocket money. He loses, and Wright thereby establishes from the outset Jake's character as that of a loser.

    Jake then goes to "Bob's place," the home of his friend and working companion. They are later joined by Al and Slim, and the foursome spends most of the remaining time before work playing bridge, followed by a "bout of the dozens" between Jake and Al. Even in this game, in which the pair take turns making less than favorable remarks about each other's ancestry, Jake cannot win: "Jake screwed up his eyes, bit his lips, and tried hard to think of a return. But, for the life of him, he could not. Al's last image was too much; it left him blank."

Wright then takes his four characters through a tedious day of work at the post office, where they are subjected to a shift of sorting mail under the scrutiny of white supervisors who go out of their way to inflict stress and tension on the four black employees. During the day, Jake manages to borrow one hundred dollars from a loan shark so that he can treat his friends to a night on the town when they get off work.

Jake's night on the town turns into disaster when he and his friends go to a local bordello for a night of drinking, eating, and carousing with the women. In the course of the evening, after they are well-fed and drunk, the foursome's hopes for some time with the women are shattered when a pickpocket makes off with Jake's wallet. Jake's protests to the management are to no avail and only gain a beating for him and his friends, followed by their being expeditiously and unceremoniously thrown out of the place.

On his way home, Jake becomes more drunken, finishing off a bottle before finally arriving to take his frustrations out on Lil. The novel's final scene, in which Lil slashes him in self-defense, completes the downward arc begun in the book's opening pages. Bleeding, confused, only half comprehending what has happened to him, Jake is utterly defeated: "He shuddered from the chill that was seeping into the marrow of his bones as darkness roared in his brain."

The Characters

Jake Jackson is a Southern black man who, like many other Southern blacks, escaped his Southern roots in Mississippi to transplant himself into what was perceived to be a more desirable environment for blacks, Chicago. The lure was not that Chicago was desegregated but that there was at least the possibility of work for blacks. Jake is fortunate to be employed as a postal worker during a time, the Great Depression, when jobs were scarce for everyone. Nevertheless, Wright makes clear that Jake and the other black postal workers suffer under extreme conditions of discrimination in their work environment; Jake's job is as much a part of the trap in which he finds himself as are his marriage, his debts, and his lust.

Jake is self-indulgent, he is mean, he is a wife abuser, he is an alcoholic, he is a womanizer. Wright presents Jake as a loser and gives no clue that he would have been any different in a more favorable situation. At the same time, however, Jake is an archetypal figure who vividly symbolizes the dilemma of many black American families from a sociological perspective. It is in that sense that Jake becomes a tragic figure, not because of who he is or his failures in life, but because he has met the destiny of so many like him.

Lil, unlike Jake, is a character with whom the reader can empathize and identify. She, too, is an archetypal figure, representing abused women—not only black women but all women. In the end, she is courageous in her battle with Jake and, if only for the moment, victorious over his assault if not the circumstances of her unfortunate situation.

Al, Bob, and Slim offer an interesting counterpoint to Jake's character. Each is single and therefore, in Jake's view, not caught in the trap of marital responsibilities that he believes is dragging down his life. Unlike Jake, Al, Bob, and Slim do not have mounting debts that they are unable to pay; they are, in Jake's estimation, "free." Nevertheless, Jake's buddies are as unsavory in their behavior as Jake. Wright pointedly plays on Al's case of gonorrhea, as well as other attributes—his bragging, his overeating, and his stinginess—to make him the brunt of the others' jokes. Slim, meanwhile, has a chronic cough, the result of tuberculosis; as Jake observes to Bob, "Ain't it funny about folks what's got T.B. They hound for women. . . ." Wright uses these characters in comedic relief against his tragic backdrop, but the technique does nothing to lighten the tragedy of Jake and Lil.

Wright captures exquisitely the black dialect of his characters and accurately preserves the language of the ghetto. A number of minor but colorful characters convey the black world of Chicago's South Side and give the reader a realistic insight into a world infrequently seen, much less understood, by whites. Wright's characters, all of them, live on the edge of survival. For those who have not been there, their actions are difficult to comprehend.

Themes and Meanings

Lawd Today focuses on the life of Jake Jackson as he is confronted time after time with his failure in life. Wright does not make clear whether Jake's flaw is the result of discrimination, learned behavior, or something inherent in the man; the reader may choose to see Jake as a product of his environment, but the evidence is so scanty as not to provoke any outpouring of sympathy for the protagonist, especially in view of the way he treats his wife. Rather, the reader is made to see Jake from more than one perspective—as both victim and victimizer.

Wright's realistic portrayal of black ghetto existence carries this theme forward, as victim is pitted against victim in a world where the law of survival prevails. Jake is not very good at the game, whether it is the numbers game, a "bout of the dozens," or a night on the town; the social prominence which he imagines his job at the post office affords him depends entirely on how much money he has in his pocket, and he is not adept at keeping it there very long.

Wright underscores the irony of Jake's situation in the Lincoln's birthday radio broadcasts which are heard throughout, confronting Jake with a nominal legacy of freedom, whereas, in reality, he remains a slave, to his environment, his lusts, and his fellow blacks.

Critical Context

Although *Lawd Today* was his first novel, Wright was unsuccessful at having it published, and it was not until after his death that the work finally reached the printer. Certainly, *Lawd Today* is inferior to his masterpiece, *Native Son* (1940); Wright did, however, accomplish several things of note in the novel which make it invaluable for understanding his work in a larger context.

First, Wright captured superbly the language of the black ghetto in all of its color and shades of meaning. Second, the book is extremely interesting structurally. It is compact, compressed into a tight little drama. Description is at a premium, and most of the story is seen through the eyes of the characters in dialogue. Indeed, one can surmise that much of Wright's early development as a writer took place in *Lawd Today*. Ultimately, however, the novel's legacy is its portrait of the brutal world of ghetto life.

Bibliography
Baldwin, James. *The Price of the Ticket: Collected Nonfiction, 1948-1985*. New York: St. Martin's Press/Marek, 1985. The essays "Everybody's Protest Novel" and "Alas, Poor Richard" provide important and provocative insights into Wright and his art.
Bloom, Harold, ed. *Richard Wright*. New York: Chelsea House, 1987. Essays on various aspects of Wright's work and career, with an introduction by Bloom.
Fabre, Michel. *The Unfinished Quest of Richard Wright*. Translated by Isabel Barzun. New York: William Morrow, 1973. The most important and authoritative biography of Wright available.
_____. *The World of Richard Wright*. Jackson: University Press of Mississippi, 1985. A collection of Fabre's essays on Wright. A valuable but not sustained full-length study.
Hakutani, Yoshinobu. *Richard Wright and Racial Discourse*. Columbia: University of Missouri Press, 1996. Chapters on *Lawd Today*, *Uncle Tom's Children*, *Native Son*, *The Outsider*, and *Black Boy*, as well as discussions of later fiction, black power, and Wright's handling of sexuality. Includes introduction and bibliography.
Kinnamon, Keneth, ed. *Critical Essays on Richard Wright's "Native Son."* New York: Twayne, 1997. Divided into sections of reviews, reprinted essays, and new essays. Includes discussions of Wright's handling of race, voice, tone, novelistic structure, the city, and literary influences. Index but no bibliography.
_____. *The Emergence of Richard Wright*. Urbana: University of Illinois Press, 1972. A study of Wright's background and development as a writer, up to the publication of *Native Son* (1940).
Walker, Margaret. *Richard Wright: Daemonic Genius*. New York: Warner Books, 1988. A critically acclaimed study of Wright's life and work written by a respected novelist.
Webb, Constance. *Richard Wright: A Biography*. New York: Putnam, 1968. A well-written biography which remains useful.

Cecil Costilow

LEAF STORM

Author: Gabriel García Márquez (1928-   )
Type of plot: Magical Realism
Time of plot: The late nineteenth and early twentieth centuries
Locale: Macondo, an imaginary town in Colombia
First published: La hojarasca, 1955 (English translation, 1972)

> *Principal characters:*
> THE COLONEL, a retired military officer
> ISABEL, his daughter, thirty years old
> THE CHILD, Isabel's son, eleven years old
> THE DOCTOR, a suicide by hanging
> MEME, an Indian servant in the colonel's house and later the doctor's
>   mistress

The Novel

Leaf Storm is narrated through three alternating interior monologues: those of the colonel, his daughter Isabel, and her son. Through this structure, García Márquez chronicles the founding of the imaginary coastal town of Macondo in the late nineteenth century, its prosperity during the 1910's, and its decadence after 1918. This is the story of the arrival and exit of the "leaf storm," the hordes of outsiders and foreigners who descended on the Colombian coast as the region grew rich on the banana industry during a short period of wealth that ended as quickly as it had begun.

As the novel begins, the doctor has hanged himself and the colonel prepares to oversee the burial of the body. It is learned that ten years earlier, the rest of the townspeople had sworn to oppose this burial, and that the colonel is honoring a personal pledge he had made earlier to the dead man to defy the will of the others. The reason for the town's hostility is only made clear later, as each of the three narrations goes back in time and tells the story of the doctor's twenty-five-year stay in Macondo. At the novel's close, the family prepares to form a funeral cortege with the coffin: What the reaction of their neighbors will be is left unknown.

The three ongoing monologues do not proceed in a linear manner. Many incidents mentioned by one character are taken up later by another, and thus the reader is engaged in a constant process of reevaluation and reconsideration of prior clues. The effect is somewhat like that of a mystery novel, in which facts are revealed by one character and corroborated later by another, but in *Leaf Storm* there is no suspense. The plot is circular, for as the twenty-five years between 1903 and 1928 unfold, little changes for the people who describe the events. The colonel and Isabel relate dispassionately the events of those years in a matter-of-fact tone that reveals little emotion. The child provides the perspective of an innocent observer who understands nothing of the facts, while intuitively seeing what exists beneath the controlled exterior of his elders.

Leaf Storm, then, serves as an allegory for the broader upheaval in the life of the Colombian coast brought on by foreign investment in the early part of the twentieth century. Through the memories of the colonel and Isabel, the class structure of this society, and its patterns of daily life, customs, and religious beliefs are described. The doctor's suicide and his years in Macondo provide the framework for those memories.

The Characters

The characterization of individual voices in *Leaf Storm* is not its author's primary goal. These characters represent larger forces in Colombian and Latin American society; their individual development is less important. Yet as each interior monologue progresses, certain details do emerge. Often, these details are revealed more through the musings of others than in the way a character may describe himself.

The colonel is a proud representative of an older order which has passed in Macondo, that of the founding families who built the town. He is a man to whom honor is paramount; thus he goes through with the doctor's burial although doing so pits him against his own neighbors. Such unquestioning acceptance of a strict moral and ethical code of behavior is expressed in words recalled by Isabel, as her father tells her she must accompany him to the doctor's house: "And then, before I had time to ask anything, he pounded the floor with his cane: 'We have to go through with this just the way it is, daughter. The doctor hanged himself this morning.'"

Isabel is also a member of the upper class of Macondo, but, as a woman, she enjoys lower social status and has suffered many personal limitations. This fact emerges most clearly in the story of her engagement and marriage, at the age of seventeen, to a man named Martin, who later disappeared from Macondo. The marriage is completely decided and arranged by the colonel; on her wedding day, Isabel has never spent time alone with her new husband; she has scarcely even spoken to him in the company of others. The product of a certain rigidly defined class system, she sees her own destiny in fatalistic terms: "My punishment was written down before my birth," she thinks, accepting without question her lot in life.

The child, through his ingenuous observations, provides an opportunity for García Márquez to show the world of Macondo through another, more wondrous perspective. The boy's monologue begins the novel with the following: "I've seen a corpse for the first time. It's Wednesday but I feel as if it was Sunday because I didn't go to school." His description of the appearance of the dead man is made in very realistic terms; he reacts directly and physically to the heat, the dark, and the generally stifling atmosphere of the doctor's long-closed house. The child, too, sees himself as controlled by forces beyond his power; he accepts the authority of his mother and grandfather. He lives in the present, rather than the past; he is a normal child who prefers playing with his friends to attending funerals.

The doctor arrives and leaves Macondo shrouded in mystery. His name and origins are never learned; it is said several times that he was a native speaker of French, though no definite country is mentioned. One day in 1903, he presents a letter of introduction to the colonel and stays on in the house for eight years. The doctor is a strange man: For his first meal as a guest in the colonel's home, he asks for grass to eat. During the years preceding the economic boom of Macondo, he does well as a medical practitioner, but when the banana companies move in, they bring their own physicians. His business drops off and eventually dies, and from that point onward he becomes more and more reclusive. At the time of his suicide, he has not been seen by anyone in four years.

The townspeople have vowed to refuse the doctor a final resting place because of an incident that occurred ten years earlier. He refused medical assistance to wounded men although he was the only doctor left in town, an act that the inhabitants of Macondo will never forgive. His reasons for this refusal, however, are never explained; they form one more mystery with which the reader must grapple. The portrait of the doctor is not a sympathetic one, though it would be unfair to characterize him as a villain. He is a totally self-involved individual who makes concessions to no one.

Meme, an Indian servant who is part of the colonel's household, is part of a great underclass of poor, illiterate people. She is a protected member of the family until it is discovered that she is expecting a child which may or may not be the doctor's. At this point, she is expelled from the colonel's house for her transgression—as is the doctor—and they begin to live together openly. Defying morality, Meme appears one Sunday at Mass, dressed in gaudy finery, and dares to sit with the ladies of Macondo; afterward, she is surrounded by a threatening circle of men but is escorted to safety by the colonel. The doctor opens a shop for Meme with his savings, and for a while she continues to be part of the town's life, but eventually she disappears from sight just as the doctor does. Her end, and the fate of her expected child, are two more unanswered questions. Meme inspires pity and sympathy but at the same time shows courage as the only character who tries to change her social status in Macondo.

Themes and Meanings

In *Leaf Storm*, as in many other works of García Márquez, the principal themes are those of the effect of economic forces in the shaping of society in Latin America and of the position of the individual within that society. In Macondo, the class divisions never change, although the town goes through a great upheaval. There is here a somewhat pessimistic view of individual control over destiny, but, at the same time, Macondo is a magical place in its everyday life, and that magic overcomes the harsh realities. The novel begins García Márquez's experimentation with themes of Magical Realism, a kind of writing begun earlier in the twentieth century by Latin American writers and which is still important. This style incorporates elements of the fantastic (for example, a man who eats grass, a priest who takes his sermons from almanacs instead of the Bible) and combines them with details from daily life. The meaning of this combination is that life in Latin America is, indeed, often fantastic and somewhat magical, and that those elements of society are accepted as normal in a town such as Macondo, which serves as an archetype.

The narrative structure of *Leaf Storm*, the interior monologues that develop the plot and the characters, are inseparable from these themes. The structure reminds the reader at all times of the historical progression in the larger society, juxtaposed with the stagnation of individual lives. García Márquez constructs a narrative to be read both for the pleasure of the story it tells and for its broader message.

Critical Context

Leaf Storm was García Márquez's first novel, following the publication of various short stories. Its themes and characters mark the beginning of the saga of Macondo, a town created in its author's imagination much as William Faulkner created the locales of his novels. Indeed, Faulkner has been recognized by García Márquez as one of his most important literary influences.

This novel is considered by critics of Latin American fiction to be a prefiguration of its author's great work, *Cien años de soledad* (1967; *One Hundred Years of Solitude*, 1970). Along with other shorter tales and novels, *Leaf Storm* introduces characters and situations that will return, in much expanded form, in *One Hundred Years of Solitude*. The story of the doctor's arrival and suicide, for example, is explained in the longer novel. Macondo, at the end of *One Hundred Years of Solitude*, disappears as retribution for its tremendous growth and decadence, providing a final end to the allegory.

In 1982, Gabriel García Márquez was awarded the Nobel Prize in Literature, following other Latin American writers such as Gabriela Mistral and Pablo Neruda. He is recognized as one of the leading modern novelist/story writers, and he is an active commentator of contemporary Latin American culture, especially in its relationship to society, a theme so well begun in *Leaf Storm* and carried out in his later works.

Bibliography

Bloom, Harold, ed. *Márquez*. New York: Chelsea House, 1989. A collection of eighteen essays by various authors on different aspects of Márquez's works. Covers the whole range of literary criticism and offers in-depth analysis of several of Márquez's novels.

Dolan, Sean. *Hispanics of Achievement*. New York: Chelsea House, 1994. A solid introduction to Márquez's work, featuring photographs and quotations. Discusses Márquez's family background, literary influences, and personal politics and how these shaped his writing.

McMurray, George R. "Gabriel García Márquez." In *Latin American Writers*, edited by Carlos A. Solé and Maria I. Abreau. Vol. 3. New York: Charles Scribner's Sons, 1989. Offers a comprehensive and critical discussion of Márquez's life and works, including *Leaf Storm*. Provides a selected bibliography for further reading.

Márquez, Gabriel García. Interview. *UNESCO Courier* 49 (February, 1996): 4-7. Márquez offers his views on the teaching and protection of culture. He also discusses his daily writing discipline and how it has influenced and enhanced his work. An informative and interesting interview.

Styron, Rose. "Gabriel García Márquez, Carlos Fuentes, and Kenzaburo Oe: From the Rose Styron Conversations." *New Perspectives Quarterly* 14 (Fall, 1997): 56-62. A revealing interview with three world renowned authors. They share their views on topics such as women and power, first and lost love, journalism as literature, spirit and faith, and multiculturalism.

Kathleen Ross

THE LEAN LANDS

Author: Agustín Yáñez (1904-1980)
Type of plot: Allegorical realism
Time of plot: The early 1920's
Locale: A typical, isolated, high-plain, sparsely populated region of Jalisco,
   Mexico, called Tierra Santa (Holy Land)
First published: Las tierras flacas, 1962 (English translation, 1968)

> *Principal characters:*
>> DON EPIFANIO TRUJILLO, one of three protagonists, a landowner, and
>> the father of Don Felipe, Don Jesús, and Miguel Arcángel,
>> half-brothers to one another
>> MIGUEL ARCÁNGEL/JACOB GALLO, the antagonist, who overthrows his
>> father and his two half-brothers
>> RÓMULO, the second protagonist, a peasant, the father of Teófila,
>> husband of Merced, and the "voice" of the people
>> DOÑA MATIANA, the third protagonist, a *bruja* (seeress), the "voice" of
>> faith/spirit
>> PLÁCIDA, Don Epifanio's willful daughter, who replaces him on his
>> death

The Novel

The Lean Lands portrays a transitional moment in the history of the Trujillo family, the sociopolitical center of the region. The action involves an internecine war among three half brothers to gain access to the power center held by their ill father, Don Epifanio (Pifanio, Don Pifas).

Consistent with the *hacendado* system (a parafeudal system of land ownership), throughout his life, Epifanio has conformed majestically to the traditional functions of the *cacique* (chieftain), the Arawak term for tribal chief. Arrogantly, he has subjugated all in the region to his arbitrary and willful nature in various ways. Chief among them is the long-held prerogative of having multiple "wives" to create an enormous progeny. Sensuality is totally lacking in the "conquests," which are motivated strictly by sociopolitical considerations. Nor is sentiment valued, for Epifanio selects from the children those whose characters promise the same uncompromising attitude that he holds toward the weak. These chosen few are brought to the Big House for watchful training to polish their ruthlessness. It seems pleasingly ironic, then, that, though the region is impotent to withstand him, it is his own potency as prolific father and his deficiencies as a guide which are the seeds of his demise and of the destruction of the region.

Two of his sons, Don Jesús, "the Snake," and Don Felipe, "the Tiger"—nicknames which delineate their basic characters—remain in the Big House until they reach majority. They then occupy two extensive ranches and solidify the family's hold over the

mountain plain. Quickly, however, they begin to vie for their father's favor and undercut each other's power.

The third son, Miguel Arcángel, "the King of Diamonds," has left the valley, changing his name to Jacob Gallo (his mother's surname), and immersed himself in the political world of the immediate post-Revolutionary period. He becomes an officer in
the army, establishes himself with the state government, embraces the fruits of progress, such as electricity, and, eventually, gains immense power. Wearing fox's clothing, he returns to his birthplace and quickly intensifies the tension between his two
half brothers. The peasants, sensitive as victims are to changing forces, give, in varying degree, their allegiance to this Prodigal Son, whose promise of a better life with
technology—electricity, irrigation, and better agronomy—they seem to accept. Thus,
the outside world has conquered the valley.

At this level, the novel's general movement is toward Progress as the antidote to the
Old Way and suggests an allegorical treatment of good triumphing over evil. Yet
Yáñez, a moralist and an intense observer of history, deepens the novel's significance.
In fact, Jacob Gallo's purpose is the same as that of his father and brothers—to win
dominance over the valley. This view, which the peasants begin to express in murmurs, increasingly sharpens until the final scene, when, etched against a gathering
storm of lightning and thunder, Gallo's baser character stands revealed. As he prepares to switch on the electrical current initiating Progress, the voice of the Old Way,
belonging to the blind *bruja*, Doña Matiana, prophesies God's punishment for Gallo's
hypocrisy and deceit: "I come . . . Miguel Arcángel to remind you that the higher you
rise the greater your fall will be. There are no short cuts in the straight and narrow
path."

The Characters

There are three gravity points in this novel, each represented by a major character:
the powerful, the disfranchised, and the spiritual. At the social level, they are created
as stereotypes. At the individual level, each acquires his own voice through the techni-
cal device of the internal monologue. While this baroque characterization tends to dis-
orient the reader, much of the novel's vitality derives from the interplay between the
external and internal experience of the characters.

Don Epifanio has dominated the landscape. A victim himself of the *cacique* image,
he now carries on the tradition of the cardinal sins. He is gluttonous, greedy, insensitive, envious, proud, hard, and, ultimately, evil.

His cultural inheritance continues in Felipe and Jesús. There are no redeeming features in Felipe; his vengeance and malice are of a piece, and he fulfills adequately
Yáñez's design for him—as a projection of the external, cultural side of his father's
personality. Jesus is a loss, for his carefully wrought portrayal as the Snake reflects a
lively intelligence, sensitivity, and psychological insight gone mad. In the language of
the peasants, he is the devil's very tongue.

With Jacob Gallo, the author completes his study of the various facets of the *mano
dura* (ruthless justice) mentality. He suggests that this ingrained pattern not only re-

fuses to yield to civilizing influences, but also seems, rather, to turn the benefits and promise of Progress into even more subtle forms of manipulation and dominance. Gallo beguiles the peasants with hope and an *abrazo* (hug) while he ravages them.

Yáñez broadens his study of the thwarting of human potential with the last figure under this category, Plácida. A half sister to the three men, she becomes the dominant personality in the Big House in the last years of Don Epifanio's life. She matches any of the men for will, dominance, and greed; not for her is the sentimentality of her sisters as they wail over the dead body of their father. She pays dearly, however, for distancing herself from her female and human base—for, in the end, she becomes insane.

Only Epifanio speaks of the inner turmoil that this position at the top has exacted from his humanity. Through his internal monologue, the stone is turned over and the reader finds pathos. The "I" voice meanders from its origins, back four generations, and up to its current state exploring life's meanings. The tone is plaintive. There is none of the strident pride of the external, perceived, social self. Epifanio ruminates over lost opportunities to be "authentic" with his children, mistresses, and his one true love, Teófila. There is no satisfaction in what he has achieved; he worries about the unhealing wounds of political failures, of his inability to control his sons, of his status as the prisoner, in his own home, of a ruthless daughter. A picture emerges, then, of a man caught in the power of evil and ending as the flotsam of time and history.

In juxtaposition to this portrayal of the powerful, Yáñez characterizes the collective voice of the weak, the victimized, in the figure of Rómulo. He is a peasant, the husband of Merced, and father of Teófila. In varying degrees, these three roles constitute his makeup, with that of the peasant/male predominant. As with Epifanio, the author presents him through the duality of his acts and his internal monologue. His social role as the disenfranchised is defined and criticized through the eyes of his wife. She sees him as weak physically and, particularly, morally. While the reader does empathize with this single individual whose demands for restitution are fruitless, the statement of his "failures" through his wife's comments further attests the isolating, divisive power of the *hacendado* system.

Rómulo's internal monologues, in tone and content, reveal the degree to which he shares his wife's view of himself. Yet he cannot be blamed for his humiliation, for his ability to be part of the land, to live with it in harmony, is as fragile as a spider's web in a storm. In his story, then, is recapitulated the denigration of the life of a peasant in a harsh environment.

The third constituting voice of this world is the eternal, spiritual one of the *bruja*, Matiana. In her extensive monologues, she draws on the wisdom of all seers. In the main, she is a witness-observer, filling gaps in the large mosaic of this world. At critical moments, she enters into the power struggle, the final time to recover Teófila's magical sewing machine. Although Matiana is attacked in the night, and her eyes are torn from her face, she foresees the future more clearly than ever. Through her, Yáñez suggests that the light of electricity—standing for Progress and ambition—will blind the people to the spiritual purity which she achieves in her final acts.

Themes and Meanings

The principal themes of this novel are suggested in the character study: the nature of power, the persistence of feudal patterns, the implications of technology, the dignity of the individual and the family in the face of corruption, and the eternal effort to wrest from the thin soil a life of peace. In the opposing motif to these temporal concerns, Yáñez presents a mystical, spiritual backdrop against which to evaluate and criticize the insanity which is Mexico's inheritance.

Ultimately, this novel's impact rests on the moral view that Yáñez holds. His novel transcends its local limits and presents a universal statement about man, his relationship with God, and his ultimate personal responsibility. Certainly, Matiana, the blind seer, serves as one signpost in the connection of this local world to the larger, deeper one. The tragic tone is a second link. The innumerable folk sayings, related as they are to both the collective wisdom—achieved in the eternal crucible of experience—and their specific metaphorical relation to nature, represent the penultimate bridge. (One critic estimates that more than a third of the novel is composed of these sayings, substitutes for rational thinking and binding in their ritualistic observance by all the characters save Jacob Gallo, who cuts off his roots to this world as surely as he did when he changed his name. Intentionally or not, Yáñez ensured this novel's place in history, for it will serve as a resource for historians and social critics who are seeking an account of a Mexico quickly disappearing.)

The last relationship of this local story to the universal world is in the retelling of Old and New Testament patterns (that is, Cain and Abel, the return of the Prodigal Son) and in the naming of the different places in the region (such as Bethlehem, Babel, Jerusalem, Damascus, and Galilea). This powerful parallel is extended through the people's response to the Church Calendar of Holy Days. Specifically, the novel is structurally divided by the fiesta celebration of the Easter reenactment, which falls roughly in the middle of the narrative and marks Miguel Arcángel/Jacob Gallo's return to his homeland.

Critical Context

Yáñez is a major figure in the development of both Mexican and Latin American narrative. Particularly significant were his efforts to assimilate international literary techniques to the distinctive materials of Mexican history and culture. He was fascinated by experimenting with simultaneity (as did John Dos Passos), with incorporating the past as a living influence in the present and the blending of subjective and objective reality (as did James Joyce), with the transference of universal myths and complexes as rationale and foundation for character (as did Sigmund Freud). In addition, his attention to unique structural devices to tie together a broad narrative panorama—the music in *Al filo del agua* (1947; *The Edge of the Storm*, 1963), critically considered his best novel, the religious calendar in *The Lean Lands*—instructs other novelists of similar epic tendencies on how to integrate their works. Finally, in the figures of *The Lean Lands*, he was to achieve a humanistic breakthrough for his countrymen by destroying the stereotypes that distance people from one another.

Bibliography

Clark, Stella T. "Agustín Yáñez." In *Latin American Writers*, edited by Carlos A. Solé and Maria I. Abreau. Vol. 3. New York: Charles Scribner's Sons, 1989. Offers an in-depth profile of Agustín Yáñez's life and career. Many of his works are discussed in detail, including *The Lean Lands*.

Detjens, Wilma E. *Home as Creation: The Influence of Early Childhood Experience in the Literary Creation of Gabriel García Márquez, Agustín Yáñez, and Juan Rulfo*. New York: Peter Lang, 1993. Examines the influence of Yáñez's childhood experiences in the formation of his novels.

Flores, Angel. "Agustín Yáñez." In *Spanish American Authors: The Twentieth Century*. New York: H. W. Wilson, 1992. A good overall view of Yáñez's work. Offers a brief critical analysis of selected novels and common themes that thread through Yáñez's fiction.

John Knowles

LEAVING HOME

Author: Lionel G. García (1935-   )
Type of plot: Psychological realism
Time of plot: The early 1940's
Locale: Southern California
First published: 1985

> *Principal characters:*
> ADOLFO, a former major-league baseball pitcher who realizes too late
> that he has wasted his life
> MARIA, Adolfo's cousin, who wants to keep all of her family at home
> CARMEN, the daughter and favorite child of Maria, an intelligent young
> woman who wants and achieves a better life than anyone in her
> family
> THE PROFESSOR (MANUEL GARCIA), a sidekick of Adolfo, a former
> elementary-school teacher
> ISABEL, Adolfo's former lover, who takes in Carmen and helps her find
> a job

The Novel

Lionel G. García's *Leaving Home* offers an intimate view of one Latino family in the early 1940's. The novel examines the pain of breaking family ties, identity crisis, and racism.

In *Leaving Home*, García is the narrator, telling the story almost entirely in a third-person omniscient voice. At one point in the novel, the author intrudes into the action using the first-person voice, and at another point, he addresses the audience directly in the second person.

As the novel opens, the aging Adolfo, a former major-league baseball pitcher who ruined his career with alcohol, is preparing to move to San Diego, away from the home of his cousin, Maria, in the Imperial Valley. He is a poor man who has little to live for but his memories. He hopes to move in with his former lover, Isabel, the mother of his son. Carmen, Maria's daughter, goes with Adolfo, hoping to move in with an aunt in order to find a better job. Maria, determined to show her family that no one loves them as much as she does, has burned the letters that Adolfo and Carmen asked her to mail to announce their respective arrivals. Maria hopes that the two will have to move back in with her.

Turned away by her aunt, Carmen is allowed to stay with Isabel. Adolfo, however, is forced to return to Maria's house. Upon his return, Adolfo discovers that he has been swindled out of his beer joint and that he has no prospects for work. Maria promises to help Adolfo find a job, but he is a proud man who considers himself to be a celebrity, and he refuses to work in the fields. Adolfo finally agrees to work as a gardener for a priest, but he soon finds the work demeaning and quits.

Adolfo then travels to Los Angeles, planning to stay with some old friends. On the trip, he meets Antonia, a con artist who easily persuades Adolfo to move in with her so she can get his pension checks. He lives unhappily with Antonia until he gives in to his craving for alcohol, after which she throws him out.

Adolfo then moves in with the Professor, another victim of Antonia's scam. When the health department condemns the men's house, Adolfo and the Professor move into a boarding house, at which they pay their rent in the form of sexual favors to the owner, Anna, a widow.

After the United States enters World War II, the Professor decides that he wants to return to Tijuana to avoid the draft. Even though he is much too old to be drafted, he remembers that during World War I, Hispanics were drafted before whites. The Professor plans to live with his sister, Yolanda. Adolfo accompanies him. In Tijuana, after another failed attempt at love, Adolfo marries a prostitute. He soon leaves her, however, and returns to Maria's house.

While Adolfo travels, Carmen succeeds in improving her life. She contracts tuberculosis while working at a film theater and must go to a state sanitarium to heal, but she discovers through this misfortune that she wants to be a nurse.

Upon her release, Carmen applies for a job at the Navy hospital in San Diego. After some struggle because of her race and her former illness, she is hired to wash pots. She is soon promoted to orderly and shortly thereafter is recommended for nurses' training in the U.S. Navy. She is graduated at the top of her class and becomes an officer. Although Carmen is capable, her promotion is based on the fact that she is Hispanic. The Department of Defense uses her as a symbol.

While visiting her mother, Carmen realizes the differences between the clean, organized military base and her mother's dusty house. Although she loves her mother dearly, Carmen suggests that Maria has not been keeping the house clean. Maria knows that the family tie to Carmen has been broken. When Carmen becomes engaged to a white naval officer in the Philippines, Maria believes that she has lost Carmen.

Maria experiences significant changes. She begins to question God's judgment when Carmen gets sick. When Arnoldo, one of Maria's sons, is killed in battle, she loses her faith in God. As her family falls apart, so do her beliefs. She is left alone and lonely. When Adolfo returns, Maria feels happy again. The two agree that Adolfo has wasted his life, but they are happy to have each other. The novel ends on this positive note.

The Characters

Adolfo, the former baseball pitcher, is full of contradictions. At once comic and pathetic, he cannot see himself as others see him, as an old man who lives in the past and talks too much. He is absurdly fastidious, as can be seen when he is offended by the sound of his lover urinating, yet he wants to project a macho image. He sees himself as a ladies' man, but at one point he is described as wearing a shrunken wool suit and canvas shoes with holes purposely cut in them to allow room for his corns. He frequently fails to wear his dentures. He is disgusted by ignorance but can barely read. Adolfo is a dreamer, and as such, he leaves the stability of Maria's house in search of a better, more prosperous life of love and leisure. Having been born talented, he believes he deserves such a life. He also believes that Carmen deserves a better life and encourages her to stay with Isabel to gain opportunities. By the end of the novel, Adolfo recognizes himself as a failure and returns to Maria's house. García uses interior monologues to show Adolfo's development.

Maria is the hub of the family, trying to keep the family connected. She does not have strong matriarchal qualities, but she is a strong woman who survives many hardships, including the judgment of the Hispanic community against women such as herself who become pregnant out of wedlock. She wants desperately to keep her family together to keep from being alone. Through her conversations, she reveals a belief in witchcraft that coexists with her belief in God. She sees herself as able to punish God by ignoring Him or breaking a promise to Him, but she fears divine power. She relies on God to keep her family safe, and when she thinks that God has begun taking family members from her, she becomes angry with Him. She begins not to care what her children do because she believes that they have forsaken her. By the end of the novel, Maria has grown bitter.

Carmen changes from a shy, indecisive child to a mature woman who knows what she wants. Carmen is Maria's favorite child. Although she loves her mother, Carmen feels no sadness when she leaves Maria. Carmen understands that in order to break out of the poverty in which she has grown up, she must move to the city and find more profitable work. In the sanitarium, she meets Luz, who tells her to do more than is expected of women, to make something of her life rather than accept the common fate.

The Professor, Adolfo's friend, is a flat character, but he is important in advancing the plot. The former elementary-school teacher shares his money with Adolfo, listens to Adolfo's stories, and takes him to Tijuana, where Adolfo meets a woman whom he believes he loves more than he loves Isabel. After being spurned by the Professor's sister and marrying a prostitute, Adolfo decides to return to Maria's house.

Themes and Meanings

Leaving Home is an examination of poverty, racism, and the family. García presents a group of related individuals in the midst of a changing society. Hispanics had begun to achieve equal rights in the 1940's but were not yet considered to be equal to whites, and hostility against them remained. Not all the characters in the novel want to break away from traditional lives of working all day and drinking all night.

In his novel, García shows a family of diverse personalities. Adolfo was born with talent, a cruel fate according to Maria. Because of his ability to pitch well, Adolfo is able, temporarily, to rise above the expected poverty of his race. His experiences as a famous pitcher cause him to continue to seek better things for himself and his family. After his baseball days, however, Adolfo is never again able to rise above poverty. Maria, on the other hand, is willing to accept her fate. She believes that she should not ask for anything more than she has. She cannot understand Adolfo's pride. When she helps him find a job, it is clear that she does not see a job as a measure of a person's worth.

García presents the plight of farmworkers and those forced to live on pensions. Farmworkers work long hours, yet make barely enough money to live on. Maria lives next to a dump where the children use old tires for toys. Adolfo is not surprised by the shabby furniture at Antonia's house because that is what he is accustomed to. People do not paint their houses, and junked cars litter yards.

The author also shows that Hispanics were treated as second-class citizens, citing the U.S. military's supposed policy of drafting minorities before whites. In the job market, García depicts blatant racism, as Carmen is told that not many people of her race become nurses.

Leaving Home is also about breaking family ties and about abandoning the predictable for the unpredictable. García presents various leave-takings throughout the novel. Adolfo and Carmen leave Maria's house to improve their lives. Carmen, unlike Adolfo, almost completely severs the tie to Maria. Another of Maria's daughters, an illegitimate child also named Maria, leaves home several times because she gets angry with her mother, but she always comes back. The death of Maria's son Arnoldo causes a further breakup of the family, almost pushing Maria to insanity. Adam, Maria's other son, also takes permanent leave. Arnoldo dies a hero, but Adam, a victim of syphilis, dies a scoundrel. Arnoldo's death gives Maria much pain, while Adam's gives her relief.

García's novel reveals that in a society of growing equality, people must be willing to take chances, to ignore the fate of their race, to leave home. Doing so may result in success and greater happiness. Such action, however, may also result in anxiety and unhappiness.

Critical Context

Leaving Home is García's first published novel. While the novel was in progress, García won the 1983 PEN Southwest Discovery Prize. *Leaving Home* was well received by critics, who forecast a promising future for García. His ability to create believable, sympathetic characters can be seen in his short stories.

In this novel, García uses several literary techniques. A shifting point of view is evident in the author's use of third-person omniscient, first-person, and second-person points of view. The author also uses indirect interior monologue. Fragmented time sequences add complexity to the novel.

García's theme of moving out of poverty is prevalent in his other novels *A Shroud in the Family* (1987) and *Hardscrub* (1990). The author bases his works on human experiences and is inspired by his own familial experiences. *Leaving Home* is part of the body of literary social criticism that examines racism, poverty, and the family.

A practicing veterinarian in Seabrook, Texas, García writes and publishes regularly. Several of his short stories have been published in various magazines. By the early 1990's, he had begun writing and publishing reminiscences revealing the strong ties in his own family.

Bibliography

García, Lionel. "Table Manners." *Texas Monthly* 18 (October, 1990): 44-45, 49-50. Although this article does not directly relate to *Leaving Home*, its reminiscences describe real people who bear a strong resemblance to the characters in the novel. For example, the depiction of Tío Nano carrying two heavy suitcases is similar to a scene in which Adolfo carries suitcases for Antonia. The grandmother in the reminiscence, always willing to help the less fortunate, is very much like Maria.

_____. "The Wedding." In *Cuentos Chicanos: A Short Story Anthology*, edited by Rudolfo A. Anaya and Antonio Marquez. Albuquerque: University of New Mexico Press, 1984. A short story by García. The section of this anthology describing the contributors provides valuable information on García's life but contains no information on *Leaving Home*. The information is useful for some types of criticism.

"Leaving Home." *Booklist* 81 (August, 1985): 1630. This favorable review gives a brief summary for a general audience. The review is helpful for understanding the plot and suggests that the work is important because it is about a group of people who need more attention from society.

Southwell, Sam "Lionel García, American Novelist." *The Americas Review* 22 (Fall/Winter, 1994): 110-113. Profiles García and details the themes and motifs in his novels that juxtapose myth and contemporary realism. Southwell asserts that García's works are tributes to his ethnic heritage but are also laments for the death of the traditions and culture of his southwestern Texas homeland.

Taylor, Pat E. "Sons and Lovers." *Texas Observer*, April 20, 1990, 16. Ellis's review focuses on García's novel *Hardscrub*, but there is some discussion of *Leaving Home*. The review suggests a common theme of the two novels of upward socio-economic mobility.

Wilson, Patricia J. "An Interview with Lionel G. García." *Texas Library Journal* 68 (Spring, 1992): 22-24. Provides insight into García's writing techniques. The article contains little information on *Leaving Home*, but García discusses where he gets ideas for his characters.

Wilma Shires

A LESSON BEFORE DYING

Author: Ernest J. Gaines (1933-   )
Type of plot: Social realism
Time of plot: 1948-1949
Locale: The former slave quarter on a plantation in rural Louisiana
First published: 1993

> *Principal characters:*
> GRANT WIGGINS, a young black teacher in the quarter school
> JEFFERSON, a young man convicted of murder and awaiting
>   electrocution
> TANTE LOU, Grant's aunt and benefactor
> EMMA GLENN, Jefferson's godmother and friend to Tante Lou
> REVEREND MOSE AMBROSE, the pastor of the quarter church
> MATTHEW ANTOINE, a Creole, Grant's former teacher
> VIVIAN, Grant's love, a Creole teacher in Bayonne
> HENRI PINCHOT, the plantation owner and brother-in-law to Sam
>   Guidry
> SAM GUIDRY, the St. Raphael Parish sheriff
> PAUL, a humane deputy

The Novel

In *A Lesson Before Dying*, Ernest Gaines once again takes his reader to a familiar fictional setting based on his boyhood home in Point Coupée Parish near New Roads, Louisiana, which becomes the fictional St. Raphael Parish, with Bayonne as its parish seat. A small town of about six thousand inhabitants, Bayonne is one of the two main settings in the novel. The other is the old slave quarter on an antebellum plantation owned by Henri Pinchot located a few miles away, near the St. Charles River. The year is 1948, a time when segregation and racial injustice were oppressive realities for Southern blacks, a time, too, when most of them did not know that the winds of change, if ever so slightly, were beginning to stir.

The basic plot is simple. A young, semiliterate black man, Jefferson, is tried for the murder of a white store owner, old Mr. Gropé; although Jefferson is innocent, the all-white, all-male jury sentences him to death in the electric chair. In pleading for his client's life, Jefferson's white lawyer argues that it would make no more sense to electrocute Jefferson than it would to execute a hog or some other dumb animal.

That assessment of Jefferson's human worth deeply troubles his godmother, Emma Glenn, who enlists the aid of her friend, Tante Lou, to pressure Tante Lou's nephew, Grant Wiggins, into trying to help Jefferson face death like a man, with dignity and courage. Grant, the sole teacher at the church school in the quarter, is reluctant to help, but he yields in the face of his aunt's strong moral cajoling and the insistence of his friend Vivian, with whom he is in love.

Before he can even visit Jefferson at the jail in Bayonne, Grant must approach the plantation owner, Henri Pinchot, who, because he is Sheriff Sam Guidry's brother-in-law, can intercede to obtain Guidry's permission. The prospect of asking Pinchot for help rankles Grant, because he knows he will have to pay a steep price—some of his fragile pride.

But even more troubling are his own persistent doubts about the efficacy of any effort to transform Jefferson into a man. Grant's sense of purpose as teacher, like his pride, is very brittle. His former teacher, Matthew Antoine, preaching nihilistic futility, had already severely damaged it, and it is soon apparent that Grant would likely bolt and run were it not for Vivian, who cannot leave with him until she has obtained a divorce from her estranged husband.

Grant's biggest problem, however, is Jefferson himself. During the initial visits to the parish courthouse in Bayonne, when Miss Emma accompanies Grant, Jefferson is almost catatonic, unwilling to communicate with either of them. When, in a subsequent visit by Grant, he does break out of his shell, his behavior shows that he has accepted his lawyer's conception of him as subhuman. He snorts and grunts, rooting on the floor of his cell and gobbling his food like a hog—behavior that greatly distresses Grant, for it seems to confirm everything that Antoine had said.

Still, Grant does not give up. Although he has no idea of how to go about restoring some pride in Jefferson, his resolve to do so gradually grows. He opts for simple kindness, believing that Jefferson's sense of self-worth must come from a belief that others care. Grant's nemesis, the Reverend Ambrose, chagrined by Grant's apparent agnosticism, pulls against him, convinced that Jefferson can find comfort only in the revealed word of God.

With patience, Grant finally begins to break through to Jefferson. He gives the condemned man a small portable radio, which Jefferson takes as a kind, caring gift, more, in fact, than he had ever before received. Then Grant encourages him to write down his thoughts and feelings, which Jefferson, in halting words, does, finally confirming his humanity. Clearly, before his date with Gruesome Gertie, the portable electric chair, he redeems his manhood; in the process, Jefferson helps Grant to find himself and earn the respect and proffered friendship of Paul, a white but sympathetic deputy. Thus, despite the awful miscarriage of justice that is the central fact of the novel, *A Lesson Before Dying* ends on a hopeful note.

The Characters

Grant Wiggins, the protagonist, is also the novel's primary narrator, so it is chiefly his thoughts that the reader audits. He is a seeker cut adrift from his communal moorings by his education, which, ironically, seems to limit rather than expand his options. Given his time and place, he can be little other than a teacher, but his doubts about the value of trying to help the quarter children make him harsh and perfunctory, almost a martinet. Initially, he seems destined to fulfill the fate that Matthew Antoine has told him is in store for him, to become "the nigger" he was "born to be."

For Grant, Jefferson's plight is all too typical of what a young, ignorant black male might expect in a white man's world, and Grant sees little point in trying to help him. He gradually warms up to his charge, however, not so much from the moral cross Tante Lou has tried to make him shoulder as his desire to prove Sheriff Guidry and others wrong. Blinded by pride, palpable resentment, and doubt, Grant does not fully understand that, in helping Jefferson, he has set out on his own spiritual odyssey, one that finally proves Matthew Antoine wrong. The reader understands, however, and knows that Paul's visit to the quarter, made from respect and admiration for Grant, signals an enduring, hopeful change.

Although Grant is hostile to Tante Lou's moral arm-twisting, she is the first important catalyst in his transformation. She will not let Grant wheedle out of what she perceives as both his Christian and communal responsibility. His education has led him to question her beliefs, but Grant's residual sense of guilt is tapped by his aunt, for whom he has both affection and grudging reverence. She, of course, is bound to the community by traditional ties based in an abiding faith that Grant, in his modern enlightenment, has almost entirely rejected. He cannot, however, refuse her on a personal level.

Vivian is the other important catalyst. Her love offers Grant solace and hope in his darker moments, when the pointlessness of trying to help seems confirmed by Jefferson's actions. She also keeps Grant anchored to his job, because she is not free to leave with him until she obtains her divorce. Her own strong sense of responsibility, rooted in more private feelings of pride and dignity, nicely balances Tante Lou's.

While Grant's main conflict lies within, it is to an important degree objectified in the person of Jefferson, the novel's victim. To raise him up, Grant must overcome Jefferson's self-loathing, inculcated by whites who have repeatedly told him that he is no better than an animal. It is that same self-effacement and contempt from which Grant has tried to run, evading rather than coping with it. In helping Jefferson, he is at last forced to face up to and triumph over it. Jefferson, going to his death with manly dignity, provides an outer measure of Grant's own spiritual growth.

Themes and Meanings

In *A Lesson Before Dying*, the personal problems of the black and Creole characters are the bitter fruit grown from seeds sown in the soil of racial bigotry. For them, the injustice of the caste system is the central, inescapable burden that weighs them down with poverty and ignorance, often with little hope of amelioration. That fundamental fact of their life is gleaned at the novel's outset, when, with prophetic resignation, Grant explains that he did not go to Jefferson's trial because he knew what the verdict would be, what it inevitably had to be.

What Gaines shows is that even in the face of such abysmal conditions, a man or woman can reveal courage and dignity—or even, like Jefferson, regain them when they are lost. Some of the novel's characters, especially Tante Lou, define their humanity by their faith both in God and tradition. Others, such as Grant, must define it on their own terms through personal exorcism, not of the devil, but of doubt and despair, and through contact with their own innate decency.

A Lesson Before Dying reads a bit like a sophisticated morality drama. It is not, of course, a religious allegory in the mode of the medieval morality plays, but like them, it involves an outward test that reflects the psychomachia, or mind struggle, within the protagonist. Grant's inner conflict is between despair, articulated by Matthew Antoine, and hope, held out by Vivian. At stake is his secular redemption, and the challenge he must meet and overcome in achieving it is objectively manifest in Jefferson, who has been reduced to the very thing that Antoine had claimed Grant was fated to become. Grant must redeem Jefferson to redeem himself, and he must accomplish this from an initial condition of existential uncertainty that approaches despair.

Through education, Grant has distanced himself from the faith that steadies Tante Lou and fires the righteous anger of Mose Ambrose. He is the new Southern black, struggling to redefine himself in the face of changes that are eroding a way of life that for prior generations had at least allowed a modicum of pride and self-respect. The time is not yet right for collective action, the boycotts and sit-ins of the next generation; for Grant, therefore, the only hope seems to lie in his love for Vivian and their anticipated flight.

Ironically, it is Vivian's situation that keeps him at his school, not any sense of self-sacrifice or humanistic concern for his charges. In fact, at first he seems to have accepted Antoine's assessment of his worth, much as Jefferson, in jail, accepts the view of himself as hog. Like Jefferson, Grant must learn in his own prison, his racially inherited place under a brutal Southern sun, that it is possible to find both dignity and hope.

Critical Context

In some important ways, the artistic antecedents of *A Lesson Before Dying* lie in Gaines's first novel, *Catherine Carmier* (1964). There are, for example, close parallels between character pairs, notably Tante Lou and Grant Wiggins and the earlier book's Aunt Charlotte and Jackson Bradley. The two spinster aunts, spiritually identical, are moral preceptors for their searching, disillusioned nephews, both of whom attempt to find themselves in romantic entanglements with Creole women.

The principal locales of the two novels are much the same, except that *Catherine Carmier* is set in the early 1960's, when a young, educated black man such as Jackson had some alternatives to teaching. Despite the pain it causes for his aunt, Jackson rejects the option in his quest for a new, personally rewarding identity. Grant, facing the less hopeful world of 1948, at least goes through the motions of teaching, though he longs, however vaguely, for something better.

Racial injustice permeates both novels. Both books relate that injustice to a generational change and conflict between the older, tradition-bound members of the community and the increasingly alienated youth, who can find nothing to bind them to their heritage. Further, both works treat that passing of a way of life with a mixture of relief, sadness, and some compensatory humor.

In *A Lesson Before Dying*, Gaines also returned to a simpler method of presenting his story. In the novel's immediate predecessor, *A Gathering of Old Men* (1983), he used the collective point of view of more than a dozen voices, but in *A Lesson Before Dying*, he confines point of view primarily to the single voice of Grant Wiggins. The novel thus shares the narrative directness of *Catherine Carmier*. It is similar, too, in its plain but lyric style—rich in colloquial speech, understatement, and bare diction—and in its characteristically even-tempered handling of the passionate issue of racial intolerance.

Bibliography
Auger, Philip. "A Lesson About Manhood: Appropriating *The Word* in Ernest Gaines's *A Lesson Before Dying*." *The Southern Literary Journal* 27 (Spring, 1995): 74-78. Auger explores the issues of dignity and self-worth in Gaines's novel, focusing on the problems black men face when attempting to define their manhood. His discussion also includes an examination of Gaines's other works that deal with the same theme.
Babb, Valerie M. *Ernest Gaines*. Boston: Twayne, 1991. A major critical introduction to Gaines, with a chronology and bibliography. The best general introduction to Gaines published before *A Lesson Before Dying*. Strongly recommended as starting point for further study.
Rubin, Merle. "Convincing Moral Tale of Southern Injustice." *The Christian Science Monitor*, April 13, 1993, 13. A review for the general reader. Gives a synopsis of the novel and an upbeat appraisal typifying the book's reception in most reviews. For Rubin, *A Lesson Before Dying* is an important "moral drama."
Senna, Carl. "Dying Like a Man." *The New York Times*, August 8, 1993, p. G21. An enthusiastic review that helps illuminate the racial lines and tensions among the book's black, white, and Creole characters. Senna does claim that the novel has an occasional "stylistic lapse" but gives no specific examples.
Sheppard, R. Z. "An A-Plus in Humanity." *Time* 141 (March 29, 1993): 65-66. Reviews *A Lesson Before Dying*, giving a short plot synopsis. Praises the author's level-headed ability to convey the "malevolence of racism and injustice without the usual accompanying self-righteousness."
Wardi, Anissa J. Review of *A Lesson Before Dying*, by Ernest Gaines. *MELUS* 21 (Summer, 1996): 192-194. A highly favorable review that explores the "role of language in symbolic enslavement." Wardi also offers a brief plot synopsis and character analysis. She praises the novel as "an extraordinary literary accomplishment."
Yardley, Jonathan. "Nothing but a Man." *The Washington Post Book World* 23 (March 28, 1993): 3. A brief but excellent explication of the novel. Focuses on Grant as protagonist and notes that the lesson referred to in the work's title is one learned by him as well as by Jefferson. Also remarks on Gaines's admirable restraint in treating racial themes.

John W. Fiero

LET THE CIRCLE BE UNBROKEN

Author: Mildred D. Taylor (1943-   )
Type of plot: Historical realism
Time of plot: The 1930's
Locale: Rural Mississippi
First published: 1981

> *Principal characters:*
> DAVID LOGAN (PAPA), the head of a landowning African American
>   family in rural Mississippi
> MARY LOGAN (MAMA), David's wife, the mother of Stacey, Cassie,
>   Christopher-John, and Little Man
> CASSIE LOGAN, the nine-year-old narrator
> HORACE GRANGER, the white owner of a large plantation
> LEE ANNIE LEES, an elderly African American woman
> WADE JAMISON, a white lawyer and friend of the Logans
> STACEY LOGAN, Cassie's older brother
> T. J. AVERY, Stacey's best friend

The Novel

Based on experiences typical of those endured by the author's parents, *Let the Circle Be Unbroken* is a fictionalized portrayal of how a rural Mississippi community, and the Logan family in particular, faced adversity and survived during the Depression of the 1930's.

The novel contains fourteen chapters that separate major episodes or denote passage of time. Cassie Logan, the nine-year-old daughter of David and Mary Logan ("Mama" and "Papa"), narrates the story.

The opening chapter establishes a theme of discrimination and abuse of the community's black families. T. J. Avery, Stacey's classmate, is unjustly accused of killing a white store owner. The black families wonder whether T. J. can get a trial at all, and, if so, whether it can possibly be a fair one. Wade Jamison, a white lawyer whom the Logans respect, attempts to get T. J. acquitted, but he is unsuccessful; T. J. is sentenced to death.

As winter comes, the plight of both black and white sharecroppers and day laborers is revealed. Most of the area's families live in one-room shacks with dirt floors. Even Papa, a landowner who has a nice five-room house and admits to being better off than many others, is worried about paying the taxes on his land. Papa has been cheated out of payment for his cotton crop by Horace Granger, the wealthy white plantation owner.

Meanwhile, Lee Annie Lees, the sixty-five-year-old aunt of a local black family, announces as she turns sixty-five that she will study for the voter-registration test. Cassie helps her to memorize all laws in the Constitution in preparation for the test, aware, however, that Horace Granger, for whom Lee Annie's relatives are sharecroppers, can control her fate.

When representatives of a Farm Workers' Union solicit Papa's support for an effort for "both black and white" he promises to "think it through," but his enthusiasm for the union is diminished by his suspicion that black farmers would not really be protected by the organization.

As tax-payment time approaches, Papa considers working temporarily on the railroad and later does so. Stacey realizes that times are hard and begs to quit school to get a job, but the Logans forbid it, insisting that they will make ends meet somehow.

Several times Papa's brother Hammer comes from the North to visit, as does Bud Rankin, Mary Logan's nephew. When it becomes known that Bud has a white wife, there is tension between Bud and Hammer in particular, but Bud asks the Logans if his daughter Suzella can visit. Encouraged by her mother, Suzella has often passed for white so things "won't be so hard" for her. Cassie has trouble accepting her: she resents giving up her bed and seeing Stacey give Suzella all his attention, but she grudgingly tolerates her.

Things worsen when the county agent requires some families to plow up the parts of their cotton crop that are over the quota. Stacey finally feels compelled to do something to help, so he and a friend, Moe, run away to take jobs cutting cane. The family is distraught; Mama sends for Papa, but it is difficult to know how to look for the boys. Cassie questions how the adults can pretend that everything is all right, but Mama reminds her that "life goes on no matter what."

As feared, Granger sees to it that Lee Annie is told that she has failed the voter registration test she had vowed to take. On New Year's Day, news finally comes that Stacey and Moe have been located. Again, Mr. Jamison helps the Logans; he finds Stacey, who is reunited with his family. Cassie remembers her mother's saying that one day Stacey would be her friend again, and she sees that her mother's prediction is true.

The Characters

David Logan (Papa) is a fully human man with a strong sense of values and strength of character that have earned him the love and respect of his family and his community. While fortunate to have acquired four hundred acres of land, he is never arrogant or indifferent to the needs of his less fortunate neighbors. He possesses the wisdom to know when and how to speak up and when to remain silent. Although he is a thoroughly admirable character, his goodness never seems contrived or artificial.

Mary Logan (Mama) is the author's mouthpiece for voicing her feelings about the unjust treatment of blacks in the 1930's. Moreover, Mama is a warm, loving mother who wants her children to understand what it means to be black in a white-dominated world and to learn to deal with it. She believes in education and in self-improvement, and she hopes that one day the children will be spared the racial discrimination she has known.

Cassie, a fifth-grader at the beginning of the story, experiences the gamut of feelings that a young girl coming into adolescence has. Capable of hurt feelings and jealousy, she is also sensitive: to harmonica music, to T. J., even to Suzella at times. She is clever; in a game of marbles, she plots to win the prize blue one, risking punishment afterward since Papa has said that "marbles might lead to gambling." She feels the sting of being treated like a child by her eldest brother when he becomes a teenager.

Stacey is a lovable, serious-minded preteen. He feels a responsibility to family, even to the point of sacrificing his own comfort and disobeying and worrying his parents in order to try to help them. He shows courage in taking the necessary risks to do what he feels is right.

Wade Jamison is a truly sympathetic character. Though shunned by other white people in the community for trying to get justice at T. J.'s trial, he has a genuine sense of justice. He faces reality squarely, however; he knows that his just behavior toward the black families cannot cancel the years of abuse they have received from other whites.

Horace Granger, the white plantation owner, is predictable. He is a prejudiced, powerful white man who seems truly to believe that racial equality is unthinkable. Perhaps a product of his own upbringing, he measures success in terms of power over, and manipulation of, both black and white sharecroppers.

Suzella Rankin experiences the dilemma of one who must live in two worlds. She admits the advantages of being able to pass as white, but she loves her black father even when she feels ashamed of him. The fact that she is too advanced to remain at her grade level in the rural Mississippi school demonstrates the contrast in education and opportunity between the North and the South.

Lee Annie, though aunt to the Ellis family by blood relationship, is "aunt" to the community. Loved by all, she shows courage and strength of character when she decides that, at age sixty-five, she will do what she has always longed to do: register to vote.

Themes and Meanings

Based on experiences of the author's own parents' generation, *Let the Circle Be Unbroken* depicts perceptively the plight of black families in rural Mississippi during the Great Depression. The book shows the clash between well-intentioned New Deal politics, the politics of white Mississippi, and the threat of unionism in this context.

The novel is a powerful and moving story of strength, love, dignity, and integrity against almost unbeatable odds. David and Mary Logan, well acquainted with the injustice of racial prejudice, provide the love and support that will help their children to know the truth about growing up black and not being defeated by it.

The sting of injustice runs throughout the novel. The black families who dare to attend T. J.'s trial see him sentenced to die for a murder he did not commit. Sharecroppers weep as they plow under cotton because a county agent has miscalculated the quota, and they see their meager profit being destroyed. Lee Annie dares to take a stand by memorizing the laws of the Constitution for a voter-registration test, only to be rejected and see her family dismissed from the Granger plantation. Stacey, determined to help his family, is not paid for his ceaseless labor.

David Logan demonstrates dignity and wisdom in managing his affairs. Knowing

Horace Granger's power in the community, Papa thinks things through before making decisions. He does not accept offers that do not ring true; under difficult circumstances, he works to pay the taxes and keep his land. In spite of injustice, Papa is fair. He is able to separate strength of character from color of skin, recognizing that Wade Jamison is "a rare man" who, though white, is a friend and is fair. He knows that T. J. has acted foolishly in going with two white boys to break into a store, although he dares to hope that the boy can have a fair trial and keep his life.

Suzella portrays the dilemma of being caught in two worlds; having mixed blood isolates her in both groups. She recognizes the social advantages of passing as white, and she feels the strength and love of her black relatives. Ultimately, however, she returns North to her white mother because she cannot cope with being black in a white world.

The novel is also a story of growing up. Stacey longs to be grown and to help support the family, while Cassie resists the inevitable and longs for things to remain the same. Each learns in time that the wisdom of their parents is to be trusted.

Through all the misery and mistreatment, the families learn that, by looking to the traditions and the heritage of their past, the community members can sustain one another even in times of trial. One endures for the sake of the next generation. The Logan family learns that love is stronger than adversity even in the difficult environment of rural Mississippi.

Critical Context

Let the Circle Be Unbroken is the third of Mildred D. Taylor's books; her first, *Song of the Trees*, was published in 1975. The next year, she published *Roll of Thunder, Hear My Cry*, and *Let the Circle Be Unbroken*, which followed in 1981, is a sequel to that book. Additional novels including *The Friendship* (1987) and *The Road to Memphis* (1990) continue the story of the Logan family.

Rather than experimenting with innovative techniques, Taylor opts to use her natural language skills to let the young Cassie Logan tell her story. The novel flows with a smoothness and clarity that helped to establish Taylor's reputation. It is both humorous and capable of evoking deep emotional reactions. The fact that the author bases her novels on the kinds of experiences that her own parents lived through may well contribute to the power and compassion that she brings to her work. Also, Taylor's own Peace Corps experience in Ethiopia as a teacher further broadened her base of knowledge and sensitivity.

Some critics have suggested that *Let the Circle Be Unbroken* and the Logan family series belong alongside other classics such as Mark Twain's *The Adventures of Huckleberry Finn* (1884) and Laura Ingalls Wilder's *Little House on the Prairie* (1869). Taylor has received formal recognition for the Logan family series, including *The New York Times* Outstanding Book of the Year Award for her first work, *Song of the Trees*. *Roll of Thunder, Hear My Cry* won the American Library Association's Notable Book award and the Newbery Medal in 1977 and was a finalist for the National Book Award.

Bibliography

Bosmajian, Hamida. "Mildred Taylor's Story of Cassie Logan: A Search for Law and Justice in a Racist Society." *Children's Literature* 24 (1996): 141-160. A perceptive essay that explores the treatment of racism and justice in Taylor's works, especially in relation to Cassie Logan. A solid examination of themes common to Taylor's writings.

Eiger, Melanie. Review of *Let the Circle Be Unbroken*, by Mildred D. Taylor. *Best Sellers* 41 (February, 1982): 444. Eiger suggests that *Let the Circle Be Unbroken* could have a positive influence on the younger reader, white or black, in dealing with problems of racial discrimination and injustice. She notes that the example of the Logan family provides instruction in courage, dignity, and the value of passive resistance.

Harper, Mary Turner. "Merger and Metamorphosis in the Fiction of Mildred D. Taylor." *Children's Literature Association Quarterly* 13 (Summer, 1988): 75-80. Harper identifies the rich oral tradition of African American folktales as a source for Taylor's works. The characters draw courage and strength from such folk songs as the one that inspires the novel's title.

Heins, Ethel L. Review of *Let the Circle Be Unbroken*, by Mildred D. Taylor. *The Horn Book Magazine* 58 (April, 1982): 173. Comments that Taylor demonstrates sensitivity in her treatment of the injustice and suffering that African Americans endured during the Depression. The reviewer observes that Cassie's narration captures something of the transition from childhood innocence to an awareness of the black condition.

Jordan, June. "Mississippi in the Thirties." *The New York Times Book Review* 86 (November 15, 1981): 55, 58. Jordan praises Taylor's ability to deal with the effects of New Deal politics and 1930's racial discrimination in language and style that is appropriate for the younger reader. The sharing of true community, the risk-taking, and the courage of the Logans even in the face of humiliation, Jordan says, make the novel worthy of being called a classic.

McDonnell, Christine. "Powerful Lesson of Family Love." *The Christian Science Monitor* 73 (October 13, 1981): B1, B11. Notes that *Let the Circle Be Unbroken* appeals to readers of all ages, although its main thrust is toward the young. Observes that Taylor uses contrast as a major means of organizing her commentary on the cruel conditions of the rural black family in Depression Mississippi.

Smith, Karen. "A Chronicle of Family Honor: Balancing Rage and Triumph in the Novels of Mildred D. Taylor." In *African American Voices in Young Adult Literature: Tradition, Transition, Transformation*, edited by Karen P. Smith. Metuchen, N.J.: Scarecrow, 1994. Smith explores the treatment of the African American family in Mississippi during the Depression.

Victoria Price

LETTING GO

Author: Philip Roth (1933-   )
Type of plot: Satiric realism
Time of plot: The 1950's
Locale: Chicago, New York, Iowa, and Pennsylvania
First published: 1962

> *Principal characters:*
> GABRIEL (GABE) WALLACH, a young literature professor at the
>   University of Chicago
> PAUL HERZ, Gabe's friend and colleague at the University of Chicago
> MARTHA REGANHART, Gabe's mistress, a divorcée and the mother of
>   two children
> LIBBY HERZ, Paul's wife

The Novel

    Letting Go is a book about literature, filled with literary references. The characters in the novel partially define themselves by the books that they have read. The novel focuses on the young academic crowd of the decade of the 1950's—particularly on three characters: Gabe Wallach, a young instructor in the humanities, and his friends Paul and Libby Herz.

    Apparently, Philip Roth intended Gabe to be a Jamesian hero: the man with an independent income, living a good life, with a career that he cares about, but always wrestling with a vague guilt. The story of Gabe's tribulations with his family and friends is complex and compassionate, but the telling often is bogged down in excessive detail. Roth displays here, as he would again and again throughout his career, his infallible ear for American and Jewish-American dialogue. Too much of a good thing, however, can weigh down the best-conceived story.

    Much of the story is told in flashbacks, as the reader learns how the characters reached the points where the narrative picks them up. The lives of these characters have not been easy. The Herzes, particularly, have been disaster-prone. A mixed marriage (Paul is Jewish, Libby, Catholic) has built-in stresses, but these are part of a larger pattern: The Herzes struggle endlessly with every aspect of their lives. Although Libby is Catholic, when she becomes pregnant she has to have an abortion because of their economic situation and her own precarious health. Roth treats this episode at great length and with a Dreiserian relentlessness that would surprise readers who know him only by his later fiction.

    Indeed, Roth has a remarkable gift for representing the nightmarish disasters that befall those who leave themselves defenseless by living with what he considers complete sincerity. The book is often powerful, as well as brilliantly perceptive. At the end, however, the reader is not certain whether Roth likes his characters—or even if he likes humanity very much. Although the reader follows Gabe and his friends from

Iowa, where they were graduate students, to Chicago and New York, and learns about all the sordid details of their lives, they remain somewhat unconvincing as human beings.

The Characters

Gabe Wallach is meant to be a complex and thoughtful character, but actually he is overshadowed by the other characters in the book. When the reader first encounters him, he is brooding over the death of his mother and involved in a moral and psychological struggle with his father. He later has an affair with Martha Reganhart, a young divorcée who loses custody of her two small children because of her relations with him. Later, when one of the children accidentally kills the other while they are away with their father, Martha breaks off the affair. Gabe feels heartbroken, guilty, and wounded. Meanwhile he has been involved with his friends Paul and Libby Herz. He is drawn to the thin, neurotic Libby, although Paul is his best friend. Finally, after he has helped Paul and Libby adopt a baby, he embarks for Europe, to mend his emotional wounds and continue his search for his identity.

Paul Herz, however, passes through even greater tribulations. Married to the intense, hysterical Libby, who is always suffering from physical and emotional problems, Paul wants to accomplish something great but never seems to be able to make any progress. The Herzes suffer from both poverty and a kind of will to doom; their marriage often seems grim and cannibalistic, despite the few moments of real affection that creep into the narrative. After her abortion, Libby develops kidney trouble which makes it dangerous for her to have a child. Eventually, Paul lands a good job in Chicago, but he immediately antagonizes the chairman of the department. When they decide to adopt a baby, the waiting lists are too long, and Libby cracks up in front of the social worker who is sent by the adoption agency to interview her. Libby's efforts at psychoanalysis with a Dr. Lumin in Chicago are not fruitful, and she continues to dwell on thoughts of suicide.

Martha Reganhart is a much more dynamic, sensible person than the others. She is a full-blown woman, with two children and a pragmatic view of life. When she encounters troubles, she fights back rather than moaning and wailing about her fate. One feels that she is the only character in the book of whom Roth really approves.

Many of the minor characters in the book, such as Paul's two uncles, Asher and Jerry, and his cousin Claire, emerge as vivid personalities with their own foibles and peculiarities. They vanish from the story all too abruptly, however, never to be heard from again, and the reader wonders why so much space was lavished on them. Indeed, when reading about yet one more aspect of Paul or Libby's misery, the reader wishes that Uncle Asher would make a reappearance and lighten the narrative for a while.

Themes and Meanings

Letting Go is a novel about human responsibility, a novel that asks what we owe to those around us. Gabe Wallach spends the four years that are chronicled in this novel rushing this way and that, trying to find a proper relationship between his own good fortune and the misfortune of others. His behavior is a sort of frenetic contest between his sympathies and his instinct for self-preservation. Through comic and tragic and often melodramatic events, Gabe tries to rescue others without drowning himself. What he cannot see is the difference between ephemeral attention to others' needs, and genuine commitment to their future. Only at the end of the book is Gabe able to release himself from the self-centeredness of his well-ordered existence and plunge into the turmoil of human life on an equal footing with everybody else.

The odds are too heavily weighted against Roth's characters. He seems to be saying that the present condition of things in the United States is so inexorably negative that there is no point in struggling. Certainly, his attitude about the United States is vividly presented. As he has said elsewhere, in an essay, Roth believes that American society is essentially insane. This point of view underlies much of his writing, even in the later books, and is the foundation for much of his humor and satire. This country is, in other words, no place for a rational man to live. Yet people do live, and they somehow make the best of it; at times, Roth seems to be scolding his characters for their struggles rather than admiring them.

Critical Context

Letting Go, Roth's first novel, was one of the most eagerly anticipated novels of the last several decades. Roth had demonstrated such brilliance at such a young age with his first book, *Goodbye, Columbus*, a collection of five short stories and the title novella, that it was believed that there was almost no limit to what he could achieve. That first book received the National Book Award, but when this vast, six-hundred-page novel appeared, the critical reaction was mixed. Many readers were disappointed by its diffuseness and by the long, dull stretches that separate the brilliant passages. Line by line, the writing was admired, but it was thought that much of the narrative simply was superfluous; the novel's parts were considered more successful than the whole. Yet, as one reviewer noted, it was one of the more ambitious novels published in 1962, and certainly one of the most memorable.

In this first novel, Roth was trying to achieve very specific literary goals. The book is structured around a mixture of irony and affirmation such as is found in the books of Saul Bellow, Norman Mailer, and Bernard Malamud. Roth may not have been entirely successful in sustaining that mixture, but the effort pointed his work in a profitable direction. This novel is much looser and freer in construction than are the stories in *Goodbye, Columbus*; the writing of it was a liberating experience for Roth. From this, he went on to write *When She Was Good* (1967), in which he focused on characters other than the Jewish Americans about which he usually wrote, and then, his most famous book, *Portnoy's Complaint* (1969).

Thus, although Gabe Wallach's philosophical and spiritual quest bogs down in Freudian ponderings, *Letting Go* was an important step in the development of Roth's career. Gabe wallows in his past, unable to come to terms with it. He seems to be a whining and ineffectual hero, afflicted by encroaching despair and an inability to move forward. By contrast, Portnoy, Roth's most celebrated protagonist, seizes his existence and wrenches meaning from it. When he looks at his past, he comes to grips with it. Roth learned a great deal from *Letting Go*, and his later books are the richer for it. After one more experiment with realism (*When She Was Good*), Roth focused increasingly on satire, which is where his genius lies. Although he still portrayed the angst of the human condition, he never again made the mistake of allowing his characters to tell one another for page after page how much they were suffering.

Bibliography

Cooper, Alan. *Philip Roth and the Jews*. Albany: State University of New York Press, 1996. Cooper explores the spectrum of Roth's writing, including his early works, the "post-Portnoy seventies," and the Zuckerman novels. An excellent overall critical view.

Gentry, Marshall B. "Ventriloquists' Conversations: The Struggle for Gender Dialogue in E. L. Doctorow and Philip Roth." *Contemporary Literature* 34 (Fall, 1993): 512-537. Gentry contends that both Doctorow and Roth are different from other Jewish authors because of their incorporation of feminist thought into traditionally patriarchal Jewish literature. He notes that their reconciliation of feminism and Judaism could alienate them from both groups, but he commends their attempt.

Greenberg, Robert M. "Transgression in the Fiction of Philip Roth." *Twentieth Century Literature* 43 (Winter, 1997): 487-506. Greenberg argues that the theme of transgression pervades Roth's novels and allows the author to penetrate places where he feels socially and psychologically excluded. An intriguing assessment of Roth's work.

Halio, Jay L. *Philip Roth Revisited*. New York: Twayne, 1992. Halio offers a brief biographical sketch of Roth as well as in-depth discussions of his works. Includes a chapter entitled "*Letting Go*: Varieties of Deadly Farce." Also includes helpful notes and a selected bibliography for further reading.

Halkin, Hillel. "How to Read Philip Roth." *Commentary* 97 (February, 1994): 43-48. Offering critical analyses of several of Roth's books, Halkin explores Roth's personal view of Jewishness, as well as other biographical elements in his works.

Podhoretz, Norman. "The Adventure of Philip Roth." *Commentary* 106 (October, 1998): 25-36. Podhoretz discusses the Jewish motifs in Roth's writing and compares Roth's work with that of other Jewish authors, including Saul Bellow and Herman Wouk. He also voices his disappointment concerning Roth's preoccupation with growing old as expressed in his later novels.

Rodgers, Bernard F., Jr. *Philip Roth*. Boston: Twayne, 1978. Rodgers provides a critical and interpretive study of Roth, with a close reading of his major works, a solid bibliography, and complete notes and references.

Bruce D. Reeves

LIBRA

Author: Don DeLillo (1936-   )
Type of plot: Psychological realism
Time of plot: The 1950's and the 1960's
Locale: The United States, Japan, and the Soviet Union
First published: 1988

> *Principal characters:*
> NICHOLAS BRANCH, a retired member of the CIA
> WALTER "WIN" EVERETT, JR., a member of the CIA relegated to teaching college
> DAVID FERRIE, a flamboyant pilot with connections to the CIA
> T. J. MACKEY, a renegade CIA agent
> LEE HARVEY OSWALD, a maladjusted young man
> MARGUERITE OSWALD, Lee's manipulative mother
> LAURENCE "LARRY" PARMENTER, a CIA agent
> JACK RUBY, a Dallas nightclub owner with connections to the underworld

The Novel

Libra is Don DeLillo's fictional re-creation of the life of Lee Harvey Oswald, alleged assassin of President John F. Kennedy, and of the conspiracy that many believe lay behind the assassination.

DeLillo has woven his novel from three major strands. The first is the story of Oswald himself, from his childhood in New York City until his death at the hands of Jack Ruby. The second strand follows the growth of a conspiracy to commit some act that will focus the anger of the U.S. government on Cuban dictator Fidel Castro. The plot is originally intended to fail; as DeLillo notes, however, "There is a tendency of plots to move toward death." In the third and simplest strand of the novel, retired CIA analyst Nicholas Branch is trying years later to write a classified history of what took place.

As *Libra* opens, young Lee Harvey Oswald is living in the Bronx with his widowed mother, Marguerite Oswald. Her efforts at finding another husband have failed, as have her attempts to make a home with relatives. In what will become a familiar pattern, Lee and his mother always seem to be on the move to increasingly cheaper apartments. Eventually, mother and son return to New Orleans. Lee was born there, and Marguerite's sister still lives there, but once again there seems to be no home for them.

Along the way, Lee discovers Marxism, which offers him an explanation for his marginalized situation in society, but he also enlists in the Marines. He is assigned to Atsugi Naval Air Station in Japan, from which U2 spy flights are launched over the Soviet Union. In Japan, he also begins an affair and makes contact with Soviet agents, expressing his belief in Marxism and offering to defect.

When he learns that his unit is scheduled to leave Japan, Lee shoots himself in the arm in a vain attempt to remain behind. A second incident—a fight with a sergeant—earns him a court martial and a brief sentence in the brig.

When Marguerite suffers a minor accident, Lee secures an early separation from the Marines. Rather than take care of his mother, however, he travels to the Soviet Union to defect. There, he marries but fails to find a meaningful role. Repeating the pattern established in his youth, he returns to the United States only to pass through a series of dead-end jobs. He becomes obsessed with making a place for himself and becoming a part of history. His attempt to assassinate right-wing General Edwin A. Walker fails, but he attracts the attention of conspirators plotting a far more important crime. The group needs a patsy with ties to the Communist world, and Oswald seems made for their purposes.

The conspirators are Win Everett, Larry Parmenter, T. J. Mackey, and David Ferrie. Bitter at American failure to support a rebel invasion of Cuba at the Bay of Pigs, Everett concocts a phony assassination attempt, complete with carefully planted clues that will lead to Fidel Castro's doorstep. Parmenter uses his contacts in the Central Intelligence Agency (CIA) to identify a likely patsy, a young man with increasingly violent tendencies who has recently returned from the Soviet Union. Mackey assembles a backup team of assassins. Unknown to Everett and Parmenter, however, Mackey neglects to explain to his team that they are supposed to miss.

Years later, CIA historian Nicholas Branch concludes that the assassination of JFK was largely a matter of chance. The conspirators focus their plans on Miami, but chance dictates that the Secret Service increase its security in Miami. Chance then takes the President to Dallas, placing him in a motorcade scheduled to pass by the very building, the Texas School Book Depository, where Oswald now works. Conspirator David Ferrie, who knew Lee as a child, persuades the increasingly unbalanced young man that fate is handing him his next target.

By November 22, 1963, Lee has fallen in with Ferrie's plan. From his window in the depository, he fires three shots at the presidential motorcade. The first hits Kennedy near the neck, the second strikes Texas governor John Connally (riding in the limousine with Kennedy), and the third misses completely. A member of Mackey's team actually fires the fatal shot to Kennedy's head. Lee flees the building for his rendezvous point, the Texas Theater. On the way, he is stopped by Patrolman Tippit, whom he shoots. Mackey plans to have Lee murdered in the theater, but police apprehend him before the murder can take place.

Suddenly in need of help, the conspirators approach Dallas nightclub owner Jack Ruby. Knowing that Ruby owes thousands of dollars in back taxes, they promise to loan him money and forgive the debt. Genuinely distraught over Kennedy's death, Ruby is easily persuaded that the public will idolize him for murdering the president's assassin. Ruby slips into the Dallas jail, where he is a well-known local figure, and shoots Lee. *Libra* concludes with a rambling, embittered soliloquy by Marguerite Oswald over the grave of her dead son.

The Characters

Lee is the "Libra" of the novel's title, the primary character around whom DeLillo builds his plot and its meaning. The astrological sign for the Libran is a pair of scales, a highly appropriate symbol for Lee, who by novel's end is ready to be tipped either way. Ambivalence has marked much of Lee's life. An avowed Marxist, he nevertheless joins the U.S. Marines. He longs for life in the Soviet Union, but once there is disappointed and returns to the United States. He admires and identifies with Kennedy, and in his growing delusional state, he believes that assassinating the president will irrevocably complete the identification.

Marguerite Oswald is, next to Lee, the novel's most compelling character. Even more than Lee, she sets the novel's tone. She is presented not so much through her actions as through her distinctive manner of speech. She often addresses some ultimate judge ("your honor") to explain her poverty and her son's problems. She is both fascinating and repellent; early on, readers sense Lee's need to escape the manipulative web of words his mother seeks to spin around him.

Conspirators Win Everett, Larry Parmenter, and T. J. Mackey exemplify varying degrees of divergence from the controls of the CIA. Attempting to carry on the work of invasion after the disastrous Bay of Pigs episode, Everett has been found out and banished to Texas Woman's University, ostensibly to identify potentially friendly students. Equally guilty but less conscience-stricken, Parmenter has managed to carry on smoothly within the agency. Mackey (who reminds Everett of a cowboy) also retains the agency's full confidence, but Mackey has given himself over completely to the Cuban rebels' cause. Conspirator David Ferrie operates as a free agent. A commercial pilot until his sexual involvement with boys costs him his job, he is obsessed with patterns, signs, and methods of control. At one point he assures Lee that he believes in everything.

Nightclub owner Jack Ruby is, like Lee, an essentially weak individual ripe for manipulation. Like Lee, he comes to identify with his target; after his imprisonment for shooting Lee, Ruby becomes convinced that he himself is responsible for assassinating the president. Like Marguerite Oswald, Ruby comes alive for the reader through his peculiar and idiosyncratic speech patterns.

Nicholas Branch is a puzzled, wary researcher who finds himself—perhaps like many readers—drawn into the mystery of the assassination. Overwhelmed by a library of data, he nevertheless comes to the tentative conclusion that Kennedy died as a result of a combination of conspiracy and chance. Within the fictional world DeLillo has created, the reader comes to the same conclusion.

Themes and Meanings

At its most obvious level, *Libra* recounts the life of Lee Harvey Oswald. DeLillo clearly has studied the vast assassination literature carefully. Those familiar with the case will recognize many of Lee and Marguerite's actual words, but even informed readers will have a hard time determining where the public record ends and DeLillo's fiction begins. On another level, *Libra* provides a plausible psychological and social context in which Lee's character could have developed and the assassination could have taken place. The novel succeeds brilliantly on both levels, offering as it does so a penetrating critique of a society controlled by new and little-understood forces.

In broad terms, Lee's life is a search for some system, political or otherwise, that will give his life meaning. American capitalism seems to offer him only a marginal existence, so his discovery of Marxism provides him with a measure of hope. Once in the Soviet Union, however, he finds only a grayer version of life in the West. By the end of the novel, he is fantasizing that there may be a place for him and his family in Fidel Castro's Cuba.

Yet nonpolitical systems are what snare Lee and in the end define his life. Marguerite Oswald's web of words, her litany of excuses and grievances, constitute one such system—one that Lee strives constantly to escape.

Without quite realizing it, however, Lee has already defined himself through another pattern, that of the images constantly projected by the media. Lee frequently conceives of himself in B-film terms. At one point, he attempts to commit suicide rather than be expelled from the Soviet Union. He sees himself draw the razor across his wrist while (as he describes it later in his diary) a violin plays somewhere offstage. After being shot by Jack Ruby, Lee sees himself on television, imagining how the shot must have looked to the cameras. As his consciousness fades, he watches himself from "a darkish room, someone's television den."

Three other forces define Lee. The first is the conspiracy itself, in which Lee is only dimly aware that he is playing an important role. This particular, rather limited action scarcely qualifies as a system, of course, but DeLillo clearly intends it to be emblematic of wider, perhaps even more mysterious forces. The assertion that "there is a world within the world" runs like a refrain through the novel.

The mirror image of the conspiracy concocted by Everett and Parmenter and Mackey is coincidence. In *Libra*, coincidence is elevated to a principle. It is by coincidence that Lee fits the profile required by the conspirators, by coincidence that the presidential motorcade passes by his new place of employment. At one point early in the novel, a character remarks that the science of coincidence is still waiting to be discovered.

Lee exists in one final pattern: He is a character in history. Known all of his life as Lee or Lee Oswald, he is transformed at the moment of his arrest into Lee Harvey Oswald, the character familiar from television and newspaper reports and the seemingly endless stream of books that have been written about the assassination. Lee senses something of this as he sits in his cell in Dallas, planning his encounters with lawyers, historians, and psychologists. While he may be wrong about the details, Lee is correct about finally having entered history.

Critical Context

Upon its appearance in 1988, *Libra* became Don DeLillo's most successful novel. DeLillo's earlier novels had explored the various forces responsible for shaping and misshaping contemporary American society, including advertising, the media, technology, and drugs. This first phase of his career culminated with the publication of

White Noise in 1985. *White Noise*, which described the effects of an "airborne toxic event," won the American Book Award and a nomination for the National Book Critics Circle Award.

Libra was nominated for both these awards and became a best-seller as well, perhaps in large part because of its subject. Polls confirm that most Americans discount the verdict of the Warren Commission—which concluded that Kennedy was killed by a lone gunman—and believe instead that a conspiracy was involved. In an author's note, DeLillo stresses that his novel is "a work of imagination," but he goes on to explain that it provides "a way of thinking about the assassination." Clearly, many readers have welcomed this opportunity.

Bibliography

Cain, William E. "Making Meaningful Worlds: Self and History in *Libra*." *Michigan Quarterly Review* 29 (Spring, 1990): 275-287. A long, thoughtful, detailed review aimed at readers somewhat familiar with DeLillo's other novels. Praises DeLillo's "astute, off-beat, defamiliarizing curiosity about everyday life."

DeLillo, Don. "American Blood: A Journey Through the Labyrinth of Dallas and JFK." *Rolling Stone*, December 8, 1983, 21-22. An early article by DeLillo stressing "our uncertain grip on the world." Provides an opportunity to examine the materials the author would assemble into a novel five years later.

_____. "The Art of Fiction, Part 135." Interview by Adam Begley. *The Paris Review* 35 (Fall, 1993): 274-306. DeLillo talks about the creative process of his works, including his visualization of scenes, which leads to the formation of sentences. He considers the language and architecture of a book to be important. His characters are often paranoid and complex, as in the case of his characterization of Lee Harvey Oswald in his novel *Libra*. A portion of the manuscript draft of *Libra* is also included with this interview.

_____. "'An Outsider in This Society': An Interview with Don DeLillo." Interview by Anthony Curtis. In *Introducing Don DeLillo*, edited by Frank Lentricchia. Durham, N.C.: Duke University Press, 1991. An expanded version of an interview that appeared in *Rolling Stone* magazine in 1988. DeLillo discusses *Libra* in relationship to his other work. DeLillo grants few interviews, making this example especially important.

Keesey, Douglas. *Don DeLillo*. New York: Twayne, 1993. A thorough introductory study of DeLillo. Covers DeLillo's major works and includes a chapter devoted to *Libra*.

LeClair, Tom. *In the Loop: Don DeLillo and the Systems Novel*. Urbana: University of Illinois Press, 1997. LeClair asserts that DeLillo should be acknowledged as one of America's leading novelists. In this study, LeClair examines eight of DeLillo's novels in detail from the perspective of systems theory.

Lentricchia, Frank. *Introducing Don DeLillo*. Durham, N.C.: Duke University Press, 1991. A collection of critical essays that form a solid overview of DeLillo's art and the social and intellectual context of his writings.

_____. "*Libra* as Postmodern Critique." *South Atlantic Quarterly* 89 (Spring, 1990): 431-453. Examines *Libra* as a novel of "social destiny," but one in which images have come to play a more important role than such factors as class and race. Also appears in Lentricchia's *Introducing Don DeLillo*.

Michael, Magali Cornier. "The Political Paradox Within Don DeLillo's *Libra*." *Critique: Studies in Contemporary Fiction* 35 (Spring, 1994): 146-156. Examines the complex proliferation of conspiracies whose plots interweave in the novel. Michael also analyzes the function of Oswald's mother, Marguerite, who figures centrally as a means of grounding characters and events.

Mott, Christopher M. "*Libra* and the Subject of History." *Critique: Studies in Contemporary Fiction* 35 (Spring, 1994): 131-134. An analysis of DeLillo's use of American mythology and ideology in *Libra*. Examines DeLillo's belief that the assassination brought into focus a new way of perceiving reality.

Tyler, Anne. "Dallas, Echoing Down the Decades." *The New York Times Book Review*, July 24, 1988, p. 1. A long, accessible review by a fellow novelist. Stresses DeLillo's mastery of the commonplace events of his characters' lives and calls the book "a triumph."

Willman, Skip. "Traversing the Fantasies of the JFK Assassination: Conspiracy and Contingency in Don DeLillo's *Libra*." *Contemporary Literature* 39 (Fall, 1998): 405-433. An analysis and response to George Will's criticism of *Libra* as "an act of bad citizenship" and "smacking of paranoia." Explores DeLillo's recurrent theme of conspiracy, culminating with *Libra*.

Grove Koger

LIKE WATER FOR CHOCOLATE
A Novel in Monthly Installments with Recipes, Romances, and Home Remedies

Author: Laura Esquivel (1950-   )
Type of plot: Romance
Time of plot: The 1910's to the early 1930's
Locale: Near Piedras Negras, Mexico
First published: Como agua para chocolate, 1989 (English translation, 1992)

Principal characters:

>TITA DE LA GARZA, the novel's heroine, a fabulous cook
>PEDRO MUZQUIZ, Tita's true love, who marries her sister Rosaura
>MAMÁ ELENA, Tita's tyrannical widowed mother with a dark past
>ROSAURA, Tita's unattractive sister, Pedro's wife and the dutiful
>   daughter of Mamá Elena
>GERTRUDIS, the rebellious illegitimate daughter of Mamá Elena
>JOHN BROWN, the family's kind doctor, Pedro's rival for Tita's love
>NACHA, an Indian cook at the ranch, a maternal figure for Tita

The Novel

Like Water for Chocolate combines the story of a forbidden romance between Tita de la Garza and Pedro Muzquiz with a collection of traditional, mouth-watering Mexican recipes. The title, from a Spanish expression meaning "boiling mad," refers to Tita's anger that an absurd family tradition prevents her from marrying and dictates that, as the youngest daughter, she remain at home to care for her mother, Mamá Elena. Like the title, all the incidents in the novel are related to cooking.

Organized like a recipe calendar, each chapter corresponds to a month of the year and begins with the name and list of ingredients for one of Tita's recipes along with the method of preparation. In its form, the book also imitates the romantic novels presented in monthly installments in women's magazines; each chapter ends with the note "to be continued. . . ." The narrator is Tita's grandniece, who reconstructs Tita's recipes and her love story from the diary in which the protagonist recorded her recipes along with the events that occurred when she prepared each of them.

The novel's plot revolves around the tension between Tita's love for the kitchen, where she creates magic with food, and her rebellion against the tradition that confines her there. The novel opens with the proper method of chopping onions for the January recipe and connects the tears caused by the onions to the flood of tears that accompanied Tita's birth on the kitchen table. The narrator explains that Tita cried her way into the world because she somehow knew her fate, and her tears at birth produced ten pounds of salt for cooking. This beginning typifies the relationship between cooking and the events in Tita's life and introduces into the narrative the recurrent Magical Realism common in modern Latin American fiction.

In the first chapter, Tita's true love, Pedro Muzquiz, requests her hand in marriage. When Mamá Elena explains that Tita cannot marry and suggests Tita's sister Rosaura instead, Pedro accepts in order to remain as near to Tita as possible. The rest of the novel recounts Tita and Pedro's attempts to be together in defiance of authoritarian Mamá Elena and how Tita rebels through her culinary artistry and the unexpected and dramatic reactions her recipes provoke. For example, Tita sheds tears in the batter when forced to prepare Rosaura and Pedro's wedding cake. Her sadness, baked into the cake, afflicts the wedding guests with desperate nostalgia for lost love that causes a mass eruption of vomiting that spoils the wedding reception. One casualty of this nostalgia is the ranch's Indian cook, Nacha, who had nourished and entertained Tita in the kitchen and taught her the secrets of cooking. Later, when Pedro presents Tita with roses to celebrate her first anniversary as the ranch's new cook, the dish Tita prepares with the flowers unleashes such erotic euphoria in Tita's sister Gertrudis that she abandons her family and rides off on horseback, naked, with a revolutionary soldier. Gertrudis ultimately satisfies her lust as a prostitute, then marries the soldier and serves with him in the army.

Tita's sister Rosaura, inept and fearful in the kitchen, cannot even produce milk to nurse her first child, Roberto. Tita rescues him from starvation, but Mamá Elena, suspicious of Pedro and Tita's love, sends Rosaura's family to Texas. Roberto, deprived of Tita's milk, soon dies. Tita suffers a nervous breakdown but recovers in the care of the family's physician, John Brown, who falls in love with and proposes marriage to Tita. Mamá Elena represses Tita until her death from the emetic she uses to counteract poison that she suspects Tita is putting into her food. With Mamá Elena gone, Tita is free to marry John but refuses his offer because of her love for Pedro. Meanwhile, Rosaura attempts to perpetuate the family tradition with her own daughter Esperanza. Tita feeds her from infancy and instills in her an independent spirit. Rosaura eventually suffers a horrid death from intestinal disorders. Esperanza then marries John's son, and at the sumptuous wedding feast prepared by Tita, Tita and Pedro are at last united. Their flames of passion, fanned by the food Tita serves, engulf the lovers in a fire that destroys the entire ranch. Only Tita's diary survives intact. The narrator, Esperanza's daughter, closes the novel with the promise that Tita will live on as long as people continue to prepare her recipes.

The Characters

Tita de la Garza, the youngest daughter in her family, wins the reader's sympathy immediately as the victim of the repressive family tradition that prevents her from marrying. Like most of the characters in the novel, in certain respects she resembles someone from a fairy tale. Beautiful, desirous of pleasing her mother, enormously talented, but cursed by an unfortunate destiny and a wicked mother and sister, Tita can be likened to Cinderella. She propels the novel's action forward through the effects produced by the dishes she prepares. Tita represents a model of female liberation because, rather than rejecting the domestic space that confines her, she employs the resources of the kitchen to obtain self-fulfillment.

Mamá Elena, Tita's cruel mother, like most female characters in the novel, is characterized largely by her relationship to the activities of the kitchen. In contrast to Tita, who uses ingredients creatively and generously, Mamá Elena displays and demands rigid obedience to rules in cooking. She is the principal villain, notorious for loving any destructive culinary activity, such as dividing, dismembering, detaching, or carving. She inspires a modicum of sympathy after her death, when Tita discovers Mamá Elena's secret: Before and during marriage, she had enjoyed an affair with a mulatto until her scandalized family had the lover murdered. Readers interpret her authoritarian ways as the tragic result of being so severely punished herself for defying repressive societal rules.

Rosaura, the unattractive and inept sister obsessed with keeping up appearances, resembles a fairy-tale wicked stepsister and thus gains virtually no sympathy from the reader. Diametrically opposed to Tita, she shows her lack of creativity in her fear of the kitchen. Her death is an act of poetic justice, punishment for unquestioning allegiance to societal norms.

Gertrudis, the rebellious, unfettered daughter of Mamá Elena and her mulatto lover, is depicted in stark contrast to Rosaura. She fully appreciates Tita's talents and observes that an entire family history is contained in Tita's recipes. She is the receptacle for the erotic response that one of Tita's recipes provokes and is the embodiment of unbridled female freedom.

Nacha, the ranch's Indian cook, serves as a kind of surrogate mother to Tita. She is the representative of a centuries-long tradition of culinary art that is transmitted only orally until Tita begins writing down her recipes. Through this character, Esquivel pays tribute to the contributions of Mexico's indigenous female population.

Pedro Muzquiz, Tita's lover and Rosaura's husband, like all the male characters in the novel, remains relatively undeveloped. He exists principally as the object of Tita's quest for romantic happiness and as the lens through which to admire Tita's beauty and talent.

John Brown, the family doctor and Pedro's rival for Tita's affections, is a relatively bland stock character, as his name might suggest. His kindly presence serves to highlight Tita's virtues and to introduce tension into Pedro and Tita's love story.

Themes and Meanings

Like Water for Chocolate playfully imitates the steamy romances included in Hispanic women's magazines and simultaneously pays tribute to the arts of the kitchen. The novel begins and ends in the kitchen, where Tita's grandniece prepares one of Tita's recipes, illustrating that the plot is above all a vehicle for the author to celebrate food and cooking as the center of daily lives and destinies. This message is also evident in the fact that cooking is the root cause for the events of Magical Realism or fantasy that pervade the novel. The importance of freedom for women is the novel's central feminist theme.

Tita learns the most important lessons about life in the kitchen from the Indian cook Nacha. As in the book's title, descriptions of how characters feel in various situations are presented in imagery from food and cooking. In addition, the unique ways in which food is prepared and the ingredients employed are shown as determining or re-defining people's fates, as with the wedding cake prepared by Tita that spoils Rosaura's reception and destroys Nacha's life. The novel equates understanding these secrets of the power of food with understanding life. In its language, food-related events, characterization in terms of attitudes toward food and cooking, and cookbook-like form, this novel makes culinary activity itself the captivating stuff of literature.

Central to conveying a message of liberation for Mexican women is the choice of a traditionally female space in Mexican society, the kitchen, as defining characters' lives. To this end, the novel's action is set temporally around the time of the Mexican Revolution, when women's rights in Mexico were also being redefined and reevalu-ated. Clearly, however, it is not the kitchen but societal codes that have restricted women's independence. Mamá Elena's miserable death from poisoning and Ro-saura's grotesque demise testify to the evils of unquestioning allegiance to tradition in the name of keeping up appearances. The novel suggests that Gertrudis's uninhibited happiness, by contrast, is the direct consequence of her rebellious freedom. The plain-est evidence of this novelistic message of liberation, even if it applies principally to amorous freedom, appears in the marriage of Rosaura's daughter Esperanza, who, through Tita's guidance, refuses to succumb to the family tradition that has enslaved her aunt.

In the end, the blending of culinary and literary arts, which triumphs most obvi-ously in the survival of Tita's cookbook and diary at the novel's conclusion, offers would-be cooks and writers new recipes for creative expression.

Critical Context

Like Water for Chocolate, Laura Esquivel's first novel, was a runaway best-seller in both the Spanish original and in English translation. In addition to its wide acclaim among nonacademic audiences, the novel was embraced by feminist scholars as a unique and significant contribution to the burgeoning field of Latin American women's writing. In its focus on the kitchen, Esquivel's work finds antecedents in her compatriot Rosario Castellanos's 1971 short story "Cooking Lesson," which denounces how the kitchen imprisons and stereotypes women, and in Puerto Rican writer Rosario Ferré's 1984 essay "The Writer's Kitchen," in which she acknowl-edges the parallels between recipes for cooking and for creative writing. Esquivel's book introduces novelty both in her narrative technique, which artfully blends reci-pes into an archetypal love-story plot, and in her lighthearted appropriation of literary genres typically associated with women, the recipe collection and the ro-mance. Other writers who explore the similarities in the creative processes of writing and cooking have not achieved the widespread appeal among diverse audiences that Esquivel enjoys; however, this topic has attracted the attention of female writers both in Latin America and in the United States. Esquivel joins these women in marking a new phase in feminist thought. Instead of rejecting the kitchen as a space that impedes women's freedom, they adapt the kitchen's secrets to literary production.

Esquivel established her reputation as a screenwriter before embarking on her successful foray into fiction writing. In 1985, her screenplay for *Chido One* received a nomination for the Ariel Award from the Mexican Academy of Motion Picture Arts and Sciences. Esquivel also collaborated with her husband on the screenplay for the film based on *Like Water for Chocolate*, which has also enjoyed great praise, capturing eleven awards in Mexico in 1992.

Bibliography
Dobrian, Susan Lucas. "Romancing the Cook: Parodic Consumption of Popular Romance Myths in *Como agua para chocolate*." *Latin American Review* 24 (July-December, 1996): 56-66. Dobrian argues that Esquivel parodies many genres in her novel, including the romance novel and its popular myths. Instead of the female character finding herself through submission to the male, she gains her sense of identity by rebelling against her mother. Dobrian cites one of the primary characters who becomes a female warrior in the Mexican Revolution as an example of the "new woman" in Latino literature.
Esquivel, Laura. "Revolucion Interior al Exterior: An Interview with Laura Esquivel." Interview by Claudia Loewenstein. *Southwest Review* 79 (Autumn, 1994): 592-607. In this interview Esquivel discusses the use of her novel by psychotherapists to explore mother and daughter relationships. She shows how masculine norms have been transmitted by women, and how the three daughters in the novel respond: one seeks liberation publicly which leads to masculinization, one seeks change within the family, and one seeks balance. Cooking represents an inversion of sexuality in which the male is passive and is penetrated by the woman's nurturing.
Ibsen, Kristine. "On Recipes, Reading, and Revolution: Postboom Parody in *Como agua para chocolate*." *Hispanic Review* 63 (Spring, 1995): 133-146. Ibsen claims that the magical realism in Esquivel's novel was inspired by Gabriel García Márquez's *One Hundred Years of Solitude,* but demonstrates that the two novels are very different in terms of perspective. Ibsen asserts that Esquivel presents the individual experience of history (an example would be that Esquivel's heroines exhibit traits not traditionally associated with women), while Márquez's novel reexamines historical trends.
Jaffe, Janice A. "Hispanic American Women Writers' Novel Recipes and Laura Esquivel's *Como agua para chocolate (Like Water for Chocolate)*." *Women's Studies* 22 (March, 1993): 217-230. Esquivel's use of the kitchen is depicted as liberating and creative for women. The novel is placed in the context of literature by female writers that envisions the kitchen as a space of female repression or, alternatively, of community and creativity. Concludes that Esquivel's positive appropriation of the kitchen was possible only after earlier feminist writers' denunciation of how domestic chores enslaved generations of women.
McMurray, George. "Two Mexican Feminist Writers." *Hispania* 73 (December, 1990): 1035-1036. McMurray briefly outlines the novel's plot, emphasizing the

Magical Realism. He attributes the book's popularity to Magical Realism and traces this aspect of the novel to the work of Gabriel García Márquez. Also discusses a novel by Mexican writer Angeles Mastretta that McMurray views as representative of contemporary feminist trends in Latino literature.

Janice A. Jaffe

LINCOLN

Author: Gore Vidal (1925-   )
Type of plot: Historical chronicle
Time of plot: 1861-1865
Locale: Washington, D.C.
First published: 1984

> *Principal characters:*
> ABRAHAM LINCOLN, sixteenth President of the United States
> MARY TODD LINCOLN, his wife
> JOHN HAY, his secretary
> WILLIAM SEWARD, United States Secretary of State
> EDWIN STANTON, United States Secretary of War
> SALMON P. CHASE, United States Secretary of the Treasury
> JOHN WILKES BOOTH, Lincoln's assassin
> DAVID HEROLD, a follower of Booth

The Novel

   Lincoln: A Novel begins and ends with the Civil War president's term of office. It is a study in the way political power is captured and maintained. Although the novel contains a subplot that focuses on the reasons for Southern disaffection with the Union, the main concern is always with the great politician himself and with how his subordinates connived to support or to undermine his authority. It is clear that Gore Vidal regards Abraham Lincoln as the greatest of American presidents, who not only preserved the Union but, in effect, re-created it. In order to comprehend fully the monumental task Lincoln confronted, Vidal follows the intricacies of cabinet and congressional politics. Many of the politicians who served and opposed the president seriously underestimated him and mistook his mild manner for weakness and passivity. As a result, Lincoln was generally perceived in his time as an ineffectual president overmatched by his demanding office.

   One of the finest qualities of Vidal's narrative is the way he gradually builds up evidence of Lincoln's shrewdness and deviousness, both of which, the novelist demonstrates, are indispensable characteristics of a leader who has to rely on ambitious politicians, vain generals, and avaricious businessmen and journalists who seek his favor but who will profit from his failures if he is too open with them.

   Much of Lincoln's success, as this novel reveals, stems from keeping his own counsel, compromising when he absolutely has to, but making sure that no one has a complete reading of his mind. Lincoln also has a knack for avoiding subjects and issues that he can do little about—such as his wife's extravagant spending, politically compromising behavior, and fits of madness. He has a way of economizing his attention for problems that he understands and can successfully resolve or at least cope with—such as the rivalries within his Cabinet and Congress. On other issues, such as the currency and the administration of the Treasury Department, he is hopelessly and even comically naïve, but he dismisses his ignorance and cheerfully delegates the responsibility for such matters to others, except where, as in the prosecution of the war, he must learn how his generals fight and why they are so inept in engaging the Confederate forces.

Lincoln's politics in this novel might be called centrist, since he sides neither with radical Republican abolitionists nor with conservative Democrats, although he makes use of both parties in his government. Yet for all his show of consulting conflicting opinions, he will often act unilaterally and even dictatorially, invoking his "inherent powers" to suspend sacrosanct democratic principles such as *habeas corpus*. His main goal is to reunite the Union, even at the cost of "bending the Constitution," as he puts it.

The Characters

Vidal's way of characterizing Lincoln's genius is one of the finest achievements of his novel. The president is often viewed through the fresh eyes of his young secretary, John Hay, who first learns about politics from his employer. Because Lincoln is so careful not to disclose too much of his strategy or of his emotions, his secretary is forced to scrutinize the politician's posture, his gestures, the small physical signs of his state of mind: "As a hundred men saluted, the President raised his hat, eyes on the road, head and neck pushed slightly forward, always a sign of anxiety, Hay now knew."

Another way of characterizing Lincoln, especially his sly side, becomes available through the many pages devoted to Salmon P. Chase, a fierce abolitionist, Christian ideologue, and pompous aspirant to the presidency. Chase disdains Lincoln's apparent lack of command, his unwillingness to confront directly the major issues of his time and to take the initiative away from his opponents. Chase prides himself on his public stands and on his astute management of his political career, which are abetted by the bold maneuvers of his devoted daughter Kate. In private, he often compromises and is at least as hypocritical as Lincoln—if not more so, since Chase lacks his competitor's self-knowledge. The secretary of the Treasury eventually destroys his chance to be his country's leader by failing to restrain the clumsy efforts of his supporters, and Lincoln, who has patiently bided his time with Chase, is rewarded with the pleasure of observing the collapse of his rival's political fortunes.

David Herold and John Wilkes Booth are the major representatives of the plots against Lincoln's life. Much of the material on Herold has been invented, Vidal notes in his afterword, and though he is given a credible psychology, particularly in the matter of his attraction to histrionic figures such as Booth who evoke the rich romanticism of the South, Herold is a pale figure compared to Lincoln and to politicians such as William Graham Sumner, Thaddeus Stevens, Edwin Stanton, William Seward, and others who appear with so much panache in wonderfully orchestrated scenes of political intrigue and argument.

In only a few sentences, Vidal is often able to capture characters in motion, working out their historical destiny as they express their personalities and political positions. There is, for example, the scene between General McClellan, the "young Napoleon," who for all his strutting fails to engage the enemy in battle; General Winfield Scott, the aged warrior approaching senility and losing touch with the planning of the war; Secretary of State Seward, the consummate politician who has more facts and figures at his disposal than the chagrined Scott; Secretary of War Simon Cameron, an inept, ignorant, and purely political appointee; and Lincoln, who, as usual, is not giving away his reactions in an embarrassing situation: "Like some ancient arcane engine of warfare, Scott swiveled round to face Cameron, whose tricky eyes were now at rest upon a chandelier. Seward found himself sweating. He glanced at Lincoln, and saw that that usually restless body was unusually still in its chair." This is the historical imagination operating in peak form, dramatizing and clarifying characters and events, and making readers experience, in an almost visceral fashion, the dynamic of the life it re-creates.

Themes and Meanings

The theme of Vidal's novel is the theme of Lincoln's life. The president makes clear, in one of his few truly frank statements, that it has been the objective of his life to hold the highest political office. A man of fierce, undeviating ambition, Lincoln could only hold on to the presidency by holding on to the nation. As Hay puts it at the end of the novel:

> The Southern states had every Constitutional right to go out of the Union. But Lincoln said, no. Lincoln said, this Union can never be broken. Now that was a terrible responsibility for one man to take. But he took it, knowing he would be obliged to fight the greatest war in human history, which he did, and which he won.

It is the political and the human example which Lincoln set that prompts Hay to say that Lincoln remade the country "in his own image." It is against this sense of "terrible responsibility" that all other presidents since Lincoln have been measured. There was much that Lincoln could not do, much that he was not competent to do, but he never wavered in his pursuit of unification and never compromised on this one principle.

After nearly three years of Lincoln's administration, William Seward, one of the president's chief doubters, is forced to recognize that he has been manipulated by a "political genius," one who has played the "joking, timid backwoods lawyer, given to fits of humility in the presence of all the strutting military and political peacocks that flocked about him," only to conceal his single-minded role of "Lord Protector of the Union by whose will alone the war had been prosecuted." Lincoln's assassination at the end of the war, when the Southern cause was truly hopeless, was not simply the last gasp of rebellion, Vidal insists, but a recognition of how powerful he had become as a political force. He had, indeed, presided over the "bloody and absolute" rebirth of his nation, as Hay says at the end of the novel—a rebirth, he speculates, which required Lincoln's own death "as a form of atonement for the great and terrible thing that he had done."

Critical Context

Lincoln takes a distinguished place among Vidal's historical novels about American politics, which include *Washington D.C.* (1967), *Burr: A Novel* (1973), and *1876: A Novel* (1976). With this tetralogy, Vidal covered all the major periods in American history, and when one includes his essays and plays, he has dealt with most of the major American political figures. Like its predecessors, *Lincoln* is noteworthy for its author's sure grasp of political personalities. Unlike other major American novelists, Vidal has patiently and shrewdly followed the careers of American politicians and explored their lives in historical fiction, a genre now usually consigned to second-rate, popular writers.

Vidal's idea of historical fiction is to follow the documented record closely. He rarely deviates from the chronology of history without informing his readers of doing so, and historians have generally complimented his fiction for its accuracy. Even secondary characters and much of the dialogue are the product of historical research. The author delights in exposing the foibles of great figures such as George Washington and Lincoln without in the least demeaning their deserved reputations. Vidal is always the realist, with great sympathy for romantic characters and dissenters such as Aaron Burr.

Bibliography

Baker, Susan, and Curtis S. Gibson. *Gore Vidal: A Critical Companion.* Westport, Conn.: Greenwood Press, 1997. The first full-length study to include Vidal's most recent works. A biographical sketch precedes a general discussion of Vidal's early writings, followed by critical discussions of individual novels. The discussions include sections on plot and character development, thematic issues, narrative style, and critical approaches. Includes an essay on *Lincoln.*

Goodman, Walter. "History As Fiction." *The New Leader* 71 (May 16, 1988): 11-12. Vidal defends himself against critics who charge that his books are "unhistorical or antihistorical exercises." Although Goodman believes that the harsh criticism is unwarranted, he argues that Vidal's novels should "best be taken for what they are, which is something different from history."

Parini, Jay, ed. *Gore Vidal: Writer Against the Grain.* New York: Columbia University Press, 1992. A collection of essays by various critics that covers the important works of Vidal's career. An interesting overview that places Vidal's historical fiction within the context of the entire body of his work. Includes an essay by Harold Bloom on *Lincoln.*

Vidal, Gore. "The Importance of Being Gore." Interview by Andrew Kopkind. *The Nation* 257 (July 5, 1993): 16-19. Vidal discusses the influence of his same-sex orientation on his work. He reveals his dismay at the adverse critical reaction that *Lincoln* received.

_____. Interview by Jay Parini. *The New England Review* 14 (Fall, 1991): 93-101. Vidal talks about his career as a novelist and television scriptwriter. He cites writers who have influenced him, including Jonathan Swift and William Golding. He also shares his views on contemporary literary criticism. A revealing interview that offers valuable insight into Vidal's artistic motivations.

Carl Rollyson

LINDEN HILLS

Author: Gloria Naylor (1950-   )
Type of plot: Psychological realism
Time of plot: The 1980's
Locale: The fictional community of Linden Hills
First published: 1985

>   *Principal characters:*
>   LUTHER NEDEED, the descendant and namesake of the founder and
>   owner of Linden Hills
>   WILLA NEDEED, the wife of Luther, locked in the basement of their
>   house with her dead son
>   LESTER TILSON, a poet and a resident of Linden Hills who refuses to
>   subscribe to its middle-class values
>   WILLIE K. MASON, Lester's best friend

The Novel

Linden Hills explores the lives of affluent African Americans who have attained the American Dream of material success, but at the expense of humanistic values. Luther Nedeed is the owner of the Tupelo Realty Company, which holds the mortgages and leases on all the homes in Linden Hills, and is the undertaker for the African American community. He lives at the bottom of the hill. The most affluent families live at the bottom of the hill, while the less affluent live at the top.

The novel begins with an introductory chapter and is then divided into sections identified by date, from December 19 to December 24. The first chapter explains the history of the Nedeed family. Luther Nedeed, an ancestor of the current character, bought Linden Hills from its white owners during the antebellum period. It was offered for sale because the white owners considered the hills unsuitable for farming. Realizing that the bottom of the hill bordered the cemetery, Nedeed became an undertaker. He built shacks on the hills and rented them to local black families. He then went to Mississippi and brought back an octoroon wife, Luwana Packerville, who produced a son who grew up to inherit his father's name, looks, and business. To keep the government from taking his land, the second Nedeed sold the land cheaply to the people already living there, on a lease of a thousand years and a day. The lease also provided that they pass their property to their children or sell it only to other black families.

The first chapter also examines the circumstances of the present Luther Nedeed's marriage and the birth of a light-skinned son who does not look like him or his male ancestors. This child causes Luther to suspect his wife, Willa, of adultery and to lock her in the basement, along with the child.

The first dated section, for December 19, chronicles the relationship of Willie K. Mason and Lester Tilson. It also introduces Ruth, who has rejected residency in Linden Hills. Ruth remains married to Norman despite the fact that he loses his mind once a year with an attack of "the pinks." In this chapter, Willie and Lester first hear the mournful screams of Willa Nedeed.

In the December 20 section, Willa's son dies. She begins to will herself to die until, while looking for a shroud for her son, she discovers the diary of the unhappy Luwana Packerville Nedeed in a basement trunk. Willie and Lester take their first job of the season, as kitchen helpers at the wedding of Winston Alcott. The homosexual relationship of Winston and his friend David is confirmed when David recites a poem at the wedding. Willie and Lester recognize how David has altered the poem to announce his departure from the relationship, which Winston does not have the courage to acknowledge. As a wedding present, Nedeed gives the newlyweds a coveted mortgage on a property on Tupelo Drive, at the bottom of the hill.

The section entitled "December 21st" examines the relationship of Roxanne Tilson and Xavier Donnell. Donnell is upset because he finds himself falling in love. He asks his colleague at General Motors, Maxwell Smyth, for an opinion. Lester and Willie, hired to clean the garage, observe the meeting between Donnell and Smyth. The chapter focuses on the life of the superficial Smyth and the lifestyle he has adopted to rise in his career. Smyth advises Donnell against marriage to Roxanne because of her inferior social standing. Willie and Lester then go to work for Mr. Parker, whose wife, Lycentia, has just died. They are to help prepare Lycentia's bedroom for a new woman on the eve of Lycentia's funeral. Meanwhile, Willa discovers the recipes of the unhappy Evelyn Creton Nedeed.

On December 22, Willa examines the recipes of her predecessor while Lester and Willie work for the Reverend Michael T. Hollis, who is preparing to preside at the funeral of Lycentia Parker. The Reverend Hollis seeks refuge, from both his memories and his cold church, in alcohol. During the Parker funeral, he gives an unusually emotional sermon that causes discomfort among his cold parishioners. Next, Willie and Lester prepare to go to the home of Laurel Dumont. They are rescued from a police patrol by Norman, who has been sent by his wife, Ruth, to check on Mrs. Dumont. Ruth is concerned about Mrs. Dumont's mental health.

On December 23, as Willa discovers fading photographs of Priscilla McGuire Nedeed, it is revealed that Laurel Dumont's husband has left her and Linden Hills, thereby nullifying his lease with Lester Nedeed. After being informed by Nedeed that she must leave her home, Laurel commits suicide by jumping into an empty pool as Nedeed watches secretly. Nedeed hires Willie and Lester to trim his Christmas tree. Before going to the Nedeed house, the young men meet Dr. Daniel Braithwaite, a historian who has collected the history of the Nedeed family and observed the history and lives of the inhabitants of Linden Hills. Willa decides to live and begins to clean the basement that is her prison.

On December 24, Willa Nedeed decides to walk back up the basement stairs. Willie and Lester arrive at the Nedeed house. The door to the basement is accidentally unbolted, and Willa comes up, carrying the corpse of her son. Lester and Willie are terrified and run out of the house. Luther Nedeed enters into a futile struggle with his wife, and the shroud in which she wrapped her son's body is ignited by a candle on the tree. All three Nedeeds are consumed by a raging fire.

The Characters

Luther Nedeed is the villain of the novel. His love for power provides the catalyst for the demise of humanistic values and the triumph of materialism in the lives of the people of Linden Hills. Like the devil he symbolically represents, his delight is in the destruction of lives of the inhabitants of Linden Hills. The first Luther Nedeed lives on in the person of each of the descendants who carry his name; they also carry his personality and his physical appearance. Willa's son, who inherits the recessive genes of his light-skinned grandmothers and does not look like his father, serves as the catalyst for the destruction of the Nedeed dynasty. The modern Luther's inhumanity and selfishness are revealed through his treatment of his wife and son and through his delight in the destruction of the lives of the inhabitants of the lower regions of Linden Hills. Luther is unable to select a wife in the same way that his ancestors did because of changes in the status and expectations of women in contemporary society. Therefore, he waits until his college reunion to pick from the single women uncomfortable with their independent status and desperate enough to consider marriage to him. The purpose of Luther's matrimonial search is simply to find a woman to bear him a son, who must be conceived in a ritual prescribed by his ancestors. Thereafter, he has no sexual contact with his wife.

Willa Prescott Nedeed is the wife of the last Luther Nedeed and the vehicle of his destruction. After being locked in the basement with her son for her supposed adultery, she discovers the plight of her predecessors while looking for a shroud to wrap the body of her son. Willa, however, is unlike the Nedeed wives before her; she is not a weak woman without personality. She has definite tastes and preferences that will not be denied, and she loves her son and mourns his useless and unjust death. Through looking at the diaries and pictures of the Nedeed wives, she gains the courage to go up the steps in an attempt to take control of her destiny.

Lester Tilson is half of the team that directs the reader through the enclave of prosperous, well-behaved, and spiritually dead people that is Nedeed's created community. Lester, whose family lives at the top of the hill, has chosen poetry as a way of life instead of joining the race for wealth and career success that his mother and sister value. Lester saw his father die early from working two jobs in order to provide the symbols of prosperity that his wife desired; he vowed never to follow that pattern. As his friend Willie points out, however, Lester is unwilling to leave his home and its comfort.

Willie Mason is Lester's best friend. He dropped out of school and the middle-class race for success. He is the child of an alcoholic father who, unable to provide suitably for his family, abused his wife, Willie's mother. Lester has great insights into the weaknesses and deceits of the people of Linden Hills. As Lester and Willie work their way through the holiday season, they reveal the foibles of the inhabitants.

Themes and Meanings

Naylor's novel examines the negative consequences of achieving the American Dream. The African Americans of Linden Hills attempt to realize this dream at the expense of their souls and their sense of history. The author presents a series of vignettes in the lives of middle-class African Americans who have sacrificed their sense of racial identity in order to achieve material and career success. The importance of Dante's *Inferno* from *La divina commedia* (c. 1320; *The Divine Comedy*) as a source for the narrative structure of this novel is evident. The topography of Linden Hills resembles Dante's hell, with the evil angel, Luther Nedeed, residing at the bottom, surrounded by a frozen lake.

Naylor constructs the primary narrative line around Willie and Lester's odyssey through the hills, juxtaposing their adventures with the story of Willa Nedeed. The names Willie and Willa are deliberately similar. Willie and Willa's journeys through hell are set in different typefaces to highlight the parallel themes. As Willie passes through Linden Hills, he recognizes and analyzes the moral failures of the lost souls he meets. At the end of Willie and Lester's journey, they have a spiritual awakening, realizing the significance of all they have seen and heard.

Willa also has a spiritual awakening, realized through her discovery of the tragic lives of the previous Nedeed wives. After producing a Nedeed heir, each became a nonentity within her own household. The first Mrs. Nedeed, Luwana Packerville, was bought as a slave and never manumitted, although her husband saw to the legal freedom of her child. She wrote in her Bible in 1837, "There is no God." Likewise, Priscilla McGuire Nedeed's image fades from view as her son's image grows in succeeding years, negating her physically and spiritually into a mere blur on family portraits. Willa's awakening comes when she recognizes her spiritual kinship with these women, which she first denied by labeling them as crazy. At the moment of her awakening, she makes the decision to enter and reclaim her home and her own identity. At this point, the power of the Nedeed men is overcome. Death of the dynasty by fire ensues.

The dating of the chapters is significant to the meaning of the novel. Naylor marks each section by the dates from December 19 to December 24, the time of the winter solstice. As Willie and Lester work on their odd jobs, they encounter the lost souls of Linden Hills. Of all those encountered, the most elaborate caricature is Maxwell Smyth, who has even changed his name from Smith to achieve a complete blending into mainstream society. Smyth attempts to deny any vestige of color in his quest to maintain his "Super Nigger" image. Maxwell's entire life is spent denying not only his racial and ethnic identity but also his natural humanity.

Critical Context

Linden Hills is Naylor's second novel, coming after the extremely successful *The Women of Brewster Place* (1982). *Linden Hills* examines a second panel of twentieth century African American life. *The Women of Brewster Place* reflected the faults, passions, and culture of a poor community. *Linden Hills*, on the other hand, is a representation of the affluent and spiritually dissolute upper class. *Linden Hills* is also a modern version of Dante's *Inferno*; souls are damned here because they have offended human nature and themselves rather than any religious system. Naylor's novel is thus an allegory based on the physical and moral topography of the *Inferno*, covering five days in the life of a twenty-year-old black poet, Willie Mason.

Like Dante, Willie analyzes the lives of the inhabitants of the hills as he works his way from the top to the bottom as a handyman. When he finally escapes from the frozen lake at the bottom of Linden Hills, Willie decides to give up his aimlessness and take charge of his life. Dante's model universalizes the novel and also gives a mythic dimension to what otherwise would have been a narrow subject. Naylor's bow to Dante's work puts her within a long literary tradition. *Linden Hills* is also a part of an explosion of noted works by African American women, including Naylor and her prominent contemporaries Alice Walker, Toni Morrison, and Paule Marshall.

Bibliography

Andrews, Larry R. "Black Sisterhood in Gloria Naylor's Novels." *College Language Association Journal* 33 (September, 1989): 1-25. Andrews examines the female characters in Naylor's novels and shows how African American women form support systems to ensure survival in challenging conditions.

Collins, Grace E. "Narrative Structure in *Linden Hills*." *College Language Association Journal* 34 (March, 1991): 290-301. Collins emphasizes the juxtaposition of the narrative of Willie's physical journey through Linden Hills with Willa's mental journey to self-realization.

Felton, Sharon and Michelle C. Loris, eds. *The Critical Response to Gloria Naylor.* Westport, Conn.: Greenwood Press, 1997. Felton and Loris's volume presents a comprehensive view of Naylor's life and works. This excellent critical study offers seminal articles and whole chapters devoted to each of Naylor's novels. Features an exclusive interview with Naylor.

Fowler, Virginia C. *Gloria Naylor: In Search of Sanctuary.* New York: Twayne, 1996. A valuable overview of the life and work of Gloria Naylor. Offers an in-depth critical treatment of several of Naylor's novels including *Linden Hills*. Features a revealing interview with Naylor, as well as a selected bibliography.

Jones, Robert. "A Place in the Suburbs." *Commonweal* 112 (May 3, 1985): 283-285. Places the novel in the context of traditions in American literature, comparing it to classic and contemporary works.

Puhr, Kathleen M. "Healers in Gloria Naylor's Fiction." *Twentieth Century Literature* 40 (Winter, 1994): 518-527. Puhr discusses African American ancestry, generational conflicts, and broken dreams in light of female characters that practice the art of physical or psychic healing. Compares *The Women of Brewster Place, Mama Day,* and *Linden Hills*.

Russell, Sandi. *Render Me My Song: African American Women Writers from Slavery to the Present.* New York: St. Martin's Press, 1990. Russell's work places Naylor's novels in the context of the overall themes presented by African American women writers.

Toombs, Charles P. "The Confluence of Food and Identity in Gloria Naylor's *Linden Hills*: 'What We Eat is Who We Is.' " *CLA Journal* 37 (September, 1993): 1-17. Focuses on the way Naylor uses food images to convey African Americans' attempts to integrate into white society. Although the inhabitants of Linden Hills are well educated, their cultural malnourishment and loss of identity is the price they pay for embracing white culture. For example, they may choose caviar over deep-fried catfish to bolster their social position.

Ward, Catherine C. "Gloria Naylor's *Linden Hills*: A Modern Inferno." *Contemporary Literature* 28 (Spring, 1987): 67-81. Ward, in great detail, compares the plot, setting, and characters of the *Inferno* to *Linden Hills*.

Betty Taylor-Thompson

LITTLE BIG MAN

Author: Thomas Berger (1924-   )
Type of plot: Picaresque
Time of plot: 1852-1876 and 1952-1953
Locale: The western United States
First published: 1964

> *Principal characters:*
> JACK CRABB, the protagonist, the only white survivor of the Battle of
>   the Little Bighorn
> OLD LODGE SKINS, his adoptive Indian father
> GENERAL GEORGE ARMSTRONG CUSTER, the leader of the United States
>   Seventh Cavalry, Jack's nemesis
> WILD BILL HICKOCK, a gunfighter, Jack's friend
> MRS. PENDRAKE, Jack's adoptive white mother, the only woman whom
>   Jack truly loves
> OLGA, Jack's white wife
> SUNSHINE, his Indian wife
> CAROLINE CRABB, his sister
> AMELIA, a prostitute who claims to be his niece
> RALPH FIELDING SNELL, his editor

The Novel

In *Little Big Man*, a white man becomes an Indian but eventually fits into neither white nor Indian societies. The novel is 111-year-old Jack Crabb's episodic account of his life from 1852, when he is ten and most of his family is killed by drunken Indians, to 1876, when he becomes the only white survivor of the Battle of the Little Bighorn.

In between, he lives for five years with Indians as the adopted son of Old Lodge Skins, chief of a small band of Northern Cheyenne (earning the name Little Big Man because of the proportion of his courage to his small stature); is adopted by the Reverend Mr. Pendrake and his beautiful young wife; falls in love with Mrs. Pendrake, but leaves when he discovers that she is unfaithful to him and the reverend; and runs away into a turbulent adulthood.

Jack crisscrosses the Western states innumerable times while working as outhouse cleaner, guide for a mule train, prospector, wagon master of a supply train, storekeeper, army scout, mule skinner for the Union Pacific, freight hauler, gambler, confidence man, and buffalo hunter. At other times, he is a kept man, a drunk, a beggar, and a Cheyenne warrior. All this time, Jack aspires to the comforts of the middle class, but circumstances and his restless nature always get in the way of his success.

Jack lives the life of a professional victim. Except for his business partners' swindling him during his storekeeping period, all of his bad luck results from violence. His white wife, Olga, and child are stolen by Indians and later killed by the cavalry, as are his Indian wife, Sunshine, and their newborn son. All of his Indian friends except Old Lodge Skins are killed—one, ironically, when he is about to kill Jack. (He is always being saved by his enemies.) Jack is shot four times, twice by Indians and twice by the victims of his skill at the poker table, and only his roguish trickery saves him from being killed in a gunfight by Wild Bill Hickok, who eventually becomes one of his few friends. He achieves peace only during his brief time with Sunshine; that harmony ends tragically when General George Armstrong Custer's troops slaughter the Indians at the Washita, one of three massive battles re-created by Berger, who thoroughly researched the history of the period.

Despite the presentation of the West as violent, melodramatic, and absurd, *Little Big Man* is a genuinely comic picaresque novel full of the greatest number of coincidences this side of Charles Dickens and a multitude of colorful characters. In addition to Custer and Hickok, historical figures such as Kit Carson, Wyatt Earp, Calamity Jane, and Sitting Bull make appearances. The novel builds up to Custer's fiasco at the Little Bighorn and to the death of Old Lodge Skins, who chooses to die when he recognizes that the destruction of the Indian way of life is inevitable.

The Characters

The "man of letters" who "edits" Jack's tape-recorded story, Ralph Fielding Snell, describes the protagonist in his epilogue as "a cynical man, uncouth, unscrupulous, and when necessary, even ruthless." Jack is a rogue, but unlike most heroes of picaresque novels, he admits his roguishness, explaining that he has had to be "shifty" to survive. Jack steals to prolong a stay in Saint Louis, lies to get a job, and runs up bills that he does not intend to pay. Worse, he leaves his pregnant Mexican mistress, gives up on Olga and their child after he discovers that they have adopted Indian ways, and decides to abandon his Cheyenne family as Sunshine is about to give birth. He never tries to justify such actions; they are merely part of daily life in the unidealized, cut-throat West. For all his sympathy for the Indians and mistrust of white civilization, he can be flexible, as when he briefly begins to prosper: "I thought it swell that white enterprise was reclaiming the Indian wastes." He resents the Indians for not sharing his materialism: "Old Lodge Skins had spent more than seventy years on the prairies and what did he have to show for it?" This man with the ironic initials will not die for anyone's sins but his own.

Berger gives Jack such flaws to make him a traditional picaro, both a victim and a victimizer, to make him a complex, believable character. Jack may be a rogue, but he has a conscience. He tries to rescue Amelia, the Kansas City prostitute who claims to be his niece, from her wayward life to atone somewhat for his own. After Sunshine is killed, Jack tracks down Custer to obtain revenge but is unable to act when an easy opportunity presents itself: "Call me a coward, but I wasn't able to slit the throat of a man while he was writing to his wife and fixing to drink coffee."

Of the dozens of secondary characters, the most important are Custer and Old Lodge Skins. Custer is vain, cruel, and paranoid, becoming especially deranged at his Last Stand, delivering a wild monologue that Berger adapted from the general's *My Life on the Plains* (1874), proclaiming the Indian "a subject for thoughtful study and investigation" as arrows whiz by. Custer can also be brilliant, rational, and magnanimous—a paradox which seems indicative of the positive and negative extremes in the American character. Old Lodge Skins, the novel's most admirable character, is Custer's equal in courage and almost his equal in foolishness. He can be as superstitiously mystical as a medicine man, as sentimentally compassionate as a grandmother, as perceptive and logical as a philosopher. He can also be the epitome of a dirty old man. Old Lodge Skins is convincing both as a savage and as a moralist.

Themes and Meanings

Any truly picaresque novel is satiric, and Berger tries to explode certain Western myths in *Little Big Man*. The heroes of legend are not all that heroic. Kit Carson denies hard-luck Jack a handout, Wyatt Earp knocks him out for belching, and Wild Bill Hickok is a tired, sad, paranoid man. Berger makes fun of naïve acceptance of the clichés of Hollywood's version of the West. Mrs. Winifred Burr, nurse to the hypochondriac Ralph Fielding Snell, does not believe Jack's claim about surviving Little Bighorn because she has seen a film in which all whites are killed, and Snell knows that Crazy Horse wore a war bonnet of feathers because he bought it from a dealer "of the highest integrity."

Although Berger presents a positive view of Indians, he debunks the image of the noble-savage. Jack sees them as "crude, nasty, smelly, lousy, and ignorant." Their camps stink, they eat dogs, and their women and children mutilate wounded enemies. Their arrogance annoys Jack: "The greatest folk on earth! Christ, they wouldn't have had them iron knives if Columbus hadn't hit these shores. And who brought them the pony in the first place?" Berger's point is that the West is so beclouded by myth that the truth about it can never be known. Eyewitness accounts—even Jack Crabb's—are untrustworthy because of the way things are twisted to make them fit preconceptions and fulfill stereotypes.

Little Big Man satirizes romantic illusions in general. After their wagon train is attacked, Jack's sister Caroline follows the Cheyenne because she thinks that they are lusting after her and because she wants to be an Indian princess. Her illusions are intact even after she has seen members of her family raped and murdered by drunken Indians. The savages dispel her misconceptions by failing to recognize that she is a woman. Years later, she reminds Jack of how the Indians "brutally stole" her "maidenhood." Since the truth is not interesting enough, she has invented her own myth and comes to believe it. Even Jack is not immune to such illusions. Thirteen years after running away from his adoptive parents, "I was still in love with Mrs. Pendrake as ardently as I had ever been, after all them years and battles and wives. That was the real tragedy of my life, as opposed to the various inconveniences." Berger implies that it is man's nature to ignore or embellish the truth and that, while such lies may comfort him, they can also cripple him.

The main theme of *Little Big Man* is perhaps the presentation of Jack Crabb as an alienated outsider. The true tragedy of Jack's life is that he is sent into exile from his relatives and friends, both white and Indian, so many times that he never has a sense of fitting in anywhere. With the Cheyenne, "[I] kept telling myself I was basically an Indian, just as when among Indians I kept seeing how I was really white to the core." He becomes "a person tending to go by the custom of wherever he's stuck," losing all sense of his identity. The economic progress of the expanding West alienates Jack further, making him feel like a premature old-timer. He is the American innocent in search of himself, in search of the meaning of America; he is modern man trapped in a chaotic, often meaningless universe. The natural order of the Indian world is attractive but unrealistic in the face of inevitable progress, while the imposed order of the white world, in which all a man can aspire to is respectability, seems superficial by comparison. The only true order or meaning is that created by the individual, but he must recognize its limitations.

Critical Context

Little Big Man is the American picaresque novel which comes closest to emulating the original picaresque and pseudopicaresque works. In its violence, in its hero who switches, usually involuntarily, from one side to another during a long period of warfare, it recalls *Der abenteuerliche Simplicissimus* (1669; *The Adventurous Simplicissimus*, 1912), by Hans Jakob Christoffel von Grimmelshausen. Berger names Ralph Fielding Snell in acknowledgment of his debt to Henry Fielding, author of *The History of the Life of the Late Mr. Jonathan Wild the Great* (1743) and *The History of Tom Jones* (1749); Amelia is named after the title character in Fielding's 1752 novel.

The novel is also firmly in the American picaresque tradition. Berger uses historical figures in the same way as Herman Melville in *Israel Potter: His Fifty Years of Exile* (1855) and John Barth in *The Sot-Weed Factor* (1960). Jack Crabb resembles Israel Potter in being an unsung hero and a permanent exile, and Berger's goals are similar to Barth's with his debunking of American myths. Berger's use of the vernacular and exaggerated humor evokes Mark Twain, whom Jack says "wasn't noted for understatement." Jack's epic journey recalls that of Twain's Huck Finn; like Huck, Jack receives a moral education in the world's duplicities. He is a Huck who has been to the Territory and turned cynical by what he has found there. In his treatment of the American innocent exploring the virgin wilderness, Berger combines the James Fenimore Cooper and Mark Twain versions of the American frontier, filtering them through an ironic contemporary sensibility.

Little Big Man also exemplifies Berger's parodic approach to literary genres. He does to the Western what he does to science fiction in *Regiment of Women* (1973), the detective story in *Who Is Teddy Villanova?* (1977), the Arthurian romance in *Arthur Rex* (1978), and the spy novel in *Nowhere* (1985).

Little Big Man remains Berger's best novel. It presents one of the most complete views of America in all of fiction. It is a powerful, entertaining exploration of the ambiguous nature of American values: the difference between the beliefs Americans profess and the way they act on those beliefs. Something is missing from life, and man does little but drift from one experience to another, not looking for a frontier since there is no longer any frontier to which he can escape. By setting these picaresque adventures in the past, Berger shows that modern man is not merely a victim of his time and implies that something may be deficient in the American experience itself.

Bibliography

Brooks, Landon. "The Measure of *Little Big Man*." *Studies in American Fiction* 17 (Autumn, 1989): 131-142. An insightful study of the treatment of Native Americans in Berger's novel.

_____. *Thomas Berger.* Boston: Twayne, 1989. Presents a brief biography of Berger and features various critical essays on his major works. Includes helpful bibliographical references for further reading.

Madden, David W. *Critical Essays on Thomas Berger.* New York: G. K. Hall, 1995. A collection of essays by various scholars that cover the spectrum of Berger's writings. Includes an essay by Michael Leary entitled "Finding the Center of the Earth. Satire, History, and Myth in *Little Big Man*."

Swayze, Carolyn. *Hard Choices: A Life of Tom Berger.* Vancouver: Douglas & McIntyre, 1987. A interesting look at Berger's life, career as a lawyer, and development as a writer. Includes an index and bibliography.

Wallace, Jon. "The Implied Author as Protagonist: A Reading of *Little Big Man*." *Western American Literature* 22 (February, 1988): 291-299. Wallace explores Berger's characterization of the narrator, Jack Crabb.

Michael Adams

THE LIVING

Author: Annie Dillard (1945-   )
Type of plot: Historical realism
Time of plot: 1855-1897
Locale: Various sites around Bellingham Bay, Washington
First published: 1992

> *Principal characters:*
>> ADA and ROONEY FISHBURN, a couple who set out from Council Bluffs,
>> Missouri, with a wagon train to settle in Whatcom, Washington
>> CLARE FISHBURN, their son, who grows up to be a possibly powerful
>> political figure in Whatcom and who is the target of Beal
>> Obenchain's plot
>> MINTA and EUSTACE HONER, a couple from prominent Baltimore
>> families who come to Washington to become farmers
>> JOHN IRELAND SHARP, the grandson of an early settler, a devotee of
>> philosophy and liberal causes
>> BEAL OBENCHAIN, a cruel social outcast, murderer, and wild man

The Novel

Based in part on Annie Dillard's experience of the northern Washington landscape as she lived there from 1975 to 1980, *The Living* recounts the early days of several settlements on Bellingham Bay from 1855 to 1897. The historical epic traces the fortunes and vicissitudes of three fictional families—the Fishburns, the Honers, and the Sharps—through several generations as they negotiate with the landscape, with the native peoples, with Chinese immigrants, with new waves of settlers, and with ever-changing economic fortunes.

The Living is divided into six long sections, each focusing on a major character, family, or event; the book also includes a brief afterword. The stories are told in third-person omniscient narration, with many flashbacks into the thoughts and events of characters' pasts. The epic weaves a tapestry of pattern and variation in the struggles of these early settling families.

The book begins dramatically, with the arrival by boat of Ada and Rooney Fishburn and their two remaining children, Clare and Glee, in Whatcom. The landscape is desolate, wet, and primitive. The heavy evergreen growth seems oppressive; the native inhabitants, primarily of the Lummi tribe, seem strange and exotic. All customary values seem irrelevant in this new land, and Ada obsessively remembers the losses, especially of her small son, Charley, that she had to endure to settle here.

Eventually, the children thrive, and the Fishburns begin to learn the joys of Northwest life. They both respond to the landscape—most notably to towering, snow-capped Mt. Baker—and set out to conquer the land, clearing away with fervor the dense evergreen growth. The native inhabitants become inextricably linked to the daily lives of the Fishburns, participating in sharing their lore and mechanisms for survival with the new settlers. Clare, who is of the first generation of white settlers to be reared here, feels marked for a heroic life. This section ends with Rooney's death by poison gas as he is digging a new well.

Book 2 recounts the formation of the personality of John Ireland Sharp, primarily through his early experiences. As a young man, he participates in a scouting expedition into the Cascade Mountains to seek a route for the Northern Pacific Railroad. During this expedition, the party discovers the evidence of racial hatred and torture: The staked body of a Skagit tribe boy who had been cruelly used by the Thompson tribe. John gets beaten up by Beal Obenchain in a random act of tyranny; ironically, he later is adopted into the Obenchain family when his own family drowns. He witnesses Beal's senseless killing of a newly born calf and the exhilaration it brings the bully. John, who has learned to love socialist causes while working in New York City, in Whatcom witnesses xenophobia in action. He comes to seek the pristine inspiration of the sight of Mt. Baker and prefer it to the cruelty he experiences among humans. The town's economic situation becomes precarious when the train terminus is set for Tacoma rather than Whatcom; there is an immediate financial slump.

In book 3, Whatcom shrivels in the economic depression. The widow Ada Fishburn moves with her son Clare to Goshen, a neighboring settlement, and there they meet Minta and Eustace Honer. Goshen is a thriving farming community where Clare, now a tall and joyful man, lends a hand with Kulshan Jim, of the Nooksack tribe, to help Eustace with clearing more of the land for farming. Ada remarries, and all goes well until there is an enormous logjam on the Nooksack River. All citizens, native and new settlers alike, set about to clear the jam, but Eustace is drowned in the effort. The vulnerability of life in this hard environment begins to affect young Hugh Honer, especially when his two young siblings die in a house fire after the rest of the family has left briefly to meet the Randalls, Minta's visiting relatives. After the tragedy, Minta's sister June remains in Goshen to be courted by Clare Fishburn, but the other Randalls return to familiar ways in Baltimore.

By the beginning of book 5, readers feel at home with the Northwest ways and the variety of people the land creates. In another vivid episode, Beal Obenchain performs the senseless and sadistic murder of Lee Chin simply because the victim is Chinese. Whatcom thrives because the Great Northern Railway proposes to have its western terminus there. Clare Fishburn returns and becomes a prosperous land speculator, and everyone believes in progress. Ironically, at the ceremony to honor the Canadians and their railroad, the citizens get involved in a petty water fight and lose the contract.

Beal Obenchain, at loose ends, decides (in the central plot event of the novel) that mere murder of the inferior does nothing to prove his own superiority. He lights upon a plan to humiliate someone: Beal will draw a name from a hat, and he will simply threaten to kill the person, with no intention of actually doing so. Thus, he will gain supreme power over that person's spirit and future, which he will control. The name he draws is that of Clare Fishburn. Clare has a wife, June Randall, whom he adores; he has children; he has a thriving career as a teacher and land speculator and a possible political future. Beal's threat at first pushes him into a kind of poignant despair and fear, yet Clare ultimately resists June's urging that they escape to Portland, Oregon, and begins to undergo a deep interior philosophical investigation about the meaning of life.

Books 5 and 6 show the settlers maturing and vast changes occurring in the political and economic spheres as the land gets civilized. Patterns begin to fulfill themselves: Minta replaces her lost children by adopting some needy Nooksack waifs. She becomes a liberated woman and a highly successful hops farmer, and she votes proudly in 1884, when Washington grants women suffrage. Ada (now Tawes) feels the days getting long and wonders how she can sustain her life after so much living. The novel's events have moved from the primitive burning of trees to clear the land to sophisticated civic festivals such as the launching of a racing sloop built by a new Swedish immigrant. At this festival, Beal Obenchain realizes that his threat has not fazed Clare Fishburn, and he decides to rescind his threat, just to drive Clare mad. At the same time, Johnny Lee sees Obenchain with a handkerchief that is twin to his own; the twin had belonged to Lee's murdered brother.

Meanwhile, in St. Paul, Minnesota, lumber entrepreneur Frederick Weyerhaeuser and railroad magnate James Hill make a mutually beneficial deal to ship immigrants west on trains and to ship lumber in the empty cars coming back. In Whatcom, the land rush is over; once again, the train terminus is set for another locale. Everyone is broke except for the Sharps, who have inherited the Obenchain estate; a stock-market crash is caused by a run on the banks during the debate over the gold standard. The news of the crash comes to Whatcom on the day of the town festival and beach picnic, when everyone feels unified, nostalgic, and full of life.

The final section reveals the ironies that history ushers in with its cycles. Ada Fishburn Tawes dies with the words of her original crossing of the plains on her lips. Clare Fishburn is humiliated that he has lost the fortune of his wife, who had excellent prospects as a senator's daughter yet chose him. Women begin to replant trees in the town that men had spent so many years trying to clear of timber. Minta's son Hugh plans to return to Baltimore to study medicine, a decision that makes the Honers' time in the West seem a detour rather than a commitment. John Ireland Sharp, despite his learning, his social prestige, and his inheritance, feels more and more alienated from his family. As his wife, Pearl, is planning to take over the abandoned grand house that was being built during prosperous times, John wants to retreat to an island in Puget Sound and live simply.

By accident, Johnny Lee's son Walter finds, in the hollowed-out tree that is Beal Obenchain's home, the porcelain dragon that the murdered Lee Chin wore around his neck. Beal has found no comfort in reading the works of Friedrich Wilhelm Nietzsche, and he is filled with despair at the turn his life has taken. Simultaneously, John Sharp seeks Beal to give him his share of the inheritance. Beal is found dead near the spot where Lee Chin's body was found. Whether his death was suicide or revenge remains unclear.

The afterword recounts the continued coping of the remaining characters. In the final scene, Hugh Honer throws himself off a platform in the dark into a pool, venturing into the unknown as his ancestors had.

The Characters

Annie Dillard develops the first half of the book by focusing on the individual sagas of single characters, family groups, or thematically linked pairs of characters. Each subsequent section also moves forward in time in terms of the waves of settlers who come to Bellingham Bay. Each of these introductory sections gives a history of how individuals related to the land upon their arrival, and how their characters and relationships developed as they encountered new hardships in the strange landscape.

Ada Fishburn, who is depicted in the first section, survives until the end of the novel, although the focus will shift to her sons and their generation. She is marked primarily by memories of loss—of her children and husband—and by her progress in accepting the native inhabitants and their ways as familiar. Dillard often presents Ada's character in third-person omniscient narration; sometimes, she shows Ada's emotional response to a scene. Ada is an intrepid pioneer and admirable survivor.

John Ireland Sharp, who is depicted in the second section, has ties to both the East and the West, and he is simultaneously an orphan and a man with historical roots in Whatcom. An educator who is greatly moved by the plight of the Chinese in America, John in his early years devotes himself to liberal social causes. His character is defined primarily by the events that shape him and his response to duties placed on him. Ironically, he becomes hermetic by the end of the novel.

Minta Honer, who loses her husband Eustace after they settle in Goshen, is portrayed as a strong and dedicated frontierswoman with a heart large enough to embrace the destitute and the alienated. She is revealed through the eyes of the omniscient third-person narrator in her response to challenge and tragedy in her life. The daughter of Senator Green Randall of Baltimore, Minta remakes herself entirely in the Western mode and is the model of a woman working toward becoming modern and liberated.

Beal Obenchain is the idiosyncratic villain of the novel. He is presented rather dispassionately and objectively, but his inability to live in society is everywhere clear. Obenchain's inhumanity is even more insidious because of his intelligence and education. He in fact builds his power game against Clare Fishburn on Nietzschean philosophy.

Clare Fishburn, along with John Ireland Sharp, is the most sympathetically presented character in the novel. He is a man of feeling, aspiration, depth, and responsibility who, because of Obenchain's plot against him, changes markedly as he learns what is valuable in life. He faces death and stares it down, releasing himself from fear and intellectual tyranny back into life.

Themes and Meanings

The Living is less a repository of meaning than it is a reclaiming of the experience of the early Western settlers. Dillard investigates the relation of individuals to their past and their heritage as well as to the strange, novel, synthetic society that begins to form them anew. She recounts the incidents in such a way that the reader begins to perceive the recurring patterns of nineteenth century life in Bellingham Bay: racial hatred and tyranny, personal loss, both human and economic, and the ways in which characters respond to and internalize the landscape.

Dillard immerses readers sensually into the Western milieu. Readers smell the omnipresent smoke of smoldering tree trunks, feel the mist and fog that shroud the mountains during most of the year, mire down in the mud of the town and the woods, and feel the horror of the exotic in the discovery of a badly mummified native corpse or the unknown perils of going about daily business (as when a tree falls and kills a child).

Similarly, the portrait of each character shows the internal mental workings, the particular slant that this individual gives to interpreting the new Western life. Telling philosophical patterns recur. Several characters display a strange combination of social conscience and desire for seclusion, symbolized respectively by Mt. Baker (as hope, aspiration) and by the canopy of evergreens that entraps and isolates. All the characters feel that the West offers them both an opportunity and a test of their personal mettle. The novel is simultaneously about the changes that individuals can and do make in the long run and also about how impervious nature and history are to these minuscule personal efforts. Patience, suffering, and hope are embodied in recurring biblical and poetic quotations that emerge at crucial points and give the novel its title: "I believe that I shall see the goodness of the Lord in the land of the living." Human effort is always new and admirable; it is also never original and doomed to be stunted by perverse human nature and the impersonal forces of history, time, and landscape.

Critical Context

Annie Dillard has been well received and highly acclaimed. Her work includes *Holy the Firm* (1977) and *Pilgrim at Tinker Creek* (1974), which are responses to nature in the transcendentalist tradition; *An American Childhood* (1987), her early autobiography; *Tickets for a Prayer Wheel* (1974), a collection of poems; and *Living by Fiction* (1982), which discusses in essay mode concerns of the modern writer. *The Living* is her first novel. Reviews of the novel have been full of praise for the scope and humanity of *The Living*, for its ability to invoke in seamless prose the atmosphere of its inhabitants, and for its skillful weaving together of the seemingly disparate plot lines.

Although *The Living* has no real models, it resembles in intent other fictionalized historical epic narratives, such as Barbara Tuchman's *A Distant Mirror* (1978), and it perhaps imitates the naturalistic fiction of the turn of the twentieth century. Dillard's novel, however, is remarkable for being an American epic and for focusing on a specific area not often centrally included in the story of the building and settling of America. The novel is also animated by her personal experience of life in the area and is reinforced by extensive historical research.

In *The Living*, Annie Dillard proves her diversity as a writer who has mastered the grand epic sweep of imagination. She is fast becoming a stalwart of American letters, having won grants from the Guggenheim Foundation and the National Endowment for the Arts as well as the Pulitzer Prize, the Washington Governor's Award, the New York Press Club Award, and the Ambassador Book Award in Arts and Letters from the English-Speaking Union.

Bibliography
Albin, C. D. "What the Living Know in Bellingham Bay." *The Christian Century* 109 (October 7, 1992): 871-873. Focusing on the omnipresence of death and hardship in the novel, Albin sees the characters' responses to the land as an education in how to accept the random irony of suffering. Albin praises Dillard's techniques for revealing the inner lives of the characters. This is an admiring review, which ultimately decides that readers are strengthened by participating in the epic struggle.
Ames, Katrine. Review of *The Living*, by Annie Dillard. *Newsweek* 119 (June 8, 1992): 57. An enthusiastic review. Ames focuses on the authentic effect of the nineteenth century writing style that Dillard emulates. She compares Dillard to E. L. Doctorow in terms of the romantic sweep of the novel.
DiConsiglio, John. "Annie Dillard." *Literary Cavalcade* 50 (March, 1998): 22. DiConsiglio examines Dillard's family background, career highlights, literary style, and major published works. Although this essay does not specifically address *The Living*, it does provide penetrating insight into Dillard's works.
The New Yorker. Review of *The Living*, by Annie Dillard. 68 (July 6, 1992): 80. Notes how Dillard's attitude toward the natural world differs from its treatment in her earlier works. Here, nature is antagonistic to humans rather than in harmony with them. The reviewer deplores the many deaths in the novel as well as what is perceived as weak plot and character development.
Parrish, Nancy C. *Lee Smith, Annie Dillard, and the Hollins Group: A Genesis of Writers*. Baton Rouge: Louisiana State University Press, 1998. Parrish focuses on the southern women's school, Hollins College, and explores how a women's writing community evolved within the college. She also praises the writers who helped launch it, including Annie Dillard.
Scheese, Don. Review of *The Living*, by Annie Dillard. *The Georgia Review* 47 (Spring, 1993): 193-197. Scheese tries to contextualize the novel in the light of Dillard's own body of work and in the light of the turn-of-the-century fiction by Theodore Dreiser and Frank Norris. His primary observations concern Dillard's use of the ideas of Social Darwinism and Manifest Destiny. He believes that the land is a major character in the novel and that Dillard has written her own self into the piece. Finally, Scheese praises the deep religious response that the novel evokes.
Smith, Pamela A. "The Ecotheology of Annie Dillard: A Study in Ambivalence." *Cross Currents* 45 (Fall, 1995): 341-358. Smith argues that Dillard's works elucidate ecology worship as a theological concept, although the philosophy is silent about the destruction of nature. Implicit in the decay of nature is that God and nature are equally important and elusive.

Stewart, Albert B. Review of *The Living*, by Annie Dillard. *The Antioch Review* 50 (Fall, 1992): 772. Stewart praises Dillard for the power of her details in the novel. He finds enough matter in *The Living* for twelve novels and admires the way Dillard has synthesized the many stories into a patterned whole. The details bring the novel a sense of reality and genuineness, a historical accuracy. With wit and subtlety, Dillard reveals many of her characters to have spiritual energy to overcome the inertia of overwhelming loss and death.

Sandra K. Fischer

THE LIZARD'S TAIL

Author: Luisa Valenzuela (1938-   )
Type of plot: Social morality
Time of plot: The reign of José López Rega, 1975
Locale: Argentina
First published: Cola de lagartija, 1983 (English translation, 1983)

> *Principal characters:*
> THE SORCERER, based on José López Rega, also referred to as Eulalito, Lord of the Black Lagoon, Master of the Black Lagoon, and Thousandmen Flower
> ESTRELLA, the twin sister of the Sorcerer, his third testicle
> GENERALISSIMO, based on Juan Perón
> MADAM PRESIDENT, the Intruder, based on Isabel Perón
> EGRET, the aide-de-camp of the Sorcerer, a eunuch
> DEAD WOMAN, based on Eva Perón
> ALFREDO NAVONI, a revolutionary, the leader of the people of Umbanda
> LUISA, the narrator of portions of the novel, the voice of the author

The Novel

The Lizard's Tail is divided into three parts. The first hundred pages of the novel are narrated by an enigmatic figure known as the Sorcerer, with interruptions by unidentified characters in the capital and an omniscient narrator. The Sorcerer claims to be indispensable to the government; it is clear from the beginning, however, that this is not a realistic political novel but rather a symbolic, mythic, and at times deliberately cryptic allegory of modern Argentina.

The novel opens with a prophecy about a river of blood which will bring twenty years of peace. The first part relates the Sorcerer's childhood in the land of the ants. (He amused himself by sitting on anthills.) Expelled from the anthills at age two, the Sorcerer is taken by Don Ciriaco to Doña Rosa, who rears the orphaned boy. Later, Dona Rosa is raped by the police, who are searching for the Sorcerer. In the capital, two observers decide that the Marshland, both a swamp and a "representation of the human unconscious," must be conceived of as a metaphor: The surface represents the repressive superego/government while the swamp represents the inverted-image underground of the Sorcerer. The Sorcerer says that he is writing a novel in which the present day will take place at all times.

The Intruder, Isabel Perón, organizes a group to determine with certainty that the corpse thought to be that of Eva Perón is in fact Eva's. A reference is made to the burial of Eva by Perón and the disappearance of her body: The Sorcerer says that he and others hid the body after a coup and after the "cult" was forbidden. The Sorcerer says that he is bringing Eva back to life. The Generalissimo, Perón, dies. The Sorcerer decides to make Isabel, Perón's wife, his ally. He makes plans to create a new kingdom which he will rule, the Kingdom of the Black Lagoon. The government begins to persecute him. Rather than fight them, he decides to build a pyramid. In his pyramid, he will have his wedding with his sister, and together they will have a son. In the capital, a plan for National Reconstruction is formulated to counter the negative images in the foreign press, which include accusations of torture and disappearances condoned by the government. The Sorcerer suggests a masked ball as a preparation for the government's campaign of disinformation. He prepares for the Grand Ball of the Full Moon and plans to invite government officials and journalists.

The second part of the novel, narrated by Luisa, is a declaration of her intention to be a politically committed writer and an examination of the compromised position in which she finds herself while trying to write a biography of the Sorcerer. At the time she receives an invitation to his masked ball, she herself has been planning a party, where she wants to introduce certain guests to the ambassador of a foreign country. Her friend Alfredo Navoni, a revolutionary, tells her to continue to write her biography of the Sorcerer. At the Sorcerer's party, guests are to be given terra-cotta masks, which will be broken with clubs distributed among the guests. Meanwhile, a counter-ceremony is being planned by Navoni's followers. At his own ball, the Sorcerer wears the mask of an ant. Crop-dusting planes cover the area with locally processed cocaine. At dawn, all masks have been broken and the guests are bloody and beaten. Luisa is advised to get rid of her devil and devil paraphernalia, which she does. In preparation for their imitation of the masked ball, the Popular Festival, the people of the town of Capivari build a pyramid and a representation of the Sorcerer.

It is said that the Sorcerer's power has grown while Luisa has written about him, which causes her great concern. The Sorcerer decides to annex Capivari into his kingdom and to cut off its water supply if the townspeople do not agree. Navoni tells Luisa that she should kill the Sorcerer in her novel. She believes that it is impossible to do this, although she thinks it would be a good idea to kill the military in her writing, since they use the Sorcerer as a shield. The Sorcerer commands that all photographic equipment and mirrors be confiscated. He covers the inside of the pyramid with the mirrors. Luisa's ambivalence about her role finally leads her to make the decision to stop writing altogether: Fearing that even writing about the Sorcerer will increase his power, she erases herself and, thereby, him.

In the third and final part of the novel, the Sorcerer believes that someone has stopped writing about him. After a ritual with the Egret in which his body is covered with mud and he becomes a woman, he has the pyramid's mirrors covered with white cloth by workers, men blind from birth.

Meanwhile, three mysterious characters move up the river, a teacher who participated in the imitation of the Sorcerer's ball, Luisa, and Navoni. The Sorcerer consummates his marriage to Estrella by injecting his third testicle with sperm and impregnating his sister (himself). In his delirium, he feels the tent closing in on him. Once his protection, he says it is now his torture chamber. The Egret travels to the foot of the pyramid and collapses, exhausted. Something explodes and blood appears. The woman with curly hair (Luisa) says it must be the sign of the twenty years of peace promised by the prophecy. The heavyset man, Navoni, disagrees and says that once one president falls, another is ready to take over, and that the little thread of blood is not the one mentioned in the prophecy.

The Characters

The characters double one another and historical figures. There are two writers, Luisa and the Sorcerer, as well as two witches, Machi and Caboclo de Mar. After Juan Perón's death, in 1974, Isabel Perón ruled the country with José López Rega, leader of a conservative Peronist faction and Minister of Social Welfare. He was forced into hiding, and Isabel was overthrown a year later. A minor police official during the first Peronist regime, he later offered his services to the exiled president and became Perón's personal secretary during his last years in Spain. Though he occupied the post of secretary of welfare, he was a close personal adviser to Perón and his wife during and after their return to Argentina and was relied upon heavily by the latter after her husband's death. He received much attention in the foreign press for his devotion to astrology and the occult, but it was his ruthless power struggle within the Peronist movement that concerned Argentines. He attacked both moderate and left wing movements.

The Dead Woman is based on Eva Perón, who was born to an unwed mother with the help of an Indian midwife in the pampas near Los Toldos. Eva met Perón and married him in 1945. Perón ruled Argentina from 1946 to 1955 and from 1973 to 1974. Isabel, Juan Perón's wife after Eva's death, was selected as his running mate in 1973. Valenzuela parodies Isabel's conscious imitation of Eva's style as she attempted to evoke the myth of Eva after Perón's return to power. Navoni is a composite of various revolutionaries Valenzuela has known. Although the generals and other political figures are depicted in detail to make them recognizable to an Argentine audience, what is more essential are the metaphors.

Themes and Meanings

The symbols of the novel are rather difficult to understand without some historical background. Valenzuela found it strange that Argentina, such a European country (ninety-eight percent of the population is of European descent), could have fallen under the power of a sorcerer. It appeared to her that Argentina was more "Latin American" than the Argentines had supposed. For this reason, she chose the structure of a myth for her book in order to show the absurd extremes that could be reached when a people allows itself to be ruled by an insane leader. As she writes, "what more obvious metaphor than that of the Marshland" could be used to describe the relationship between the government, the repressive superego on the surface, and the sorcerer, the government's repressive inverted-image underground? Valenzuela wrote *The Lizard's Tail* to cure Argentina of its conspiracy of silence, its inability to speak out against the torture of dissidents and the *desaparecidos* (the "disappeared ones").

Valenzuela had begun to write another book, about an ambassador and a woman, before she wrote *The Lizard's Tail*. This book was inspired by her own experiences of helping Argentines to leave the country. After leaving Buenos Aires, however, where she had been writing, to spend some time in Mexico, she decided to stop struggling against the preliminary narrative and to write three shorter works using some of the same material, resulting in *Cambio de armas* (1982; *Other Weapons*, 1985), *Donde viven las aguilas*, 1983), and *The Lizard's Tail*.

. Having decided to focus on López Rega in *The Lizard's Tail*, she formulated a response to his discourse and to that of the generals, some of whose language appears in the book. Yet Valenzuela does not pretend to be a physician or healer who is unscathed by the disease. She, too, has been tortured by the memories of the disappeared, whose silhouettes have been stamped on the walls of Buenos Aires. Her cure is based on the practice of deconstruction: "We should deconstruct the textuality inscribed in the para-official discourse." In other words, the reader must seek the underlying assumptions of this discourse.

In *The Lizard's Tail*, the reader participates in the creation of and is cured by the poetic text. Valenzuela chooses to exorcise the demons that have destroyed the country from within. Rather than rid the country of subversives, she would rid the consciousness of her reader of identification with the repressive regimes that have countenanced the torture and the disappearances of the 1970's. In her novel, the sick body of Argentina is transformed into a symbolic landscape upon which Valenzuela performs the exorcism. She creates an allegory in which the Argentine psyche can view the pain that the body can no longer tolerate.

Critical Context

The critical context for Luisa Valenzuela's work must be defined to include the political situation in Argentina in addition to works of other writers. In France, Valenzuela came into contact with the group of poststructuralist critics associated with the avant-garde literary journal *Tel quel*. Poststructuralists in France were critical of orthodox Marxism and its failures. The rise of French feminism coincided with the breaking away from orthodoxy on the Left. In Argentina, women made gains in terms of working conditions and democratic rights during the Perón period. Ideological contradictions in the movement allowed a broad spectrum of women, from traditional to radical, to call themselves Peronists. At the time Valenzuela wrote *The Lizard's Tail*, Argentine women were engaged in political struggle not only as family members of revolutionaries in the home, but also as an integral part of the struggle. The military government did not make allowances for gender in its torture of women.

In an interview in 1983, Valenzuela mentioned that Jacques Derrida, Michel Foucault, and Roland Barthes had been her colleagues at the New York Institute for the Humanities. It is within this context of postmodernist debates about language and the political situation in Argentina that Valenzuela chooses to situate herself as a writer.

Valenzuela's work is also grounded in the contemporary writing of Argentina, including the work of such writers as Jorge Luis Borges and Julio Cortázar. These writers also incorporate the themes of dream, death, magic, and desire. In fact, it was not until *Aquí pasan cosas raras* (1975; *Strange Things Happen Here*, 1979) and *Como en la guerra* (1977; *He Who Searches*, 1979) that Valenzuela began to address political issues in her work. Existentialism and psychoanalysis have become woven into the fabric of contemporary letters in Argentina. Valenzuela's attitude toward these traditions is irreverent on occasion, and at least equally informed by feminism and a belief that only truth and justice can exorcise the phantasms in her country. Several critics have noted that it is very important that one not read Latin American literature as merely symbolic or magic; Latin American writers are faced with the problem of conveying a political reality that is frequently "unbelievable," especially to readers from another culture. Nevertheless, Valenzuela wishes her work to be read for its metaphors, as literature, not only as political commentary.

Bibliography
Bach, Caleb. "Metaphors and Magic Unmask the Soul." *Americas (English Edition)* 47 (January/February, 1995): 22-27. Offers a fascinating look at Valenzuela's life and writing career. Briefly explores some of her themes and examines some of the writers who have influenced her, such as Jorge Luis Borges.
Garfield, Evelyn P. "Luisa Valenzuela." In *Latin American Writers*, edited by Carlos A. Solé and Maria I. Abreau. Vol. 3. New York: Charles Scribner's Sons, 1989. Offers an entry on Valenzuela that covers her life and career. Presents in-depth readings of many of her works and includes a selected bibliography.
Kadir, Djelal. "Focus on Luisa Valenzuela." *World Literature Today* 69 (Autumn, 1995): 668-670. A revealing profile of Valenzuela that covers her tenure as a Puterbaugh Fellow at the University of Oklahoma, the quality and style of her writing, and her focus on human potential and failures. Although this essay does not address any particular work, it offers interesting background information.
Pinto, Magdalena. *Women Writers of Latin America: Intimate Histories.* Austin: University of Texas Press, 1991. A collection of interviews with Latin American women writers, including one with Luisa Valenzuela. Features helpful bibliographic references for further reading and an index.
Pye, Geralyn. "Political Football: Sports, Power, and Machismo in Luisa Valenzuela's *The Lizard's Tail.*" *Studies in Latin American Popular Culture* 13 (1994): 115-127. Pye examines the political aspects of football in Argentina as portrayed in Valenzuela's novel. She explores the relationship between sports, power, and masculinity; Valenzuela's use of symbolism in her novel; Argentina's hosting of the 1978 World Cup Soccer Tournament; and the military government's use of sports in political affairs.

Emily Hicks

LOCOS
A Comedy of Gestures

Author: Felipe Alfau (1902-   )
Type of plot: Magical Realism
Time of plot: The 1920's
Locale: Toledo and Madrid, Spain
First published: 1936

> *Principal characters:*
> DR. JOSÉ DE LOS RIOS, medical attendant to the Crazies
> FULANO, a character in search of an identity
> DON BENITO, the prefect of police
> GASTON (EL COGOTE) BEJARANO, Don Benito's nephew
> JUAN CHINELATO, a Spanish-Chinese strongman
> DON BAEZ, a professional beggar
> SISTER CARMELA, also known as CARMEN and LUNARITO, Gaston's
>   sister
> GARCIA, a beggar and fingerprint expert

The Novel

Locos: A Comedy of Gestures consists of a prologue with interconnected stories narrated by an unnamed writer who observes prostitutes, gamblers, and thieves gathering at a café, where writers may choose from among them for characters in their stories. "Identity" concerns Fulano, a persona who searches for recognition as a real character. Dr. José de los Rios suggests that Fulano fake his suicide, then return to Madrid, where he and the writer will help make him a more substantive character. Fulano does as the doctor instructs but does not realize that an escaped convict then assumes Fulano's identity, becoming better known than Fulano himself was. Fulano jumps successfully to his death following promises of literary immortality.

In "A Character," Gaston (El Cogote) Bejarano observes a beautiful woman (Lunarito) walking alone in the rain. After they exchange kisses, the girl then disappears, and Bejarano returns to his lover, Carmen. The doctor takes the author to visit El Cogote, who, having learned of Lunarito's murder, has become ill. He recounts a recurring dream in which his sister, Carmen, whom he retrieved from a convent following a family scandal, has Lunarito's face. El Cogote provides one ending, the writer another.

In "The Beggar," Garcia is devastated to discover that he has accidentally given another beggar his gold coin. Garcia tracks down the beggar, Don Baez, in a sumptuous house. Although he initially tries to retrieve the coin dishonestly, Garcia is taken aback at Baez's generosity. Breaking down, he confesses his lies. Baez forgives him and promises Garcia future assistance.

In "Fingerprints," Don Gil Bejarano, in order to compel Spanish citizens to have their fingerprints on file, offers his own, but the effort fails. He continues to insist to Prefect Don Benito that if fingerprints belonging to a man in China were found at a crime scene in Spain, he would nevertheless be found guilty. Later, as Don Gil plays cards at home, his wife, Felisa, catches their daughter, Carmen, and son, Gaston, being intimate together. Benito calls on Gil to accompany him to his office, where he explains that his fingerprints were found at the site of a grisly murder. He has unwittingly become "the man from China."

"The Wallet" takes place during a police convention while a citywide power outage affords criminals an opportunity to rob. Pepe bets his uncle, Prefect Don Benito, that Benito will be robbed as soon as they part company on their way home. Later, someone bumps into Pepe on the street. Realizing that his wallet is missing, Pepe beats the man to get it back. Later, Pepe discovers that the wallet is not his. The following morning, Benito tells Pepe that someone robbed him of his wallet. Pepe offers Benito back the wallet he had wrested from the man. Having stolen his own brother's wallet the previous night, El Cogote returns it, with apologies. Overcome by the morning's events, Don Benito tries to sit down, but he is in too much pain.

"Chinelato" involves a Chinese boy who learns how to cheat, gamble, and steal. Juan Chinelato becomes well known for his powerful physique and later weds Senorita Iturbe, whom he delights in tormenting. Once she gives birth, Chinelato cooks and serves their child to her. He later becomes Olózaga, a butterfly charmer in his own circus, resells suits from corpses, and finally fades from memory.

In "The Necrophil," Dona Micaela Valverde is fixated on death so much that she attends a score of funerals daily and goes into a prolonged rigor mortis state. Dr. de los Rios tells Micaela that suicide is the only cure for her morbid fascination. After a failed suicide attempt, she is done with death.

"A Romance of Dogs" concerns Garcia, a boy tormented by hours of religious study and merciless beatings by Catholic priests. While he is walking home, a dog threatens him, while at school a second dog attacks tardy students. Things brighten when Padre Inocencio and Sister Carmela join in their instruction. While Garcia is occasionally confused by Carmela's sexual manner, she and the padre make his life bearable until her brother, El Cogote, elopes with her and Padre Inocencio jumps to his death. The writer periodically visits Garcia who, as an adult, goes mad and blind.

The Characters

The majority of the characters who populate *Locos* are on the periphery of society, either by their own design or because they overstep boundaries of acceptable behavior. Dr. de los Rios and the unidentified writer function as complementary halves that comment to one another and constitute the whole of one who observes the strange behavior of others with very little direct involvement. Alfau, clearly intrigued with the thin line between crime and the law, often uses his characters to play out this fascination rather than develop them fully. The focus is more on plot in some of the stories. In "The Wallet," Prefect Benito's sore bottom indicates that Pepe mistakenly beat up his own uncle the night before, thinking that Benito had stolen his wallet. The lack of specific character development places an emphasis on the power of the wallet itself as a source of corruption. Even family members are susceptible to the lure of financial gain at the expense of their blood relations. Repeatedly, Alfau drops clues along the way, impelling the reader to pick up the scent and pursue answers. Chinelato, the Philippine-born Chinese man, is afforded a long thirty pages in this slender book. Without parents and a minority against whom others vent their racist wrath, he becomes increasingly more violent and misogynist. Like necrophil Micaela Valverde or even fragile Garcia, Chinelato endures to the bitter end. When he becomes too old for acts of physical bravado, he starts a business hawking dead people's clothes. Relatively little space is devoted to the appearance of the characters except as their various eccentricities become personified: Micaela is cadaverous; Chinelato is enormous and musclebound. Just as life is unpredictable, there is an underlying danger of any one of these creations wresting the narrative away from the author. Readers first meet Garcia as an adult beggar, then (in one of many time twists) in "A Romance of Dogs" as a child forced to toil under the Machiavellian tutelage of Spanish priests. It is this character that reads closest to authentic experience, as his sexuality is awakened by Sister Carmela. When her pimpish brother, El Cogote, whisks her away and Padre Inocencio, heartbroken, leaps to his death, such events are never discussed, either by the priests or amongst the male students; the incident is buried, along with any possibility of young Garcia's being allowed to fathom it or grieve for the loss of the two people dearest to him. The narrator meets Garcia years later in Madrid; he is living alone but across from the ever watchful de los Rios. Garcia slowly loses his mind, embracing trees and repeatedly crying, "Spring is coming!" His attendant is the omnipresent Lunarito, the near-silent woman who tends to male needs without complaint. Some characters in *Locos* descend into madness rather than die, as though they have made a pact with the devil to exchange their mental stability for their physical presence on earth.

Themes and Meanings

    Locos: A Comedy of Gestures is a sly, well-constructed mosaic of stories that indicts the Spanish people, enslaved by Catholicism and their own inability to choose between self-interest and the common good. The author also comments, in a larger fashion, on human foibles and their attendant problems as well as the subjective quality of truth and reality. Perhaps most touching is the last story, "A Romance of Dogs," as the boy Garcia struggles futilely against his Catholic education that insists on mindless absorption of arcane material, thus depriving him of the joys that learning can bring. Although the adult Garcia dies insane and blind, he is nevertheless a poet in love with spring. Alfau cautions the reader both to reserve judgment about the characters and to refrain from taking the following events too seriously. While his inventions do double duty as multiple personas, the themes of criminality and justice intertwine. What dominates in *Locos* is the inherent conflict between religious purity and religious totalitarianism. Children are terrorized, and women are abused; strutting about at the center, nostrils flared, is a dangerous kind of Spanish machismo, one which imposes itself on other countries as well as on the "weaker" sex. Nevertheless, many of the stories manage to underscore a certain affection for the national character. One feels inclined toward accepting the melodrama of such women as Tia Mariquita, one of Chinelato's wives, as a foil against a harmful reality. Giving in to passion in a less condemning society, Alfau indicates, may produce happier people. Despite the tales' dark qualities, such as the outrageous abuse many of the women suffer at the hands of their less than loving men, a sense of playfulness prevails. Alfau understands that the human mind receives satisfaction from piecing together parts of a picture, and he uses his abilities as a writer to give or withhold information. In "Fingerprints," Don Gil is the one who hires Garcia as a fingerprint expert. Later, Prefect Benito declares that even Garcia checked the murderer's prints for verification of Don Gil's culpability. Regardless of the hard physical evidence, did Don Gil really commit murder? How can a womanizing baby killer like Chinelato also be capable of charming butterflies into spelling out his name? As in life, appearances in *Locos* are deceiving, and the reader is invited to play detective.

Critical Context

Written when Felipe Alfau, a Spanish immigrant, was twenty-six years old and living in New York, *Locos: A Comedy of Gestures* was published eight years later in 1936. Alfau's *Old Tales from Spain*, a collection of children's stories, was published in 1929. Although he produced a second novel, *Chromos: A Parody of Truth* (1948), Alfau faded from view, although *Chromos* was later nominated for a National Book Award in 1990. Dalkey Archive Press reissued *Locos* in 1989, publishing *Chromos* and a collection of his poetry three years later.

The structure of *Locos*, in which characters' names change as they intrude on one another's dramas, gives the book a dreamlike, surreal texture. Like Luigi Pirandello's 1921 play *Six Characters in Search of an Author*, in which related characters have an unstoppable need to have their story articulated by the writer, Alfau's creations step out of the action to comment on or even attempt to redirect events. Critics have further compared Alfau's book to the works of Italo Calvino, Gabriel García Márquez, and Jorge Luís Borges, who share similar qualities of Magical Realism and postmodernism. *Locos* also resembles Flan O'Brien's *At Swim-Two Birds* (1939), which also employs a story-within-a-story structure. Two facts make *Locos* a phenomenon unto itself: None of these writers appears to have had any knowledge of Alfau's anachronistic stories, and a half century of obscurity elapsed before the book was republished to greater acclaim than had met its original printing.

In *Chromos*, a fictionalized Alfau gazes by matchlight at old pictures from a Spanish calendar. He imagines a novel about the same characters as those in *Locos*, living lives quite separate from that of their adopted home, Manhattan. This ability to write of separation from the outside world has finally earned Alfau a long overdue reputation as a complex and clever storyteller.

Bibliography

Alfau, Felipe. "Anonymity: An Interview with Felipe Alfau." Interview by Ilan Stavans. *The Review of Contemporary Fiction* 13, no. 1 (Spring, 1993): 146-153. A revealing talk with the author in which he discusses his philosophy, politics, and life as a writer. Provides a telling glance into Alfau's wry sense of humor.

Dirda, Michael. "Crazy Like a Fox." *The Washington Post Book World* 19, no. 17 (April 23, 1989). Along with a detailed review of *Locos*, Dirda also provides some background on Felipe Alfau and puts the novel into literary context.

McCarthy, Mary. Afterword to *Locos: A Comedy of Gestures*, by Felipe Alfau. Elmwood Park, Ill.: The Dalkey Archive Press, 1988. An unabashed fan of Alfau, McCarthy revisits *Locos*, having originally reviewed the book in 1936 for *The Nation*. She also helps in untangling some complex plot points.

Shapiro, Anna. "Sixty-one Years of Solitude." *The New Yorker* 65 (June 5, 1989): 105-108. A luminous review of *Locos*, along with a succinct overview of Alfau's life.

Stavans, Ilan. Introduction to *Sentimental Songs*, by Felipe Alfau. Elmwood, Ill.: The Dalkey Archive Press. 1992. Stavans, who also interviewed Alfau in *The Review of Contemporary Fiction*, provides contextual information on Alfau's work, including his relationship to the Romantic movement.

Nika Hoffman

THE LONE RANGER AND TONTO FISTFIGHT IN HEAVEN

Author: Sherman Alexie (1966-   )
Type of work: Short stories
Time of work: Late twentieth century
Locale: The Spokane Indian Reservation in Washington State
First published: 1993

> *Principal characters:*
>   VICTOR, the main character, sometimes the narrator, in most of the
>   stories
>   VICTOR'S FATHER, a heavy drinker
>   JAMES MANY HORSES, a mystic and seer, nearly a Christ figure
>   THOMAS BUILDS-THE-FIRE, a storyteller, symbol of Native American
>   tradition
>   JUNIOR, another "typical" Indian youth, a diabetic

The Stories

Set on the Spokane Indian Reservation in eastern Washington State, *The Lone Ranger and Tonto Fistfight in Heaven* is a collection of loosely related stories featuring a recurring cast of characters. In these twenty-two stories, the young male protagonists, usually in their late teens or their twenties, struggle with poverty, alcoholism, and the despair of everyday life on and off the reservation. They also try to come to grips with what it means to be Indian (as the characters exclusively refer to themselves) in the late twentieth century.

Though these stories have no chronological order, vary wildly in style, and use different narrators, the author manages, with thin plots, sketchy characterization, and "artless" language, to build stories of great cumulative power and understanding. The reader is well advised to read the book through to experience the full effect.

The first story in the collection, "Every Little Hurricane," describes a New Year's Eve party as seen through the eyes of nine-year-old Victor. Images of bad weather metaphorically represent the emotional storms of the party, where Victor's drunken uncles, Adolph and Arnold, fight viciously for no apparent reason. "He could see his uncles slugging each other with such force that they had to be in love. Strangers would never want to hurt each other that badly." A flashback then recounts a Christmas of four years before, when there was no money for gifts and Victor had seen his father cry in despair. The narration then moves back to the party, with the emotional storm prompting other memories of pain, poverty, and humiliation among the partygoers. In the final scene, Victor crawls between the unconscious forms of his parents, passed out in their bed. He feels the power of love and the family there, and the power of survival.

Another story that explores Victor's family relationships is "Because My Father Always Said He Was the Only Indian Who Saw Jimi Hendrix Play 'The Star Spangled Banner' at Woodstock." A series of family memories in this plotless sketch describe

Victor's relationship with his father, his father and mother's unusual love story, and Victor's father's relationship with alcohol. All of this is set against the ever-present background of the Native American's relationship with modern America.

In "This Is What It Means to Say Phoenix, Arizona," Victor and his lifelong but estranged friend Thomas Builds-the-Fire travel to Phoenix to collect the personal effects of Victor's father, who has died of a heart attack. In the course of the journey, some episodes in the earlier life of Victor and Thomas are recounted, and their friendship is reborn. Thomas, a visionary storyteller and link to traditional Indian ways, suggests that they throw Victor's father's ashes in the Spokane River so that he can "rise like a salmon . . . and find his way home." In the story, therefore, three things are, like the phoenix, reborn from the ashes: the relationship of Victor and Thomas, some small part of Indian tradition, and Victor's father's Indian spirit.

Many of the themes and symbols of the book are brought together and underscored in the final story of the collection, "Witnesses, Secret and Not." Thirteen-year-old Victor accompanies his father on a trip to the Spokane Police Department to answer questions about a man who had disappeared ten years earlier. In the car, they discuss those who have died and those who have disappeared into the cities, but a dangerous near-accident on the ice goes unremarked. They see a drunken Indian man that they know, give him a couple of dollars, and leave him "to make his own decisions." They are treated cordially but with little respect by the police, who have called the father in to the police station for little reason, requiring a long journey on dangerous, icy roads. Returning home, they join their strong and apparently happy family, the redeeming quality of their lives. The story is simple, even superficial, but in the course of it, the issues of white-Indian relationships, alcoholism and personal responsibility, death and disappearances, and the warm bond of the family are subtly yet effectively explored.

Other stories deal with the narrator's relationship with a white woman ("The Lone Ranger and Tonto Fistfight in Heaven"), the trials of schooling ("Indian Education"), illness and death ("The Approximate Size of My Favorite Tumor"), and alcoholism ("Amusements"). Still others adopt a more mystical tone and experimental style to examine the art of storytelling ("A Good Story," "The Trial of Thomas Builds-the-Fire"), alternate history ("Distances"), and dreams of the future ("Imagining the Reservation").

The Characters

Victor is either the narrator or the main character of most of the stories in the book. He becomes the reader's eyes and ears in the world of the Spokane Reservation, from the first glimpse of the disturbing New Year's party when Victor is nine, to the quiet summing up of the themes of the book in the final story. He is perhaps the "typical" Native American youth, recounting his view of his society and his struggles with identity, alcohol, and family relationships.

Thomas Builds-the-Fire is a near mythical character, a storyteller and thus a symbolic link to the past. The stories he tells are usually historical, casting one of his present-day friends into a historical situation—as in "A Drug Called Tradition," in which he starts a round of storytelling by imagining his friend Victor raiding the camp of a rival tribe to steal a horse named Flight. In other stories, Thomas is ridiculed for telling too many stories, stories that the others do not want to hear anymore. Thomas's strongest appearance is in the surrealistic piece "The Trial of Thomas Builds-the-Fire." In it, he "testifies" by telling stories, casting himself first as a horse among a herd captured by the cavalry in 1858, then as a warrior in a similar battle. Though he is originally charged with "telling the truth," by the end of the trial, his crime is the murder of two soldiers in the story he told of events of a century before. Thomas represents the pull of tradition among Native American people. He becomes the scapegoat for the "crimes" of the past and is the nagging conscience of modern Native Americans, reminding them of the past and the traditions that they often do not want to remember.

James Many Horses is the mystic of the stories, the fountain of wisdom and guidance. His near divinity is revealed in the title of his first story: "Jesus Christ's Half-Brother Is Alive and Living on the Spokane Indian Reservation." He was born near Christmas, and his mother claimed to be a virgin, "even though Frank Many Horses said it was his." The infant James survives a fire that kills his parents and is adopted by the anonymous narrator of the story. James fails to develop normally and cannot walk, talk, or even crawl, but he is a supportive companion to the narrator through years of physical trials and alcoholism. James finally begins speaking at age eight, but his comments could possibly be only in the imagination of the narrator. The boy is wise and prophetic; his visions and counsel support the narrator for much of his life. In a poetic, visionary story, "Imagining the Reservation," an "Indian child," apparently James, figures strongly, counseling the anonymous narrator to "break every mirror in my house and tape the pieces to my body," a marvelous metaphor for the act of becoming a writer who reflects his environment. In "The Approximate Shape of My Favorite Tumor," an adult James Many Horses faces death from cancer with humor and love. James indeed becomes a Christ figure in life and death.

Themes and Meanings

The Lone Ranger and Tonto Fistfight in Heaven deals primarily with the Native American quest for identity. The characters in the stories constantly run up against what it means to be an American and an Indian, with the twentieth century cultural icons of soft drinks, television, and convenience stores played off against the Native American values of family, community, and tradition.

In the story "The Lone Ranger and Tonto Fistfight in Heaven," Victor lives with a white woman in Seattle, and the story chronicles the inevitable failure of the relationship as well as the suspicion he faces and the dislocation he feels in the city. In "Crazy Horse Dreams," the question becomes one of trying to live up to the model of an ideal Indian. Victor's relationship with an unnamed Indian woman fails because she wants the ideal. She is "waiting for Crazy Horse," while Victor finds that he must tread the steeper path of being "just another Indian."

The broader issue of the Native American quest for a cultural identity is also a major theme of these stories. The Indian society portrayed here is caught between two worlds. On one hand, Indians desire the modern America of fancy cars and cable television, even though they realize that this is a world in which they will never feel at home. At the same time, they feel a mixed nostalgia and embarrassment toward the pull of their Native American heritage and the ingrained values and traditions of thousands of years. This double ambivalence stops the characters in their tracks at every turn.

Alexie pulls these complex emotions together in simple symbolic sentences. For example, in "This Is What It Means to Say Phoenix, Arizona," Thomas, the storyteller who annoys the people with his incessant historical or mystical tales and is thus the symbol of traditional culture, gets in a fight with Victor when both are fifteen years old. Alexie writes, "That is, Victor was really drunk and beat Thomas up for no reason at all." Under the influence of the white cultural symbol of alcohol, Victor, the young Indian everyman, attacks the symbol of thousands of years of Native American tradition.

Indeed, alcohol nearly becomes another character throughout the stories. Characters in one story measure their lives by whether events happened before or after they had their first taste of alcohol. Alcoholism is accepted fatalistically: It is simply part of life, an irresistible temptation. In a subtle but powerful scene in "All I Wanted to Do Was Dance," Victor has recently been paid and is standing in front of the beer cooler in a store. A bystander comments that it seems that Victor has been standing there his whole life; another says that he thinks it has been five hundred years. The Native American culture has been corrupted with money and alcohol since the arrival of the first Europeans, almost exactly five hundred years before the writing of the story.

In spite of all of this, Alexie opens the door for rays of hope. At the end of several stories, characters are left wanting, or intending, to change the world. Other stories close with the family together in love, even if drunk or in tears, waiting for the future.

Critical Context

The Lone Ranger and Tonto Fistfight in Heaven is Sherman Alexie's first full-length work of fiction. His previous books, all published between 1991 and 1993, consist of two volumes of poetry and two books of poems mixed with short prose pieces. His conversational style and major themes are common to all of his work, and even some of the characters in *The Lone Ranger and Tonto Fistfight in Heaven* are introduced in earlier books.

Alexie's concern with the issues of contemporary Native Americans—their search for identity in modern America and their often ambivalent feelings about their disappearing traditional culture—places him in the mainstream of Native American fiction at the close of the twentieth century. Though this genre has emerged as a significant literary force only since the 1960's, Indian writers are working with and against a heritage of thousands of years of oral literature. The structure of this traditional literature was quite different from the European tradition into which most modern writers try to fit. The oral Indian tale was generally authorless, passed down through generations from storyteller to storyteller, altered and personalized, but never claimed. The storytellers "cared for" the stories, but never owned them. The stories therefore tended to be mythical and timeless, descriptive of the culture as a whole, as opposed to character studies of individual people. Alexie refers often to this tradition of storytelling, and his work, too, seems to consist of timeless stories of rather generic characters who confront problems, feel pain, and experience joys common to many people, yet are in many ways unique to the situation of Native American culture.

Out of this tradition, then, Sherman Alexie has risen to present his view of life on the modern reservation. His stories show the young Native American man, in conflict with himself and the world in which he finds himself, getting by on love and trust and treading the narrow line between the past and the future.

Bibliography

Alexie, Sherman. Interview by Dennis West and Joan M. West. *Cineaste* 23 (1998): 28-32. Alexie responds to questions about the similarities and differences between his novel *The Lone Ranger and Tonto Fistfight in Heaven* and his movie *Smoke Signals*. His comments on the autobiographical elements of both are particularly interesting.

Egan, Timothy. "An Indian Without Reservations." *New York Times Magazine*, January 18, 1998, 16-19. Profiles Sherman Alexie and his Indian background. Covers Alexie's comedic look into the hardships of being a Native American; his vocal attacks on author Barbara Kingsolver; the making of film versions of his books; and the life on the reservation where he was raised.

Low, Denise. Review of *The Lone Ranger and Tonto Fistfight in Heaven*, by Sherman Alexie. *American Indian Quarterly* 20 (Winter, 1996): 123-125. Low discusses the postmodern characteristics of Alexie's novel, focusing on his use of humor and irony. She praises the book for its deft mingling of popular and Native American cultures.

Price, Reynolds. "One Indian Doesn't Tell Another." *The New York Times Book Review*, October 17, 1993, 15-16. Price, a short-story writer himself, finds moments of monotony and obsessive gloom in some of Alexie's stories. He also expresses disappointment at the spare plots and lack of detail, which others might consider Alexie's mythic voice. Finally, though, he praises the "lyric energy" and "exhilarating vitality" of these stories and looks forward to a more mature, broader vision from the writer.

Schneider, Brian. "The Lone Ranger and Tonto Fistfight in Heaven." *Review of Contemporary Fiction* 13 (Fall, 1993): 237-238. This review focuses on Alexie's use of myths and mythmaking to describe and support the Native American culture. Schneider especially praises Alexie's ability to juxtapose humor and pathos with brutally honest prose.

Velie, Alan R. "World Literature in Review: Other European & American Languages." *World Literature Today* 68 (Spring, 1994): 407. Favorable review of *The*

Lone Ranger and Tonto Fistfight in Heaven. Velie compares Alexie's novel to Louise Erdrich's *Love Medicine*, pointing out the similarities in characterization and the use of humor. Concludes that "Alexie has turned the lives and dreams of the people of his reservation into superb literature."

Joseph W. Hinton

LONESOME DOVE

Author: Larry McMurtry (1936-   )
Type of plot: Western
Time of plot: The late nineteenth century
Locale: The Great Plains of the United States, from South Texas to Montana
First published: 1985

Principal characters:

AUGUSTUS MCCRAE, a former Texas Ranger, the co-owner of the Hat
    Creek Cattle Company in Lonesome Dove, Texas
WOODROW F. CALL, also a former Texas Ranger and co-owner of the
    Hat Creek Cattle Company
JAKE SPOON, a former Texas Ranger and old friend of Augustus and
    Woodrow
LORENA WOOD, the town prostitute of Lonesome Dove
CLARA ALLEN, a housewife, the former lover of Augustus
JOSH DEETS, a black trailhand and longtime friend and companion of
    Augustus, Woodrow, and Jake
NEWT, a teenage trailhand, Woodrow's unacknowledged son
BLUE DUCK, an evil Indian raider

The Novel

Lonesome Dove is the story of a cattle drive from far South Texas through the central Great Plains and hostile Indian country to virgin grazing land in Montana. Along the way, the characters either grow and change or deepen to reveal further elements of themselves.

Part 1 introduces the characters and begins the cattle drive. Augustus McCrae and Woodrow Call are two middle-aged former Texas Rangers who for several years have been operating a cattle ranch headquartered in the town of Lonesome Dove on the Rio Grande River. Lorena Wood, the beautiful town prostitute, works at the Dry Bean saloon; most of the men are in love with her. Lorena herself is fond of Jake Spoon, also a former Texas Ranger and friend of Augustus and Woodrow, who has drifted into a life of grifting and low companions. Jake, who is on the run from Arkansas, where he killed a man accidentally, turns up in Lonesome Dove and renews his relationship with Lorena. Jake proposes to Woodrow that they enlarge the cattle herd and take it to Montana, where there is choice unused grazing land. In fact, Jake wants to stay on the run and be near his former ranger friends so that they will protect him if the law catches up with him. Lorena makes Jake promise that he will take her to San Francisco, and she plans to accompany the herd for part of the way. Woodrow and Augustus also have hidden reasons for going on the drive; Woodrow wants to see and conquer new territory for one more time in his life, and Augustus hopes that he will meet his great love, Clara Allen, along the way.

Woodrow and Augustus increase the number of their herd by raiding a Mexican ranch across the river and rustling the stock of a Mexican bandit who has stolen from them in the past. Among the hands who go on the trail drive are Josh Deets, a black cowboy who rode with Woodrow and Gus in their rangering days; Dish Boggett, who is in love with Lorena; the Irish immigrant O'Brien brothers; Newt, Woodrow's son by a prostitute; and the cowhands Jasper Fants and Pea Eye. The men begin the drive with the ominous knowledge that they have a long way to go and will be beset by dangers both unknown and known (most obviously hostile Indians, including the psychopathic loner Blue Duck).

Part 2 introduces a major subplot. July Johnson, the young sheriff of Fort Smith, Arkansas, knows that the killing Jake committed was accidental; Jake fired his gun in self-defense but missed and hit the victim, July's brother Ben. Ben was the mayor of the town, however, and his wife Peaches forces July to track Jake down. To do so, July must leave his recent bride, Elmira, who has already grown tired of July and is happy to see him leave. July is joined on his trek through Texas following Jake's trail by his middle-aged deputy Roscoe Brown, Joe Boot, who is July's stepson, and a young orphan girl, Janey. While July heads southwest into Texas, Elmira, who is pregnant, leaves Fort Smith and goes northwest in search of her former lover, Dee Boot, who is Joe's father.

As soon as the cattle drive begins, tragedies and disasters overtake the cowboys. While the cattle ford a river, one of the O'Brien brothers rides into a nest of water moccasins and is bitten to death. Hailstorms, rain, and drought alternately plague the herd and its owners. Blue Duck, the Indian Woodrow and Augustus had dreaded they would meet, kidnaps Lorena and takes her away to a gang rape by Indians and comancheros. Augustus rescues Lorena from her captors, and in response, she falls in love with him. July Johnson and his friends also run afoul of Blue Duck, who kills all of them except July.

Jake, ashamed that he has allowed Lorena to be taken, runs away from his friends and begins to ride with a group of outlaws who are not only thieves but murderers. When Woodrow and Augustus catch up with Jake, they have no choice but to hang him with the rest of the criminals, a shocking event that ends part 2.

Part 3 features the end of a number of relationships and the flowering of new ones. Elmira, July, Augustus, and Lorena all wind up in succession at the farm of Clara Allen, which is conveniently located where many trails cross. Elmira has her baby there and then goes to the nearby town where Dee is awaiting hanging. After his death, she heads back across the plains, but she is killed by Indians. July arrives, and Clara, whose husband lies dying after having been kicked in the head by a horse, tries to convince July that Elmira's baby is his and that he should stay on the ranch and help her run it. Augustus and Lorena come to Clara's house, and Clara refuses Augustus's romantic overtures. Augustus leaves Lorena at Clara's for her recuperation.

When Augustus rejoins the herd, the novel moves to its climax. Deets is suddenly and mistakenly killed by an angry Indian. While Augustus and Pea Eye are out exploring, they are attacked by a band of hostile Indians. Augustus is seriously wounded by an arrow in his leg, and he sends Pea Eye back to the herd for help. Augustus makes it to a town, where his leg is amputated, but gangrenc has set in, and he begins to die. Woodrow, whom Pea Eye reaches, is there for the death of his friend, and he promises Augustus that he will return Augustus's body to a spot by a river in Texas where Augustus had a memorable picnic with Clara.

When the herd reaches Montana, Woodrow selects a site for a ranch, and both cattle and men prosper, with Newt gaining more and more responsibility and growing into a man in the process. When spring comes, Woodrow begins to fulfill his pledge to Augustus; before leaving, he gives his beloved horse, the Hell Bitch, to Newt. He also stops at Clara's, where she castigates him for not living up to his responsibilities to Newt. Woodrow also witnesses the demise of Blue Duck, and when he returns to Lonesome Dove after burying Augustus, he finds that the owner of the Dry Bean has burned it down, disconsolate over the loss of Lorena.

The Characters

Augustus McCrae is the dominant and most memorable character in *Lonesome Dove.* An engaging combination of rustic philosopher and confidence man, Augustus displays both humor and an adaptability to any circumstances, including physical danger, that make him likable and trustworthy. Augustus talks more than anyone else in the novel, a point about which his taciturn partner, Woodrow, reminds him frequently, but Augustus is not all blarney; when he rescues Lorena from a gang of desperadoes, he kills several men in a matter of seconds. When Augustus dies, it is as if a pillar supporting the structure of the novel has been removed.

Woodrow Call is similar to Augustus only in his ability to handle any physical trouble. Trouble of the other kind, devils of the mind and relations with other people, paralyze Woodrow. At the end of the novel, it is clear why Woodrow has been so quiet and withdrawn throughout; this behavior is a retreat from involvement and a defense against those who need him. He is friends with his apparent opposite, the affable Augustus, because both share a sense of honor and integrity, as well as many years and miles.

Jake Spoon shows what might happen to a person with the rough frontier skills of Woodrow and the slyness of Augustus but without the sense of principle that defines his former ranger pals. Jake uses Lorena, since he has no plans to take her to San Francisco; furthermore, he abandons her in her hour of greatest need. When Jake falls in with a gang who murder for fun, he knows that he will be blamed for riding with them, but he is too cowardly either to confront them or to break away. This weak behavior leads to his death at the hands of his best friends.

Clara Allen is the pioneer woman par excellence; when her husband falls into a coma, she takes over and runs their ranch more efficiently than he did. She is the only person capable of standing up to both Augustus and Woodrow. She refuses to renew her relationship with Augustus for a classic reason: She admires Augustus for his independence, and a lengthy romance would hurt either her (because Augustus would roam) or him (because his basic personality trait would be smothered). She also chastises Woodrow for his failure to live up to his responsibilities to Newt, and she is successful in making July stay with his son.

Lorena is, like Woodrow, a frozen character. While in Lonesome Dove, she is indifferent to the men who pay her for sex (except for Augustus, whom she finds amusing), behavior that may be an emotional defense. Her desire to go to San Francisco with Jake reveals her dissatisfaction. She does not care much for Jake, but he is a ticket to a more exciting life. Traumatized after her abduction and rape by Blue Duck, she hardly speaks again, but her actions and passionate attachment to Augustus show that she has found what she needed all along—understanding, tenderness, and protection.

Newt slowly emerges from the background characters to become, at the end of the novel, the strongest character. A boy as the drive begins, Newt gains more and more knowledge and ability. When Woodrow savagely beats a soldier who attacked Newt, Augustus tells Newt that Woodrow is the boy's father. Just before Woodrow leaves to take Augustus's body back to Texas, he turns over the operation of the ranch to Newt, and this time Newt is able to handle a physical challenge to his authority by himself. Yet Woodrow's failure to accept Newt as his son leaves Newt bitter.

Themes and Meanings

Hidden behind the stock Western novel device of the epic trail drive are basic themes of the novel, love and death. Several of the characters are either seeking lovers or are haunted by absent lovers. (This motif explains the title; doves mate for life, and a lonesome dove is one that has lost or is searching for its partner.) Elmira thinks that she can find happiness with Dee Boot, and she leaves both husband and baby in a search for a reprobate who will be hanged the day after she is reunited with him. Dish Boggett hangs around Lorena, to whom he is devoted, like a panting puppy. Even the remarkably resourceful and self-contained Augustus rides hundreds of miles to plead his case to Clara. Although Lorena reveres Augustus as a rescuing knight, she fails to understand that Augustus really is a knight: He helps her not because he has designs on her body or soul but because she is in danger, so he saves her as a good knight or Texas Ranger should. Dish Boggett's passion for Lorena is a reminder that emotion alone cannot sustain deep love. Lorena's attitude toward Dish passes from indifference to annoyance to scorn, perhaps because in Boggett she sees a reflection of her own moon-eyed pining over Augustus. Lorena is too weak to inspire more than affection in Augustus. He can only love someone who is as strong and independent as himself—and for that reason, ironically, there can be no permanent relationship between Clara and Augustus, since they are too strong for each other.

Lonesome Dove is also a reminder of mortality. The deaths begin as soon as the drive begins, when the O'Brien brother is bitten by the snakes. Because this character had scarcely been introduced, his death is more shocking than affecting. The deaths continue to come, however, and to characters of more significance; the deaths of Deets and Augustus are almost unbearable. Since the drive itself moves through ever-changing and unpredictable circumstances, the deaths are the final test of the characters' ability to change and adapt. The novel thus is an account of what happens when a group of people whose characters and relationships are fixed are placed in new circumstances and forced to adjust. Malleable and fluid characters such as Augustus thrive; those whose characteristics are set and unchangeable are destroyed or suffer reduction.

Critical Context

Much of Larry McMurtry's work is a continuing examination of life in modern Texas, both rural (as in *The Last Picture Show*, 1971, and *Texasville*, 1987) and urban (as in *All My Friends Are Going to Be Strangers*, 1972, and *Terms of Endearment*, 1975). Much of the remainder, including *Lonesome Dove*, is an attempt to understand the frontier past. Other McMurtry novels set in the nineteenth century include *Anything for Billy* (1988), an account of the life of Billy the Kid, and *Streets of Laredo* (1992), a sequel to *Lonesome Dove*.

The characters Augustus, Woodrow, and Deets are based on the real plainsmen Oliver Loving, Charles Goodnight, and Bose Ikard. Many of the features of the trail drive are suggested by events described in Teddy Blue's *We Pointed Them North* (1939), but McMurtry's novel is an ironic account of these lives and adventures. McMurtry's modern Texas novels are filled with a sense of frustration and dissatisfaction, as if Texas had once been a place where one could find fulfillment but, because of the collapse of frontier values, one no longer can. *Lonesome Dove*, most of the characters of which remain frustrated, suggests that the root of the problem may lie not in historical changes but in the male psyche, since Clara, with her self-reliance and her happiness in her involvement in the lives of those around her, is the most fully developed and fulfilled character.

Bibliography

Busby, Mark and Tom Pilkington. *Larry McMurtry and the West: An Ambivalent Relationship*. Denton, Tex.: University of North Texas Press, 1995. Offers a comprehensive overview of McMurtry's fiction, including a chapter devoted to *Lonesome Dove*. Also includes bibliographical references and an index.

Cawelti, John G. "What Rough Beast—New Westerns?" *ANQ* 9 (Summer, 1996): 4-15. Cawelti addresses the revival of the Western in print, film, and on television. He notes that the new genre reflects the loss of the mythic West of the past and shows how the contemporary Western, instead of glorifying the American spirit, now criticizes America's shortcomings. Offers a brief assessment of *Lonesome Dove* from a mythic point of view.

Mogen, David. "Sex and True West in McMurtry's Fiction: From Teddy Blue to Lonesome Dove to Texasville." *Southwestern American Literature* 14 (1989): 34-45. Traces the sources of *Lonesome Dove*, particularly Teddy Blue's account of an old-time cattle drive. Mogen also relates the book to the rest of McMurtry's work.

Reynolds, Clay, ed. *Taking Stock: A Larry McMurtry Casebook*. Dallas: Southern Methodist University Press, 1989. An exhaustive survey of McMurtry's career up to 1989. Contains a section featuring several essays on *Lonesome Dove*.

Thorburn, David. "Interpretation and Judgment: A Reading of *Lonesome Dove.*" *Critical Studies in Mass Communication* 10 (June, 1993): 113-127. Comparing and contrasting McMurtry's novel and the TV miniseries which was based on it, Thorburn argues that media texts, like literary works, can be critiqued and interpreted according to the criteria of "formal mastery" and "intellectual coherence." He also asserts that critics' reluctance to engage in comparative evaluation of non-canonical works impoverishes scholarship.

Jim Baird

THE LONG DREAM

Author: Richard Wright (1908-1960)
Type of plot: Bildungsroman
Time of plot: The late 1930's and the 1940's
Locale: Mississippi
First published: 1958

> *Principal characters:*
>> REX (FISHBELLY) TUCKER, the central figure of the novel
>> TYREE TUCKER, Fishbelly's father, a prosperous black entrepreneur
>> GLADYS, Fishbelly's mistress
>> DR. BRUCE, a black doctor, co-owner with Tyree Tucker of a dance hall
>> GLORIA, Tyree Tucker's mistress
>> CANTLEY, the white chief of police of a small Southern town

The Novel

The Long Dream is set in Clintonville, a Mississippi town of twenty-five thousand people, ten thousand of them black. The narrative is told from the point of view of Rex Tucker, nicknamed Fishbelly, a name his friends have shortened to Fish. The story begins when Fishbelly is a young child. He is the son of a prosperous black businessman whose undertaking business provides a front for his other enterprises, including ownership of many dilapidated rental properties, a bordello whose prostitutes and customers are black, and coownership with Dr. Bruce, a prosperous black professional, of The Grove, a dance hall frequented by blacks.

As a child, Fishbelly accidentally sees his father in a compromising situation with Gloria, his father's mistress. Fishbelly is intrigued by what he sees. He does not want to look, but he cannot make himself turn away. The event causes the boy to have a highly symbolic dream, which strongly suggests that Fishbelly has a castration complex, a problem that is to figure significantly in his later life.

Fishbelly is relatively protected in his early youth. He knows little of the racial tensions that characterize the Mississippi of his youth. His parents have a comfortable existence, as secure an existence as black people in the Deep South of the mid-1930's could have. Thus, only gradually does the boy become aware of the underlying dangers that face blacks in a racist society.

Fishbelly is first brought face-to-face with these realities when the body of Chris Sims is brought to his father's mortuary. Chris had been caught alone in a room with a white woman, and a mob of enraged white men killed him. As Fishbelly sees Chris's body on the embalming table, he notices that the genitals have been cut from it. He winces and puts his hand to his own genitals.

Richard Wright and other black writers often drive home the point that blacks living in subjection to whites are emasculated by their subjection, but nowhere is the point more poignantly made than in this scene from *The Long Dream*. Fishbelly's castration complex is heightened by this traumatic experience, which brings the boy to his first adult understanding of the society in which he lives and in which he has been brought up.

The incident also leads to another step in Fishbelly's perception of his world, because shortly after it, he is arrested for the quite innocuous crime of trespassing on a white person's property. While he is being held, the police threaten his genitals with a knife, and Fishbelly is so completely panicked by this threat that he passes out.

Tyree Tucker comes to the police station and grovels before the white policemen in order to have his son released. Fishbelly loathes his father's subservient attitude to these ignorant, unfair captors. He loathes even more his own terror in this threatening situation. Through this episode, Fishbelly gains a new awareness of what his father is, and this awareness does not lead to his having increased respect for him.

Despite his unfortunate brush with the white authorities, Fishbelly loves the white world because it represents to him a world in which people can progress according to their abilities, a luxury that he believes is not available to American blacks.

The next crucial event in Fishbelly's coming of age occurs when The Grove, the dance hall his father and Dr. Bruce own, burns down. Forty-two people die in the fire, among them Fishbelly's mistress, Gladys. This event, based on an actual dance hall fire at the Rhythm Club in Natchez, Mississippi, leads to a revelation of far-reaching consequences for Fishbelly.

It is revealed that through the years, Tyree and Dr. Bruce have been paying regular monthly bribes to Chief of Police Cantley so that he will overlook fire-code violations at the Grove. They have paid the bribes by check, and Tyree has had his mistress, Gloria, hold the canceled checks so that he might use them against Chief Cantley should the need ever arise.

Chief Cantley has also been Tyree's partner in the bordello that Tyree owns, so he is deeply involved in illicit activities that Tyree can document. Tyree decides that he must make public the bribes Cantley has been taking, and he turns the canceled checks over to a white reformer, who decides that he must deliver them to a grand jury. Cantley, however, has the checks snatched as they are on their way to the grand jury, and Tyree now fears that Cantley will take from him everything he has worked his whole lifetime to acquire.

Cantley, however, wants more than Tyree's money. Knowing that he can never have peace of mind while Tyree is alive, he sets up an ambush, and Tyree is killed. As he lies mortally wounded, Tyree expresses his relief that at least his holdings have not been taken from him.

Fishbelly inherits his father's property and has the financial means to leave Clintonville if he so desires. He finds that he cannot bring himself to leave behind the thriving enterprises that his father has developed over many years, however, and he decides to replace his father as head of these businesses. Fishbelly was never one to admire his father's business tactics or his subservience in dealing with whites, but now he is willing to become like his father, a role that will necessitate resorting to Tyree's exploitative and hypocritical tactics.

Fishbelly, however, is not destined to serve as his father's replacement. In the novel's final section, "Waking Dreams," he comes into possession of some of the incriminating canceled checks that Gloria had been holding. Gloria and Dr. Bruce flee to Memphis, and Chief Cantley, fearing that Fishbelly has evidence that could incriminate him, trumps up a rape charge against Fishbelly, who serves more than two years in prison.

Upon his release, Fishbelly leaves not only the South but also the United States. He goes to Paris to join his childhood friends, Tony and Zeke, who are there serving in the American military. Wright leaves his readers with the message that salvation for the American black does not lie in leaving the South and going to the North but rather that the black's only realistic solution is to leave the country altogether.

The Characters

Most of the characters in *The Long Dream* are overshadowed by Fishbelly and his father, Tyree Tucker. Fishbelly's story, like that of most protagonists in a *Bildungsroman* or in an *Entwicklungsroman*, concerns loss of innocence. A black child from a prosperous family in a small town in the Deep South, however, endures more than a typical child does in coming of age. Fishbelly has the identity crises and the sexual adventures of any adolescent, but superimposed upon them is his coming to realize what it means to be a second-class citizen, a person who enjoys neither the opportunities nor the basic protections afforded white citizens.

Fishbelly's illusions are chipped away steadily as he comes to realize that white human beings are capable of castrating and murdering black human beings and that their society will protect them from retribution for having committed such acts. Even after Fishbelly sees Chris Sims's mutilated corpse in his father's embalming room, the boy has some illusions left. His father, after all, is a prosperous and successful businessman. He presumably has some standing in his own community.

Fishbelly comes to see Tyree's real standing in the community, however, when his rather humiliates himself in order to reclaim the boy after his arrest. Simultaneously, Fishbelly realizes how the terror of physical mutilation, of castration, has turned him into a coward. In this scene, Fishbelly begins to see himself as a person who will eventually be forced into being the subservient black that his father of necessity has become.

Finally, Fishbelly is totally co-opted when he decides to replace his father after his murder. Fishbelly and all the blacks with whom he associates have been forced by the dominant society to hate themselves. The only way that they can feel any sense of human superiority is by demeaning someone inferior to them, and early in the book, they find this person. Angie West is an effeminate black boy whom Fishbelly and his buddies, Tony and Zeke, humiliate. This humiliation is a foreshadowing of the kind of humiliation that Tyree perpetrates upon his black tenants, his whores, and his customers in the various enterprises that are making him rich.

As interesting as Fishbelly is, Tyree is even more complex. In Tyree, one sees a man who has been so corrupted by the system, which he has in his own way joined, that he has lost every shred of dignity and self-respect. He has sold out to such an extent that he prefers death to losing his material possessions. His spiritual emasculation is total, and for Wright, Tyree is the symbol of every black man who benefits from cooperating with and supporting a racist society. Tyree has bought the American Dream, but this dream, Wright seems to be saying, is for blacks the most terrifying nightmare imaginable, because they can achieve their dream only by allowing themselves to be totally demeaned and only by demeaning other members of their race who are less affluent than they.

Themes and Meanings

In *The Long Dream*, Wright repeats the themes and employs the metaphors of several of his earlier works. He uses the castration metaphor continually to emphasize the emasculation of an entire race of American citizens held in subjugation by the people in whose hands power resides. He is concerned with the questions of manhood and the loss of manhood both by individuals and by a race of people. In his development of Fishbelly, Wright builds on the castration metaphor to the point that it becomes the controlling image of the novel.

Akin to the theme of emasculation is the theme of self-hatred. Wright demonstrates this theme in many ways: Early in the book, for example, when the young Fishbelly and his friends attend a fair on "Colored Folks' Day," they throw balls at a "nigger head," a grotesque face that in essence is their own.

The Long Dream was the first volume of a projected trilogy, but only it and five episodes from the second volume were ever written, so it is impossible to know precisely what Wright would have done with the themes that figured so prominently in this work. The long dream to which the title refers alludes to Fishbelly's childhood sexual dream early in the book, but it alludes more broadly to the nightmare faced by black people in the United States.

Critical Context

The Long Dream was Wright's fifth novel and was preceded by his enduringly popular *Native Son* (1940) and *Black Boy* (1945). Wright wrote *The Long Dream* when he was a decade into his exile in France, and he was somewhat out of touch with his sources at that time. His growing remoteness from his American roots is evident in the book's language, particularly the slang, which is somewhat dated, reflecting usages of the middle and late 1940's rather than those of the late 1950's.

The Long Dream is angry, born of incredible personal pain, as many of the books of the protest movement of the 1960's were to be, but for the most part Wright allows the events of the novel to speak for themselves, rather than using fiction as a forum for polemics. Wright's work anticipates some of the black fury that was represented in the protest literature of the 1960's: Works such as *The Autobiography of Malcolm X* (1965), James Baldwin's *Notes of a Native Son* (1955), and the LeRoi Jones (Amiri Baraka) plays *Dutchman* (1964), *The Slave* (1964), and *The Toilet* (1964) owe much to the spirit of social protest that Wright exemplifies.

Bibliography
Baldwin, James. *The Price of the Ticket: Collected Nonfiction, 1948-1985.* New York: St. Martin's Press/Marek, 1985. The essays "Everybody's Protest Novel" and "Alas, Poor Richard" provide important and provocative insights into Wright and his art.
Bloom, Harold, ed. *Richard Wright.* New York: Chelsea House, 1987. Essays on various aspects of Wright's work and career, with an introduction by Bloom.
Fabre, Michel. *The Unfinished Quest of Richard Wright.* Translated by Isabel Barzun. New York: William Morrow, 1973. The most important and authoritative biography of Wright available.
_____. *The World of Richard Wright.* Jackson: University Press of Mississippi, 1985. A collection of Fabre's essays on Wright. A valuable but not sustained full-length study.
Hakutani, Yoshinobu. *Richard Wright and Racial Discourse.* Columbia: University of Missouri Press, 1996. Chapters on *Lawd Today, Uncle Tom's Children, Native Son, The Outsider,* and *Black Boy,* as well as discussions of later fiction, black power, and Wright's handling of sexuality. Includes introduction and bibliography.
Kinnamon, Keneth, ed. *Critical Essays on Richard Wright's "Native Son."* New York: Twayne, 1997. Divided into sections of reviews, reprinted essays, and new essays. Includes discussions of Wright's handling of race, voice, tone, novelistic structure, the city, and literary influences. Index but no bibliography.
_____. *The Emergence of Richard Wright.* Urbana: University of Illinois Press, 1972. A study of Wright's background and development as a writer, up to the publication of *Native Son* (1940).
Walker, Margaret. *Richard Wright: Daemonic Genius.* New York: Warner Books, 1988. A critically acclaimed study of Wright's life and work written by a respected novelist.
Webb, Constance. *Richard Wright: A Biography.* New York: Putnam, 1968. A well-written biography which remains useful.

R. Baird Shuman

THE LONG GOODBYE

Author: Raymond Chandler (1888-1959)
Type of plot: Hard-boiled detective
Time of plot: The early 1950's
Locale: Los Angeles and its suburbs
First published: 1953

> *Principal characters:*
> PHILIP MARLOWE, the narrator and protagonist, a Los Angeles private
>   investigator
> TERRY LENNOX, a war hero and a drifter
> SYLVIA LENNOX, Terry's wealthy wife
> ROGER WADE, a successful author of historical novels and an alcoholic
> HARLAN POTTER, a multimillionaire newspaper publisher, the father of
>   Sylvia Lennox and Linda Loring
> LINDA LORING, a doctor's wife, eventually Marlowe's lover
> EILEEN WADE, the wife of Roger Wade
> BERNIE OHLS, a sheriff's deputy

The Novel

Private investigator Philip Marlowe has casually befriended Terry Lennox, a "man it is impossible to dislike," and when Lennox comes to him in trouble, Marlowe takes him across the border to Tijuana. The same night, Lennox's wife, Sylvia, is found brutally murdered, and Marlowe is arrested for refusing to talk about his connection with Lennox. He is released from jail when Lennox's death in a small Mexican town is reported and the police receive his written confession. The police, the lawyer of Sylvia's father, Harlan Potter, Sylvia's sister Linda Loring, and Harlan Potter himself, as well as a gangster friend of Lennox, all warn Marlowe to leave the case alone since he is still vulnerable to a charge of being an accessory after the fact of murder, and for a time he seems to do so.

Marlowe is then hired by Eileen Wade to find her husband and bring him home from a seedy, illegal clinic for wealthy alcoholics. Roger Wade, despite his success as a writer of historical novels and his marriage to a beautiful woman, has lately become a periodic drunk, reportedly given to violent outbursts. Marlowe finds him and, after a violent encounter with the owner of the clinic and his unbalanced assistant, rescues Wade and returns him to his wife. Eileen Wade tries again, as she has previously, to hire Marlowe to stay in the house and watch over her husband to prevent him from drinking and becoming violent or wandering off. Wade himself, revealing to Marlowe that he is troubled by an event that he does not consciously recall, urges him to stay, but Marlowe refuses.

Marlowe is nevertheless present in the Wade house when Roger Wade, after an afternoon of drinking, is found shot in circumstances which point strongly to suicide. It has been revealed that he had been one of Sylvia Lennox's many lovers, and after his death Marlowe and others at first believe that he was also her murderer; it has become more and more unlikely that Terry Lennox was the real killer.

Sheriff's deputy Bernie Ohls, who has investigated Wade's death, is dissatisfied with the official verdict of suicide, and points out to Marlowe the suspicious circumstances which suggest that Eileen Wade was her husband's killer. Reluctant at first to believe Ohls, Marlowe nevertheless undertakes an investigation. With Wade's publisher, he confronts Eileen Wade with the evidence that he has uncovered, that she and Terry Lennox were married in England, early in World War II. She assumed that he was dead after he was captured on a Commando mission in Norway, and she did not realize that he was alive until years later, when she saw him accidentally after Lennox had married Sylvia. She eventually breaks down and acknowledges the truth of Marlowe's accusation that she murdered Sylvia Lennox, whom she regarded as a slut who had taken both of her men away, and that she also killed Roger Wade, thinking that his suicide would be taken as a tacit confession of guilt in Sylvia's murder. She has also come to hate her husband for having been one of Sylvia Lennox's lovers.

After Marlowe and the publisher leave, Eileen Wade commits suicide with Demerol, having written a full confession. The district attorney tries to suppress the confession, but Ohls and his superior in the sheriff's office arrange for Marlowe to take a copy, which he then gives to an independent newspaper, chiefly to clear Terry Lennox's name. In the end, Lennox reappears, having taken a new name and identity; his suicide had been faked, with the help of his gangster friends and perhaps of Harlan Potter. Marlowe no longer regards him as a friend.

The Characters

Philip Marlowe is at the center of the action, as he is in all seven of Chandler's detective novels. He conforms to Chandler's dictum, in the essay "The Simple Art of Murder," that a fictional private eye should be a kind of knight amid the grim decay of the modern city, a conscientious man who tries to right the wrongs of society. In *The Long Goodbye*, Marlowe and the world through which he moves are less tough and gritty than in the earlier Chandler novels. Marlowe makes several sentimental gestures when he thinks that Terry Lennox is dead; he pursues his investigations only because of his interest in Lennox; he never has a paying client; and he moves with ease in a more affluent social world than that of the earlier novels.

Among the other characters, Terry Lennox and Eileen Wade are the most interesting. Lennox has irresistible charm, and once in his life has performed an instinctive, heroic action, earning the gratitude of two powerful gangsters whose lives he saved. He is, however, without any moral sense, and it is this lack that leads to his decay, his connivance in the phony suicide, and Marlowe's eventual rejection of him. Eileen Wade is a woman of "paralyzing" beauty who cannot accept the loss of her youthful romantic marriage. Until confronted with Marlowe's evidence, she believes that her murders are justified and that her beauty and power over men will enable her to escape the consequences of her actions.

The other characters are vividly delineated. Linda Loring's physician husband is a jealous man, a snob overconfidently sure of his social and professional position. Harlan Potter is suitably austere and tough. Marlowe's policeman friend, Bernie Ohls, engages in angry exchanges with Marlowe, disagrees with him about the nature of crime, and cynically uses him to trap one of Lennox's gangster friends. The minor policemen, gangsters, and petty crooks are stock types, but each has identifying characteristics.

Themes and Meanings

As in all of Chandler's novels, the overriding theme of *The Long Goodbye* is the corruption of society, and the lengths to which people, especially the rich, will go to preserve the appearance of virtue. Harlan Potter, who appears only briefly, is the key figure in this regard. An imposingly wealthy man, he will use his intermediaries to go to any lengths to maintain his privacy and to keep the taint of negative publicity from touching him or his family. People may be killed, lives destroyed, public officials corrupted, as long as Potter's privacy is maintained. The homes of the rich—isolated, carefully guarded, too large for human comfort—are an important symbol of this aspect of the novel.

At the same time, this novel is explicit in stating that corruption and crime are an inevitable product of the American ethos. In an extended dialogue, Bernie Ohls tells Marlowe that he hates gambling of any kind because it is one of the ways in which money and power go to organized crime and therefore contributes to corruption. Marlowe responds that "Crime isn't a disease, it's a symptom." He goes on to say that police fail to understand their society: "We're a big rough rich wild people and crime is the price we pay for it, and organized crime is the price we pay for organization. We'll have it with us a long time. Organized crime is just the dirty side of the sharp dollar." Marlowe seems to see his role as the preservation of more humane values; his dogged pursuit of the truth is valuable for its own sake, but he is not under any illusion that it will change society.

Critical Context

Along with Dashiell Hammett, Raymond Chandler is credited with having originated the hard-boiled private-detective novel. Chandler located his novels in Los Angeles, not only because he lived there but also because it seemed to embody the worst traits of the emerging American society of the 1940's and 1950's; Hammett's novels are, for the most part, located in San Francisco and its vicinity, while the authors' most important disciple, Ross MacDonald, placed Lew Archer's adventures in Chandler's Southern California territory. Today, hard-boiled private-eye novels are written about Seattle, Boston, Indianapolis, Miami, and virtually every other real or fictional city in the country.

These novels are a distinct departure from the traditional detective story, since their interest lies not in solving a puzzle but in the adventures of the protagonist and in what they reveal about the brutality and evil of the society in which they are placed. *The*

Long Goodbye is typical in this respect. The clues which the reader would need to solve the mystery are not presented until Marlowe's confrontation with Eileen Wade; while her actions are sometimes irrational or suspicious, there are only a few hints that might link her to Terry Lennox before the final revelations. Marlowe does not reveal even a suspicion that her motive for trying to employ him in the first place might be related to some connection between her and Lennox.

This is the sixth of the seven Philip Marlowe novels, and, as noted above, it differs in some respects from the earlier books. The action of *The Long Goodbye* takes place almost entirely in the homes and haunts of the rich, with little of the contrast between those locales and the seamier side of Los Angeles life which characterized the five previous novels. Marlowe has even moved from his grimy urban apartments to a small but pleasant house on a hillside. At the same time, perhaps sensitive to critical observations that Marlowe's celibacy was suspect, Chandler has given him a sex life. He escapes seduction by Eileen Wade only by accident, and at the end he spends a night with Linda Loring. Finally, Marlowe's streak of sentimentality is more pronounced in this novel. With the exception of Hammett's Sam Spade and the Continental Op, fictional private eyes are universally sentimental about small animals, children, and society's victims, but Marlowe's actions in *The Long Goodbye* are motivated entirely by an unabashed sentimentality.

In this longest of Chandler's novels, much space is given to Marlowe's explanations—to the reader and to the other characters—defending his actions as protector of the helpless. The action and much of the dialogue are presented in the clipped, spare style typical of this kind of novel, but Marlowe's thoughts and some of his exchanges with other characters are more wordy. Yet if this novel is in some ways the talkiest of the Philip Marlowe novels, it is also the richest in its depth of characterization and the most detailed in its examination of the means used by the rich and powerful to protect themselves from reality.

Bibliography
Babener, Liahna K. "Raymond Chandler's City of Lies." In *Los Angeles in Fiction*, edited by David Fine. Albuquerque: University of New Mexico Press, 1984. The chapter on Chandler is a study of the image patterns in his novels. The volume as a whole is an interesting discussion of the importance of a sense of place, especially one as mythologically rich as Los Angeles. Includes notes.
Hamilton, Cynthia S. "Raymond Chandler." In *Western and Hard-Boiled Detective Fiction: From High Noon to Midnight*. Iowa City: University of Iowa Press, 1987. This study provides unusual insight into Chandler's detective fiction from the historical and generic perspective of the American Western novel. Includes three chapters on the study of formula literature, a bibliography, and an index.
Hiney, Tom. *Raymond Chandler: A Biography*. New York: Atlantic Monthly Press, 1997. Supplements but does not supersede Frank MacShane's biography. Hiney makes good use of memoirs, critical studies, and new archival material documenting Chandler's life and career.

Jameson, F. R. "On Raymond Chandler." In *The Poetics of Murder: Detective Fiction and Literary Theory*, edited by Glenn W. Most and William W. Stowe. San Diego: Harcourt Brace Jovanovich, 1983. Starts with the observation that Chandler's English upbringing in essence gave him an outsider's view of American life and language. A useful discussion of the portrait of American society that emerges from Chandler's works.

Knight, Stephen. "A Hard Cheerfulness: An Introduction to Raymond Chandler." In *American Crime Fiction: Studies in the Genre*, edited by Brian Docherty. New York: St. Martin's Press, 1988. A discussion of the values and attitudes which define Chandler's Philip Marlowe and which make him unusual in the genre of hard-boiled American crime fiction.

Lehman, David. "Hammett and Chandler." In *The Perfect Murder: A Study in Detection*. New York: Free Press, 1989. Chandler is represented in this comprehensive study of detective fiction as one of the authors who brought out the parable at the heart of mystery fiction. A useful volume in its breadth and its unusual appendices: one a list of further reading, the other, an annotated list of the critic's favorite mysteries. Includes two indexes, one of concepts and one of names and titles.

Skinner, Robert E. *The Hard-Boiled Explicator: A Guide to the Study of Dashiell Hammett, Raymond Chandler, and Ross Macdonald*. Metuchen, N.J.: Scarecrow Press, 1985. An indispensable volume for the scholar interested in tracking down unpublished dissertations as well as mainstream criticism. Brief introductions of each author are followed by annotated bibliographies of books, articles, and reviews.

John M. Muste

LOOKOUT CARTRIDGE

Author: Joseph McElroy (1930-   )
Type of plot: Epistemological intrigue
Time of plot: 1971, with occasional flashbacks
Locale: London, Corsica, Stonehenge, the Hebrides, and New York City
First published: 1974

> *Principal characters:*
>> CARTWRIGHT, the narrator and protagonist, a man of many occupations who is engaged in seeking out those who have destroyed his experimental film
>> DAGGAR DIGORRO, along with Cartwright (who serves as sound man), the maker of the lost film
>> INCREMONA, apparently a hit man for organized crime who may be the ringleader of a large political conspiracy involving Cartwright and the production of his film
>> JENNY, Cartwright's daughter, who may be dangerously and unwittingly implicated in Incremona's conspiracy
>> SUB, Cartwright's childhood friend and the representative of all the novel's innocent bystanders
>> LORNA, Cartwright's wife
>> MONTY GRAF, a crooked businessman who is interested in Cartwright's film
>> CLAIRE, Jenny's double and secretary to Phil Aut, the president of Outer Film
>> TESSA ALLOT, Cartwright's former lover
>> PAUL,
>> JACK, and
>> GENE, the Flint brothers, who are vitally interested in Cartwright's film and involved in Incremona's conspiracy

The Novel

   Lookout Cartridge begins on Halloween, 1971, with Cartwright's description of a ride in a damaged helicopter above New York City, where he observes below the sudden flash of an explosion. From these mysterious beginnings, Cartwright's story of his experiences in the previous months as he searches for those who have destroyed his film unfolds. Through flashbacks and montage (indeed, *Lookout Cartridge* might be "read" as a film), Cartwright recounts the making of the film with his coauthor, Daggar DiGorro, speculates on the reasons for its destruction, and describes the labyrinthine entanglements of plots and personalities which have led him to the discovery of, possibly, an international political conspiracy that endangers his own life and that of his daughter. McElroy's novel contains dozens of characters, scenes, and stories which seem to have been "cut together" by the narrator in a frustrating search for the logic and order behind seemingly unconnected appearances and events. Cartwright might be seen as a contemporary detective, except that his quest for the solution to the mystery is thwarted by the nature of the clues themselves, which are so multiple and ambiguous as to defy interpretation. As Thomas LeClair has suggested, *Lookout Cartridge* is a novel of excess. Readers of the novel (like the protagonist) are exposed to such a barrage of unassimilated information (one learns, for example, about the Mayan calendar, the origins of Stonehenge, Frederick Catherwood's explorations in Central America, Isambard Kingdom Brunel's engineering feats, the structure of liquid crystals) that they are hard-pressed to discover the nature of the mystery, much less what its solutions might be. More than simply a parody of the detective novel, *Lookout Cartridge* questions the value and purpose of knowledge in a technological universe overexposed to information.

Understanding the mystery behind *Lookout Cartridge* might well involve understanding the Daggar-Cartwright film, purportedly an avant-garde attempt to capture "English life" from an American point of view. Daggar insists on envisioning the film as a series of *mises en scène*: a softball game involving American expatriates in an English park, a meeting of druids at Stonehenge, the activities of inhabitants and visitors at a circular English country house, a conversation between an American draft-dodger and his friend in a room stripped bare of furnishings, the doings of vacationers on Corsica. As Cartwright recounts the filming of each sequence, he realizes that Daggar has managed the casting and production in such a way that the same characters appear in widely scattered shots, seemingly meeting for some dark purpose or to exchange secret messages. Cartwright begins to suspect that Daggar is using the film as a pretext for his complicity in some revolutionary plot which may involve anything from the hiding of American war resisters to a terrorist explosion that may kill a room full of singing children.

The political causes and effects of this dimly perceived conspiracy are never made clear, but, in his attempt to find out why the film has been destroyed, Cartwright crisscrosses the Atlantic and encounters numerous characters who, in the end, all seem to bear a relation to one another in terms of the conspiracy. Even Cartwright's daughter Jenny may be implicated in the plot and, for unknown reasons, threatened by it (her double, Claire, is mistakenly and brutally killed by parties looking for Jenny), though whether she is an agent or a victim of the plot is unclear. It is clear that Cartwright's friend Daggar has betrayed his fellow filmmaker by involving him in whatever secret activities are at hand to the extent that Cartwright is hounded and physically threatened by those who want his diary, a verbal transcription of what Daggar has filmed, containing information harmful to those who are supposedly controlling these events. Even Cartwright's own wife and his friend and former lover, Tessa, may somehow be part of the mosaic of conspiracy. Other characters also become mysteriously involved: Who are the Flint brothers (bearing resemblances to the Marx Brothers and the brothers Kennedy) and what is their interest in the film? Why should a hustler such as Monty Graf have any interest in an obscure experimental film? At times, like a paranoid, Cartwright believes that everything is connected, but the flow of information in McElroy's novel is so vast and dispersed that any single solution to "the mystery" is undermined. Almost by accident, at the novel's end, Cartwright kills the mysterious Incremona, who haunts the novel as the brains behind the plot; yet the meaning of this tragicomic action (Cartwright and Sub drop a television from Sub's flat onto a passing taxicab, which proceeds to run over Incremona) is never made clear. Cartwright's last words reveal the obscurity that shadows the novel's conclusion: "Everyone was looking up at me and Sub, and I was not sure what I had seen but I knew what we had done." Similarly, the actuality of the novel's fragmented events is apparent, though their purposes are ever-hidden.

The Characters

Depending upon one's view, there may be dozens of characters in *Lookout Cartridge* or only one, that represented by the voice of Cartwright. As the purposes behind events are ambiguous, so are the motives usually associated with the activities and personalities of traditionally defined characters. Why, for example, should so many people be interested in a cheaply made, seemingly disorganized film shot by two completely unknown amateur filmmakers? Characters in *Lookout Cartridge* bear names (sometimes, confusingly, two characters share the same name) and engage in activities but never emerge from the matrix of plot and cross-purpose to become Forsterian "rounded characters." Cartwright himself often questions his own status as an actor in an unseen plot or a discrete self in an overcomplicated world; at times, he compares his being to a crystal in an LED display, a stray signal in a noisy system of communication, or a "lookout cartridge"—a device which merely records, rather than sorts out, whatever information is fed into it.

It is precisely what he decides his function to be within a novel which is an assemblage of scattered facts and actions that defines Cartwright's "character" and his position as protagonist. Like the familiar hero of an Alfred Hitchcock film, the innocent "who knows too much," dragged into a mystery not of his making and beyond his powers of comprehension, Cartwright is often simply the victim of a world that has gone out of control, as he vainly attempts to organize and make logical that which is impossibly contradictory, disconnected, and irrational. Yet there are times when he believes that his privileged position in the plot as uninformed witness confers upon him a special kind of power:

> And at this instant, hearing Sub come out of the kitchen and stand on the threshold of the littered living room and not speak, I found that though my power to prove my feeling about computers—about miles of memory, or abstract numbers switched out of the blue into the real angular turns of a machine or the actual relation of two electric currents—stirred inchoate though contained inside a circle of broken connections that could get long or short or acquire right angles and stern diagonals while being still this circle of known emotions and words and people, my power to turn that inchoate into a statement was, as if half unwilled, finding itself in the new movements after the ruin of the film that my pulses from moment to moment were deciding to make.

The power that Cartwright believes he has is that of the detective in McElroy's epistemological wonderland: As recorder of all the novel's scattered information, he has the opportunity to understand, in new and creative (if partial) ways, the connection between "emotions and words and people"—though these ways will defy the logic and expectations that usually inform the detective novel or the novel of character.

Themes and Meanings

It is exactly the "ways of knowing" that formulate the subject of *Lookout Cartridge*. McElroy's novel is filled with references to information theory, computers, and film production—all of them the results of modern technology, and all requiring new languages while conferring upon society new modes of perception in order to understand what they do. McElroy is interested in redefining the nature of meaning in the novel, and in portraying a world which has already reached the point of achieving an overabundance of information while possessing scarce means of assimilating it into knowledge. In a universe populated by such "advances in knowledge" as Einsteinian physics, the Heisenberg principle of indeterminacy, and the structure of the liquid crystal (which Cartwright describes as "organic chemicals having the uniform molecular patterns of crystal systems, yet in the way they flow to conform to their containers they seem not solids but liquids"), the modes of perceiving reality—indeed, reality itself—have been radically altered so that old ways of perception, seeing something as either a solid or a liquid, a wave or a particle, will no longer work.

One metaphor which the author uses to make this point is that of the film montage, which is paralleled by the "montage" of Cartwright's scattered, partially destroyed diary. Montage works by association, rather than by syllogistic logic; it breaks up chronology through the use of flashback and flash-forward; it may exist as a series of disconnected sequences, as if someone had made a film from the leftovers on the cutting room floor; it may make use of such devices as the split screen or the jump cut, which force the observer to regard two projections at once, or instantly to assimilate disparate phenomena. In the same way, *Lookout Cartridge* forces the hero and the reader to partake of its information in such ways that the traditional devices of the novel—plot, scene, chronology, and character—are transformed. These are either sundered or made new as the reader (like Cartwright) is forced to assemble the pieces of the novel's puzzle by reading analogically, rather than logically, by accepting fragmentation and excess, rather than form and substance, as the significant gifts which the novel confers upon its readers.

In reading the novel, one is compelled to accept the idea that there may be many partially entangled plots and mysteries here with multiple solutions—or no mystery at all, merely one's need to make sense out of an overload of information. McElroy wishes to suggest that such is the nature of human mental activity in a technocratic society. By situating much of this novel, as well as several of his other novels, in the urban environment of New York City, McElroy portrays the plight of the contemporary self, which defines itself in terms of the ways in which it processes information or negotiates the complexities of the city-labyrinth. McElroy's heroes thus experience the sense of alienation and lost community represented in *Lookout Cartridge* by the loosening of Cartwright's family ties and the ironic nostalgia for the kinds of scientific-religious communities that might have created a Stonehenge. On the other hand, Cartwright is clearly part of a larger international community which, for better or worse, is that of the global village in contemporary technocratic society.

Critical Context

Without exaggeration, it is fair to say that Joseph McElroy has been one of the most ignored of major contemporary American novelists. While his novels have been generally well reviewed, he has not acquired a large reading public despite the range and intelligence of his work. This is partially attributable to the difficulty of his writing: His novels make considerable demands on the reader's knowledge and purposefully fracture traditional expectations regarding plot, sense, and meaning. In his first novel, *A Smuggler's Bible* (1966), McElroy portrayed a protagonist in the process of revising the eight sections of his memoirs; hence, the novel is replete with "unedited" and unassimilated materials which the reader must assemble in order to understand the patterns of David Brooke's life. In *Hind's Kidnap: A Pastoral on Familiar Airs* (1969), as in *Lookout Cartridge*, a detective-protagonist enters a complicated verbal universe and attempts, like a lexicographer, to sort out its etymologies and allusions in order to understand its significances. In the "science fiction" novel *Plus* (1977), McElroy created the image of a human brain floating in space, self-supporting, becoming conscious of itself, its past, and the earth. Each of these novels, like McElroy's others, is an experiment in form as well as an encyclopedic incursion into the languages of information and technology; each, in its way, attempts to represent processes of perception and knowledge as they unfold in the present and future. Like Thomas Pynchon in *Gravity's Rainbow* (1973), William Gaddis in *JR* (1975), or John Barth in *Letters* (1979), McElroy is concerned with how communication operates in contemporary America, and in what ways the contemporary novel is a form of communication. While his work has not been as widely recognized as the work of these others, McElroy has continued, perhaps in ways more boldly experimental than their approaches, to probe the limitations of our capacity to understand the world we have made.

Bibliography

Buckeye, Robert. "*Lookout Cartridge*: Plans, Maps, Programs, Designs, Outlines." *The Review of Contemporary Fiction* 10 (Spring, 1990): 119-126.

Campbell, Gregor. "Processing *Lookout Cartridge*." *The Review of Contemporary Fiction* 10 (Spring, 1990): 112-118.

Hantke, Steffen. "God Save Us from Bourgeois Adventure: The Figure of the Terrorist in Contemporary Fiction." *Studies in the Novel* 28 (Summer, 1996): 219-243. An analysis of terrorists as portrayed in McElroy's *Lookout Cartridge* and Don DeLillo's *Players* and *Mao II*. Hantke notes that the image of the terrorist in the novel since World War II has shifted from Communist conspirator to religious fanatic, and the traits of the terrorist are not as monolithic as when Communism reigned.

Johnston, John. "'The Dimensionless Space Between': Narrative Immanence in Joseph McElroy's *Lookout Cartridge*." *The Review of Contemporary Fiction* 10 (Spring, 1990): 95-111. A discussion of the narrative technique in the novel.

O'Donnell, Patrick. "Engendering Paranoia in Contemporary Narrative." *Boundary 2* 19 (Spring, 1992): 181-204. Examines a number of novels since the 1960s including *Lookout Cartridge* which share the common theme of paranoia.

Siemion, Piotr. "Chasing the Cartridge: On Translating McElroy." *The Review of Contemporary Fiction* 10 (Spring, 1990): 133-139.

Stonehill, Brian. "Intimations of Human Divinity in Joseph McElroy's *Lookout Cartridge*." *The Review of Contemporary Fiction* 10 (Spring, 1990): 127-132.

Patrick O'Donnell

LOON LAKE

Author: E. L. Doctorow (1931-   )
Type of plot: Bildungsroman
Time of plot: The 1930's
Locale: New York and Indiana
First published: 1980

> *Principal characters:*
>> JOSEPH KORZENIOWSKI, the protagonist, a young man from Paterson, New Jersey
>> WARREN PENFIELD, a poet at Loon Lake, Joe's surrogate father
>> F. W. BENNETT, a wealthy industrialist with an estate at Loon Lake
>> LUCINDA BENNETT, a famous aviatrix and wife of Bennett
>> CLARA ZUKACS, the girlfriend of gangster Tommy Crapo, Bennett and Joe's romantic object
>> RED JAMES, an undercover agent in an automobile assembly plant
>> SANDY JAMES, Red's wife
>> SIM HEARNE, a carnival owner
>> FANNY, the fat woman in the carnival, who is exploited by Sim

The Novel

In many ways, E. L. Doctorow's *Loon Lake* is a *Bildungsroman*, a book about a young person's adventures in moving from childhood to adulthood. After his 1918 birth in Paterson, New Jersey, the protagonist, Joseph Korzeniowski, becomes a young hoodlum alienated from his parents. He moves to New York City, where he becomes a grocery boy, but after hearing about idyllic life in California he hops on a freight train with other impoverished youths and heads west. He does not go far before he leaps from the train and finds employment at a broken-down carnival that features freaks. At the end of the summer, he discovers that Sim Hearne, the carnival's owner, allows paying customers to gang rape Fanny, the fat woman, before she dies. Joe leaves the carnival with Hearne's wife and a bankroll, but he throws the money away, leaves Hearne's wife, and begins a long trek through the upstate New York woods.

As he walks through the woods, he sees a naked woman in a private railroad car. He follows the railroad tracks to the lavish Loon Lake estate of F. W. Bennett and is attacked by a pack of wild dogs. Although he escapes, he is seriously mauled. He recovers at Bennett's estate, where he presumptuously signs the guest book as "Joe of Paterson," the first of many identity passages in the novel. While an employee of Bennett, he meets Warren Penfield, a poet who had earlier come to Loon Lake and been similarly attacked by wild dogs. A deep bond develops between Penfield and Joe, who also is attracted to Cara Lukacs, whom gangster Tommy Crapo has given to Bennett. Both Penfield and Joe love Clara, but since Penfield knows he cannot escape with her, he aids Joe in taking Clara away in Mrs. Bennett's Mercedes-Benz convertible. As they travel west, Joe becomes obsessed with making Clara "recognize" him as a person; this further develops Joe's concern with identity. Joe and Clara switch cars to throw off would-be pursuers and eventually stop in Jacksontown, Indiana, where Bennett has one of his automobile assembly plants. Because there is some labor unrest, Joe gets a job on the assembly line and meets Red James, another plant employee. At first, Joe sees him as a "rube" or a "cracker" who is not very intelligent. Red ostensibly is working for the union, but after he and Joe are attacked and Red is killed, Joe comes to the belated conclusion that Red was actually a double agent working for Bennett's company. Crapo's thugs murder Red because he is no longer useful. When he is questioned by the police, Joe fabricates a narrative that will allow him to extricate himself from possible murder charges. He tells the police that he is Bennett's son and challenges them to phone Bennett. As he is questioned, he sees Clara leave in a car driven by Tommy Crapo. After Joe is freed, he has Sandy, Red's wife, collect Red's insurance policy; he and she pack up the furniture, and he is determined to take her back to her family. However, he abandons her, as he had Mrs. Hearne, and returns instead to Loon Lake. He has seen a newspaper article about Lucinda Bennett's death while on a flight, like Amelia Earhart's, over the Pacific Ocean; from the photograph that accompanies the story, he learns that Penfield also has died.

When he returns to Loon Lake, he ingratiates himself with Bennett, whom he despises, and he becomes another person—one not like Penfield, whom he resembles, but one like Bennett. Half a year after leaving Indiana, Joe enrolls at Williams College; after his graduation in 1941, his name is changed to Joseph Paterson Bennett. Although his post-Loon Lake life is only provided in annotated form, readers do discover that he essentially assumes his "father's" persona, holds the same posts, has failed marriages, has no children, and, in the last words of the novel, is "Master of Loon Lake."

The Characters

As a *Bildungsroman*, *Loon Lake* focuses on one character, Joe Korzeniowski, who denies his parentage when he gives up his birth name and becomes Joe of Paterson. "Paterson" itself contains the words "pater," or father, and "son," and when Joe changes his last name to Bennett, he retains Paterson as a middle name. In his quest to become famous, to become someone, he is an archetypal figure who must enter the allegorical dark woods, endure trials, and then assume his place as the master of Loon Lake. When he leaves New York for California, he is determined to find or create a self, but he in fact becomes what he has to become. He assumes identities, impersonates people, and is torn between the two surrogate fathers, Penfield and Bennett. While Penfield claims that his life is Joe's life, Joe chooses to become Bennett, although Joe's role of narrator would seem to ally him with Penfield. Both Penfield (who has written three books of poetry, including one entitled *Loon Lake*) and Joe (who inherits those works and memories) annotate their texts. Since the fictional narrative ends with Joe's becoming Bennett, it is tempting to see Joe's real life, his story, ending when he becomes Bennett and his "life" is reduced to lists of posts, offices, achievements, and failed marriages. Like Bennett, he has no offspring, thereby adding to the idea that sterility is the price of Bennett-like success.

Warren Penfield is also a symbolic character, the person Joe resembles in his narrative attempt to control his story and explain his choice of identity. Joe may, like Penfield and the loon, dive deep and then emerge from the depths; but Joe, who says he wants freedom, does not take flight like the loon and Penfield. Flight, for Penfield, comes to mean death, but Joe is interested only in security. Unlike Penfield, who is a creative and complex character as well as a symbolic one, Bennett is strictly symbolic, the capitalist par excellence: "His dramatization suggests life devoted almost entirely to selfish accumulation of wealth and ritual use thereof according to established patterns of utmost class." Sim Hearne is a cheaper version of Bennett; both exploit, and in this novel, it is the exploitation of women that is stressed.

Clara is the blonde goddess, the idealized woman that Joe seeks. Like F. Scott Fitzgerald's Jay Gatsby, however, he finds that the goddess has feet of clay. She is passed, like Fanny, from one man to another and is thus a commodity. Yet Penfield and Joe, as they tell their stories, desire to link her with the three child-women figures that appear in the novel. Since Clara cannot literally be a little girl, the identification reflects Joe's determination to create his own reality.

Themes and Meanings

The exploitation of women is one metaphor for the capitalistic exploitation of workers and nature. In an ironic chapter of "data" about Bennett's life, the narrator discusses capitalism, damning with faint praise the high living standards under capitalism and offering a version of the trickle-down theory from the wealthy to the poor: "And while we may not admire always the personal motives of our business leaders we can appreciate the inevitable percolation of the good life as it comes down through our native American soil." In the next chapter, Joe describes the power of business leaders such as Bennett: "Mr. Antobody Bennett was a big man who . . . made the universe punch in like the rest of us." Bennett can control not only time but also nature, in the form of Loon Lake. He imposes his will on it, plumbs its depths, and makes an isolated fortress of his estate.

In *Loon Lake*, Doctorow suggests that the American Dream is really a nightmare. Attaining the dream does not necessarily depend on diligence and thrift; and when the dream is achieved, the "dreamer" is isolated from society and is morally and emotionally barren (neither Joe nor Bennett produces any children).

In order to convey these themes, Doctorow experiments with narrative. He includes many narrative threads, annotated poems, accounts of the impending death of Penfield and Lucinda, sociological analyses, résumés, and letters; Joe, though, is the narrator. He switches from first to third person to describe himself, eliminates punctuation in stream-of-consciousness passages, and intersperses poems with prose, all in an effort to suggest not only a character but also a narrative in the process of becoming. Since the novel is not chronological and perspectives are not easily identified, the reader is forced to be an active participant in the creation of the narrative. The novel is about characters, but since the reader sees characters narrating, it is also about the writing of fiction.

Critical Context

In his treatment of Joe's quest, desire for fame, and obsession with creating his own identity, Doctorow has created an updated *The Great Gatsby. Loon Lake*, though, is an even more cynical parody of the search for the American Dream. *Loon Lake* focuses not only on how the American Dream is attained but also on the negative effects, isolation, and emptiness that accompany the successful quest. Success destroys Doctorow's protagonist. It is in his narrative experimentation, however, that Doctorow is most contemporary. The concern with metafiction—fiction about the writing of fiction—can also be found in the works of Jorge Luís Borges, Donald Barthelme, and John Barth, among others. This kind of fiction forces readers to become interpreters, creators of a narrative that blends fictional events and characters with historical ones. In that process, it is difficult to determine Doctorow's own view of the 1930's, for he mixes cynicism with sentimentality. Doctorow's narrative experiments in *Loon Lake* are more radical than those in his earlier, more popular, and more accessible novels such as *The Book of Daniel* (1971) and *Ragtime* (1975), but readers of *Loon Lake* are offered a complex reading of America's Depression years and the American Dream.

Bibliography

Barkhausen, Jochen. "The Confusing Recovery of History in E. L. Doctorow's *Loon Lake.*" In *E. L. Doctorow: A Democracy of Perception*, edited by Herwig Friedl and Dieter Schulz. Heidelberg: Verlag Die Blaue Eule, 1988. Study of the relationship between history and experimental narrative technique in the novel.

Fowler, Douglas. *Understanding E. L. Doctorow.* Columbia: University of South Carolina Press, 1992. Short biographical chapter followed by chapter-length analyses of Doctorow's novels. Chapter 5 focuses on *Loon Lake* as *Bildungsroman.*

Gross, David S. "Tales of Obscene Power: Money and Culture, Modernism and History in the Fiction of E. L. Doctorow." In *E. L. Doctorow: Essays and Conversations*, edited by Richard Trenner. Princeton, N.J.: Ontario Review Press, 1983. Analysis of the relation of money, power, and isolation.

Harter, Carol C., and James R. Thompson. *E. L. Doctorow.* Boston: Twayne, 1990. Short biography, supplemented by helpful chronology of Doctorow's life. Provides an overview and assessment of the novel. Chapter 4 examines the synchronicity in the *Loon Lake* narrative and the ties between Joe and his two surrogate fathers, Bennett and Penfield.

Parks, John G. *E. L. Doctorow.* New York: Continuum, 1991. Doctorow's early life is discussed, followed by analyses of Doctorow's novels. Chapter 5 focuses on the Depression-era content of the novel and Joe's search for identity.

Thomas L. Erskine

LOS GUSANOS

Author: John Sayles (1950-)
Type of plot: Political realism
Time of plot: The 1980's
Locale: Miami, Florida
First published: 1991

 Principal characters:
   Scipio de la Pena, an aging and ailing Cuban exile who fought at the
    Bay of Pigs
   Marta de la Pena, Scipio's daughter
   Blas de la Pena, Scipio's eldest son
   Ambrosio de la Pena, Scipio's youngest son, killed at the Bay of Pigs
   Felix de la Pena, Scipio's brother
   Guillermo Nuñez (El Halcón), a professional killer
   Luz, a Cuban exile who works in a nursing home
   Serafín, Luz's brother
   Rufo, Luz's boyfriend, a small-time criminal
   Narciso Villas, a Cuban exile and former professor
   Walt, a CIA agent
   Dewey, an orderly at the nursing home
   Roosevelt, an orderly at the nursing home
   Duckworth, a Miami police detective
   Rivkin, a Miami police detective
   Padre Martín, a defrocked Catholic priest and Cuban exile

The Novel

Los Gusanos takes place primarily in the 1980's, though the narrative frequently flashes back to the 1960's and to events surrounding the failed Bay of Pigs invasion. The novel centers on a family of Cuban exiles and on the attempts of one member of that family to organize another invasion of Cuba to strike at least a symbolic blow at the object of their personal and political hatred, Fidel Castro.

The novel is narrated in the third person, but it includes sections of one character's journal and the recorded imaginings of another. The narration shifts its focus through a number of characters, taking the reader into their various consciousnesses. The story begins in 1981 in Miami, Florida, in the heart of the Cuban exile community of Little Havana. Scipio de la Pena, a leader of the ill-fated 1961 Bay of Pigs invasion, lies dying in a nursing home bed. He is rarely coherent, but he is faithfully attended by his daughter, Marta de la Pena, who talks to him of the invasion. Marta is the one child of Scipio who did not take part in the attack on Castro's Cuba. Her oldest brother, Blas, survived the attack but has lived outside the United States, a criminal exile, for several years. Marta's younger brother, Ambrosio, a poet, was killed in the invasion but left behind a diary that forms part of the novel's narrative and becomes a part of the invasion's history. The novel's central plot details Marta's attempt to mount a second (and more or less symbolic) invasion of Cuba.

One of the novel's secondary plots involves another young woman and Cuban exile, Luz, who attends to Scipio in the nursing home. Luz moves through a number of relationships with local men, and in the course of doing so finds herself involved with Rufo, who looks to involve himself in the political and criminal activity of Little Havana. Luz's brother, Serafín, meanwhile finds himself romantically attracted to Marta, who has little time for anything that is not political.

Around these two plots swirl a number of lesser but related plot lines. A Central Intelligence Agency (CIA) agent works to manipulate Marta and her recruits to the best advantage of the agency and of U.S. interests in the region. Two local police detectives investigate a murder that seems to be connected to the local exile community and to the gangs that have sprouted from that community. A man known as El Halcón haunts the edges of this community; he is a killer, willing to work for whoever best pays him for his services—CIA, Castro loyalists, or exiles.

As the story moves through these various narrative angles, characters move in and out of one anothers' lives, sometimes touching only obliquely, sometimes growing to be profound parts of those lives. Marta de la Pena stands outside most of these relationships as she concentrates on pulling together the threads of her invasion plan and on recruiting members to her cause. Various forces—internal and external—exert themselves on Marta, who finds herself learning more and more about the political machinery that once ran the anti-Castro movement in Cuba and which now operates out of the realm of exile. She also learns—and the reader learns—of the histories of betrayal and falsehood that inform this movement.

Eventually, Marta realizes her dream, taking her small band out of Miami and to the shores of Cuba. There, they make what is effectively a symbolic (and in some ways a tragically ironic) strike against Castro and against the history that claimed her brother's life twenty years earlier.

The Characters

In *Los Gusanos*, John Sayles assembles an expansive cast of characters, all of whom bear some relation—whether acknowledged or not—to the political events that marked the 1961 Bay of Pigs invasion. Moreover, most of these characters lead lives still defined by that invasion; even in exile from their homeland, these *Cubanos* participate in the past and the present of the world from which they were severed.

Marta de la Pena has inherited the revolutionary fervor from her father, Scipio, who is now bedridden by a stroke. Exempted from the original invasion because of her age, and never taken quite seriously because of her sex, Marta looks to redeem her father's "heroic failure" by organizing a second attempt at the island. She is, in effect, a Cuban Joan-of-Arc-in-exile who looks to become her father's third "son." At heart, Marta probably aspires to martyrdom, but her immediate aim is to strike a blow against the

Castro regime that took her father's heart and her younger brother's life and that turned her older brother from a political exile into a criminal thug. Marta collects the history of her island and of the revolution, taking to heart the idealism that spurred her family—and other like-minded Cubans—to political action.

Marta's youngest brother, Ambrosio, comes closest to capturing the pure spirit of the rebellion. He is a poet and a historian; he records the experience of his training, of his indoctrination, of his brief fight for the Fulgencio Batista movement in his diary. This diary serves as one of the alternative narratives in *Los Gusanos*; it becomes the voice of Ambrosio, speaking to Marta and to the reader from the time of the invasion. Interleaved among Ambrosio's prose recollections are his poems, which present both a portrait of *los gusanos*—"the worms," as Castro himself called those Cubans who sided with Batista and against him—and a self-portrait of the poet-warrior. Ambrosio finally becomes a victim of the dark web of betrayal that confounds the Brigade; on the verge of actually facing battle in the invasion, Ambrosio is murdered—for vague and shadowy political reasons—by the vicious and amoral El Halcón.

It is partly to avenge that murder that Blas de la Pena returns to Miami. Risking discovery and arrest for his own various crimes, Blas lands in Miami to search out the killer of his brother and to exact a certain degree of revenge for both the death of Ambrosio and the failure of the revolution. All the idealism of his father and his brother has been drained from Blas by the long, disillusioning string of betrayals; played false by the CIA and the U.S. government, Blas places his political and personal faith in himself only. As ugly as his nature is, he does manage to bring El Halcón to a deadly accounting for his sins against the family and the movement. Blas de la Pena stands diametrically opposed to his brother in his nature and his sensibilities. He is, at the beginning of the struggle, the true fighter for the true cause. By its end, however, he has become a bitter, sometimes brutal realist who reads his country's history with a jaundiced eye.

All this history catalyzes Marta de la Pena toward renewal of the fight. She moves about Little Havana trying to collect recruits and arms for her mission, her quest. She enlists her Uncle Felix, who himself fought against Castro at the Bay of Pigs and whose boat carries Marta and her band toward Cuba once again. Persuaded to join Marta as well is Padre Martín, a defrocked Catholic priest who feels the dual loyalties of church and homeland tugging at him. She also attracts Dewey, the young orderly at her father's nursing home. Distracted by masculinist, militarist fantasies, Dewey constructs an elaborate dream life as a sort of mercenary without a cause; his own "journal" functions as a second alternative narrative in *Los Gusanos*, and it records his gradual psychological disintegration. Before he can actually live out his fantasy as a member of Marta's rebel band, Dewey breaks down and shoots up his apartment, an act that gets him arrested and removed from the action.

Themes and Meanings

Los Gusanos is a study of the political nature of history and of human action. In the world of this novel, every act is colored by some sort of political intent or influence.

As the novel remarks at one point, *Toda la vida es política*: All of life is political. Behind every act (even the most idealistic and pure), argues Sayles, stands a political
motive.

The novel is also an examination of the making and meaning of history. *Los
Gusanos*, in its own way, is a history itself, attempting as it does to write a version of
the Bay of Pigs invasion and its legacy. History is written, is textual, suggests Sayles;
what matters is who happens to be writing the current version of that history.

Sayles is also interested in the problems of culture and of cultural crossings. His
portrait of the Cuban exile population of Miami is, among other things, a portrait of a
community in transition; its people move between the world they knew (and were
forced to leave) and the world that has become their temporary (or, for some, permanent) home. Character, Sayles contends, is defined by culture, and the characters in
Los Gusanos find themselves struggling to establish or understand the very nature of
the exiled self.

Critical Context

John Sayles is a writer who perhaps is better known popularly as a filmmaker.
However, his fiction has been consistently acclaimed by scholars of contemporary
writing for its realistic imaginings of the political and social lives of its characters. In
Los Gusanos, Sayles extends his vision to include the broadly historical stories of the
Cuban American community, stories inherently wrought by various geopolitical di-
mensions.

The novel is critically interesting, as well, for its narrative adventuresomeness.
Sayles filters his novel's action through the imaginations of several different characters, and he offers alternative narratives (diaries, imagined journals) that complement
or compete with the dominant narrative in the novel. Sayles also attends to the fidelity
of language, strategically sprinkling passages of Spanish throughout *Los Gusanos*,
challenging the reader to enter the very cultural milieu of his characters and to make
sense of what initially might be foreign and obscure.

Finally, Sayles takes on the serious and much-argued question of history—its
textuality, its reliability, its very nature as truthful narrative. In some ways, *Los
Gusanos* might be considered a historical novel, taking as it does the complex story of
Fidel Castro, Fulgencio Batista, the Brigade, and the Bay of Pigs invasion as its narrative backdrop. Sayles also takes into account the multitude of personalities who contribute to the shaping and the telling of history, who contribute their fictions, their bi-
ographies, their lies to the larger story that is labeled as history. It is perhaps on this
level—as historical critique and as a critique of historical writing—that *Los Gusanos*
operates most significantly.

Bibliography

Davis, Thulani. "Blue-Collar Auteur." *American Film* 16, no. 6 (June, 1991): 18-25. A
     discussion of Sayles's oeuvre in the context of his film work. Includes an excerpt
     from *Los Gusanos*.

Goodwin, Jo-Ann. Review of *Los Gusanos*, by John Sayles. *New Statesman and Society* 4, no. 171 (October 4, 1991): 36-37. An interesting British perspective on the novel.

Kenan, Randall. Review of *Los Gusanos*, by John Sayles. *Nation* 252, no. 24 (June 24, 1991): 856-858. A provocative discussion of the novel.

Sayles, John, and Gavin Smith. *Sayles on Sayles*. London: Faber and Faber, 1998. Contains a series of interviews with Sayles, each of which takes up a separate work of fiction or film. An indispensable source.

Simpson, Janice C. "Neck Deep in the Culture." *Time* 138, no. 5 (August 5, 1991): 64. A discussion of Sayles's work in literature, films, and television. Focuses on his penchant for championing underdogs and outsiders.

Gregory L. Morris

LOSING BATTLES

Author: Eudora Welty (1909-   )
Type of plot: Comic and ironic pastoral
Time of plot: The 1930's
Locale: The rural Mississippi hill country
First published: 1970

> *Principal characters:*
> > GRANNY VAUGHN, the presiding matriarch of her large family, whose ninetieth birthday is the occasion for the reunion that brings its members together
> > JACK RENFRO, the hope of the family's survival, just out of prison to rejoin them
> > BEULAH RENFRO, his mother, who will become the new matriarch of the family
> > MISS JULIA MORTIMER, the community schoolteacher whose values are antagonistic to those of the family
> > GLORIA SHORT RENFRO, Jack's wife, who represents the tension between the values of family and the values of Miss Julia
> > JUDGE MOODY, a former student of Miss Julia who sent Jack to prison

The Novel

Losing Battles is not an easy novel to read, not because it is philosophically demanding or because it has a complex plot, but rather because of its style (it is written almost entirely in dialogue) and because of the large number of characters (twenty-eight listed in the cast at the front of the book) who populate it and who join in the talk that makes it up. It is precisely the talk and tale-telling of the rural family, however, that constitute the novel's essence, as it attempts to capture the spirit of a tight-knit oral culture.

The plot is so simple as to be nonexistent, even though this, unlike many of Eudora Welty's earlier works, is a long novel of more than four hundred pages. The action takes place on the day of Granny Vaughn's ninetieth birthday—the occasion for a reunion of the family that includes the Renfros and the Beechams—and the following day, which is the day of the funeral of the old schoolteacher of the rural area, Miss Julia Mortimer. Indeed, although Miss Julia does not figure in the novel in actuality, her legend and her influence dominate the last half of the book, much as the clan of Granny Vaughn dominates the first half.

The central event which unites these two strands is the return of Jack Renfro, who has just been released from prison; Jack, the oldest son of Beulah Renfro, one of Granny's grandchildren, is the central hope of the family—an innocent but brave and loving young man who has chosen to stay with the family instead of making his fortune elsewhere. Jack has been in prison because of a fight he had with Curly Stovall, the town storekeeper, over Granny's gold ring, which Curly took in payment for a family debt. After Jack fights Curly and carries off the safe in which the ring is kept (which is lost on his trip home), he is sent to prison by Judge Moody for "aggravated battery."

The story of Jack's trial and adventures surrounding his return home from prison is presented in great detail by the symphony of voices of the characters themselves, in such a way that, as is typical of an oral culture, the past blends with the present. On Jack's way home to the reunion, he helps pull a man's car out of a ditch, only to find out when he arrives that the man is none other than Judge Moody himself. When Jack returns to undo his Good Samaritan deed, his wife and child barely escape being run over by the judge, who swerves off the road to avoid hitting them; as a result, the judge's car is stuck in a precarious position perched on the edge of a precipice. Because Jack claims that the judge saved the life of his wife and child, he vows to help him free his car and then brings him and his grumbling wife back to the reunion with him.

Jack's wife, Gloria, is the schoolteacher who has succeeded Miss Julia; she fell in love with Jack when he was one of her overgrown students. She had his child, Lady May, while he was in prison. Gloria is in many ways at the very center of the tension between the rural world of the clan and the sense of progress and ambition that Miss Julia represents. Miss Julia has been set against her star pupil and protégée, who married Jack Renfro and thus became merely a wife and mother in the midst of the clannish backwardness of the rural world. When the clan checks its genealogy in the family Bible, it discovers that Gloria is actually a cousin of Jack and thus she is welcomed into the family much more warmly than when she was considered to be an outsider aligned with the foreign world represented by Miss Julia.

Following the freeing of the judge's car, a comic masterpiece of description, the novel comes to a close rather quickly with the funeral of Miss Julia. At the end, Jack, Gloria, and Lady May walk off together, presumably to a new life somewhat freed from both factions, with Jack singing "Bringing in the Sheaves" so loudly that "all Banner could hear him and know who he was."

The Characters

Character and a sense of place are the two most important elements in this pastoral novel, with the wide cast of characters who represent the clan constituting the very sense of place that is Banner, Mississippi, and its rural environs. Although Jack is the central figure in the work, and his return from prison signals that he will carry on the family tradition, Granny herself is always there as the presiding matriarch, prepared to hand down her leadership role to Jack's mother, Beulah Renfro. Opposing the values represented by Granny and Beulah is Miss Julia Mortimer, the teacher who tries to bring the new values of education and progress into this rural world.

Representing both sides are Judge Moody, Miss Julia's first protégée, who, although he has aligned himself with the side of progress, has remained to adjudicate the actions of the rural world, and Gloria, Miss Julia's last protégée, who is caught be-

tween Miss Julia's realm and the realm of the clan. Gloria, however, has her own
aims—to be with Jack and their child, Lady May, without the support of Miss Julia's
plans for her as a schoolteacher and also without subsuming herself within the all-
encompassing family life of the clan.

The novel focuses not only on a multitude of individual characters but also on character in the ultimate sense—that is, the strength of character to withstand the many
losing battles that constitute life. Although the rural people distrust Miss Julia and all
she represents, they must admit that she, like themselves, understands the need to endure, and they begrudgingly admire the strength of her character. Although they know
that she was "St. George and Ignorance was the dragon," they also affirm their own
values of personal strength and endurance. As Uncle Curtis says, "There ain't no end
to what you can lose and still go on living."

Themes and Meanings

The basic theme of the book centers on the conflict between two different cultures—the oral culture of the rural South and the written culture of the modern world.
(The tension is also between the related values of remaining at home within the protection of the family as opposed to striking out on one's own.) *Losing Battles* is thus a
book about cultural survival, but, ironically, the oral culture which the book celebrates
exists only in the written work that *Losing Battles* is.

Welty takes a great artistic risk in this novel, for she tries desperately to present it as
an oral work. The book, filled as it is with so many different voices, departs so much
from the conventions of writing that it is difficult to follow. Judge Moody is the immediate representative of the written word, and it is the letter of the law that sends Jack to
prison, but, still, it is talk that dominates the book. When the judge reads the family a
last letter from Miss Julia, someone asks if he cannot simply tell them what the letter
is about rather than read it. The letter from the dying woman, now deserted and deprived, is the center of the irony that gives the book its title. She writes that, all of her
life, she has fought a hard war with ignorance: "Except in those cases that you can
count off on your fingers, I lost every battle. Year in, year out, my children at Banner
School took up the cause of the other side and held the fort against me."

Although Miss Julia says that she has lost the battles, the novel itself indicates that
ultimately she has won the war, for even as this novel celebrates the oral culture, it also
is an elegy for its inevitable loss. As Miss Julia continues in her last words, one hears
the death knell of the oral culture itself: "It's the desperation of staying alive against
all odds that keeps both sides encouraged. But the side that gets licked gets to the truth
first." The truth is that although it seems as if the oral culture has won the battle, it has
indeed lost; for the world of Miss Julia ultimately dominates.

Critical Context

Losing Battles was published to the great anticipation of those discriminating readers who had valued Welty's short stories and novels since the late 1930's and early
1940's. Few American writers with a relatively small body of work such as Welty's

have been so honored by their literary peers. Although Welty had published several novels before *Losing Battles*, her reputation rested (and still rests) on her short stories, and only in the 1970's and 1980's has she gained a wide readership commensurate with her critical standing.

Losing Battles, her first long novel, is radically different from the style and structure of her short stories. It does not have the tight mythic and symbolic pattern of the stories or their usual metaphoric structure. It is rather epic in intent, focusing less on the individual lives of her Southern grotesques than on the collective life of the culture from which they all spring. Thus, it is diffuse rather than tight; moreover, its attempts to replicate the oral culture which it both celebrates and laments make it seem idiosyncratic and therefore inaccessible to the general reader.

Losing Battles was enthusiastically received by many critics and praised as a masterpiece; some reviewers, however, suggested that it was a masterpiece that would remain largely unread. Misunderstanding the values of the rural culture from which it springs, many critics tended to identify with Miss Julia. They generally saw the family clan as more suffocating than supporting. Indeed, it is difficult to unseat oneself from the modern, print-oriented world of fragmentation and separation and understand the values of the oral world of family unity on which the novel focuses. One not familiar with the culture Welty depicts may find it difficult to understand why the clan sees education as so threatening, why they take it to be an evil, a mystery, a threat. The real issue underlying this fear, however, is the conflict between the concrete world of the family, which is presented as the real natural world, and the world of abstractions propounded by education, which is seen by the folk as artificial.

Welty does not really take sides in this novel, for she understands the absurdity of the dedicated Miss Julia as well as the pettiness of the devoted family; rather, she attempts to present a balanced view of these two worlds, the primitive-mythic and the progressive-modern, locked in a comic-epic battle for survival. The work falls into the tradition of the folktale or tall tale, although it is presented within the conventions of realism—a combination that makes it difficult for the reader to know how to approach it. Because of this generic confusion, it did not gain for Welty the recognition that she had long deserved. That honor was reserved for her next book, *The Optimist's Daughter* (1972), which won the Pulitzer Prize and which started a series of celebrations of Welty and her work that extended from Mississippi to New York—a long overdue recognition for a great writer who embodies the simple virtues of her oral culture while having consummately mastered the demands of her writing craft.

Bibliography

Bass, Eben E. "The Languages of *Losing Battles*." *Studies in American Fiction* 21 (Spring, 1993): 67-82. Bass explores the opposing feminine modes of communication which serve the common goal of challenging male authority in Welty's novel. Bass compares the effectiveness of Julia's written and bookish modes of communication to Granny Vaughn's spoken word.

Champion, Laurie, ed. *The Critical Response to Eudora Welty's Fiction.* Westport, Conn.: Greenwood Press, 1994. In her introduction, Champion presents an overview of the criticism on Welty's fiction. Five separate essays by different scholars are devoted to various aspects of *Losing Battles.* Includes a helpful bibliography of works for further reading.

Gray, Richard. "Needing to Talk: Language and Being in *Losing Battles.*" *The Southern Literary Journal* 29 (Spring, 1997): 72-86. Gray contends that Welty's novel is similar in style to Faulkner's works in that Welty and Faulkner both portray life as a series of dialogue that creates an open-ended chain of discourse with no possibility of finalization. Gray characterizes this style as "folk-speech" and shows that all of Welty's characters have a need to tell their stories.

Gretlund, Jan Nordby. "Welty's *Losing Battles.*" *The Explicator* 51 (Fall, 1992): 49-50. Gretlund argues that several critics who admire Welty have misinterpreted passages in her works that reflect the dark or evil side of human nature. She uses the example of the instance when 90-year-old Grandma Vaughn invites her 12-year-old grandson into her bed. Gretlund contends that Grandma's action could have been an innocent mistake.

Kornfeld, Eve. "Reconstructing American Law: The Politics of Narrative and Eudora Welty's Empathic Vision." *Journal of American Studies* 26 (April, 1992): 23-49. Kornfeld examines the contention of some legal scholars that Welty's novel shows that American law should be reformulated to overcome bias against minorities, women, and the poor. Welty's book reflects an empathic point of view by having the judge reinterpret the law based on sympathy for a family's troubles.

Charles E. May

THE LOST LANGUAGE OF CRANES

Author: David Leavitt (1961-   )
Type of plot: Family
Time of plot: The mid-1980's
Locale: New York City
First published: 1986

> *Principal characters:*
> PHILIP BENJAMIN, a twenty-five-year-old gay man who edits paperback
> romances
> OWEN BENJAMIN, Philip's father, the dean of admissions at a
> prestigious boys' school
> ROSE BENJAMIN, Philip's mother, a copy editor at a small literary
> publishing house
> ELIOT ABRAMS, Philip's lover, a young, wealthy, and enigmatic
> entrepreneur
> JERENE PARKS, Eliot's roommate, an African American lesbian and
> pe-rennial graduate student

The Novel

The Lost Language of Cranes is a naturalistic, contemporary novel about a small, upper-middle class intellectual family in New York City in which the son's acknowledgment of his homosexuality transforms his parents' marriage in unexpected ways.

The novel is divided into four sections: "Voyages," "Myths of Origin," "The Crane Child," and "Father and Son," with the third significantly shorter and the last significantly longer than the others. The section titles are thematic; chronologically and stylistically, the novel flows as a unified whole. It is presented in a third-person narrative voice that often enters the thoughts and feelings of the main characters.

As the novel opens, the reader sees Owen and Rose Benjamin in their separate exploits on a Sunday afternoon. They are a happily, or at least tranquilly, married couple who have comfortable jobs and live in a rent-controlled apartment on New York City's posh Upper East Side. The security of their shared life is threatened by news that their building is to become a cooperative apartment house, leaving them the equally unattractive options of buying or moving out.

The reader then meets their son Philip, a twenty-five-year-old editor who is in love with a golden and capricious young man named Eliot. Philip dotes on Eliot but always feels uncertain and unsatisfied; he is also uncomfortable with the secrecy of his homosexuality and the distance it creates between him and his parents.

The novel weaves in and out of the Benjamins' lives as they travel the streets of New York, share meals, work, converse, make love, and face challenges large and small. Along the way, readers observe Owen in his secret life, furtively frequenting adult motion-picture houses where he indulges in homosexual fantasies and barely resists constant temptations. Readers are also introduced to Jerene, Eliot's roommate, an African American graduate student estranged from her parents because of her lesbianism.

Leavitt fills in details through flashbacks—about the Benjamins' marriage, Rose's extramarital affairs, Philip's childhood and sexual development—and constantly shifts among the characters to establish the connections between them and their stories. The novel's background is a New York populated by cab drivers, doormen, and street people and a media culture defined by television shows, books, and celebrities. Leavitt portrays his protagonists intimately, penetrating the isolation of their separate lives.

The main story lines of the book develop simultaneously. Philip's love for Eliot, and his fascination with Eliot's adoptive father Derek, ultimately result in Eliot's sudden departure. The real-estate dilemma creates a sense of despair in the Benjamins' apartment. Desperate and in search of love and identity, Philip seeks his old friend Brad and faces his need to be honest with his parents about himself. Jerene meets and becomes involved with a new woman, and she feels the need to seek out her parents once again. Owen finds it harder and harder to suppress his homosexual desires.

In the novel's critical scene, Philip informs his parents of his homosexuality. Rose responds with pain and a sincere effort to understand; Owen closes off and sobs silently to himself. Both know implicitly that Philip's is not the only sexuality at stake, and that his honesty unwittingly threatens the fragile foundation of their marriage.

In the brief third section of the novel, Leavitt explores a case study from Jerene's research in linguistics. The case involves a neglected, possibly retarded, teenage boy who was fascinated by some distant construction cranes and who would interpret and respond to their movements as if in a strange language. The case provides the novel's title and a central metaphor about the need for communication and love.

After encountering the Crane Child, Jerene seeks out her paternal grandmother Nellie in a Long Island nursing home. The reunion, a brief encounter in which she portrays her life as secure and normal for her simple, doting grandmother, is Jerene's first step toward reestablishing a link with her past and her estranged family.

The last section focuses on Owen and Philip, their individual transformations, and the growing affinity between them. As the gap between him and Rose widens and his homosexual yearnings grow, Owen looks to Philip, ironically, as a role model. A family dinner at which an English teacher from Owen's school is guest of honor invokes telling behavior and triggers the mostly silent but painfully honest confrontation between Rose and Owen, where his secret is acknowledged by both and the peace of their coexistence is irrevocably shattered. In the end, Owen seeks comfort and refuge in Philip's apartment.

The Characters

Philip is the central and most sympathetic character of the novel. His story is a coming-of-age and a "coming-out" tale, and he is the main conduit for emotional understanding. Philip is a sincere and sensitive young man whose journey takes him from self-doubt and obsessiveness toward self-knowledge and authentic love. It is through a more rigorous examination of his lovers and his parents that Philip ultimately finds himself. At the same time, he provides an interesting foil and gloss to Owen; at numerous points, scenes from their lives—meals, sexual encounters, phone conversations—are effectively juxtaposed.

Owen, an older, more confused, and more repressed man, is much more enigmatic. While on the surface potentially despicable for his deception and indecision, Owen is not an unsympathetic character, for Leavitt is careful to convey Owen's pain, guilt, and sincere desire to do what is right for both himself and those he loves. He is portrayed as a man lost and confused, a representation of the bluntness that results from the repression of desire and honesty.

Rose, though not as repressed or deceptive, has also been living with lies. While seemingly a victim, she is also a wife guilty of infidelities who prefers to avoid confrontation. She is a sympathetic character, but one with a complex layering of feelings, thoughts, desires, and self-deceptions. That her journey is determined primarily by the desires and actions of others indicates the passive nature of her personality.

Jerene provides both a contrast to the Benjamins, in her distance from them and the different issues that concern her, and a touchstone by which to understand their stories. The account of her parents' response to her lesbianism creates a tension in anticipation of Philip's eventual disclosure to Rose and Owen. Her interest in lost languages amplifies the significance of the characters' private worlds.

The narrative voice rarely penetrates the other characters, but they provide valuable links in the overall structure of the novel. The sharp contrast between Eliot and Brad helps to define Philip's emotional growth. Winston Penn, the dinner guest, becomes, essentially, a lens through which Rose confirms Owen's true nature.

Leavitt also uses character to establish the complexity of New York life, through a variety of serendipitous, and often undiscovered, connections. When Owen desperately calls a hotline for advice, Jerene is the volunteer who answers. Eliot's adoptive father Derek is one of Philip's favorite childhood authors, one whose books Rose edited. Owen discovers that the cinema he frequents is one Philip has visited as well. These links heighten the tension, irony, and emotional logic of the novel and contribute to the sense of complexity throughout.

Themes and Meanings

The Lost Language of Cranes is a novel, above all, about identity and empathy. The main characters face the challenges of defining themselves as clearly and honestly as possible and of choosing the terms, the aspects of life—relationships, jobs, sexuality, race, gender—by which their sense of self is established.

For Rose and Owen, marriage and home are implicit to identity. When they tell Philip that they might give up their apartment, he says that he simply cannot imagine them living anywhere else. Rose examines herself in the mirror, imagines herself in others' situations, and thinks about how people perceive her. While she and Owen both know that their intimacy has faded, neither is willing to question the basic value of their relationship.

For Philip and Owen, homosexuality is the issue through which identity is explored. In his secret life, Owen assumes the anonymity provided by gay film houses and bars; his self-image merges with those of the sex-driven men in the pornographic films he watches. He is painfully aware of playing roles in his marriage and job, of hiding his true identity in subtle but telling ways.

Philip at first locates his identity wholly in his love for Eliot, a love that is self-degrading and ultimately based in fantasy. It is only through the process of understanding himself and, more important, expressing himself more honestly to the world around him that he arrives at a way of loving that does not destroy his sense of self.

Communication becomes important as the manner in which identity is expressed. When Owen builds enough courage to call a man whom he encountered anonymously, the man misunderstands Owen's name and calls him "Bowen"; the mistake symbolizes the inevitable distortion of identity that comes with repression and deception. Philip searches through Derek's books for clues to Eliot's elusive identity. Jerene's false description of her life to Nellie is both poignant and pathetic; it is the only real language she can use.

Language, then, comes to define the individual. In describing Jerene's response to the Crane Child case, Leavitt gives the novel's clearest and most compelling articulation of this theme:

> How wondrous, how grand those cranes must have seemed to Michel, compared to the small and clumsy creatures who surrounded him. For each, in his own way, she believed, finds what it is he must love, and loves it; the window becomes a mirror; whatever it is that we love, that is who we are.

Furthermore, identity becomes a question of finding one's place. Philip is strikingly conscious of where he and Eliot spend their nights together. For Rose and Owen, the imminent change in living situation is a metaphor for the challenges that their marriage faces. The home that was once safe for Owen has become a place of danger, yet it is still preferable to living on the street, an unlikely scenario that he and Rose both fear. Early in the novel, Philip and Rose step over a homeless person asleep in Philip's entryway; at the end of the novel, Philip comes home to find his father in the same spot. Yet Owen's descent to such figurative poverty represents liberty and clarity, not bankruptcy. He becomes one with, and brings empathy to, the many poor and nameless faces of urban life.

Such a transformation suggests the empathetic understanding that suffuses the novel. As the characters face their own needs and idiosyncrasies in the pursuit of authentic identity, they need more than anything the empathy of others. *The Lost Language of Cranes*, despite the highly emotional nature of the conflicts and situations it examines, never explodes into anger, hatred, or vitriol. Rather, Rose, Philip, Owen, and the others consistently extend compassion to others; they strive not to judge but to understand.

This theme is underlined in various smaller events of the novel. At one point Rose, frustrated by incessant phone calls from opportunistic real-estate agents, lashes out at one caller only to receive an overpowering description of the caller's own miserable life. It is a reminder that all have burdens to carry, and that the best one can do is to accept others as they are. Such empathy can be the key to understanding such very human phenomena as homosexuality, infidelity, poverty, and emotional need.

It also can be the key to functioning in the complex and confusing society of the modern cityscape. Leavitt's New York is not merely a backdrop but a character in itself that constantly challenges and reflects on the protagonists. It is a world so vast and overwhelming that knowing one's place in it requires the utmost honesty, energy, generosity, and commitment.

Critical Context

At the age of twenty-three, David Leavitt burst on the American literary scene with a collection of short stories entitled *Family Dancing* (1984). The stories dealt with issues of sexuality and terminal cancer. *Family Dancing* received the PEN/Faulkner Award and was a finalist for the National Book Critics Circle Award. Because of his youth, Leavitt received much attention and was hailed by some as the new voice of his generation.

Two years later, *The Lost Language of Cranes*, Leavitt's first novel, appeared to mixed reviews. Focused more clearly on homosexual themes and characters, it established him as a gay writer. During the mid-1980's, the gay rights movement was well into its second decade and approaching a certain maturity; Leavitt's novel was noted for dealing with gay themes in a very accessible and universal manner. Despite the critical response, *The Lost Language of Cranes* spent many weeks on best-seller lists and was a popular success. In 1992, the British Broadcasting Corporation filmed an adaptation of the novel, transferring the story to London.

Leavitt's other works include *Equal Affections* (1988), a novel about a family facing its matriarch's slow death; a second collection of stories, *A Place I've Never Been* (1990); and a novel set in wartime England entitled *While England Sleeps* (1993). Leavitt has lived in Europe, and his work enjoys great popular and critical success there.

Bibliography

Hubbard, Kim. "*The Lost Language of Cranes*." *People Weekly* 26 (November 3, 1986): 19-20. After a brief synopsis of the novel, Hubbard considers the humorlessness of the characters and their preoccupation with sexual identity. The reviewer also questions the novel's lack of attention to AIDS.

Jones, Adams-Mars. "*The Lost Language of Cranes*." *New Republic* 195 (November 17, 1986): 43-46. A balanced appraisal of the novel on several levels. Jones examines the larger themes and metaphors and the use of pathos, irony, tone, and tempo. He criticizes Leavitt for underdevelopment of certain characters and the lack of a mature central protagonist.

Leavitt, David. "The Way I Live Now." *The New York Times Magazine* 138 (July 9, 1989): 28-32. Inspired by Susan Sontag's story "The Way We Live Now," Leavitt discusses AIDS with candor and conviction. He looks at AIDS in his own writing and reviews the history of AIDS activism. Includes criticism of society's stereotypes in fighting the epidemic.

Lo, Mun-Hou. "David Leavitt and the Etiological Maternal Body." *Modern Fiction Studies* 41 (Fall/Winter, 1995): 439-465. Examines the correlation between mothers and homosexuality in Leavitt's written works. Discusses excerpts of books with themes similar to Leavitt's subjects, the influences of a maternal figure in the development of homosexuality, and the portrayal of acceptance by mothers of homosexual children. Offers a framework for a better understanding of the relationship between Philip and Rose.

Lopate, Phillip. "Sexual Politics, Family Secrets." *The New York Times Book Review*, October 5, 1986, 3. Lopate favorably reviews the novel, commending Leavitt's female characters and the freshness and suspense of the story. He takes issue with the novel's emphasis on sexual identity and politics. The review is accompanied by an interview box in which Barth Healey quotes Leavitt's views on the novel.

Staggs, Sam. "David Leavitt." *Publishers Weekly* 237 (August 24, 1990): 47-48. An intimate article based on an interview with the author. Leavitt discusses his work from a dispassionate, objective viewpoint. He also comments on the challenges of youthful success, his popularity in Europe, and his responsibility as a gay writer in the AIDS era.

Time. "A Family Reveals Its Secrets." 139 (June 29, 1992): 85. Reviews the BBC adaptation of Levitt's novel, noting the change in location from New York City to London. The reviewer praises the adaptation, but contends that "the change of locale distances the already remote characters and undercuts the work's emotional force."

Barry Mann

THE LOST STEPS

Author: Alejo Carpentier (1904-1980)
Type of plot: Psychological realism
Time of plot: The late 1940's
Locale: An unnamed metropolis (probably New York City), a South American city, and the South American jungle
First published: Los pasos perdidos, 1953 (English translation, 1956)

Principal characters:

THE NARRATOR, a composer and musicologist, now working in an advertising agency

RUTH, his wife, an actress

MOUCHE, his French lover as the novel begins

ROSARIO, the mestizo woman who becomes his lover in the jungle

THE ADELANTADO, the explorer who leads the expedition into the jungle, founder of Santa Monica de los Venados

The Novel

The Lost Steps narrates a journey, through space and back through time, to the most remote origins of Latin American history. The novel, which is written in the first person, can be read as a diary kept by the unnamed narrator-protagonist as he flees mechanized civilization in search of a more primordial existence. The dated entries which provide the basic structure for the novel are augmented by the narrator's fragmented recollections of the past and his meditations on art, culture, and history.

As the novel begins, the narrator is surveying the set of a long-running play about the antebellum South; in this play, his wife, Ruth, has a leading role. The play is a resounding commercial success despite its banality, and as he surveys the soiled costumes and the dwarf magnolias the narrator is overcome by boredom and loneliness. Once a promising young composer and musicologist, he now prostitutes his talents in an advertising agency. Neither the automatic nature of his weekly sexual relations with Ruth nor the frenetic, pseudo-intellectual gaiety of Mouche and her friends can satisfy him. Every aspect of his life seems mechanical and uninspired. Faced with the beginning of a three-week vacation, he feels empty and disoriented.

A chance encounter with his old friend and employer, the Curator, whom he has not seen for several years, presents the narrator with a unique opportunity. The Curator reminds him of his earlier work on primitive instruments and of his theories on the origins of music and asks him to travel to South America during his vacation to acquire a number of indigenous clay instruments for the museum. The narrator initially rejects the offer, but finally Mouche convinces him to go, announcing that she will accompany him.

The second chapter opens with their arrival in an unspecified South American city. The central role that geography will play in the novel becomes more explicit. The narrator hears once again the language of his childhood and is haunted by memories of his early years. In these new surroundings he begins to feel more alive, to recover his spiritual equilibrium. At the same time, Mouche's urban pretensions and protestations of trendy modernity strike him as increasingly false and ridiculous. When he meets the mestizo woman Rosario during the bus ride to the interior, he is captivated by her strength, simplicity, and obvious connection with nature. He and Rosario become lovers and Mouche, bedraggled and weak with malaria, is dispatched home.

The small group—which now consists of the narrator and Rosario; a Capuchin friar; Yannes, a Greek prospector and miner; and their guide, the Adelantado— presses its way by boat into the jungle. They pass through remote, almost mythic regions. When the Adelantado appears with magnificent specimens of the primitive instruments for which he has been searching, the narrator is suddenly overcome by the realization of "the first outstanding, noteworthy act of my life to that moment." He decides to continue on the expedition. Then, in a small village which seems to exist before time and before history, the narrator hears a funeral lament which convinces him that he has witnessed the birth of music. He resolves to remain in the jungle, never to return "back there." With Rosario, he sets up housekeeping in Santa Monica de los Venados, the town founded by the Adelantado, and begins to compose a new work, *Threnody*, based on the text of Homer's *Odyssey*.

The narrator is increasingly troubled, however, by a number of misgivings: the Adelantado's establishment of a civilized order in what has been an idyllic, natural place; his own failure to deliver the prized instruments to the Curator; Rosario's refusal to marry him; and, most important, the growing scarcity of the paper he desperately needs in order to complete his composition. The unexpected arrival of a small plane, part of an expedition sent by Ruth to find her lost husband, offers him the irresistible chance to return briefly to the city in order to settle his affairs and stock up on those items he considers indispensable for his new life in Santa Monica de los Venados.

The return occasions a series of personal and professional difficulties: a messy divorce from an embittered Ruth, loss of both job and credibility, and financial troubles brought on by his mounting legal expenses. The "tentacular city" alienates him more than ever; he stumbles through an almost apocalyptic landscape which underscores the bankrupt quality of the city's inhabitants and their art, religion, work, and relationships.

When the narrator is finally able to return to the jungle, it is too late. The incision which marked the path to Santa Monica de los Venados has disappeared beneath the rising waters of the river. Yannes tells him that Rosario is now pregnant by another man. The narrator immediately recognizes his error: "One day I had made the unforgivable mistake of turning back, thinking a miracle could be repeated, and on my return I found the setting changed, the landmarks wiped out, and the faces of the guides new."

The Characters

The narrator-protagonist of *The Lost Steps* is to some extent an autobiographical figure. Like his character, Carpentier grew up in Latin America, studied musicology, and found himself trapped by necessity in a large, hostile city, working in an advertising agency. While living in Venezuela in the 1940's, Carpentier made several trips into the jungle and was awed by the geographical and ethnological richness he encountered there. Carpentier's protagonist is a man caught between two cultures, between two languages, between "here" and "back there." His chaotic memories of his earlier life—his childhood, the war, his adulterous courtship of Ruth, his disillusionment with his artistic efforts—confirm and explain the rootlessness that seems to be his identifying characteristic. Although the expedition into the jungle begins as an escape, it soon becomes a pilgrimage to personal and cultural origins. The narrator sees the trip as a new beginning and believes that he is traveling not only through space but also back in time.

Yet he cannot escape the inherent tension between "here" and "back there" that is the heart of the novel. He is unable to express his wonder at the exuberant beauty of the jungle without resorting to allusions to Western culture. Thus a natural rock formation recalls "the world of Bosch, the imaginary Babels of painters of the fantastic, the most hallucinated illustrators of the temptations of the saints," and finally, "an incredible mile-high Gothic cathedral."

Before he can arrive at Santa Monica de los Venados, he must pass through a series of trials—first, the nocturnal terrors of the jungle and then a cyclone which hits as he is traveling on the river. The third and final trial is the arrival of the rescue plane. The narrator confesses: "I did not want to go. But I admitted to myself that what I lacked there could be summed up in two words: paper, ink." He leaves behind both Rosario and his unfinished composition. Later, he is unable to return, in part because of his own blindness: He cannot find the incisions in the tree trunk. Yet he also understands that he has tried too hard to understand life in the jungle; instead of feeling and living life, he has insisted on thinking about it. Certain forces of the world that he has been trying to escape pull him back toward modernity and history.

It must be confessed that the women in the novel serve mainly to illustrate different stages in the narrator's journey. Ruth is described solely in terms of her profession; the fact that she is an actress underscores the essential falseness of the narrator's life in the city. Even as she anxiously awaits her husband's rescue she seems to be playing the role of Penelope, the faithful wife. Mouche (whose name in French means "fly") represents decadent modernity. The animal sensuality which the narrator once admired loses its attractiveness once they have arrived in the South American capital. Unlike Mouche, who is totally alien to the jungle surroundings, Rosario is at one with them. Her high cheekbones, thick black hair, and sensual mouth reveal her to be the living sum of Indian, Mediterranean, and black races, and the narrator senses that her intimate knowledge of plants and herbs somehow provides a link between him and the jungle. Rosario is the ultimate Earth Mother, who refers to herself in the third person as "Your woman" and watches the narrator leave Santa Monica de los Venados with contemptuous indifference.

The minor figures in the novel appear more as archetypes than as fully rounded characters. The Curator, who reminds the narrator of his musical interests and sends him on the mission to the jungle, is identified only by his title. The Adelantado's name (in Spanish it means "he who goes ahead") is a reference to his explorations in the jungle and to the city he has founded there. Yannes, the Greek sailor, reads with great pleasure a bilingual copy of the *Odyssey* that the narrator has given him and, at the close of the novel, tries to interpret what has happened in terms of that epic.

Themes and Meanings

Recapturing lost origins—of man himself, as well as of his art, his language, and his history—is a central theme in *The Lost Steps*. Yet, as both the title and the conclusion of the novel suggest, such a recuperation is impossible. The narrator is driven by the need to discover in the past some essential truth about himself and his culture but is prevented from doing so by his commitment to the present. Thus, in the final pages of the novel, he comes to the realization that "the only human race to which it is forbidden to sever the bonds of time is the race of those who create art." The novel examines the relationship between the artist and his creation, as the narrator-protagonist struggles to find a balance between his desire for an audience for the *Threnody* and his painful awareness of the pitfalls of perverting his creation to suit an uncomprehending public.

The Lost Steps presents a Spenglerian view of modern civilization as decadent and moribund, especially when contrasted with the exuberant fertility of the New World jungle, although, given the truncated nature of the narrator's idyll in Santa Monica de los Venados, the novel cannot be read as a Utopian romance. The narrative is divided among three readily distinguishable locales—the modern city, a civilized zone in Latin America, and the marvelous and mysterious jungle—in the manner of many works which trace a symbolic journey, and the epigraphs which introduce each chapter mirror the narrator's thoughts and emotions.

Indeed, Carpentier is a highly symbolic writer, and his novel is also structured around three mythic figures who bear some resemblance to the protagonist: Sisyphus, condemned to spend his life pursuing an endless and fruitless task; Prometheus, the rebel who is condemned to eternal suffering because of his godlike aspirations; and Ulysses, whose long journey home takes him to far-off lands and unimagined adventures.

Finally, Carpentier examines the relationship between humanity, nature, and history. The protagonist realizes that nature, like history, is a text to be read, a text which Rosario can read but which he cannot. Thus his concluding meditation on his own odyssey: "I had lived to make straight a destiny that was crooked because of my own weakness, and a song had welled up in me—now cut short—which had led me back to the old road, in sackcloth and ashes, no longer able to be what I had been."

Critical Context

The Lost Steps is Carpentier's most important work, and it represents a turning point in his development as a writer. Latin America in the 1940's beckoned to avant-garde writers as a place of artistic and spiritual rebirth. Carpentier took the surrealist concept of magic realism and attempted to redefine it as a purely Latin American phenomenon. His theories were published in the form of a prologue to *El reino de este mundo* (1949; *The Kingdom of This World*, 1957). In *The Lost Steps*, Carpentier confronts this issue directly within his narrative; the protagonist struggles to come to terms with questions regarding the origins of language and tradition. *El siglo de las luces* (1962; *Explosion in a Cathedral*, 1963) represents a further attempt to write Latin American fiction based on the history of the New World. In *El recurso del método* (1974; *Reasons of State*, 1976), Carpentier paints a hilarious yet biting portrait of a Latin American despot caught between his European pretensions and the reality surrounding him.

The Lost Steps is often mentioned as one of the forerunners of the "boom" in Latin American literature, the explosion of literary activity in the 1960's and 1970's—writing, publishing, and translating—that brought authors such as Gabriel García Márquez and Jorge Luis Borges to the attention of readers outside Latin America. Finally, the language of *The Lost Steps*, rich in metaphor and cultural allusions, is as dense and prolific as the jungle it describes, making the novel a primary example of the Latin American neo-Baroque.

Bibliography

Echevarría, Roberto González. *Alejo Carpentier: The Pilgrim at Home*. Ithaca, N.Y.: Cornell University Press, 1977. Explores what seems like a radical disjunction between Carpentier's fiction and nonfiction. Echevarría finds unity, however, in certain recurring themes, which he illuminates by discussing Carpentier's debt to writers such as José Ortega y Gasset and Oswald Spengler. The novelist's penchant for dialectical structures and for allegory is also explored. Includes a bibliography and index.

Harss, Luis, and Barbara Dohmann. *Into the Mainstream*. New York: Harper & Row, 1966. Includes a chapter often cited as a succinct introduction to Carpentier's work up to the early 1960's.

Janney, Frank. *Alejo Carpentier and His Early Works*. London: Tamesis, 1981. An introductory survey that is still useful.

Kilmer-Tchalekian, Mary. "Ambiguity in *El siglo de las luces.*" *Latin American Literary Review* 4 (1976): 47-57. An especially valuable discussion of Carpentier's narrative technique and handling of point of view.

King, Lloyd. *Alejo Carpentier, Caribbean Writer*. St. Augustine, Fla.: University of the West Indies Press, 1977. Often cited for its perceptive introduction to Carpentier's work.

Shaw, Donald L. *Alejo Carpentier*. Boston: Twayne, 1985. Chapters on Carpentier's apprenticeship, his discovery of the "marvelous real," his handling of time and circularity, his fiction about the Antilles, his explorations of politics, and his last works. Includes chronology, notes, and annotated bibliography.

Souza, Raymond D. *Major Cuban Novelists: Innovation and Tradition*. Columbia: University of Missouri Press, 1976. Should be read in conjunction with Harss and Dohmann.

Karen Stolley